An Historical Detail

of

Seven Years Campaigns

In North America

From 1775 to 1782.

With an introductory Review

Of the Progress of the Discontents in the Colonies,

From the Stamp Act, to the Commencement of Hostilities.

To which

Is added An Appendix,

Containing Extracts from the Public Correspondence

And other important and interesting Papers.

By Lieut. General Sir Henry Clinton K. B..

In three Volumes.

Vol. I

Veniet Tempus, quo Ista quæ nunc latent

In Lucem Dies extrahet   Seneca

THE AMERICAN REBELLION

SIR HENRY CLINTON'S NARRATIVE

OF HIS CAMPAIGNS, 1775–1782, WITH AN

APPENDIX OF ORIGINAL DOCUMENTS

EDITED BY WILLIAM B. WILLCOX

ARCHON BOOKS, 1971

Copyright 1954 by Yale University Press
Reprinted 1971 with permission
in an unaltered and
unabridged edition

Library of Congress catalog card number: 72–150768
International Standard Book Number: 0–208–01022–X
The Shoe String Press, Inc., Hamden, Connecticut 06514

Printed in the United States of America

CONTENTS

MAPS

The end paper map and the Chorographical Map of the Province of New York are reproduced by courtesy of the Map Collection, Yale University Library, the other maps by courtesy of the Clements Library.

ACKNOWLEDGMENTS

THE PUBLICATION of Sir Henry's narrative has been financed jointly by the Yale University Press, the Yale University Department of History, and the Horace H. Rackham School of Graduate Studies of the University of Michigan; the entire editorial work has been financed by a series of grants from the Rackham School. My thanks are due also to Dr. Richard W. Hale, Jr., and Miss Josephine Corriveau for making available to me a partial transcription of the text, and to Miss Roberta Childs for work on transcription; to the staff of the New-York Historical Society for assistance in locating place names; to Professor Edward Earle for reading and criticizing the editorial introduction; to Professors Lewis Curtis and Leonard Labaree and the staff of the Yale University Press for deeply appreciated advice on preparing the manuscript for publication; and to my two successive research assistants, Messrs. Jack Upper and George Knepper, for their scholarly labors and for a companionship that enlivened what might otherwise have been a tedious task. Above all I am grateful to the various members of the Clements Library staff during the past decade, whose hospitality, patience, and helpful interest have contributed as much as the documentary riches in their charge to making the Clements the most enjoyable research center in my experience.

W. B. W.

Ann Arbor, Michigan
October 16, 1953

I. *The Man and the Manuscript*

IN THE familiar story of the War of the Revolution Sir Henry Clinton is inconspicuous. While other British commanders—Gage and the Howe brothers, Burgoyne and Cornwallis—stand out in the foreground, he remains for the most part in the background. Yet Washington is the only general on either side who held a crucial position as long: Clinton was second in command to Sir William Howe from the autumn of 1775 to the spring of 1778, and for the four years thereafter was commander in chief. For that reason alone his obscurity is puzzling, and the puzzle is deepened by his achievements. He led the British advance in the Battle of Long Island and claims (with apparent truth) to have planned that brilliant envelopment; in the autumn of 1777 he stormed the American forts on the Hudson, and in the following spring began his term as commander in chief with a dexterous and successful defensive; in 1780 he gained the one solid British triumph of the war by capturing Charleston and its garrison. This is not the record of a military nonentity.

Clinton also failed, of course, both as subordinate and as commander in chief. For the culminating disaster at Yorktown he had a large measure of responsibility, although scarcely the full measure that the British public assigned him in its need for a scapegoat. History has no such need, and its neglect of him is difficult to understand. Burgoyne and Cornwallis, who scored no such successes as he did, made lasting names for themselves by being captured. He, who was either too competent or too cautious to share their fate, has been virtually forgotten.

Forgetfulness began in his lifetime. He was recalled a few months after Yorktown, as Howe had been recalled after Saratoga, and like him tried to obtain a parliamentary inquiry. It was refused—because, he felt, Cornwallis had too much political influence—and phamphleteers began to saddle him with the whole disaster. He fought long and hard to vindicate himself, but unsuccessfully; while Cornwallis went on to win new laurels in India, Clinton was left to cool his heels in obscurity and frustration.

He spent the remaining twelve years of his life in composing the narrative that follows, which he entitled as shown in his frontispiece on p. ii. The book was written to redeem his military reputation at the cost of others, primarily Cornwallis, and its purpose determined its structure: about half of it deals with the five years from June of 1775 to June of 1780 and the remaining half, except the final chapter, with the campaigns of 1780–81, upon which his critics had concentrated. The structure is also affected by the fact that he is describing his war, not the war as a whole, and therefore glosses over campaigns in which he was not concerned. His attitude toward what he does describe is obviously biased; if he had not been convinced of his own consistent good judgment, he presumably would never have put pen to paper.

With all its shortcomings, his apologia has great historical value. Memoirs of military men in the 18th century were not the commonplace that they are today. We are accustomed to generals' and admirals' writing books to explain a war in terms of their own roles. The victorious write of their contributions to victory, the defeated of why they were powerless to avert defeat. In either case the author is more concerned with broad contours of strategy and logistics than with the details of individual actions; he consequently provides evidence that the historian must have and analyze if he is ever to get beyond details. But the leading commanders in the War of the Revolution did not publish such books. Aside from occasional, and usually polemical, narratives of particular campaigns, they left their stories to be told by those who had not experienced their difficulties, which is perhaps a reason why the war has been described far more than it has been analyzed. Clinton is the exception: he alone told his story himself. Because defeat prompted him to tell it, he tried to analyze the factors that had brought about defeat. However suspect his analysis, in the process of making it he composed a study in the problems of command—not only strategy but logistics and finance, politics and personal relations—that is unique in the literature of the war.

He died before his manuscript was ready for the printer. It remained unnoticed with his papers, an enormous aggregation of private and official documents that was kept together by his descendants. In 1925 William L. Clements purchased the collection, and in the following year deposited it in the Clements Library of the University of Michigan. The original narrative then became accessible to scholars, many of whom have since consulted parts of it. Few, however, have had occasion to read it all (two large folio volumes), and only one excerpt of a few pages has been printed; with that exception the entire manuscript has remained unpublished. Clinton, in short, has not yet succeeded in putting his case before the public, and it is high time that he should be allowed to do so.

The editing of the manuscript raises a number of questions. The most important is that of Sir Henry's reliability: to what degree is his view of events, described years after they happened, distorted by hindsight and afterthoughts? The answer lies in his papers. The bulk of the editorial work has been collating his narrative with the voluminous letters and memoranda that he wrote at the time the events occurred, and explaining where the story in one is clarified or contradicted by the story in the other. The papers, it will be seen, frequently clarify the text. But they seldom contradict it. The facts of the narrative are almost never mistaken. Its opinions are substantially unaltered; they may be expressed more lucidly than Clinton was able to do at the time, but he rarely claims to have held one for which there is not contemporary evidence. This does not mean that his opinions were necessarily sound or free from self-deception, but only that they were the same during his retirement as they had been during his command. If the test of reliability is the accurate reporting of events and views, his narrative is as reliable as the most exacting scholar could desire. The extent to which his outlook was distorted by his peculiar personality is quite another question, which will be dealt with in its place.

Some lesser editorial problems need mention. One is how to handle Sir Henry's prose, which no one could call transparent. He preferred elegant involutions to clarity; he was fond of pronouns and cavalier about their antecedents; he cared little for sentence unity and less for paragraph unity. To reproduce the manuscript unaltered would perpetuate confusion, but to rewrite it would be presumptuous. It has therefore been altered only in ways that make it more readable. Foreign words and phrases and the names of ships have been italicized (all other italics are in the original), and spelling and capitalization have been modernized throughout. Long paragraphs have been divided, and long sentences broken up wherever grammatically feasible; bracketed insertions have occasionally been made to clarify the meaning. The original chapter divisions and the analytic tables of contents have been retained, but chapter titles are an editorial addition.

The problem of the author's footnotes is discussed at the beginning of the appendix. All that needs mention here is that his notes are of two sorts, in his manuscript and on loose sheets among his papers. Of the former, a few of the shortest have been incorporated in the text; the others are either printed as Clinton's notes or, if they are excerpts from correspondence, relegated to the appendix. The loose notes, when they add anything substantial, are embodied in whole or in part in those of the editor. The bulk of the material in these editorial notes is drawn from the Clinton Papers (abbreviated throughout as CP), which are arranged chronologically in the Clements

Library. All references are to them unless otherwise indicated; to avoid redundance, the citation CP and all other superfluous details are omitted whenever they are obvious in context. Thus a note about Clinton's opinion of Captain Elphinstone in March, 1780, contains the following quotation: " 'You are so much of a soldier,' he wrote him on the 22d, 'that you know our wants and can best state them.' " The implicit reference here is Clinton to Elphinstone, Mar. 22, 1780, CP.

No discussion of Clinton's correspondence, or even of his narrative, can ignore his handwriting, which was odd at best and almost illegible at worst. The narrative was fortunately written by a secretary, and most of it is crystal clear; when Sir Henry added a phrase or sentence, it is usually in his best hand. But much of the most important material quoted from the CP is in his worst: when he was under the influence of strong emotions, he rarely bothered to sharpen his quill or to form individual letters, so that his most impassioned comments are usually his most illegible. His own secretaries could not read them; their transcriptions are studded with blanks, queries, and wrong guesses. The editor must rush in where they feared to tread. But he has the advantage over them of ten years spent with Sir Henry's peculiar turns of phrase as well as pen, and submits his readings as substantially accurate; if in some cases they are not the only possible ones, they are at least as probable as any.

The oddity of Clinton's hand is one of many signs that he was an odd person. His character, although it determined in great measure the part he played in the war, scarcely appears at all in the pages of his narrative. There he tries to be the conventional 18th-century gentleman-soldier, who is soundly trained, intelligent, and gifted with keen strategic insight; he admittedly has feelings, which are sometimes hurt, but their intensity is muffled in the cotton wool of his style. This is Sir Henry on public view, and he is concealing more of himself than he shows. Sir Henry writing to his few friends, or scribbling memoranda for his own eye, is a different person, who is incredibly repetitious, sensitive, and suspicious of everyone except— and sometimes including—himself. These are two men. One is the military rationalist, reserved and dignified; the other is torn between timidity and aggressive self-confidence as if the furies were at work on his psyche. The interaction between the two is the clue to Clinton's generalship.

The clue is complex and elusive. The official Clinton is clear enough from his own story. He pleads his case, attempting to clear himself of guilt for all his failures by laying it on others; and the editor's task is to evaluate the pleading. This can be done only in the light of evidence furnished by the private Clinton, writing off the record, because that evidence suggests, by omission as much as by statement, the personal failings that were failings in the general. The suggestion is not mere historical gossip. The fact that a man is inadequate for his job is in itself commonplace. But, when the job is commanding a major army in a war whose importance surpassed the wildest dreams of those who waged it, the man's inadequacy becomes an appreciable force in the working of destiny.

The remainder of this introduction, therefore, will be a biographical study of Sir Henry, based upon his narrative and papers: first a sketch of his background before the war; then a critical survey of his American career and the fluctuations in his generalship; lastly some conclusions about the effect of his character upon his official conduct. The conclusions will be tentative, partly because they trespass on the field of the psychologist, partly because the data contain no more than hints, and most of all because the historian cannot pretend to a definitive interpretation. Clinton's history, like history in general, resembles the detective story in the tangle of personalities, motives, and evidence, but differs from it in the absence of a clear-cut solution. The question of *how* can usually be answered. The question of *why* cannot be answered either by Sir Henry or his editor; it comes to rest at last in the lap of the reader.

II. *Preparation for Command*

Henry Clinton was born into the aristocracy. His father, Admiral George Clinton, was the younger brother of the Earl of Lincoln. The Earl had married a sister of Thomas Pelham, the first and most famous Duke of Newcastle-under-Lyme; the son of this marriage, young Henry's first cousin, likewise married a Pelham, and succeeded his father as Earl of Lincoln and his maternal uncle as Duke of Newcastle. Clinton was thus a cadet of the House of Lincoln, which traced its peerage back to Henry VII, and was within the orbit of the newer and greater dynasty of the Pelhams, so that he had the connections needed for a successful military career.

His father the Admiral abandoned the sea to become governor of New York, where he took up his duties in 1743. He had two daughters. The elder, who died in 1750, married Robert Roddam, a naval officer of some distinction; the younger, Mary, married in 1778 Sir Francis Willes, a son of the Bishop of Bath. Henry, Admiral Clinton's only son, was apparently born in 1738 (although on this point there is some doubt), and grew up in New York at a time when his father was tak-

ing a prominent part in King George's War. In 1751 the family returned to England, and ten years later the Admiral died. Although
he had supposedly been rich, his estate turned out to consist of few
assets except tracts of New York and Connecticut land, and a claim
against the government for unpaid salary; his debts, on the other hand,
amounted to £1500. His son spent almost twenty years in trying to
capitalize on the land and collect on the claim; after the Revolution the
first was confiscated, and the second was compromised for some £3700.
Henry was never well off by the standards of his class, and financial
worries harassed him throughout his career.

His connections, however, ensured him a good start. In the Seven
Years' War he served as aide-de-camp to the Prince of Brunswick, distinguished himself for gallantry, and rose to be a colonel. During the
interim between the Peace of Paris and Bunker Hill his military career
was as uneventful as that of most well born officers in peace time. In
1764 he was appointed groom of the bedchamber to the Duke of
Gloucester, the King's brother, and held this post for a number of
years; he was also in attendance on the Duke of Newcastle, who
in 1772 secured his election to Parliament. With the two Dukes for
patrons, his professional success ought to have been ensured. But in
the years to come they both failed him. An unfortunate marriage put
Gloucester out of favor at court; although Clinton wrote him assiduously from America, his letters apparently netted him nothing.
As for Newcastle, he was irascible, flighty, and far from intelligent—
unfitted by nature and inclination to carry on the Pelham tradition of
wire-pulling. He controlled so many votes in the House of Commons
that his political dabblings could not be ignored, and he probably did as
much for Clinton as a man of his stamp could do. But, when it came
to the crucial point of getting the government to accede to his cousin's
wishes, the Duke was a broken reed.

Clinton's two principal friends in the services were, like him, members of Newcastle's entourage. One was John Jervis, then a naval captain and later First Lord of the Admiralty and Earl of St. Vincent, a
name second only to Nelson's among the admirals of the Napoleonic
period. Clinton corresponded with Jervis throughout the war, and
once suggested him for command on the American station; [1] but the
Admiralty rendered the Americans the great service of keeping him
in Europe. The other friend was William Phillips, almost the only
man to whom Clinton could open his heart. Phillips was an artillery-
man, who had also served in Germany; he was reputedly fat and easy-

1. For the relationship between the two see Marie M. Hatch, ed., "Letters of
Captain Sir John Jervis to Sir Henry Clinton, 1774–1782," American Neptune, 7
(Apr., 1947), 87–106. For Clinton's suggestion see below, pp. 142–143.

going, and his military gifts were not outstanding. But he did have a
gift for friendship. The affection between the two men was mutual, and
lasted until Phillips died of fever on the Chesapeake in 1781.

In February of 1767 Clinton married Miss Harriet Carter, who came
of a well connected family. Letters from the bridegroom's friends
indicate that the match was a surprise to them, and it does not seem
to have improved his professional or financial prospects. But it
brought him the deepest attachment of his life. He was almost equally
devoted to his wife's family: Mr. Carter, as long as he lived, was a
second father to him; Elizabeth Carter, his sister-in-law, became closer
than most sisters, brought up his children during his absence in America, and was still living with them when he died. He had five children: two daughters, Augusta and Harriet; two sons, William Henry
(doubtless named after the Duke of Gloucester) and Henry, both of
whom grew up to be generals; and a third son, Frederick, who presumably died in childhood.[2] Five pregnancies in five years may have
been too much for Mrs. Clinton. She died in August, 1772, eight days
after Harriet's birth.

At this blow Clinton, in the eyes of his friends, virtually went out of
his mind. He ignored his business affairs; he neglected to take the
seat in Parliament to which he had just been elected; he shunned
Newcastle's ménage to the point of offending the Duke. He apparently
reproached himself so bitterly, for reasons unknown, that he could
not maintain even a semblance of the stoicism that society expected,
or reorganize his life unaided. "I will endeavor . . . to assist you in the
pursuit of *some* system," Phillips wrote him almost four months after
his wife's death. "What will be best cannot be ascertained but by a
serious, or rather many serious, conversations. But it is absolutely
[necessary] for you to fix on a system, or your life will pass in continual
anxiety and endless suffering." [3] His life improved, and its surface was
never again shattered by disaster. But the episode suggests strong
forces working under the surface.

In the spring of 1774 Clinton set out on a trip to the Balkans. His
ostensible purpose was to examine the Russian army assembled there
for Catherine the Great's war against the Turks; another reason, conscious or unconscious, may have been the desire to escape from a clut-
ter of unpleasant memories. In any case he left in company with a
Welsh general in the Russian service and two young English noble-

2. The only extant reference to Frederick seems to be in a letter from Jervis to
Clinton, June 28, 1774.

3. Phillips to Clinton, Dec. 18; see also P[hillips] to Clinton, undated and filed at
the end of 1772. The only evidence about Clinton's state of mind is in these two letters, and it is tantalizingly incomplete.

men, one a son of Newcastle. They traveled overland to the Danube, where Clinton bought a canoe and went ahead of the rest, reveling alone in the beauty around him—"woods all in bloom, all sorts of birds in high song, nightingales in every bush, a most enchanting scene." In Vienna the travelers were entertained for weeks and received by the Emperor. Eventually they reached Moldavia, but saw no action; the Treaty of Küchük Kainarja was signed in July. They presumably observed the Russian army, however, for Clinton later wished to see Russian instead of Hessian mercenaries sent to America.[4] The trip may have broadened his horizon, and certainly increased his fund of military anecdotes, of which he was a collector; but otherwise it achieved little except distraction.

By the time he returned, the government was making plans for coercing Massachusetts. Clinton, who by now had been promoted to major general, was ordered to service in America.[5] Soon afterward he sailed for Boston in the frigate Cerberus. He was on the threshold of his real career. The professional connections that he had made were good, his family connections were better, and his military judgment was ripe enough to justify the confidence that he had in it. The auguries for success appeared excellent.

But he was also on the threshold of middle age. He had never held an independent command, and had not seen active service for more than a decade, during which his military life had been largely unmilitary. He had shown signs, furthermore, of a characteristic that might confound the best of professional auguries: an aloofness, particularly under strain, that insulated him from his fellows and made the give and take of collaboration singularly difficult.

III. From Bunker Hill to Sullivan's Island, 1775–76

With Clinton on the Cerberus were two generals with whom his career was to be closely linked, John Burgoyne and William Howe. Their rank was the same as his; Burgoyne was his senior in age but his junior in the army, Howe his senior in both. The voyage threw them

4. "We must be reinforced, not with Germans (I fear they will desert), [but with] . . . my friends the Russians. They have no language but their own; they cannot desert." (Clinton to Edward Harvey, Adjutant General of the British army, [summer, 1775,] "Memoranda" [for which see below, p. 24 n. 11], fol. 9.) The quotation earlier in the paragraph is from Clinton's day-to-day account of his trip in ibid., fols. 82–87. The account breaks off in Hungary, but later references in the CP show that Clinton reached Moldavia. The year of the trip appears from internal evidence and from Jervis to Clinton, Apr. 4, 1774.

5. Viscount Barrington to Clinton, Feb. 3. Clinton subsequently emphasized the point that he had not volunteered but had been ordered to service.

into close contact, but Clinton left friendly overtures to his ship-mates. "At first (for you know I am a shy bitch) I kept my distance, [and] seldom spoke till my two colleagues forced me out." [6] The parenthesis is revealing, especially in conjunction with a later con-fession that his diffidence "gave an appearance against me some-times." [7] He was conscious of his shyness, in other words, and of its disadvantages.

Soon after landing he showed another side of his character. The discovery that the British were besieged in Boston led him to recon-noiter; he promptly worked out a plan for seizing Dorchester Heights, presented it to his commander in chief General Gage, and pressed it on him with more enthusiasm than tact. Gage did not adopt it. Clin-ton had his first indication, but not his last, that a superior officer might prefer muddling through on his own to accepting even the best ideas of a subordinate. A wholly diffident man would doubtless have absorbed this lesson and learned to keep his own counsel. But the "shy bitch" was also aggressive, in planning and conduct; and his com-bination of diffidence and self-assertion was a trial to his colleagues and himself.

The combination came out in the Battle of Bunker Hill. Clinton disobeyed the letter of his instructions in order to take part in the ac-tion; he was of great assistance to Howe, the field commander, and his gallantry was warmly praised. But for months afterward he worried that he might be taken to task for disobedience. Both his courage and his worry are typical: he could defy orders, but could not really believe that success would justify defiance; when he acted boldly, therefore, he paid a price in fear of consequences. Audacity is a gam-ble. If an officer worries about the results to himself of winning as well as losing the gamble, he is unlikely to be often audacious.

In the autumn of 1775, when Gage was recalled, Howe became commander in chief and Clinton his second in command. Immediately signs began to appear of the trouble that soon became endemic at British headquarters—friction between the commander and his princi-pal subordinate. This friction developed steadily during the two and a half years that Howe and Clinton were together; it developed much further after Clinton had taken Howe's place and Cornwallis had taken Clinton's, until by 1781 it was paralyzing British strategy. The cause of trouble was not merely personal; to a large extent it lay in the nature of the situation. Throughout the war the second in command

6. Clinton to unknown, June 13, [1775].
7. Clinton's memorandum of his conversation with Sir William Howe, July 8, [1777].

used great latitude in advising his chief. The latter probably could not have accepted the advice often without derogating from his position; in any case he commonly rejected it for a plan of his own. His subordinate had equal latitude in criticizing this plan, and no responsibility for its success. Quite the contrary: its resounding failure would tend not only to vindicate his own views, but to advance his fortunes. For he was the obvious successor, and the succession would be open as soon as his chief made one egregious misstep. This situation was calculated to breed mistrust between any two commanders, and only men of real stature could keep their relationship from being poisoned by it. Such stature Clinton did not have, but his shortcomings merely accentuated difficulties that were inherent in the system.

He and Howe were soon at odds. They could never agree on any professional question, as they later admitted to each other. Clinton thought the reason might be that they had had different military backgrounds: his had been the German phase of the Seven Years' War, Howe's the American.[8] A more likely reason is that Clinton was at once so touchy and so insistent on his opinions that even his chief's good temper was ruffled. "[He] esteems me [as] being [a] good officer, known [to be] zealous; but perhaps [I] speak too freely. In general [I] *have a right* [as] second in command." [9] He may have had the right, but he certainly did not have the tact that makes free speaking effective. Howe, perhaps in the interests of tranquillity, first removed him to command of the outpost at Charlestown, then detached him on an expedition that he had been ordered to send to the south.

Clinton welcomed the escape that the expedition offered. He had already concluded that he could not win Howe to his ideas, and would have to submit passively; "while I have the mortification of being under his command, [I] will do my utmost to fulfil his wishes and intentions." [10] The expedition would at least temporarily free him from this mortification. At the last moment, however, he was only half convinced that he wanted freedom. He argued with his chief that his instructions were not sufficiently precise, and expressed fear that the King might not have authorized open war against the southern provinces by declaring them in rebellion; to friends he complained that Howe was uncooperative, the force assigned him insufficient, and the government's design full of pitfalls. He even confessed that his desire for an independent command was extremely impertinent, because he

8. Clinton's memorandum of Clinton-Howe conversation, July 6, 1777.
9. Clinton to Phillips, Dec. 12, [1775,] "Memoranda," fol. 22. This entry, like others in the volume, is jottings for a letter that has not survived.
10. Clinton to Harvey, [Dec. or Jan., 1775/76,] *ibid.*, fol. 27v.

had never before had one. "This business I feel [the] weight of. [It] does not crush me, but [it is] rather too much merely to steady me." [11]

In early January, 1776, he sailed from Boston with a small force, expecting to make a prompt rendezvous on the Cape Fear River with a larger force, military and naval, coming from England. The purpose was not to conquer, but to make a demonstration in the south that would evoke strong loyalist support; the government had already reached the conclusion, to which it held throughout the war, that such support would germinate magically wherever the King's troops appeared, and would soon grow into a force sufficient to be self-sustaining without their aid. The site of the demonstration was not stipulated; Howe suggested Charleston, but the choice was left to Clinton and the naval commander from England, Commodore Sir Peter Parker. In any case the expedition was expected to finish its work by summer, establish a post for the loyalists to hold, and return northward to join in the projected attack on New York.

Clinton conferred en route with the Governor of Virginia, and at the Cape Fear he met the Governors of North and South Carolina. Their reports and his own observations convinced him that the southern loyalists would never rise in sufficient numbers to maintain themselves, but would need continuing protection; either the regulars would remain to provide it, or, by retiring, they would betray Britain's friends to the vengeance of the rebels. This conclusion, which was squarely at odds with that reached in London, meant that a short-lived demonstration in the south would be worse than useless. Before the expedition was assembled, in other words, Clinton had lost faith in its underlying premise.

He was consequently disinclined to attack Charleston, which if conquered would require a large garrison. He looked instead toward the Chesapeake, primarily for geographic reasons. The area bounded by the bay, the sea, and the Dismal Swamp was a strategic island, where a small, permanent garrison of regulars could maintain an asylum for the loyalists of the region, and could blockade the rebels' commerce and attack their land communications between New England and the south. This prospect, it seems, was what excited Clinton to uncharacteristic optimism. He envisaged such success that the government would promote him to an independent command: the theater of war was growing too large for unitary control, and who, after all, was better qualified for independence? "I believe I know better than any single person in this continent what

11. Clinton to Phillips, [Jan., 1776,] *ibid.*, fol. 30v; see also Clinton to Burgoyne, Jan. 20, and to Harvey, [Dec. or Jan., 1775/76,] *ibid.*, fols. 25v–26v, 27–28, 29v.

military plans should be followed in it. If I do not, I ought—I have seen all, conversed [?] with all, and had opportunities that no other could have had." [12] These were bold words. They did not, however, spring from solid confidence, and his conduct soon belied them.

When the reinforcements arrived, weeks after they had been expected, Clinton found that his new colleague Sir Peter Parker was much more interested in South Carolina than in the Chesapeake. The Commodore soon suggested seizing Sullivan's Island, at the entrance to Charleston harbor. Clinton surrendered his own scheme, apparently without protest, and fell in with this idea. Such docility was unusual. It may have been due to unsureness, but it could scarcely have been due to the force of Parker's logic. For logic, at this point, virtually disappeared from the campaign.

On the government's premise about the loyalists, an argument could have been made for capturing and holding Charleston. But Clinton did not expect to capture it, except in the unlikely event that resistance was negligible; he hoped merely to occupy the island as a base for future operations. This hope was fantastic. He could spare only a small garrison, and its nearest supplies would be in the West Indies; if it were not captured and did not starve, what conceivable purpose could it serve? Future operations in the area were hypothetical; the island was an unlikely rallying point for loyalists, had little strategic value, was remote from the main theater of war, and was in every way inferior to the Chesapeake position. If Clinton had had the courage of his earlier convictions, he would never have sailed southward from Cape Fear.

Once he had done so, he and Parker piled error on error. Their first was in attacking the island instead of Charleston, whose inhabitants, when the fleet arrived off the bar on June 1, were panicky, short of ammunition, and without confidence in their leaders; the British might have run past the two weak forts that guarded the harbor, and either stormed or surrounded the town.[13] Their second error was in trying to seize the island by a leisurely *coup de main*, which is a contradiction in terms. They spent weeks outside the harbor, discussing and reconnoitering, while General Lee arrived with American reinforcements and began to organize the defense. The moment for attack had passed long before the attack was made.

The third error was Clinton's alone. He eventually disembarked

12. Clinton to unknown, [Mar. or Apr., 1776,] *ibid.*, fol. 57.
13. This argument, which all the evidence seems to corroborate, was advanced by an anonymous eyewitness of the attack; see Frances R. Kepner, ed., "A British View of the Siege of Charleston, 1776," *Journal of Southern History, 11* (Feb., 1945), 93–103.

his troops on an island adjacent to Sullivan's, without discovering (as he might have done by any reconnaissance worth the name) that the intervening channel was too deep for them to ford, and without enough boats to ferry them across. For another fortnight they remained inactive and useless, until Parker suddenly lost patience and—with no clear idea of whether they could support him—attacked the fort. The army looked on while the navy was repulsed with heavy losses. One service was now disheartened by inaction, the other by action; the campaign was abandoned. Britain had worse defeats in the course of the war, but no more egregious fiasco.

Clinton's generalship was at its worst. Once he gave in to Parker's enthusiasm for a move against Sullivan's Island, his initiative virtually disappeared. Instead of settling on an objective and formulating a coherent plan for reaching it, he drifted halfheartedly from one scheme to another, while his mood oscillated between confidence and foreboding. His sense of urgency, never his strongest point, grew as weak as the Commodore's; he wasted time before and after the landing, waited on developments that did not develop, evolved an implausible design for turning the American position by way of the mainland, and finally did nothing at all. Parker was equally dilatory, and his action, when it came, was ill advised. But at least he acted.

Clinton was obsessed by the need for avoiding a repulse. He realized that war depends as much upon psychological as military factors, and that even a minor reverse might have disproportionate effects. So far, so good. But he saw only half the truth. If the danger was real, so was the opportunity; he stared so hard at one that he did not notice the other. In this early phase of the war American morale was as unreliable as American militia, and a handful of regulars, used with decision and daring, might have achieved a triumph that flouted all the rules. Instead, fearing failure, Clinton hoarded his strength and wasted it, so as to produce just the psychological setback that he had feared. His caution was self-defeating, but he did not learn the lesson and change his ways. Whenever he was in independent command during the rest of the war he followed, as far as he could, the policy of minimum risk —which in the long run is the riskiest policy of all.

The blame for the southern debacle was not entirely his. The government had assigned him a vague and difficult task, and the difficulty was increased by circumstances beyond his control. He was unsure how much latitude he had; loyalist support had been weakened, before he arrived, by the suppression of several premature risings; his available time was limited at one end by the late arrival of the troops from England, at the other by the necessity of returning to New York. Last but not least, he had his first experience of sharing command with a naval officer. The campaign depended on his and Parker's ability to plan together, and it failed primarily because they failed to do so.

The Commodore was patient and polite. But the English language was an even more unsatisfactory medium for him than for Clinton, and gave him particular difficulty when he had to communicate by letter or messenger—which was most of the time, because the two commanders rarely met face to face. Their understanding of each other diminished until no teamwork was left. When Parker decided that honor required bold action, he apparently took it without forewarning his colleague or giving much thought to his position, and must consequently share the blame with him for reducing the troops to helpless spectators.

This breakdown of cooperation with the navy recurred time and again throughout Clinton's career. Like the friction in the army command, the cause lay as much in the nature of the system as in personalities. If one commander in chief had trouble in collaborating with his subordinate, two commanders in chief had even more in collaborating with each other, essentially because they were two. Combined operations, which constituted the bulk of the British effort in America, are jeopardized in any war by a divided command. The ranking naval officer has had a different training from that of his army colleague, and is consequently unlike him in the bent of his tactical and even strategic thinking, in his service loyalties, and in the superiors upon whose favor he depends and whose prejudices he must respect. No matter how agreeable two such commanders may be, their professional background and position fix a gulf between them. To give them equal authority, and expect them to cooperate like the right and left hand, is to expect a continuous miracle. This is substantially what the British government expected. The difficulties that resulted at Sullivan's Island were only a faint foretaste of those to come.

Clinton's reaction to his fiasco was typical; he acquired a grievance. To be more accurate, he acquired two simultaneously: one against Lord George Germain, the new Secretary of State for the Colonies, who he felt had distorted his report of the campaign when editing it for publication; the other against the Commodore for implications in his published account. The grounds for resentment are less significant than the resentment. In retrospect Clinton had misgivings about his part in the expedition, but at the time his impulse was to avoid self-reproach by reproaching others. This escape into accusation, repeated over the years, made him a colleague who would have tried the patience of a saint. And the British armed services were not staffed with saints.

IV. *Second Fiddle to Howe and Burgoyne, 1776–77*

Clinton rejoined the main army in time for the campaigns around New York. Failure had not taught him humility: he bombarded headquarters with suggestions for the maneuvers on Long Island, for seizing Manhattan, for the movement that fizzled out at White Plains, and for the pursuit of Washington across New Jersey. Some of the suggestions were accepted in part; most were rejected. In the text he puts them all in the best light, and gives no hint that Howe may have had valid reasons for not embracing them. But they remain, after allowance is made for a creator's bias, remarkably interesting plans, both for themselves and for the light they throw on Clinton's capacity.

During the voyage from Sullivan's to Staten Island some curious alchemy seems to have transformed his generalship. Instead of slipshod thinking and dilatory execution, he now had the will to conquer and a precise idea of how to do it. His purpose in all his plans was not to seize territory but to destroy Washington's army; his method was a flanking movement to surround the enemy. In the Battle of Long Island he urged a double envelopment, and Howe for once accepted it. If it had been pressed home, it would presumably have annihilated the enemy; even executed as it was, it produced as great a tactical triumph as any in the war. Clinton next urged seizing Kings Bridge, to bottle up the Americans on Manhattan; instead Howe maneuvered them into a strong position on the Harlem. During their subsequent retreat across New Jersey Clinton made three proposals for getting ahead of them: first, that the main army sail to the Delaware while he marched on Philadelphia from the Chesapeake; second, that he land on the Jersey coast, engage the south wing of the enemy, and hold it until the overland pursuit from the Hudson caught up; third, that he land in the Delaware to seize Philadelphia. Any one of these maneuvers might, as he suggests, have proved decisive. Each amounted to strategic envelopment, which was certainly more promising than the direct and uninspired advance that took place.

Howe's behavior during this campaign is a mystery, which the narrative highlights but does not explain. Whether he was reluctant to win, grossly overconfident, or merely inept, he missed golden opportunities to end the war on Long Island, on Manhattan, and in New Jersey. On each occasion he preferred the occupation of territory to the method Clinton suggested for destroying the American army; on each occasion Washington slipped through his fingers, and nothing was settled. Whether Clinton would have done better if he had been in command may be questioned, on the ground that his reluctance to take bold action increased in proportion to his responsibility for the consequences. But his proposed envelopments did not require boldness so much as common sense. If he had had the superb chances to apply his favorite maneuver that Howe had that autumn, Washington's army might well have disintegrated.

Some of the staff apparently admired Clinton's plans, but Howe did not. He seems to have had occasional difficulty in getting his subordinate to comply with orders, and to have decided to get rid of him by the method he had used the year before. Clinton was detached on a mission (of which he thoroughly disapproved) to seize Rhode Island as a naval base. Before leaving he presented his chief with a final bit of advice, not to maintain an extended chain of winter cantonments in New Jersey. Howe paid no attention, and the ensuing disaster at Trenton could scarcely have deepened his affection for the man who had warned him.

Clinton occupied Rhode Island in a tidy operation, and then asked and was given leave to go home. He did not intend to come back. He was still angry with Germain and Parker, and now he was at outs with Howe; his solution was to quit the army. "If I cannot serve with them I like," he had written a year earlier, "I had rather not serve at all." [14] Such an attitude in a general on active service was less extraordinary than it seems today, but even by the standards of the time he carried it to extremes. For the next four years he tried periodically to resign, and one of his reasons was usually that he disliked the men he served with. He wanted to play a lone hand in a game that required partners; rather than meet the requirement he preferred to give up the game.

His reception in England was most cordial. In the spring of 1777 great plans were in the making, and officers competent to execute them were scarce; his success at Rhode Island, furthermore, had wiped out the memory of his earlier failure. Germain received him with open arms and soothed him with a knighthood. His name was suggested for command of the army that was to invade New York from Canada, an appointment that would have meant independence with a vengeance. He does not seem to have lifted a finger to get this plum, which went instead to Burgoyne. Until the following July he imagined that he might still have it for the asking as soon as Burgoyne came within reach of New York; when he discovered that Howe thought differently, he at once acquired another grievance—that Burgoyne, his junior, had been promoted over his head. For not grasping at the chance when offered

14. Clinton to Harvey, [Dec. or Jan., 1775/76,] "Memoranda," fol. 28.

in London he had only himself to blame, and that was the one person he could not blame; instead he concocted a slight put upon him by the government. This devious working of his vanity predisposed him from the start against Burgoyne's ill-starred expedition.

The government had no intention of slighting him. He was offered, as an alternative to the northern army, the command in chief in Canada; this he declined because he would have nothing to do with displacing the incumbent, Sir Guy Carleton. The King, Germain, and his friends then pressed him to return as Howe's second in command. He yielded, apparently because he was persuaded that it was the only honorable course; in matters of honor he leaned on his friends' opinions like crutches. But he went reluctantly, and the hope of resigning stayed with him.

His arrival in America brought him a rude shock. How much he had been consulted by the government about the impending operations is not clear—apparently not enough to foresee (if, indeed, anyone in London foresaw) their precise design, but enough to realize that they were expected to end the war; he knew that they included an attack on Philadelphia, which he had told Germain ought to end, not open, the campaign. When he landed at New York on July 5, he discovered two things: first, that the main army had not budged, although the campaigning months were far advanced; second, that it was about to go by sea to Pennsylvania while he remained as garrison commander of Manhattan. Howe and Burgoyne were to have their chances of winning fame in the field; he was to be relegated to what he called "a damned starved defensive," which would be at best inglorious and at worst disastrous.

Personal disappointment was only part of his shock. The campaign that was opening was strategic stupidity, as he recognized at once. Pennsylvania in summer was unhealthful and a trap; holding it would immobilize the entire field army, while Washington would be free to move, if he chose, either against New York or Burgoyne. Howe could succeed in his plan only at the cost of penning up his army in a cul-de-sac and of imperiling the two other British armies, which were separated from each other and from him. Nor was this the worst of it. Although in July Clinton, like Howe, never dreamed that the northern army might be advancing toward serious trouble, he knew, as Howe did not, that the government expected the campaign to be decisive. It could not be, he was convinced, unless the main army cooperated with Burgoyne. The key to cooperation was the Hudson, and the key to the Hudson was the American forts in the Highlands. A move against them from New York was the first prerequisite, and it would require Howe's entire force; the attack on Philadelphia would therefore have to be postponed until the end of the campaign. This was substantially Clinton's argument, as it can be reconstructed from his narrative and from his notes at the time. It was based, like his plans of the previous autumn, not on brilliance but on sense.

The question at issue that July was not whether to support Burgoyne, as has sometimes been assumed, but how to win the war. No one, least of all Gentleman Johnny himself, expected serious difficulty in the north. Even if it had been expected, the prospect of forcing Washington to a decision in Pennsylvania might have outweighed the risk. But Howe had no such prospect, and he knew it. This was the crux of his blunder. His plan patently would not impale Washington on the horns of a dilemma, and force him to choose between losing an area that was vital to him and risking everything on a battle to defend it; the plan consequently could not win the war in one campaign. Clinton's plan of an advance up the Hudson, on the other hand, to make contact with Burgoyne and threaten the crucial American communications with New England, promised to create just that dilemma, and so to make a decision possible. Once more, as in the previous autumn, Howe was intent upon a territorial objective, while Clinton was aiming at the destruction of the enemy.

For three weeks Sir Henry tried to persuade his chief. At moments Howe seemed to waver, particularly when he learned that the government expected this campaign to be the last; but the wavering may have been in Clinton's imagination. Sir William had submitted his plan, London had approved it, and he was not the man to change it on the spur of the moment—especially when the spur was personified by a subordinate who had roweled him for a year and more. Clinton's records of their interviews show that they were both under great strain; their disagreement on immediate strategy brought into the open every past disagreement. They discussed their relationship with the humorless candor of adolescents, raking over every annoyance, misunderstanding, and grievance, and concluded that they simply were not made to collaborate. "By some cursed fatality we could never draw together." [15] The fatality was a godsend to the American cause. At that juncture no one, perhaps, could have diverted Howe to the Hudson. But the one man who tried was the one least likely to succeed, and his failure deprived Britain of her last great opportunity to win the war.

In the denouement of the Saratoga campaign Sir Henry played a slight but controversial part. His primary obligation was the defense of New York, for which he feared that his force was inadequate; he was

15. Clinton's memorandum of Clinton-Howe conversation, July 6, 1777.

perhaps right as long as Washington was free to move against him, but the fear persisted long after the danger had passed—the first sign of what later became almost an obsession for the safety of his base. After he had become anxious about Burgoyne, he delayed moving up the Hudson toward him until reinforcements arrived from England. The moment they did, he moved with energy and skill; his capture of the forts in the Highlands, if it could be considered as an isolated operation, was as neat a *coup de main* as the war produced. It was not isolated, but part of a campaign; and as such it came too late to be effective.

After it he was feeling his way, as the text makes clear, in a strategic fog. He did not know Burgoyne's full peril or the whereabouts of Washington, and feared that a precipitate move would expose New York. He sent a small reconnaissance expedition up river, and prepared methodically to follow as soon as he had established his communications. At that point Howe, who knew as much as he did of Burgoyne's plight, sent a demand for reinforcements that stopped the advance, and soon afterward ordered the forts abandoned. By then Burgoyne had surrendered, and the British had paid their exorbitant price for the conquest of Philadelphia.

Could Clinton have prevented the surrender? Modern historians have criticized him for not pushing on immediately after the capture of the forts.[16] But at that late date the chance of his doing anything effective would have been negligible; a more cogent charge is that he might have been in the Highlands sooner. He has an answer: the move would not have been justifiable until the reinforcements arrived, and could not have succeeded before the bulk of the American forces was withdrawn. Perhaps. But the conclusion is hard to escape that a more farsighted commander would have realized that disaster threatened Burgoyne, outweighing any danger to New York, and that a rescue force might even be sacrificed if it permitted him to escape; or that a hard-driving commander, ridden by his sense of urgency, might have scraped together the force for opening the Highlands by mid-September and then, trusting to the navy for his needs, pushed on regardless of rule-book logistics. Sir Henry was not such a commander.

When the situation called in reality for improvisation, he remained the general of regular approaches. The Saratoga campaign involved him in his first large-scale crisis, and he met it with almost pedestrian de-

16. Sydney G. Fisher, *The Struggle for American Independence* (2 vols., Philadelphia and London, 1908), 2, 101–102; Willard M. Wallace, *Appeal to Arms: A Military History of the American Revolution* (New York, 1951), p. 164.

liberation. For this there were, it is true, particular reasons. He was correct in insisting that he was not responsible for the troubles of the northern army, and neither Howe nor Burgoyne had expected him to assist it. He was annoyed with both men, and annoyance may have heightened his sense of irresponsibility. In any case, although he convinced himself afterward that he had taken a desperate gamble at the first possible moment, and had succeeded beyond his fondest hopes, his notes and letters at the time indicate that he looked on Burgoyne's "scrape" with the eyes of a concerned but half-complacent spectator. He certainly had no inkling of what was at stake in the north, or that it might call for anything more than deliberation.

This kind of shortsightedness was routine in 18th-century warfare. If Clinton's thinking was as firmly tied to orthodox calculation as his army to supply lines, the same was true of most professional generals of his day. A garrison commander was not expected to see the war as a whole, or risk everything on his own initiative to redeem a colleague's blunders, but to act as effectively and promptly as possible. The accepted standards of the possible were unexacting, and Sir Henry more than satisfied them. He struck, when ready, with precision and power; he achieved a brilliant local success, which accorded with the proprieties of making war and for which he was acclaimed. Neither he nor his contemporaries paused to consider why his local success was part of a far-reaching strategic failure.

V. *Commander in Chief: The Northern Campaigns, 1778–79*

After Saratoga the British public craved a successful commander. Howe, although he was ensconced in Philadelphia, was held responsible for the campaign that had lost an army. Burgoyne was a prisoner. Cornwallis' reputation was still clouded by the memory of Trenton, Carleton's by the memory of his unsuccessful invasion of New York. Only Clinton was left. He had redeemed Sullivan's Island at Newport, and had won the most spectacular victory of the recent campaign. His star consequently rose as his chief's declined. The effect on him was interesting: when the prospect of succeeding to the command became a likelihood, his timidity got the better of his ambition. He again tried and failed to resign; he then assured his friends that he would prefer even detached service in Florida to the command in chief. Appointing a man against his will made Lord North understandably dubious, but he had little choice. Clinton had none; in April he received orders to go to Philadelphia and take over from Howe.

He could scarcely have assumed the reins at a more disheartening moment. In March the intervention of France had transformed the whole character of the war, and the cabinet had embarked on a combined political and military retreat. The Carlisle Commission was sent to America to negotiate almost any settlement short of independence; Clinton was ordered to evacuate Philadelphia and authorized, if he saw fit, to give up New York and Rhode Island and fall back on Canada. He was commanded to display weakness, in other words, at a moment when the only hope of political settlement depended upon displaying strength.[17]

He dared not disobey the tenor of his instructions; but he was emboldened, perhaps by annoyance, to alter important details. At the risk of disrupting the government's strategy he kept with him until late autumn a large force that he had been ordered to detach at once to the West Indies; he evacuated Philadelphia not by sea, as commanded, but overland through New Jersey. On the march he was encumbered by an enormous baggage train; the heat was broiling, and the Americans were in close pursuit. As soon as they came within range, near Monmouth Court House, he attacked them. The battle— the only one worth the name in which he ever commanded—was indecisive, but it permitted him to finish his retreat unmolested.

He had no more than reached New York before a new storm gathered. A French squadron under Comte d'Estaing appeared off the town, and seemed about to join Washington in attacking it. Clinton for once had a naval colleague who knew his business and liked to fight: Lord Howe (who had not yet followed his brother home) was thoroughly outnumbered and thoroughly unperturbed; he had confidence in his ships, his men, and himself. D'Estaing observed his preparations, and then sailed off to attack the British post on Rhode Island. When Howe and Clinton moved to its relief, a storm supervened and drove the fleets to sea. The French had had enough. Their first attempt to help their American allies ended in rounds of mutual recrimination.

The Clinton of this campaign seems to have been again transformed. He was not the Clinton who had dreaded promotion a few months earlier; once responsibility was forced on him, he took it and used it to the full. He refused to detach the troops ordered to the West Indies; he refused to send the army by sea from Philadelphia. After conducting a skillful retreat through New Jersey, he turned on his pursuers at the first opportunity; the battle that followed, although it did not fulfill his hopes, showed that he was more aggressive than the supine strategy imposed upon him from London. During the subsequent crisis at New

17. See William B. Willcox, "British Strategy in America, 1778," *Journal of Modern History*, 19 (June, 1947), 105–110.

York he was confident and energetic, and for once he achieved real teamwork. He was never intimate with Lord Howe. But their correspondence in those weeks shows that they respected and understood each other as Clinton and Sir William never had, and worked together hand in glove.

Why was the best of Sir Henry uppermost? One reason may have been that he was stimulated, for all his irksome instructions, by the novelty and independence of command. A more likely reason is that a series of defensive problems kept him too busy for introspection. When he was called upon to take the initiative, as he had been in the previous autumn, his timidity came out in worries about the weakness of his force and the risks he might run. In this campaign the initiative lay primarily with the enemy and secondarily with the Royal Navy. Clinton was forced to meet each successive enemy threat with the means available, and he had rare good fortune in the naval command. He was never able to infuse energy into a lethargic admiral, and often dissipated his own in the attempt; but Lord Howe had energy to spare, and a confidence that may have been contagious. In any case Clinton never showed to better advantage than in these weeks of defensive collaboration with him.

D'Estaing's withdrawal began a long strategic hiatus. For almost a year neither Washington nor Clinton made any move of consequence. Sir Henry planned great things for the moment when his promised reinforcements arrived for the campaign of 1779. They did not come in time, and consequently his plan never materialized. But it is worth examining, because it is one of the clearest proofs that his strategy, although orthodox, was also competent. Its purpose was simple: to bring Washington to the choice with which he might have been confronted two years earlier, of abandoning the line of the Hudson or fighting a decisive battle under disadvantageous terms. Its method was complex: Sir Henry dared not risk battle until he was reinforced, and the part of the campaign that he carried out was a series of minor maneuvers to draw the enemy into position for the climactic battle. First he sent a raid into Virginia to destroy supplies and distract attention; next he seized Stony and Verplanck's Points, which commanded the main route across the Hudson below the Highlands. Washington reacted by occupying West Point in force. Once established there he was dependent, Sir Henry believed, on his supply depots at Trenton and Easton; if the British moved either against them or directly against the Point, he would have to fight or abandon the Highlands. The campaign, in short, had reached its scheduled climax.

There it stopped, for lack of reinforcements. Clinton could do little more than mark time. He ordered a raid on the Connecticut coast, hoping that Washington would move to the rescue and be open to attack if the troops arrived. Instead came a requisition from Canada for 2000 men, and news from London that a French fleet was again expected on the coast. Sir Henry thereupon threw in the sponge. He felt that his campaign had been soundly designed and had failed through no fault of his own, and for this opinion he had some basis. His series of related moves to draw the enemy off balance, typical of 18th-century warfare, was articulated with a skill that deserved a better fate.

The upshot was a wasted season, which Britain could ill afford. Clinton may have been unwise in devoting it to a campaign that hinged on the arrival of reinforcements, but to what better use could he have put his army? He felt that it was too weak to engage in major land operations without risking counterattack, and two American successes against his outposts support his point. He might have concentrated upon raids planned solely for devastation, rather than as parts of a larger scheme, and in that case would have accomplished far more than he did in Virginia and Connecticut; but this was a policy that he abhorred, and it would have sacrificed the hope of decisive victory to the long gamble of attrition. He might have launched an offensive in South Carolina. This idea, which had been in the wind since the fiasco of 1776, had been envisaged in Germain's initial instructions to him as commander in chief; and the recent British successes in Georgia had paved the way. He did play with the idea of joining troops from the West Indies for an attack on Charleston. But he was not confident of holding the town, and his old fear of betraying the loyalists seems to have led him to postpone the move until he had been reinforced from Britain and had made a final effort to settle scores with Washington. The decision was reasonable, even though it resulted in squandering precious time.

The reinforcements finally arrived in August, when the season for an offensive in South Carolina was opening; but naval developments kept them cooped up in New York. First d'Estaing appeared in the West Indies, ending hope of reinforcement from there. Then he set out for North America, and the British busily prepared to defend New York and Halifax. Instead he besieged Savannah, and was repulsed. But he forced Clinton and his new naval colleague Admiral Arbuthnot to defend themselves against a danger that did not materialize, and hence to postpone their southern move. The strategic pause was thereby prolonged until the end of the year. Clinton managed not to blame himself, but he realized that others were blaming him. Morale was low on Manhattan, and he was the focus of grievances that were in turn a grievance to him; he hoped to be quit of the whole business. "I am by no means the fashion here with civil or military. . . . My successor, if I am permitted to resign the command, will start fair with both." [18]

He was referring to Cornwallis. The Earl and Admiral Arbuthnot, the two men with whom he was most closely associated and most disastrously at odds for the next two years, arrived a month apart in the summer of 1779. Cornwallis, who had been at home on leave, rejoined the army as second in command, with the usual dormant commission to succeed if his chief were incapacitated. Clinton immediately asked the King's permission to resign in his favor, but did not receive an answer until the following spring. Throughout the planning and execution of the attack on Charleston, consequently, the two men were in an anomalous relationship. Sir Henry felt, doubtless with reason, that he was less popular than Cornwallis, not only on Manhattan but with the army at large and with Admiral Arbuthnot. This feeling may have increased his reserve; in any case Cornwallis sought more congenial companions, and his search looked to his chief like intriguing for popularity. The gulf between the two widened rapidly.

Vice Admiral Marriot Arbuthnot also brought with him seeds of trouble. Why this aging and undistinguished officer was selected to command on the American station is one of the enigmas of Admiralty politics. Even if the station was considered subsidiary, the crisis of 1778 had shown the need for resource and resolution in its chief. Arbuthnot's long career had not demonstrated either quality, and in fact he had neither. At one moment he was stubborn, at the next vacillating; he was sometimes ebulliently overconfident, sometimes plunged in gloom, and always slow to take responsibility and quick to take alarm. His tactics were uninspired, if dogged, and his strategic ideas often ludicrous. Anyone who knew him ought to have realized his unfitness for a critical spot at a critical time.

The appointment was also a direct rebuff to Clinton. He had pointed out to Germain the need for close harmony between the two commanders in chief, and had begged that he might either resign or have a cooperative colleague; he had even named five flag officers, with any one of whom he would gladly serve. This nomination of a slate was presumptuous, but Lord Sandwich at the Admiralty should have been more concerned with facts than etiquette. Clinton's character was reasonably well known in Whitehall, and the government would have been well advised either to get rid of him or to satisfy him. He might have been replaced by a general with more gift for collaboration; he might

18. Clinton [to Adm. Keppel?], Nov. 10.

have been sent an admiral who was, if not one of the five suggested, at least a man of tact and equanimity. Instead he was refused permission to resign, and was sent a colleague whose talents were mediocre, and whose irritability was as waspish as his own. A surer recipe for trouble would be hard to imagine.

In the autumn of 1779 Clinton and Arbuthnot, although already eyeing each other askance, finished their preparations for the southern expedition. Stony Point and Verplanck's were abandoned, and Rhode Island had already been evacuated. The troops from these posts, combined with the Manhattan garrison and the reinforcements Arbuthnot had brought, gave Clinton an army that he felt was large enough to be safely divided between New York and South Carolina. On the day after Christmas he sailed with more than 7000 men, and a new phase of the war began.

VI. The War in the South, 1780–81

The opening of the southern campaign changed the whole strategic picture. Ever since Bunker Hill the British had adhered reasonably well, if unconsciously, to the principle of the concentration of force. They had had numerous posts but only one main army, except during the attempted invasions from Canada—the first of which had ended in the repulse of Carleton, the second in the capture of Burgoyne. From the end of 1779 to the end of 1780 the British force was divided, for a defensive in the north and an offensive in the south; the two parts depended entirely upon the sea for supplies and mutual support. Then Cornwallis broke away from his base at Charleston to invade North Carolina, and thereby created a third independent army; Clinton, trying to assist him, gradually built up a fourth on the Chesapeake, which Cornwallis joined in the late spring of 1781. Thereafter there were three again, at New York, in Virginia, and in South Carolina. The result of this dividing and subdividing was what might have been expected. The various armies lost touch with one another and with New York, and their commanders had to assume such freedom of action that Clinton was soon faced with the insuperable problem of imposing integration on strategic anarchy.

This in itself was bad enough; what made it far worse was the naval situation. Ever since the spring of 1778 the danger of a superior French fleet had hung over the British like the sword over Damocles. When they divided their army between New York and the Carolinas, they began to convert the danger into potential disaster. But Clinton, for all his awareness of sea power and passion for safety, does not seem to

have been aware of the fundamental risk. D'Estaing's two visits had
shown him that an enemy fleet from the West Indies might paralyze
his strategy and imperil his posts unless he had a covering British
squadron, and he realized that Arbuthnot fell far short of Lord Howe.
Yet he staked everything on the assumption, which he never seems to
have examined, that the royal navy could control coastal waters. He
not only should have known better; he did know, from firsthand experience. His later reiterated insistence on the need for naval superiority
may have been his way of atoning to himself for a gamble based on
oversight.

He carried out the reduction of Charleston with supreme competence. His approach was quite different from that of four years before:
he bypassed the forts by landing southwest of the harbor, moved
around it to a position north of the town, and occupied the neck of the
peninsula. There he opened his siege, while flying corps severed the
enemy's remaining communications with the back country. Progress
was slow but sure, and on May 12 Charleston and its garrison of more
than 5000 capitulated—a revenge for Saratoga, and the most complete
British victory of the war.

Clinton's crowning triumph occurred almost within sight of where
he had suffered his worst fiasco, and one was as richly deserved as the
other. At Sullivan's Island he had been planless and timid; at Charleston
he was methodical and confident, and executed without a hitch the kind
of envelopment that he had urged on Howe at New York. Fortune for
once favored him in every way. He had ample superiority of force and
ample time: before the end of the siege roughly 14,000 men were under
his command, and the only chance of interruption—the arrival of a
French fleet—was never imminent enough to be a real consideration.
The geographical accident that the town was on a peninsula between
two rivers, and the enemy's decision to defend it at all costs, gave him
the perfect setting for his trap. When he had sprung it, all that remained was a conventional siege, complete with sap and parallel. His
generalship, in sum, was wholly orthodox. And orthodoxy, when conditions are right, can yield dazzling results.

The fall of Charleston was only the beginning of his design. He intended to use the town as a base for reducing the back country, then
invade North Carolina, and eventually subdue everything from Georgia
to the Chesapeake. But he was unable to direct these far-flung operations himself. Word had reached him that a French armament was
bound for America, and he and Arbuthnot felt that their proper post
was New York. He consequently turned over the campaign to his second in command, who was left with a force that he admitted was ample,

and with instructions that bound him to almost nothing except the defense of Charleston. In early June Sir Henry sailed for the north. When he and Cornwallis next met, seventeen months later, the Earl was a prisoner on parole.

Clinton had well-founded misgivings about leaving him in what was virtually an independent command. The relationship between the two had been deteriorating for months past, and particularly since they had heard of the King's refusal to make Cornwallis commander in chief; the Earl was sulky at this rebuff, Sir Henry was convinced, and busy intriguing against him. During the siege friction had become so acute that Clinton had taken a leaf from Sir William Howe's book, and detached the Earl on a mission to the back country. Now he was detaching himself, leaving his subordinate with a large army, a free hand, and hundreds of miles between them. It was an extremely dangerous move. The smooth integration of his and Cornwallis' strategy depended upon a degree of understanding that they had not achieved when together, and could scarcely hope to achieve when separated by half the Atlantic seaboard. The fruit of Clinton's decision to divide his force between north and south was that he was cutting himself off, physically and strategically, from a large part of that force.

He was probably right that he had no alternative. He could scarcely remain in the south, or turn over operations there to anyone but Cornwallis; he had to leave him a free hand, if only because the time that dispatches took between New York and Charleston precluded effective control. He had another reason, of more doubtful validity: because he still hoped—or thought he did—that the Earl would replace him, he was anxious to impose plans upon him. His perennial desire to resign was beginning to affect his conduct, and to add its force to the complex of geographical and personal factors that in the end produced a breakdown of command.

His disagreement with his other principal colleague was also developing ominously. He and Arbuthnot had maintained a semblance of harmony, and appeared to the public as sharing gracefully the laurels of their joint conquest. But in private they had been clashing with greater and greater frequency, and by the time they sailed for the north each was full of complaints about the other.[19] The emergency that confronted them when they reached New York, far from bringing them together, destroyed irreparably the chance of their collaborating.

In July the French seized Rhode Island. This development, which Clinton's narrative treats almost casually, changed the complexion of

19. See William B. Willcox, "Rhode Island in British Strategy, 1780–1781," *Journal of Modern History*, 17 (Dec., 1945), 307–308.

the war in the north. For the first time a Bourbon army was established in the American theater, and a naval squadron based on Newport threatened British sea communications. Arbuthnot, reinforced in mid-July, was still superior to the enemy; but the control of American waters that the Royal Navy had exercised almost unchallenged for the past five years was now in jeopardy. It could be saved in only one way, by destroying the French before they were securely established. Speed was of the essence.

Clinton and Arbuthnot began to plan a *coup de main*. Sir Henry drew up three schemes and sent them to his colleague (who by then was cruising off Rhode Island) for a decision on which, if any, was feasible. Arbuthnot was on the spot in both senses, and to avoid the responsibility of choosing he retired into a fog of vagueness. He managed to ignore or dismiss all Clinton's ideas without producing one of his own, and then to blame Sir Henry for pestering him with aides-de-camp instead of reaching a decision. By the end of August the mere passage of time had been decisive: Rochambeau was entrenched on Rhode Island, and the Americans were in position to support him. The attack was abandoned. It had achieved nothing except to set the British commanders at loggerheads.

For this result Clinton was partly to blame. During the critical weeks he stayed at or near New York, and communicated with the Admiral by letters and messages that were not so explicit or emphatic as they should have been; when he finally became enough concerned to travel the length of Long Island for a personal conference (only to be left to cool his heels on the seashore), the time for effective action had already passed. He does not seem to have realized the stakes involved, or the absolute necessity for speed; he squandered time with a prodigality reminiscent of Sullivan's Island. He did, however, have ideas. Arbuthnot refused to adopt them, produced none of his own, and then blamed him for inaction. Sir Henry's grievance is understandable.

It took the form of a demand, made in late August, that the government should remove either Arbuthnot or himself. The demand was reasonable but unfortunate; it produced months of uncertainty at New York, during which Clinton did not know who was to command the army or navy in the forthcoming campaign. The war was moving toward a climax. In the autumn Cornwallis opened the offensive that finally led him to Virginia; simultaneously his chief, after the failure of the Arnold conspiracy, began to detach in force to the Chesapeake. The army was more widely dispersed than ever before, from Florida to New York, and consequently clung for its life to the navy. At that

moment the chiefs of the two services gave up hope of working together, and Sir Henry asked Whitehall to resolve their quarrel.

Whitehall refused to oblige. In October the cabinet decided that
Arbuthnot should be removed some time and replaced by some one, but
the vital details were left open. This shilly-shally in the face of facts,
which is even more incomprehensible than the initial appointment
of Arbuthnot, was so far from a victory for Clinton that he was expected, at least by Lord Sandwich, to resign. Instead he kept his post.
He may have been as deeply addicted to the fleshpots of New York
as his critics charged.[20] He may have hoped that Newcastle's influence would still secure him a clear-cut endorsement. He may have
distrusted Cornwallis too much to take the final step that would give
him the command. In any case he did nothing, but remained until the
following summer yoked to an admiral in whom he had lost all confidence. The effect was paralyzing.

A short-lived relief from paralysis came in the autumn of 1780, when
the unexpected arrival of Admiral Rodney from the West Indies coincided with the maturing of the Arnold conspiracy. Clinton had been
working long and patiently on the plot to seize West Point, hoping to
gain by strategem what he had failed to gain by strategy in the campaign of 1779, control of the Highlands. But his disappointment at the
collapse of the plot was apparently submerged in his grief over the
resultant death of André. The Major had been far more than his
adjutant general. Despite the difference in age and position Sir Henry
made him his confidant, particularly during the difficulties with Cornwallis at Charleston, and felt for him something much nearer friendship than he usually permitted himself to feel. André's execution seems
to have been a more telling blow than the loss of West Point.

While bad luck and personal frictions were vitiating British strategy
in the north, the rift between Clinton and Cornwallis was growing
wider. The two men were working on different premises, and neither
understood the other's. Clinton expected the southern offensive to advance northward, by deliberate stages, until it could be integrated
with his own operations. The first stage would be the subjugation of
the coastal region of the Carolinas, after which the rebels could be dislodged from the back country and the safety of Charleston secured
once and for all; then, and only then, a substantial part of Cornwallis'
army might be available for service in the Chesapeake. Meanwhile
Sir Henry began his own Chesapeake operation, which was intended

20. See Adm. Rodney to Germain, Historical Manuscripts Commission, *Report on
the Manuscripts of Mrs. Stopford-Sackville, of Drayton House, Northamptonshire*
(2 vols., London, 1904–10), 2, 191–195.

to serve one or both of two purposes, depending on how strongly he was reinforced from England. (He had had enough of tailoring a campaign to fit Germain's promises, and was tailoring this one elastically to fit whatever developed.) If he had had the strength, he would execute a pincers movement against Pennsylvania, one force striking north from the Chesapeake and one west from New York. If he lacked the strength for this, he would establish a post in Virginia, raid enemy communications with the south, and so assist Cornwallis. He hoped that the Earl would appear eventually, but not until and unless he had secured the territory between himself and Charleston.

Cornwallis had other ideas. After his victory at Camden in August of 1780, he concluded that the back country of South Carolina was sufficiently subjugated to make Charleston secure, and that he might now safely advance northward. But the coastal plain, he was convinced, was too unhealthful for major operations; instead of moving by the Cape Fear, as Clinton had suggested, he struck overland into the highlands of North Carolina. For this decision he paid a heavy price. Because he was out of touch with the navy, he was chronically short of supplies; because supplies were short, he could not stay long enough in one spot to win loyalist support; because he was unsupported, he could not hold territory; because his army held nothing, he could not force the enemy to a decisive battle. His campaign, like Burgoyne's, turned out to be a blow struck at the air.

He had no understanding of his chief's plans for Virginia, and believed that troops were being sent there solely for his benefit. This illusion was strengthened by the fact that the first expedition from New York, led by General Leslie in the autumn of 1780, was put under his command. It had no more than established itself at Portsmouth when he summoned it to join him by way of Charleston. "This is an end," Clinton commented, "of all golden dreams in Chesapeake." [21] But the fault was largely his own; he had not made clear to Cornwallis what he had in mind. This fault he compounded over and over again in the succeeding months, until his "golden dreams in Chesapeake" gave place to a nightmare.

He was discovering that distance, far from lending enchantment, exacerbated his differences with Cornwallis. Although the Earl had charm and self-confidence, he was given to fits of bad-tempered sulking, which Clinton did not know how to ignore, discipline, or understand; instead he resented them, and looked behind them for an evil motive. In December of 1780, for example, a letter from Cornwallis lashed out

21. Quoted in William B. Willcox, "The British Road to Yorktown: A Study in Divided Command," *American Historical Review*, 52 (Oct., 1946), 9.

at the quality of the troops he had summoned from the Chesapeake. He was being encouraged from London, Clinton at once concluded, to criticize his chief as a prelude to succeeding him. Sir Henry could do nothing about his conclusion, whether or not it was true. Embracing it only increased his annoyance, at a time when he needed all the patience he could muster.

At the beginning of 1781 Cornwallis disappeared on his offensive into North Carolina. From January until late April no direct word from him reached Clinton, who had to make his dispositions for the Chesapeake without knowing what to expect from the south. He and the Earl were fighting independent wars, in which neither supported the other or knew of the other's progress. Simultaneously Sir Henry and Arbuthnot were busy fighting each other; during the spring they achieved nothing except the rescue of their new general, Benedict Arnold, from capture in Virginia—and this by a dangerously narrow margin. By the time the campaigning season was at hand, Clinton was still groping with uncertainties. He was waiting for his removal or the Admiral's, for reinforcements, for news from Carolina. His elastic plans were intended to fit whatever situation materialized, but he reckoned without Cornwallis and without the enemy.

VII. *The Final Campaign, 1781*

In late April news from the south began to come thick and fast. First Cornwallis reported that he had reached Wilmington, on the Cape Fear, after a "uniformly successful" campaign in which three-quarters of his army had melted away. He had paid for his defiance of logistics, and had barely reached the sea in time to save a remnant of his force; but his confidence was unimpaired. A return to Charleston, which would have savored of defeat, he found reasons to dismiss. Virginia now obsessed him; he urged Clinton to make it the strategic focus—at the cost, if necessary, of abandoning New York—and announced that he was marching there himself. He set out before Clinton could stop him, and reached the Chesapeake in early May. He thereby set the stage for the final phase of the war.

His explanation of his move does not make sense, and his real reasons are conjectural. Clinton seizes on what may have been a relatively minor point, that the Earl did not wait to see dispatches from his chief that were waiting at Charleston, and deduces from this that Cornwallis was determined to force his own plan and hoped, once in Virginia, to succeed to the command. Sir Henry is again jumping to a conclusion on inconclusive evidence. But the Earl's conduct certainly warrants suspecting either his intelligence or his integrity. He was leaving the garrison of South Carolina to fend for itself before North Carolina was subjugated, and was enormously increasing the British commitment to Virginia, all without consulting Clinton or knowing his plans. The subordinate, in other words, was arrogating to himself the function of the commander in chief.

To what end? If his purpose was to conquer Virginia, his actions after his arrival there gave little sign of it. He rejected Clinton's suggestion of a move northward against Pennsylvania, and reiterated that Virginia was the key to the war, but did nothing of consequence to secure the key. It was not to be had for the asking, as he discovered in a month-long chase of the little American army under Lafayette. Thereafter he settled down at Williamsburg, and waited to hear Clinton's intentions. This novel curiosity was not satisfied. Sir Henry's letters, perhaps because of his resentment, were even more involved and obscure than usual. As the final climax of the war approached, the two commanders were so far out of sympathy that they were out of touch.

By June, after learning the results of the Wethersfield conference, Clinton expected that New York would be attacked in force. He had no thought of giving it up; all his plans were aimed at defending it. At first he hoped to forestall attack by striking at Philadelphia, using Cornwallis' army for one half of the pincers movement that he had long had in mind. The Earl would have none of it. Sir Henry then attempted to integrate the two armies in the defense of New York, by suggesting that Cornwallis hold a post on the Chesapeake and send the bulk of his troops to help defend Manhattan. A post Clinton was determined to have, partly for naval operations and raids on American supply lines, partly for the Pennsylvania campaign that he still hoped to wage in the autumn. Although a series of commanders had failed to find a site defensible by a small force, he persisted in believing that Cornwallis could find and fortify one, and at the same time detach most of his army. In a tone that was almost peremptory he ordered him to do so.

He should have known his man better. The order infuriated Cornwallis, and drove him in an unexpected direction. He was convinced that he needed his entire force to hold a post (an idea that had never entered Clinton's head), and therefore that he could not both hold one and detach as ordered. Which half of his instructions was he to obey? He chose the second, and decided to abandon the Chesapeake. His army marched to Portsmouth to embark for New York, and he himself asked permission to return to South Carolina. Clinton, when he heard what was happening, was flabbergasted, and countermanded the embarkation. He later concluded that the Earl had deliberately misunderstood, to teach him to keep hands off; but this is unlikely. The order, it is true, asked for only such force as could be spared, and this qualification may have implied that establishing a post took priority over sending any troops. The implication was far from obvious, however; and Cornwallis was not a logician, but a ruffled general.

This misunderstanding cost the Earl almost a month, in addition to the one already lost in his wild-goose chase after Lafayette. Not till late July did he receive categorical orders to take a post and hold it, if necessary, with his entire army. He reluctantly selected Yorktown as the best site available, and began to fortify a position that he had never wanted to take. His design for conquest had broken down, primarily because Clinton had refused to concentrate both British armies in the Chesapeake. Sir Henry's hope of integrating those armies had also broken down, because his subordinate had refused the means suggested. There now could be no integration. The entire army in Virginia was busy digging in behind fortified lines, and the army on Manhattan was equally immobile; the enemy was free to attack whichever he chose. Each commander had refused to reinforce the other while the navy commanded the sea; now neither could do so if the navy lost command. The chickens hatched at the beginning of the southern campaign were coming home to roost.

Clinton meanwhile was absorbed with another and quite different possibility, which he glosses over in the text. This was a second plan for a *coup de main* against Rhode Island. Arbuthnot had finally sailed for home, and Rochambeau's army had left Newport for a junction with Washington. These two developments had made an attack feasible, and throughout July and August Clinton was busily planning one. If he had succeeded in it, he might have deranged the allied concentration and even saved Cornwallis; if he had tried and failed, he would at least have justified his expense of time and effort. But the scheme dragged on as it had the summer before; it was never put to the test, and only distracted him from the crucial danger in the Chesapeake.[22]

The final act there opened in August with the march of the Franco-American army and the arrival of de Grasse, and ended on October 19 with the surrender of Cornwallis. The intervening events are familiar, and Clinton describes them at length. In the process he underlines Cornwallis' shortsightedness, blunderings, and insubordination so heavily that they need no further emphasis. His indictment is formidable, and the accused is unquestionably guilty in some degree. But

22. See Willcox in *Journ. of Mod. Hist.*, 17, 324–331.

is the prosecutor above reproach? His chief purpose in prosecuting is self-vindication; he conceals from himself, and therefore from the reader, his own inadequacies and their effects. Evaluating his responsibility, in consequence, involves weighing factors of which he was unconscious.

One of these, as already implied, was his use of the English language. His suggestions to Cornwallis were often put so deviously that they can be discovered only by a reader with leisure and a willingness to understand. The Earl had little leisure in the heat of the campaign; and his headstrong self-confidence, which made him bridle at direct orders, also made him unwilling to find indirect ones. He had neither the time nor the temperament to follow a thread of unwelcome thought through a labyrinth of words.

Sir Henry's plans were as involved as his style. He wanted Cornwallis to attack Pennsylvania, to establish a post on the Chesapeake, to detach to New York. He was dallying with the idea of raiding Philadelphia himself. He was scheming to capture the French squadron at Rhode Island. He had so many irons in the fire that he could not concentrate on any one, and his varied and numerous plans give in sum the impression of planlessness.

They give an even stronger impression of timelessness. Before Arbuthnot left in early July, delay was understandable. Once the naval command devolved upon Rear Admiral Graves, Sir Henry began bombarding him with ideas. The two commanders discussed them most amicably, and for various reasons postponed them repeatedly, until they all evaporated. Then came the crisis. Graves tried to reach Cornwallis, fought the French fleet, and returned to New York to refit. He and Clinton resumed their discussions, this time on ways and means of rescue, and held frequent councils of war. Even in this supreme emergency their pace was unhurried, and they did not move until their preparations were complete to the last possible ship. On the day they finally sailed, Cornwallis surrendered.

Only the navy could have rescued him, and it was responsible for the delays at New York. Clinton, on the surface, had nothing to do but prepare the troops and wait. Yet he had an underlying duty to hurry on the preparations in every way he could, and to galvanize the Admiral. This he neglected. With every passing week he retired deeper into fatalism, until he became again what he had been four years before, a spectator of catastrophe. He was unquestionably in shock. The discovery that someone—the government, or Rodney in the West Indies —had betrayed him by providing inadequate naval protection seems to have been shattering, and may have induced him to push off the problem onto the navy. He was resentful, it must be remembered, of the whole development in the Chesapeake. Although he never suggested, as he had with Burgoyne, that Cornwallis had got himself into his scrape and ought to get himself out of it, he felt that his own plan for the war had been largely superseded and his warnings ignored. Now that the consequences were glaring, he would have been phenomenal if he had thrown himself heart and soul into the effort to avoid them.

That he had in any way contributed to them apparently never crossed his mind. An objective review of his conduct, however, suggests that he had a large measure of blame—not so much because of what he did as because of what he failed to do. The failure is not obvious from his narrative, but the facts are there. They are hidden in the story not of the Chesapeake crisis itself but of the preceding months, from April to July. At that time, when Cornwallis was taking the bit in his teeth, Clinton had two obvious alternatives. He might have resigned the command, or he might have exercised it. He did neither, but accepted a division of authority between himself and the Earl. If this division was unnecessary, it was certainly unjustified. It ran counter not merely to his own interests, as he suggests in the narrative, but also to the King's, because it sacrificed the best hope of integrating the two principal British armies. If a feasible alternative was open, therefore, Clinton ought to have taken it.

Why did he not resign? He claims that he wanted to, and he had received permission. He had abundant grounds: Arbuthnot had not been recalled, but remained until summer; and an unusually rude letter from Germain, received in late June, made clear that the cabinet endorsed Cornwallis. Sir Henry stood alone, at odds simultaneously with the Admiral, the Earl, and the government. He professed to believe that the army, as well as Arbuthnot and Whitehall, would support Cornwallis. His way of escape was patent. When he argues that he could not properly take it as long as New York and the Chesapeake were in danger, he is unconvincing: a change of command in crisis does not necessarily have serious results, and is always preferable to the breakdown of command.

Why did he refuse the other alternative, of exerting his authority? He admits that he did refuse, but argues that he had no choice because he intended soon to turn over the command to Cornwallis. Here his argument is even more unconvincing. Future prospects do not condone abdicating present responsibility, no matter what the difficulties. He would, it is true, have had a hard task if he had tried to bring the Earl to heel. The situation in Virginia was not clear enough in New York for Clinton to give unconditional commands, even if he had been able to express them; and Cornwallis would doubtless have reacted with the vigor of a prima donna. But Sir Henry might have arranged a conference, as he thought of doing, and either won his subordinate's agreement on strategy or ordered him back to South Carolina. Instead he did nothing. He, who formerly had advocated a unified command for the army and navy, tolerated within the army a degree of insubordination that subverted its whole hierarchic structure. He failed to resign. He failed to be in fact, as well as name, commander in chief. No sense of propriety, however quixotic, can explain this refusal of the responsibility that inhered in his position.

The most plausible explanation is in terms not of his narrative but of a deterioration in the fiber of the man. Two years earlier he had made the revealing comment that inactivity and worry had undermined his constitution; "in one campaign more I shall probably be fitter for Chelsea than any other service." [23] The next campaign had been in South Carolina, where for six months he had been at his best. But he had returned to New York, and never thereafter went farther afield than Long Island. He had a physically inactive and soft life, cheered by a mistress and surrounded by sycophants; he was frustrated by continually planning great things that failed to materialize. It would be small wonder if this combination of creature comforts and professional disappointments clouded his apprehension of a crisis and sapped his power to meet it. Certainly the Clinton of 1781 was not the man who had been eager to destroy Washington in 1776, or even who had tried to save Burgoyne in 1777. The years between had accentuated his caution and slowed his pace. If he was not yet fit for Chelsea, he was less fit than he had been for the command in chief.

VIII. *Conclusions*

This survey of Clinton's career suggests that his generalship, for all its fluctuation, had certainly reasonably stable characteristics. Some of them were obviously virtues, some shortcomings; a few were now one, now the other, depending upon circumstances. An evaluation of his record as a whole may well begin with a summary of these characteristics, and conclude with an attempt to strike a balance between them. Any evaluation, as already mentioned, must be tentative. It must also be complex, if it is to fit Sir Henry's tortuous personality. Last but not least, it must be in terms of the period. Clinton was wholly a man of his times, for whom war was a business conducted on established principles, and to whom the ideas of a Clausewitz or du Picq, the tactics of

23. [Clinton to] William Eden, Sept. 4, 1779.

a Suvorov or Jackson, would have seemed fantastic aberrations. This is clear from every line he writes and every question he formulates, and he must be judged accordingly.

He was at his best as a planner. At several points he drew up plans that might, if executed, have won the war. They developed to the full the resources that he expected to be available. They were almost invariably based upon the idea of strategic envelopment, which doubtless appealed to his caution; because the purpose of envelopment is to win a battle before it is joined, the enveloping army, although it may fail, runs relatively little risk of defeat in the field. His plans were based, above all, upon sound geographical premises. He had the strategist's instinct for a map. He was continually advising his friends to look at one, and assuming that they would see in it what he did, an outline of future operations. His concern with the Hudson and Chesapeake are examples in point. He had not been in America six months before deciding that these areas were crucial, and he never changed his mind. His plans for the Hudson were frustrated in 1777 by Howe, in 1779 by the tardiness of Arbuthnot's arrival, and in 1780 by Arnold's failure to deliver West Point; his plans for the Chesapeake were frustrated first by Cornwallis, then by de Grasse and Washington. But the plans were inherently sound, because they rested upon the facts of Britain's strategic position.

Throughout the war British land campaigns depended upon sea power. The armies drew sustenance from the sea, and could not venture far from it without risking disaster—the disaster that was overtaking Burgoyne in upper New York before he lost a battle, and Cornwallis in North Carolina before he won a battle. This fundamental relationship between logistics and sea power Sir Henry understood. Hence his concern with the Hudson and Chesapeake, the two regions where the navy could penetrate deeply into enemy territory and where sea-based armies could operate to best advantage; hence also his recurrent idea of attacking Pennsylvania by a pincers movement, which could be supported from the sea on three sides. His eye for a map, in short, was not that of a mere landsman. He was the son of one admiral and the brother-in-law of another, and had a wide acquaintance among naval officers; he was doubtless correct in saying that he knew more about their service than most of them did about his. He certainly knew enough to realize that any successful strategy had to accord with the war's amphibious character.

By the same token he saw the war in broader terms than those of his own command. He did not, it is true, understand how much French intervention decreased the importance of the American theater, or how great a strain the expansion of the struggle put upon Britain's resources; he was constantly clamoring for more troops and deploring (even when he purported to recognize) the necessity of weakening his army in order to strengthen Canada or the West Indies. But a theater commander in a world war is unlikely to see the contest as a whole. He is doing well if he grasps its true character in his own theater, and in this respect Clinton compares favorably with most of his contemporaries.

He recognized not only the role of sea power but the sovereign importance of using political means to convert nonbelligerents into active supporters. A large part of the population held aloof, waiting to throw in its lot with whichever side showed signs of winning; and military acts—a proclamation, a skirmish, the execution of a prisoner—were parts of a struggle for the allegiance of the waverers. This fact Clinton clearly understood. His understanding affected his strategy, but whether on balance for good or ill is an open question. The effect was to increase his caution, a quality that was sometimes sensible and sometimes self-defeating.

The sense appears in his conclusions about the military potentialities of the loyalists. From the spring of 1776 until the end of the war he held that effective support would be forthcoming only where the loyalists were persuaded that the King's forces had come to stay, and could never be elicited (as London persistently imagined) by the mere appearance of the royal standard. He was therefore contemptuous of a fly-by-night expedition, such as Leslie's turned out to be in Virginia, or a cross-country race like Cornwallis' through North Carolina. He never wanted to occupy territory before he could be sure of holding it, as witness his plans for the southern campaign and for the Chesapeake, and his resentment at having to evacuate Philadelphia in 1778. If he did not invariably adhere to his convictions, nevertheless they do him credit. They were politically sounder than the wishful thinking of Germain and Cornwallis.

The self-defeating aspect of Sir Henry's caution appears in his worry about the political repercussions of failure. That worry helped to keep him motionless at Sullivan's Island. It contributed to his obsession for preserving New York from affront, and so to his delaying the attempt to rescue Burgoyne, and later refusing numerous chances to strike at Washington. It militated, along with his genuine distaste for ruthlessness, against what he called the policy of "conflagration"—the coastal raids that might, if pushed to the hilt, have altered the balance of the war. His political sense, in summary, both sharpened his insight and weakened his determination.

The other aspect of his generalship that is particularly hard to evaluate is his capacity as a tactician. Despite his seven years of service in America he saw action remarkably seldom. As a subordinate he participated in two major engagements, Bunker Hill and Long Island, and carried out a *coup de main* on the Hudson; as commander in chief he fought one battle and conducted one siege. He was not a great combat leader who inspired devotion or prodigies of effort. Although he had abundant courage and handled his men skillfully, he was never popular with them, like Burgoyne or Cornwallis; he regarded them much as a chess-player does his pieces. But he used them well, and was an antagonist to be taken seriously, as the Americans found at Monmouth—a battle, ironically, that was not at all in his style. His favorite maneuver, in tactics as in strategy, was envelopment. It was no monopoly of his, as witness the Brandywine; but he used it with almost monotonous regularity, and sometimes with great success. His tactical competence, in short, was midway between the brilliance that snatches victory where none should be and the passivity that earns disaster.

The shortcomings that clouded his reputation were of a different sort, and the best way to approach them is to summarize his own presentation of his failures. At Sullivan's Island he did nothing because Parker took the initiative without consulting him or enabling him to give support. In 1777, left at New York with an inadequate force, he failed in his gamble to relieve Burgoyne but made a most promising wedge in the American position; Howe refused to drive it home. In 1779 the offensive against Washington collapsed, when on the verge of success, because Clinton was meagerly and tardily reinforced. In 1780 and 1781 the breakdown of his attempted *coups de main* against Rhode Island was due to procrastinating admirals. In the Yorktown campaign his strategy was overruled by the government in favor of Cornwallis' ideas; the Earl blundered into an untenable position, and was trapped there when the navy failed to afford the protection promised. This, in slightly oversimplified form, is the story that emerges from Clinton's narrative. If examined objectively, what does it show?

One conclusion is obvious: Sir Henry is always trying to vindicate himself for not acting, never for acting unsuccessfully. *If* he had cornered Washington in 1779, *if* he had destroyed the French at Rhode Island, *if* his Chesapeake plan had been tried in 1781—these *ifs* are the highlights, except for Charleston, in his career as commander in chief; they prove that his best laid plans had a way of not being carried out. Here he is in striking contrast to Cornwallis. The Earl planned badly, but until the final crisis in Virginia he acted audaciously; his instinctive response to finding himself in a tight spot was to do something, sensible or foolish—after Cowpens to invade North Carolina, after reaching Wilmington to invade Virginia. Clinton's response, frequently before Charleston and invariably thereafter, was to make elaborate plans and then wait. The one thing his record lacks is the daring failure.

His reasons for inaction are often impressive. Attempting to concert operations simultaneously with Cornwallis and Arbuthnot was like trying to guide a wild horse while carrying the Old Man of the Sea. Sir Henry's luck, also, was appallingly bad: his best troops were commandeered for other theaters when he needed them most; reinforcements did not reach him on schedule, while French fleets did. His colleagues and his luck, however, are insufficient to explain the caution that sapped his initiative. He frequently delayed striking a blow, or acquiesced in the navy's delay, until the maximum possible strength had been built up—and the opportunity had passed. He was amply intelligent enough to know that time is as important in war as strength, and that meager force at the right moment may do more than enormous force at the wrong one. Yet he repeatedly chose to ignore this truism for a course that seemed to promise safety. There was no safety. His labor was lost by eating, in the psalmist's phrase, "the bread of carefulness."

The narrative suggests a second conclusion. Although Clinton won cooperation from most of his army subordinates (with the conspicuous exception of Cornwallis) and from junior naval officers such as Hotham, Collier, and Elphinstone, he was never able to get on more than briefly with men who were his superiors or equals. Gage and Howe, good-tempered as they were, found his insistently proffered advice a trial, and rarely took it; he was perennially at outs with Germain, and tried the patience of North and the King. In dealing with his equals his touchiness raised even greater havoc. As commander in chief he had to work hand in glove with his naval colleague, and this he could not do for long. He succeeded with Lord Howe for four months in 1778, and with Rodney for two in 1780, but these are the only exceptions; his dealings with the others, from Gambier to Graves, show the growth of much the same misunderstanding as that with Commodore Parker. When Clinton was thrown into long continued association with any admiral, his reserve seems to have tightened into a strait-jacket.

The blame, as usual, was not entirely his. During the first years of the war the friction inherent in dual command had been concealed by the accidental relationship of the commanders in chief. If the two Howe brothers were separated, Clinton commented, "their equals are to be found in either profession; but together they are irresistible, and to be equaled only by two such brothers." [24] He himself, lacking a brother, tried when he took over from Howe to secure his brother-in-law or a particular acquaintance for his colleague, and as an alternative suggested unifying the command. The government ignored these ideas and sent him flag officers who were as undistinguished, professionally and personally, as any in the service. Responsibility for the results lay with Whitehall as well as with New York.

If Clinton had been a more understanding man, nevertheless, he might have got on with even these colleagues, condoning their foibles for the sake of harmony. But he had no sympathy with others because he had none to spare; he spent it all upon himself. It was his substitute for self-understanding, which he never achieved. Such glimpses as he had of his imperfection were undoubtedly painful and seem to have been infrequent; here his analytic power, in other areas far from contemptible, simply did not operate. He was unable to admit that he might have substantial faults or, by the same token, that he might be outgeneraled by the enemy. His failures therefore deserved and received his heartfelt sympathy, because they had to be due to bad luck or to the shortcomings of his associates. Only the latter explanation was emotionally satisfying. Every plan that miscarried left him, in consequence, aggrieved against whoever else had been most concerned in it—usually his naval colleague. The longer he was teamed with him the more numerous were the miscarriages, the greater his cumulative grievance, and the more fragile the teamwork. If this interpretation is sound, it means that Clinton's antipathy was not to admirals as such but to anyone with whom he had to share prolonged responsibility.

His record contains hints of a third conclusion, that he was afraid of responsibility in itself. When he submitted his plan to Arbuthnot for a *coup de main* against Rhode Island, or to Graves and Digby for rescuing Cornwallis, he did not offer to take the blame if the plan failed, but insisted that the navy must guarantee to do its scheduled part or the army would not budge. When he realized the implications of commanding the southern expedition in 1776, or of succeeding Howe in 1778, the prospect dismayed him. Once he became commander in chief, he submitted his resignation with a regularity that even Lord North must have envied. Yet, when he finally received permission to turn over his burden to the insubordinate Cornwallis, he could not steel himself either to do so or to assert his authority. All this was more than the mere application to his own career of the safety-first policy that he so often applied to strategy. The implication is hard to escape that he was essentially, when the chips were down, a timid man.

24. [Clinton to Gen. Benjamin Carpenter,] Jan. 18, [1778].

How is timidity to be reconciled with other parts of the record? During his first year in America he gave bold advice to his chiefs, and was eager for an independent command; as commander in chief he had fleeting but grandiose hopes of extending his authority. His plans to trap Washington in 1776, and his efforts to redirect Howe's strategy in the following year, exude self-confidence. These pieces of evidence seem scarcely compatible with timidity. But they are misleading: they consist either of plans for which others (usually Howe) would have borne the brunt, or of hopes for himself that had no immediate prospect of being realized. Being bold for others, or for oneself in the conjectural future, is no test of boldness. The test for a general comes with the actual opportunity to seize the initiative, above all when he is responsible to no one but his god and his government. Clinton never passed this test.

He had, in summary, solid military virtues, but his generalship did not last the course. He was intelligent. He understood the map and the role of sea power, and had a better than average conception of the war's true character. In its earlier years he could sometimes be adaptable, as in the expedition into the Highlands and the retreat from Philadelphia; his bent, however, was always for developing his resources with careful deliberation. Only once, at Charleston, did deliberation bring success; for the most part it was a dangerous drawback. In his later campaigns he became so addicted to the bread of carefulness that he lost what taste he had ever had for audacity, and at the same time he was increasingly alienated from the two men, Arbuthnot and Cornwallis, upon whom he chiefly depended for implementing a slow, methodical strategy. Months before the final crisis burst upon him in Virginia, his leadership was bankrupt.

The underlying causes of bankruptcy were in him. He was utterly self-centered, but the center was out of focus; he never attained the integrated, ruthless egoism that often makes a general great. Instead his intellect pulled him in one direction, his emotions in another. He built impressive and admirable plans, but most of them existed only in his mind; he could not get them executed. The reason was sometimes bad luck and sometimes the counterdesigns of the enemy. Equally often it seems to have been that his blend of pushing assertiveness and morbid sensitivity made his colleagues distrust him. But most of all it was that he distrusted himself. His caution bordering on procrastination, his insistence on the absolutely full measure of naval support, his reluctance to take the command and repeated attempts to resign it, his failure to assert his authority over Cornwallis—all these

are signs of a basic unsureness, which grew until it rotted out the core
of his generalship. The pages that follow are his apologia for a career
that failed. But the failure, in the last analysis, came from a cause that
he would have died rather than admit. His nemesis was himself.

GREAT BRITAIN, on her first sending colonies to North America, appears not to have had an adequate idea of the power and magnitude to which they were to rise, or of the consequent advantages which might be derived from their increasing population and commerce. Else she might probably have been more provident in taking the necessary measures, on their establishment, to secure their permanent dependence upon her, and not have so readily given them the forms of government which the first settlers solicited, and which seem to have had no other object in view but to encourage and allure emigrations for the quicker peopling that vast wilderness. Though the fatal consequences of this error were afterward suspected, the suggestion came too late for an effectual remedy to be applied without great difficulty and danger. The intention was, however, retained until a proper opportunity should offer for bringing it forward. And, as every administration for fifty years back had foreseen that America sooner or later might become too powerful to remain quietly under an external government, various measures were from time to time consulted upon for preventing or at least retarding the apprehended evil. But administration, through a timidity and caution naturally occasioned by a subject of such great nicety and importance, unfortunately neglected to make the attempt while the situation of circumstances in that country was such as to render its success probable.

Being in a manner surrounded by the colonies of an enemy who diligently watched every opportunity of distressing them, and exposed to the merciless ravages of the Indians on their frontiers, our American colonies naturally looked to their mother country for protection and support and were, it is presumable, prepared by their apprehension of impending evils to have cheerfully obeyed whatever laws and regulations she was pleased to impose. But, when these terrors were removed by the conquest of Canada, and the peace that followed had reconciled all the jarring interests of the different colonies (who were now become sensible of their own strength from the share they were acknowledged to have in that event), the moment for introducing new systems of government was passed. Even the smallest innovation would now require the most experienced and cautious hand to direct it.

As Great Britain had incurred a heavy debt by this very war, which had been engaged in merely for the protection and preservation of the colonies, it was judged but equitable that the colonists themselves should contribute something toward its liquidation. For this purpose Mr. Grenville (who was unquestionably a very able minister, though he happened to be unfortunate in this particular instance) hardily attempted to extort a revenue from them by force of an act of the British Parliament. Unluckily, previous to this, orders had been sent to the King's ships on the American coast to be vigilant in suppressing a contraband trade at that time carried on with the Spaniards, which had been hitherto connived at on account of the considerable advantages derived from it to Great Britain as well as her colonies. And this measure, with the burdens just laid on their trade with the French West India Islands, had already caused no small disturbance and put the colonists very much out of temper. Their alarm was therefore extreme when they heard that the Parliament had come to a resolution of further oppressing them by charging certain stamp duties in the colonies and plantations.

This resolution, being not immediately followed by a bill but only held out as an intention for the next year, gave time to the colonies to consult together and prepare their objections. Petitions to the House of Commons against it were accordingly transmitted by some of their assemblies to the Board of Trade, who referring them to the Privy Council, the King was advised to order them to be laid before Parliament. The American agents, too, had been instructed to oppose the bill whenever it should be brought into the House of Commons, by petitions against the right of taxing America without the consent of its inhabitants. But every effort turned out ineffectual. The bill passed notwithstanding a very spirited opposition, and threw the whole continent of America into a ferment, which soon raised an army of writers in her cause, whose nervous productions contributed not a little to make her sensible of her rights and ability to support them.

The opposition was begun by the Province of Virginia, whose House of Burgesses came to several resolutions asserting that their general assembly had alone a right to lay taxes and impose duties on the people of that province. This example was in general followed by the other colonies, and in consequence of a circular letter from the assembly of Massachusetts Bay a general congress met at New York on the 7th of October, 1765. This convention, after coming to several spirited resolutions on their rights and grievances, prepared petitions to the King and House of Commons and a memorial to the House of Lords complaining of the restrictions lately laid on their trade, the duties imposed on them by an act of the British Parliament, and the too extensive jurisdiction and powers given to Courts of Admiralty in the plantations, and claiming an exclusive right of granting their money themselves when it should be wanted. Therefore, though it was reckoned derogatory from the dignity of the legislature to receive addresses coming from a body not legally assembled and unknown to the constitution, yet the representations, transmitted at the same time by the governors, of the universal discontents excited by the Stamp Act were so alarming that the King judged it proper to recommend the affairs of America to the consideration of his Parliament.

This measure brought on very warm debates in both houses; and, petitions being at the same time presented by London and Bristol and other great trading towns against the act, it was deemed expedient to repeal it—but not totally to relinquish the right. A bill was therefore soon after passed for the purpose of securing the dependence of America on Great Britain, and of asserting the right of the British Parliament to bind the colonies in all cases whatsoever. A temporary calm was by this means restored to the colonies, and universal rejoicings followed throughout America for the victory their firmness had obtained, though they were not very well pleased with the Declaratory Act with which it was accompanied. However, as they imagined no future administration would venture, after what had happened, to renew the attempt of taxing them, they judged it prudent to let the matter rest and not agitate it further.

The Parliament, however, made another essay the next year [1767] to draw a contribution from America toward defraying the expenses of the public, by laying duties on certain enumerated articles imported into the British colonies and plantations. The factious spirit of America was in consequence put again in motion, and a great deal of ill blood was generated. Associations were formed and nonimportation agreements entered into, which considerably affected the merchants and manufacturers of this country and furnished the opposition in both houses of Parliament with the means of clogging the wheels of government. The friends to it were therefore obliged at last to give way. But, to preserve an appearance of consistency and to vindicate the legislative power of Parliament over every part of the realm, a small duty on teas imported into America was still continued, perhaps under a persuasion that its insignificancy as an object of revenue might secure it from notice amidst the acclamations which the abolition of the rest was expected to excite. The colonies, however, were by no means satisfied with this condescension. They still firmly denied the right which the British Parliament had assumed of taxing them for the purpose of raising an internal revenue, and resolutely declared that any duty, ever so trifling, unless imposed by their own legislatures, was unconstitutional and not to be admitted. New associations and combinations were therefore universally entered into against the importation of British manufactures or permitting the landing of teas from Great Britain until the duty was taken off.

The great diminution in the consumption of teas, which this resolution had occasioned, could not fail to be seriously detrimental to the English East India Company. The directors were consequently induced to petition for a remission of the duty, and administration, being desirous of gratifying them, obtained an act of Parliament to empower the Lords Commissioners of the Treasury to grant licenses to the Company to export teas duty free—which, vesting in them a sort of monopoly of the sale of that article in America, it was expected might make them some amends for the injury they had sustained and help to retrieve their affairs, thought at that time to be on the decline. The directors, being consequently prevailed on to avail themselves of this indulgence, established factors or agents in America to dispose of their teas, and consigned to them cargoes of that commodity for sale there. This spread a universal alarm through the colonies, and, the committees in the different ports being vigilant in preventing its being landed, several vessels after their arrival were obliged to return back without breaking bulk. But unfortunately the inhabitants of Boston were urged by some peculiar circumstances to carry their opposition to a more pernicious length; for three of the Company's vessels, which had come to that port and lay aground at the wharves, were boarded by a number of men in disguise, who in a couple of hours effectually destroyed all the tea they contained, to the amount of 340 chests.

When an account of these proceedings arrived in England, the Parliament was sitting. And administration, being sensible that something ought to be done not only to stop but to prevent the repetition of such acts of violence in future (which seemed to threaten the abolition of all legal government in the colonies), caused them to be communicated without delay to both houses in a formal message from the King. Consequently, certain papers being at the same time laid before them which seemed to evince an inimical disposition in America toward this country, the Parliament was exceedingly incensed at the unwarrantable and seditious conduct of the colonies, and almost unanimously acquiesced in the vigorous measures recommended from the throne for compelling a more respectful obedience to the sovereignty of Great Britain. Therefore, as the Colony of Massachusetts Bay and the town of Boston had shown the most turbulent forwardness and had proceeded to greater degrees of defection than the other colonies, it was determined to inflict such a punishment on the inhabitants of its capital as might strike a terror into the rest of America and restore order and submission to the laws. For this purpose a bill was passed to shut up the port of Boston and remove the seat of government and the public offices from thence to Salem, until the inhabitants should make restitution to the East India Company of the full value of the tea which had been destroyed, and the people of the province were rendered sensible of the great impropriety of their past conduct.

The great majority with which this bill made its way through both houses of Parliament, and the general satisfaction it seemed to give to the nation, encouraged the Ministry soon after to bring forward others, for annulling the charter and new-modeling the government of Massachusetts Bay and for altering the government of Canada and enlarging its boundaries. No sooner did news of these bills and of the military preparations for supporting them reach the shores of America but a flame of discontent and opposition spread with the utmost violence through every colony. A universal defection seemed to take place, and even those who had before been inclined to be friendly, or were at least wavering, now took a decided part and joined the most zealous opponents of government. Consolatory and encouraging letters were written from the committees and meetings assembled in the towns of the other provinces to those in Boston, assuring them of their utmost support; and subscriptions were set on foot and contributions collected for the relief of its inhabitants. In short, the cause of Massachusetts Bay and its capital soon became the general cause of the whole continent.

The 1st of June having been appointed for the Boston Port Bill to take place, the general assembly of Virginia directed public prayers to be offered up to heaven on that day in behalf of America, imploring the Diety to grant them one heart and one mind to oppose all encroachments on their native rights. Their example was universally followed, and the 1st of June observed as a day of fasting and prayer throughout the British colonies. A general congress of the whole was likewise recommended and agreed to, for the purpose of deliberating on their present very critical circumstances and directing the conduct they ought to pursue. Each colony also appointed committees of correspondence for mutual communication on public concerns, and a cessation of all commercial intercourse with Great Britain was again solemnly covenanted until a repeal of the late oppressive acts should be obtained.

In the midst of these disorders General Gage, who was at the time commander in chief of the army in America, and a gentleman universally beloved and respected, arrived in Boston in quality of Governor of the Province of Massachusetts Bay. This officer was chosen by the Minister on account of his general good character, and perhaps on a supposition that he might be more agreeable to the Americans from his having married a lady of that country and resided many years among them.[1] But the turbulent inhabitants of that province were not now to be soothed by lenitives. The taking away their charter was considered by them as an act of injustice they ought not to brook, and they were consequently determined to resist what they deemed an infraction of their rights at every hazard.

Accordingly the general assembly, which had been summoned by the Governor to meet at Salem in conformity to the Boston Port Bill, gave the highest proofs of their dissatisfaction, and were so violent in the several resolutions they came to on the necessity of a general meeting of all the colonies in congress, and [in] a declaration they drew up expressive of their sentiments on the present occasion, that it was found requisite to put an immediate end to their proceedings by a dissolution. The Boston Committee of Correspondence also (which was composed of men of the most violent principles), in order to propagate and keep up the spirit of resistance and rebellion for which they saw the minds of the people everywhere prepared, took this opportunity of framing an instrument, under the old Oliverian title of a Solemn League and Covenant, to which they exhorted all their countrymen to set their names. By this covenant the subscribers solemnly bound themselves to break off all commercial intercourse with Great Britain, after the month of August, until the late acts should be repealed and the colony's charter restored, and to reject all trade or dealings with whoever purchased, used, or imported any British goods after that period. They also renounced every connection with all who should refuse to join them, and threatened to make their names public as enemies to their country. The consequence, of course, was that not only the inhabitants of the New England provinces immediately signed the agreement, but almost every other part of America soon followed their example.

The Governor of Massachusetts Bay could only show his disapprobation of these extraordinary proceedings by issuing a proclamation to prohibit the people from entering into such illegal and traitorous combinations, and the magistrates were directed to apprehend the publishers, subscribers, and abettors of them. But the trumpet of sedi-

1. For the circumstances of Gage's appointment in the spring of 1774 see John Richard Alden, *General Gage in America: Being Principally a History of His Role in the American Revolution* (Baton Rouge, 1948), pp. 202–203.

(Proper names, whether of persons or of ships, are normally identified in the Index rather than in footnotes.)

tion blew too loud, and turbulence and discord had taken too strong a hold of the populace, for proclamations to be listened to. The Governor's commands were consequently disregarded and his menaces treated with contempt and defiance, the executive powers of government being no longer able to stem the torrent of sedition, which now began to overflow the bounds of all order and law.

Preparations having been for some time in forwardness for holding the proposed general congress, and each province having selected from their present or old members of assembly the deputies to compose it, it met on the 5th of September at Philadelphia, and proceeded immediately to business. One of their first steps was to publish a declaration to commend the conduct of Massachusetts Bay, lament the distresses brought on the inhabitants of Boston, and recommend liberal supplies for their relief; firmly declaring at the same time that, should force be used for carrying the late oppressive acts into execution, all America would join to oppose it; and assuring the citizens of Boston that, should any of them be forced to leave the town for their personal safety, they should be indemnified by a general contribution for whatever losses and injuries they might sustain by abandoning their property. This was followed by a letter to General Gage announcing their deputation and business, and beseeching him to abstain from all military operations that could have the slightest tendency to produce hostilities.

The Congress then issued a kind of manifesto, setting forth the claims and rights of British America but avowing that to preserve the connection between Great Britain and her colonies upon a firm basis they were still willing (as they ever had been) to pay due submission to such acts of the British Parliament as should be framed for the mere regulation of commerce and securing to her the benefits arising from the American trade. And, after recommending a general association throughout the provinces to abstain from the importation and consumption of British goods until an entire repeal of the obnoxious acts of Parliament should take place, they drew up a petition to the King and an address to the British nation in the united name of all the inhabitants of America, strongly expressive of their attachment to their parent state and duty, affection, and loyalty to the King's person, family, and government, but complaining in firm language of the late encroachments on their rights, and beseeching His Majesty and the Parliament to renounce all such unconstitutional claims and place the colonies in the situation they were in at the close of the last war—which, they said, was all that was wanting to re-establish the happiest order and harmony between them.

These acts were followed by an address to the inhabitants of Canada and another to their constituents. The former they endeavored to inspire with an ardent love of liberty and a jealousy of the danger to which they said it was exposed by the Quebec Act, and invited them to join their brethren of the other colonies in the glorious struggle they were making in support of their common rights. The latter they advised to observe the strictest moderation and abstinence from every act of violence until they could know the effects of their petition and remonstrance to their King and parent state.

Without presuming to enter into any discussion on the validity of the right to which the British Parliament laid claim, we may venture to suggest that perhaps it would not have been an unwise policy to have unbent a little at the present moment. For, though some of the colonies may possibly have given just cause of offence by the insulting manner in which they conducted their opposition to the legislature, none of them had yet denied their obligations and dependence; and their united resistance began now to assume a more awful and regular form. It was no longer a seditious, turbulent rabble which Great Britain had to contend with, but the united wisdom and deputed voice of all her colonies, whose prayers and remonstrances it surely could not derogate from her dignity to listen to, though perhaps the mode of conveyance might have differed from what had been customary in like cases. For the sword had hitherto slept in the scabbard, and nothing as yet had happened which ought to have obstructed the path to a reconciliation on which the future peace, dignity, and happiness of both countries so much depended.

But the demon of discord, or the evil genius of America as well as Britain, had otherwise decreed. The dignity of the nation appeared to be insulted, and the obstinacy with which the transatlantics had combated the measures of administration was thought to call aloud for chastisement. The Ministry, therefore, though not unaware of the many difficulties and immense expense to which the transporting, recruiting, and feeding a large army at 3000 miles' distance from the seat of government must be necessarily exposed, were by the misinformations of overzealous loyalists induced to flatter themselves that the malcontents in America were greatly inferior in number to the friends of the old constitution, and that the resources of that country were so unequal to any effectual resistance against the power of Great Britain that, when they found her seriously determined to reduce them, they would be very soon humbled into submission and obedience. This persuasion, of course, induced them to advise His Majesty to call upon his Parliament for assistance to break the seditious and disobedient spirit of his American subjects, and with firmness to support the supremacy which this nation ought ever to retain over her colonies.

While Great Britain was engaged in these measures, disaffection and revolt were hastening fast to maturity in America, particularly in the New England provinces, where the standard of rebellion was already raised. For, a rumor having been spread through the country that the King's troops had some bad designs against the citizens of Boston, thousands of the inhabitants from the neighboring counties assembled in arms, and sent messengers into the town with offers of assistance in case of extremity. Though this tumultuous rising was soon dispersed without any consequence of moment, it had very justly excited in General Gage the most alarming apprehensions. He saw himself cooped up in a large, defenseless town with a small garrison, exposed to the insults of its numerous and seditious inhabitants within (who were kept in a continual ferment by the inflammatory discourses of their preachers) and the menaces of a disaffected and armed multitude without, while the laws were violated and trampled on in every part of the province and the ministers of justice obliged to hide their heads and fly before the rage of popular fury. Prudence consequently pointed out the necessity of immediately throwing up entrenchments and other defensive works on the neck of land which connects Boston with the country, and of securing the arms and other military apparatus in the arsenal at Cambridge and the public and private gunpowder in the magazines of Charlestown.

These proceedings quickly excited a universal alarm through the country, which the different committees did not fail to avail themselves of to inflame the minds of the people. The provincial congress immediately called out the militia, formed them into companies, and advised that a number of ablebodied, trusty persons should be selected from each under the denomination of Minute Men, to be in constant readiness to turn out on the first alarm. And, as a further preparation against what might follow, the cannon and military stores at Rhode Island, Fort William and Mary in [Portsmouth,] New Hampshire, and everywhere else not immediately guarded by the King's troops, were seized for the use of the colonists. Uncommon exertions were likewise made in the other provinces to provide themselves with everything necessary for resisting the coercive measures with which they were threatened, and their respective committees were equally assiduous in persuading the people that the devastations of war or unconditional submission were the only alternatives they had to expect.

Thus was this unfortunate dispute hastening fast to an awful crisis, which held both sides of the Atlantic in anxious suspense for the issue, as on it depended to Great Britain the continuance or loss of three millions of subjects to her prince, and to her merchants and manufacturers of an annual export and import trade of full four millions of money, the loss of which might eventually involve that of near five millions more from the West Indies; [2] and both [America and the West Indies were] contributing to the support of government an immense revenue, which flowed into her treasury without a murmur. But, above all, [at issue for her was] the sovereignty of a country which supplied to her fleets naval stores in abundance and a never-failing nursery of hardy seamen, to her armies a faithful associate and a strong and trusty support, and to all her measures and operations stability and vigor—resources which, under the guidance of wisdom, promised her not only a permanence of internal felicity but, in process of time, such a preponderating weight in the scale of empire as might render her the arbiter of Europe and admiration of the world. But to the inhabitants of British America [the crisis threatened to bring] all the manifold miseries and calamities of civil war in immediate exchange for the peaceful comforts and happiness with which a fertile soil, an extensive and flourishing trade, and an easily attainable competency had abundantly blessed them, and which they enjoyed in security under the protection of the mildest government under heaven —without the prospect of any one future advantage (likely to result from an almost hopeless success) but an imaginary independence ages before they were ripe for it, and to which they must wade through decreased population, taxes accumulated beyond their ability, a total alteration in manners and dissevering of connections which long habit, the ties of blood, and a mutual intercourse of kind offices had strongly endeared to them! And, to sum up the whole, perhaps it may not be too bold to assert that a most unaccountable madness appears to have seized both countries, urging them blindly on in pursuit of phantoms, the attainment of which cannot greatly benefit either; and numberless political and domestic evils were likely to be the destructive consequences of not only their failure but success.

But, to be capable of judging of the wisdom of the measures administration had now resolved on, it will be requisite that we should have some knowledge of the military face of the theater of the war, and the ability of its inhabitants to defend it. With this view the following short sketch is offered to the reader. The five North American

2. *Clinton's note:* This loss is happily not yet felt. But who can promise how long we shall retain our possessions in the West Indies after the commencement of another war with France, should America (as she most probably will) be against us?

governments to the eastward of Hudson's River teem with a robust and hardy race of men, who are seated in general in a mountainous and a strongly defensible country, accessible, however, from the sea by numerous bays and inlets, which afford most excellent harbors for shipping. The other eight to the south and westward of that river are somewhat less difficult for military operations, especially to a naval power, as the lands from the falls of the rivers to the ocean are mostly level (except in some few parts of Pennsylvania and the Jersies) and intersected with large navigable waters which are capable of supplying commodious and extensive communications with cooperating fleets; and the white inhabitants (who from constitution and climate are less qualified for war than their northern neighbors, and in the five more southern provinces are inferior in number to the blacks) cannot be so readily or in such force collected for their internal defense, from the comparative inferiority of their armed strength and their more scattered situation, having but few towns and living in general on their respective plantations. The southern provinces also were alone capable of furnishing the means of purchasing the necessary supplies for the war, their staple produce being the only wealth the Americans had to carry to European markets or to give them consequence with the princes of this hemisphere. And these two districts are entirely separated from each other by the River Hudson, which falls into the sea at New York after forming a broad navigable communication for 170 miles between that city and Albany.

From this short description, which, it is presumed, is a pretty just one, the River Hudson naturally presents itself as a very important object, the possession of which on the first breaking out of the disturbances might have secured to Great Britain a barrier between the southern and eastern colonies, which would have most effectually divided the strength of the inimical states by depriving those to the southwest of all assistance from the populous and hardy eastern provinces unless by a difficult, circuitous inland intercourse through the mountains. For, as long as a British army held the passes of that noble river and her cruisers swept their coasts, the colonists would have found it almost impossible to have joined or fed their respective quotas of troops. And, indeed, the inhabitants of the countries on each side must in that case have experienced the greatest distresses, on account of the scarcity of bread corn in those to the east and of black cattle and horses in some of the others, with which they had been accustomed mutually to supply each other. A ready intercourse would have also been by this means obtained with Canada by the lakes, from whence many obviously important advantages might have been derived.[3]

But a combination of circumstances had early drawn the attention and arms of Britain to Boston, whose unruly inhabitants had long been troublesome to government. Administration, therefore, in hopes that the chastisement of that town might prove the means of humbling the rest of America without further expense or trouble, directed General Gage to draw to him all the troops which could be spared from the other posts under his command. These, added to the regiments already in Boston and Castle William together with the marines of the squadron, formed a body of nearly 4000 effectives. Several other battalions and a regiment of light cavalry were also ordered to join him from Great Britain and Ireland.[4]

These hostile preparations could not fail to alarm the colonists very much, especially those [colonists] in Massachusetts Bay against whom they appeared to be principally intended. The leaders of the people consequently redoubled their diligence in arming and disciplining the militia, erecting foundries for the casting of cannon, and establishing manufactures of muskets, saltpeter, and gunpowder. Magazines of the like articles were likewise formed in the other provinces, and every other preparation made for war. So that instead of shrinking from the attack, as was expected, the colonists seemed determined to meet it with firmness and resolutely return blow for blow.

This inimical disposition had been, indeed, for some time showing itself in the New England provinces on every occasion that offered. But the conduct of the malcontents became everywhere now so daring and alarming that, upon intelligence that a quantity of cannon and military stores was collected at Concord [5] for the avowed purpose of acting hostilely against the King's troops, General Gage judged proper to endeavor by an unexpected and rapid move to seize or destroy them before the defection of the country became more general.

3. This strategic possibility, with which the British experimented fumblingly in 1777, attracted Clinton as early as the autumn of 1775. He was then writing of what might be done by a two-pronged offensive southward from the St. Lawrence and northward from New York. See Clinton to Gen. [Harvey] and the Duke of Newcastle, Nov. 15.

(As explained in the Introduction, the year of a document is omitted when it is obvious from the context. All references not otherwise identified, such as that above, are to the chronological file of the Clinton Papers; these papers are referred to when necessary by the initials CP. The Clinton, Gage, and Germain Papers are in the Clements Library of the University of Michigan.)

4. The most recent authority estimates that Gage had not more than 3500 troops available at Boston when hostilities began. (Alden, *General Gage*, p. 221.) Castle William was the principal fort of Boston, built on an island in the harbor some three miles from town.

5. *Clinton's note:* A small town about twenty-one miles from Boston.

The grenadier and light infantry companies were accordingly assembled with as much privacy as possible about nine o'clock in the evening of the 18th of April at the bottom of Boston Common. From hence they were sent in boats under the command of Colonel Smith of the Tenth Regiment and landed a few miles up Charles River. The detachment had not, however, marched far on the road toward Lexington before the firing of cannon and ringing of bells gave Colonel Smith reason to suspect that his destination was discovered and the country collecting to oppose him. He therefore, without loss of time, dispatched notice of his suspicions to the Commander in Chief, and sent forward six companies of light infantry (under Major Pitcairn of the marines) to secure two bridges that were on the roads beyond Concord, with a view of preventing the removal of the stores, or the strength of the country from coming against him. The Commander in Chief, as soon as he received Colonel Smith's note, immediately ordered out a brigade with two pieces of cannon to his support; and Lord Percy, who commanded the reinforcement, fortunately met him at Lexington on his return from performing the service he was sent upon, at a moment when his detachment had nearly expended all their ammunition and was almost overpowered by the armed multitudes that pressed them on all sides or had hung in their rear all the way from Concord. But the enemy's impetuosity was checked by the sight of the reinforcement, and, His Lordship's judicious disposition of it obliging them to keep at a distance, proper accommodation was provided for the wounded and a fresh supply of cartridges distributed to the men.

When the troops had been a little refreshed, Lord Percy made the best arrangement of them possible for their return to Boston. Nor did it require a small share of prudence and military skill to escape material affront or loss in a retreat of fifteen miles through a country which on both flanks was exceedingly strong, and appeared to be almost covered with armed men as far as the eye could reach. But His Lordship's prompt decision on the march, in striking suddenly into the Charlestown road, considerably lessened the effect of the dangers that surrounded him. For, as soon as his troops had reached the heights of that peninsula, the commanding eminence of Bunker Hill and the fire from the King's ships in the river forbade all further pursuit and annoyance.

This unfortunate excursion cost the King's troops two hundred and seventy-three men in killed, wounded, and missing, and the colonists by their own account about sixty. The loss was, however, much less than might have been expected when it is considered that the militia of that populous province were in arms from forty miles round, and the King's troops exposed to their fire the whole day with very few opportunities of returning it to any purpose, on account of the extreme closeness of the country and the many covers it consequently afforded to the enemy. The transactions of the day had also such an extensive effect that the militia of the neighboring counties, assembling under their respective leaders, very soon formed an army of above 20,000 men.[6] These immediately advanced to Boston, and by running a line from Roxbury to the Mystic and occupying with cannon the heights that commanded the avenues to the town precluded the garrison from all access of provisions or intercourse with the adjacent country. It is, moreover, astonishing with what rapidity the news of them [the transactions of the day] spread from one end of the continent to the other, and what influence they had in diffusing the spirit of revolt through the provinces. In some the populace seized upon the money in the public treasury, in others they possessed themselves of the arms and other military stores in the arsenals, and in all they prepared for war with the greatest ardor. And, though the King's governors were not yet expelled from their governments, their authority was totally gone and scarcely any respect paid to their persons, the people being entirely ruled by the provincial congresses, who now began openly to raise corps of horse and foot and form magazines of every sort for their supply. Even commerce was for a while suspended, and in many places a stop put to the exportation of all provisions. In short, every man now threw off his usual occupation and became either soldier or committeeman, being urged by principle or a regard to personal safety at least to appear active in the public cause—though it must be confessed that many were actuated by the sincerest and most ardent enthusiasm. Of this the surprising the forts of Crown Point and Ticonderoga by private individuals about this time may be adduced as a very serious instance, the revolters being thus by one bold and successful stroke not only put in possession of above 200 pieces of ordnance and a large quantity of gunpowder and military stores which they then very much wanted,[7] but they became masters of the nearest and strongest door

6. Modern estimates of the American losses at Lexington and Concord are approximately ninety men. (Willard M. Wallace, *Appeal to Arms: A Military History of the American Revolution* [New York, 1951], p. 25; Alden, *General Gage*, p. 246.) By late May the besieging army numbered at most 16,000; see Charles Martyn, *The Life of Artemas Ward, the First Commander-in-Chief of the American Revolution* (New York, 1921), p. 108.

7. The desperate shortage of artillery, arms, and ammunition in the American camp persisted until midwinter, when the heavy guns arrived from Ticonderoga. See Martyn, *Artemas Ward*, p. 115; John C. Fitzpatrick, ed., *The Writings of George Washington from the Original Manuscript Sources, 1745–1799* (39 vols., Washington, 1931–44), 3, 458; Wallace, *Appeal to Arms*, pp. 30, 55–56, 61; Allen French, *The First Year of the American Revolution* (Boston and New York, 1934), p. 309.

to Canada, which they might open or shut at their pleasure as defensive or offensive policy should require.

The affair of Lexington had likewise a considerable share in adding the Province of New York to the confederacy, an accession which gave no small strength to the union from its lying on the Hudson—that important link, as before observed, which separates or connects the eastern and southern colonies. For this province had hitherto kept aloof and preserved some small appearance of respect for government. The patriotic party, it is true, had been numerous from the beginning of the discontents; but they seemed disposed to wait the issue of a memorial and remonstrance transmitted by their assembly to the King and two houses of Parliament which, they had reason to flatter themselves, might become the groundwork of a reconciliation.[8] On the first news, however, of this fatal business the voice of sedition grew louder; and, the approach of some Connecticut regiments to the neighborhood of New York animating the disaffected in that city, the mask was soon forced from every countenance, and it was no longer in the power of the moderate party to stem the torrent. Delegates were now voted to the general Congress, and a stop was put to all exportations to those colonies which still adhered to Great Britain. The disaffected in the other colonies were also indefatigable in taking advantage of the present moment. Committees met, provincial congresses were convened, associations formed, and the most inflammatory and seditious proposals adopted. So that nothing but the cry of war and liberty was anywhere heard, diffusing an enthusiastic frenzy through all ranks and ages of both sexes that raised them above the dread of every consequence.

As it was in the midst of this ferment that the conciliatory proposition from Parliament of the 20th of February [9] was laid before some of the provincial assemblies, the popular demagogues had no great difficulty in obtaining its almost unanimous rejection, on the principle of its being unsatisfactory and more calculated for undermining the confederacy than removing the grievances complained of. The same causes likewise gave vigor and success to all the debates and motions of the general Congress which met soon after at Philadelphia; and, as the raising an army for the common defense and establishing a fund for its support were among the first measures proposed and carried,

8. See Peter Force, ed., *American Archives, Containing a Documentary History of the English Colonies in North America, from the King's Message to Parliament, of March 7, 1774, to the Declaration of Independence by the United States* (4th series, 6 vols., Washington, 1837–46), *1*, 1313, 1316, 1318.

9. Lord North's controversial proposal, passed over the opposition of many of his own followers, that any colony that contributed a satisfactory sum for internal government and imperial defense should be exempted from taxation by Parliament.

they serve to mark the hostile tendency of their intentions, as also their artful policy in thus early securing the strenuous support of their constituents by involving them all so equally in the crime of rebellion that none could afterward well recede with safety.

It was now the general expectation that, as soon as the reinforcements arrived at Boston, the General would immediately attempt something to convince the revolters that Great Britain was sufficiently powerful to punish their temerity and ingratitude, especially as no part of America was more exposed to chastisement than the very provinces in which the disturbances first began—as all the New England coast abounds with little seaport towns which lay at the mercy of conjunct expeditions of fleet and army, by which the sources of that piratical depredation which soon afterward so much infested the British trade might easily have been crushed in the shell. But the war was unfortunately of so singular and unprecedented a nature that, it must be confessed, the chiefs of the two services had a very difficult part to act.[10] And they were, moreover, probably restrained from making hostile attempts against the harbors on the coast by humanely considering that the loyalists might possibly suffer in the indiscriminate destruction which would inevitably follow. They may also have had some apprehensions of the clamor which the burning a town in that early stage of the quarrel might possibly excite in England as well as [in] the colonies. Nor was, perhaps, their line of conduct as yet sufficiently marked, or their instructions so comprehensive, as to provide for every contingency and preclude error.

General Gage, however, judged it right to prepare for whatever offensive operations he might be hereafter forced into. And as a preliminary measure he issued a proclamation in his capacity as civil governor, enumerating the many acts of rebellion which had been committed by the insurgents and, after denouncing the penalties of high treason against them if they persisted, offering a free pardon in the King's name (with some exceptions) to whoever should lay down their arms and return to their duty. He likewise took into his consideration the best means of putting the town of Boston into a proper state of defense, that its garrison might be exposed to as few inconveniences as possible from the machinations of the malcontents. Nor did it escape his judgment that to this end the two adjoining peninsulas should be laid hold of, as the heights of both, commanding

10. The two chiefs were Gage and Vice Admiral Samuel Graves, who had been appointed naval commander in chief on the North American station in 1774. This officer is not to be confused with Thomas Graves, his cousin, who was in temporary naval command on the same station in 1781.

most parts of the town, might put it in the power of any enemy that should attain possession of either to be at least a very troublesome neighbor. But the carrying this salutary purpose into execution happened unfortunately to be too long deferred, and the neglect was productive of much bloodshed and other consequent evils, which a little timely precaution might most probably have prevented.

CHAPTER 1

Bunker Hill to Sullivan's Island, June, 1775, to June, 1776

Battle of Bunker Hill. General Gage returns to England. Sir William Howe commander in chief. Sir Henry Clinton detached to the Carolinas. King's troops evacuate Boston and remove to Halifax. Sir Peter Parker attacks the fort on Sullivan's Island. The public were not then nor never have been properly informed of the part the army took in that business. King's army assembles before New York.

ADMINISTRATION having come to the resolution of augmenting the army in Boston, Sir William Howe, General Burgoyne, and I received His Majesty's commands to repair thither and act as major generals on that staff.[1] On our arrival we found, to our great astonishment and concern, that hostilities had been already begun and that the King's troops were in consequence confined within a circle of scarcely two miles diameter, as the insurgents had seized every avenue from the surrounding country, whereby all supplies of fresh provisions by that course were cut off from the garrison.[2] The move to Lexington most probably accelerated this mortifying extremity. I do not, however, presume to give an opinion on the policy of that ill-fated measure, as I am not competent to judge of General Gage's reasons for adopting it. But I should humbly conceive that the first stroke in such a war ought to have been important and certain of success. The ferment excited by

1. "I could not have named two people I should sooner wish to serve with in every respect. We of course differ often in opinion, but in such a manner as, I am sure, I receive great benefit from." Clinton to unknown, June 13.

Clinton, here and elsewhere, refers to Howe as "Sir William," and numerous historians have done likewise. In fact, however, he was merely Gen. Howe until the autumn of 1776, when he was made a Knight of the Bath. See Germain Papers: Germain to Howe, Oct. 10, 1776; Bellamy Partridge, Sir Billy Howe (London, New York, and Toronto, 1936), pp. 135–136.

2. "Dans une situation aussi bizarre, il ne nous reste qu'une chose à faire: d'ouvrir nos coudes un peu, par là de nous procurer les commodités de paysage." (Clinton to unknown, dated May and filed at the end of the month.) "Ouvrir nos coudes" is strikingly similar to the remark that Burgoyne is supposed to have made at the same time, and from which he derived his nickname of "Elbow-Room." See Christopher Ward, The War of the Revolution, ed. John Richard Alden (2 vols., New York, 1952), 1, 73 and n. 1.

it gave the disaffected colonies an army, which, though badly armed, as ill appointed, and without discipline or subordination, was, it must be confessed, respectable for its numbers and the enthusiasm by which they were actuated.

We had soon to manifest a proof of the above observation in this raw undisciplined body boldly projecting to lay hold of Charlestown Heights, though we had the command of the waters on both sides of the peninsula, and consequently their only communication with it (by the short neck which joins it to the continent) [was] liable to be intercepted by the fire from our ships, galleys, gunboats, and other water batteries. They, however, attempted it; and it cost us the lives of many valuable officers and more men than can be well apprehended to force them from the works which, with astonishing perseverance, they threw up there in the course of only one night. A few more such victories would have shortly put an end to British dominion in America.

Having been directed by the Commander in Chief to remain on the Boston side, at a battery we had on Cobb's Hill, for the purpose of forwarding reinforcements to General Howe, it does not become me to say anything more of the movements of the troops employed in the attack of the rebel works than what is contained in the *Gazette* account of the action. I shall, therefore, only just mention that upon matters' beginning to assume a very serious appearance, and observing one of those critical moments which sometimes happen in military operations, wherein I thought it possible I might be of use, I ventured to exceed the limits of my orders by crossing the water to the Charlestown side.[3]

3. "On seeing our left give totally way I desired General Burgoyne, who was with me, to save me harmless to General Gage for going without his orders, and went over to join with Howe. I landed under fire from the town; two men were wounded in the boat before I left it. I wrote to General Gage, informing him of the critical state of matters. I then collected all the guards and such wounded men as would follow—which, to their honor, were many—and advanced in column, with as much parade as possible to impose on the enemy. When I joined Sir William Howe he told me that I had saved him, for his left was gone. The enemy about this time quitted. I desired I might go forward with the light troops, but [said] he might rest assured I should not go further than I found he chose to sustain me. He called me back, I thought a little forcibly, but gave words expressive of the service I had done." Clinton memorandum in the MS history, dated Apr. 13, 1785, and quoted by French (with significant differences of reading) in his *First Year of the Revolution*, pp. 243, 252.

Although Clinton's conduct was acclaimed in England and rewarded by the government, he long remained anxious about having crossed to Charlestown without orders. (See Maj. Gen. Frederick Haldimand to Clinton, Sept. 2, 1775; Gage to Clinton, Jan. 3, 1776.) Howe, in turn, remained anxious about the burning of Charlestown; Clinton assured him six months later that the action had been justified and that "we all had our little share in it, and I as well as any of them—that

After the insurgents were driven from all their holds on Charlestown Neck and the business appeared to be at an end, as I was only a volunteer on that side, I returned to Boston, which I thought it not unlikely that the heavy loss we had sustained and the absence of so large a detachment from the garrison might encourage the enemy to attack in the course of the night. I was also anxious to forward an important service I had much at heart, and which it had been intended I should have the direction of the next morning. This was the seizing the heights on Dorchester Neck, the possession of which I looked upon as absolutely necessary for the security of Boston, as they lay directly on our water communications and more seriously annoyed the port of Boston than those of Charlestown did. And it had in consequence been agreed on (in a council held on the 15th) to lay hold of them first. But having discovered some symptoms of the rebels' intention to entrench on those of Charlestown and reported them to Sir William Howe and General Gage, the preference was given for the present to the latter. This plan, however, did not take place after all; [4] and the dropping it, even after we were embarked in boats for the purpose, excited in me no small concern. For I foresaw the consequence, and gave it formally as my opinion at the time *that, if the King's troops should be ever driven from Boston, it would be by rebel batteries raised on those heights.* Subsequent events have unfortunately shown that I was not altogether mistaken, and indeed Sir William Howe has all but confessed it in his letter to me on that subject.[5]

In the early part of the quarrel various causes had undoubtedly given us many friends in the revolted colonies, whose disposition in our favor might have been turned to good account had it been made proper use of. And with becoming submission I will venture to say that, had Mr. Gage been permitted to go at first with his whole force to New York (where persons of that description at that time abounded) and Crown Point and Ticonderoga been put into a proper state of defense and suitably garrisoned, that whole province and Canada would have

his officer came to me [and] told me General Howe's message, and I told the officer to obey it." "Conversation with Sir William Howe relative to the southern expedition," Jan. 3, 1776.

4. Clinton's grammar is obscure. His meaning is that the design on Dorchester Heights was adopted, then postponed for the attack on Charlestown Heights that led to the Battle of Bunker Hill, then abandoned altogether.

5. Clinton apparently refers to Howe's letter to him of Mar. 21, 1776, which confessed nothing, even by implication; Howe merely gave a factual account of the operations on Dorchester Heights and the evacuation of Boston. For Clinton's warning about the heights see below, p. 23 n. 9.

As mentioned in the Introduction, all italics in the text or the Appendix are Clinton's, except ships' names, foreign phrases, or where specifically indicated.

been secured. We should then have had little to apprehend from the inimical efforts of the colonies to the eastward and southward, who, as has already been stated in the Introduction, could never afterward have assisted or communicated with each other while our fleets commanded the ocean. But the taking those forts by surprise threw a quantity of ordnance and military stores into the hands of the rebels, which they had not yet found the means of obtaining from other quarters. And, indeed, we are not without suspicion that they were but ill provided with either ammunition or arms.

This, together with my opinion of the kind of troops which such an army as theirs must at that period of the contest be composed of, induced me to propose to our two chiefs a joint night attack along the whole extent of the rebel lines, with a view of trying their countenance and pushing to the utmost any advantage that might offer in the course of it. The General had the goodness to listen to me and to order a move to take place agreeable to the plan I had given in, and notwithstanding there happened a malapropos firing from our right (through some misconception, I presume, of my design), by which the enemy's left was kept in constant alarm, the detachment I was with succeeded to my utmost expectations. For we penetrated with facility into the rear of Roxbury; and, had the Commander in Chief not called me back but permitted the impression to be improved, there is no saying how fortunate the consequences might have been, as I never saw stronger symptoms of confusion, dismay, and total incapacity of acting than appeared at the moment in that part of their camp. But I fear Mr. Gage had not that confidence in me I flatter myself he would, had he known me better. I proposed also, without effect, another alert or two and a cannonade for the purpose of exercising our own troops and harassing those of the enemy. But neither the importance nor use of such movements seemed to strike the General in the same light they did me.[6]

The strict defensive which was adopted after the Battle of Bunker Hill furnishes little worth relating during the remainder of General Gage's command, except an expedition to Canada sent from the rebel camp under Mr. Arnold, which for the boldness of the undertaking and the fortitude and perseverance with which the hardships and great difficulties of it were surmounted will ever rank high among military exploits. Intelligence of the enemy's intention having been early brought into Boston, I made a proposal to endeavor to frustrate it by sweeping the coast from Newburyport to Kennebec River, and offered myself for that service if 1000 men could be spared to accompany

6. See French, *First Year of the Revolution*, pp. 329–330 and nn.

me. Upon which Admiral Graves, whose zeal was unquestionable, seeing the importance of the service proposed, very readily promised 500 marines and every other naval cooperation. But, it being judged inexpedient to draw as many men from the defenses of Charlestown and Boston as would make up the remainder, the enterprise unfortunately could not take place.[7]

I very early indeed saw that nothing solid could be attempted from Boston, and that sickness and decrease of numbers must be the inevitable consequences of our wintering there. I therefore took the liberty, with others, of advising General Gage to remove his army from thence to New York or some of the southern provinces, where the large navigable rivers gave room for the exertion of our naval strength and the assistance of friends might enable us to seize and fortify the Hudson, which would effectually separate the eastern from the southern colonies and at least impede, if not prevent, their uniting against us. And, should it be judged necessary to hold Dorchester Neck and Fort William, I offered to remain there entrenched with 3000 men for the purpose of obliging Boston to observe a neutrality—though it must be confessed we should have had a most severe climate to contend with, without a stick of wood to either cover us or to burn but what we could lay in before the army left us [or] get out of the town afterward. The General likewise seemed to be fully sensible of the expediency of the measure as well as the great advantages to be derived from it. But, not thinking himself just then at liberty to evacuate Boston or change his post, it was not adopted.[8]

On the 26th of September Mr. Gage received His Majesty's orders to return to England and lay before him the state of his command and to assist in the consideration of what might be necessary to the

7. Clinton wished to push his raids along the Maine coast as far as Machias, to crush a party of rebels there that threatened Halifax; "on the salvation of Halifax depended our own." Howe was persuaded to agree, although initially "he was by no manner of means clear that anything ought to be done." Clinton memorandum, Sept. 4.

8. Throughout this period the British Generals in Boston were arguing their next step. In August Clinton proposed the move to New York, while Burgoyne advocated seizing Rhode Island even at the cost of evacuating Boston. At the beginning of October, in answer to a query from Gage, Clinton advised holding Boston through the winter, until reinforcements arrived, and then establishing 6000 men at Rhode Island and 10,000 at New York. By early December the American drive on Canada seemed to threaten Quebec. Howe, the new Commander in Chief, felt that the loss of Quebec might make Halifax untenable, and that he would then have to attack New York; meanwhile he would wait at Boston for reinforcements. See French, *First Year of the Revolution*, p. 332; Wallace, *Appeal to Arms*, p. 60; Clinton memoranda of Sept. 4 and Dec. 3, CP; Burgoyne to Gage, Aug. 13, Oct. 2, Gage to Clinton with enclosed questions, Oct. 1, and Clinton's answers, Oct. 8, Gage Papers.

future plan of operations. Therefore, upon his resigning the chief command to Sir William Howe, that on the Charlestown side devolved of course on me, where I had the good fortune to conduct it in such a manner as to keep our camp perfectly quiet by constantly alarming that of the enemy. The troops, indeed, suffered much from the severity of the weather by being obliged to continue in camp until the 15th of December, which, with an almost total want of fresh provisions, sent numbers to the hospital in the scurvy. But their winter cantonments could not be prepared sooner, and I must do them the justice to say they, both officers and soldiers, bore their hardships with becoming fortitude and patience.[9]

Defensive situations are at all times unpleasant. But ours in Boston and on the heights of Charlestown was accompanied with some mortifying circumstances which heightened the satisfaction I felt at finding myself released from it by an order from Sir William Howe to take upon me the command in the southern district, and to proceed to Cape Fear River to meet an armament coming from Ireland in order to support the loyalists and restore the authority of the King's government in the four southern provinces. For it seems the governors of those provinces had sent home such sanguine and favorable accounts of the loyal disposition of numbers of their inhabitants, especially in the back country, that administration was induced to believe "that nothing was wanting but the appearance of a respectable force there to encourage the King's friends to show themselves, when it was expected they would soon be able to prevail over those who, having contrived to get the sword into their hands, had hitherto kept them in awe and effected their rebellious purposes without control."

This force, the Commander in Chief was told, would be sent from Cork by *the 1st of December,* so as to arrive on the Carolina coast sufficiently early for operations in that climate and to finish the services expected from it in time for its joining the northern army before the campaign opened. He was accordingly directed to instruct the general officer who should be sent thither "to leave each colony, as

9. "The weather has been very bad for these five weeks past, scarce a day without rain, high winds, or hard frost. It now, indeed, seems to declare for snow, and by tomorrow morning I expect to find my tent covered with it. The troops bear it tolerably well—a glass of rum extraordinarily reconciles it." Clinton to Gen. [Harvey], Nov. 15.

The troops were stationed at Charlestown because Howe feared an attack from that quarter. Clinton differed: "it had been early and ever my opinion," he told the Commander in Chief, "they would attempt to burn the town on Dorchester side." Howe answered that he was sure they would not attempt it, because they would not dare risk their mortars on Dorchester Heights; "if they did, we must go at it with our whole force." Clinton memorandum, Dec. 3.

it should be reduced to obedience, to the support and protection of the well affected provincials that might take up arms in the King's cause, and to join him with the whole of the regular troops as soon as the navigation of the northern coasts of North America became practicable." [10]

Instructions conformable to these commands were delivered to me by Sir William Howe on the 6th of January. And as soon as the ships could be got ready I embarked in the *Mercury*, frigate, and sailed from Boston on the 20th, in company with two transports and a store-ship having on board the light companies of the Fourth and Forty-fourth Regiments and a few officers for a corps intended to be raised among the Highland emigrants in North Carolina.[11] It had been part of my instructions to call at the different ports in my way to the southward, that I might have an opportunity of picking up pilots, consulting governors and other officers of government, and collecting intelligence. We consequently put in to Sandy Hook, where we arrived on the 4th of February, and immediately ran up to New York through the ice.[12] Here we found the *Asia* and *Phoenix*, men-of-war, lying in the East River, and the Governor (Tryon) residing on board ship, none of them very pleasantly situated. For, though they had been hitherto regularly supplied with fresh provisions from the shore, the tumult of the times rendered it rather dangerous for any person to venture from them into the town, the inhabitants of Long and Staten Islands having been disarmed a little before our arrival by a detachment of Jersey militia under Lord Stirling, and New York being kept in awe by a body

10. This and the preceding quotation are free paraphrases of instructions to Howe from Lord Dartmouth, Secretary of State for the American Colonies, Oct. 22. For a further account of this letter see Eric Robson, "The Expedition to the Southern Colonies, 1775–1776," *English Historical Review*, 66 (Oct., 1951), 541–543.

11. Rumor in England expanded these officers into a mythical company of Highlanders and deserters (*ibid.*, p. 551 and n. 3). Clinton, knowing his true strength, was gloomy. The prospects of effecting a rendezvous with the troops from England seemed to him remote, and he himself had only 1200 or 1500 "boys" (his estimates varied); "risk that handful I *dare* not, [and] must ever have one foot in my ships." [Clinton to Gen. William Phillips, early Jan.,] in "Memoranda," fols. 25v–26v. This volume in the CP is a letterbook in which Clinton entered—in a hand that is bad by even his standards—drafts of his personal correspondence. He rarely named the recipient and almost never dated the letter; these details, however, can often be deduced from internal evidence. The letters contain much valuable material, especially for the year 1776, which is not extant elsewhere.

12. Clinton had been instructed to call at ports on his way, and to go to the Cape Fear River as rapidly as possible—an obvious contradiction. He wished to go directly, but the commander of the naval escort had orders to put in at New York. Entry of Feb. 2 in "Journal of an Expedition to the Southern Colonies under the Command of Major-General Clinton," a separate MS volume in a case entitled "Miscellaneous Correspondence, 1776–1782," CP.

of those from Connecticut, who were also just joined by General Lee from the rebel army before Boston.[13]

Having been detained by contrary winds, it was the 12th of February before we could sail from Sandy Hook; and on the 17th we took the advantage of a favorable breeze to pay a visit to the Earl of Dunmore in Virginia, where we found His Lordship on board a ship in Hampton Road, driven from the shore, and the whole country in arms against him. On which account, I must confess, I could not see the use of His Lordship's remaining longer there, especially after the failure of his attack on the rebel post at the Great Bridge.[14] I, however, let His Lordship retain the detachment of the Fourteenth Regiment then attending him, as he seemed to flatter himself that some opportunity might yet offer for his acting to advantage. Unfortunately the day after our arrival a gale of wind had considerably damaged our transport by driving her foul of the *Mercury*, which made it necessary to get her repaired before we could move. This accident and contrary winds detained us within the capes until the 27th, when we at last took our departure for Cape Fear.

From this day to the 9th of March we were buffeted by violent storms, in shoal water and on the most dangerous coast. The frigate, too, in which I sailed did not appear to be in very fit condition for combating so boisterous a season, having been some time before thought in too bad a condition to be trusted on a voyage even to Halifax for repair! The tediousness of the passage, however, gave me most anxiety, as Lord Dunmore had informed me that the Regulators and Highlanders of North Carolina were embodied and then on their march to Wilmington,[15] and I had every reason to expect that the

13. For the difficulties that had forced Tryon to take refuge on shipboard see French, *First Year of the Revolution*, pp. 454–455. At New York Clinton was involved in abortive peace negotiations through James Drummond, a claimant to the Earldom of Perth. "Lord" Drummond had been at Philadelphia conferring with some members of Congress who, he assured Clinton, were eager to go to England if they could receive safe conduct, and was simultaneously sounding out Washington. Clinton suspected that the overtures were inspired by American anxiety about his expedition. He had no power to act, but kept communications open after he left New York. See his memoranda, Feb. 7, Feb. [8 and] 10, and [Clinton to Howe] filed under Feb. 12; [William Smith,] *The Candid Retrospect, or the American War Examined, by Whig Principles* (New York reprint, 1780), p. 16 n.; I. N. Phelps Stokes, *The Iconography of Manhattan Island, 1498–1909* (6 vols., New York, 1915–28), 4, 984–985, entries of Feb. 4 and 12; Fitzpatrick, *Writings of Washington*, 4, 330–331 and n. 93.

14. For this skirmish and its background see Wallace, *Appeal to Arms*, p. 90; French, *First Year of the Revolution*, pp. 576–578; Ward, *War of the Revolution*, 2, 845–848.

15. For the origin of the Regulators, their march toward the coast, and their defeat at Moore's Bridge on Feb. 27 see Ward, 2, 656–659, 662–664.

fleet from Ireland must be by this time on the coast. Being now joined by the *Syren*, frigate, with Lord William Campbell on board, we had the pleasure at last of coming to an anchor within the cape on the 12th without loss or accident. There was no sign, however, of the Irish fleet, and to add to my mortification Governor Martin [16] communicated to me the melancholy tidings that the King's friends in the back country, whom he had invited to arm in January in full confidence of its arrival, had been attacked by the rebels on the 27th of February, and after meeting with some loss were now totally dispersed and many of them in confinement. I found also from Lord William Campbell's account of his province that the loyalists there, overflowing with zeal and elated by some advantages they had gained over the rebels, had been equally precipitate in showing themselves [and] consequently [had been] overpowered, disarmed, and many imprisoned.

These were but gloomy forebodings of my future success. I had the pleasure, however, to find that the Governors were not dispirited, though they had both been driven for shelter on board ships of war. I was therefore happy I had it in my power at least to give them an opportunity of stretching their legs on shore by landing the few men I had with me, two light companies. Here I continued for above a month, sometimes on board, sometimes on shore, casting an anxious eye every day toward the cape in expectation of a signal for the fleet. But neither that nor any vessel from the northward appeared, so that I had the mortification to see the sultry, unhealthy season approaching us with hasty strides, when all thoughts of military operation in the Carolinas must be given up; while my ignorance of the Commander in Chief's proceedings and intentions rendered me incapable of forming any plan of junction or cooperation, and, to add to our apprehensions, not a fortnight's provision left to either men-of-war or army.[17]

In this state of uncertainty, and under a well founded conviction that the friends of government in the Carolinas were at too great a distance from the coast to afford any reasonable ground for hope that

16. Josiah Martin was Governor of North Carolina, Lord William Campbell of South Carolina. The *Syren*, a new frigate, had reached Cape Fear from England on Jan. 7 with the cheering but erroneous news that the transports had sailed from Ireland a month before. (Capt. Evelyn [to Clinton], Feb. 19; Martin to Lord George Germain, Dartmouth's successor, Mar. 21.) The frigate had then apparently sailed to Charleston and brought Campbell back to Cape Fear.

17. Clinton complained that he was "literally almost starved." The two Governors, when they did not dine with him or the captains of the men-of-war, depended on whatever fish their Negroes could catch; many of the officers dined on biscuits and such oysters as they could dig up on the shore. The only other staple food was wild cabbage, which "when boiled [tastes] like artichoke bottom, when raw [like] finest chestnut." [Clinton to unknown, early Apr.,] "Memoranda," fols. 48v–49.

order and the King's authority could be re-established in those provinces through their means, especially at that advanced season of the year, I revolved in my mind the possibility of seizing some situation which might be held with a small force, and where the King's persecuted subjects and his officers might find an asylum until the proper season for a southern American campaign returned, and His Majesty's troops were in fitter capacity for commanding success and consequently of yielding them effectual support.[18] For to bring those poor people forward before that was the case would have only exposed them to the resentment and malice of their enemies, and multiplied our difficulties by putting the rebels so much the more on their guard.[19]

The provinces bordering on the Chesapeake being by much the most accessible by means of the large navigable rivers which, after branching through them, fall into that bay, they naturally attracted my attention. And I had intended, if the troops should join me in any seasonable time, to endeavor to lay hold of two posts there— the one in Perquimans River, which discharges itself into Albemarle Sound, the other on the southeast branch of Elizabeth River in Virginia, particularly at Mill Point, that place having struck me very forcibly when I was there with Lord Dunmore as an excellent position for covering the King's frigates and other small vessels which might be employed in those waters. By these stationary posts a secure asylum would for the present have been opened for whatever loyalists in the lower parts of Carolina and Virginia might be disposed to join the King's standard, in a country abounding with provisions and in situations covering and communicating with each other behind the great Dismal Swamp, where the force left there would be perfectly safe from affront and might be reinforced or withdrawn at pleasure (as we could have the command of both waters), and from whence the three adjoining provinces might be kept in constant alarm by desultory excursions along their shores, for the purpose of distress-

18. *Clinton's note:* Administration had recommended the port of St. Augustine as a place of asylum, rendezvous, and retirement. But it is presumed that it did not then occur to them that the bar to that harbor, besides being a very dangerous one, has not above six feet [of] water over it!

19. Clinton was convinced that the loyalists would never be able to maintain themselves once the regular troops were withdrawn; on this crucial point he differed with Gov. Martin as well as with the administration. He wrote Germain, the new Secretary of State for the American Colonies, that any move to encourage the friends of government to show themselves must be followed up in force; otherwise "you abandon [them] to the rage and fury of an incensed multitude. Upon this principle, My Lord, I shall proceed warily during the time it may fall to my lot to command in the southern provinces." Letter of May 5 in "Copy Book of Letters Commencing 11th January 1776," CP. See also his memorandum, Mar. 14; [Clinton to John Pownall,] Mar. 20; Martin to Clinton, Mar. 20, and to Germain, Mar. 21.

ing the disaffected and collecting together the well affected inhabitants.[20] But unfortunately neither this nor any other operation which involved a possibility of delaying a junction with Sir William Howe, when called upon, could be engaged in without waiting to receive his approbation. I therefore lost no time in communicating to him my ideas and plan, and requesting to be honored with his commands as soon as possible.[21]

On the 18th of April the first transport of the Irish fleet joined me, and they continued to drop in every day after this by single ships to the 3d of May, when Commodore Sir Peter Parker with the bulk of his fleet at last made his appearance. It seems he did not leave Cork before the 13th of February, and the reasons for this extraordinary delay he can best explain; but Sir William Howe was assured by the Minister the armament should sail from thence by the 1st of December. There were, however, several ships still missing, nor did the last of them join us before the 31st of May.

Our first care after the arrival of the fleet was to land the troops, who stood much in need of that refreshment after being so long cooped up in transports, particularly the Forty-sixth Regiment, which was very sickly. But how to employ them afterward to the best advantage for the King's service was a subject which required much consideration. The advanced season of the year and the depressed state of the King's friends in the two Carolinas forbade our looking to the southward; and, as I was expecting every moment to receive the Commander in Chief's summons to join him, I became apprehensive that I should not have time to put my Chesapeake scheme into any sort of train. I proposed, however, as soon as the fleet could be got in readiness for sailing, to proceed to Virginia and there wait Sir William Howe's ultimate directions.

20. *Clinton's note:* It is much to be lamented that this plan (which Sir Henry Clinton uniformly recommended to all the general officers he afterward sent to Virginia, particularly to Lieutenant Colonel Dundas, who accompanied General Arnold) was not adopted. And there can be little doubt that, had Lord Cornwallis done so [in 1781] and encouraged the building of boats, etc., in Albemarle Sound, no attempt of the enemy against him, even by conjunct expedition, could have in the least hurt him.

21. Sullivan's Island, guarding Charleston, was reputedly garrisoned by fifteen hundred men with thirty heavy guns. For this reason, and because he did not believe that a self-supporting body of loyalists could be created in South Carolina, Clinton suggested the plan for the Albemarle-Chesapeake area that is outlined in the text. He had been interested since the previous autumn in the strategic possibilities of the Chesapeake; he apparently expected a small force to remain there indefinitely, as a nucleus for loyalist volunteers and as a means of harassing the vicinity. Clinton to Howe, Mar. 23, in "Copy Book of Letters Commencing 11th January 1776"; Clinton to John Pownall, same date, *ibid.;* [Clinton to unknown, *ca.* Nov. 15, 1775,] "Memoranda," fol. 19.

But, Sir Peter Parker having in the meantime procured intelligence from whence it appeared the rebel work on Sullivan's Island (the key to Rebellion Road and Charleston) was in so unfinished a state as to be open to a *coup de main* and that it might be afterward held by a small force under cover of a frigate or two, and [I] having about the same time received a private letter from Sir William Howe in which he seemed to intimate a wish I could get possession of Charleston without expressing any hurry for my joining him, I was tempted to accede to the Commodore's proposals for a joint attempt upon that island. For, though neither the season of the year, the orders under which I acted, the short time allowed me, nor the number of troops I had under my command would warrant an expectation of *suddenly* getting hold of Charleston and keeping it afterward with the small garrison I was at liberty to leave there, yet I thought Sullivan's Island, if it could be seized without much loss of time, might prove a very important acquisition and greatly facilitate any subsequent move we should be in a condition to make in proper season against that capital.[22] Preparations were accordingly made for re-embarking the troops, and on the 31st of May the fleet sailed to the southward.

Within a few leagues of Charleston harbor we were joined by the remaining transports, which, having separated from Sir Peter Parker, were driven into an English port and sent after him under convoy of the *Ranger,* sloop. I received a letter by this ship from the Secretary of State dated the 3d of March, signifying to me His Majesty's commands "not to engage in any attempt whereby the troops under my orders might be *exposed to great loss or the service to the northward disappointed,* and to proceed immediately to join Major General Howe

22. Clinton's logic is obscure. His earlier arguments against going south must have gained weight as the season advanced, and the "private letter" from Howe did not controvert them; it suggested Charleston, but left the decision to him. (Howe to Clinton, Apr. 12.) In early May Clinton felt that little could be achieved in South Carolina, and that Virginia was the sensible objective. (Clinton to Germain, May 5.) Then came the volte-face. On May 16 Parker sent a schooner and frigate to reconnoiter the Charleston defenses; the ships returned on the 26th, with such an encouraging report about the fort on Sullivan's Island that the General readily acquiesced in the Commodore's proposal to attack it. "Instructions to Lieut. Caulfield," May 6; Clinton memorandum filed under June 28.

The underlying purpose is not—and presumably was not—clear. The island, not the town, was the primary objective, and Clinton does not seem to have made up his mind what he would do if he gained it. He had no intention of attacking Charleston itself "without a moral certainty of rapid success." (Clinton to Germain, July 8, below, Appendix, p. 373.) Such a success might well have been achieved, but only if the British had at the start sailed past Sullivan's Island and assaulted the town; in the early weeks it seems to have been wide open to attack. See Frances R. Kepner, ed., "A British View of the Siege of Charleston, 1776," *Journal of Southern History, 11* (Feb., 1945), 93–103.

with my whole force if, upon the arrival of the armament at Cape Fear, I should be of opinion (upon mature consideration of all circumstances) that nothing could be *soon* effected that would be of great and essential service and advantage." [23] However, the Commodore and general officers, whom I consulted on this occasion, agreeing with me in opinion that the object before us promised very great advantages and was likely to be accomplished without much delay, we determined to proceed upon it now we were so near the port. But hard gales and contrary winds prevented our passing the bar before the 7th of June,[24] when the frigates and great part of the transports got over into Five Fathom Hole,[25] leaving the Commodore's and a few other heavy ships without.

I had now an opportunity of reconnoitering the islands to the northward of Charleston, and immediately embarked in a small sloop for that purpose. It took me two days to make the necessary observations, the result of which was that a landing on Sullivan's Island without the bar, in face of the enemy, would be attended with considerable hazard on account of a violent surf which constantly beat on the shore, but that we might easily get possession of Long Island, which was not held by the rebels in any force and (communicating with the main[land] by creeks navigable by boats of draft) was but a small distance to the northward of the other, to which it was confidently reported by the pilots to be in a manner joined by a ford passable on foot at low water.[26] Therefore, upon consultation with the Commodore, Lord Cornwallis, and the [other] generals, this was looked upon as the properest place to forward our cooperations from with the fleet; and our whole force was accordingly assembled on Long Island on the 16th of June except

23. A summary of this letter is in "Précis of the Expedition to the Southern Colonies," Germain Papers, Supplement, Vol. 1.

24. This is not strictly accurate. On the afternoon of June 1 the fleet was eight leagues off the bar and the wind favorable; Clinton urged Parker to cross at once, but the wind veered before the ships were ready. Memorandum, June 1; Parker to Clinton, same date; same to same, No. 1 of June 2, 1776, CP.

25. *Clinton's note:* Two vessels ran aground in this attempt, one of which unfortunately filled and was lost.

26. See the map facing p. 158. The choice of Long Island (now known as the Isle of Palms) instead of Sullivan's was fatal to the whole operation. When Parker realized that the bar would delay the fleet, he advised landing on the north end of Sullivan's; Clinton refused unless he could be sure that there was no surf, and that the navy could cover a possible retreat. (Parker to Clinton, Nos. 1 and 2 of June 2.) The landing could scarcely have been more difficult than that on Long Island, which was made "through a very heavy surf." (Memorandum filed under June 28.) The reason behind Clinton's choice seems to have been the hope that by-passing Sullivan's Island would enable him to cut off and capture its entire garrison: "the business, thus finished, would be more complete, as not only the island fell but everything in it." [Clinton to unknown, no date,] "Memoranda," fol. 63v.

some recruits, who were left on board the transports for a deception. Violent and contrary winds preventing the transports and other craft from getting up to the island, this was the soonest it could be affected.

The first object of our attention after landing was to ascertain the situation and depth of the ford. But to our unspeakable mortification and disappointment we discovered that the passage across the channel which separates the two islands was nowhere shallower at low water than seven feet instead of eighteen inches, which was the depth reported. This of course rendered it impracticable for the troops to take that share in the attack of the fort on Sullivan's Island which had been at first intended, and [which] was agreed on only under the presumption of there being a ford.[27] For, having only fifteen flat-bottomed boats left, not more than seven hundred men (with the assistance of every additional aid) could be thrown on shore at a time. And these would have to land in face of an entrenchment well lined with musketry exceeding themselves in number, exposed at the same time to a heavy fire from batteries of cannon as they rowed up, without a possibility of being covered while landing by either battery, frigate, armed ship, galley, or gunboat. After this, even if they could effect a landing, they would have their ground to maintain under every disadvantage while the boats were returning and bringing back another freight of troops. Consequently the attempt appeared to the general officers as well as myself so full of temerity that it was resolved on the 18th, which was the soonest we were certain of the fact, to send Brigadier General Vaughan to the Commodore to state our situation and consult with him upon the best means of employing the troops, under these circumstances, in support of the attack by the King's ships whenever he should judge proper to begin it. General Vaughan was likewise directed to offer to the Commodore two battalions to act on his side if he and General Vaughan, who was to command them, thought they could be covered in their landing and were likely to be of any essential service.

It may well be supposed that I suffered no small uneasiness on seeing myself thus enticed by delusive information (which offered an important object to my grasp) to turn my face to the south, so contrary to the opinion I had but a few days before given to both the Minister and Commander in Chief; then drawn on in its pursuit by unforeseen delays and accidents, considerably beyond the time I had prescribed to myself or the tenor of my instructions admitted; and now,

27. During his two-day reconnaissance before the landing Clinton presumably did not go ashore on Long Island; otherwise he could scarcely have failed to examine the "ford" for himself. After the landing he spent many nights "in fording and reconnoitering those infernal bogs and creeks that lay contiguous to Sullivan's Island," and returned in the mornings "wet and miry." Richard Reeve to Clinton, Aug. 27.

after all, likely to be foiled by this discovery, which, from the confident assurances I had received, there could not have been the slightest suspicion of.

Sir Peter Parker, in the answer he sent me by General Vaughan on the 21st, seemed to imply that he thought himself fully equal to the attempt with the ships alone, and only expected from the troops the best cooperation in their power when he made it.[28] The 23d of June was accordingly named for the day of action. Unfortunately contrary winds prevented the ships from moving for some days, whereby the rebels had time to perfect another battery and entrenchment that was begun on the 22d. This, being 500 yards back from their first position on the point, in very strong ground with a much more extended front, having a battery on the right and a morass on the left and abatis in front, obliged us to make an entire change in the plan of operations on our side. For it was apparent that the few men I had boats for, advancing singly through a narrow channel uncovered and unprotected, could not now attempt a landing without a manifest sacrifice. Lord Cornwallis and I therefore took some pains to explain and point out the circumstances of our situation to Mr. Whitworth, one of Sir Peter Parker's lieutenants, supposing that his description (from having been on the spot) might make the Commodore more clearly sensible of them than any we could send him in a letter. We at the same time informed him that the troops could now do nothing more in support of his attack than to cause a diversion as occurrences should arise, and that we should probably with this view land on the main, apportée for an attack on the rebel battery at Heddral's Point, if the Commodore would be pleased to send a few frigates to the westward to enfilade the communication between the main and Sullivan's Island.[29]

28. Parker later implied that he had been drawn into the attack against his better judgment. He had told Clinton and Cornwallis, after reconnoitering the fort, that an assault with the naval force he had would be unjustifiable against Frenchmen or Spaniards; even against Americans it was dangerous enough so that he felt impelled to lead it in person. "I will appeal to yourself as a man of honor and nice feelings," he wrote to Clinton on Jan. 1, 1777, "whether any propositions for declining an attack, however hazardous, could come from me consistently with the honor of the navy or consistently with my own honor." Clinton's subsequent view of his own conduct was that he might have been overcautious, "never having had a command [and being] fearful of a blunder [in] the first I attempted." Memorandum of Clinton-Howe conversation, July 8, 1777.

29. The development of Clinton's ideas is not clear from his description. He had landed on Long Island with two alternatives in mind: either to cross to Sullivan's Island, or to land at Mt. Pleasant (on the mainland immediately to the north of Sullivan's) and advance on Heddral's Point, thereby isolating the fort and its garrison. He bandoned the first scheme, as he explains, when the American position on the northern end of Sullivan's grew too strong to be attacked. He then suggested the second scheme if Parker could support it with frigates, but gave it up as too

The Commodore, in his answer to this message, says "Mr. Whitworth has given me a very unfavorable account of your situation, and I see many difficulties for you to surmount. The *Experiment* is off the bar, and I have ordered her to be lightened and to come over as soon as possible. She may be of great service in the course of our operations here. But, as I think we *shall succeed in the intended attack without her assistance,* I shall not delay a moment in putting our determination to begin (the instant the wind, etc., will suffer us) into execution." And in another part of his letter, "I hope *to enfilade their works from the ships stationed to the westward,* and to cut off the retreat of many of the rebels. *This may be of use should you have formed a scheme on Mount Pleasant.* I intend also, *should I silence their batteries and find it [the fort] enclosed* so that it may be defended from within, *to land seamen and marines (which I have practiced for the purpose) under the guns to get in through the embrasures.* Should this happen, *we may keep possession* till you send as many troops as you may think proper, *who may enter the fort the same way.*" [30] This letter was also accompanied by some signals, by which I was to know *when the battery was silenced, when the Commodore took possession of the fort, when he landed his seamen and marines,* and in short everything he was about.[31]

I have transcribed these extracts from Sir Peter Parker's letter only to show that he expected nothing more from the army *than a descent on the main in cooperation with the frigates he was to send to the westward,* and *a detachment from it to receive the fort from his seamen*

---

dangerous when the frigates went aground during the assault. "In short," he concluded later, "I congratulate myself (and so do the fleet and army) that I was not mad enough to make the attempt." Clinton to his "sisters" (Mary Clinton and Elizabeth Carter), [June 29,] "Memoranda," fol. 62; see also Clinton to Gen. Harvey, Nov. 26, CP.

30. Parker to Clinton, June 25. The italics throughout are Clinton's.

31. *Clinton's note:* Signals enclosed in the above letter:

"1. If I would have the marines of the squadron prepare for landing and rendezvous at the off side of the *Bristol* from the batteries, I will hoist a flag half red, half white, at the fore-topgallant masthead. 2. If I would have the companies of seamen *that have been disciplined by my order on board the ships for the purpose of making descents* prepare for landing and rendezvous at the off side of the *Bristol,* I will hoist a blue flag pierced with white at the fore-topgallant masthead. 3. If I would have the companies of seamen and all the marines prepare and assemble at the off side of the *Bristol,* I will hoist a flag striped red, white, and blue at the fore-topgallant masthead.

"Should only the marines land, they are to put themselves under the command of Captain Boisrond [?] of the marines on board the *Bristol.* Should the companies of seamen only land, they are to be under the command of the lieutenant that goes from the *Bristol.* But, should both seamen and marines land, the whole body will be under the command of Captain Morris of His Majesty's ship *Bristol.*"

and marines after he had silenced the batteries with his ships and
taken possession—which he seemed not to entertain the least doubt
they alone were capable of effecting without the assistance of the troops,
or he certainly would have accepted the offer I made him of two battalions to act under General Vaughan on his side. But, how much
soever I might have differed from Sir Peter Parker in opinion with
respect to the facility of this acquisition and the mode of accomplishing it, I could not explain to him my sentiments on the subject more
fully than I had already done. I had now, therefore, only to wait his
hour of attack and hold my few boats and troops in readiness to
catch at advantages as they should happen to offer in the course of it,
intending in the meantime to make every demonstration of landing
that was likely to deceive the enemy, until an opportunity should occur *through the cooperation of the frigates of doing so effectually
on the main,* and thereby supporting the attack of the squadron to
the full extent of our abilities. And I was not, indeed, altogether without hopes that our joint efforts might even yet prove successful if
the ships should bring up as near the fort as the pilots assured Sir
Peter Parker in my presence was possible (about seventy yards),[32]
as the fire from the ships' tops, being so much above the enemy's
works, would probably at that distance soon drive raw troops (such
as those assembled there were certainly at that time) from their guns,
and it was not unlikely that our moving into their rear at that critical
moment might cause them suddenly to evacuate the island.

This long menaced attack took place at last on the 28th of June.
About eleven o'clock in the morning we saw the *Active, Bristol, Experiment, Solebay,* and three other frigates moving toward the fort
on Sullivan's Island (in the order in which they are here placed),
but no signal whatsoever as agreed on to prepare the troops. Everything was, however, got in readiness on our side for the troops' acting
as events should suggest. Every demonstration was accordingly made
of an intention to land on the island, and every diversion by cannonade and other ways as long as the sands remained *uncovered.*
Small armed vessels were at the same time ordered to proceed near
the shore as if to cover a descent (which, however, all got aground);
the boats were drawn up and the troops so disposed that in an instant they could attempt a landing on either the island or the main,
as circumstances during the attack by the ships should direct. But,

32. *Clinton's note:* Sir Peter Parker acknowledged to Sir Henry Clinton that,
on bringing up, he found the *Bristol was rather too far off,* and he hailed the *Experiment* to go in nearer. Sir Henry Clinton has since sounded the depth of water off
Sullivan's Island, and found five and a quarter fathoms at low water within seventy
yards off the shore and one hundred off the fort.

soon after the leading ships had taken their stations, we had the mortification to discover that the three frigates (which were intended to favor the attack by the troops on the battery at Heddral's Point) were stuck fast on the bank behind the Commodore, and that the ships engaged with the battery on Sullivan's Island had brought up at too great a distance (800 yards at least) to avail themselves of the fire from their tops, grapeshot, or musketry.[33] From hence we soon grew apprehensive that no serious impression could be made, and even every instant expected to see the ships draw off. To our great surprise, however, the cannonade still continued (without any favorable appearances that we saw) until night, while the troops remained all the time on the sands anxiously looking out for some signal to let them know what the squadron was doing.

But, not suspecting that the King's ships could have suffered so materially, and supposing that the attack would be renewed the next morning, the troops were held in readiness. And the best disposition possible was made of all our light ordnance to enable them at the proper time of tide to risk one effort on the island should necessity require it—which I must, however, confess would have been a step not to be justified but in case of the success or distress of the King's ships, to take advantage of the one or to relieve the other. Break of day discovered to us that the squadron had given up the contest and retired, leaving one of the frigates aground, which was afterward burnt; and to this was soon added the melancholy intelligence that their attack was attended with very considerable loss, which fell principally upon the two fifty-gun ships. Nothing, therefore, was now left for us to do but to lament that the blood of brave and gallant men had been so fruitlessly spilt, and prepare for re-embarking as soon as possible.

33. Clinton subsequently blamed the failure of the whole attempt on the position taken by the larger ships and on the frigates' running aground. (Clinton to Gen. Harvey, Nov. 26.) Parker believed that the range had been 450 yards or less, but admitted that even that had been too great. The *Bristol*, he said, had anchored during his absence from the quarterdeck; on his return he had protested, but the pilot had refused to go nearer the shore. Parker had then ordered the *Experiment* to anchor inshore of the *Bristol*; her pilot in turn had refused until high water, and then had "only got a little within us." (Parker to Clinton, Jan. 4, 1777.) The fort was in any case well within range of the ships: their shot fell on the other side of the island, "raising a perfect surge in the sand." (Memorandum filed under June 28.) Modern estimates of the range vary from 800 to 400 yards: Robson in *Eng. Hist. Rev.*, 66, 559; John Richard Alden, *General Charles Lee: Traitor or Patriot?* (Baton Rouge, 1951), p. 125.

After the capture of Charleston in 1780 Clinton made the soundings that he speaks of in the preceding note. His comment was "what say you now, Sir Peter Parker?" Journal of the siege of Charleston (fol. 45), in a slip case entitled "Notes," CP.

I should not have been so diffuse on this unsuccessful affair had it not been in general much misunderstood, owing to the manner in which Sir Peter Parker represented it in his public letter to the Admiralty and the misstated or misconceived (for it certainly was not a just) abstract or abridgment of my letter to the Secretary of State given in the *Gazette*. By the first it seemed to be implied that the fort, being *silenced by the squadron and evacuated for one hour and a half,* might have become an easy prize to His Majesty's arms *had the troops crossed over to the island and taken possession.* And the other was so strangely drawn up that it caused a universal opinion that, though induced to land on Long Island by information that there lay a shallow ford of eighteen inches between it and Sullivan's Island, *I continued there for twenty days without making the necessary search to ascertain whether there was one or not,* and that I consequently *did not know the channel was impassable on foot until the instant I was preparing to cooperate with the attack of the King's ships.*[34] Now this conception of the matter was so very opposite to the real fact, and so injurious to the reputation of the army as well as myself, that the instant I saw the *Gazette* I complained of it to the Secretary of State, and requested that he would do me the justice only to publish my letter. At the same time I prevailed upon Sir Peter Parker to acknowledge under his hand (as may be seen in the appendix[35]) that I informed him ten days before his attack that, there being no ford, the troops could not take the share in it that was first proposed; that I offered him troops for acting on his side if he and General Vaughan were of opinion they could be safely landed and of any use; that I requested him to send frigates to cooperate with the troops

34. Clinton sent his secretary, Richard Reeve, to England with news of the operation. Reeve immediately forwarded him the *Gazette* account, and pointed out that in it Parker not only seemed to take all credit but omitted such crucial circumstances as the range of the bombardment, Clinton's offer of troops, and the necessity of frigates to support them. (Reeve to Clinton, Aug. 27.) These omissions were the crux of Clinton's grievance against Parker. His grievance against Germain was not at the time what he suggests in the text, but that his letter had been edited before publication so as to imply that he had had no alternative plan once the "ford" had proved impassable, and that he had merely folded his arms and waited on Long Island, offering the navy nothing but good wishes. Clinton to Gen. Harvey, Nov. 26.

35. See below, pp. 371–379 and nn. This correspondence is not included in the MS; it is in a draft, filed under June 25, which seems to be what Clinton intended to use. He published much the same material in *A Narrative of Sir Henry Clinton's Co-operations with Sir Peter Parker, on the Attack of Sullivan's Island, in South Carolina, in the Year 1776, and with Vice-Admiral Arbuthnot, in an Intended Attempt against the French Armament at Rhode-Island, in 1780* (4th issue, New York, 1781). Four copies of this rare pamphlet, with Clinton's marginal notes, are among his papers.

in an attempt I proposed making on the battery at Heddral's Point, and that the three he sent to the westward were intended to have done so had they not got aground; that, had the fort been silenced and evacuated, it was his sailors and marines (whom he had practiced for the purpose) who he expected were to take possession, and not the troops, who were seven miles by water from him, had two bars to cross and without boats; that no signal was made to let the troops know the fort was silenced and evacuated; and, in short, that I gave the King's ships every assistance which my very limited powers of acting could possibly admit.

Thus have I fairly and candidly stated the Sullivan's Island business, without presuming to claim merit from my conduct on the occasion. Indeed the troops had unfortunately no opportunity of doing anything which might deserve praise. But, as I am conscious that we are at least undeserving of censure, I could not help feeling with honest indignation that wanton injustice which had been done to us both. And, as I humbly conceive we had a right to have our part of that transaction explained, I have taken the liberty to do it here simply as it was, without extenuation or gloss—though I must at the same time acknowledge that His Majesty was graciously pleased to honor me with the fullest approbation of my conduct through his Secretary of State, and to invest me with the red ribband soon after my arrival in England.[36]

The purpose that carried us to the southward having thus proved abortive, I requested Sir Peter Parker that he would lose no time in conveying the troops under my command to Sir William Howe. But contrary winds and various other impediments prevented our sailing from South Carolina before the 21st of July, and it was the 31st before we arrived at Sandy Hook. Here we found the Commander in Chief and army arrived from Halifax, and immediately joined them

36. The red ribband was that of the Order of the Bath; see below, p. 59 and n. 1.

Reeve, on his arrival in England, did his best to justify Clinton's failure to Lord North and Germain. The Prime Minister said that "he wished Sir Peter Parker had been as prudent as General Clinton." Germain asked why the expedition had gone to South Carolina instead of to Virginia. He was told that Clinton had been swayed by the reconnaissance report and by the Commodore, and remarked that this coincided with the King's understanding of the matter; he himself, he added, found no fault with Clinton's conduct. (Reeve to Clinton, Aug. 27.) The Minister expressed himself similarly in a letter to Clinton on Aug. 24, but without mentioning Parker.

These private assurances explain Clinton's bitterness at the public treatment of the episode in the *Gazette*. He protested to his friends in England, and in the autumn the government was vigorously attacked in the House of Commons for its treatment of him. *The Parliamentary Register; or, History of the Proceedings and Debates of the House of Commons . . . during the Third Session of the Fourteenth Parliament of Great Britain* (17 vols., London, 1802), 5, 31, 46.

on Staten Island, where they were waiting for the Hessians and Guards, whose appearance was hourly expected.[37]

37. The first contingent of Hessians sent to America consisted of 7800 men under Lt. Gen. von Heister; with them were 1000 British Guards. The troops left Spithead in late May, touched at Halifax after Howe had departed for New York, and joined him on Staten Island at the beginning of July. The arrival of Parker's squadron at the end of the month, fresh from its defeat in the south, is said to have encouraged the Americans by showing them what shore batteries could do against ships. See [George Collier,] *A Detail of Some Particular Services Performed in America, during the Years 1776, 1777, 1778, and 1779. Compiled from Journals and Original Papers, Supposed To Be Chiefly Taken from the Journal Kept on Board of the Ship* Rainbow, *Commanded by Sir George Collier, While on the American Station during That Period* . . . (New York, 1835), pp. 2–7.

CHAPTER 2

New York, White Plains, and Rhode Island, August, 1776, to January, 1777

> First division of Hessians arrive. King's army lands on Long Island. Battle of Brooklyn. Landing on New York Island. Rebels retire to Kings Bridge. Army removes through Hell Gate to Frog's [Throg's] Neck. Obliged to re-embark and land on Rodman's Point. Advances and attacks the rebels at White Plains. Falls back to the North River. Takes Fort Washington. Lord Cornwallis pursues the debris of Mr. Washington's army to Brunswick. Expedition under Sir Henry Clinton to Rhode Island. Sir Henry Clinton returns to England.

HAVING the honor to be second in command, my rank in the line gave me, of course, the *avant* and rear guards of the army when acting in the field, according to the situations of the enemy. Being consequently not seldom one of the principal actors in the operations of the campaign, it sometimes fell to my lot to be consulted respecting them. If on these occasions my opinions, which were ever given with the most candid freedom, happened at any time to differ from those of my chief, he will, I am persuaded, do me the justice to acknowledge that my zeal and exertions, even in moves which I did not approve, were unquestionable. For it has been ever a maxim with me in council to point out every difficulty I see, in the field to obey orders and make as few [difficulties] as possible. Actuated, therefore, by no other principle than to contribute my utmost toward the speedy extinction of the rebellion, I could not be satisfied with being a mere passive machine that was only to act as directed; but I thought it my duty likewise, though a subordinate officer, to sometimes exercise my own eyes and understanding in examining the face of the country and the positions and strength of the enemy, and to take the liberty of humbly submitting to the Commander in Chief, when he permitted me, such measures for that purpose as my observation suggested. My zeal may perhaps on these occasions have carried me so far as to be at times thought troublesome, nor will I presume to say that my plans were always best or even practicable. I was never, therefore, offended at their not being adopted. On the contrary, as I was sensible that the Commander in Chief could alone possess the power of procuring every information requisite for guiding his judgment, I never doubted but he was influenced by the most potent reasons whenever he declined following my opinions, which on that account I ever offered with the utmost diffidence.[1]

Observing that the summer was passing away fast, and that the enemy was active in availing himself of the time our present delay gave him to strengthen his positions and throw every possible obstruction in our way, I was encouraged by our having got some ships of war up the North River, and nearly 10,000 troops in high health and spirits, to propose to the Commander in Chief the landing of a sufficient corps at Spuyten Duyvil in order to lay hold of the strong eminence adjoining, for the purpose of commanding the important pass of Kings Bridge and thereby embarrassing the rebel operations. It might also, with the assistance of our armed vessels, have possibly put it in our power to cut off the retreat of many of the enemy on the attack of York Island. And indeed I once thought he seemed inclined to follow my advice. But he afterward told me he had no intention of acting offensively before the arrival of the Hessians, nor did he think it advisable to stir a day's march from his cantonments before the troops had their camp equipage.

On the 12th of August the long expected reinforcement at last made its appearance; and on the 22d the elite of the army disembarked under my orders, without opposition, near to New Utrecht in Long Island. Lord Cornwallis was now immediately sent forward to take post at Flatbush. This was a measure I did not altogether approve, as

---

1. Clinton had offered advice on the campaign before it began. During his brief visit to New York in January he had conferred with Gov. Tryon and drawn up a plan of attack, which he subsequently communicated to Howe. The gist of his ideas was that the enemy was unlikely to try to defend New York but that, if he did, the British should occupy Long Island; from there they might maneuver him out of Manhattan by threatening his communications with the mainland. See Clinton memorandum, Feb. 8; Clinton to Howe, Apr. 29, "Copy Book of Letters Commencing 11th January 1776"; Clinton to Howe, [early spring,] "Memoranda," fols. 40–42.

For full modern descriptions of the ensuing campaign see Troyer S. Anderson, *The Command of the Howe Brothers during the American Revolution* (New York and London, 1936), chaps. viii and x; Ward, *War of the Revolution, 1,* 202–274.

A CHOROGRAPHICAL MAP OF THE PROVINCE OF NEW
Y O R K , *by Claude Joseph Sauthier, London, 1779*

I *knew* it would bring on skirmishing to our disadvantage, which happened as I expected the next day; and some loss was sustained by us without any one good end likely to be answered by it. For by this means the rebels were acquiring courage, confidence, and service, while we lay exposed to affront in a very awkward situation.

The enemy in our front being in possession of some rocky, woody heights (which they had fortified) at the distance of about two miles from their lines at Brooklyn, round which they made a bend to the left,[2] and there being but few passes through them by which they could be penetrated, I took some pains to reconnoiter them. And, discovering a pass to their left about a night's march from us which I thought practicable, I drew up a plan for laying hold of it, which I requested Sir William Erskine (if it met with his approbation) to show to the Commander in Chief.[3] Sir William was pleased to make me some compliments and undertook to carry it to headquarters, where, however, it did not seem to be much relished. But two or three days afterward I was sent for and desired by Sir William Howe to take under my orders the *avant garde* of the army and march with them in the evening, at what hour I pleased by whatever route I thought proper; and, having seized the gorge I mentioned in the plan I sent him, [to] wait there until he joined me in the morning. Major General Grant was also detached with the Fourth and Sixth Brigades and

---

2. Clinton's meaning is presumably that the American lines followed the curvature of the heights, which at their southern extremity bend to the west—or left as viewed from the British position—near the Narrows. See Henry B. Carrington, *Battles of the American Revolution, 1775–1781: Historical and Military Criticism, with Topographical Illustration* (New York, etc., 1876), p. 201 and map facing p. 214.

3. *Clinton's note:* Copy of the plan sent to headquarters by Sir Henry Clinton:

"The position which the rebels occupy in our front may be turned by a gorge about six miles from us, through a country in which cavalry may make the *avant garde.* That, once possessed, gives us the island; and in a mile or two further we shall be on the communications with their works at Brooklyn. The corps which attempts to turn this flank must be in very great force, for reasons too obvious to require detailing. The attack should begin on the enemy's right by signal; and a share [should be] taken in it even by the fleet, which (as the tide will then suit) may get under way and make every demonstration of forcing by the enemy's batteries in the East River, without, however, committing themselves. The efforts to be made by the army will be along the *dos d'âne* at the points of Flatbush, New Utrecht, etc. These the principal [attacks]; many other small ones to cooperate. They should all be vigorous but not too obstinately persisted in, except that which is designed to turn the left of the rebels, which should be pushed as far as it will go. The moment this corps gets possession of the pass above Howard's House, the rebels must quit directly or be ruined. I beg leave also to propose that this corps may begin to move at nightfall, so that everything may be at its ground by daybreak; and that light infantry and chasseurs may cover its left flank in such strength as to effectually prevent the enemy's patrols from forcing them and thereby making a discovery of our intentions."

Forty-second Regiment by our left (not along the ridge, as I recommended, but along the coast) to try to make an impression on the enemy's right and thereby draw off their attention from the flank I was to act against.

Accordingly, having first properly posted the Seventy-first Regiment for the purpose of drowning the noise of our cannon over the stones, masking our march, and preventing the enemy's patrols from discovering it, the *avant garde* moved from Flatlands at eight o'clock in the evening in one column by half-battalions, ranks and files close. Between eleven and twelve o'clock, being in a lane, we heard much firing in the rear of the column, which made me hasten to get into the open fields which cross the country to the Jamaica road. It, however, turned out nothing, and we continued our march unmolested until my guides informed me we were within a quarter of a mile of Howard's House, which was only a few hundred yards from the gorge I wished to lay hold of. Upon this I immediately sent forward a patrol to examine if it was occupied, which, falling in with another belonging to the enemy composed of five officers, had fortunately the address to take them all without noise. Finding by their report that the gorge was not occupied, I immediately posted a detachment there; and, ordering parties to be distributed along the Bedford and Newtown roads, which pass through it, I waited for daylight to take possession in force.

As soon as the dawn appeared I made my disposition against any opposition I might possibly meet with from the enemy, and laid hold of the pass with the whole *avant garde*. The head of the army column, with Sir William Howe, joining us in about two hours afterward, the line then moved forward. The Commander in Chief seemed to have some suspicion the enemy would attack us on our march, but I was persuaded that, as they [had] neglected to oppose us at the gorge, the affair was over.[4] When we reached the village of Bedford we observed some parties of rebels endeavoring to cut from one wood to another on our left, upon which we advanced with the cavalry, just to try their countenance and judge from thence whether they were supported. But as we approached they precipitately plunged back

4. "In all the opinions he ever gave to me, [General Howe] did not expect any good from the move. And during the march [he] seemed not anxious of passing beyond the gorge of Howard's; and even when in the village of Bedford he did not seem to know we were there." (Clinton's "memorandum of the affair of Brooklyn," filed under Aug. 29.) The significance of the final sentence is that the British forces at Bedford, 10,000 strong, were in the *rear* of the American right wing, so that in effect the battle was already won. For an account of this "masterpiece of secrecy and silence" see Ward, *War of the Revolution, 1,* 222–223.

into the woods in the greatest confusion, which was a manifest proof they were not.[5]

On our return, therefore, I immediately joined the light infantry and began the attack, after I had first seized a breastwork the enemy had on the Bedford road. From this instant the enemy showed no disposition to stand; but, having lost their direct retreat by our getting thus into their rear, their whole left was thrown back in the utmost disorder on their right. And had our left under General Grant, instead of marching along the shore, taken up and continued its march along the summit of the hill (as I had taken the liberty of recommending and [as] might, I believe, have been done) every man of this detached corps of the rebels must have been killed or taken. As it was, the victory was certainly very great, for that part of the rebel line which was opposed to General Grant in a strong country, hearing our cannon in their rear, immediately broke. This, easing him, gave him an opportunity of pressing forward and taking many prisoners, whereas before he had found it very difficult to penetrate— which occasioned the heaviest loss to fall on his detachment, though in truth the loss suffered by our whole army was not great, if we except the death of Colonel Grant of the Fortieth and of one or two other excellent officers. But that of the rebels was very severe according to Lord Stirling's account, who told me that out of thirty battalions which they had in front of their works most of their generals, cannon, and colors fell into our hands; and a great number of other officers, with about four thousand men, were either killed, drowned, or taken.[6]

General Vaughan, who led the grenadiers, having pressed after the enemy up the hill beyond a road which Sir William Howe was unwilling we should pass, was called back by his orders. I must confess that (notwithstanding I knew the Commander in Chief's wishes) I had permitted this move, and I had at the moment but little inclination to check the ardor of our troops when I saw the enemy flying in such a panic before them. I was also not without hopes that His Excellency, who was on a neighboring hill and, of course, saw their confusion, might be tempted to order us to march directly forward down the road to the ferry, by which, if we succeeded, everything on the island must have been ours. I do not mean, however, by this to

5. Clinton did not order the cavalrymen to pursue the enemy into the wood, "as I did not choose that their first *coup d'essai* should be under such disadvantages." [Clinton to Gen. Harvey,] Sept. 3 and 4.

6. Washington's estimate of the total number killed, wounded, and missing was 700 to 1000; a recent historian concludes that the figure was nearer 1500. Fitzpatrick, *Writings of Washington, 6*, 21; Wallace, *Appeal to Arms*, p. 111 and n. 12.

insinuate that Sir William Howe was in the least wrong in not doing so. On the contrary I am persuaded that he acted from intelligence, and, had I at the time possessed the same information he was master of, I should possibly, like him, have judged it prudent to wait for the less hazardous certainty of regular approaches. Nor can any after-knowledge of the fallacy of that information invalidate the propriety of his conduct under it.[7] It is, therefore, without the smallest intention to detract from his merit that I only mention the circumstance—though it has since, indeed, been very well known that the rebels had not at that very moment above 800 men behind that great extent of line (which would have required at least 6000 to defend the different works along it) [and] not a single close work that commanded the landing at the ferry (which Sir William Howe from his intelligence was suspicious of); and that the ground leading to it, being greatly cut with ravines, is unfavorable for defense and offers a number of covers to shelter an advancing army. Could this, therefore, have been but known at the time—had, therefore, the attempt been made—the completest success would most likely have been the consequence. For there is no saying to what extent the effect resulting from the entire loss of that army might have been carried in that early stage of the rebellion, or where it would have stopped.

We encamped that evening in front of the enemy's works, and the next night broke ground at a few hundred yards' distance from a redoubt on their left. But in the course of the subsequent night they wisely evacuated them, and very ably effected the retreat of their whole army over the East River. I took the liberty, on being asked, upon this to advise that we should march as soon as possible to Hell Gate (as our raising batteries at that place would be the most likely to give jealousy), make every appearance of intending to force a landing on York Island, and when everything was prepared at Montresor's Island (which I would have laid hold of for the purpose) throw the troops on shore from thence at Morrisania, and move forward directly to mask Kings Bridge by occupying the heights of Fordham.[8] Had this been done without loss of time, while the rebel army lay broken in separate corps between New York and that place,

7. Anderson quotes this passage to indicate that Clinton defended Howe's actions. (*Command of the Howe Brothers,* p. 139.) Sir Henry meant to do nothing of the sort; in context his criticism is thinly veiled. Its justification is the fact that Howe lost as good a chance as Britain ever had of winning the war at a stroke.

8. Montresor's was the present Randalls Island, Morrisania the southwestern Bronx, and Kings Bridge the point of exit from Manhattan across the Harlem River. Clinton was developing the strategy that he had sketched to Howe in the spring (p. 40 n. 1): a turning movement to seize the line of the Harlem, thereby either surrounding the American army on Manhattan or forcing it into a pell-mell retreat.

it must have suddenly crossed the North River or each part of it fallen into our power one after the other.

The arguments adduced for landing on York Island proved, however, most prevalent. And it was in consequence at first concerted that the King's army should land there in two divisions—the one which I was to lead at Horen's [Hoorn's] Hook as soon as the fort there could be silenced, and the other under the Commander in Chief at Kipp's Bay.[9] But some difficulties being discovered in the crossing at Hell Gate, the strength of the rebel fort there (the ground behind being very commanding), and the pilots' refusing to bring thither the ships of war that were intended to cover the descent, all induced a determination to land the whole army at the latter [Kipp's Bay]. I must confess that I strenuously opposed this in council. My reasons were that the shore at that place was entrenched and full of troops and the landing practicable only on projecting points of rocks or in muddy bays [10] entirely exposed to the enemy's fire, which the frigates could not throw a shot among them to stop after we got on shore; that the ground above the landing place was favorable for batteries against our shipping, and we should consequently have run the hazard of being beat in detail; and finally that the loss of time and delay of operations by this course must be very great [even] though we should be lucky enough to succeed, because we should after all have to remove the rebel army from Kings Bridge, whereas according to the plan I had proposed the whole, I thought, might have been finished at one stroke.

On receiving my orders to prepare for landing with the first embarkation, I immediately went on board the *Roebuck* to reconnoiter; and from her decks I could plainly discern that the rebel entrenchment (which was about 300 yards from her) was well lined with men, whose countenance appeared respectable and firm. On my return from the ship I met the boats with the troops coming out of Newtown Creek; but, being told that the tide of flood ran so strong just then in the channel that they would be carried above Kipp's Bay, I advised Commodore Hotham to order them up alongside the transports and wait

9. Hoorn's Hook is in the present Carl Schurz Park, on the East River at 89th Street; Kipp's Bay is a large cove on the East River between 34th and 38th Streets.

10. *Clinton's note:* It had been reported to the Commander in Chief that the landing in these bays at the pitch of high water was on firm sand, and it is not impossible we should have found them so could the landing have been effected exactly at that instant. But, the flood tide running a sluice in the channel two hours after the ebb takes place along the shore, the flatboats could not cross the channel until the slack had taken place there; consequently they could not possibly arrive in the bays before the fall of the water would have left them in the condition above described.

until the slack. As soon as the rebels saw this movement, concluding that we proposed to wait for the ebb in order to land lower down at Stuyvesant's Cove, they hurried away out of their entrenchments thither to oppose us.[11] But, becoming immediately sensible of their mistake when they perceived the boats making for Kipp's Bay on the slack, they endeavored by a short cut to hasten back to them. Suspecting, therefore, their intention and the route they were going to take, I requested the Commodore to order the frigates to load with round shot instead of grape and point their guns toward a windmill, between which and the shore I knew they must pass in their return. This had the desired effect, as they were immediately checked and reduced to the necessity of making a considerable detour to reach us. Through this means the landing was made without opposition, though it had at first the appearance of leading to serious consequences if the rebels had not luckily committed this blunder.[12]

As soon as the troops were all on shore, in obedience to my orders I laid hold of the height of Inclenberg [Murray Hill] and sent forward Colonel Donop with four battalions of Hessian Grenadiers, with a view of intercepting the retreat of different parties of rebels who appeared before us in motion from all quarters.[13] On this service the Hessians fell in with two of the enemy's battalions who were in a redoubt and seemingly disposed to lay down their arms; [they] might have been made prisoners had it not been for the impetuosity of an officer who, by hastily throwing in a fire, brought on a skirmish which cost some lives on both sides, and gave many an opportunity of escaping, so that only a very few, with the two pieces of cannon in the work, fell into our hands. It happened unfortunately, too, that much time was lost before the second embarkation landed (it being some hours after the first), as by our stretching immediately across the island great numbers of the enemy must have been taken prisoners.

11. Newtown Creek is an inlet on the Long Island shore of the East River, opposite Kipp's Bay; Stuyvesant's Cove, on Manhattan, was at the eastern end of the present 15th Street.

12. "My advice has ever been to avoid even the possibility of a check," Clinton had written early that morning. "We live by victory. Are we sure of it this day? J'en doute. These people are assembled in force. Their entrenchments are not exposed to the fire from our ships; those, on the contrary, are much so to the rebels' fixed [?] batteries. In short, I like it not. No diversion, no demonstration but what a child would see through, little prospect of victory without buying it dear, some apprehension of receiving—what we might have given—a defeat en détail." (Memorandum, Sept. 15.) The "entrenchments" were in fact so trifling that the Americans did not try to hold them, but fled in confusion; see Ward, War of the Revolution, 1, 242, 244–245.

13. Washington attempted to rally these fleeing troops and came within an ace of being captured. See Ward, 1, 242–243.

But, my orders being to secure the Inclenberg, I did not think myself at liberty to attempt it before Sir William Howe joined us; and indeed I do not know but, had we made such a move, even then we should have cut off many of them who had not yet got over the river or to Kings Bridge.[14]

A detachment of the King's troops now marched into the city of New York, which the enemy had abandoned on our first landing; and the gross of the army formed in front of the town, the line extending from Horen's [Hoorn's] Hook to near Bloomingdale on the North River.[15] On my going the next morning to take the command of the foreposts, I found that the light infantry, having with rather too much impetuosity pursued some parties of rebels toward their works, had got themselves somewhat disadvantageously engaged under a heavy fire of grape, upon which I directly advised the officer who led them to fall back a few yards to more favorable ground. This was effected with certain precautions but not without some loss, as the rebels were in considerable force—not less than 7000 men. It, however, since appears that we might have held this post, which would have probably been a better one than that we took afterward, as it might have saved us the dangerous passage of Hell Gate.[16] But the Commander in Chief had, without doubt, very sufficient reasons for ordering me to retreat to Apthorp's, which we did at dusk without receiving a single shot from the enemy.

The army continuing in this position for near a month, little else was done in all that time but the taking possession of Paulus Hook without a contest on the 23d of September.[17] For, there being no chance of stirring the rebels from their strongholds at Kings Bridge by any but a direct attack as long as we continued in New York Island, it took up some time to determine upon the means of doing it

14. I.e., had the British moved west to the Hudson as soon as Howe came up. Instead their principal moves were north and south, and were made only after considerable delay. This pause on Murray Hill was later explained by the story that the British commanders had been beguiled by Mrs. Murray's hospitality. Clinton's account, however, is only part of the evidence that disproves that pleasant legend. See *ibid.*, 2, 937–939.

15. Bloomingdale was an area on the west shore of Manhattan, between the present 90th and 100th Streets.

16. Clinton minimizes what was considered at the time a major action and an American victory; see Ward, 1, 247–252. His meaning seems to be that the British, if they had held their position, might have established themselves on the Harlem and subsequently crossed it to Morrisania; from there they could have advanced on New Rochelle by the coast road instead of by water through Hell Gate.

17. Apthorp's House was Howe's headquarters; it stood approximately on the present 9th Avenue, between 90th and 91st Streets. Paulus Hook was on the right bank of the Hudson, in what is now Jersey City; it subsequently became the principal western outpost in the British defenses of New York.

by a move to the continent. For this purpose many different plans were suggested, among which my former one of landing at Morrisania was mentioned. That, however, I could not now support, as the situation of the enemy was very materially altered—because, when I proposed the move to Morrisania, the rebel army was dispersed in separate posts between Amboy and Kings Bridge; but now they were collected in the latter in great force, and had above six weeks given them to complete their works there. My present opinion, therefore, was that our landing should be made at such a distance from the enemy's gross that our whole army might have time to be disembarked before they could come upon us in numbers sufficient to disturb us, yet at the same time so near their three communications with the continent [that] they must be obliged to fight us on our own terms or fall back.[18]

Conformable to these ideas I proposed to the General and Admiral [19] that, having first given the enemy every jealousy for Jersey, the boats should drop down silently by night to Whitestone or Haviland and, the army being marched thither, suddenly passed from thence to Myer's Neck and moved on to [New] Rochelle, where we were directly upon their great communication with New England, and nearer to the principal points of the other two (Croton and Pine [Bridge] on the Croton, and White Plains) than they were, which with the assistance of our armed vessels in the Hudson would enable us to embarrass the enemy's supplies both from the eastern and southern colonies.[20] But—as Lord Howe thought the ships of war, transports, etc., could not lie in safety off Myer's Neck—this plan was overruled; and we had to lament that what His Lordship proposed could not be adopted, viz., to land the troops at Wilkins' Point or Castle Hill [21] under cover of a single frigate. For (this place being situated within three miles of the rebel army, the ground favorable for them and not to be approached by a ship of war nearer than three-quarters of a mile, and the shore of such a nature that a landing could be made on it only at certain times of tide, which did not include above five hours in the twelve) the Commander in Chief concurred with the

18. Clinton deleted parts of this passage but did not substitute another version.
19. Lord Howe, the General's brother, had assumed command of the naval forces in America in February.
20. Whitestone was on the Long Island shore, in what is now Flushing; Haviland was the present Hewlett Point, Long Island, and Myer's Neck the present Davenport Neck at New Rochelle. The three routes of communication for the American army were: (1) the coastal road by New Rochelle to Connecticut; (2) the inland road by White Plains to Connecticut; (3) the road that forked northward from 2 at White Plains, crossed the Croton at Pine Bridge (on the south shore of the present Croton Reservoir), and followed the east bank of the Hudson to Albany.
21. Two points at the mouth of Westchester Creek, directly opposite Whitestone.

other Generals in adopting a proposal made by Sir William Erskine to land on Frog's [Throg's] Neck, which, being equally convenient to Rochelle, Rodman's Point,[22] or the Bronx, I acceded to because, though roundabout, it led finally to the object I had in view.

The first embarkation of the army intended for this service got into the boats at Kipp's Bay at three o'clock in the morning of the 12th of October. But a variety of accidents prevented our moving before broad daylight, and just as we were entering the very dangerous passage of Hell Gate an excessive thick fog came on, which enveloped us with utter darkness. The Admiral, who was present, persisted notwithstanding in the prosecution of the move at every hazard, and by his own excellent management and that of his officers the whole got through, almost miraculously, without any other loss than that of an artillery boat with a few men and three six-pounders, and even that by an accident not in the least imputable to His Lordship or the navy. About eight o'clock we arrived off Frog's Point, where we found a frigate stationed to cover our debarkations. A few rebels made their appearance as we approached the shore; but some scattering shot soon dispersed them, and the landing was effected without loss. As soon as the troops could be formed, we pushed for Westchester Bridge in hopes of securing it. But the enemy had been too quick for us, having already destroyed it in their retreat.[23]

As we had now, therefore, no other *débouchée* but over a narrow neck of meadow, which was masked by a strong work belonging to the enemy [and] occupied in some force, we found ourselves after all our trouble and loss of time under a necessity of re-embarking and landing either at Wilkins' Point, protected by our artillery from Frog's Point, or at Rodman's. The latter I preferred as leading to Rochelle, which I constantly considered as the fittest position for answering the object of the move. The want of provisions, however, preventing our stirring for some days, it was the 18th of October before this plan could be carried into execution. At two in the morning of this day the *avant garde* under my orders embarked; but we could not move till

22. The present Rodman Neck, between East Chester Bay and Pelham Bay.

23. *A loose note by Clinton:* On our landing from Frog's Neck Lee is supposed to have gone to Washington and prevailed on him to have moved. But, had it been possible for us to have been at Rochelle by Myer's Neck three days sooner, Washington must have attacked us on our own terms or lost *all* his communication and laid down his arms, probably. [For Lee's part in the American retreat see Alden, *General Charles Lee*, p. 144 and n. 18; on the time element in Washington's escape see Carrington, *Battles of the Revolution*, pp. 236–237. Clinton subsequently stigmatized the landing as "a tweedledum business," and complained that Howe had annoyed him by contradictory and needless messages by his aides-de-camp. Memorandum of Clinton-Howe conversation, July 6, 1777.]

five, and the frigate which had been ordered to Tom Pell's Point[24] to cover us got aground. However, six pieces of cannon, which Sir William Howe had judiciously placed for the purpose on Frog's Point in case of accidents, gave us full protection by obliging the rebels to keep under shelter until we got abreast of the landing place. They then began to fire a few shot. But, as I was certain they could not be in any great force, I ordered the debarkation to proceed; and we took possession of the ground on the end of the neck as they quitted it. The moment the whole *avant garde* was ashore I passed the defile and detached Lord Cornwallis with the grenadiers, light infantry, and First Chasseurs to our right, with directions to cover that flank and preserve the communication open between us. As we advanced, we found the enemy strongly posted behind stone walls, from whence they might have greatly obstructed our march had it not been for the corps I had detached to the right—the number of the enemy being said to have been at least 14,000.[25] The Commander in Chief joined us here and, the rebels being forced to quit the high-road, the gross of our army lay this night on their great communication with New England.

Many plans for our further proceedings became now again the subject of deliberation. Mine, still inclining for Rochelle, was at last adopted, and the grand depot removed in consequence to Myer's Neck. For, though Lord Howe had formerly objected to this place as dangerous for the ships, it was now, upon being examined more minutely, judged to be the most commodious that could be found; and all our supplies were accordingly landed there. On the 25th of October the *avant garde,* under my orders, was directed to make a forward move to within three miles of the rebel camp at White Plains; and the rest of the army following (except the corps which had been detached to Parson's Pass and Rochelle) we encamped in that position and drew our supplies from Myer's.[26]

By this move, which had forced the enemy to pass the Bronx and gain the White Plains passes[?], we reduced the enemy to a single

24. On the shore of the present Pelham Bay Park.

25. A fantastic exaggeration. The American force—the famous "amphibious" Marblehead Regiment under Col. John Glover—was about 750 men. See Ward, *War of the Revolution, 1,* 257–258.

26. Parson's Pass was in East Chester, on the coast road from New York to New Rochelle.

A loose note by Clinton for his history seems to belong at this point: "The impetuosity of a new corps of Jägers had nearly drawn us into an action with Washington's army on a march to White Plains. It was necessary to sustain them and bring them off with credit, lest a lasting impression should be made to their prejudice." On this incident see Carrington, *Battles of the Revolution,* p. 236.

communication. But, not knowing the ground about White Plains or how the rebels had posted themselves on it, I could not think an immediate attack of their camp there prudent, and therefore advised the Commander in Chief, if he had any such intention, to first reconnoiter in force and, having formed his plan in consequence, fall back to Rochelle and detach along the road to Ma[ma]roneck as if intending to strike a blow toward Rye, then (after having made himself perfectly acquainted with the roads) move, in as many columns as he could form in, by a night's march directly to White Plains and attack the enemy's camp at daylight.

The General seemed at first to incline to my opinion. But, being induced, perhaps, by more general information to alter it, he ordered me on the 27th to take out a part of the army to reconnoiter. I accordingly did so and made my report, but could not from what I saw recommend a direct attack, as I suspected that the enemy's lines at the White Plains shouldered to the Bronx and to the mountains, whereby their flanks were safe and their retreat practicable when they pleased. The next day, however, the army was ordered to advance toward White Plains, upon which I requested the Commander in Chief would allow it to move at least in two columns, and offered to lead that on the right with whatever guides I could procure. This was accordingly permitted; and, as we advanced, upon seeing the enemy in motion he sent me word they were forming to attack. But I was certain, the instant they discovered my column, they would retire; and I therefore halted the head of it and detached Lord Cornwallis from its rear with some battalions and cannon, with a view of getting round them. This, however, was prevented by the enemy's advance [guard] continuing to retire. For after a cannon shot or two, and posting a corps on their communication behind the Bronx, they fell back to their lines and gave the march to the whole.

Part of the left column was now directed to cross the Bronx, and I happened by it to have an opportunity of observing an inconvenience which I had long apprehended might result from officers' carrying fuzees, which was then and had been the general practice on the American service. Two British regiments, having very spiritedly passed the river, suddenly found themselves exposed to a very heavy fire from a body of rebels posted on the top of an adjacent hill. The officer who led them immediately formed in column for attack and advanced; the instant I saw the move I declared it decisive. But when the officer had marched forward about twenty paces he halted, fired his fuzee, and began to reload (his column remaining during the time under the enemy's fire), upon which I pronounced it a *coup manqué*, foretelling at the same time that they would break. It happened as I said, and I could not help remarking to Sir William Howe that, if the battle should be lost, that officer was the occasion of it.[27] I had scarcely done speaking when Lord Cornwallis came up with the same observation. The matter being, however, quickly recovered, the hill was carried, and the rebel corps posted there was driven back to their lines with some loss.[28]

After this little brush we paused a while, the army remaining astride of the Bronx. The Commander in Chief now desired me to examine the enemy's right and rear; and, after having reconnoitered it with some care, my report was that the position was to be forced by seizing with his left a bald hill that lay on our side the river and threatened and commanded a passage of it, [and by] making a diversion at the same time with the center but following it up with caution, and the right cooperating as far as possible. My reason for giving this caution with respect to the center was because, the attack from thence being over a single bridge against a double entrenchment on commanding ground, it might probably miscarry, or be at least severely handled, unless both wings attacked in force at the same moment.

The attack being afterward determined on, I received orders late at night to lead it from the center the next morning. I own this resolution surprised me, after the report and opinions which I had given in, and the more so as no previous notice had been given me, that I might have an opportunity of taking another look at the ground. Finding, therefore, that it was not intended that either of the flanks should cooperate to any effect (the left having orders not to advance beyond the river and the right not to stir until I had succeeded), I took the liberty of intimating to the Commander in Chief that it might prove rather hazardous to make any attack from center or right until we saw what would be the effect of one from the left as far as the Bronx, and that even then they ought to be pressed with caution, as the enemy

27. *A loose note by Clinton:* General Burgoyne and I have often represented the absurdity of officers' being armed with fuzees, and the still greater impropriety . . . by which they neglected the opportunity of employing their divisions to advantage. These [divisions] had no confidence in them, and they [the officers] became in fact as the worst soldiers in their divisions. [Clinton uses "division" in the generic sense of a part of the army. A fuzee, or fusil, was a flintlock musket.]

28. Clinton's movements during the battle are obscure in his description. He first led the right wing; Howe then arrived and ordered him to command the left, which was to attack the American position on Chatterton's Hill. Clinton and Cornwallis reached the Bronx, and the former was about to give his orders for the assault when Gen. von Heister came up with the Hessians. Clinton felt that the German should be left in command, and remained as a spectator. See his memorandum on the battle, Feb. 9, 1777.

had a very strong position in the gorges of the mountains behind them.

Bad weather, however, having afterward much swelled the river, Sir William Howe sent for me about two in the morning to ask my opinion respecting the present expediency of the proposed attack. I made answer that His Excellency was already possessed of my opinions with respect to the general expediency, but that rain could be no objection with me while the river remained passable for the left, and I should be ready to obey his commands whenever he thought proper to order the attack. The center was accordingly soon after put in motion. But the rebels, having quitted their lines in the night, had fallen back to the mountains about a mile in their rear (just as I supposed they would), and it was judged inexpedient to follow them. The Hessian Grenadiers were therefore directed to march into the ground they had quitted and take post there.

It being now impossible to turn either the enemy's left or right or to attack them in front to any effect, and ignorant as we were of the progress of the northern army,[29] it was deemed proper to avail ourselves of the direct communication we had thus opened with the North River and approximate to New York Island. For, though we might possibly have determined the enemy's retreat over the Bronx River to New England by placing the King's army on the right of the Bronx, where it made a bend round their right, difficulties in getting up provisions and other supplies, as I was told, rendered a longer stay inexpedient.[30]

The whole army consequently passed the Bronx at daybreak on the 3d of November, the rear guard being composed of the reserve, the Guards, First Brigade, light infantry, cavalry, and Hessian Grenadiers under my orders. As these last were supposed still to hold the rebel camp at White Plains, I was ordered to march close under the lines covered by them. But, through some mistake, they had quitted that position, and consequently the march of the rear by that route became *sujet à caution*. Upon finding, therefore, that the Hessian Grenadiers were no longer in possession of that ground, I ventured (after consulting Lord Cornwallis, who was near me) to make a slight alteration in the route allotted for the rear. But, the Commander in Chief having thought proper to let me know by an aide-de-camp that he ex-

29. *Clinton's note:* That Sir Guy Carleton had by wonderful exertion raised a navy, by a noble decision taken the command of it, gained a most decisive victory, regained the lakes, uncovered Crown Point, and threatened Ticonderoga and consequently all the northern frontier, which made a most powerful diversion in our favor.

30. For a discussion of the ambiguities in this paragraph see Anderson, *Command of the Howe Brothers*, pp. 192–193.

pected his order of march was not to be altered, I had nothing to do but make my bow and obey.[31] Accordingly the head of the column had no sooner got upon the bridge but, as I suspected, they were saluted with a running fire of musketry, which continued until the whole got over. However, we fortunately suffered little, as the enemy had neglected to run down cannon, and the numbers who got into the lines happened to be very inconsiderable.

Soon after this I received orders to take upon me the command of an expedition against Rhode Island. Consequently I cannot detail with precision the subsequent movements of the main army. As I did not, however, embark for some time afterward, I had sometimes an opportunity of knowing what was going forward, and of being of course an occasional spectator. On these occasions I still took the liberty, whenever I was called upon or permitted, to contribute my mite of advice as the course of circumstances and events suggested. The attack of Fort Washington being one of the transactions which occurred in this interim, I happened to be present when the arrangement of the move was under consideration; and, foreseeing the obstructions a single attack—which was at first proposed—might have to encounter, I ventured to recommend two others in cooperation. But indeed I believe the Hessians would have succeeded of themselves if they had divided and made two attacks instead of one.[32]

I must confess that I never approved of the Rhode Island expedition, as I looked upon the time of year as more favorable for a move to the southward, which appeared to me of the utmost importance in that early stage of the rebellion, before time had been given to those provinces to strengthen themselves. On the contrary, had the rebels in Rhode Island done what they might, I should have found them in an entrenched camp, strong by situation, and at a season of the year when the ground in that climate is generally too hard for penetrating, the country covered with snow, and not a possibility of building huts or procuring straw or even wood for firing. These I judged to be sufficiently strong reasons for disapproving that expedi-

31. *Clinton's note:* Sir Henry Clinton, being hurt at the little confidence the Commander in Chief seemed to place in him, was provoked to express himself rather peevishly on the occasion to Lord Cornwallis, who was close by him. This gave rise to a singular anecdote, which will be noticed in its proper place. [Clinton has deleted part of this note but made no substitution. For the anecdote see below, p. 65 n. 15.]

32. This sentence is obscure. The attack was made in three divisions, with a fourth participating before the end; the Hessians took a leading role, and for the final assault they did in fact divide into two columns. See Ward, *War of the Revolution, 1,* 271–274.

tion; and I took the liberty of laying them in the most forcible point of view before the Admiral and General, making a separate proposal at the same time to each of them, viz., to defer the expedition to Rhode Island and send the corps allotted for that service under convoy up the Chesapeake to within forty miles of Philadelphia, and the Commander in Chief to march thither at the same time by land along the Delaware with 10,000 men while the fleet sailed up that river accompanied by an adequate body of troops for landing occasionally and removing impediments.[33] But I very soon perceived that the plan of possessing Rhode Island had been too strongly determined on to be laid aside. The Admiral wanted a winter station for his large ships, and every other consideration must give way.

After Fort Washington surrendered a new field opened to our view, the rebel army being greatly diminished by losses in battle and desertion, the debris split into separate small bodies, and the time for which the men had enlisted on the eve of expiring, and Sir Guy Carleton's successful operation to the northward being felt. In this unpromising and shattered state of their affairs I proposed that my detachment, being at that very time embarked and ready for any move, should be thrown on shore in the Jerseys either at Elizabeth Town or Amboy for the purpose of cooperating with Lord Cornwallis, who had crossed the North River a little above Fort Lee in chase of General Washington—who, being reduced to nearly 3000 men, was retiring to his magazines at [New] Brunswick and from thence to the Delaware. Failing likewise in this, I finally proposed to Lord Howe to take me with him up the Delaware and place me at Philadelphia. This in all probability would have dispersed the Congress, and consequently at that moment have deranged all their affairs. But it is possible the lateness of the season and a thousand other substantial reasons, which I knew nothing of, prevented the two chiefs from adopting any of my plans, though from my ignorance of them I could not help lamenting at the time that they were not carried into execution, and which I now am convinced must have proved decisive.

Lord Cornwallis' success in striking a panic into and dispersing the affrighted remains of Mr. Washington's army was so great before I left New York that I had little doubt, and told Sir William Howe so, of His Lordship's overtaking them before they could reach the Dela-

---

33. A few days, Clinton felt, would give the British control of the Delaware and of New Jersey. "Should it be difficult afterward to penetrate on the east of Hudson's River, you may by the west." Memorandum of Nov. 8; see also Clinton to Gen. Harvey, Nov. 26.

ware, or of his at least crossing the river with them and laying hold of Philadelphia.[34] (For I could not possibly have the most distant suspicion that His Lordship's orders were not to pursue farther than Brunswick.) And I own these favorable appearances flattered me with expectations that the rebellion was on the brink of being wholly crushed by the annihilation of that corps. For, though we had not hitherto any considerable victories to plume ourselves with (except that of the 27th of August), the rebel General had not a single advantage to carry to Congress. And I therefore presume I was justified in conceiving that, if some extraordinary reverse did not soon happen, there was good ground to hope the disaffected colonies, upon finding it impossible to raise another army on account of the general dejection such an event must occasion, would be compelled to give up the contest, and that this campaign would consequently be the last.

When I communicated these sentiments to Sir William Howe, in a consultation he honored me with on the present posture of affairs, I was much concerned to find his expectations not quite so sanguine.[35] And, upon his hinting to me his intention of running a chain of posts across east Jersey, I took the liberty of cautioning him against the possibility of its being broken in upon in the winter, as he knew the Americans were trained to stratagem and enterprise, that they knew every trick of that country of chicane and would quickly catch at any opening that might offer in that way. I even advised him, after having pushed [36] Washington to the utmost, if he could not succeed in taking his army, to evacuate the Jerseys altogether in preference to any such measure, and either act with them to the southward or withdraw his troops to Staten Island until the spring, as the few friends we had in the province might be brought away with them and more easily protected there and at New York than by having established posts dispersed at a distance from each other in the Jerseys, where no offensive move of éclat could be undertaken in winter but a misfortune might be followed by the most serious consequences, as we should most probably in that case have the whole business to begin over again.

On the 26th of November Sir William Howe delivered to me his

34. *A loose note by Clinton:* On Sir William Howe's telling me Lord Cornwallis had landed in Jersey and was pursuing Washington, I proposed to him that instead of going to Rhode Island Lord Percy and I should be landed at Amboy, and endeavor to intercept Washington in his retreat to the Delaware. I proposed it afterward to Lord Howe, but it was not approved of. It was alleged that a place of safety was absolutely necessary for the navy, and Rhode Island the only one; in return for the zeal which had been shown by the Admiral and the whole navy it became us to pay them every attention and, if Rhode Island was the only safe post, to occupy it.
35. See Anderson, *Command of the Howe Brothers*, pp. 209–212.
36. "Passed" in the MS.

final instructions, to proceed to Rhode Island "and, in conjunction with the officer who should be appointed to command the naval part of the expedition, to make a descent on that island in the most effectual manner for the full possession of it, and for the security of the town and harbor of Newport; and to take such other posts as should be necessary for its preservation, and for other purposes I might judge expedient for the advancement of His Majesty's service and for distressing the enemy." [37]

Accordingly we sailed from New York on the 1st of December with two brigades of British and two of Hessian troops, under convoy of a squadron of His Majesty's ships commanded by Commodore Sir Peter Parker; and on the evening of the 7th we anchored in Weaver's Bay on the west side of that island. The troops being disembarked the next morning without the least opposition, Major General Prescot, with the grenadiers and light infantry, was immediately sent forward with a view of intercepting a body of rebels who had fled from the works in and about Newport toward Bristol Ferry, and Lieutenant General Earl Percy followed at the head of the heavy battalions to sustain him; but the rebels, who retired with precipitancy, had abandoned their fort at the ferry and crossed over to the continent before the King's troops could overtake them, so that only two pieces of cannon and a few prisoners fell into our hands.[38] A battalion had been also detached to take possession of Newport, where we found some artillery and stores which the rebels had not time to remove. But the most material prize unluckily escaped us, as the rebel privateers under Hopkins, consisting of three large ships and several other armed vessels,[39] had run up Providence River on the first appearance of our fleet.[40]

The facility with which we had obtained this important acquisition might have tempted me to have proceeded further. But I was

37. The quotation is a free rendering of Howe to Clinton, Nov. 26. See also same to same, Dec. 3, and a day-by-day·account of the expedition, from Nov. 25 to Dec. 15, at the end of "A Journal of an Expedition to the Southern Colonies under the Command of Major-General Clinton," CP.

38. Weaver's Bay, or Cove, is just north of Newport; the ferry to Bristol Neck was at the northern tip of the island.

39. This was the American fleet under Esek Hopkins. It was blockaded in Narragansett Bay, and in the spring of 1777 Hopkins was suspended from his command.

40. Clinton's note: A council of sea and land officers had been held on the expediency of a move against Providence; and a small one against Bristol was directed in consequence, merely to try the enemy's countenance. But such a violent storm of snow came on in the course of the preceding night and [such] a severe frost the day following that all the Generals, Sir Peter Parker, Commodore Hotham, and all the other sea as well as land officers declared that nothing of the sort ought to be risked in that climate so late in the year.

aware of the great risk I should run should I place large waters between divisions of my little army at that time of year in so rigorous a climate, wherein a violent snowstorm or frost, catching me suddenly in the midst of a move, might have put it out of my power either to advance or fall back. For, though report magnified the number of the rebels collected at Providence and Bristol to several thousands, yet, as I knew they were mostly militia except two or three artillery companies, no apprehension from them would have withheld me had the season been less critical.[41] These considerations induced me, therefore, to lose no time in putting the troops under cover and laying in magazines of fuel, which the severity of the cold began already to make necessary.

Having now given directions for constructing such works as I judged necessary for securing the different posts I established in Rhode Island and its dependencies, and [having] ascertained the number of men they would require to garrison them, I made my report of everything to the Commander in Chief, and availed myself of the permission he had given me to return to Europe in the *Asia*, which was ordered to England for repair.[42] I therefore delivered over to Earl Percy the command of the King's troops in that district and left to His Lordship the completing the defenses of the posts and the prosecuting such further operations as he might find conducive to the good of His Majesty's service.

41. Soon after his arrival Clinton reported his dispositions to Howe. The Americans, he was convinced, were profoundly disturbed by his success; but he was also convinced that he could not push it further at that time of year. To attack the enemy at Providence with his small force would be to risk a repulse, "which to them would be a victory." [Clinton to Howe, late Dec. or early Jan.,] filed at the end of Dec., 1776.

42. Clinton's aide, Capt. Duncan Drummond, preceded him to England with news of the capture of Rhode Island, and was most cordially received. The King expressed his satisfaction with Clinton's conduct, his affection for him, and his desire to keep him happy. Drummond and Reeve assured the General that the Sullivan's Island business was forgotten, and urged him in consequence to lay aside his quarrel with Parker. Reeve to Clinton, Feb. 2; Reeve and Drummond to Clinton, Feb. 15, 1777.

CHAPTER 3

The Journey to England and the Command
on Manhattan, March to October, 1777

Sir Henry Clinton graciously received by His Majesty and his conduct approved. Returns to America. Left in the command at New York. Expedition to Philadelphia. Rebels attack Sir Henry Clinton's posts and are repulsed. His descent in the Jersies. Forts Montgomery and Clinton carried by storm. General Vaughan detached up the North River and burns Esopus. The Highlands evacuated by Sir William Howe's order. Sir Henry Clinton solicits leave to return to England.

On my arrival in England in March I had the satisfaction to receive from His Majesty the most gracious marks of his royal approbation of my whole services and conduct.[1] And, having sometimes the honor of being asked by the new Minister [Germain] my opinions of past and the intended plans of future operations, I thought it my duty to give them candidly though with diffidence, as far as my little experience—aided by some knowledge of the theater of the war and the strength and resources of the enemy—could enable me. In these conversations, though I could not say a great deal in approbation of the extensive cantonments of the army in Jersey at the close of the last year's campaign,[2] I did not fail to justify the Commander in Chief

1. Germain took credit for obtaining Clinton the Order of the Bath. The King had remarked that the General, despite all marks of approval, still felt hurt; Germain had replied by suggesting the knighthood, even though there was no vacancy in the Order. George had hesitated for fear of offending Howe. (Clinton, when told this, "looked very grum.") But Lord George had persuaded him that Howe "had no right to monopolize all the red ribbons nor anything else." The Minister retailed this to Clinton in a courtly interview, in which "His Lordship said a thousand civil one-two-threes, and I as many polite four-five-sixes." Clinton memorandum, undated and filed at the end of Apr., 1777.
    The King's version of the episode was different. Clinton had let it be known among the officers in America that he insisted on publication of his entire dispatch about Sullivan's Island; if this were not done, the army would think he was in disgrace. George and Lord North agreed that publication would be unwise, and decided upon a knighthood as the only means of re-establishing Clinton's prestige. See two letters from the King to John Robinson, Mar. 11, Additional MS 37,833 (British Museum), fols. 155, 159.
2. Clinton believed, before he left for Rhode Island, that he and Howe were agreed on not extending these cantonments. When he later heard that Sir William had ex-

for placing the Hessians at Trenton, as that was their proper post in the line, and no troops could have behaved better than Colonel Rall's Brigade did in the attack of Fort Washington. And, notwithstanding the too great distance between the links of the chain which formed them, I was persuaded that, had the officer whom Sir William Howe entrusted with the command in that province ordered Rall to fall back on Donop, or Donop to have supported, or both to have fallen back on himself in case of being pressed, or that he had marched in time to sustain them, or had he directed a close work to have been thrown up at Trenton (which perhaps would have been the most judicious measure), Mr. Washington would have never made the attempt, or having made it must have failed.[3]

I could not, however, help lamenting that so good an opportunity as soon afterward offered of punishing the rebel General's temerity was lost. I mean when his little army was hemmed in by Lord Cornwallis at Trenton between the Assanpink, an unfordable creek whose only bridge was masked in force by His Lordship, and the Delaware, which was rendered at that time unpassable by floating ice. From such a situation he could not possibly have escaped with impunity had only a single patrol been sent to feel for him, from either Lord Cornwallis' camp or General Leslie's, toward Allentown or Cranbury. For His Lordship, holding the string of the bow, could have easily met Mr. Washington before he finished his circuit. Whereas his being deceived by the lighted fires and regularity of sounds, etc., in the rebel camp, which seem to have lulled him in[to] security, prevented His Lordship from knowing anything of his retreat until he heard his guns attacking Colonel Mawhood's Brigade several miles in his rear.[4]

When the design of employing an army under General Burgoyne on the upper Hudson was mentioned to me, I took the liberty of sug-

tended them, and before he knew of the resultant disaster, he criticized his chief so freely that Howe later taxed him with disloyalty. Memorandum of Clinton-Howe conversation, July 6, 1777.

3. I.e., in the first Battle of Trenton. See Anderson, *Command of the Howe Brothers*, pp. 201–209, for a justification of Howe's preceding strategy, and Alfred H. Bill, *The Campaign of Princeton, 1776–1777* (Princeton, 1948), for a lucid and lively account of the American offensive.

4. Clinton's loose notes contain comments on this second Battle of Trenton which, though pungent, are too repetitive to quote in full. He was convinced that the Americans had escaped solely through the negligence of Cornwallis, who had been duped by an elementary ruse: Washington had moved "so awkwardly that the youngest ensign in the [British] army was convinced he was marching, as he filed off before his fires and not behind them." In British military circles in America the Earl's blunder was notorious. In England Clinton tried to cover it up; he could not go into detail for fear of exposing "the most consummate ignorance I ever heard of [in] any officer above a corporal."

gesting the hazard of a miscarriage unless it was supported from below, and the consequent propriety of directing an early cooperation of Sir William Howe's whole force on the lower district of that river. For, as the attacking Philadelphia (which I understood to be the object of that general officer's first operations in the ensuing campaign) could be undertaken only upon the principle of drawing on a general action with the rebels, I humbly presumed that end, if anything could effect it, was more likely to be obtained by a vigorous exertion of the two British armies on the Hudson, the passes of which must consequently fall under their power (to the entire dissevering of the eastern from the southern colonies) unless the rebels should happen to be successful in an attack on either. Whereas Philadelphia, though the possession of it would certainly be of the utmost importance, was from its southern situation and from its requiring an army to keep it a fitter object to close than to begin the campaign with.

The many circumstances which occurred in the course of the last campaign to hurt my feelings made me very desirous of retiring. But the reasons assigned for the necessity of my return to America seemed to have more force than my objections. I was consequently obliged, in compliance with my friends' wishes, to recross the Atlantic and resume my former situation in Sir William Howe's army.[5] I was determined, however, to request I might not be forced to retain it any longer than the present campaign.

On my arrival at New York on the 5th of July I found that I was to be left in the command of that garrison and its dependencies, while the grand army under the Commander in Chief was employed on an expedition against Philadelphia, to which place they were to proceed by sea. I lost no time, therefore, when asked, in delivering to Sir William Howe my opinions upon the intended southern move with the same freedom I had done in England to the Minister. I stated the probable risks and delays it would be exposed to from the sickness and southerly winds generally prevalent in that climate in the summer

5. Sir Henry's principal reason for returning arose from the peculiar command situation. In the spring of 1776 he had received a dormant commission as general in America, to take effect if Howe were incapacitated; by it he would outrank the Hessian generals. (Germain Papers: Germain to Clinton, Apr. 25, "Military Dispatches, Secret, 1775–1782," Appendix.) The King, Germain, and Clinton's friends agreed that this commission necessitated his return. Otherwise—if anything happened to Howe, the command would fall to Gen. von Heister—a possibility, it seems, that no one dared contemplate. (Clinton to Burgoyne, Dec. 11; to Gen. Harvey, Dec. 19, 1777.) Howe's reputation for exposing himself recklessly in battle is suggested in Germain to Howe, Oct. 18, 1776, Historical Manuscripts Commission, *Report on the Manuscripts of Mrs. Stopford-Sackville, of Drayton House, Northamptonshire* (2 vols., London, 1904–10), 2, 42.

months, and with all deference suggested the many great and superior advantages to be derived at the present moment from a cooperation of his whole force with General Burgoyne on the River Hudson.[6] And I took the liberty at the same time to say that it was highly probable, the instant the fleet was decidedly gone to sea, [that] Mr. Washington would move with everything he could collect either against General Burgoyne or me and crush the one or the other, as neither would be very capable of withstanding such superior force unless timely intelligence should fortunately bring the fleet back to our relief.

My arguments were at first but little attended to, though from a conviction of the solid ground on which they were founded [they were] repeated perhaps oftener than was agreeable. By degrees, however, I thought I was listened to; and—though the momentary suspense which seemed to have been occasioned by what I said soon yielded to the predilection Sir William Howe had for his own plan, which he told me could not now with any propriety be laid aside on account of its having been approved of at home—I so far convinced him of the weak state he was leaving me in (6095 rank and file fit for duty and 1117 sick) that he made an addition of three thin battalions, and promised to lend me the Fourth Brigade until Mr. Washington removed to a greater distance, he being at that time within a day's march of the west side of the North River.[7]

But on the 18th of July the Commander in Chief informed me by

6. Clinton's initial preference seems to have been for a junction of the two armies, until he discovered on reaching New York that the campaign was late in opening. The American force to the north, consequently, "may have been so reinforced as to be able to hold against Burgoyne long before he gets to Albany." (Clinton [to Harvey], July 11.) He therefore urged indirect support, by a move in full force against the Highlands to open communication with Burgoyne. He was not, he pointed out to Howe, arguing from self-interest: his own plan would make him directly subordinate, whereas the move against Philadelphia would leave him a large measure of independence at New York. (Memoranda of Clinton-Howe conversations, July 8 and 13.) For Clinton's subsequent role see Jane Clark, "Responsibility for the Failure of the Burgoyne Campaign," *American Historical Review*, 35 (Apr., 1930), 542–559.

7. The memorandum of Clinton-Howe conversation of July 8, if accurate, reveals the Commander in Chief in a gloomy mood. He had less a predilection for his own plan than a sense of obligation to carry it out; he did not believe that the war could be won that year, and hoped that it could be the next. Clinton assured him that victory, in the opinion of the government, must be won before winter, and added his opinion that it could not be won in Pennsylvania—which might perhaps be conquered, but could not be kept. "If the ministers would not carry it on another year," Howe answered, "they had better give it up now."

The original memorandum is in Clinton's hand. His secretary's copy is legible but faulty, and its errors have produced misinterpretations. One of the most notable is in Partridge, *Sir Billy Howe*, pp. 172–174: the words that Partridge considers crucial are attributed to Howe, but were actually spoken by Clinton.

letter that this arrangement was "altered in consequence of intelligence that the rebel General had no intention of crossing the North River unless his army moved up it, and only waited in the mouth of the Clove to attend its motions—and that he had besides detached Sullivan with 3000 men to Albany. That these considerations, therefore, determined him to take the Fourth Brigade with him."[8] I still, however, complained that my defensive was too much starved, my force being barely adequate to the garrisoning the numerous and extensive works raised and raising, and posts on Long, Staten, and York Islands and Paulus Hook which, comprehending a circuit of considerably more than 100 miles, would afterward leave no surplus whatsoever for offensive operations. And I had, moreover, but a scanty proportion of artillerymen, no chasseurs, and no cavalry which I was at liberty to use, the Seventeenth Dragoons being ordered to be held in constant readiness for embarkation.

I am well aware that the statement Sir William Howe has given in his *Narrative* of the amount of the force he left with me[9] differs greatly from the idea I have here given of it. And I can reconcile the two in no other way than by supposing that Sir William Howe drew that statement from the gross effectives of the corps left with me—in which are included those on *public employ,* on *command recruiting,* and *prisoners with the enemy.* which at the time alluded to amounted to above 1100—none of which can properly form any part of an army's strength for the field. For by the exactest returns I could procure after the General left me my rank and file fit for duty, which is the standard he says in his *Narrative* he means to measure his own strength by,[10] did not exceed 7200 (including 325 artillerymen, nearly 3000 new-raised provincials, and much about the same number of foreign auxiliaries) until I was joined on the 24th of September by 1700 British and German recruits, which, being included in my return of

8. A free paraphrase of Howe to Clinton, July 18. Sir William had said earlier that he hoped, if the expedition succeeded as he wished but dared not expect, to send back half his army to act under Clinton. Memorandum of Clinton-Howe conversation, July 6.

9. *Clinton's note:* "Eighty-five hundred, exclusive of the sick and convalescents of the corps in New York and those belonging to the army I carried with me." *Vide* Sir William Howe's *Narrative* [*The Narrative of Lieut. Gen. Sir William Howe, in a Committee of the House of Commons, on the 29th of April, 1779, Relative to His Conduct, during His Late Command of the King's Troops in North America: To Which Is Added, Some Observations upon a Pamphlet, Entitled, Letters to a Nobleman* (London, 1780)], page 23. In confirmation of this Sir William Howe refers to a return from Sir Henry Clinton dated the 1st of October, stating the force under his command at 10,167 rank and file. But this return was made after the junction of 1700 recruits from England on the 24th September.

10. *Clinton's note: Vide* Sir William Howe's *Narrative,* page 13 [note b].

the 1st of October, swell my numbers to the amount Sir William Howe notices in his *Narrative*.

With so small a defensive, therefore, I must say I had the strongest reasons for thinking my situation most critical, especially while Mr. Washington continued in such force near me. Because, should he have possessed himself of the heights of Morrisania (near which, or any of those between City Island and Hell Gate, no ship of war can possibly lie), how easily might he have landed—under cover of batteries raised there—on the plain of Harlem? And, when there and in possession of Brooklyn and Staten Island, it will be readily admitted, I believe, he could without much difficulty have rendered my hold of New York very precarious, or at least have destroyed my magazines and burnt the town.[11]

Notwithstanding that my instructions and many other unequivocal demonstrations tended to show that Sir William Howe's army was destined for an expedition to the southward, I own I could not to the very last bring myself to believe it. For I was satisfied in my own mind that it was all a feint, particularly after the receipt of General Burgoyne's letter from before Ticonderoga, which other credible accounts at the time asserted he was in possession of.[12] I could not, therefore, help telling the Commander in Chief on his taking leave of me that I was persuaded *he intended to deceive us all, and, though he was pleased to say he was going to sea with the present northerly wind, I should expect to see him return with the first southerly blast and run up the North River.*[13]

11. I.e., by artillery fire from Staten Island or Brooklyn. Clinton has been charged with excessive fear for the safety of New York (Anderson, *Command of the Howe Brothers*, p. 266). But neither he nor Howe expected Washington to defend Philadelphia in force (memorandum of Clinton-Howe conversation, July 6; Clinton [to Harvey], July 11); Sir Henry therefore had to take into account the possibility he mentions. It was actually in Washington's mind as late as Aug. 21; see Fitzpatrick, *Writings of Washington*, 9, 108.

12. *Clinton's note:* A letter came from General Burgoyne, giving an account of his taking possession of Ticonderoga, which Sir Henry Clinton forwarded to Sir William Howe on the 21st July, two days before he sailed from Sandy Hook. But Sir William, in his *Narrative*, says he received it on the 16th [August], for reasons obvious. [The last sentence is from Clinton's note in "Memoranda," paper-bound supplement, p. 5.]

13. Talk with Burgoyne's messenger convinced Sir Henry that Howe should make a diversion in full force to help the northern army, and would so decide. Clinton felt that the Highlands could not be forced quickly enough to help, and wrote his chief that moving the army into the Connecticut Valley might win the war. Just after sending the letter he learned that Howe, to throw Washington off the scent, was circulating the rumor of a similar move, and thereupon recalled his letter for fear of looking ridiculous. "Not sent," is his endorsement on it; "I repent I did not." Clinton to Howe, July 21; for Sir William's planted rumor see Sydney G. Fisher, *The Struggle for American Independence* (2 vols., Philadelphia and London, 1908), 2, 17.

But I soon found I had conjectured wrong, as the fleet disappeared on the 23d. And I must confess I was not a little mortified at seeing myself thus left, on the opening of a most important campaign, with such a fettered and starved defensive that I could not have the smallest prospect of doing anything either to serve my country or advance my own fame, while my junior in rank was placed in the high road to glory and enjoying all the agremens of an active and separate command. It is true, indeed, that I was offered a very high command, and it was perhaps possible that I might have had this; but General Burgoyne was certainly the fittest for it from having served in Canada the preceding campaign, and the other I could not by any means accept before the very able General in possession should think proper of himself to resign.[14] However, when I was about to return to New York I was very far from suspecting that the chief I was going to serve under could possibly have any motives for acting toward me with the coolness which I afterward experienced.[15]

14. Clinton was suggested for two positions, the command in chief in Canada and the command that Burgoyne received. The first he declined because it would be a slight on Sir Guy Carleton. The second he did not actively seek in London, partly because he believed that Howe would give it to him, if asked, as soon as the northern army was in touch with New York. When he did ask, on July 13, Sir William refused because the shift would disgrace Burgoyne. Clinton acquiesced, in some confusion, and remained embittered about the whole affair.

The skeleton of the story is in Jane Clark, "The Command of the Canadian Army in 1777," *Canadian Historical Review, 10* (1929), 133–135. For details see John W. Fortescue, ed., *The Correspondence of King George the Third from 1760 to December 1783* (6 vols., London, 1927–28), 3, 421, 427; Partridge, *Sir Billy Howe*, p. 175 (in which the memorandum is misdated); memoranda of Clinton-Howe conversations of July 8 and 13; undated Clinton memorandum filed at the end of 1777; Clinton [to Harvey], July 11; [to Newcastle,] undated and filed under July 11; to Percy, July 12–13; to Phillips, Dec. 12; [to Drummond,] Dec. 23, 1777 (filed under Jan. 26, 1778); [to Carpenter,] Jan. 18, 1778.

15. *Clinton's note:* When the Commander in Chief informed Sir Henry Clinton that he proposed leaving him in the command at New York, he also said he had no doubt he would be much pleased with such an arrangement, as he understood from Lord Cornwallis *Sir Henry Clinton would gladly prefer the heading of three companies at a distance from him to serving in any capacity immediately under him.* Though Sir Henry Clinton was struck with astonishment by this unexpected speech, he candidly acknowledged that it immediately brought to his recollection some words of that tendency which he had once uttered in a peevish mood in the presence of Lord Cornwallis, at a moment when he happened to be a little ruffled by a message from His Excellency; but that he had long since totally forgot the circumstance. Nor could he conceive what could be His Lordship's motive for troubling His Excellency with the repetition of a private conversation, which he must have known was not meant to go farther.

This speech discovered also to Sir Henry Clinton the source of the Commander in Chief's unfriendly hint in one of his letters to Lord Percy, which he could not before that account for. As Sir Henry Clinton's reasons for not going to Providence had been fully explained to Sir William Howe, and received his fullest approbation in a letter in which he unequivocally declared it to be his own opinion *"the season was too far advanced to attempt anything further,"* yet after this Sir Wil-

Soon after the sailing of the fleet I received a letter from Sir William Howe to tell me that, if the wind continued fair for running down the coast, he might be tempted to take the route to Chesapeake Bay; but that I was nevertheless to send all expresses after him to the Delaware until I should know more certainly of his destination. I was now, therefore, perfectly convinced he was decidedly gone to the southward. And Mr. Washington, who had his spies in New York who gave him the earliest intelligence of all our movements, lost no time in putting his army into immediate motion. The gross of it marched with himself directly toward the Delaware, after detaching a considerable body of men to join the northern corps under Schuyler; and Putnam was left with about 4000 at Peekskill, where and on Rattlesnake Hill they had begun throwing up works for the defense of the Highlands on the east side the Hudson.

All this I immediately communicated by express to the Commander in Chief, and was much surprised by the purport of his answer in the following words, dated July 30th: "We are proceeding to the head of Chesapeake Bay, and I cannot possibly determine when I shall be able to send you reinforcement. *But, if you can in the meantime make any diversion in favor of General Burgoyne's approaching Albany (with security to Kings Bridge), I need not point out the utility of such a measure.* The regular troops on Staten Island may certainly be withdrawn from thence, leaving the defense of it to Skinner and his provincials, if the enemy do not show anything to put it in danger from the Jersies after Washington's departure." [16] For when Sir William Howe left me he declared that he expected nothing from me, it being impossible for me to stir even a patrol until I knew he was landed and Mr. Washington was decidedly gone to meet him. [17] It could not, therefore, but appear singular that he should now propose to me an offensive operation, though he very well knew no change had happened since his departure to put me in a fitter condition for it. [18]

---

liam Howe tells Lord Percy "it is reported here the enemy had no force whatever at Providence when you took possession of Rhode Island. It would have been a most important stroke if you had taken possession of that place at the same time."

16. The first sentence of the quotation is a free paraphrase, which omits a promise to send the reinforcements as soon as expedient. The remainder is accurate.

17. Howe reached this conclusion after long argument. His orders to Clinton did not mention a diversion to assist Burgoyne, but in conversation he often recurred to the idea of seizing and holding the Highlands. While the enemy was present in strength, Clinton argued, this could not be done with anything less than the entire army. Howe finally and reluctantly agreed. Howe to Clinton, July 9; Clinton memorandum, July 10; memoranda of Clinton-Howe conversations, July 9, 11, and 13.

18. *Clinton's note:* It appears by a return of the army belonging to the New

Had the Commander in Chief, indeed, received the Secretary of State's letter of the 18th of May before the date of his to me, this might in some measure be accounted for.[19] But as he says he received that letter on the 16th of August, which was above a fortnight afterward, I cannot guess any other reason for the earnestness he then showed for my cooperating with General Burgoyne but his being apprehensive that general officer might meet with difficulties in obtaining supplies for his army after it reached Albany. And, lest any subsequent miscarriage should happen in consequence, which might possibly be imputed to the neglect of attempting a cooperation with it from the side of New York, he may have wished that something should be on record to show that he gave hints to that purpose. However, my total incapacity to do anything of the sort was very soon after rendered manifest by the enemy's attacking me in three parts of my command at the same time.

The first intimation I had of the enemy's intentions was by intelligence that they were in movement toward Rye, and that boats were prepared for making a descent on the east end of Long Island. Upon this I immediately requested that a frigate might be sent to reinforce the armament in the sound, and all necessary orders were dispatched to Brigadier General DeLancey of the provincials, who commanded on Long Island. Next day Major General Tryon reported to me from Kings Bridge that a considerable body of rebels [had] made their appearance near his foreposts and had cut off part of his advanced picket. And at three in the afternoon an express arrived from Brigadier General Campbell with notice that the enemy had landed in force on Staten Island.

Not knowing at what particular part the enemy aimed their chief blow, I instantly caused a proper number of boats to be collected at Greenwich in New York Island to take two battalions and some artillery to either Paulus Hook, should it be attacked, or to Staten Island on the

York district, dated the 15th of August, that Sir Henry Clinton had only 7006 rank and file fit for duty.

19. Germain's letter left Howe freedom of action, but emphasized the importance of his finishing the Pennsylvania campaign in time to cooperate with Burgoyne; on Aug. 30 Howe answered that he could not do so. (Fisher, *Struggle for American Independence*, 2, 15–16 and nn.) The letter may well have disturbed Sir William. He had previously envisaged the northern invasion as a bait to draw off Washington, and had neither expected nor wished Burgoyne to get beyond Albany. Clinton, on the contrary, feared that Burgoyne would be checked and threatened with destruction by Washington and his army, and that Howe might then have to come to the rescue at the cost of relinquishing his gains in Pennsylvania. Memorandum of Clinton-Howe conversation, July 13; Clinton to Lord Percy [July 23]; [to Newcastle?], July 27.

ebb, and act as emergency should require. But, the appearance of the enemy before Kings Bridge proving to be a feint by their falling back (on General Tryon's marching out to observe their motions) and Paulus Hook not being threatened, I ordered the Seventh and Twenty-sixth Regiments, with a company of Anspach Grenadiers, to fall down the river to Staten Island and, landing under the redoubts there, wait General Campbell's commands. The Commodore [Hotham] was so obliging to accompany me thither at break of day the next morning, and I had just given orders for the march of the detachment toward Richmond when it was stopped by intelligence from General Campbell that the rebels had been driven from the island the evening before. The troops were consequently immediately re-embarked and sent back to New York, to be in readiness for carrying assistance to any other quarter that might want it. But I found, by a report from Brigadier DeLancey which met me on my return, that the attempt of the rebels against Long Island had been equally unsuccessful.[20]

These moves of the enemy were certainly most admirably well combined. And, if Mr. Washington had made them with fourteen instead of seven thousand men, they might probably have succeeded in one or the other of his two principal objects,[21] or perhaps in both, which would have undoubtedly obliged Sir William Howe to return. And I cannot but from thence conclude that Mr. Washington looked upon the southern move as favorable to the then situation of the rebel

20. *Clinton's note:* General Parsons' attack of the post at Setauket on Long Island was, after a brisk cannonnade and five hours' perseverance, repulsed by Lieutenant Colonel Hewlett of DeLancey['s Regiment], who commanded there with only 150 provincials. But General Sullivan's descent on Staten Island, being made with less alarming preparation and in greater force, might have been attended with the most serious consequences had not the vigilance and excellent conduct of Brigadier General Campbell at once stopped his career by rapidly marching against him, the moment he heard of his landing, with the Fifty-second Regiment supported by that of Waldeck. For the corps that first landed had effected an almost total surprise of two provincial battalions belonging to Skinner's Brigade, and after setting fire to the magazines at Decker's Ferry were on their march to Richmond; while another corps, that had landed on the west part of the island for the purpose of cutting off three other provincial battalions, had taken Lieutenant Colonel Lawrence, with great part of his battalion, prisoners, and only missed of the remainder by Lieutenant Colonels Dongan and Allen having the presence of mind to throw them into some old rebel works at Prince's Bay. These corps consisted, too, of chosen detachments from Sullivan's, Smallwood's and De Borre's Brigades, headed by their respective brigadiers, and Dayton's and Ogden's battalions. The greatest part of the boats attending the west attack fell into the hands of the King's troops, and the number of prisoners taken in the whole amounted to 259, including officers; their killed could not be ascertained. And what heightened the satisfaction resulting from General Campbell's success was that the loss sustained was nearly confined to the provincials who had been swept off on the enemy's first landing.

21. I.e., Long and Staten Islands.

affairs, and was not altogther willing to turn Sir William Howe wholly from it by too serious an attempt against my posts, though he was tempted to affront them and knew he could do so.[22]

Mr. Washington continued in the Jersies for some time after this, marching and countermarching as if undetermined which way to bend his course. But, upon hearing at last that the British fleet had entered the Chesapeake, he immediately crossed the Delaware. And I received intelligence about the same time that Putnam, who lay at Peekskill with four brigades, intended to pay a visit in person to Long Island, his boats being prepared for that purpose at Fairfield and a considerable body of militia assembled under Parsons at New Haven; and also that Sullivan was come to the neighborhood of Elizabeth Town (at the head of two brigades and the Jersey militia) with a view of making another descent on Staten Island, which a number of boats collected in that creek seemed to give some color to. Notwithstanding, however, all these threatening appearances, I was determined to proceed on a little excursion I had meditated in the Jersies, on which I proposed taking with me 2000 men, which were the utmost I could spare from the necessary defense of my posts, and even those liable to be hurried back by the first alarm of any one of them being attacked.

But, before any such step could be attempted, I wished to ascertain the amount of the force Mr. Washington had left on the east side of the Delaware, and to be certain that Sir William Howe was actually landed; for I had not had any letter from him since that of the 30th of July. For, though I was certainly under no apprehension for the safety of New York Island unless the enemy should happen to be in very great force near me, the rebels might, notwithstanding, have done me irreparable injury by possessing themselves of either Staten or Long Island. And, the provincials on the latter being barely sufficient for garrisoning Setauket and Huntington, it was only in the navy's power, not mine, to prevent their landing there—which once accomplished, every evil was to be apprehended from their arming the numerous disaffected on the island together with the prisoners who were quartered in King's County, the loyalty of a great part of whose inhabitants I had some reason to be very doubtful of.[23]

22. Clinton reached this conclusion in retrospect. At the time he expected that, "if Washington is not a blockhead, he will leave our chief where he is and exert his whole force against Burgoyne or me." (Clinton [to Hotham], Aug. 27.) Washington has been criticized at length for not doing just that; see Wallace, *Appeal to Arms*, p. 136 and n. 9.

23. The last two sentences are drawn almost verbatim from Clinton to Howe, Sept. 1, in which Sir Henry concluded that the enemy opposed to him "might do

Under these circumstances I thought it behooved me to be cautious. And I had accordingly written to General Burgoyne about the 10th of August, to apprise him of my present inability to make a diversion in his favor, but assuring him that I should not neglect to attempt something the first moment it was in my power.[24] As I had not heard anything of the progress of the northern army since its being in possession of Ticonderoga, I began to be very anxious about it. But I must, however, own that I did not wish to hear of its advancing to any distance from the lakes unless its communication with Canada could be secured by the Mohawk River, Wood Creek, and the Oneida and Ontario Lakes, as the other by Lakes George and Champlain appeared to me to be rather too long after it should get to Albany; and it was, moreover, exposed to the attack of all the populous eastern provinces.[25] Besides, I did not perceive any possibility of my ever being in a condition to escort supplies to him from New York.

I was at last relieved from my suspense by a letter from General Burgoyne dated from Fort Edward on the 6th of August, wherein was described his march thither from Skenesboro and his expectation of reaching Albany by the 23d at farthest. This letter showed him to be in the highest spirits, and did not contain an expression that indicated either an expectation or desire of cooperation from the southern army. But, having heard soon after through other channels of Colonel Baum's defeat at Bennington, and that the rebel northern army had detached considerably that way in consequence (under a supposition that corps was General Burgoyne's *avant garde*), I wrote to him on the 11th of September to say that, if he thought his operations could be assisted by it, I should in about ten days make an attempt on the forts in the Highlands with about 2000 men, as I was in hourly hopes of seeing a reinforcement from Europe to that amount.[26]

such things as I dare not whisper." Summary of Clinton's correspondence with Howe and Burgoyne, filed under July 9.

24. One of the well known "masked" letters, in which the message appears only when a mask is laid over the written page. This one is discussed and reproduced in Partridge, *Sir Billy Howe*, pp. 193–194.

25. The route by the Mohawk and Lake Ontario was shorter and safer than the other. There was water carriage all the way except for short portages, and the country until a few miles from Albany was controlled by friendly Indians. Clinton to Harvey, Sept. 16.

26. For the effect of this letter on Burgoyne see Ward, *War of the Revolution*, 2, 521. Clinton interpreted Bennington as a successful feint, which had drawn the enemy into Vermont and opened the road to Albany. His offer of an attack on the Highlands seems to have been intended partly to buttress this success, partly to serve his own ends. He wanted Burgoyne's sanction for a move that he had long hoped to make but dared not, because of the risk to New York, unless it were specifically requested. See Clinton to Harvey, Aug. 18; Clinton to Howe, Sept. 6, in

Hearing likewise about this time through the rebels that Sir William Howe's army was landed at the Head of Elk and marching toward Philadelphia, I thought I could not employ the intermediate time better than by a desultory move into East Jersey, which, besides throwing into our hands a quantity of cattle and other refreshments (which both the ships and troops very much wanted, and I knew the two rebel armies greatly depended upon), might at so critical a moment possibly operate in favor of either Sir William Howe or General Burgoyne, or might at least draw off some part of the force that protected the Highlands, which were the destined object of my next move. I had, moreover, some little hopes that an opportunity might offer of making a blow at two of the Jersey brigades which, I was told, were then on their march to the northward, if they should in their route happen to pass by the neighborhood of New Bridge.

The detachments allotted for this little combined move were accordingly put in motion on the evening of the 11th, and descents made much about the same time at Elizabeth Town, Schuyler's Ferry, Fort Lee, and Tappan, the different corps that landed being so disposed as readily to cooperate with and assist each other. The detachment that landed at Elizabeth Town was proposed to be the acting one, and the others stationary to cover and support its operations. Accordingly Brigadier General Campbell, who commanded it, was directed to march into the country and make a sweep for cattle and disarm the inhabitants in his route through Newark to Acquackanonck [Passaic], where Major General Vaughan lay ready to receive him. After this service was performed, as the troops had gone out without either tents or blankets and the weather began to wear a threatening appearance, I now judged it best to fall back with the little booty we had collected—amounting to some horses, about four hundred head of cattle and the same quantity of sheep, together with twenty milch cows, which afforded a seasonable refreshment to the squadron and the army (amongst whom they were all distributed) without costing either them or the government a shilling.

This little excursion happened to take place on the day of the Battle of Brandywine. But I cannot presume to say it was really of service to either Sir William Howe's or General Burgoyne's operations.[27] It

---

"Correspondence with Sir William Howe" (Clinton letterbook), pp. 22–23; memorandum, June 9, no year, filed under Clinton to Peter Russell.

27. If he had known Howe's situation or plans, he commented at the time, he might have pushed his raid further to assist him. He convinced himself afterward that the move had in some unexplained way been of assistance. Clinton to Harvey, Sept. 16; to Phillips, Dec. 11.

is sufficient to know my intentions were good, and I had the satisfaction to see most of its other objects accomplished without affront or material loss.[28] It is not improbable, also, that the fewness of the numbers I carried with me might have contributed materially to my subsequent success, by exciting in the enemy such a contempt for my force as to tempt them to uncover the Highlands and detach to the southward. For in about twenty-four hours after my return General McDougall came down from Peekskill with five regiments, three brigades, and all the militia he could collect, while a movement was made at the same time toward the coast on our right. And after parading in our neighborhood for a few days he turned his face to the westward and marched on to join Mr. Washington.

The long expected fleet arriving from England on the 24th of September with about 1700 British and German recruits,[29] I prepared without delay to perform my promise to General Burgoyne, though I remained still ignorant of the exact situation of Mr. Washington's and Sir William Howe's armies. But, before I moved, I thought it right to let Sir William Howe know of the arrival of the English fleet and the expedition I had resolved on in consequence, lest he should have occasion to call for any part of my force, and that he might be prepared to avail himself of whatever advantages my success might possibly offer to him. On the 29th a note was brought to me from General Burgoyne, dated the 21st of September in answer to mine of the 11th, saying that "an attack or even the menace of one upon Fort Montgomery would be of great use to him." And the messenger who came with it informed me that his army had only thirty days' salt provisions, that the communications with Canada could not be preserved, and that it was therefore the General's intentions to endeavor at a junction with the southern army.

This intelligence, of course, confirmed me with respect to the necessity of the attempt I had meditated, and I consequently lost no time in making the proper arrangements for it with Commodore Hotham.[30] On the 3d of October, therefore (the tides not suiting sooner), I began my move up the North River with about 3000 men.

28. *Clinton's note:* Eight rank and file killed, one lieutenant and seventeen rank and file wounded, one dr[ummer?] and nine rank and file missing, five rank and file missing [*sic*].

29. *Clinton's note:* Major Generals Robertson, Pattison, and Sir Thomas Spencer Wilson arrived in this fleet.

30. The Commodore was skeptical about the expedition. He did not want to seize the Highland forts unless they could be kept, and he consented to make the attack only reluctantly and at the last minute. "Memoranda," supplement, p. 12.

I had before this given the enemy jealousy for every object but the true one,[31] and it was generally believed, even within the King's lines, that the armament was intended against some place in the sound. Its appearance off Verplanck's on the morning of the 5th being consequently unexpected, they [the enemy] were not in force there or at Stony Point to oppose it. They therefore retired without firing a shot, leaving a twelve-pounder in their confusion behind them. Sir James Wallace, who preceded us with the galleys, was immediately sent forward to block up Putnam's boats in Peekskill, from whence lay their only pass over the river on our side the Highlands. General Putnam had about 3000 men then with him on the east side the river, ready to throw over to the forts when wanted.

The instant I was preparing to land at Verplanck's for the purpose of securing that post and drawing the enemy's attention from the west side of the river, I received a note from General Burgoyne, dated the 28th of September from his camp above Stillwater, referring me for information to the bearer, Captain Campbell, and desiring my orders. The intelligence this officer gave me was "that General Burgoyne's whole army did not exceed five thousand men, having lost between five and six hundred men in the action of the 19th; that the rebel army was very strongly posted to the amount of above twelve thousand men within a mile and a half of his camp, and had besides another considerable body hanging in his rear; that his provisions would not last him longer than till the 20th of October, his communications with Canada being entirely cut off;[32] that though he had no doubt of being able to force his way to Albany yet, being uncertain if he could subsist after he got there, he wished before he attempted it to know whether I could open a communication with that town, at what time I expected to be there, and whether I could procure supplies from New York for him afterward; and requesting that I would send him as soon as possible by triplicates my most explicit orders, either to attack the enemy in his front or to retreat across the lakes while they were clear of ice—hinting at the same time *that he would not have relinquished his communication with them had he not expected a cooperating army at Albany.*" The messenger further

31. *Clinton's note:* On the 23d of September, Major General Tryon had proposed the attacking the rebel General Parsons and opening Westchester County. This Sir Henry Clinton readily, in appearance, gave in to as a blind to his real intention, which he communicated to no one but the Commodore, General Vaughan, and a very few confidential officers whom he was under a necessity of employing.

32. *Clinton's note:* It is supposed that General Burgoyne heard on the 27th of September of his boats being taken [on Lake George, imperiling his retreat].

told me that, as the General could not remain in his present position longer than the 12th of October, if he did not hear from me by that time he should retire and repass the lakes.[33]

This account of General Burgoyne's real situation, which I had neither heard of nor suspected until the present moment, filled my mind with the most anxious reflections, as I instantly saw all the difficulties and dangers that surrounded him. It, however, surprised me not a little that after the receipt of my letter to him of the 11th of September (wherein I fully described my poverty) the General should seem to entertain hopes of my being able to force my way to Albany with only 2000 men, which, being the most I had promised him, was all that he could count upon; and of course they ought not to have excited much hopes of my being able even to seize the forts in the Highlands. For without proper artillery or the possibility of dragging them over mountains of difficult ascent (the passes through which would have been impracticable if defended) no great success could have been expected, from the handful of troops which prudence permitted me to draw from New York, against fortifications defended by nearly 170 pieces of cannon, fully garrisoned, and as strong as art and nature and the most difficult approaches could make them.

Yet, had the reinforcement from Europe arrived in time to have enabled me to make the move sooner, I had little doubt that even the attempt might have so alarmed the enemy as to have called off some part of the multitude opposed to our northern army, and have thereby perhaps eased its retreat—[a retreat] which, if I could presume to have advised, would have been my wish before the enemy had time given them to lay hold of and fortify the fords and passes in its rear. But, as matters were circumstanced, I greatly feared it was now too late. However, as from my having the command of the lower Hudson I had not much to apprehend for my own corps in case of a miscarriage, and I knew I could always on an emergency send 1400 men back to New York in at least eight hours, I determined to proceed and try the event. I therefore immediately dispatched a messenger [34] to General Burgoyne to let him know where we were.[35]

33. Burgoyne communicated by messenger, and entrusted almost nothing to paper. On the 28th he sent Campbell, who arrived on Oct. 5; on the 27th he had sent the same report by a Capt. Scott, who arrived on the 9th. When these men left him, Burgoyne was desperate: "I saw . . . that nothing but a successful action could enable me to advance or retreat." Burgoyne to Clinton, Oct. 25. See also summary of Clinton's correspondence with Howe and Burgoyne, filed under July 9; "Correspondence with Sir William Howe," Clinton letters, pp. 42, 47–48.

34. And a written message. See Clinton to Burgoyne, Oct. 6, below, pp. 379–380.

35. As the stiffness of his reply indicates, Clinton resented the attempt to foist responsibility on him. Burgoyne's conduct was "neither military nor liberal": he had

After having given the enemy every jealousy for the east side, [I] landed the troops suddenly on the west, at Stony Point, the 6th of October at break of day.[36] As soon as they were all on shore the *avant garde* (consisting of the Fifty-second, Fifty-seventh, and Loyal American Regiments, the New York Volunteers, and Emmerich's Chasseurs, under Lieutenant Colonel Campbell of the Fifty-second Regiment) directly began their march over the mountain with orders to secure pass of Thunder Hill [Dunderberg] and, having made a detour of seven miles round the hills, to form in the rear of Fort Montgomery. The main body (consisting of the grenadiers and light infantry, Twenty-sixth and Sixty-third Regiments, one company of the Seventy-first, a troop of dismounted dragoons, and a few German chasseurs, under the command of Major General Vaughan) followed immediately after and, continuing their march straight on to Fort Clinton, not only covered that of the *avant garde* but, by their attack of this fort, were expected to facilitate Colonel Campbell's attempt against the other; while in case of misfortune they would be ready to favor his retreat. And Major General Tryon had orders to bring up the rear (consisting of the Seventh and Trumbach's Regiment), after leaving a battalion at Thunder Hill to keep open the communication with the armament on the river.

These two forts had been constructed by the rebels upon the high steep rocks which form the western border of the Hudson at its passage through the mountains, about sixty miles above New York, and were at that time their northern barrier of that river, being intended to cover a large chain, or boom, which they had run across it under them to obstruct the navigation. They had likewise another chain and a *chevaux-de-frise* higher up. The forts, which were called Montgomery and Clinton, were separated from each other by a creek that flowed from the mountains between them, and they communicated by means of a narrow bridge thrown across it. The approaches to them on the land side were rendered almost impracticable by steep, craggy mountains; and the high upright rocks on which they were placed made all

---

had in effect an independent command; how he had got into his scrape he and Howe best knew, but now that he was in it he was trying to climb on Sir Henry's shoulders—to ask orders of a man who was a hundred miles away, and totally ignorant of the country and the plan of campaign. Clinton [to his sisters], Oct. 14.

36. A full contemporary account of the ensuing attack, from the American side, is in *Public Papers of George Clinton, First Governor of New York, 1777–1795, 1801–1804* (10 vols., New York and Albany, 1899–1914), 2, 389–395. For modern accounts see Carrington, *Battles of the Revolution*, pp. 355–361 and map facing p. 362; Hoffman Nickerson, *The Turning Point of the Revolution, or Burgoyne in America* (Boston and New York, 1928), pp. 341–353.

access to them by water still more difficult, while the numerous redoubts that covered them had all the regular appendages of ditch,
picket, fraise, and abatis, lined by an adequate proportion of troops
for their defense and connected by an entrenchment.[37]

The tremendous precipices and other natural impediments opposed
to the progress of the King's troops over the mountain, with a circuit
of about seventeen miles, prevented Colonel Campbell from getting
to his ground before five o'clock in the afternoon. His arrival being
that instant made known by signal, General Vaughan (who, by having a somewhat shorter route, had got to his [ground] earlier) was
directed to dislodge the enemy from a stone breastwork that lay a
little in front of their works, under the range of their cannon and
covered for half a mile by a strong abatis. This the General very soon
accomplished, and by my directions waited for a favorable moment
in Colonel Campbell's attack on Montgomery before he began his on
Fort Clinton. This latter was a circular height lined with musketry,
having a battery of three guns in barbette in the center, a redoubt
on each flank, and the approaches to it through a continued abatis
of four hundred yards, every inch of which was defensible and exposed
to the fire of ten pieces of cannon.

Agreeable to my wishes, General Vaughan seized a critical instant
of the assault on Montgomery and advanced, trusting by order to the
bayonet only. The order was punctually obeyed, the troops not firing
a shot; and much about the same instant both redoubts were stormed
and carried, the ardor of the assailants being greatly animated by seeing the galleys pressing forward with their oars and the frigates crowd-
ing every sail to support them. Unfortunately Colonel Campbell did
not live to enjoy the glory of this success, as he was killed in the first
of the assault. But the attack on his side was afterward conducted with
very proper spirit and judgment by Colonel Beverly Robinson of
the provincials, who was next in command, and to whose knowledge
of the country and very useful information I must acknowledge myself
to be indebted in the arrangement of my plan.

The rebels, finding we had succeeded against the forts, set fire about
ten o'clock to their frigates, *Montgomery* and *Congress*, and some galleys and other armed vessels that lay a little higher up the river; and
in the morning the Commodore joined me in a summons to Fort Con-

37. An abatis was a barricade of felled trees, with the sharpened ends of their
branches projecting toward the enemy. A fraise was a line of inclined and pointed
stakes set in the rampart. For the *chevaux-de-frise*, booms, and chains, see E. M.
Ruttenber, *Obstructions to the Navigation of Hudson's River, Embracing the Minutes of the Secret Committee Appointed by the Provincial Convention of New York,
July 16, 1776* . . . (Albany, 1860), pp. 64, 97, 117.

stitution. But, the rebels having thought proper (contrary to the practice of civilized nations) to fire on the flag that carried it, we were under a necessity of ordering an embarkation of troops under General Tryon and Sir James Wallace—who, however, on their landing there the day after found the storehouses, etc., burned and the works evacuated. The destruction of the rest they completed; and, as soon as they had removed the small chain which was run across the river in that place, Sir James proceeded to explore the *chevaux-de-frise* between Polipals Island and the main, and everything in the river beyond it.

The loss of the King's troops sustained in the whole of this service was trifling when weighed against its possible importance and the strength of the works assaulted, as it did not exceed one hundred and ninety men in all—of which only forty-one lost their lives on the spot, though some valuable officers who fell in the attack cannot, certainly, be too much lamented.[38] I had also the pleasure to find that the number of the enemy who were unavoidably sacrificed in the ardor of assault was comparatively small, their dead who lay within and without the works not exceeding one hundred, though I am credibly informed the two state regiments added to the militia engaged in the defense of them amounted to more than one thousand. It must, however, be confessed that only 263 were taken prisoners,[39] from whence it is presumed great numbers must have escaped under the darkness of the night.

Another letter was now dispatched to General Burgoyne, to inform him of our success and let him know that all the obstructions on the river between us and Albany were removed. But I told him likewise that I must still hold myself excused from either ordering or advising, though I should not relax in my exertions to facilitate his operations.[40] General Tryon was afterward detached to Continental Village

38. *Clinton's note:* One lieutenant colonel, two majors, one captain, two lieutenants, one ensign, three sergeants, thirty rank and file killed. Four captains, five lieutenants, two ensigns, four sergeants, one dr[ummer?], one hundred and twenty-six rank and file killed. Five rank and file missing. Count Gabrouski, a Polish nobleman who acted as a volunteer aide-de-camp to Sir Henry Clinton, was killed in the assault.

39. *Clinton's note:* One colonel, three lieutenant colonels, three majors, four captains, nine lieutenants, three ensigns, one assistant deputy quartermaster general, one director of ordnance, one quartermaster, and two hundred and thirty-seven privates.

40. This was the letter of Oct. 8, sent in a silver bullet and intercepted; see Wallace, *Appeal to Arms*, p. 164. On the 9th Clinton wrote Howe that the way to Albany was clear, but that he dared not attempt it with his small force; Campbell's report, furthermore, indicated that any such attempt would probably be too late. On the 10th Sir Henry sent another message northward, with no advice to

on the east side the river, where he burned a range of barracks for 1500 men and several storehouses and loaded wagons, this being the only establishment the rebels had in that part of the Highlands from whence their troops in the vicinage could draw their supplies.[41]

But, if I was to speak of this enterprise as it deserves, I very much fear that, when all the difficulties and danger of it are maturely considered, there may be found rather too much ground for calling it a desperate attempt. And, indeed, though I had certainly everything to expect from the discipline, vigor, and intrepidity of the small corps I had the honor of commanding, as also from the ardent zeal, cool resolution, and judicious conduct so conspicuously displayed by the experienced officers who led it, I must confess that its very complete success far exceeded the most sanguine hopes I had the presumption to entertain on my setting out. It should, however, be recollected that the occasion which determined my progress was also a little desperate, and demanded exertion.

And I had, besides, a prospect of catching the enemy in an unguarded moment, having much about that time received intelligence that the rebel General, presuming on my weakness, had drawn off a considerable body of troops from the protection of the Highlands to reinforce their army in Pennsylvania. And by letters which fell into my hands afterward I found that McDougall had been actually detached by Putnam with about 2000 men to join Mr. Washington,[42] and that Governor Clinton was so alarmed for the forts in consequence (on whose safety, he says, that of the state depended) that he sent orders on the 29th of September to a militia colonel to throw half his battalion immediately into Fort Montgomery, and hold the remainder in readiness for following at a moment's warning. The dates, too, of these events mark the move to have been so critically timed that, had it been made six days sooner or a few hours later, there is the greatest probability it must have failed. For, though I had taken the precaution to block Putnam's boats in Peekskill, yet, had our operations been protracted much longer, he might by a detour have effected his passage of the river higher up, and by occupying the passes of the mountain put it totally out of my power to get to the forts.

There not being now a gun left in the Highlands, all the rebel

Burgoyne but merely the assurance that Wallace controlled the river far beyond the Highlands. "Correspondence with Sir William Howe," Clinton letters, pp. 56–58.

41. Continental Village was just above Peekskill, on Canopus Creek.

42. *Clinton's note:* This was the 1st of October, and Sir William Howe in his published letter says that the junction of this reinforcement enabled Washington to attack him at Germantown on the 4th!

craft on the river destroyed, and a fair prospect opening of our being able to remove every obstruction as far as Albany, I began to extend my views beyond the limits they were at first confined to. However, the small number of men which would remain to me for further operations, after garrisoning the extensive posts I had taken—which I was obliged either to defend or dismantle—and securing my communications with New York, precluded every idea for the present of penetrating to Albany, especially as my total ignorance of the situation and strength of Mr. Washington's army prevented my forming a judgment how far it might be practicable for him to detach in force to Stony Point and thereby force me down the river.[43] Therefore, to obviate the latter, I lost no time in ordering the engineer to carefully examine that ground, that with the Commodore's assistance measures might be taken for securing it. And as a remedy for the former I took the precaution, by dismantling Fort Montgomery and strengthening Fort Clinton, so to reduce our defenses in the Highlands as to be able to hold this strong position with a few men. I proposed likewise to leave General Vaughan with a sufficient corps at Verplanck's or on the Croton, from whence he might readily either succor the Highlands or fall back to Kings Bridge, as emergencies should require.

But, happening to receive a letter about this time from General Pigot informing me he could spare 1000 men from the defense of Rhode Island, I began to entertain hopes that I should even be able to support General Burgoyne, should he incline to force his way to Albany. Therefore, while Sir James Wallace was employed in exploring a passage through the *chevaux-de-frise* and removing the booms across the river, I went back to Kings Bridge to make some arrangements respecting the command there which required my presence.[44] And, availing myself of General Pigot's offer by requesting him to send 1000 men to New York, I ordered the Second Battalion of Anspach, Koeler's Grenadiers and the Forty-fifth Regiment to proceed from thence to the Highlands, and six months' provisions for five thousand men to be directly put on board vessels of proper draft for running up the river to Albany. After making this arrangement I immediately returned, and detached General Vaughan with nearly 2000 men under the escort of Sir James Wallace with the galleys up the Hudson, giving him orders to feel his way to

43. At the time he feared more than a detachment in force. He had heard nothing from Howe since Aug. 30, and thought that Washington and his entire army might be approaching. Clinton to unknown, Oct. 26.
44. The reason for his return was news from New York that Generals Robertson and Leslie were ill. This meant that the command would devolve on an untrustworthy Hessian: "nobody but drunken General Schmidt to trust the foreposts to; I therefore determined to return myself." "Memoranda," supplement, p. 11.

General Burgoyne and do his utmost to assist his operations, or even join him if required.[45]

This little armament got up to Esopus [Kingston] on the 15th; and General Vaughan informed me he judged it proper to stop and destroy the place, lest the works and troops there might interrupt his communication with Fort Clinton or harass him on his return. He afterward proceeded to Livingston's Manor, about forty-five miles from Albany, where the vessels were obliged to come to anchor by the pilots' absolutely refusing to take charge of them further. From hence the General sent me information that he had not been able to communicate with General Burgoyne, as Putnam with 5000 men had taken posts on his right and Parsons with 1500 on his left; but that all accounts agreed in representing his situation as desperate.

Though this intelligence destroyed all my hopes of being in the least serviceable to the northern army, whose fate I now feared was inevitable, it yet was very much my wish to be able to retain the footing we were now possessed of in the Highlands. Every view of that sort was, however, dissipated by my next dispatches [46] from the Commander in Chief, as I was thereby ordered to send him "*without delay* the Seventh, Twenty-sixth, and Sixty-third Regiments, two battalions of Anspach, and [the] Seventeenth Dragoons, together with all the recruits and recovered men belonging to the southern army and the Jägers and artillerymen which came by the English fleet—*even notwithstanding I might be gone up the North River, agreeable to the intimation I had given him of my intentions in my letter of the 29th of September*—except I should be on the eve of accomplishing some very material and essential stroke, being left at liberty *in that case* to proceed upon it *provided I judged it might be executed in a few days after the receipt of his letters.*" [47]

45. Tryon suggested a more daring plan. The bulk of the army would move northward in two detachments, one for a time by forced marches up the river bank and the other on shipboard; the two would then change places, to rest the men who had been marching. Empty transports would follow as soon as possible, to receive Burgoyne's army if it could fight its way to the river. If, instead, it had to fall back on Ticonderoga, Howe might be induced to send enough support to permit a junction near the lakes. Tryon to Clinton, Oct. 8; see also Clark in *Am. Hist. Rev.,* 35, 557.

46. *Clinton's note:* Received by Sir Henry Clinton on the 18th of October.

47. The quotation paraphrases parts of two letters from Howe, of Oct. 8 and 9; the second merely reiterates the instructions in the first. Between writing the two, however, Howe had received from Clinton Burgoyne's notes of Sept. 21 and 23, accompanied by the man who had brought them to New York. A covering letter from Clinton, dated Oct 1, sketched the situation that this man's oral message revealed: the northern army was losing its communication with Canada, was short of provisions, and intended to attempt a junction with the force at New York. ("Correspondence with Sir William Howe," Clinton letters, pp. 41–42.) This oral

These orders being too explicit to be misunderstood or obedience to them *even delayed*, and several of the corps with General Vaughan being particularized in them, I wrote to that general officer on the 22d of October to direct him to return with all speed. And, receiving soon afterward another order from Sir William Howe to dismantle Fort Clinton,[48] I was under the mortifying necessity of relinquishing the Highlands and all the other passes over the Hudson, to be reoccupied by the rebels whenever they saw proper. For, even had General Burgoyne been fortunately in a situation to have availed himself of my success and been tempted to trust to my support at the time I received these orders, I believe there is no military man who will not allow that I should have had no small difficulty in reconciling the delay an effort of that consequence must have necessarily occasioned with the obedience I owed to so explicit and pressing an order from my Commander in Chief.

I must confess, indeed, that I was not a little hurt and disappointed when I found my move up the North River so contrary to the Commander in Chief's views (for he not only weakened me by these immediate drafts from my own corps, but countermanded the thousand men I had called for from General Pigot) [49] because I had, on the contrary, flattered myself with hopes that, as soon as he found I had opened the important door of the Hudson, he would have strained every nerve to keep it so and prevent the rebels from ever shutting it again—even though he had been obliged to place the back of his whole army against it. And I hope I shall be pardoned if I presume to suggest that, had this been done, it would have most probably finished the war. And Sir William Howe's southern move, instead of being censured, would perhaps have been extolled as one of the operative parts of a judicious and well combined plan, and even the loss of General Burgoyne's army looked upon as a necessary sacrifice, as having both essentially contributed to draw off the two grand armies of the enemy

---

report was Sir Henry's first inkling of Burgoyne's true position, he said later, and "determined me to risk everything to serve him." (Clinton [to his sisters], Oct. 14.) Howe, in short, *before* he confirmed the orders that he knew would vitiate any rescue attempt, had in his hands the information that had persuaded Clinton to make one at all costs.

Sir Henry's understanding of the situation, although more accurate than his chief's, still fell far short of the reality. He believed that Howe was sacrificing not an army but the chance of a great victory; and he shared Sir William's conviction that Burgoyne (after he had in fact surrendered) could still make good his retreat. Clinton [to unknown], Oct. 13 [and after], to Vaughan, Oct. 18; Howe to Germain, Oct. 22, Hist. MSS Com., *MSS of Mrs. Stopford-Sackville*, 2, 79–80.

    48. Howe to Clinton, Oct. 25.
    49. Howe to Clinton, Oct. 26.

to a distance from that very strong and important hold, which might possibly have been placed beyond our reach had either remained in its neighborhood.[50]

Although the brilliant success His Majesty's troops under my command fortunately met with on this occasion had excited universal admiration and applause, there were not wanting malevolent spirits who did all in their power at the time to lessen its merit, by throwing out hints that the attempt ought to have been made sooner, as the deferring the move so long had totally defeated the purpose for which it was intended. I shall, therefore, beg leave to trouble the reader with a further explanation of my conduct, in addition to what I have already said respecting the extensive posts I had to guard and the danger to which the principal depot of all our magazines might have been exposed in the absence of any portion of the troops left me for their defense.[51]

Let it be supposed for argument's sake that Sir William Howe had left ten thousand regular troops for the defense of New York and its dependencies, and had *positively* ordered the officer commanding them to attack the enemy's strongholds in the Highlands with five or six thousand men, whenever General Burgoyne should invite him to cooperation or he should judge that his situation required it. Could he with propriety have done it before? For, until that was really the case or other information told him that his assistance was wanted, he might by such a measure (notwithstanding his 10,000 men) have put the safety of New York in danger without any great prospect of success in the object for which it was risked. For, if in his absence the enemy without the lines (who were sufficiently near and numerous to take such an advantage until the latter end of September) assisted by those within (for I fear there were such) had seized upon that city, I need not, I believe, point out the fatal consequences of such a catastrophe! But it is well known that the Commander in Chief left me, on the contrary, in a most starved defensive; that General Burgoyne, so far from calling for assistance, scarcely even hinted that he expected cooperation before his letter of the 21st (in answer to mine of the 12th), which I did not receive until the 29th of September; and that

50. Clinton convinced himself that his expedition had had one positive result: it had threatened the Americans' rear, strengthened Burgoyne's hand in negotiating with them, and thereby enabled him to get better terms than he could otherwise have had. Clinton to Burgoyne, Dec. 16; for a later discussion of this point see Fisher, *Struggle for American Independence*, 2, 101–103.

51. *Clinton's note:* It is also to be recollected that the redoubts Sir William Howe had ordered to be constructed in front of Kings Bridge were not finished before October.

every account of him and from him to the 5th of October represented his progress, except in the check at Bennington, as most flourishing.

Nay, had I had twice the number of troops supposed, I will venture to assert that an attempt against the forts in the Highlands before they were uncovered must have been fruitless, and would have justly exposed me to censure. For, even as it was, the success appeared to be hopeless; and [it was] consequently one of those extraordinary events which may happen once in a century, and therefore to be attributed only to a combination of fortunate circumstances, some tolerable arrangement, and wonderful exertion and spirit in the execution. Wherefore I flatter myself the reader will readily agree with me that all I could offer, or General Burgoyne expect from me, was barely a menace of the forts as soon as the situation of the enemy and my own strength permitted me to risk a move to any distance from Kings Bridge.

And, indeed, from the very instant Sir William Howe abandoned the possibility of cooperating with that General it was my anxious wish he might not advance beyond Fort Edward, much less pass the Hudson. For the only success I could flatter myself with afterward, from any diversion that was in my power to make, was the possibility of easing his retreat back to Ticonderoga, as I had not the most distant idea of his being able to subsist his army at Albany before a communication was opened with New York—which, requiring a previous removal of every obstruction on the Hudson, I saw little probability of accomplishing with less than Sir William Howe's whole force. But, after I had so very unexpectedly succeeded, not knowing how far the tenor of General Burgoyne's orders or the complexion of his neighbors (particularly the Vermonters) might urge or tempt him to advance to Albany, I sent General Vaughan forward, as related, to endeavor to communicate with him; and I instantly freighted a number of small vessels with provisions to carry with me thither for his support.[52]

The campaign on the side of New York being thus, after so promising an opening, in a manner fruitlessly closed, and Sir William Howe's

52. When he sent the expedition, Clinton said afterward, he hoped that Vaughan and Burgoyne could join forces at Albany, and that the provision boats could reach them from New York. (Clinton to Phillips, Dec. 11.) But he apparently despaired of opening the river for their retreat unless Howe came in full strength; at least he nowhere mentions Tryon's suggestion of empty transports. Did he, then, expect Burgoyne and Vaughan to fall back on Ticonderoga, as he said later? ("Private memorandums to follow campaign [of] '77," filed at the end of 1777.) In that case the idea mentioned in the text, of pushing to Albany himself, would have been madness. The truth seems to be that he was groping in the dark: he did not have the information about Burgoyne, let alone about Howe and Washington, on which to build a plan.

late requisition having left me too low to admit of more than the strictest defensive (6142 rank and file fit for duty), I renewed my solicitations for leave to return home, as I plainly saw that my continuance in America was not likely to contribute to the service of my country or the advancement of my own honor. But the Commander in Chief being of the opinion that my services could not be dispensed with for the present—especially as General Burgoyne's late misfortune had left the enemy at liberty to employ the whole army which had been opposed to him, either against General Pigot or me—I was obliged to submit to the mortification of enduring my situation somewhat longer.[53] However, I must confess that his reasons for not indulging me were very properly founded, as the rebels made their appearance soon afterward before both our posts, and even made an attempt upon me in two places. But, observing that we were well prepared for their reception, they precipitately fell back again with some little loss. Indeed, being aware of the probability of their doing so, I had taken such good precautions that nothing but a very sudden *coup de main* could offer them a prospect of the most trifling success. And I did not apprehend I was much exposed to anything of that sort before the Harlem River should be frozen, which not happening before a reinforcement of 1500 men joined me from Philadelphia, I was in perfect security for the rest of the winter.

53. In August Clinton had told friends in England that he was again anxious to resign. In October he raised with Howe the question of returning home, and the two debated it throughout the winter; Sir William eventually refused permission without the King's leave. Meanwhile hints were multiplying that Clinton would soon be named commander in chief. He tried to avoid the honor by having Drummond, who was still in London, work for him on the Duke of Newcastle. The Duke attempted to have Cornwallis named instead, and was besieging the King and Prime Minister with requests for his kinsman's recall a month after Sir Henry had been given the command. See Percy to Clinton, Nov. 5; Harvey to Clinton, Nov. 5, Dec. 12; Gen. B[enjamin] C[arpenter] to Clinton, Dec. 8, 1777; Clinton's memorandum of his correspondence with Howe, Feb. 15; Drummond to Clinton, Jan. 10, with Clinton's note; Newcastle to North and North to Newcastle, Mar. 3, 4, 1778.

CHAPTER 4

The Command in Chief and the Monmouth
Campaign, May to June, 1778

Sir Henry Clinton is appointed commander in chief. He joins the army in Philadelphia. The King's Commissioners arrive there from England. That city is evacuated by His Majesty's troops, who march through the Jersies to New York. The rear of the line of march is attacked at Monmouth by the advance [guard] of Mr. Washington's army under General Lee. The enemy is repulsed and driven back four miles. The King's troops cross over to Sandy Hook Island and are sent from thence to their respective stations in Long, New York, and Staten Islands.

As I HAD sent an aide-de-camp to England to solicit the King's leave for my return, and the winter and spring had not produced anything material on the side of New York, I continued in anxious and hourly expectation of my recall until the month of April—when to my very great concern the packet brought me intelligence that, Sir William Howe having asked and obtained permission to return home, His Majesty had been graciously pleased to appoint me to relieve that general officer in the chief command of the army. The great change which public affairs had undergone, in Europe as well as America, within the last six months had so clouded every prospect of a successful issue to the unfortunate contest we were engaged in that no officer who had the least anxious regard for his professional fame would court a charge so hopeless as this now appeared likely to be.[1] For neither honor nor credit could be expected from it, but on the contrary a considerable portion of blame, howsoever unmerited, seemed to be almost inevitable. I was, notwithstanding, duly sensible of the confidence with which the King had honored me, and I consequently

1. For an analysis of the situation at the time see William B. Willcox, "British Strategy in America, 1778," *Journal of Modern History*, 19 (June, 1947), 97–102. This article, based primarily upon the CP, covers the period that Clinton discusses in this chapter and much of the next; footnote references to the CP will therefore be kept to a minimum.

prepared with all diligence to obey His Majesty's commands to the fullest extent of my ability.[2]

The day after my arrival at Philadelphia a frigate from England brought me two sets of instructions signed by His Majesty, dated the 8th and 21st of March. The latter, which superseded the former, signified to me that, "in consequence of a treaty of amity and commerce entered into by the French King with the American states, a resolution had been taken to make an immediate attack on the Island of St. Lucia, and directing me to detach 5000 men to the West Indies for that purpose, so as to arrive there before the hurricane season set in. I was also desired to send at the same time 3000 men to St. Augustine and West Florida, and to return the 600 marines in garrison at Halifax to their respective ships. And, as my army would be much weakened by these detachments, etc., I was commanded to evacuate Philadelphia and proceed by sea with the remaining troops and stores to New York, there to wait the issue of a treaty to be proposed to the American Congress by Commissioners whom His Majesty had nominated for that purpose. And I was further instructed, if the proposed treaty should prove unsuccessful and I should find myself in danger of being overpowered and forced by superior numbers, or my retreat likely to be cut off, to withdraw the troops in either of these cases from New York and proceed with them and the stores, etc., to Rhode Island, and from thence, after leaving there what might be necessary for its defense, to Halifax—which place I was to put into a proper state of security and then send what troops, ordnance, and stores remained (after these services were provided for) to Quebec."

I was also at the same time informed by the Secretary of State "that no more than the three regiments destined for Nova Scotia could be spared me from Britain, and that, the recruits raised for the regiments in America having been otherwise disposed of, the weakest corps must be drafted to fill up the remaining; and that I was consequently to look upon these orders as necessarily superseding the measures which had been recommended to me in his last dispatches."

The dispatches which the Minister refers to in the above letter

2. On the reasons for Clinton's appointment, and his reluctance to accept it, see *ibid.*, pp. 108–109.

THE AREA OF THE MONMOUTH CAMPAIGN, *from a* MS *map in the* Clements Library (*John Hills, "A Complete Plan of Part of the Province of Pennsylvania [and] East and West Jersey, . . . August, 1778"*)

contained the instructions of the 8th of March, noticed before as having been delivered to me at the same time with those of the 21st.
Those instructions (after informing me that Parliament had repealed
the Tea Act and the one for the better regulating the government of
Massachusetts Bay and passed a bill to enable His Majesty to send
Commissioners to America fully empowered to treat with Congress,
suspend acts of Parliament and hostilities, grant pardons, restore
colonies to their former constitutions, and nominate governors, etc.)
recommended to me, in case the commission did not produce the effect expected, "to endeavor without delay to bring Mr. Washington
to a general action. And, if that could not be soon accomplished, to
give up every idea of offensive operation within land and employ the
troops under my command only in desultory expeditions in conjunction with the King's ships of war, for the purposes of attacking the
rebel ports between New York and Nova Scotia and seizing or destroying all their vessels, wharves, docks, and naval and military stores
along that coast. And after the month of October to proceed to the
conquest of Georgia and the Carolinas, and make at the same time
every cooperating diversion in Virginia and Maryland, in the expectation they might lead to the entire reduction of all the colonies to the
southward of Susquehannah." In case of this event, I was further told,
"the intention was to leave those to the northward to their own feelings, and make them suffer every distress which the cutting off their
supplies and blocking up their ports might occasion." And to enable
me to carry these designs into execution a reinforcement of 7000 British troops to my own army was promised me, besides 3000 men to
Canada and 2700 to Halifax.

Such, in short, were the plans proposed and reinforcements intended
before it was known that France had decidedly joined the Americans.
But, as soon as that event was announced in form by the French court,
administration seems to have relinquished all thoughts of reducing the
rebellious colonies by force of arms, and to have determined to trust
the decision of the quarrel to negotiation, that the collected strength
of the realm might be more at liberty to act against this new enemy.[3]
Consequently nothing remained for me to do but to accommodate myself to the present views, and to prepare to forward them in the best
manner I could, without exposing His Majesty's arms to insult in the
course of the arrangements I should adopt for that purpose.

Sir William Howe having now delivered up to me the command of

3. For the background of the commission and an analysis of the two sets of
instructions see *ibid.*, pp. 102–106. Anderson gives a slightly different interpretation
of the instructions of Mar. 8: *Command of the Howe Brothers*, pp. 306–307.

the army, and the King's Commissioners [4] (who arrived on the 6th of June) having announced the purpose of their mission to Congress, I lost no time in communicating to the loyalists the orders I had received to evacuate Philadelphia and retire to New York.[5] But, the dispersed state of Lord Howe's fleet rendering it impossible for the present to obtain from His Lordship sufficient convoys for the West India and Florida embarkations, I was under a necessity to postpone my compliance with this part of my instructions until my arrival at that port [New York], from whence I also judged they might be dispatched with more secrecy and convenience than was possible from the Delaware.

I took the liberty, however, of discouraging every idea of our intending to withdraw all the troops from America, although administration had thought proper to propagate such a report in England and the Secretary of State had recommended it to me to assign the same reason for the proposed embarkations in order to conceal their destination. For I was not a little apprehensive that, if a notion of that tendency should once happen to gain ground in America, it would soon excite the most dangerous alarm among the well affected colonists both within and without the lines—and even among the provincial troops, who, looking upon their cause as lost and themselves abandoned, might perhaps be urged by the first workings of their resentment and despair to make their peace with Congress by any sacrifice in their power. And, indeed, many of the principal loyalists [6] in Philadelphia solicited me for passes to sound the American government upon the terms they might be inclined to grant them, which I took

4. *Clinton's note:* The Earl of Carlisle, Governor Johnstone, and Mr. William Eden, to whom were joined in the commission Lord Howe and Sir Henry Clinton.

5. With the Commissioners came Lord Cornwallis, who had been on leave in England. He was to be second in command, and held a secret dormant commission as Clinton had done under Howe; his purpose in coming, he had written Sir Henry on Mar. 3, was to "do all in my power to contribute to your ease in a situation which, I fear, you will not find a bed of roses." Soon after landing he realized how bad the situation really was, and tried unsuccessfully to resign; at the end of the year, because of his wife's illness, he secured leave to return to England. See Charles Ross, ed., *Correspondence of Charles, First Marquis Cornwallis* (3 vols., London, 1859), *1*, 33–34.

6. *Clinton's note:* Mr. Gal[lo]way, with several others, consulted Sir Henry Clinton upon the expediency of sending a deputation to Congress to know the terms they had to expect if they submitted to the new government. This Sir Henry Clinton strongly opposed, contrary to the sentiments of the Admiral and Sir William Howe, who seemed rather to advise it.

One of Clinton's loose notes: Lord Howe not only advised the loyalists to send out to Washington, but advised me to *consent* or *wink* at it. But His Lordship seemed at last convinced of the danger to us, and bad policy to them, in making such a proposal at such a time; and it did not take place.

some pains to dissuade them from, though both Lord and Sir William Howe seemed to think it right to permit them.

As a deficiency of transport tonnage put it out of my power to take away the whole army and stores at one embarkation, and the Admiral told me it could not take place nearer than New Castle (about forty miles distant from Philadelphia), I judged it most prudent to retreat to New York by land through the Jersies, in preference to the attempting to get thither by sea as my instructions directed me.[7] For every circumstance of the moment rendered it highly probable that the latter course might endanger the whole armament and even the safety of that very important post, should contrary winds or other causes happen to procrastinate its arriving there. I was influenced also by the consideration that this measure would enable me to afford a comfortable refuge to the distressed loyalists, whose attachment to the royal cause justly entitled them to every protection I could give them, especially as they were become thereby too obnoxious to the rebel rulers to expect the smallest chance of even personal safety should they be left behind. The saving the cavalry and provision train, which I had not the means of conveying by water, was likewise another circumstance which determined my choice.

And I was, moreover, not altogether without hopes that Mr. Washington might be tempted by his superior numbers and many other advantages to measure his strength with me in the field. (For his army then at Valley Forge amounted to at least 14,000 regulars, besides the 4000 that were under Gates in the Jersies, ready to join or cooperate as he pleased to direct them; and he could further swell his numbers to any magnitude he chose by calling out the militia of the neighboring populous provinces, who were little inferior in perseverance and courage to his best soldiers.) For, though I was prepared to expect from such a multitude every obstruction which their numbers and knowledge of the country might enable them to give me in so long a march, yet I had so full a confidence in the spirit and discipline of the troops I led that I had little doubt respecting the issue of a general and decisive action with them. I had, therefore, only to guard against the enemy's catching the little triumph of some partial blow, which the unavoidable length of my line of carriages and the several strong defiles I had to pass through might possibly expose me to. I must, however, confess that Mr. Washington had just

---

7. The Admiral was still Lord Howe. Although his brother left for England on May 25, the Viscount waited for his successor until Sept. 22—a delay that was one of Clinton's rare strokes of good fortune. Few admirals in the service could have risen so effectively to the naval crisis of the summer.

now much stronger motives of policy for declining a general action than he ever had with Sir William Howe, because the late alliance with France and his knowledge of the near approach of a superior French squadron [8] gave him strong reason to expect that the wishes of the colonies were on the eve of being accomplished without his risking so hazardous an expedient.

Accordingly, when the baggage, artillery stores, merchandise, and the friends of government were all got on board the transports, together with the sick of the army and the Anspach battalions which were sent to reinforce New York, I evacuated Philadelphia. This event took place about three in the morning of the 18th of June, and, marching to Gloucester Point without being followed by an enemy, everything was transported across the Delaware in less than seven hours through Lord Howe's most excellent arrangements—who, together with all his officers, showed the utmost attention to our security and accommodation. As soon as the line of march was formed, the troops were put in motion and proceeded by easy day's stages to Allentown, without meeting with any other interruption than what was caused by the rebel militia and light troops filling up the wells and breaking down and destroying the bridges and causeways before us.

Even the difficult and strong pass of Mount Holly was not disputed, the rebel troops that were posted there having precipitately abandoned it on our approach. This being the most commanding position I had to pass over, I fully expected that, if I was to meet with opposition in my route, Mr. Washington would have made choice of it. And I had laid a plan accordingly—with the assistance of some guides I had in my army who were natives of that country, and whom necessity had made acquainted with the passes through the swamps—to play over again much the same game with him as on Long Island in '76, by turning his left and cutting off his retreat. But, as I met with no molestation at this place, and his main army kept at a distance from me, I was convinced he had no thoughts of risking a general action.

My route hitherto had pointed equally to the River Hudson and Staten Island by the Raritan, and the enemy was consequently kept in suspense with respect to my intentions. But I could now no longer avoid to mark it more decidedly. The encumbrances, therefore, with which an indispensably enormous provision train had necessarily clogged me being of themselves a sufficient motive for shunning the difficult passage of the Raritan while one army lay in my front and another on my flank, I did not hesitate to order the troops to take the road which leads through Freehold to the Navesink, especially

8. The force under the Comte d'Estaing. See below, p. 99.

when I considered that from Sandy Hook I could most commodiously prepare to carry the King's further commands into execution. I had also in view by this move to draw the enemy down from the hilly country, in the hope that an opportunity might offer of getting a fair stroke at him before I finally took my leave. And, as he would be thus thrown behind me, I should, by placing the elite of my army between him and my baggage, have it more effectually in my power to defend it from insult and to seize at advantages as they offered. For, though the principle of my march was unquestionably retreat, I wished to avoid every appearance of a precipitate one. And, as I have just noticed, I had hopes Mr. Washington might possibly be induced to commit himself at some distance from the strong grounds of Princeton, along which he had hitherto marched. But, finding on my arrival at Cranbury that he still observed his usual caution (though joined, as I then imagined, by Gates), I gave up that expectation.[9] And, as my provisions were nearly expended and I knew I could not procure three days' supply in that country, I judged it best to prosecute my march without further delay.

When the King's army reached Freehold, I determined to halt there for a day and look about me. For, strong reconnoitering parties of the enemy having shown themselves to our rear on the 25th, I judged that their gross was not far behind and would take the route of Cranbury, where I afterward found they halted on the 26th. My hopes, therefore, began to revive that Mr. Washington might yet afford me an opportunity of having a brush with him. But when, upon reconnoitering on the 27th all the ground that lay between the apparent march routes of the two armies, I found that the stream we had passed the day before at a ford about three miles from Freehold was one of four branches of the South River—[branches] which, laying between us and the enemy and running through so many marshy, boggy bottoms, could be passed by them only at single narrow defiles, [and] that on the left, next them, [only] over a small bridge—I immediately relinquished every idea of a decisive action, which I saw was altogether impracticable on that ground. For I could not entertain so bad an opinion of Mr. Washington's military abilities as to suppose he would risk his *avant garde* over those difficult passes without the support of his gross, or that he would even venture to support through such a country.

9. Gates commanded the American army covering New York. Although he had offered to cooperate with Washington before the Battle of Monmouth, he did not join forces with him until late July. See Samuel W. Patterson, *Horatio Gates, Defender of American Liberties* (New York, 1941), p. 276 and n.

And, indeed, the evidence given on General Lee's trial plainly proves that I was not mistaken in my opinion of this ground.[10] For it appears that General Dickinson, who was appointed the enemy's Quartermaster General for this march on account of his being perfectly acquainted with the country, expressed himself to General Lee on his crossing the first ravine (which I distinguished by *the left branch*) in these remarkable words, "General Lee, you may believe me or not. But if you march your party beyond the ravine now in your rear, which has only one passage over it, you are in a perilous situation."

I was not, however, without jealousy that Mr. Washington might meditate a blow at my baggage, or might perhaps endeavor to push a considerable corps by me for the purpose of seizing the heights of Middletown (which lay in my route), from whence I could not expect to force him without loss. To guard, therefore, as much as possible against either, I had intended to march in two columns: the one to the right, having the charge of the baggage, by a road which crosses the river at a ford near Jews Town; and that on the left by another, almost parallel to it, over Plain Dealing Bridge. But Sir William Erskine, my Quartermaster General, bringing me intelligence in the night of the 27th that the enemy had thrown parties toward Jews Town, this disposition was changed; and the right column with the baggage was now ordered to take the lead of the left as far as the crossroads, then proceed to the Hope River and, halting on its verge, remain there until the left column was past the three branches of the Hope on the Middletown road.

The right column began its march, as ordered, very early in the morning of the 28th. And, being convinced by the report of the Queen's Rangers and the observations I made myself in reconnoitering the branches that morning that the enemy had not yet passed 1000 men, the left column (forming now the rear guard) was put in motion about ten o'clock, by which time I judged the *avant garde* under General Knyphausen was sufficiently advanced on its march. But soon afterward, observing that the enemy was moving in great force by Scots Meeting House, I gave General Knyphausen directions to proceed to Polhemus Ford, pass it, and halt.[11] And hearing likewise

10. At this point Clinton appends long extracts from American accounts of the battle. See Lee to Washington, June 28, Washington to the President of Congress [July 1], and Lee's testimony at his trial [Aug. 9], below, pp. 381–385, 388–390. The most modern description of the battle from the American side, and one of the most lucid, is in Alden, *General Charles Lee*, pp. 212–227; see also Carrington, *Battles of the Revolution*, pp. 422–445, and William S. Myers, ed., *The Battle of Monmouth, by the Late William S. Stryker* . . . (Princeton, 1927).

11. Clinton's manuscript maps make it possible to locate most of the place names in the preceding description with reasonable accuracy. The "ford near Jews Town"

from Lord Cornwallis (who covered the rear of the rear guard with the elite of the army) that the enemy began to appear in force on the heights of Freehold, which he had just quitted, I caused the whole rear guard to face about and return back. And I dispatched a public officer forward with a written order for the nearest British brigade and the Seventeenth Dragoons to be immediately detached to me from the *avant garde*,[12] at the same time directing my Adjutant General, Lord Rawdon, to remain there and form them (as soon as they arrived) on an advantageous piece of ground at the crossroads near Scots Meeting House as a cover to my right, of which I was a little jealous. And it appears from General Lee's trial that it had been that officer's intention to march a corps by this route in order to penetrate between what he judged to be our rear guard and gross.

I also learned by other intelligence that detachments were moving in force on each of my flanks, and that a considerable corps was now advancing on the road toward Jews Town. But, as I had been assured that the gross of Mr. Washington's army had encamped the preceding evening three miles in the rear of Englishtown, the only inference I could draw from these movements of his guard was that they proposed (as I had before suspected) to attack my baggage. I therefore came immediately to the resolution of pressing the enemy's advance [guard] so hard as to oblige the officer commanding it to call back his detachments from my flanks to its assistance, for I knew their main army was at too great a distance to sustain him.

Wherefore, finding when I got to the now head of the column that

---

was over Yellow Brook, approximately at Colts Neck; Plain Dealing Bridge was presumably over Pig Brook, near Vanderburg. The Hope River is now Hop Brook, and its three branches may have been Willow, Pig, and Yellow Brooks. Scots Meeting House was north of Freehold, near Marlboro. Polhemus Ford, on a somewhat roundabout road from Freehold to Middletown, was under Polhemus Hill at the modern village of Phalanx.

12. *Clinton's note:* Though this order was in writing (Lord Cathcart wrote it at Sir Henry Clinton's desire), carried by a public officer (one of the Adjutant General's assistants), and delivered into the hands of General Grant (who commanded the left of General Knyphausen's column), it was not obeyed. But, as Sir Henry Clinton's subsequent rapid movements had forced all the enemy's detachments back even beyond the furthest defile on their side, and his right was consequently not exposed, Sir Henry Clinton took no further notice; though he could not help complaining at the time to Lord Cornwallis and others of General Grant's very reprehensible inattention, by which an opportunity might have been lost had Mr. Washington been so imprudent to commit himself between those impracticable ravines.

From one of Clinton's loose notes: Sir Henry Calder and General Birch told me they both pressed to be detached but General Grant, under most *frivolous* pretenses, neglected doing so. Had this detachment been posted, I should probably have taken another day's trial with Washington had he remained within my reach.

the enemy's *avant garde* had passed all the ravines, I prepared to attack them as they descended into the plain. And, their right seeming to be in the air, I made a disposition to turn it, which had the desired effect.[13] For they were soon forced from the first ravine and fell back behind it. Observing, therefore, that the ground on our side rather commanded that on the enemy's, I ordered the Hessian Grenadiers to keep possession; and I advanced with the Guards, British grenadiers, and two brigades, knowing very well that I should not run the least risk in doing so (as I should always have it in my power to retrograde on the Hessian Grenadiers) and judging that Mr. Washington's situation must become critical should he venture to commit himself among those defiles in support of his advanced corps.

Upon these troops' rushing through the defile, great part of the enemy's advance [guard] (which had retired behind it) threw down their arms and were falling back in the utmost confusion on a second line of theirs that had formed on some strong ground behind them. To avail myself of this, I sent for the Sixteenth Dragoons, in the hope of entering it along with them. But their second line, throwing in upon us a very heavy fire through their own troops, galled the cavalry so much as to oblige us to retreat with precipitation upon our infantry. The King's troops, however, returned again to the charge, and at last obliged the enemy's second line to break. The enemy then formed on another rising ground [14] in front of a bridge over a morass in their rear, with a strong fence supporting their right, but soon quitted it. Therefore, as some battalions had engaged even beyond the morass, I ordered the King's troops to keep possession of this ground to cover their retreat (in which they might otherwise have been much annoyed) and rode back myself to the rear to attend to matters in that quarter. For the heat of the sun was by this time become so intolerable that neither army could possibly stand it much longer.[15]

13. *Clinton's note:* Another much larger column appeared, directing its course toward the Court House on our right. Had this column turned our right, it must have put us in a most dangerous situation. *Vide* Lee's defense in his trial [below, pp. 388–390].

14. *Clinton's note:* This is the height which, as mentioned in the trial, Mr. Washington ordered Lee to defend while he deployed his gross, that was then arriving in column from Englishtown four hours after the action began.

15. "Had I had only four regiments more, or the season been not so unfavorable, I will not scruple to say a most advantageous stroke might have been expected. But with the thermometer at 96—when people fell dead in the street, and even in their houses—what could be done at midday in a hot pine barren, loaded with everything that [the] poor soldier carries? It breaks my heart that I was obliged under those cruel circumstances to attempt it." Clinton [to his sisters], July 6.

Mr. Washington in the meantime formed his whole army behind the third ravine, and detached a corps with cannon to our left. But, as the purposes for which I made the attack were answered, I had no intention of pushing the matter further; and should have immediately ordered the advanced troops to fall back to the ground possessed by the Hessian Grenadiers had not their presence where I left them been absolutely necessary to cover the retreat of the light troops, as mentioned before.[16] For they were certainly exposed on this ground to a cross fire that annoyed them very much. However, from my intentions not being properly understood, or some other cause, all the troops had quitted it soon after me except the First Battalion of grenadiers under Colonel (now General) Medows; and the enemy began to repass the bridge in great force. Wherefore on my return I found this brave corps losing men very fast; and, as I was looking about me in search of other troops to call to their support (for the ground was not to be quitted at any rate, for the reasons before assigned) I perceived the Thirty-third Regiment, with that gallant officer, Colonel Webster, at their head, unexpectedly clearing the wood and marching in column toward the enemy. The First Grenadiers, on this, advanced also on their side; and, both pushing together up to the enemy in order to stop the cannonade from a farm on the hill, their [the enemy] troops did not wait the shock, but instantly quitted and retired again over the bridge. The First Grenadiers and Thirty-third then put themselves as much under cover as possible (by shouldering the hill on their left) until the light corps, whose usual gallantry and impetuosity had engaged them too forward, were returned. And the whole afterward fell back, without molestation from the enemy, to the first or right branch, which was the ground the enemy had first quitted and where I had posted the Hessian Grenadiers.

The loss in this brush appears by the enemy's account to have been nearly equal, ours amounting to sixty-five killed and one hundred and seventy wounded, and theirs to sixty-nine killed and one hun-

16. Part of one of Clinton's loose notes seems to belong here. He explains that Sir William Howe had retained the formations universally practiced by British troops during the French and Indian War: single file on the march, and in action "the open, flimsy order of two deep in line." Clinton had disapproved, particularly of the two-deep line, and had trembled for the consequences. On coming to the command, however, he had decided to retain the familiar line but guard against its dangers. "We have succeeded always [with] it; the enemy have adopted it; they have no cavalry to employ against it. Till a new enemy, therefore, comes, I shall content myself with supporting it always with something solid."

The reason for the note at this point is apparently that the tactical situation illustrated Clinton's use of solid support. The Hessian Grenadiers supported the advanced elements, which in turn supported the light troops making the assault.

dred and fifty-nine wounded.[17] But besides those slain in action the heat of the day destroyed us fifty-nine more; how many of theirs died by the same cause is not mentioned, though most probably they were in equal proportion according to their numbers.[18]

I beg permission in this place to observe that, notwithstanding the sentence of the court martial on General Lee for his conduct in this day's action, there will, I fancy, be little doubt after reading both accounts that his whole corps would probably have fallen into the power of the King's army if he had made a stand in front of the first defile, and not retreated with the precipitancy he did.[19] For my rear guard and the other troops then up were at that time nearly fresh, my cavalry was infinitely better and superior in numbers to his, and the quality of all my corps so far exceeded anything he had to oppose them that there cannot be the smallest doubt but they would in that case have obtained the completest success in ground so greatly in their favor—especially as the affair must have been finished long before Mr. Washington's main army could possibly be near enough to support him. And these sentiments will, I trust, be found to correspond exactly with even the facts that were proved by the evidence on that officer's trial and what may be very fairly deduced from General Washington's own account of the action.

During the time the left column was engaged, a slight attack was

17. *Clinton's note:* One lieutenant colonel, one captain, two lieutenants, four sergeants, fifty-seven rank and file killed. Three sergeants and fifty-six rank and file died of fatigue and heat. One colonel, one lieutenant colonel, one major, eight captains, five lieutenants, seven sergeants, one hundred and forty-seven rank and file wounded. Three sergeants and sixty-one rank and file missing, German and British.

Of the enemy one lieutenant colonel, one major, three captains, two lieutenants, one sergeant, fifty-two rank and file killed. Two colonels, eight captains, six lieutenants, six ensigns, one adjutant, two sergeants, one drummer, one hundred and twenty rank and file wounded. Five sergeants and one hundred and twenty-six rank and file missing. Artillery: one lieutenant, seven matrosses, one bombardier killed; one captain, one sergeant, one corporal, one gunner, ten matrosses wounded; one matross missing; six horses killed, two wounded. The militia not returned.

18. Sir Henry believed at the time that the Americans had had some 600 men killed. (Clinton [to his sister], July 6.) Disagreement about the losses has not yet been settled. See Carrington, *Battles of the Revolution,* p. 444; Fisher, *Struggle for American Independence,* 2, 186; Alden, *General Charles Lee,* p. 227, n. 42; Myers, *Battle of Monmouth,* pp. 259–262.

19. After the war Clinton discussed this point with Benedict Arnold, who had been prominent in the American army during the Monmouth campaign. He assured Clinton that his fellow-officers had disapproved "Washington's conduct, private as well as public, on that day; that Lee's was generally approved; that Washington had condemned it in a hurry, and his pride would not let him acknowledge the truth; and that all the officers in general have said since that Washington's popularity and Lee['s] unpopularity determined them to back him." Clinton's note, Aug., 1783, on the flyleaf of an alphabetized volume entitled "Notes," CP.

made on the baggage by the enemy's militia and light troops. But General Knyphausen's attention and disposition, and the vigilance of the troops under his orders, prevented any disgraceful accident from happening to it before they were called off, as I had foreseen, upon my driving General Lee over the ravines. And, indeed, it is but common justice to say that nothing could possibly exceed the intrepidity and ardor of the troops in both columns throughout the whole of this busy day—wherein, if they did not obtain a complete victory, I believe it cannot be denied that they at least repulsed very superior numbers with honor to themselves and no small disgrace to the enemy.

Nothing, surely, can be more ridiculous than the claim to advantage which both Mr. Washington and Mr. Lee have set up in their respective accounts of this day's action, wherein they are pleased to assert *"the King's army received a handsome check."* [20] For besides the manifest misapplication of that term to an army whose principle is retreat, and which accomplishes it without affront or loss, there does not appear to be the slightest foundation for a claim to advantage on the side of the enemy at any one period of the day, the transactions of which may be summed up in very few words. "The rear guard of the King's army is attacked on its march by the *avant garde* of the enemy. It turns upon them, drives them back to their gross, remains some hours in their presence until all its advanced detachments return, and then falls back, without being followed, to the ground from which the enemy had been first driven, where it continues for several hours undisturbed, waiting for the cool of the evening to resume its march. And so apprehensive are the enemy of approaching its position that not even a patrol ventured near it until twelve o'clock the next day."

In short, Mr. Washington's boasting of a victory on this occasion puts one in mind of a ridiculous story which is told of the Grand Vizier in '72. After threatening Prince Repnin to pass the Danube, attack him at Bucharest, and drive him out of the country, he passes the river, attacks the Prince as he had threatened, is beaten back, and retires again behind the Danube. But afterward (because a Turkish "bashaw" never announces a defeat, and loss of battle in that nation is generally followed with loss of head) the Grand Vizier writes a letter to Prince Repnin and dates it *de mon camp victorieux*, etc.

The King's troops, after having rested on the field of action without

---

20. The quotation is from Lee's letter to Isaac Collins, July 3, published on the 8th in the *New Jersey Gazette* and printed in *The Lee Papers* (New-York Historical Society Collections for 1871–74, 4 vols. [New York, 1872–75]), 2, 452. Washington referred to the battle as a victory in two general orders, but in his reports to Congress claimed only to have forced the enemy from the field. Fitzpatrick, *Writings of Washington*, 12, 128, 130–131, 139–146.

further molestation from the enemy until near midnight, took advantage of the coolness of the night to escape the fatal effects of another day's sun, and resumed their march without being followed by a single man of the rebel army. The next morning we rejoined General Knyphausen's column at Nut Swamp.[21] But, before I began my march, I had the precaution to send an order to the left column for a brigade of infantry, the Second Battalion of light infantry, and the Seventeenth Light Dragoons to meet me, that I might be in force to attack Mr. Washington should he think proper to throw himself in my way. For I was not without suspicion he might possibly place himself before me in some of the defiles I had to pass through, or hasten forward a corps to lay hold of a strong position on the heights of Middletown. But I soon found he had more wisely relinquished the pursuit (as he calls it in his letter) and drawn off his whole army to the North River, except a few of his light troops who were left to watch our motions. Therefore, as soon as the sick, artillery, stores, baggage, and cavalry were transported to New York and a bridge of boats thrown over the channel by which the sea had last year separated Sandy Hook from the main, the King's army descended from the high ground of Navesink, where I had caused them to encamp, and embarking in transports were conveyed to their respective stations on Staten, York, and Long Islands.

Thus was this long and difficult retreat in face of a greatly superior army brought to a happy conclusion, without being tarnished by the smallest affront. But, before I close this account of it, I beg leave to acknowledge my very great obligations to the generals and commanding officers of corps, to whose conspicuous zeal, activity, and professional knowledge I feel myself indebted for such very honorable success. And I hope they will do me the honor to accept of this small tribute of praise, only as a mark of my gratitude; for I am thoroughly conscious that no language I am master of can convey an adequate idea of the high sense I shall ever entertain of their merits, or add anything material to the dignifying applauses they have so justly received from their sovereign.[22]

21. Approximately three miles south of Middletown.
22. Clinton's private opinions were far less eulogistic. On coming to the command, he says in one of his loose notes, he found "that every officer in the army was a general—and not only gave his opinions, but acted, with an independence destructive of all order, subordination, and discipline. . . . What I call gallantry in public was in fact indecent, ungovernable impetuosity, . . . which might have engaged me, in such a country, with half the army worn down with excessive heat and fatigue, [and] with Washington's whole army arriving fresh from Englishtown. Both Lord Cornwallis and I saw many instances that day, both in conversation and conduct, that alarmed us."

CHAPTER 5

The French Offensive and the Carlisle Commission, July to November, 1778

Count d'Estaing appears off Sandy Hook. Leaves that station after twelve days' blockade. Followed by the British squadron under Lord Howe. Rhode Island attacked by a rebel army and the French fleet. Relieved by Sir Henry Clinton from New York. General Grey's successful expedition to the eastward. The King's army takes post on each side of the North River. A corps of rebel light cavalry surprised and taken. Expedition under General Grant sails for St. Lucia. Large detachments from the army sent to both Floridas, the Bahamas, and Halifax. Sir Henry Clinton solicits the King's leave to resign, after representing the impracticability of the war. Colonel Butler's expedition against the rebel settlement at Wyoming. The Congress evades complying with the Saratoga Convention. Loyalists alarmed by the large detachments sent from New York. Sir Henry Clinton endeavors to pacify them. Provincial corps do not fill; others formed on a more general plan, which succeed[s] better. Army three times in danger of starving. Lucky escape of the Cork fleet. King's Commissioners return to England.

THE PRUDENCE of my resolution to deviate from His Majesty's instructions and march the army through Jersey instead of embarking it on board transports in the Delaware became very soon manifest. For we had scarcely finished the transportation mentioned in the preceding chapter when Count d'Estaing anchored before Sandy Hook with twelve sail of the line and three frigates—a force so very superior to the few ships Lord Howe had with him that it is probable nothing could have saved the fleet and army from being captured had they been exposed to the delay which an embarkation from Philadelphia must have necessarily occasioned. And, even as it was, the King's ships and transports had a very narrow escape. For the French fleet arrived on the coast of Virginia about the 5th of July, and ours had got round from the Delaware to Sandy Hook only on the 29th of June.

But, with respect to the idea which some persons have entertained that the army also would have been very critically circumstanced if the French fleet had arrived a few days sooner and passed over the

99

bar of New York, I must declare that I should not have had the smallest apprehensions for its safety. For I am persuaded the troops could in that case have been all passed to Staten Island from South Amboy or Point Pleasant, under cover of the galleys and other armed small craft which we had in the narrow channels along that shore, whose depth of water is too shallow to admit any vessels Count d'Estaing had with him. And, indeed, had I been even caught at the Hook Island, I should not have despaired of escaping by the same means.

The very able disposition Lord Howe made of his little squadron and the land batteries I caused to be constructed at Sandy Hook, where a few battalions were placed under the command of Brigadier General O'Hara, contributed somewhat, it is presumed, to deter the French fleet from entering the harbor.[1] Matters, however, certainly bore a very formidable appearance, and seemed to indicate a design in the enemy to make a powerful combined attack on all or at least some of the posts under my immediate command. For Washington and Gates hung over New York with 20,000 Continentals, besides militia, and by credible information there were upward of 3000 troops on board the French ships; while my fit for duty amounted to little more than 21,000.

Rhode Island had been also for some time menaced, and, should the storm which seemed now to threaten us burst upon that post before I could reinforce the garrison, everything was to be apprehended for its safety. I therefore took the advantage of Count d'Estaing's remaining in a state of suspense before Sandy Hook to send thither through the sound five battalions, which, should they be fortunate enough to get to General Pigot, would, I flattered myself, enable that general officer to make a respectable stand against any force which might be collected against him—at least so far as to procrastinate and gain time until the arrival of Admiral Byron or some of his squadron should enable Lord Howe to go to his relief.

And it may be here not unworthy of remark that neither His Lordship nor I had received any official information of that officer's sailing, or even of that of the Toulon squadron, before the 1st of July.[2] Nor did Admiral Byron, who we were told was immediately to follow it with

1. For details of Howe's and Clinton's dispositions see Willcox in *Journ. of Mod. Hist.*, *19*, 111. One of Clinton's loose notes for his history adds that O'Hara had been posted on Sandy Hook because he was a good engineer and well known to Lord Howe. "But I soon found he was the last man I should have sent with a detached corps—plans upon plans of defense; never easy, satisfied, or safe; a great, nay plausible, talker."

2. See the extract of Germain to Clinton, May 4, below, p. 381.

thirteen ships of the line, leave England before some time in June, though d'Estaing took his final departure on the 13th of April. On the contrary, the rebels had been early apprised of the French fleet's destination and force, and were consequently prepared to derive every advantage from their cooperation.[3] It may, therefore, be very justly the subject of wonder to many how it happened that we sustained scarcely any injury from so complete and powerful a combination of force, especially as such a length of time intervened before any part of the promised reinforcement joined us. This can only be accounted for by doing us the justice to suppose that we were not wanting in our mutual exertions to be prepared in all parts to meet the suspended blow wherever it might fall, as well as to act in our turn with offensive vigor the instant Mr. Byron or any of his ships should arrive. And, indeed, it is but common justice to say that we were most zealously assisted by every description of persons within the British lines, the masters and crews of the transport and merchant vessels vying with each other in pressing their services on the Admiral for manning his ships, and the whole army being eager to turn out volunteers for embarking as marines.

Count d'Estaing, after having completely blocked up the port of New York for twelve days and making prize of every vessel that approached it in that time, weighed anchor at last on the 22d and disappeared. Between this event and the 30th Lord Howe had the good fortune to be joined by two line-of-battle and two fifty-gun ships,[4] which, though they did not render His Lordship's force equal to that of the French, made it so respectable that he determined immediately to seek them and endeavor to frustrate their views. And, being persuaded from the movements of the enemy that Rhode Island was now their object, I made an offer to His Lordship of embarking with him in person for its relief, having previously settled signals with General Pigot to direct his motions in concert with mine.[5] But,

3. Clinton's criticism of British blundering was well founded. But there were reasons for it; see Willcox in *Journ. of Mod. Hist.*, *19*, 106–108; 112–114 and n. 70; 120 n. 108. Sir Henry was mistaken in thinking that the Americans had the advantage of earlier intelligence. The news that a fleet had left Toulon in April was not known in Philadelphia until July 8; Washington first learned of it on the 11th, at the same time that he heard a rumor of d'Estaing's arrival off the Chesapeake. See *Lee Papers*, *2*, 474; Fitzpatrick, *Writings of Washington*, *12*, 168, 170–171, 176.

4. One ship of the line, which arrived on the 30th, was the first of Byron's squadron; the other three ships were reinforcements from Halifax and the West Indies. The ensuing campaign was primarily naval, although this fact is scarcely apparent from Clinton's description. See Willcox in *Journ. of Mod. Hist.*, *19*, 114–118.

5. Clinton [to Pigot], July 29.

that being looked upon as inexpedient for the present, His Lordship took from me only as many troops as supplied his deficiency of marines, and sailed in quest of d'Estaing on the 6th of August. In the meantime I ordered 4000 men to hold themselves in readiness for instant embarkation on board transports, which were sent into the sound to receive them. And Major General Tryon, who had been detached with a body of troops to the east end of Long Island for a particular service, was placed in a situation there either to reinforce Rhode Island or to make a descent on the coast of Connecticut, as circumstances should point out.

General Sullivan's beginning to collect troops at Providence in the month of May had given Major General Pigot early jealousy of his hostile intentions against his post. And, very much to his praise as a vigilant officer, he had seized every opportunity that offered to retard the enemy's preparations by repeated excursions to destroy boats, artillery, stores, etc., in which he happened to be very successful with little or no loss to himself.[6] But, the appearance of Count d'Estaing's fleet on the 29th of July having put the matter out of doubt, he lost no time in concentrating his force and preparing for defense. And I had the pleasure very early in August to receive information from him *"that he had secured most of his provisions and ammunition, and that he did not know that anything was wanting,"* [7] which made me perfectly easy with respect to his situation.

The day after Lord Howe's arrival off Newport the French fleet sailed out of that harbor, and on the same day the rebel army under Sullivan effected a landing on the island by Hoogland's Ferry [Howland's Ferry, from Tiverton]. From hence they cautiously advanced to the British lines in front of the town of Newport. But their batteries were not opened before the 19th, which was the day on which the French ships returned thither in a very shattered condition after the great storm that had disabled and dispersed both fleets.

Intending to proceed up the sound to be within Lord Howe's call, should His Lordship see an opportunity of landing me anywhere to advantage, I had detached Major General Grey with 4000 men to Flushing in Long Island. And, just as they were embarking from thence on the 27th, I received a letter from General Pigot to inform me that the French fleet had entirely quitted the island, but that the rebel troops were still there in force. Upon this I judged it advisable

---

6. Sir William Howe had reports of the American design as early as March. Pigot's principal raids were in May, immediately after Sullivan's arrival at Providence. Howe to Clinton, Mar. 17; Pigot to Clinton, May 27, 31.

7. Pigot to Clinton, Aug. 3; the italics are Clinton's.

to sail thither immediately, in order to raise the siege and avail myself of whatever advantages the now exposed situation of the rebels might offer. But, our passage having been unluckily retarded by calms and contrary winds, and time being consequently given for alarming Sullivan by the beacons along the coast, we had the mortification on our arrival there to find that he had quitted the island the night before—being followed, however, by General Pigot's troops and severely handled in his retreat.

The rebel General's precaution on this occasion saved him most probably from being very critically circumstanced. And, indeed, this appears to have been pretty nearly his own opinion, as may be collected from the conclusion of his letter to Congress, wherein he tells them *"the event has proved how timely my retreat took place, as 100 sail of the enemy's ships arrived in the harbor the morning after our retreat."* [8] For, having sent my Adjutant General, Lord Rawdon, forward to communicate to General Pigot my arrangements and plan for intercepting the enemy's retreat (by our runing up the Narragansett Passage to the Bristol Neck, where I proposed to land and seize their batteries, boats, stores, etc.), I had reason to hope that with the assistance of the frigates and galleys in the passage of Hoogland's Ferry, and the cooperation of General Pigot's army acting in his rear, matters might be so managed that very few of Sullivan's troops could have found means of escaping, had we been but fortunate enough to have had only a common passage.

Finding myself thus disappointed, I sailed with the troops the next day for New London, proposing thereby to draw off the enemy's attention and force from their eastern ports, against which I had meditated an immediate attack. And I had it in view at the same time to seize any advantages that might occur by making a descent even there [New London] if any object should happen to turn up of sufficient importance and facility to induce the attempt. But, the transports through some mistake not getting all up to the mouth of the harbor, I thought a partial landing might be attended with more hazard than the few vessels and stores at that time collected there could compensate. I therefore directed Major General Grey to proceed without loss of time to the eastward, and I returned to New York.

The success attending that general officer's operations was very complete, and in every respect corresponding to what I had reason

8. The quotation is from Sullivan's letter to the President of Congress of Aug. 31, for which see Otis G. Hammond, ed., *Letters and Papers of Major-General John Sullivan, Continental Army,* New Hampshire Historical Society Collections, *13–15* (3 vols., Concord, 1930–39), 2, 280–286. The italics are Clinton's.

to expect from his known activity and zeal. At [New] Bedford, Fairhaven, and in the whole extent of Acushnet River were destroyed nearly one hundred vessels of different sizes, consisting mostly of privateers and the prizes they had taken, a large number of whale boats, nearly forty storehouses filled with West Indian produce and naval stores, two large rope-walks, and a fort which defended the river mounting eleven pieces of heavy cannon with a magazine and barracks, the whole being executed in the space of eighteen hours from the landing of the troops to their re-embarkation. From hence the armament proceeded to Martha's Vineyard, where were taken and destroyed several more vessels and a considerable salt work, and a contribution collected from the inhabitants, who were likewise deprived of their arms [and] of 300 oxen and 10,000 sheep, which afforded a very seasonable refreshment to the garrison of Rhode Island and the King's ships and troops in New York.

As I wished much to employ the force under my command (while it remained with me entire) on some service of importance, I had offered to accompany Lord Howe with 6000 men to Boston Bay if His Lordship judged that any advantage was likely to be obtained by our united efforts against the French fleet in their then disabled and dismantled state in that harbor. But, the attempt being judged to be ineligible for the present and His Lordship determining to resign the naval command to Admiral Byron and return to Europe— a circumstance which caused very great regret and concern in the whole army, who as well as myself had the most unbounded confidence in His Lordship's professional abilities and cooperation [9]—I employed the troops in the only move which I was now at liberty to attempt under His Majesty's last orders, as they required my keeping them within distance for the more speedy embarkation of the West India and Florida expeditions the moment the Admiral should think proper, after the equinox, to give them a convoy.

As soon, therefore, as General Grey returned from the eastward, I requested Lord Cornwallis to take a position with a considerable part of the army between New Bridge in the Jersies and the North River,

9. Sir Henry repeatedly urged Howe to attack Boston, but the Admiral declined because of "either his want of confidence in me or in the Minister." (One of Clinton's loose notes.) The two commanders parted on the most cordial terms, and Byron inherited the cordiality. "Howe gives you such a character," were his first words to Sir Henry, "that I deliver my fleet to you. . . . You shall find every inclination in me to confide totally in you." But Clinton was cautious: he did not know Byron, and Byron did not know Boston harbor. "It required a time to consider; and, before anything could be fixed, d'Estaing sailed for the West Indies. . . ." Clinton [to Northumberland], July 29, 1796; see also Willcox in *Journ. of Mod. Hist.*, 19, 118 and n. 101.

and Lieutenant General Knyphausen to accept the direction of another respectable corps on the east side of that river between the Wepperham [10] and the Bronx. By these positions the army was placed in a situation to be assembled on either side the North River in twenty-four hours, a number of flatboats being held in constant readiness for that purpose; and, as we had the command of it by means of our galleys and other armed vessels as far as the Highlands, Mr. Washington could not draw his together under ten days. And, should he be tempted to quit his mountains to interrupt our foraging in the Jersies or support any detachments sent thither for that purpose, I had a good chance of having a fair stroke at him, the probability being very great that by such a move he must have risked a general action. This position was also intended to serve the double purpose of covering a general forage and favoring the operations of a corps I had detached, under Captain Ferguson, to destroy a nest of privateers at Egg Harbor, which had done us a great deal of mischief.[11]

Mr. Washington, however, would not be moved from North Castle, where he continued in perfect security. But, notwithstanding my views with respect to him were by that means disappointed, I had the satisfaction to find that the move had not proved altogether fruitless, Lord Cornwallis having by one of his detachments surprised and carried off almost an entire regiment of the enemy's light cavalry and a few militia, the expedition to Egg Harbor being partly successful, and considerable supplies of provisions, grain, and hay being procured for the use of the fleet and army,[12] while a door was at the same time opened to a number of loyal families from the Jersey and New York provinces, who embraced so favorable an opportunity of joining us.

The Admiral having now signified to me that the convoys were ready, I immediately caused the army to fall back; and Major General Grant was detached on the proposed expedition against the Island of St. Lucia in the West Indies with ten British regular regiments and a proper proportion of artillerymen, forming altogether a corps of

10. A stream flowing into the Hudson north of Kings Bridge, in what is now Yonkers.

11. *Clinton's note:* The rebels had considerable salt works at Egg Harbor, and a large depot of naval stores for supplying the privateers that usually rendezvoused there and from its vicinity greatly infested New York harbor. The salt works and storehouses were destroyed, but most of the privateers got out before Captain Ferguson arrived. A considerable part of Pulaski's Legion was likewise surprised.

12. Cornwallis' feat, to which Clinton refers so casually, was in American eyes one of the outstanding atrocities of the war—the attack on Col. Baylor's force at Old Tappan. For this and the raid on Egg Harbor see Fisher, *Struggle for American Independence*, 2, 219–222.

somewhat more than 5000 choice troops, most amply equipped with
a complete battering train and every other suitable appointment.[13]
Brigadier General Campbell embarked at the same time for Pensacola
with one German and two provincial battalions, and two hundred and
fifty men were sent to garrison the Bermudas and Bahama Islands.
Between two and three thousand men were likewise soon after embarked under the command of Lieutenant Colonel Archibald Campbell to attempt the reduction of Georgia and reinforce Brigadier
General Prevost, who commanded in East Florida, and about six
hundred more to relieve the marines that were doing duty in garrison
at Halifax and were now ordered to be sent to England.

These very large detachments from the army under my immediate
orders, amounting in the whole to full ten thousand men, together
with the loss of three regiments of infantry (which I had been ordered
to draft) and one of cavalry, which I was directed to send home, left
me reduced to the most strict defensive. I had, moreover, been subjected by His Majesty's command to General Haldimand's requisitions for troops whenever he pleased to call upon me; so that, had
he now made a demand for as large a reinforcement as I had reason
to expect, it is not improbable I should have found it necessary, in
obedience to the general tenor of my instructions, to have evacuated
New York and Rhode Island and retired to Halifax, by which the
Province of Canada would have been laid open to the weight of
the whole continent.[14] But that general officer having required no more
than 2000 men, and the Admiral not being in a capacity to spare a
convoy for even that number before it was too late to send them,
fortunately saved me from the mortification of adopting a measure so
destructive to all the British interests in America as that must have
been at the present moment.

I was, notwithstanding, by no means easy under my situation, while
I looked upon myself as charged with all the weight and responsibility
of the American war and exposed to every concomitant odium resulting from disappointment and the enormous expense attending it. Be-

13. The Admiral was Gambier, who commanded at New York while his superior, Byron, was trying to blockade d'Estaing in Boston. The French fleet escaped
and sailed for the West Indies at the same time as Grant's expedition, but missed
it by chance. See Willcox in *Journ. of Mod. Hist., 19*, 118–119.
14. In late July Clinton had written the government that he intended to evacuate
New York before the end of September. His dispatch, when it reached London,
caused a flurry of surprise and alarm. (*Ibid.*, p. 113 and n. 66.) Not until October
did Lord North feel convinced that Sir Henry meant to hold the city, and that
the government might make future plans without "the apprehension that all our
views will be prevented by some material step being taken in the intermediate time."
Hist. MSS Com., *MSS of Mrs. Stopford-Sackville, 2*, 117.

sides, the force I was now at the head of (13,661 rank and file fit for duty, of which above 7000 were Germans and provincials) was totally inadequate to any material object, being weaker by at least 16,000 men than that of my predecessor in command (including the army under General Burgoyne, which may without injustice be regarded as adding strength to the one under his more immediate orders). On the contrary, the rebels were every day getting stronger in numbers, confidence, and discipline, and occasionally supported by the immediate assistance or more distant—but equally effectual—cooperations of a French and Spanish fleet and army.[15] I was, however, fully sensible of the indispensable necessity administration was under of drawing from me so considerable a portion of my strength to enable them to exercise the very wise resolution they had taken to attack the French West India islands.

And, although by a cautious management of the defensive I was consequently reduced to I might preserve the King's American possessions entire during the winter, yet (as I foresaw that the necessary calls for conducting the war with France, and the great probability there was of our soon being engaged also in one with Spain, would put it out of the power of government to send such augmentations to the army in America as might place it in any sort of condition for entering upon an active campaign the ensuing summer) I flattered myself that His Majesty would not be displeased with me for wishing to retire, now that I was no longer in a situation to promote his interests. Therefore, as soon as the campaign was closed on the side of New York, I sent my aide-de-camp, Major Drummond, to England with as full and candid a representation as I could make of the present state of our American affairs, and to request the Secretary of State to lay at His Majesty's feet my most humble and earnest solicitations that he would be graciously pleased to grant me permission to resign the command of his army and return home.[16]

During the course of the preceding transactions on the side of New

15. For the period under discussion this statement is wrong; Spain did not enter the war until the following year.

16. Drummond, promoted to major, had left London in March. He returned on Nov. 29, carrying a letter in which Clinton attempted to resign. The King refused the request; Germain sweetened refusal with flattery, apologies for the past, and vague assurances for the future. (See Clinton to Germain, Oct. 8, and Germain to Clinton, Dec. 3, below, pp. 393, 397.) Drummond then tried to get Sir Henry a temporary leave, and stirred Newcastle to ask it of the King; this favor was also refused. The reason was political: the opposition was arguing that the folly of continuing the war was demonstrated by the desire of every general officer in America, including the Commander in Chief, to be permitted to come home. Drummond [to Clinton], Dec. 5, 17.

York, an attack had been made by the rebels down the River Mississippi against the frontiers of East Florida, in the early part of the summer, which was repulsed by the exertions of Governor Tonyn and Brigadier General Prevost.[17] And on our part the rebel settlements of Wyoming were laid waste by a party of rangers and Indians under the command of Colonel John Butler. But I should not have judged it necessary for me to mention the latter, which more properly belongs to the Canada command, had I not wished to refer the reader to the appendix for Colonel Butler's report, in which he will find a very different account of that transaction from that which has been given to the public by authority of the American Congress—which, by being mostly adopted by all the writers on the American war for want of other information, has diffused more horrid ideas of the barbarous cruelty of the corps employed on that expedition than I must hope it deserves. But whether the American account or Mr. Butler's is most consonant with truth I shall leave to others to determine, and have only to lament the causes which induced so much misery and destruction to the human race.

I must beg leave likewise to refer him to the extracts from the Commissioners' and my own correspondence with the Secretary of State, which he will meet with in the same useful and important collection, for information relative to our proceedings in the execution of the pacific and benevolent mission with which we had the honor to be vested, and the haughty and indecent reception which our several conciliatory advances met with from the American Congress, both on the subject of restoring tranquillity to the revolted colonies and the release of General Burgoyne's army agreeable to the Convention of Saratoga, which had been most shamefully evaded in violation of every principle of justice and good faith, evidently to serve interested and political purposes. And, indeed, General Heath's most exorbitant demand of £183,000 sterling in hard money for six months' supply of necessaries to those troops (though he knew they had been purchased for Continental paper under a depreciation of five for one) and his refusing the commissary of that army permission to make the purchases himself prove that they were determined to make every advantage of their detention.[18]

17. East is apparently an error for West Florida, where the attack was actually made. For details of the expedition see Wilbur H. Siebert, "The Loyalists in West Florida and the Natchez District," Mississippi Valley Historical Association *Proceedings*, 8 (1914–15), 107–111.

18. Clinton never made a "useful and important collection" of the material to which he refers in this and the preceding paragraph. The relevant documents are printed in the Appendix, partly from his notes in the history and partly from the

The examining into this and similar peculations even within our own lines, and the watching over the immense public expenditures which were hourly increasing in proportion as our posts grew more numerous and every necessary for the army advanced in price, would, I found, engross so much of my time that the reappointment of a commissary of accounts in the room of the one lately deceased became absolutely requisite to relieve me from the weight of a business which few military men are equal to, and which the other important matters, civil as well as military, that more immediately demanded my attention rendered it impossible for me to find time for. I therefore recommended my aide-de-camp, Major Drummond, to the Lords of His Majesty's Treasury as a fit person to fill that office.

The other objects of my care seemed likewise to multiply as our powers of extinguishing the rebellion diminished, and the alarm which was now excited among the loyalists by the large detachments sent off from the army called forth my utmost exertions to ease their minds, by convincing them that a total evacuation of the British posts was not intended. For I readily saw that the very worst consequences were to be apprehended from such an idea laying hold of them, as the number and zeal of those colonists who still remained attached to the sovereignty of Great Britain undoubtedly formed the firmest ground we could rest our hopes on for extinguishing the rebellion. Should they, therefore, happen to be shaken in the confidence they had of support from her, policy might point out to many of them the prudence of early making the best peace they could with the usurpers. And, when that dangerous door was once opened, it was impossible to foretell where the defection might stop, or how soon the entire alienation of America might follow. It was consequently incumbent upon me to obviate these fatal ideas as much as possible—for the appearances on our side were, to be sure, not very imposing.

All, therefore, that I had to do was to endeavor to turn the eyes of our friends to the distresses which their enemies were then universally deploring: the rapid depreciation of their money, the ruinous and dangerous neglect of their husbandry, and the universal discontents arising from the failure of their great ally's late effort to support their cause. Of course the natural inference to be drawn from hence was

CP. They are: (1) A letter from Butler of July 8 on the Wyoming campaign (below, pp. 386–388). (2) Clinton's extracts of the Commissioners' letters to Germain of July 7, 26, Sept. 5, Oct. 15, Nov. 15, 27 (pp. 386, 388, 391–392, 394, 396; the rest of this correspondence is printed in Benjamin F. Stevens, ed., *Facsimiles of Manuscripts in European Archives Relating to America, 1773–1783* [25 vols., London, 1889–98], *11–12, passim*). (3) A report in the CP, dated Oct. 25, on the difficulties of supplying the Convention army (pp. 394–396).

that nothing was wanting to derive the happiest advantages from the present temper of the people but a sufficient augmentation of our army to admit of a vigorous attack of the southern colonies; and, should we be so fortunate as to reduce them to obedience, the most favorable change in our affairs must quickly follow. These hopes, as it was my duty, I endeavored to inculcate, though I must confess in private I could not flatter myself with any, and often ruminated with an aching heart on the blackness of the prospect before us unless administration should strain every nerve to render the next campaign decisive.

But nothing distressed me more than the number of refugees who came in from all quarters to seek protection within the British lines. Many of these unfortunate people had been reduced from very affluent circumstances to the most abject penury by their firm attachment to Great Britain. Both humanity and sound policy, therefore, required that at least some temporary provision should be made for their support. And, as I wished to ease the public all in my power of the great expense they were exposed to from this and other causes, and at the same time with a view of adding to our strength by employing such of them as were desirous and capable of bearing arms, I had from the moment the command of the army devolved upon me sedulously endeavored to increase the provincial line by every encouragement I could devise. But, although gentlemen of the first influence among them had been placed by Sir William Howe and myself at the head of regiments and brigades, they had met with so little success in raising their respective quotas of men that many of the battalions were nearly as strong in officers as in privates. It is, however, but justice at the same time to say that in our then confined situation men were very difficult to be procured.

Seeing, therefore, that no very large portion of the friendly colonists who had taken refuge within our posts seemed much inclined to add to their other sufferings those of a military life, I was reduced to the necessity of reforming some of these nominal battalions and placing their officers either upon half pay or in a corps of guides and pioneers, which I had instituted principally with a view of affording a maintenance to the most needy. But, that nothing might remain unattempted for augmenting my force, I had recourse to those sources from whence the rebels themselves drew most of their best soldiers—I mean the Irish and other Europeans who had settled in America.

As it was difficult, however, to hold forth terms of sufficient advantage to these emigrants to incite them to quit their present service without running a risk of giving umbrage to the natives of America who had, with voluntary zeal, entered into the first provincial corps that had been raised, I made use of another lure, which I thought might prove equally effectual. This was to endeavor to work upon the national attachment of the Irish by inviting them into a regiment whose officers should all be from that country, and placing at its head a nobleman of popular character and ability. Accordingly, before I left Philadelphia, I began to form such a corps, under the title of the Volunteers of Ireland and the command of Lord Rawdon, whose zeal I knew would lead him to spare neither expense nor pains to complete its numbers and render it useful and respectable. The foundation of a legionary corps was also at the same time laid, for the reception of such other Europeans as might choose to join it, the command of which I gave to a Scotish nobleman, Lord Cathcart, with the same views and expectations that had influenced me with respect to Lord Rawdon's. These two corps afterward filled fast and, being employed on active service the rest of the war, had frequent opportunities of signalizing themselves, as will appear in the sequel of this narrative.

Observing likewise that there were several hundred invalids in the regular corps of the line, whose time of service had not yet entitled them to the benefits of Chelsea and who, though unfit for the more arduous service of the field, were capable of being very useful in garrison, whereby more active troops might be spared to augment my files for the campaign (a circumstance of no small consequence to me in the then reduced state of my army), I formed them into a garrison battalion for the defense of the Bermudas and Bahama Islands, where they might have an opportunity of benefiting themselves as well as the public by completing the time they wanted to entitle them to become Chelsea pensioners. This battalion was also rendered still more respectable by being officered either by gentlemen from the half-pay list who solicited employment, or by worthy old officers whose wounds or infirmities had obliged them to retire from more active service.

To these many difficulties which I had to struggle with was likewise, more than once, added the danger of starving, [we] having been in the hitherto short space of my command three several times reduced to less than three weeks' provisions. And nothing but the greatest good luck could have saved us from ruin by the total capture of one fleet of victualers—at a moment, too, when our stock was reduced to the lowest ebb. For this fleet had, through some unaccountable neglect in their orders, run up the Delaware after we had evacuated Philadelphia and all our ships of war had quitted that river, though that event was well known to be determined on some time before it sailed from Cork.[19] However, except in this instance, I am fully persuaded that the failures in our supplies proceeded from a concurrence of untoward incidents, which could not be foreseen or guarded against at such a distance from the seat of government. Nor do I presume to entertain the least doubt but the Lords of His Majesty's Treasury paid every possible attention to the wants of the army in America. I only state facts as they really happened, which, it must be confessed, were very alarming at the time, and make me tremble even now when I think of the very fatal consequences they might have produced.[20]

The same motives which had partly influenced me in my solicitations for leave to resign the command of the King's army in America induced also the Earl of Carlisle and Mr. Eden to retire from a situation in which they could not entertain the smallest hopes of rendering the least service to their country.[21] For, although many causes had contributed at the present period to make the colonists dissatisfied with the French alliance and heartily tired of the war, yet the strong appearances which our present measures bore of imbecility on the side of Great Britain, and the consequent probability that she might be at last driven to the humiliating necessity of acknowledging the independence of America, enabled the republican leaders in Congress to maintain their influence and power over the people and counteract the effect of the many distresses under which the whole community groaned. Consequently this could not be regarded as a favorable moment for offering the olive branch and courting the Americans to return to their allegiance. And, on the other hand, unless Great Britain should soon find herself in a condition to augment her forces by sea and land very considerably indeed, every chance of compelling them to listen to terms of accommodation seemed to be at an end.

These gentlemen having therefore thought proper to withdraw them-

19. "On the 24th March I am ordered to quit Philadelphia with the army. To show how little the offices [of government] corresponded, on the 24th May my victualers are ordered to go there; and chance only prevented their laying my supplies at the wharves of Philadelphia." Clinton's note on a letter of May 27 from Robert Gordon, Commissary of Provisions at Cork, to Capt. James Langmure, R.N. See also Willcox in *Journ. of Mod. Hist.*, 19, 112 and n. 59.

20. In January of 1779, Clinton explains in one of his loose notes, the army was saved from destruction by the unexpected arrival of a fleet of victualers from Cork. At that time the garrison was reduced to ten days' provisions; as much again might have been had from the environs of New York, and perhaps a week's supply from pillaging Philadelphia. "After that, *bas les armes* if the Delaware Neck could not have supplied us."

21. The Commissioners sailed for home on Nov. 27. See Stevens, *Facsimiles, 12,* No. 1227.

selves from the Commission in which I had the honor of being joined with them, I had the misfortune to be thereby deprived of the many important advantages I had hitherto derived from their very able and zealous assistance and advice. I must confess, however, that, influenced perhaps by the too sanguine reports of overzealous loyalists, they carried with them to England rather more flattering ideas of the abating spirit of revolt in the disaffected colonies, and of the general inclination said to be arising in the people in favor of the British offers, than I could see reason to entertain.

CHAPTER 6

Minor Operations and New Plans, 1778-79

Sir Henry Clinton moves out from his winter cantonments in hopes of intercepting the Convention army in their passage of the North River. Unfortunately his intelligence came too late for success. Takes that opportunity of reconnoitering the country about Stony Point and returns to New York. Future prospects gloomy. Colonel Campbell's success in Georgia. Unsuccessful attempt to carry off a rebel corps from Elizabeth Town. Salt pans, etc., at Horse Neck destroyed by General Tryon. Sanguine expectations raised in England by the report of the Commissioners on their return, which occasion the plan of the war to be changed. Consequent orders sent to Sir Henry Clinton, who is promised a reinforcement of 6600 men early in the spring and the 5000 from West Indies. With this addition he determines to do the best he can, and cheerfully acquiesces in the King's pleasure for him to remain in the command. Sir Henry Clinton requests the Minister to order the St. Lucia troops to join him in June, and forms his plan for the campaign accordingly.

AFTER THE departure of the Commissioners and the sailing of the aforementioned detachments, the debris of the troops under my command was distributed in the respective posts which were allotted to them during the approaching winter. But, intelligence being some little time after brought me that the Convention troops were soon to cross the North River on their march to Virginia, covered by the greatest part of Mr. Washington's army, and that two considerable bodies of loyalists and Indians had advanced to the neighborhood of Esopus, on which a large detachment had been sent from the rebel army to oppose them, I was tempted, by the chances that presented themselves of recovering at least part of those troops and attempting Mr. Washington's rear in his passage of the river, to draw a part of my army from their winter cantonments for a short excursion in the present favorably mild weather.[1]

1. In order to relieve Massachusetts of the burden of the Convention army, Congress had instructed Washington to remove the prisoners to Charlottesville, Va. They crossed the Hudson at the end of November, 1778. Meanwhile the Cherry Valley massacre on Nov. 10 had alarmed the settlements to the west of the Hudson; half the militia of Ulster and Orange counties moved westward to protect

A sufficient corps was therefore immediately embarked, under the orders of Brigadier General Mathew, with directions to proceed by water up the North River while Brigadier General Sir William Erskine marched by land as far as Tarrytown, with five battalions of infantry and a squadron of cavalry, and the light infantry and grenadiers followed in boats, ready to support as occasion should require. But the intelligence happened unfortunately to arrive too late for us to benefit from it, and an unavoidable delay of four days in our passage up the river prevented the expected attempt on Mr. Washington's rear, the last of his baggage and stores having been transported across the river the evening before our arrival at Verplanck's. However, as I had come so far and the weather was fine for the time of year, I landed the flank companies and part of the battalion of Guards, under cover of the galleys, at Stony Point in order to try the countenance of the enemy, who were in some force within a few miles of that place, and to give me an opportunity of reconnoitering the ground thereabouts, which I thought might be possibly of use on some future occasion. But, the enemy falling back and no other object occurring worth the detaining them, the troops were re-embarked and returned to their respective stations.

The completion of my instructions and the close of the campaign by both armies left me now at leisure to reflect on the state of the war, and my own particular situation as having the charge of it. And I fancy the reader will believe me very readily when I tell him that I did not derive much satisfaction from either. For, though I could not but be happy at being so repeatedly honored by my sovereign's approbation of my conduct, and was not a little encouraged by the late success of our efforts to preserve to His Majesty all the posts I found in possession of his arms when I took the command, yet I could not but look forward with the most anxious solicitude to the operations of the ensuing summer, when a second combination of the same powers and a more judicious exertion of them might, by means of a naval superiority, not only preclude every possibility of the evacuations recommended conditionally but consequently wrest from us every remaining hold we had in America, one after the other, with-

---

them, Pulaski's Legion at Minisink was strengthened, and several regiments of Continentals were detached from Washington's army. (Alexander J. Wall, "The Story of the Convention Army, 1777–1783," New-York Historical Society *Quarterly Bulletin, 11* [Oct., 1927], 87–90; *Papers of George Clinton, 4,* 277; Fitzpatrick, *Writings of Washington, 13,* 266–267.) An American deserter reported these troop movements to Beverly Robinson, who on Nov. 28 forwarded the information to Clinton; Robinson's letter is endorsed by Sir Henry: "occasioned my move to Verplanck's."

out my having the power to prevent it—while the blame of the whole would most probably in the end be thrown upon my shoulders, and perhaps the undeserved censure of my country added to the grief and mortification which so deplorable an event must necessarily give me. I flatter myself, therefore, that these considerations will justify the earnest desire I had to be relieved from a situation of so little hope and so great responsibility.[2]

But, while I waited in daily expectation of the King's leave to return home, I had the very great satisfaction to receive advice that the expedition I had sent against Georgia under Lieutenant Colonel Campbell had accomplished the reduction of that province. I ought, however, to mention that this attempt had been suggested to me by the American Minister in his letter of the 5th of August in the last year. And, being ever desirous to carry into execution His Majesty's wishes to the utmost extent of my ability, I added 1000 men to the reinforcement I was directed to send to East Florida in order to enable Lieutenant Colonel Archibald Campbell, who commanded it, to make a descent near Savannah for the purpose of attacking that capital, while Brigadier General Prevost cooperated from the side of St. Augustine, for which he had previously received my orders.

The success which that judicious officer met with was rapid, and fully justified the choice I had made of him for the command of this enterprise, having in less than a fortnight from his landing recovered not only the town of Savannah but the chief part of the province, though the enemy had the advantage of six days' alarm, from the arrival of the fleet at Tybee before he could put his troops on shore. (Lieutenant Colonel Campbell arrived at Tybee on the 23d of December, 1778, moved up the river on the 28th, and landed at Geridot's Bluff, within three miles of Savannah, the next day.)[3] This acquisition was a great detriment to the enemy and of the utmost importance to us, as it deprived the rebels of one of their principal sources of remittance to Europe and formed an excellent barrier to East Florida, while it furnished at the same time a near situation for the King's troops to assemble at in any future enterprise against the Carolinas. It also supplied

2. "I remain to public view as tenacious of a command, the patronage and emoluments of which meet everybody's eye; whilst very few will take the time to examine the detail which weighs down the opposite scale. Should the result of my endeavors be (as is most probable) below the public expectation, that patronage and those emoluments will be considered as having been the objects of my attention. And I shall sit down in my old age miserably conscious of appearing to have preyed upon my sinking country." [Clinton to Newcastle,] Apr. 30.

3. For modern accounts of this campaign see Wallace, *Appeal to Arms*, pp. 204–206; John W. Fortescue, *History of the British Army* (13 vols. in 20, London, 1899–1930), 3, 270–277.

a safe opportunity of making the so much desired experiment to prove how far the restoration of civil government might operate in calling back the disaffected colonists to the affections and sovereignty of their parent state.

My attention had been for some time directed to the drawing out of the enemy's hands by every possible means the troops of the Saratoga Convention, which it became now manifest they were determined never to fulfill. And I had consequently made a proposal to Mr. Washington for exchanging a portion of those brave and unfortunate men for the rebel officers who remained prisoners with us, which brought on a conference between commissioners mutually appointed by us for that purpose. But those of the enemy having refused to part with any of the privates until *all* the officers were first exchanged, I thought it right to put an end to the negotiation, as our soldiers would by that means have been left without officers to take care of and protect them and exposed, of course, to the operation of such arts as the enemy might use to incite them to enter into their service. Colonel Campbell's success in Georgia had, however, afforded some expectation that we should soon have a sufficiency of prisoners of every quality to effect a regular exchange of the whole.

With the hope, also, of increasing their number I was tempted by the uncommon mildness of the season to beat up the enemy's quarters. In this view an attempt was made to surprise one of their brigades that lay at Elizabeth Town under a General Maxwell, in the success of which I was much disappointed, as the troops for that service had been drawn from the interior of Long Island and put on shore in the night within three miles only of the town before any alarm could have possibly reached the enemy. But unfortunately some of those untoward accidents to which night movements are liable defeated my purpose, by retarding the progress of the detachment until the whole brigade had time given them to escape. In another little excursion from Kings Bridge under General Tryon, made much about the same time toward Horse Neck and Greenwich, a number of salt pans and a quantity of military stores and provisions were destroyed, a few vessels burned, and some cattle collected. We were not fortunate enough, however, to acquire many prisoners in either.[4]

The same illiberal policy rendered abortive likewise another meet-

4. In March Maj. Gen. Mathew was sent against Providence, to destroy the American shipping there. His raid was based on thorough reconnaissance, and Clinton had great hopes for it as the first major experiment in a "war of expedition." Mathew turned back at the last minute, however, when he learned that the ships had vanished from Providence. Clinton [to Mathew], Mar. 14; Mathew [to Clinton], Mar. 19; [Clinton to] Eden, Apr. 4.

ing of commissioners, which the enemy themselves now proposed for establishing a regular cartel for the exchange of prisoners. But Congress seems in this [proposal] to have been influenced by no other motive but to quiet the clamors of their officers, prisoners with us, who were much hurt by the miscarriage of the last.[5] For their commissioners still affected to object to the adequacy of my powers for giving permanency to a general cartel, and they even refused to enter into any agreement whatsoever that should extend to the release of prisoners taken in Georgia, pretending a total ignorance of all transactions there and paying no sort of regard to a formal return of prisoners, signed by Major General Prevost, which I had sent to my commissioners to show them.

The flattering opinions which were formed in England, soon after the return of His Majesty's Commissioners, of the difficulties the American Congress would meet in raising an army for the campaign, the discontents said to be germinating among the people on account of the French alliance, and the general disposition arising in them to return to their former allegiance, together with the facility with which His Majesty's arms had subdued the Province of Georgia,[6] excited the most sanguine expectations in administration and seemed for a while to dispel the cloud which the interference of France had spread over American politics. Instead, therefore, of the strict defensive which I had been directed to conform to by my instructions (and to which alone, in my reduced state, I was equal) of the 21st of March in the last year, and which the late detachments from my army had rendered absolutely indispensable, I was ordered to recur to the offensive plan proposed in those of the 8th of that month, before any thought had been entertained of diminishing my force. The principal objects of this plan were to endeavor to force Mr. Washington to a general and decisive action, or at least to compel him to seek for safety in the Highlands of New York or the Jersies and leave the inhabitants of the open country at liberty to follow their inclinations, and to employ two corps of 4000 men each in expeditions on the side of New England and New Hampshire, and in the Chesapeake Bay. To accomplish this a reinforcement was *promised* to be sent me, early

5. See the captured American officers' memorial to Congress in 1778, below, pp. 380–381. For the exchange negotiations in 1779 see below, pp. 401–403; Jared Sparks, ed., *The Writings of George Washington* (12 vols., Boston, 1858), 6, 512; James T. Flexner, *The Traitor and the Spy: Benedict Arnold and John André* (New York, 1953), pp. 270–271.

6. *Clinton's note:* This error prevailed throughout the whole war. The easy victories we gained to the southward induced many to suppose they would be obtained with the same facility against the northern people, a race differing as much from the enervated race of southern man as the Highlander does from the Gentoo.

in the spring, of 6600 men from Europe and the 5000 I had sent with General Grant to the West Indies.[7]

It had been from the very first my firm opinion that to crush the rebellion in one campaign (for, should it be continued longer, I ever thought a land war ruinous and unavailing) it was absolutely necessary to have, over and above sufficient garrisons for certain posts, an acting army of at least 30,000 men, and those British.[8] By employing these judiciously in separate corps cooperating on the upper and lower Hudson, on the Connecticut River, and in expeditions at proper seasons to Chesapeake and the Carolinas, I had no doubt but the rebel Congress might have been driven to such straits that they could have nowhere made head against them, and that the people themselves would have consequently soon forced them to accept of the proffered terms. But, knowing well that this was not the time for admitting so large a drain from the seat of empire when Great Britain was attacked by such powerful enemies, though I could not bring myself to think so highly of the respectable capacity the promised reinforcements would place me in as the American Minister seemed to do, I was determined to do the best I could for the King's service with what he engaged to send me—though I must own I should have felt myself more at ease if His Majesty had been graciously pleased to comply with my request of resigning the command of his army. But, as the circumstances of the times and his royal pleasure required my remaining in it, I submitted with the most dutiful acquiescence.

In expectation, therefore, that the succors, small as they were, would join me as early as the American Minister promised me, I arranged my plans for the operations of the ensuing campaign in such a series that, the one forwarding the other, they might be entered upon without loss of time and followed up in succession as my powers should increase. In the same view I had directed my aide-de-camp, Major Drummond, then in England, to press Lord George Germain to order Major General Grant to meet me with his corps from the West Indies

7. See Germain to Clinton, Dec. 3, 1778, Jan. 23, 1779, below, pp. 397–399. The first dispatch gave Sir Henry leeway; the second sketched the new plan mentioned in the text. This alteration in strategy was based upon information furnished by the Commissioners when they reached London. (Germain to North, Jan. 11, Germain Papers; and Eden to Clinton, Jan. 23, CP.) Their sanguine reports induced the government to promise Clinton reinforcements and order him to seek a decisive battle. "I opened my campaign with a move leading to this object," he comments in one of his loose notes. "Reinforcements came not till the 28th August, and then with such a pestilential fever as sent 6000 men to the hospital and put me *hors de combat.*"

8. In his note on Germain's letter of Jan. 23 Clinton gives his total force fit for duty as just under 19,000 (below, p. 399, n. 19); in a letter to an unknown on May 15 he estimated it as 18,000.

at Port Royal in South Carolina before June.[9] And I proposed in the meantime to put matters in such a train on the side of New York and in the Chesapeake that, the instant the fleet should arrive from Europe, a vigorous effort might be made to bring Mr. Washington to a decisive action, [and] in case of success to proceed in proper season to the conquest of the two Carolinas. Should we be so fortunate to succeed in this (which the distressed state of the rebel affairs gave me some reason to flatter myself might be the case) and no foreign interference again disturb us, I was not altogether secretly without hopes that the American war might possibly be yet finished in one campaign.

9. Clinton's original directions to Drummond, which are not extant, were repeated at the beginning of March. A month later Germain wrote that Grant had been ordered back to New York, as Sir Henry wished, unless a golden opportunity developed in the islands; thenceforth the field army in the West Indies would operate there during the winter and in North America during the summer. This coincided with Clinton's views, except that he also wished for a single commander in chief for the army in both theaters; "indeed, an *admiralissimo* would be equally necessary." [Clinton to Drummond,] Mar. 1–2; see also [Clinton to] Eden, Apr. 4; Germain to Clinton, Apr. 1, and Grant to Clinton, May 26, below, pp. 401, 408.

Sir Henry felt that without any reinforcement he was strong enough to seize Charleston, but not to hold it. He was therefore unwilling to make the attempt, because of his old fear of encouraging and then betraying the loyalists, and decided that an early attack on South Carolina depended upon Grant's arrival at Port Royal. Clinton to Germain, Apr. 4, and the letters to Drummond and Eden just cited.

CHAPTER 7

The Chesapeake, the Hudson, and the Penobscot, April to August, 1779

Situation of Mr. Washington's cantonments, which is too strong and his force too great to be attempted before the arrival of the reinforcements. Sir Henry Clinton resolves to endeavor to stir him in the meantime by indirect maneuvers, in hopes of an opportunity of attacking him to advantage after they come. An expedition to Virginia planned in consequence. Its object. While preparing for it an attempt is made to surprise a Continental regiment at Middletown. Miscarries. Virginia expedition sails under General Mathew and Sir George Collier. Its very great success. Another up the North River takes place immediately on its return. Stony Point and Verplanck's taken and garrisoned. Mr. Washington moves from Middlebrook to cover West Point.

Sir Henry Clinton unfortunately stopped in the further prosecution of his plan by the delay of the reinforcements. Is without money, provisions, ships, or troops adequate to any beneficial purpose. Regular part of his army discontented at the rank lately allowed to provincial officers, to their prejudice. Washington considerably reinforced. A desultory move under General Tryon and Sir George Collier into Connecticut. The rebels surprise Stony Point and carry off the garrison. The post immediately recovered and rendered stronger than before. Transactions in West Florida and Georgia. Expedition to Penobscot. The post begun there attacked by a considerable armament from Boston. Relieved by Sir George Collier, who takes and destroys all the rebel ships. Earl Cornwallis arrives at New York. Sir Henry Clinton threatened by another French armament. General Haldimand makes a requisition to him to send troops to Canada. He is obliged in consequence to assume a strict defensive until the arrival of the reinforcement expected with Admiral Arbuthnot.

MR. WASHINGTON's cantonments during the winter lay on each side the Hudson, the levies from the southern colonies being on the west and those from New England on the east. As his army, therefore, still kept the same position, and that part of it which lay in the Jersies consisted of at least 8000 Continentals, besides a numerous militia who were ready to turn out at a moment's warning, I thought his camp at Middlebrook, which was his headquarters, too strong and his numbers too respectable to be rashly attempted with my present force. My plan was consequently to endeavor by indirect maneuvers to draw him forward before the new levies from the different states should have time to join him, and then move against him while in motion, or force him into a general and decisive action by placing myself between him and his magazines at Trenton. But, as this latter might have led me too far from New York and my other posts, all that I could do for the present was to put matters in forwardness against the arrival of the expected succors.

I accordingly concerted with Sir George Collier, on whom the naval command had devolved upon the departure of Admiral Gambier,[1] a desultory expedition to the Chesapeake, with a view of retarding the levy of 2000 men whom Virginia was at that time collecting to send to Mr. Washington's army, and to destroy some considerable magazines formed there (for the march of troops to the westward and Georgia) and a quantity of naval stores which that province had provided for supplying a French fleet they were in expectation of.[2] There were also some ships of force that they were building and fitting out there, which I wished to deprive of the power of doing us a mischief.

And, when the attention of the enemy should by these operations be turned to the southward, it was planned that the armament should suddenly return and join in a move I proposed making up the North River against the rebel forts that covered King's Ferry. And, should the English and West Indies reinforcements join me at that critical moment (as was promised and fully depended on), it was my intention to extend my views even to the attacking the works at West Point. An action with Mr. Washington's army was likewise comprised within the operations I proposed. For, should he be tempted to hazard one in the defense or recovery of his Stony Point or Verplanck's forts, I very well knew he must for that purpose have met me in an angle between

1. Gambier sailed for England on Apr. 5. On the 4th Collier received his promotion to commodore and temporary commander in chief. Collier to Germain, Apr. 19, Germain Papers.
2. The reference is to d'Estaing's fleet, which subsequently attacked Savannah. Clinton's instructions to Mathew (Apr. 29, filed under May 5) merely mention American supplies intended for South Carolina; there is no indication that Sir Henry at this time expected a French attack.
Collier, in the letter to Germain just cited (n. 1), claimed to have planned the expedition to the Chesapeake; Clinton "heartily adopted" the plan. The Commodore's objectives were substantially those given in the text. He did not then expect to establish a permanent post, but did hope to return to Virginia in the autumn.

the mountains and the river, on terms replete with risk on his part and little or none on mine.[3]

While we were preparing for the Virginia embarkation, intelligence having reached us that a Continental regiment lay in an exposed situation at Shrewsbury and Middletown, the Commodore and I were induced to send thither a conjunct detachment in the hope of carrying it off by surprise. And, Colonel Hyde of the Guards (who was upon his return to England) having very spiritedly solicited to have the command of the troops, my confidence in that officer's prudence and perfect knowledge of the country and [in] the partisan abilities of Captain Ferguson of the Seventieth Regiment, who accompanied him, made me almost certain of success. But a sudden change of wind and weather unluckily delayed the boats too long in their passage up Shrewsbury River, by which, the enemy being alarmed in time to effect their escape, only about thirty of the rear guard and a small part of the regimental baggage fell into the hands of our detachment.

We had, however, most ample amends made us for this little disappointment by the subsequent success of the expedition to the Chesapeake, every object of which was fully attained even beyond my most sanguine expectations. For, besides the universal terror and alarm which this armament spread on its arrival through every part of the country bordering on that great expanse of water, the loss which the enemy sustained from its operations was prodigious—consisting chiefly of provision magazines, gunpowder, and naval stores, about 150 vessels of different sizes (several being of force and richly laden), and a quantity of cannon and ordnance stores, together with some thousand hogsheads of tobacco, all which were taken or destroyed in the short space of a fortnight, the armament not having been detained on the coast above that time altogether from the landing of the troops to their re-embarkation.[4]

As I could not be certain that the magnitude of the succors I expected or the time of their joining me would conveniently correspond with an immediate establishment in Virginia, I thought it right to

3. *Clinton's note:* Sir Henry Clinton, having long had an intention to seize the pass at Stony Point when the enemy had nearly completed their work there, [had] reconnoitered very carefully all the ground about it in 1777, and had taken another attentive look at it when he was up there last year, so that he was well prepared to draw every advantage from the situation had Mr. Washington committed himself there for the defense of the forts.

4. *Clinton's note:* The armament sailed from Sandy Hook on the 5th of May, entered the Capes of Virginia the 8th, landed in Elizabeth River near Fort Nelson on the 10th, and after fully completing their business re-embarked on the 24th and returned to New York, where they arrived in the evening of the 29th.

caution Major General Mathew, to whom I had entrusted the command of the troops on this service, against inviting or encouraging the King's friends in that province to a junction with the army, lest they should be exposed to the resentment and malice of the disaffected by his necessary departure. To provide, however, as much as possible against unforeseen events which might have rendered his continuance there eligible, I communicated to the Commodore and him the plan I had formed in 1776 for possessing two posts on each side of the peninsula between Albemarle Sound and the Chesapeake, and left it entirely to the General's discretion to adopt or not the idea of forming a small establishment there, as he should from circumstances on the spot judge its importance worthy of superseding the objects which had induced me to request his speedy return.

In consequence of this communication Sir George Collier had the goodness to inform me by letter that the inhabitants appeared to be friendly and desirous of returning to their allegiance, and that he looked upon the port of Portsmouth as a most commodious and safe harbor for the King's ships.[5] But, as General Mathew was of opinion that nothing had occurred which could warrant a deviation from the general tenor of his instructions, he came to the resolution of rejoining me as soon as he had completed the service he was sent upon. And, indeed, it was too late, when the Commodore favored me with his ideas, to stop the return of the troops had I deemed such a measure expedient. Nor was it possible for me at the time to spare the reinforcement he solicited.

The troops being embarked for the enterprise up the North River, and every other preparation ready, those from the Virginia expedition arrived just in time to join them. And the whole proceeded together on the 30th of May, accompanied by the frigates, galleys, and gunboats of the squadron under the direction of Sir George Collier, whose zealous assistance contributed very much to our subsequent success. The wind being fortunately fair, our progress was quick; and Major General Vaughan was in consequence enabled to land with the greater part of his force on the 31st about eight miles below Verplanck's, from whence he immediately marched by a detour into the

5. See Collier to Clinton, May 16, and Clinton to Mathew, May 20, below, pp. 406–407. Collier's letter is slightly amended in transcription; Clinton's bears little verbal resemblance to the original draft in the CP.

Collier was bitterly disappointed at having to abandon Portsmouth, "whose importance and utility stood higher, in my opinion, than almost any other in America." He blamed Mathew for insisting on literal obedience to his instructions, and for refusing to wait for an answer from the Commander in Chief. Collier to Germain, June 15, in Hist. MSS Com., *MSS of Mrs. Stopford-Sackville*, 2, 128–129; see also Collier, *Particular Services Performed in America*, pp. 74–89.

rear of Fort Lafayette, a small but complete work of four guns on the east side the river garrisoned by seventy men. In the meantime three battalions of infantry and a detachment of Jägers under G[eneral] Paterson (which I accompanied), moving higher up, were put on shore on the west side within three miles of Stony Point, a high rocky eminence of difficult ascent, with strong natural defenses and those of art in some forwardness. These two forts covered the passage of the river at King's Ferry, which lay immediately above them; and, being on the great communication below the Highlands between the southern and eastern colonies, the inhabitants as well as their army must by the loss of it be thrown forty miles back and obliged to cross the mountains twice by a circuit of at least ninety [miles] before they could recover the old road.

As soon as our little fleet came in view, the enemy's troops on the west side set fire to a large blockhouse at Stony Point and, evacuating their works, drew up on the hills with some show of an intended resistance. But, as the King's troops approached nearer, they fell back and left us the possession without a conflict. While this was doing, the galleys kept amusing the fort on the opposite side the river by the exchange of a few shot; and under their fire we without molestation occupied the heights of Stony Point, which commanded it [Fort Lafayette]. The necessary ordnance being afterward landed and dragged up in the course of the night, a battery of cannon and mortars was mounted (through the judicious exertions of Major General Pattison of the artillery) on the summit of this difficult rock, and opened against Fort Lafayette by daybreak. The well directed and incessant fire from hence, which was also well supported by that of the galleys, had soon such an effect on the opposite works that the garrison, seeing themselves completely invested and their retreat cut off by General Vaughan in their rear, were obliged to surrender at discretion.[6]

This pass was of such great importance to the enemy[7] that I fully expected Mr. Washington would have risked an action for its recovery. And with this view I left there a considerable part of my army, and took with the remainder a centrical position within twenty-four hours of all my principal posts, that I might be in readiness on the arrival of the promised reinforcements to seize any advantage that should offer.

6. See Carrington, *Battles of the Revolution*, p. 466; Fisher, *Struggle for American Independence*, 2, 238–239. Clinton had waited until the enemy had fortified the two posts for him because "I could not spare time, men, labor, or materials to do it for myself." Clinton [to Newcastle], June 18.

7. *Clinton's note:* The loss of this pass obliged the enemy to pass and repass the Highlands twice, and lengthened his communications between the eastern and the southern provinces at least sixty miles.

But this severe loss had no other effect on that General than to cause him to hastily assemble his troops a considerable while before he was in a condition to take the field, and march with them behind the mountains to cover Fort Defiance at West Point, into which he immediately threw 3000 men on a suspicion that it might become my next object. The same number of men had likewise occupied the east side of the river, but they retired higher up on the nearer advance of the King's troops.

Had the *promised* reinforcements arrived in any *reasonable* time, my opening the campaign thus early had given me every advantage over the enemy I could wish. For the different states had not yet sent in their respective quotas of men; and their magazines of flour, corn, and dry forage were nearly exhausted, so that they could not venture to take the field in any numbers, as the vegetation of the earth was not yet sufficiently advanced to furnish a substitute for either. It had likewise the good effect of preventing them from pursuing any scheme they might have meditated for the annoyance of Canada or the interruption of General Haldimand's arrangements for the security of that province. And, as Mr. Washington after this move to New Windsor was necessarily obliged to live from his magazines at Trenton and Easton [and] I had a body of troops afloat in the river ready to debark at a moment on either side of it, his communications with both might have been easily cut off by our seizing his former strong camp at Middlebrook, which would have placed me nearer either than he was.[8] The consequent distress from which event to his own army, as well as to Sullivan's (then on his march to the westward against the Indians), which drew its supplies from Easton, would most probably have compelled him to hazard an action—as the alternative would have presented him only a choice of difficulties, the country on the east side the Hudson being already exhausted and the harvest, as mentioned before, at some distance. This or an attempt on the forts above was the exact dilemma I wished to draw the rebel General into.

But where, alas, were the promised succors to enable me to prosecute my plan? Had they arrived at this time, which was the longest date to which I thought contrary winds or accidents could have possibly protracted their coming (as I had been informed they sailed the first of April), I have not the smallest doubt but I might have availed myself with the fullest success of the then very critical circumstances and situation of the enemy. But to have ventured at any of these with 6000 men, which was the utmost I could march out with, would have probably only exposed me to the affront of a sudden retreat, should the

8. Clinton deleted the last part of this sentence, but made no substitution.

enemy have made a movement at the same time toward New York. For I was much too weak in troops to retain that post, break in upon or even threaten Mr. Washington's communications with his magazines, and secure those with my own, all which were indispensable to insure the advantages I expected from it.

It was, however, perhaps possible by a rapid movement of cavalry for us to have seized or destroyed the enemy's heavy artillery and baggage, which had been left there under a strong guard; and I had it in contemplation to make the attempt. But, upon consultation with a cavalry officer of high rank and reputation in that line, on whose judicious and spirited conduct in its execution I should have principally depended for success, I was persuaded by him to drop my intention.

As my plans for the campaign had been formed under the presumption of my receiving early reinforcement, and their successful execution must depend upon Admiral Arbuthnot's joining me as soon as I was taught to expect him, this unexpected delay in the arrival of his fleet could not but excite in me the most serious anxiety for myself as well as the public. Another year's expense of this destructive war was now going to be added to the four which had so unprofitably preceded, without a probability of its producing a single event to better our condition or brighten our prospects. The burdens of the people were every day increasing, and their patience of course diminishing in proportion as they saw the end of their misfortunes farther removed. It was consequently a natural apprehension that the inactivity of an army on whose operations their hopes had chiefly rested might at last inflame them to a blind condemnation of the General who directed its motions. And recent history had furnished too many examples of a like injustice for me to doubt of its possibility with respect to myself, notwithstanding the utmost efforts of my zeal.[9] The American Minister's late letters had, moreover, chalked out for me expeditions and conquests much beyond anything that appears to have been expected from Sir William Howe in the zenith of his strength, though it was a third more than mine.

The discontents, too, excited about this time in the regular part of my army by the rank which I was directed to allow to provincial officers (to command as the youngest of their respective ranks in the line, when upon duty with regular corps) gave me no small uneasiness. I was, moreover, not insensible of the mortification it must give to gentlemen

9. On May 14 Clinton wrote two protesting letters to Germain, and on the 22d his pent-up feelings burst out in a long indictment of the way he was being treated; Lord George's reaction to this outburst is suggested by his letter to Drummond of June 23. See below, pp. 404–406, 407–408, 409–410.

who had made the profession of arms their study, and had acquired their ranks by long service, to see themselves liable by the *new* arrangement to fall under the orders of men, many of whom must be totally ignorant of military matters, [and of] others [who] had been taken from the regular regiments and [were] their juniors.

Of no small consequence was it also to the Commander in Chief to be thus exposed to the hazard of having his best plans disconcerted by such an event, which the chance of action might frequently occasion (notwithstanding his best precautions to obviate it) whenever the regular and provincial lines should be employed together upon the same service. My predecessor had very wisely provided against this inconvenience by directing that majors in the regulars should command all provincial lieutenant colonels, and the field officers of the latter were perfectly content under this arrangement, which for the same reasons I thought proper to continue after I came to the command. For, though no detriment may have resulted from the rank given to provincial officers under Lord Amherst in the last war, from their acting but seldom with the line (being in general employed on grass guards,[10] communications, and such kind of services), the case was very different with us, when provincials constituted a considerable portion of our acting force and were every day unavoidably joined to regular troops on services of moment.

It appeared to me, therefore, that I had reason to be displeased with two officers whom I had placed about the Secretary of State, in a confidential character, for giving that measure the sanction of my approbation when consulted by Lord George Germain upon it.[11] And I consequently thought it a necessary act of justice to myself to take the earliest opportunity, after it came to my knowledge, to disclaim their having any authority from me to do so, in order to remove the offense it had very justly given to the regular officers of the army serving under my command.

I had, moreover, other very serious causes for uneasiness. The emptiness of my military chest had been for some time very alarming, and had lately put it out of my power to give the officers of my army the usual douceur of bat and forage money on their taking the field—at

10. Grass or forage guards were detachments to protect foragers from enemy attack.

11. The two officers were Maj. Drummond and Col. Alexander Innes, both of whom returned to America during the summer. For the squabble about the provincial line see Clinton to Germain, May 14; Germain to Drummond, June 23, to Clinton, June 25; Drummond and Innes to Clinton, Sept. 13, below, pp. 404–405, 409–410, 420–421; for the discontent the issue was still engendering among line officers a year later, during the siege of Charleston, see below, pp. 184–186 and nn.

a time, too, when they were obliged even to draw their subsistence at eight or ten per cent discount, and every necessary of life was so dear that few of the highest ranks could afford to purchase them. My provisions were also running low, and the rebel privateers grown so numerous and daring that I every hour dreaded to hear of the capture of the Cork victualers, to whose arrival alone we trusted for a supply.[12] In short, without money, without provisions, ships of war, or troops sufficient to accomplish the services which seemed to be expected from me, or even the smallest intelligence from Europe for three months past, my situation was certainly not to be envied.

When the works at Stony Point and Verplanck's were nearly perfected, a respectable force (besides their proper garrisons) was left in the neighborhood of the latter, and the remaining troops fell back to Phillipsburg, where the chief part of the King's army lay encamped. This situation was within a convenient distance of all my posts and apportée for acting offensively to advantage the instant it should be in my power to do so. Therefore, as Mr. Washington's army was by this time considerably reinforced, and from the more advanced season of the year in a better condition for taking the field, and the bulk of his force lay on the west side of the Hudson—great part of it in the neighborhood of New Windsor and a considerable corps in the mouth of the Clove [13]—I proposed to remain here watching the course of events until at least some of the expected reinforcements should make their appearance.[14]

And in the meantime, as the enemy had but few troops below the Highlands on the east side of the river and those chiefly cavalry, I

12. Clinton had long been alarmed about the naval situation. Gambier, with thirty to forty fewer ships than Lord Howe, had left New York almost unprotected during the winter, and communications with Rhode Island and eastern Long Island had been most precarious. When Collier took over the squadron in April, it was impressive only on paper; a quarter of the ships had been blown off station and were unaccounted for, and half of those that remained were immobilized for lack of seamen. Gambier to Clinton, Jan. 5; [Clinton to] Eden, Apr. 4; Hist. MSS Com., *MSS of Mrs. Stopford-Sackville*, 2, 125; Collier, *Particular Services Performed in America*, pp. 72–74.

13. Phillipsburg is just outside Middletown, and New Windsor three miles southwest of Newburg. By "the Clove" Clinton presumably meant Smith's Clove, Washington's headquarters near West Point.

14. *Clinton's note:* Average strength of Mr. Washington's army: At West Point and in its neighborhood, 8600; light infantry near Fort Montgomery, 1500; Virginia regiments in the mouth of the Clove, 2720; [total] on the west side, 12,820. Massachusetts troops near Continental Village, 1150; lower down the country, mostly cavalry, 2180; [total] on the east side, 3330. Total, 16,150.

N.B. This is the average result of private information and reports of deserters compared together. On the contrary, the King's army in the New York district did not much exceed 13,000 men.

thought it very probable that, if I should send a corps into Connecticut, the cries of that province might stir him from his position and, by the suddenness of his passage across the North River, possibly afford an opening either of attacking some part of his army or executing my old intention of seizing some strong post on his communications, either of which would certainly be attended with the happiest effects should Mr. Arbuthnot critically arrive while Mr. Washington was in motion, or even the four regiments join me from the West Indies, which a letter I had just received from their commanding officer, General Grant, flattered me with the expectation of.[15]

I accordingly drew from Rhode Island what troops could be spared from its defense, and caused about 2600 men to be embarked at Whitestone in Long Island under the command of Major General Tryon, to whom I gave directions to make descents at New Haven, Fairfield, Stratford, Milford, and other parts of the Connecticut coast for the purpose of destroying public stores, privateers, etc., and doing the enemy every other injury he could consistent with humanity. To these I added such further instructions for that general officer's proceedings as a pretty accurate acquaintance with the face of the country and the strength of the enemy enabled me to give him.

Sir George Collier, who very cordially entered into all my views, was pleased to accompany this desultory expedition himself, and the armament set sail in the evening of the 3d of July. But for want of wind it did not reach the harbor of New Haven before the morning of the 5th. This unfortunately giving time for alarming the coast, the King's troops were consequently exposed to more opposition than was expected. The places that were visited suffered very severely. At New Haven all the public stores and several vessels and some ordnance were destroyed, and an armed privateer and six fieldpieces brought off. At Norwalk a few salt pans were demolished, as likewise the magazines, stores, and vessels. And both this town and that of Fairfield were consigned to the flames in resentment for the inhabitants' firing at the troops out of their dwelling houses.[16] But after the descent at Norwalk, as General Tryon found the enemy to be very considerably increased in respectability as well as numbers, he judged it best to recross the sound to Huntington Bay for a fresh supply of artillery and force. And, meeting with my orders there for his return to White-

15. Grant to Clinton, May 26, below, p. 408; the letter is a rough paraphrase of the original. See also Germain to Clinton, Apr. 1, below, p. 401.
16. This sentence is marked in a way that may have been intended as deletion.

stone, he immediately obeyed them, and the detachment was soon afterward disembarked.[17]

My reason for putting a stop to that general officer's further progress at present was that, as Mr. Washington seemed to be determined not to stir from his position and all the militia of the country were assembling in arms, a further prosecution of these desultory descents was likely now to be attended with a greater loss of men than the impression they might make on the enemy would probably compensate. And, indeed, I could not but view with concern the very afflicting damage they had been already productive of to private property, it never having been my intention to extend the destruction to houses of individuals, much less to those of public worship.[18]

Upon my dispatching the expedition up the sound I found it necessary to withdraw from Verplanck's all the troops that were not immediately wanted for garrisoning the works, and I left that post under the care of Colonel Webster, who was an officer of great experience and on whom I reposed the most implicit confidence. After this, that I might the better favor General Tryon's operations in Connecticut and be within distance to take advantage of the probable consequences of his success, I moved the army to Byram [19] and Mamaroneck, not entertaining the smallest apprehension that any attempt the enemy could make against that place [Verplanck's] or Stony Point could possibly be attended with mischief before I should be able to afford them assistance. For the natural strength of the latter (which commanded the works on the opposite side of the river), being nearly a peninsula at high water and of great height and difficult ascent, seemed to require little more than vigilance in its garrison to defend it from a *coup de main*, which was the only kind of attack the enemy dare engage in. And under this idea the commanding engineer and other officers, to whom I had consigned the fortifying those posts, formed their plan of defense. I had, however, on the 14th suggested to them the necessity of *at least one close work* to ob-

---

17. *Clinton's note:* A day or two before General Tryon sailed, a detachment of cavalry had been sent under Lieutenant Colonel Tarleton of the Legion to Pound Ridge [Bridge in MS], about thirty miles from the British camp, with a view of surprising a regiment of the rebel cavalry and about 100 Continental foot that lay in that neighborhood. The enterprise was conducted with prudence, spirit, and secrecy, but was disappointed of success by a guide's mistaking the right road. For, our troops having overshot the enemy, they being thus apprised of their danger instantly mounted and fled, by which, though closely pursued, only about forty of them were killed, wounded, and taken.

18. See the report on the raids in Tryon to Clinton, July 20, below, pp. 411–415.

19. Byram is on the coast at the New York–Connecticut line.

viate the consequences of a possible surprise; though I must, notwithstanding, confess that I looked on the place as perfectly secure with the works already there, especially as it was under the charge of a vigilant, active, and spirited officer and a very ample garrison.[20]

These precautions having been taken and matters thus circumstanced, my astonishment could not but be extreme when intelligence was brought me on the 16th that the lines of Stony Point had been assaulted and carried the night before, and the guns there [were] playing on Verplanck's, which was likewise menaced by a considerable body of troops in its rear.[21] As soon as I heard of the misfortune, I immediately ordered the army to be advanced to Dobbs Ferry and the cavalry and some light troops to press forward to the banks of the Croton, to awe the land operations of the enemy against Colonel Webster, while three regiments under Brigadier General Stirling were moving up by water with all expedition to save the garrison under his command or recover Stony Point. The progress of the latter being, however, likely to be retarded by a northerly wind which then blew, and being apprehensive that Mr. Washington might by that delay have time to collect a force at the points too powerful for Brigadier Stirling's detachment, I embarked myself with the light infantry and joined him in Haverstraw Bay, as I was anxious that no measure should be omitted for the recovery of the post and [was] not without hopes that Mr. Washington, in the course of the struggle for it, might be drawn into an engagement, the chief part of my army being at a convenient distance to be readily collected in case such an event was likely to take place.

But it is most probable, from Mr. Washington's own account of this business, that [that] wary officer suspected my intentions and saw the advantages my command of the river gave me over him in ground so critically circumstanced.[22] For, as soon as the rebels perceived the approach of the galleys and boats, they precipitately abandoned their acquisition, of which they now had held possession four days; and, setting fire to a galley which they had brought down to carry off the heavy artillery, they left us at liberty to reoccupy the post without molestation.

20. *Clinton's note:* Lieutenant Colonel Johnson, with the Seventeenth Regiment of foot, the grenadier company of the Seventy-first, one company of the Loyal Americans, and a detachment of artillery; in all, one colonel, six captains, eighteen subalterns, twenty-eight sergeants, eighteen drummers, and five hundred and forty-four rank and file, of whom there were twenty killed and seventy-four wounded in the assault.

21. See Wayne to Washington, July 17, below, p. 411.

22. See Washington to the President of Congress, July 21, below, p. 415.

The success attending this bold and well-combined attempt of the enemy procured very deservedly no small share of reputation and applause to the spirited officer (General Wayne) who conducted it, and was, I must confess, a very great affront to us, the more mortifying since it was unexpected and possibly avoidable. I do not, however, mean by this to impute blame to the garrison or the officer who commanded, who has unquestionable merit and was honorably acquitted by a court martial. I only wish to do justice to the officers who planned the defenses, who, as they depended on the armed vessels in the North River to cover the flanks, cannot with propriety be censured for the loss of the post if the one [vessel] which had hitherto guarded the left happened that night to be removed and no disposition made to stop the opening—because the works they had constructed, by being rendered thereby imperfect, had not a fair trial.[23] In other respects the consequences were only felt in the diminution of our force by the capture of the garrison, as we were very soon reinstated in a much stronger hold of the position than before.

It being foreign from the design of this narrative to detail all the operations of the different detachments from the army under my command which were acting at a distance from me (as the relation might be in many instances imperfect and perhaps not often very interesting), I thought it right not to interrupt the course of it for the purpose of mentioning in their proper places Major General Campbell's arrival and transactions in West Florida, or those of Major General Prevost in Georgia subsequent to the taking of Savannah and the revival of civil government in that province.[24] The great distance and difficulties of communication with the first placed the troops there

23. For the American side of this famous *coup de main* see Carrington, *Battles of the Revolution*, pp. 472–474; Wallace, *Appeal to Arms*, pp. 196–198; Henry P. Johnston, *The Storming of Stony Point on the Hudson, Midnight, July 15, 1779: Its Importance in the Light of Unpublished Documents* (New York, 1900), especially pp. 62–87. The naval dispositions to which Clinton refers were intended to prevent approach by the submerged bar along which the attackers advanced (Johnston, pp. 66, 79–80). The CP throw no light on why the ship was withdrawn. The records of the court martial of the British commander, Lt. Col. Sir Henry Johnson, are apparently not extant; his superior, Col. Webster, instead of trying to divert blame to the navy, concluded that "no apology can be made for the place being carried at all." (Webster to Clinton, July 29.) Collier blamed Clinton, by implication, for leaving an inadequate garrison: *Particular Services Performed in America*, pp. 99, 101.

24. At the end of 1778 Clinton detached two Campbells to the south almost simultaneously—Lt. Col. Archibald Campbell to Georgia, and Brig. (later Maj.) Gen. John Campbell to West Florida. The latter was sent at Germain's suggestion, to attack New Orleans if Spain entered the war; he was eventually besieged and captured by the Spaniards at Pensacola. For this campaign, and the activities of Prevost, see Fortescue, *British Army*, 3, 270–277, 301–302, 351–352.

beyond the reach of timely assistance from me if the strength of my army could have afforded any, and whenever I had an opportunity of hearing from General Campbell (which was very seldom) I could consequently only lament my inability to remove the numberless distresses he generally complained of. Indeed, as it was often impossible from the lateness or infrequency of my intelligence to send him even instructions for his conduct, I was happy to find that the American Minister had in great measure rendered them unnecessary by transmitting to him orders immediately from England.[25] The only means, therefore, left for me to serve him to any effectual purpose were by repeatedly representing his defenseless situation to the Admirals on the Jamaica and Leeward Island stations [Parker and Byron], and requesting they would send to Pensacola some ships of war for its protection.

The force Major General Prevost had with him in Georgia was fully sufficient to repel all attempts of the rebels to dispossess him of that province, but was not equal to more. It being, therefore, my wish that he should for the present confine his operations within the limits of his command, I was not a little alarmed at hearing he had advanced with the largest portion of it into South Carolina, because I was not without my apprehensions that he might thereby eventually expose Savannah (which was his principal hold of Georgia) to risk, and hazard the safety or at least the health of the troops he carried with him without a possibility of any essential advantage to result from the move. But, on the contrary, there was great reason to suppose that it might rouse the Carolinians to the fortification of their capital, and of course render the conquest of it more difficult when a properer season and an augmentation of our powers should induce the attempt.[26] It consequently gave me very great satisfaction to receive intelligence that, after a fruitless effort against Charleston and successfully sustaining a vigorous attack on his entrenchments at Stono Ferry on the 10th of June, that general officer had happily effected his return into Georgia by Port Royal Island with his whole force, except a corps which he judged proper to leave under Lieutenant Colonel Maitland at Beaufort for the purpose of securing a footing in Carolina.

Toward the close of the last year I had received orders from the American Minister to send a detachment from the troops in Nova

25. See Germain to the general officer commanding in West Florida, July 1, 1778, below, pp. 385–386.

26. *Clinton's note:* But this move of General Prevost was regarded by administration in a very different light, as appears from the . . . extract of a letter from Lord George Germain to Sir Henry Clinton, August 5, 1779 [below, pp. 415–416].

Scotia to take post on the River Penobscot, by way of securing a place of reception and a permanent establishment in the Province of Maine for the King's loyal American subjects who had been driven from their habitations and deprived of their property by the rebels. Accordingly, Brigadier General MacLean, who commanded in Nova Scotia and had in consequence received my directions to carry His Majesty's pleasure into execution, landed there on the 26th of June with 650 men, and immediately began the construction of a fort.[27]

This measure having, of course, given umbrage and alarm to the disaffected in Boston, they came to the resolution of crushing the infant establishment before the troops sent on that service could cover themselves. A considerable naval force was in consequence immediately equipped, under the command of a Captain Saltonstall of the *Warren*, Continental frigate; and between two and three thousand men embarked on board transports, under a militia General called Lovell; and the whole arrived off Penobscot River on the 25th of July. When General MacLean received the first intelligence of the sailing of this armament, two of the bastions of his fort were untouched; and the other two, with the curtains, were in no part above five feet in height and twelve in thickness, the ditch in most places not above three feet in depth, no platform laid, nor any artillery mounted. However, through the great zeal and exertion of all ranks, he put his post into the best posture of defense the time would admit, the commanders and crews of the King's ships in the river having cheerfully joined their efforts to those of the troops. In the meantime, information having been brought into New York on the 28th of the destination of the armament fitting out at Boston, Sir George Collier hastily collected all the naval force that was within his call and sailed with it to the relief of General MacLean on the 3d of August. Fortunately the rebel army made such slow progress in their advances that the work of the besieged was little interrupted, and they were consequently soon so well covered as to be out of all danger from an assault. The post being, therefore, in possession of His Majesty's troops when Sir George Collier's squadron came in view on the 14th, the enemy's ships and army betook themselves to immediate flight. But the former were all either taken or destroyed, and their crews, with the latter, being dispersed in the woods, had to explore their way

27. For the instructions for the expedition and the commanders' accounts of it see below: Germain to Clinton, Sept. 2, 1778; Collier to Clinton, Aug. 19, and MacLean to Germain, Aug. 26, 1779 (pp. 390–391, 416–417, 419–420); also Collier, *Particular Services Performed in America*, pp. 102–116, and Gardner W. Allen, *A Naval History of the American Revolution* (2 vols., New York and Boston, 1913), 2, 419–438.

back to Boston through the wilderness under every circumstance of mortification and disgrace.

The Minister's dispatches, delivered to me on Lieutenant General Earl Cornwallis' arrival at New York on the 21st of July, having put me upon my guard on account of an armament they informed me had sailed from France under Monsieur de la Motte-Picquet and was suspected to be destined for North America,[28] I began to think of making the necessary dispositions for strengthening the defenses of New York. But measures of this tendency required the utmost caution, as there were numbers of disaffected persons within our lines who would have gladly seized that opportunity for exciting an alarm, of which the enemy might have availed themselves to our prejudice. Wherefore I had intended to fortify gradually, and continue the army some time longer in their present camp on the North River, to prevent all suspicions of my apprehending the arrival of an enemy's fleet on the coast.

I was, however, soon obliged to relinquish this mode of conduct. For a pressing requisition from General Haldimand to send 2000 men to Canada and Sir George Collier's sudden departure for the relief of Penobscot, leaving at New York only one twenty-gun ship and two sloops (which were very inadequate to the affording sufficient naval assistance, should rapid water movements and debarkations be required) somewhat precipitated my measures, and obliged me to call in the troops rather sooner than I intended. The army was now, consequently, ordered to fall back to a position nearer Kings Bridge, and a strict defensive was necessarily assumed until the arrival of Admiral Arbuthnot might set us again in motion.

28. Germain to Clinton, May 5, 1779, below, pp. 403–404.

CHAPTER 8

The Collapse of the British Offensive, August to September, 1779

Sir Henry Clinton receives the King's fullest approbation of his services. Is appointed colonel of the Seventh Dragoons. Much mortified at the indispensable suspension of his plans. Delay of the reinforcement, and the consequent evils, to be imputed to Admiral Arbuthnot's excursion to the relief of Jersey. The West India corps stopped from coming to New York. No English fleet or intelligence of them in the middle of August. Sir Henry Clinton implores the King's leave to resign both his commissions to Earl Cornwallis. Paulus Hook attacked by the rebels and nearly carried. All active operations laid aside in the New York district, and preparations made for expeditions to the southward. Admiral Arbuthnot arrives, 25th of August, with only 3800 young troops. They bring with them a putrid fever which sends 6000 to the hospitals. Sir Peter Parker and Governor Dalling alarmed for Jamaica. Sir Henry Clinton detaches to its support 4000 choice troops, which are luckily stopped by timely intelligence that the French fleet was on the coast.

THE FAVORABLE notice the King had been pleased to take of my humble services, and the distinguishing and profitable marks of his royal approbation (the Eighty-fourth Regiment and Queen's Dragoons) with which I had been lately honored, were highly flattering to me.[1] Such unsolicited returns for the zeal I had shown comprehended every reward I could aspire to, and did not fail to strengthen my ardor for His Majesty's service. But in truth my spirits, already pressed down by many adverse incidents, began to sink under the additional weight of new disappointments. The promises repeatedly made me of early reinforcement from Europe and the West Indies had been so unequivocal that they could not be doubted. My plan of operations for the campaign had been formed on that ground, considerable advances had with some success been made in it, and hopes of carrying them on to its completion had been with no small exertion sustained even to the present hour. Any military man, then, who is actuated

1. See Germain to Clinton, Apr. 22, below, p. 402.

by honest ambition in such a cause, or tenacious of his fame, may possibly judge what were my feelings when I saw so promising a prospect gradually vanish, and the season for active service in the district I was in likely to be totally lost by the delays which Admiral Arbuthnot's self-suggested project of relieving Jersey must inevitably occasion. My late dispatches had given me intimation of this event as a circumstance which did the Admiral honor, and I hope for his sake that it may be still considered as of sufficient importance to apologize for and compensate the fatal consequences which ultimately resulted from that measure.[2]

The American Secretary had assured me in his letter of the 1st of April that, besides the European reinforcement, the whole of General Grant's command should be returned to me from the West Indies as soon as the season for offensive operations in that climate was over. And General Grant told me in May that, though the whole could not be spared, I might depend upon having four regiments sent to New York immediately.[3] But now I had the mortification of seeing the middle of August pass me without bringing any part of the English fleet; and a change of circumstances in the West Indies, by the arrival there of la Motte-Picquet, had entirely extinguished all chance of succor from thence. Thus circumstanced, I own I felt very great satisfaction from the arrival of Lord Cornwallis, as I flattered myself that every objection to my request of being released from my very arduous and unpleasant situation must now cease, since His Majesty had upon the spot an officer of rank and experience on whom to confer the command of his army. I therefore took the earliest opportunity of imploring His Majesty's leave to resign both my commissions into His Lordship's hands, as being a nobleman every way qualified to be entrusted with the King's interests in America; and of renewing my most earnest supplication to the throne to be relieved from a burden which I found myself unequal to, and a situation in which there was not any prospect at present that my personal services could be wanted.[4]

2. Arbuthnot sailed from Portsmouth on May 1, and heard on the 2d that Jersey was under attack. He sailed to the rescue, found that the French had already been beaten off, and promptly rejoined his convoy at Torbay. Contrary winds held him there until June 4, and then greatly impeded his passage. The detour to Jersey therefore cost him only one week out of almost seventeen that elapsed between his leaving Portsmouth and reaching New York. See Hist. MSS Com., *MSS of Mrs. Stopford-Sackville*, 2, 127–128; G. R. Barnes and J. H. Owen, eds., *The Private Papers of John, Earl of Sandwich, First Lord of the Admiralty, 1771–1782*, Navy Records Society Publications, 69, 71, 75, 78 (4 vols., [London,] 1932–38), 3, 122, 129.

3. See Grant to Clinton, May 26, below, p. 408.

4. Cornwallis' wife had died in February. In April he renewed his offer to serve, and it was at once accepted; he was made second in command in America, and his

The only incident worth noticing that occurred between the army's drawing nearer to New York and Admiral Arbuthnot's arrival was a well designed, though ultimately disgraceful, attempt of the enemy to destroy the works and carry off the garrison of Paulus Hook. That post had been just reinforced, and a detachment of provincials under Lieutenant Colonel Buskirk had been sent out . . .[5] to intercept some parties of rebels who made a practice of interrupting the usual supplies of provision from the country. A rebel partisan of the name of Lee, availing himself of this opportunity, advanced with a body of men about three in the morning to the outward barrier of the works —where, being mistaken by a careless guard for Colonel Buskirk's corps on its return, he entered without opposition, and through the unsuspecting security of the garrison possessed himself of a block-house and two redoubts with little or no difficulty. The alarm being now spread, the commandant, Major Sutherland, threw himself with forty Hessians into another redoubt, and by a well directed and incessant fire from thence forced the rebels out of the works before they had time to damage the cannon or set fire to the barracks.

As soon as the noise of the firing reached New York, some troops were thrown into boats as quickly as possible and passed across the river, which enabling the commandant to pursue the enemy, he came up with their rear and made a captain and some privates prisoners, but was not in time to recover about forty invalids (part of his garrison) whom they had carried off.[6] I own I was not very well pleased at this affront, happening so recently after the one at Stony Point; and, suspecting it had arisen from some relaxation of discipline, I ordered the commandant to be tried on a charge of general misconduct—for which, however, I had the satisfaction to find there was no foundation, the court martial having honorably acquitted him.[7]

---

old dormant commission was renewed. He was gloomy about the war, and anxious that the command should not devolve upon him; "I come to share fortunes with you," he assured Clinton from England on Apr. 9, "but I will not let you desert me." At the first opportunity Sir Henry tried to do just that, as he explains in the text. The King, however, turned a deaf ear. See Cornwallis to Clinton, Jan. 22, Apr. 4, 9, CP; Germain to Clinton, Apr. 11, and Clinton to Germain, July 28, Aug. 20, below, pp. 401, 415, 417–418; Ross, *Correspondence of Cornwallis, 1,* 37–42.

5. The deletion is a parenthesis, "(upon it)," which is unintelligible: the provincials were sent out from the Hook, not to it.

6. Clinton minimizes this exploit of Light-Horse Harry Lee. The American estimate of British losses was fifty killed and one hundred and fifty-eight or nine taken prisoner: Fitzpatrick, *Writings of Washington, 16,* 167; William H. Richardson, *Washington and "the Enterprise against Powles Hook," a New Study of the Surprise and Capture of the Fort, Thursday, August 19, 1779* (Jersey City, 1929), p. 60.

7. The court of inquiry found that there had been general misconduct by Maj. Sutherland, neglect of duty by the garrison, and "particular, shameful misbe-

The waste of the season and the enemy's exertions in this important interval having rendered unsuitable to the present period that part of my plan to which the past movements of the campaign had been only preparatory, it now became necessary to abandon all thoughts of offensive operations on the side of New York and turn my face to the south, whither the time of the year and the critical state of our affairs in Georgia began to invite me—the conquest of South Carolina having been judged by everyone to be almost indispensable for the securing our hold of that province. And, as in order to give the effort a fair trial it was necessary the King's troops should get there before either Mr. Washington could throw in reinforcement or any part of the French fleet in the West Indies should be detached to the American coast, I lost no time in putting New York in a proper posture of defense, judging it right to secure that important post from all possible insult in my absence.[8] And I got everything in readiness for engaging in two expeditions (in the Chesapeake and South Carolina) as soon after Mr. Arbuthnot's fleet should join me as possible, intending in the interim to mask their destination by some demonstration against the enemy's seaport towns to the eastward.

Admiral Arbuthnot's long expected fleet arrived at last on the 25th of August, bringing an addition to the army under my command of two new-raised battalions and part of another, with English recruits (the German and Irish recruits did not arrive before the 21st of September) and drafts for seven regiments, making in the whole about 3800 men instead of the 6600 which had been promised me. But even of these the numbers fit for duty were few, and they brought with them a malignant jail fever,[9] which soon spread itself among

---

havior" by the artillerymen in the fort and the guards in the blockhouses. ("Proceedings of the Court of Inquiry," Aug. 20.) These charges were quashed by the subsequent court martial, the records of which have apparently disappeared.

Clinton was in fact far from satisfied with the final verdict. "The court of inquiry . . . examined many people and did it upon the spot. The court martial examined very few, and the most material question—whether, as the place was an island, Maj. Sutherland drew up the bridge—was not asked, or at least does not appear in the trial. For which reason, though I confirmed the sentence, I did not approve it. And I have private reasons for disapproving of Major Sutherland's conduct: I cautioned him myself against surprise; I told him how to secure himself against affront, and he neglected it." Clinton memorandum, "Hints for C. Lloyd," Nov. 9.

8. The first two sentences of this paragraph are paraphrased from Clinton to Germain, Aug. 21, below, pp. 418–419.

9. *Clinton's note:* It should be mentioned to the honor of Lieutenant Colonel Thomas Dundas of the Eighty-second Regiment that, when the soldiers and sailors on board his transport were so much weakened by the fever that they were incapable of working the ship, he often stood at the helm himself, and assisted in several other acts of labor as an encouragement for those who could move to

the rest of my army and sent above 6000 of my best troops to the hospital. So that I could not look upon this augmentation as adding anything to my strength, especially after I had complied with General Haldimand's late requisition, which would take from me 2000 well disciplined soldiers. They sailed for Canada on the 10th of September.

Nor could I see any greater likelihood of our being benefited by the change which had taken place in the naval command. For, as I had constantly experienced the most hearty assistance from Sir George Collier whenever we acted together, I had naturally the greatest confidence of his willingness and zeal to forward the public service; and, being from thence persuaded that our part of the naval business would have been properly conducted under *him,* I could not but eye his removal with regret.[10] On the contrary, having never served with his successor, who was besides much advanced in years and might possibly have everything with respect to us to learn, I must rest my expectations from him entirely [11] on the character which Lord George Germain had given me of him—which was, however, indeed in terms of the highest panegyric.[12]

And I was well aware that the naval cooperations in America were of that very peculiar nature that professional abilities in the commanding admiral were not alone sufficient. A perfect intimacy with the inlets and shoals along that intricate coast, [with] the kind of vessels proper for commanding the navigation of the numerous large

---

exert themselves, and immediately on his arrival at New York was himself visited with this fever, which had nearly deprived us of that valuable officer.

10. This was one of the rare moments during Clinton's command when he was on cordial terms with the navy. His high opinion of Collier was fully reciprocated. "Your Lordship will permit me to express my entire satisfaction and pleasure in serving with this gentleman," the Commodore wrote to Germain. "*One* mind has animated us on every occasion where our royal master's service could be promoted. We are neither of us *land* or *sea* officers, but *both.* I strip my ships bare of men, even to leave scarce a boat's crew, for the purpose of dragging cannon, moving troops, horses, etc. The General frequently lends us small detachments which enable ships to go to sea that otherwise, for want of men, could not; and every other act of kindness to the navy he is always ready to perform." Collier to Germain, June 15, Germain Papers, 9; see also Collier to Clinton, June 12, CP.

11. Not entirely. He had already heard that the Admiral was honorable, well meaning, and anxious for his good opinion. "A little of a proser! But, if you can only make him act, that will not signify." Eden [to Clinton], Mar. 3.

Although Arbuthnot's selection affected the whole future of the war in America, the reason for choosing him is not clear. He had commanded for three years at Halifax, and had recently served as a judge in the court martial of Adm. Keppel. But his age alone (he was almost seventy) might well have suggested that he was not the man for the American station.

12. See Germain to Clinton, Mar. 3, 1779, below, p. 400.

rivers which intersect it, and [with] every minute circumstance relative to sudden embarkations and landings of troops, [together] with an unremitted attention to keeping the transports, boats, etc., in a constant state of preparation as well as the appointing a proper portion of active officers and seamen from the fleet to manage them whenever employed on actual service (to which those from the transports were by no means adapted [13]), and the preserving at all times free and ready communications between the several posts of the army, although that might sometimes clash with his cruisers (which, though of importance, ought not always to be considered as the principal object)—[these were] indispensable requisites to constitute a fit naval commander. To which might very properly be added a certain sensible, good-natured pliancy of temper that was disposed to follow where it might be improper to lead, particularly as (the scene of action lying in general more on the land than the water) it might not unoften happen that, when the assistance of the King's ships should be wanted for other purposes besides covering descents, the critical time for yielding it and the mode of conducting it to the best advantage might be not improperly suggested by the officer commanding the troops.[14]

And, in my conviction of the justness of these sentiments, I had very early presumed to intimate to the American Minister my ideas on the subject, and to name five officers in the naval line whose dispositions I was thoroughly acquainted with, and whose hearty and effectual cooperation I could consequently depend upon: Admirals Roddam and Barrington and Commodores Elliot, Hotham, and Sir

13. The transports were under naval control, and Clinton had a low opinion of their crews: when transferred to other ships nothing could be expected of them; when on their own ships they were little better. For the protection of New York he preferred galleys to transports. "The first move against wind and tide; the last are so ill manned that I almost doubt whether they can move with the assistance of both." Clinton to Collier, May 21, filed under June 18; see also Clinton [to Newcastle], June 18.

14. Clinton had reached the conclusion that the command should not be divided, but should rest with either the army or the navy. If the government decided upon a "war of expedition" (i.e., of raids), the navy should be in charge and the army commandant no more than a governor, responsible for defending New York and supplying the navy's requirements; most of the raids "will fail, so little do these sea gentry in general know of land operations." If the government decided upon a vigorous land campaign, the commanding general should direct it, as Sir William Howe had done. This was the sort of war that Clinton still hoped to wage, and for it the ranking naval officer "must be . . . tractable (forgive the expression). One must command, and I know—without vanity I say it—more of their service, as far as it is connected with ours, than anyone of the sea service does of ours." [Clinton to] Drummond, Mar. 10.

John Jervis.[15] But I must, at the same time, acknowledge that an equal pliancy of temper might be often reciprocally necessary in the commander in chief on shore. And I am happy in having in my power to declare that, during the time I had the honor of acting in that situation, I made it my constant study to preserve the utmost harmony between the two services, and in particular that I neglected nothing which I thought was likely to conciliate Admiral Arbuthnot's favorable sentiments and concurrence.

With these desires and dispositions I met the Admiral on his arrival. And I had, very soon after, an opportunity of evincing the sincerity of them by acceding to his and Lord Cornwallis' opinions (though they were somewhat different from my own) with respect to the immediate necessity of sending a reinforcement to Jamaica upon a requisition made to us by Governor Dalling and Sir Peter Parker, who were alarmed for that island by intelligence that a considerable French armament was assembling at Cape François.[16] My zeal for the King's service and knowledge of the great importance which our West Indies possessions were of to Great Britain would have ever prompted me to contribute my utmost to their security without hesitation. But, as there was not in the present case any appearance of Spain's joining her forces to those of France,[17] and there was but little probability the latter would attempt the supposed enterprise by herself and during the hurricane season, I thought there was good ground for suspecting the Hispaniola fleet had some other object.

And, I own, for these reasons I did not look upon the present necessity as very urgent. Wherefore I would have rather wished to decline detaching from my army at a moment when I was upon the eve of carrying into execution a scheme which I had long meditated and communicated to administration, and upon the prompt success of which the safety of Georgia seemed to depend—especially, too, as

15. Clinton's choices, with the possible exception of Hotham, were a group of distinguished officers. Roddam, his brother-in-law, was serving as commander in chief at the Nore; Barrington and Hotham were in the West Indies, where they had recently gained fame in the capture of St. Lucia; Elliot, who had been Lord Howe's second in command, had returned to Europe; Jervis, later the most famous of them all, never served on the American station during the war. Clinton apparently did not forward the five names to Germain by letter; in all likelihood they were suggested orally by Drummond or Innes.

16. See the extracts of Dalling to Clinton, Aug. 11, and Clinton to Dalling, Sept. 16, below, pp. 416, 421.

17. Clinton is here referring to Spanish naval dispositions, not to Spain's recent juncture with France. Germain's dispatch of June 17, informing him of the Spanish declaration of war, had been received on Sept. 1.

the parting with 4000 British troops (being not at liberty to send either foreigners or provincials to the West Indies [18]), added to the 2000 I had just sent to Canada, would not only oblige me to put off the southern expeditions to a late day but, considering the sickness then prevailing at New York, put every other [expedition] out of my power, perhaps for the rest of the campaign.[19] However, the motives before mentioned induced me to waive all objections, and in compliance with the wishes of Admiral Arbuthnot (who proposed sending thither all his line-of-battle ships) I embarked nearly 4000 men under the command of Lord Cornwallis, who was very anxious for the measure and with a commendable zeal offered himself to conduct it.

As it was impossible for me to give any formal instructions to Lord Cornwallis on this occasion, wherein everything must so much depend upon contingencies, I could only in general state my wishes according as he should find matters on his arrival, and recommend to His Lordship's consideration such subsequent objects as appeared to me eligible, particularly the reduction of New Orleans and reinforcement of Pensacola, with my request that he would join me afterward, with the troops that were left, at Savannah.[20] But, soon after His Lordship had sailed, he fortunately met a vessel with certain information that Count d'Estaing's fleet was seen on the 31st of August off the Bahama Islands steering for the North American coast. This information brought him, of course, immediately back—and was probably the means of saving the whole armament from being captured, as d'Estaing made his appearance off Tybee in two or three days afterward.[21]

18. See below, pp. 393, 597 and n. 98.

19. *Clinton's note:* The fit for duty in the New York district before Admiral Arbuthnot's arrival were 14,682; their amount at the present period was only 14,184. Sir Henry Clinton's strength was consequently less by 498 men than it was before the reinforcement joined him.

20. See Clinton to Dalling, Sept. 16, and to Cornwallis, Sept. 23, below, pp. 421–422.

21. *Clinton's note:* He arrived off Tybee the 2d of September.

CHAPTER 9

Defensive Retrenchment, October, 1779

Alarmed for New York, Rhode Island, or Halifax. Consequent precautions taken to defend the entrance of New York harbor, and Rhode Island evacuated on the Admiral's opinion that it was of no use to the navy and he could not spare a single ship for its defense. Posts of Stony Point and Verplanck's dismantled and their garrisons withdrawn. Expeditions to South Carolina and the Chesapeake suspended. Admiral resolves to remove his fleet to Halifax. Sir Henry Clinton alarmed by hearing he intends wintering there. Sends an officer to remind him of the operations they had concerted to take place as soon as the enemy's fleet had quitted the coast. The Admiral yields to his reasons and relinquishes that design.

THE INTELLIGENCE of so superior a fleet being near us naturally excited alarming apprehensions for New York, Rhode Island, and Halifax, one or other of which we took for granted was its object, and of course caused us to suspend the proposed expeditions until the storm we saw gathering should blow over. Troops and artillery were consequently immediately sent to the Lighthouse [Governor's] Island and the old fortifications there repaired. The Admiral also collected all his naval force at the Hook (consisting of two seventy-fours, three sixty-fours, two fifties and two forty-fours) to endeavor to defend the entrance of the harbor,[1] and submitted to my consideration the expediency of evacuating Rhode Island, as he could not spare a ship for its protection and did not think the possession of it of the smallest use to the navy.

The decided opinion which the Admiral had now given me that Rhode Island was no way useful as a situation for ships of war, for whose benefit alone it had been hitherto taken in '76 and retained

---

1. D'Estaing had twenty-two ships of the line, two fifties, and fourteen frigates. (Carrington, *Battles of the Revolution*, p. 477.) Arbuthnot was convinced that this force, so enormously superior to his own, was bound for New York. Although he adopted Lord Howe's method of defending the harbor, he lacked Howe's confidence; if the French ever succeeded in forcing their way past the bar, Clinton was told, he would have to fend for himself. Arbuthnot to Clinton, Nos. 1 and 2 of Oct. 4.

(as the post was certainly unessential to land operations in the then state of our affairs), and the rescuing from the imminent danger of so unprotected a state the artillery and stores in that post, together with its large garrison [2] (whose services would probably be required for immediate defensive as well as future offensive), were such forcible arguments for quitting it that I could not hesitate about its propriety, especially as Lord Cornwallis and the Commodore [Collier] joined in the same sentiments. Accordingly, I availed myself of an offer Colonel Stuart was so obliging to make me (of whose zeal and abilities I had had such frequent proofs) by sending him thither to arrange everything necessary with General Prescott, for a total or partial evacuation as emergencies might require. And, in the meantime, I invited the Admiral to a consultation whether it would not be more expedient to keep a small post there for the purpose of preventing the rebels from getting possession in case the French did not come, as even a partial hold of the harbor might be eventually hereafter of consequence should we happen, notwithstanding appearances, to be mistaken with respect to the destination of the French fleet. The Admiral remaining, however, steady to his first opinion, and the Commodore coinciding in it, I sent General Prescott my final orders for bringing away the garrison and dismantling the works.

But twelve days after this, when it was more than probable General Prescott had made considerable progress in the demolition of the works, the Admiral wrote to me to request I would suspend the evacuation of Rhode Island until he could hear from Halifax, which he discovered from some intercepted Spanish letters was one of Count d'Estaing's principal objects, "because the loss of that port, should it have taken place, considerably changed the question, and would give an importance to the harbor of Newport which he did not consider it to have while we held the other." [3] Therefore, as I had consented to the evacuation out of deference to the Admiral's opinion and advice, so from the same motives I now consented to send directions for everything being stopped until further orders, and even the debris of the works to be reoccupied unless the officer commanding there should see evident destruction likely to follow the attempt to retain possession. It happened, however, that the armed vessel which the Admiral sent with my dispatches was taken. But, not knowing it and being repeatedly disappointed for several days in my endeavours

2. *Clinton's note:* The Rhode Island garrison amounted to 4011 rank and file effective.

3. This is not even a paraphrase, but gives the general idea expressed in Arbuthnot to Clinton, Oct. 19.

to obtain another from him, to carry Colonel Stuart [4] thither with further instruction to General Prescott and [to] learn his situation, I suffered the most anxious apprehensions for the safety of the garrison under his command, until I had the happiness of seeing it arrive at New York. [5]

I had, a few days before this, been likewise joined by the garrisons of Stony Point and Verplanck's, whose importance of course ceased the moment I gave up offensive operations on the Hudson, which was the chief purpose that induced me to lay hold of them. For, though the possession of those stations gave us in a great degree the command of both sides of that river for nearly fifty miles up it (whereby the Indians were assisted in their excursions, and desertion from the enemy much encouraged, while our intelligence from the rebel country and Canada was greatly facilitated), I foresaw I should be under a necessity of abandoning them before I went to the southward, because there would not be afterward enough of troops left in the New York district to maintain them through the winter but at the utmost difficulty and hazard. And I knew very well that Mr. Washington would not venture to attempt preventing my retaking them whenever they should be again wanted. Therefore the present moment of apprehension and suspense urged me to take this opportunity of dismantling them, and adding their garrisons to the defensive I was forming at New York.

Having about this time received intelligence that the rebels had formed some magazines of hay and other stores, and collected together a number of large boats on carriages, in the neighborhood of Somerset Court House, a plan was formed by Lieutenant Colonel Simcoe of the Queen's Rangers to destroy them, which was communicated to me and received my approbation. He consequently landed at Amboy in the night of the 16th of October with his own corps and the Bucks County Volunteers, and, having burned seven-

4. *Clinton's note:* Nothing could possibly be more handsome than this most excellent and very spirited officer's zealous and active conduct in the whole of this business, and in every other while we served together.

5. The question of withdrawing the garrison was discussed in a month-long correspondence between Clinton and Arbuthnot, which illustrates their inability to understand one another. Sir Henry's extracts of these letters, between Sept. 26 and Oct. 25, are given below, pp. 423, 424–425, 426–431. In retrospect the evacuation of Rhode Island must have seemed a major strategic blunder, because it permitted the French to establish themselves there nine months later. No doubt for this reason, Clinton attempts to lay the sole responsibility on the navy. But he was seriously considering the move as early as Sept. 23 (before he knew that the French were on the coast), because the garrison was needed to replace troops to be detached from New York to South Carolina. See [Clinton to Cornwallis,] Sept. 23, and to Germain, Sept. 26, CP; Arbuthnot to Clinton, Oct. 6, below, p. 424.

teen boats and a considerable quantity of hay and other articles, he proceeded to the Court House and liberated a number of loyalists that were confined there. But, the enemy having laid an ambuscade to intercept him on his return to a bridge where he had posted his infantry, he had the misfortune to be wounded by an unexpected fire as he was passing through the wood where it lay, and himself and four others were taken prisoners. This being the only loss sustained in this spirited enterprise, which was achieved by eighty horse, the rest of the detachment returned the next day without further interruption to Staten Island with twenty-two prisoners.

Upon Admiral Arbuthnot's first alarm for Halifax and his determining in consequence to carry his fleet thither, I had embarked three battalions and the flank companies of the Eighty-second Regiment, under Brigadier General Stirling, to accompany him as a reinforcement to the garrison there. I took the liberty, however, to suggest to the Admiral that I thought the season of the year somewhat too advanced to render it probable Count d'Estaing would engage in offensive operations so far to the northward. And the Admiral in his answer seemed to incline to my opinion, and to be determined in consequence to give up the idea of going thither, or at least to defer it until the return of a swift-sailing vessel he had sent thither for intelligence. But in four days afterward he changed his mind, and wrote to me to let me know he should sail for Halifax the next day. Wherefore, as I had not had an opportunity of being fully informed of the Admiral's intentions with respect to the subsequent operations of the winter, I thought it right to recall his attention to the expeditions which had been interrupted by Count d'Estaing's visit to the coast, and was not a little astonished and alarmed at hearing he proposed to remain himself with the large ships of his squadron at Halifax. I therefore immediately dispatched an aide-de-camp to the Hook with a fuller explanation of my sentiments and wishes, who was so fortunate to get there just as the fleet was getting under sail; and I had the happiness to find my arguments prevailed upon him to reconsider the matter, with more attention to the season of the year, and lay aside his intended voyage altogether.

CHAPTER 10

Preparations for the Southern Campaign, October to December, 1779

D'Estaing's fleet anchors off Tybee. Savannah, the capital of Georgia, invested by the French and Americans. They endeavor to carry the town by assault and are repulsed. The French commander re-embarks his troops and leaves the coast. Sir Henry Clinton embarks 8000 men on an expedition against Charleston. Short account of the transactions in West Florida. Sir Henry Clinton complains of the great expectations raised in England of his success. Shows the false foundation on which they were built. He is appointed sole commissioner, and renews his prayer to be released from both that and the command.

WE HAD not received any certain accounts of the French fleet's operations on the American coast before the 8th of October, when a privateer arrived at New York with intelligence that Count d'Estaing was off Tybee and had taken the *Experiment,* man-of-war, which had sailed some little time before from New York for Savannah with £30,000, which I had sent by her for the use of the troops, and Brigadier General Garth, who was going to relieve Major General Prevost in that command. We, however, continued still ignorant of the Count's real intentions until the beginning of November, when accounts reached us from the rebels that the town of Savannah was invested by the united forces of France and America. And on the 19th I received letters from Governor Tonyn and Colonel Fuser, with a short account of the proceedings of the combined army, which was confirmed on the 10th of December by dispatches from General Prevost giving me a more circumstantial relation of the siege.[1]

By these I had the satisfaction to be informed that, contriving in consequence of Count d'Estaing's summons on the 16th of September

---

1. See Prevost to Clinton, Nov. 2, below, pp. 432–434. Clinton had been afraid that the loss of Georgia would unhinge the whole British plan of campaign in the south, and he was correspondingly elated to hear of the enemy's repulse. "I think this is the greatest event that has happened the whole war." (Clinton [to unknown], Nov. 8–19.) For modern accounts of the siege see Carrington, *Battles of the Revolution,* pp. 477–483; Fisher, *Struggle for American Independence,* 2, 257–260; Wallace, *Appeal to Arms,* pp. 206–209.

to gain time for consideration, he had the good fortune to be joined in the interim by Lieutenant Colonel Maitland and the chief part of the Beaufort garrison—which, amounting to nearly 1000 men, enabled him to set the enemy's menaces at defiance. Their batteries were consequently opened against his works on the 4th of the following month, and on the 9th the French and American troops advanced to the assault under cover of a thick fog, which concealed their approach. But though the attack, which was led by Count d'Estaing in person, was spirited and obstinate (two stands of colors having been actually planted on the Ebenezer Redoubt and several of the assailants killed on the parapet) the enemy was repulsed with great slaughter; and, being driven in confusion over the abatis into a swamp, the whole precipitately retired, leaving 231 dead and 116 wounded behind them, most of whom lay in the ditch and on the works.

The loss sustained by the King's troops on this occasion did not exceed sixteen killed and thirty-nine wounded, which with the very honorable issue of the affair are strong proofs what perseverance and resolution are capable of effecting behind works, even against a very superior force. For General Prevost had not above ten guns mounted in battery on the day of summons; and his garrison, including the armed inhabitants and sailors, did not consist of more than four thousand, of which not above twenty-four hundred were regimented troops. The defenses of the place were also only field works, formed of loose sand hastily scratched together on almost a dead flat. On the contrary, the besieging army consisted of about six thousand disciplined French troops and more than one thousand Americans, aided by an ample battering train and headed by officers of courage and ability, while they were at the same time covered by twenty-two sail of the line, two fifties, and several large frigates, which very powerfully assisted the operations on shore. Thus was the capital of that province (very much to the credit of its brave garrison) preserved to His Majesty, and the enemy's efforts to wrest it from him defeated by the zealous exertions of an engineer *who understood his business* [2] and the spirited resistance of a few judicious officers and a handful of men, who were not to be dismayed by the imposing parade and formidable numbers of their assailants. For on the tenth day after their disgraceful repulse the besieging army totally abandoned their lines and dispersed, the French troops re-embarking on board their fleet, which

2. Capt. James Moncrieff, who afterward served with equal distinction in the siege of Charleston. Clinton's italics are presumably intended to emphasize the contrast with the shortcomings of Cornwallis' engineers at Yorktown, for which see below, pp. 335 and n. 4, 348 and n. 31.

soon after quitted the coast, and those of America falling back into South Carolina to prepare for the defense of that province and its capital.

I had long determined, as already mentioned, on an expedition against Charleston, the capital of South Carolina, which every account I had received from Georgia convinced me was necessary to save that province from falling again into the hands of the rebels. And, indeed, having in a manner pledged myself to administration for making the attempt, I could not now go from it without justly exposing myself to censure, as I had drawn the attention of government to this as an object of importance, and I knew that its reduction was consequently looked for with anxious solicitude.[3] Besides, the universal dejection occasioned in the rebel country by the late miscarriage of the French and their combined efforts before Savannah, added to the great sufferings of the bulk of the people from the enormous depreciation of the Continental paper money (now fallen to fifty for one) and the many other grievances extending even to their army, which Congress found it impossible to stifle the complaints of, all strongly at this time invited me to it.[4]

My intention had been to put the Chesapeake and Carolina expeditions in motion together early in October, that we might have the whole winter and following spring before us to carry our operations to their proper extent. And I was not without hopes, if they were successful, that the spirit of rebellion might be thoroughly subdued in the two Carolinas, and such a hold afterward taken of the Chesapeake as should prove at least a barrier between them and the northern states. But the visit of a French superior fleet to the American coast (without being followed by a single [British] ship from the West Indies) obliged the Admiral and me to confine our thoughts, as long as that threatened us, to the security of such of His Majesty's American posssessions as were immediately near us. While we remained in the suspense occasioned by this circumstance, I kept my eye of course on Mr. Washington's motions—who, I found, was making preparations to act against New York in concert with Count d'Estaing, whom he had very strongly in-

3. A second attempt on Charleston had been under consideration almost since the failure of the first in 1776. Howe had planned such a move for the winter of 1777–78. Germain urged it on Clinton in the spring of 1779; simultaneously and independently Sir Henry decided to end that year's campaign with an attack on South Carolina. His preparations were well under way in August, and the danger from d'Estaing interrupted them only temporarily. See Germain to Howe, Sept. 3, 1777, in Germain Papers, Military Dispatches, Appendix; Germain to Clinton, Mar. [31], 1779; Clinton to Eden, Apr. 4, May 20; Clinton to Germain, Aug. 21.

4. *Clinton's note:* In the middle of December part of General Washington's army was several days without bread, and for the rest he had not, either upon the spot or within reach, a supply sufficient for four days.

vited to that enterprise. And I was determined, after my acting force
was increased by the junction of the Rhode Island and Verplanck's garrisons, to strike at him had he given me an opening for it. But that wary
General conducted himself with his usual caution, by keeping his army
in the remote fastnesses behind which he had entrenched it the whole
summer. I had nothing, therefore, to do but to adjust my arrangements
to prepare for embarking a body of troops to carry with me from thence
to the southward, as soon as I knew for certain that the French fleet had
quitted the coast.

In the calculation I was making of the number of troops necessary
to defend the many widely dispersed posts of the New York district,
I did not neglect to take into consideration the usual extreme severity
of the winters, which not infrequently renders their insular situation
useless at that season toward their defense.[5] And, as the ordinary duties
in the lines at Kings Bridge and the other works on New York Island,
those of Setauket, Huntington, Brooklyn, etc., on Long Island, the
security of Staten Island, and the garrison of Paulus Hook would take
at least eight [to] ten thousand men,[6] besides the militia which the town
of New York might furnish on an emergency, I could not well leave behind me less than twelve thousand, especially as from the best information I could obtain Mr. Washington's force (hutted near Morristown
and on the east side of the North River, together with the garrisons of
the forts at West Point) was not less than sixty-five battalions or corps,
all regular troops, besides as many militia as he pleased to embody in
the neighboring populous provinces, which were little inferior in practice and courage to the Continentals.[7] Consequently, as I had still full
6000 sick in my hospitals, many of whom could not be fit for duty before the spring, I had not above 7000 men to take with me to the southward.[8] Nor should I have had even that number if part of the detachment I had sent to Canada had not failed in their voyage and been
driven back to New York.

5. *Clinton's note:* In this very winter of '79 the North River was covered with
so strong a coat of ice that heavy-loaded wagons passed over it for several weeks
from New York to Staten Island.
One of Clinton's loose notes: The campaign at New York never could finish,
neither offensively nor defensively; for the most important moves were made from
the place (and might be made against the place) in depth of winter when the river
was frozen and passable.
6. The MS has both figures, 8000 in the text and 10,000 interlined by Clinton.
7. *Clinton's note:* Battalion[s] or corps with General Washington at Morristown
and in the neighborhood, forty-two; detached in Jersies, two; at West Point (artillery not included), seven; in the Highlands, four; near Continental Village, four;
beyond Danbury, four; cavalry in Connecticut, two. Total, sixty-five.
8. *Clinton's note:* The amount of the whole force in the district of New York
on the 1st of December did not exceed 18,538.

But, as Admiral Arbuthnot seemed now to enter cordially into the execution of the important service we had in contemplation, and had promised to accompany me himself with the principal part of his squadron, I had little doubt, if we should have a prosperous voyage and retained our superiority at sea, but these would prove fully sufficient not only to achieve the conquest of Charleston but to recover the chief part of South Carolina. And I proposed, toward the breaking up of the frost, to draw 2000 more troops from New York to occupy a commodious post in Virginia, for the purpose of cooperating with the southern army in the reduction of North Carolina, should circumstances at the time encourage such an effort.

Had it been practicable for us to have left New York so early as I had at first proposed, there is no saying to what lengths our success might have been extended. But, as it was late in December before we had any accounts which could be depended on of what was become of the French fleet, I found myself obliged by the advanced season of the year to contract my plan.[9] For, the intelligence we received rendering it probable that some of the enemy's line-of-battle ships were to winter in the Chesapeake, it became now imprudent to hazard the attempt of seizing a post there without first depriving them of the power to hurt us; and the hasty approach of the severity of winter made me cautious of stopping there to attack the ships supposed to be in Virginia, lest the delay such a measure must necessarily occasion (as we should most probably find them covered by works) should entangle us in the ice, and consequently prevent our voyage to Carolina until the spring. These considerations, therefore, determined me not to suffer myself to be diverted by any lure from my main object, though the Admiral pressed it strongly and sent Lord Cornwallis and Sir Andrew Hamond to me to blazon the *opportunity we had of destroying eight of the enemy's capital ships*, which his information had mounted them up to, though mine assured me there were only two and as many store-ships.[10]

9. In other words, to abandon his earlier intention of establishing a post in the Chesapeake on his way south. The primary reason for such a post would have been to impede the transfer of troops from Washington's army to the defense of South Carolina. " 'Tis a great distance; and, if the Chesapeake was clear of French ships, we might throw great obstructions to their march." Clinton [to Newcastle], Dec. 12, 1779.

10. Clinton here appends the following note: "The *Fendant*, an *armée en flûte*, and one frigate and two store-ships," which presumably means that the *Fendant* herself was *armée en flûte*, or incompletely armed. In an undated memorandum (filed at the end of May, 1780) he complains that "the navy to the last obtained no information. A vessel I dispatched did, and . . . reported one seventy-four [and] one old store-ship." The *Fendant* was in fact completely armed, and was accompanied by two frigates. This small squadron was important because it first

And it was very fortunate that I held to my resolution. For, had we not taken the advantage of the favorable wind which offered on the 26th of December, it is more than probable the expedition would have been totally frustrated, as a most violent snowstorm came on the next day but one, and the frost set in immediately afterward with such unremitting severity that, had we gone into the Chesapeake, we should undoubtedly have been fastened up there for the rest of the winter.[11]

As none of the [British] ships of war in the West Indies had been detached to North America after Count d'Estaing, and I had given to both our Admirals on those stations very early notice of the ruined state of the fortifications at Pensacola and had most earnestly requested their attention to the defense of that port and the Province of West Florida, I had so little apprehension of any injury being likely to happen to Major General Campbell that I even expected soon to hear that Sir Peter Parker and he had made themselves masters of New Orleans. Nothing, therefore, could equal my surprise but my concern when I received information from that general officer that Don Galvez, the Governor of New Orleans, having earlier notice of the Spanish declaration of war than he had, was enabled thereby to wrest from him all his posts on the Mississippi together with their respective garrisons, by which his whole force was reduced to 724 rank and file, and that, the Indians being somehow estranged from our interests and the inhabitants of the province averse from military service, he had not the smallest prospect of assistance from either, should Pensacola or Mobile be attacked.[12]

This most fatal inattention to the security of that important possession was much to be lamented. But it was absolutely out of my power, at the time I received the intelligence, to afford General Campbell any other relief than by repeating my solicitations to Sir Peter Parker for a frigate or two to be sent to Pensacola, to frustrate any attack of that port from the sea, whereby we might be enabled to retain at least one hold in West Florida until we should be fortunately in a condition to recover what we had lost there.

In reading my public dispatches in the latter end of October, I was sorry to observe that the most flattering expectations were still en-

---

drew British attention to Yorktown. See William B. Willcox, "The British Road to Yorktown: A Study in Divided Command," *American Historical Review*, 52 (Oct., 1946), 6, n. 7.

11. Clinton's extracts of his correspondence with the Admiral on this subject, Dec. 23–26, are given below, pp. 437–438. Arbuthnot had an additional reason for wanting to attack the French ships, the fear that they would assault New York in his absence. Arbuthnot [to Clinton], Dec. 26, CP.

12. Campbell to Clinton, Nov. 7, Dec. 15, below, pp. 436–437.

couraged in England of the great success that was to follow the junction with me of Vice Admiral Arbuthnot's reinforcement and the regiments from the West Indies, which the American Minister had calculated would take place at latest toward the close of July or beginning of August. His Lordship seemed also to have cherished very sanguine ideas of the great numbers of loyalists I should be enabled to embody in the provincial corps in consequence of the late regulations, so that no doubt was entertained but that I should in the course of the present campaign not only harass the coasts of the enemy and reduce the southern provinces to obedience, but also be able to carry with me into the field an army capable of forcing Mr. Washington to a general and decisive action or of compelling him to disband his forces. My arrangements for conducting the campaign and the few advantages which had hitherto resulted from my measures had, moreover, been applauded in the warmest language of panegyric. The most favorable prognostics were formed of their progress, and the public was taught to believe that my hands were sufficiently strengthened for carrying them into execution.[13]

After the reader has taken the trouble of perusing the foregoing chapters, he need not, I believe, be told that the foundations on which these visionary hopes were raised had moldered by degrees to nothing, and that of course I was not responsible for their failure. But, though the dispassionate eye of candor may possibly do me ample justice in the present hour of cool reflection, I could not flatter myself that was likely to be the case immediately after the unexpected disappointment of such high-wrought expectations. For it was not to be supposed that, when the people afterward saw a campaign from which they hoped so much and [which they] confidently believed would be the last thus unproductively closed, and all their dreams of conquest and the benefits to follow vanished into air, they would have patience to investigate the causes or make allowance for them. No—to the Commander in Chief alone was it to be apprehended they would impute the blame; and there is but little doubt that those, if there are any such, who really deserved it would employ all their art in his absence to fix it upon him, and thereby shift the public indignation from themselves.

I felt, therefore, the tottering ground on which I stood. And, notwithstanding the soothing commendations of my conduct which almost every packet brought me from England and the additional mark of confidence with which the King had lately honored me, by appointing me his sole commissioner for restoring peace to his colonies,

13. See Germain to Clinton, June 25, Aug. 5, and Sept. 27, below, pp. 410, 415–416, 423–424.

prudence still forcibly urged me to implore my recall. It was my resolution, however, in the meantime to exert every faculty I was master of to advance the interests of my country; and, in the certain expectation that my request, so repeatedly made, would not be refused, I communicated all my plans and designs to Earl Cornwallis, which seemed to meet with His Lordship's fullest concurrence. And I endeavored to interest him in those measures which I thought the most conducive to the King's service, to the end that the great object of all our wishes might not suffer by a change of the commander of the army in America, but that a unity of plan might notwithstanding be continued, and give all possible vigor and success to the future exertions of His Majesty's arms.[14]

14. See Clinton to Germain, Oct. 29, below, pp. 431–432.

CHAPTER 11

The Siege and Capture of Charleston, January to May, 1780

Sir Henry Clinton's present powers and prospects compared with those of Sir William Howe in July, 1777. Expedition sails. Disasters and great length of the voyage. Arrival at Tybee. Councils of war. Reasons for calling them. Lord Cornwallis' opinion prevails. Part of the army proceeds from thence by sea to South Carolina. The danger of that route in the present season. The transports enter the North Edisto Inlet and the troops are landed on Simmons [Seabrook] Island. Captain Elphinstone's knowledge of the coast and island navigation and his unremitting exertions in forwarding the supplies to the army of the greatest service. Sir Henry Clinton obliged to act different from what had been settled at Tybee. His reasons. Sir Henry Clinton sends to New York, West Indies, and the Bahamas, etc., for artillery and ordnance stores to replace those lost on the passage, and calls to him more troops from the northward and Georgia. Admiral Arbuthnot passes over the bar into Five Fathom Hole. Missing transports join.

The flatboats from the fleet pass the enemy's batteries in the night and transport the elite of the army across the Ashley to Charleston Neck. Ground broke within 800 yards of the enemy's works. The Admiral passes Fort Moultrie on Sullivan's Island and anchors under Fort Johnson. The town summoned. Summons rejected and batteries of first parallel opened. Colonel Webster detached with 1400 men across the Cooper, which the Admiral promises to occupy with an armed force. Three regiments of well appointed rebel cavalry and a body of militia surprised by the Legion and Major Ferguson's Rangers under Lieutenant Colonel Tarleton, who mounts his own corps on their horses. Reinforcement joins from New York. An addition is made to the corps detached to the other side of the Cooper and the command of it given to Lord Cornwallis.

The Admiral declines sending an armed force into the Cooper. Consequent severity of duty to the troops in the trenches. Strength of the rebel defenses described. Rebel cavalry remounted and again routed and dispersed by Lieutenant Colonel Tarleton. Sullivan's Island surrendered to Captain Hudson of the navy. Third parallel completed and town again summoned. Terms refused. Batteries opened and the enemy's guns silenced. Prepare for carrying the place by assault. The

*Admiral now refuses to place the King's ships against the enemy's
sea batteries (though his own proposal), and only promises to loose
his sails and indicate a design of doing so. General Lincoln capitulates
and his whole garrison surrendered prisoners of war. Amount of
prisoners, ordnance, killed and wounded, etc.*

THE NECESSARY arrangements being settled for the defense of New
York and its dependencies, that they might be exposed to as little
risk as possible in the absence of so considerable a portion of the fleet
and army, and the care of the whole committed to Lieutenant General
Knyphausen (on whom the command devolved in course as the senior
officer in that district), the expedition against Charleston sailed from
Sandy Hook on the 26th of December, 1779, as mentioned in the last
chapter.

But, that the reader may be qualified to judge of the many difficulties we had to encounter and the consequent strength of my motives for wishing to be released from the chief command of the army in
America, it may perhaps be not impertinent, before we proceed to the
events that followed, to take a retrospective view of the very great dis-
proportion between Sir William Howe's powers and prospects when he
sailed from the same port in July, 1777, and mine at this very critical and
important period.

That general officer's correspondence with the American Minister
shows it was his absolute opinion that nothing short of 15,000 men
in addition to what he then had would be sufficient to give him a
superiority—though he had the Americans alone to contend with and
no foreign enemy to dread, and was, moreover, assisted by a very
numerous fleet under the orders of his brother, Lord Howe, on whose
most hearty cooperation he could depend, and whose abilities and
zeal gave facility and vigor to all his measures. On the contrary, when
I undertook this move, my army was inferior to that my predecessor
actually had by at least sixteen thousand men, the ships of war serving with me were not equal to a third of the number he had, and the
Commanders in Chief of the two services were scarcely known to each
other; while the rebel forces were considerably improved in discipline
and increased in strength, and at the same time made bold with

A PLAN OF THE MILITARY OPERATIONS AGAINST
CHARLESTOWN, *London, 1780*

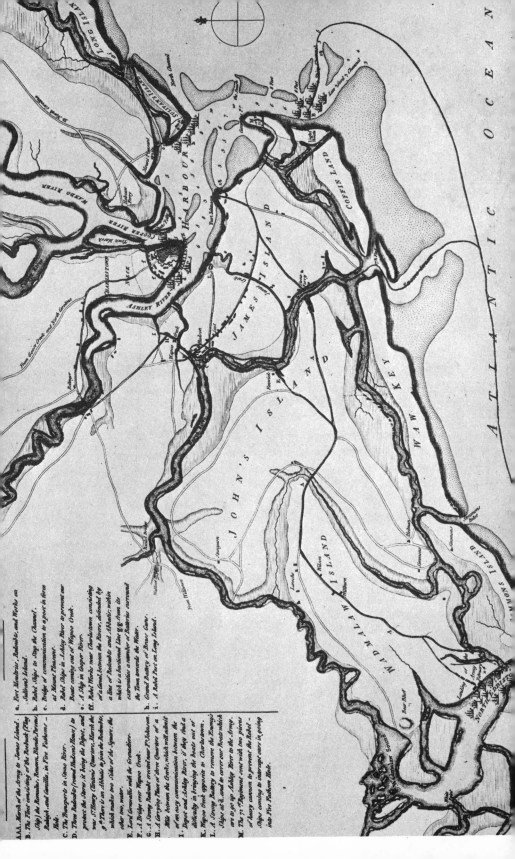

AAA. *March of the Army to James Island.*
B. *The Fleet consisting of the Roebuck (Flag Ship) the Romulus, Renown, Blonde, Perseus, Raleigh, and Camilla, in Five Fathoms Water.*
C. *The Transports in Stono River.*
D. *Three Redoubts (toward Hudson's House) to prevent the Burning & being the Depots, and near Mt Henry's Distant Quarters, distant at h. There is an Abbatis to join the Redoubts, which make one Line of the Square, the other two, water.*
E. *Lord Cornwallis with the Grenadiers.*
F. *A Bridge over Wapoo Creek.*
G. *A Strong Redoubt erected near Mt Johnson's.*
H. *A Carrying Place or three Quarters of a Mile between the Creeks, which will admit of an easy communication between the Ashley River & Stono River, if they find a Difficulty in bringing the boats out of Wapoo Creek opposite to Charlestown.*
K. *A Strong Battery to remove the Enemy's Ships at d, and to cover our Boats which are to go up Ashley River to the Army.*
M. *The 71st Regiment sent with two pieces of Heavy cannon to prevent the Rebel Ships coming to intercept our's in going into Five Fathom Hole.*

a. *Fort Moultrie, Redoubts, and Works on Sullivan's Island.*
b. *Rebel Ships to Stop the Channel.*
c. *Bridge & communication to & from in three at Mount Pleasant.*
d. *Rebel Ships in Ashley River to prevent our Boats coming out of Wapoo Creek.*
e. *A Ship in Cooper River.*
ff. *Rebel Works near Charlestown consisting of a Canal, between the Rivers, defended by a Bar of Redoubts and Abbatis; within which is a horizontal Line gg; from its extremities a number of Redoubts are carried to Town towards the Water.*
h. *Grand Battery of Brazs Guns.*
i. *A Rebel Fort on Long Island.*

confidence by the conquest and capture of General Burgoyne's army and the support given to their cause by the ships and troops of France and their late alliance with Spain. Add to this that, as the fleets of France had twice already since I came to the command rode triumphant in the American seas, the spirit of enterprise on our side must of course be damped and the plan of all subsequent operations confined within a much narrower compass, from the great hazard to which water movements were likely to be exposed by their probable return.

The safety of my widely dispersed posts being likewise rendered more precarious by these contingencies, and consequently requiring a larger portion of troops for their defense in my absence, those that were left me afterward for active service were too much limited in number to be adequate to any great design.

I had, however, such confidence in the spirit and discipline of the corps and the ability of the officers I took with me that I did not doubt of success, though it certainly required the utmost vigilance and precaution to guard against accidents and obviate the various obstacles I might consequently meet with, especially if the length of our voyage should give time for the reinforcements which Mr. Washington might detach from his army to arrive in South Carolina before us. Every delay, therefore, which we experienced in the course of it could not but excite in me pain in proportion to so critical a situation.

Nor was I without ample subject for anxiety. For scarcely a single day during the voyage passed without being marked by the foundering of some transport or other or the dispersion of the fleet, while we had the vexation at the same time of seeing ourselves hurried by the Gulf Stream to the eastward, almost beyond the hope of being able to regain the American coast. However, the Admiral's commendably zealous perseverance fortunately proved superior to the malevolence of the winds; [1] and we had the happiness at last to arrive with the greatest part of the transports in Tybee River by the last of January, after a most harassing and tempestuous voyage. But many of the transports were still missing; and loss of an ordnance store-ship with the chief part of our heavy artillery and ammunition and [the loss] of most of the horses belonging to the cavalry and the Quartermaster and Commissary General's departments (which either died on the passage or perished with the vessels that carried them) were misfortunes not likely to be soon repaired. A vessel, too, with Hessian troops on board

1. In one of his loose notes Clinton explains that the flagship lost her backstay while the fleet was running along the coast, and that Arbuthnot at once bore away to refit and ordered the other ships to follow. "Who can say I am not liberal with the old Admiral, when 'tis known that owing to his obstinacy we got into the Gulf Stream, and our voyage was delayed, and we met with great losses?"

was obliged to bear away for England, and some small craft with cavalry appointments were captured by rebel privateers.

Notwithstanding these heavy disasters I was determined to do my utmost to accomplish the objects of the expedition we had engaged in. I therefore, without loss of time, wrote to St. Augustine, the West Indies, and the Bahamas for all the artillery and stores they could spare me. And, as soon as the several necessary matters could be adjusted for conveying the troops, we prepared to commit ourselves once more to the ocean. This was, however, a measure I wished much to avoid, as our late experience of the great uncertainty of movements on that element and the storms generally prevailing at that season of the year on the American coast excited in me no small dread of being again driven from the land.

But the opinions I gave for proceeding to South Carolina through the inland navigation in order to escape these ruinous hazards, and for not diminishing my force (already too small) by detachments, were both overruled in council. For, having every reason to suppose that my request for leave to resign the weighty commissions I held to Earl Cornwallis would not be refused, and that His Lordship would most probably have in consequence the finishing of what I had begun, I thought it right to consult him on all occasions and to submit every step I proposed taking in the present expedition to the decision of a council of war. In conformity, therefore, to His Lordship's sentiments and a majority of those of the officers called into council [it was decided] to detach all the cavalry and about 1400 infantry under Brigadier General Paterson to Augusta on the upper Savannah by way of making a diversion, while the remainder of our acting force, which did not much exceed 5000 men, proceeded round by sea to lay siege to Charleston.

The Admiral had at first proposed to land us for this purpose on John's Island by Stono Inlet. But he was luckily persuaded by Captain Elphinstone to prefer the Edisto entrance to that of Stono, which would have carried us some leagues farther to the northward and detained us longer at sea.[2] The transports, having got into North Edisto harbor without

2. Arbuthnot, apparently, was not so much persuaded as overruled. He resented the change of plan as a needless delay, and subsequently blamed it on Clinton rather than Elphinstone. Sir Henry insisted privately that he had not meddled in what had been a purely naval decision, and complained in turn that the Admiral's errors had seriously delayed operations. At the beginning of their first joint campaign, in other words, the two Commanders in Chief were already at odds. See Clinton's autograph journal of the siege of Charleston (fols. 3v–6v), in a slip case in the CP entitled "Notes." This volume is cited hereafter as "Journal of the Siege," to distinguish it from an alphabetized volume in another slip case that is also entitled "Notes."

accident the day after we left Tybee, very fortunately escaped a violent tempest that arose in the succeeding night, whereby the expedition might possibly have been defeated had we been again entangled with the Gulf Stream, which would have been certainly the case had the Admiral persisted in his first design. For this piece of good fortune we were indebted to Captain Elphinstone's zealous and animated exertions, as also to his perfect acquaintance with all the island navigation of the Carolina coast, which enabled him to run the ships boldly up that difficult channel, which a person of less knowledge and decision in those matters would probably not have hazarded.

A considerable part of the flank corps,[3] which Lord Cornwallis and I had accompanied, were put on shore that evening on Simmons [Seabrook] Island, and the rest of the army followed the next day. The want of wagon horses might have now rendered it difficult to get forward the necessary supplies for the troops, especially as the galleys which had been sent from Savannah through the inland navigation did not make that expedition in their progress we expected. But through Captain Elphinstone's unremitted attention and very judicious arrangements every impediment was soon surmounted.[4] And, some victualers, ordnance vessels, and gunboats being passed between the islands into Stono, possession was taken of John's Island and a proper force advanced over Stono Ferry to the main. The occupying Fort Johnson and the rest of James Island followed within a few days after; and, the banks of the Ashley being from thence attained by a bridge over the Wappoo Cut, the entrance of that river was secured by batteries of heavy guns. But more serious operation could not go on against the body of the place until our depots were formed and the Admiral could pass a naval force into the harbor to assist us with heavy artillery and ammunition for the operations of the siege, and seamen and boats for the transportation of the troops to Charleston Neck.

In the meantime, as I found the enemy were drawing all their force from the surrounding country to Charleston and seemed determined to rest the fate of both Carolinas on the defense of that capital, which

3. Flank corps, or companies, were composed of grenadiers and light infantry. They were assigned to operations, such as this landing, that required particular skill or courage. See Edward E. Curtis, *The Organization of the British Army in the American Revolution* (New Haven and London, 1926), p. 4. For modern accounts of the ensuing operations see Carrington, *Battles of the Revolution*, pp. 493–497; Fisher, *Struggle for Independence*, 2, 264–269; Fortescue, *British Army*, 3, 307–310.

4. Clinton expressed himself even more warmly about Elphinstone in a letter to Germain of Mar. 9. Sir Henry was particularly impressed by the Captain's ability to interpret the army's requirements, and for once was not shy of saying so. "You are so much of a soldier," he wrote him on the 22d, "that you know our wants and can best state them."

they strove to render as strong as a happy situation and the labor of a vast multitude of Negroes under skillful engineers could possibly make it, I took the opportunity by Major General Robertson (who had lately joined us from England and was going to New York in the *Russell*) of requesting General Knyphausen to send me some more troops. And, without referring to the opinion of a council as had been hitherto my custom in all matters relating to this expedition,[5] I called immediately to me the corps which had been left in Georgia under Brigadier General Paterson (as before mentioned, for the purpose of trying the temper of the back settlements and endeavoring to create a diversion in favor of the besieging army), as this small addition was now become absolutely requisite to enable me even to occupy the numerous posts that were necessary for preserving our communications.

Violent gales of wind had driven out to sea some transports that were bringing to us a battalion of the Seventy-first Regiment from Savannah. The *Defiance*, of sixty-four guns, belonging to Mr. Arbuthnot's squadron, was likewise lost at the entrance of Tybee harbor. And many other untoward circumstances, the effects of the present tempestuous season, considerably retarded the movements of the fleet and kept back the cooperation and assistance we anxiously expected from them. However, as soon as the remaining line-of-battle ships could be secured in Beaufort harbor, some heavy guns, ammunition, and seamen were forwarded from them, and the rest of the ships of war assembled off Stono. A battalion was immediately upon this sent to the Lighthouse Island and two twenty-four-pounders mounted in battery to cover the boats of the fleet while laying buoys on the passage over the bar.[6] It was, however, the 20th of March before we had the satisfaction to see the Admiral's flag flying on board the *Roebuck* in Five Fathom Hole.

All our missing transports were by this time arrived, and our preparations now got forward fast. As soon, therefore, as we were joined by

5. "I had not the same reason for doing so," Clinton explains in one of his loose notes. "I had received anwers to my requisitions to resign; the Minister informed me in most flattering terms that, though His Majesty had reason to be satisfied with Lord Cornwallis' abilities, he did not wish to see the command of his army in other hands than mine, concluding very civilly indeed." This letter of Nov. 4, 1779, reached Clinton on Mar. 19, 1780 (below, pp. 434–435), a few days before Cornwallis served formal notice that he did not wish to be consulted on plans. (Undated Clinton memorandum, filed at the end of May, 1780.) For a fuller discussion of this episode see below, pp. 183–184 and nn.

6. "We could not have done anything till the Admiral got over the bar; and I appeal to him whether he had any thoughts of doing it till he had assembled his fleet, and whether he could do it before I had sent two twenty-four-pounders and the Seventy-first to occupy Lighthouse Island." ("Journal of the Siege," fol. 5v.) Lighthouse Island, now Morris Island, was just to the east of Fort Johnson.

Clinton's attempts to borrow artillery and ammunition from the navy involved him in further wranglings with Arbuthnot; see below, pp. 438–439, 440.

Brigadier General Paterson's detachment from Georgia and seventy-five flatboats had come up from the fleet, I caused the elite of the army to advance to Drayton Hall (fifteen miles above Charleston), from whence they were passed over the Ashley the next morning without any attempt from the rebels to obstruct them. For the enemy—as they did not perceive the boats coming up, which passed their batteries in the night with muffled oars—expected the landing would have taken place five miles lower down, and had thrown up a treble breastwork across the causeway leading from the ferry to obstruct it.[7] And, this being now of course abandoned when they found we had effected a landing higher up, an uninterrupted, commodious passage was opened thereby for the transportation of the stores and remaining troops. The following day the army moved toward Charleston without any other resistance from the enemy than an ineffectual scattering fire on the head of the column.[8] And in the night of the 1st of April we broke ground within 800 yards of the rebel works.[9]

The fortifications of the place we had now sat down before were by no means contemptible, as may be perceived by the following sketch of them. The defenses on the land side of the town extended in a chain of redoubts, lines, and batteries from Ashley to Cooper Rivers, into which oozed two deep morasses that lay in front of each of the flanks and were joined to one another by a broad canal. Betwixt this latter and the works of the place were two rows of abatis, all the other various obstructions usual before fortified towns, and a double-picketed ditch. The center of the line, where the natural defenses seemed to be weakest, was strengthened by an enclosed hornwork of masonry, which was converted into a kind of citadel during the siege. And through the extent of these works were mounted eighty pieces of cannon and mortars of various calibers, from which a well served fire was unremittingly kept up. On the sea side a number of ships was sunk in the mouth of

7. The help rendered by the navy in this move momentarily thawed Clinton's chilliness toward Arbuthnot. "A million of thanks to you for your assistance in boats," he wrote the Admiral on the 28th; "it is most ample indeed."

8. *Clinton's note:* The Earl of Caithness, who attended Sir Henry Clinton on this move as a volunteer aide-de-camp, was very badly wounded in the body by this fire.

9. On the same day Clinton and Cornwallis discussed the matters described in the next chapter (pp. 184–186), and their relationship reached a new low. Cornwallis denied propagating the rumor of his chief's impending resignation, and insisted that he had come to America largely in the hope of reconciling him to retaining the command; but then he delicately accused him of ignoring a royal order about the provincial corps. Clinton was furious: the injustice of the charge showed the Earl's malicious nature; "I ought to have seen through him when he betrayed my private conversation with him to Sir William Howe in '76. All since is of a piece." "'Tis not time for altercation, but I can never be cordial with such a man." "Journal of the Siege," fols. 1v–2v, 6v–7v.

the Cooper; and the batteries which guarded the entrance of each river, and commanded the navigation up to the town, appeared to be equally formidably numerous with those to the land, and well furnished with heavy guns.

The Admiral with his squadron having passed Sullivan's Island on the 8th (fortunately without much injury to the King's ships, although they were for above an hour under a very heavy fire from Fort Moultrie or Sullivan at 600 yards' distance), and the first parallel being now completed and the guns mounted, we jointly summoned the place. But Mr. Lincoln, the rebel General, having thought proper to reject our proposals, the batteries were opened of course the next day, and ground was broke for a second parallel. The attack had been planned with so much judgment by the commanding engineer, Captain Moncrieff (who had already given the most honorable proofs of his skill in the late successful defense of Savannah), that I had not the smallest doubt of my becoming master of the town without much loss. This consideration alone would have been a sufficient incitement for me to prefer the mode of regular approaches to any other, less certain though more expeditious, which might have sacrificed a greater number of lives on both sides.[10] Other important motives also influenced me on this occasion, among which *to secure the capture of all the rebel corps in Charleston* had been from the first a very principal object with me, as I saw the reduction of the rest of the province in great measure depended upon it.

But to accomplish this the place must be completely invested, which was a service that would require considerably more men than I had with me. I had, therefore, called to me the Georgia detachment and an additional number of troops from New York; and Admiral Arbuthnot of his own free motion was so good to flatter me into a belief that he would very soon pass some frigates and armed vessels into Cooper River, to enable us most effectually to shut every door of escape. They were likewise wanted to cover the left of our lines, which was otherwise liable to be enfiladed by the galleys and armed vessels that might run up it [the Cooper] from the town.

I detached in the meantime 1400 men, under Lieutenant Colonel Webster of the Thirty-third Regiment, by Goose Creek and Strawberry Ferry over the forks of the Cooper, with instructions to place himself

10. Regular approaches were greatly handicapped at this time by the shortage of supplies, particularly of ammunition. The loss of the ordnance ship at the start of operations was still keenly felt; the replacements ordered from New York had not arrived. Arbuthnot offered powder but not shot. He had plenty of both, Clinton felt, and was holding back only in order to assert himself. "I must ever be on my guard with this man, who . . . will study to dog me." *Ibid.*, fols. 11v–12v.

on the enemy's communications from Charleston with the country on that side, while my different posts on the islands and the vigilance of the squadrons which lay under Fort Johnson precluded them entirely from those by the Ashley. The general tendency of this officer's move was to circumscribe the rebels in their more essential communications (and thereby narrow the channels of escape to the garrison), divest them of great collected supplies,[11] cut the courses through which more were to flow, defeat or disperse the sole corps they had remaining to awe the country, and ultimately to direct itself to those points which the Admiral might wish as a cover to the shipping he proposed sending into the Cooper and Wando. But this detachment was liable to be a good deal harassed by the above-mentioned corps, which consisting of three regiments of well appointed cavalry supported by a considerable body of militia, the inferiority of our light dragoons (both in number and quality of their horses) could not promise much success against it. However, its destruction was indispensable, as a passage over the river could not be effected before it was at least dispersed. I therefore recommended the attempt very strongly to Colonel Webster as one of the first objects of his attention.[12]

It has been already mentioned that the horses belonging to the Legion cavalry, and [to] the detachment from the Seventeenth Light Dragoons acting with them, were lost on the passage from New York. To procure others was one of our first cares after we arrived in Tybee; and Lieutenant Colonel Tarleton, who commanded the Legion, had removed at his own request with the dismounted troopers of both to Port Royal Island for that purpose. Here by great exertion and good luck he collected a number of horses (though very poor in quality), in time to join Brigadier General Paterson as he passed by that route in his march to the army before Charleston.

The reader will consequently be pleased to hear that with these weak, undersized, ill-appointed, and untrained horses that active and gallant young officer, with the assistance of Major Ferguson (who supported him with his Rangers), effectually depressed, at least for the present, this much vaunted flying corps, on which the rebels had

11. *Clinton's note:* The rebels' principal depot was at Cainhoy. They had also another at Monk's Corner. The communication between these and Charleston, and also with General Huger (who commanded the troops that covered them), they endeavored to preserve by securing the passes of the Cooper by works. They threw up another also at Lemprieres, with an intention of facilitating the escape of the garrison of Charleston should such a measure become necessary.

12. Sir Henry had little hope that Arbuthnot would move into the Cooper, and made the detachment as the only alternative method of cutting American communications. Webster's success, he was convinced, depended entirely on surprising the enemy force covering Biggin's Bridge. "Journal of the Siege," fol. 16.

rested all their hopes of forwarding supplies and succors to Charleston and keeping alive the spirit of rebellion in the upper country. For, Colonel Webster having sent forward the Legion and Ferguson's corps to cover his march, Lieutenant Colonel Tarleton—contriving to obtain accurate intelligence of the position General Huger had taken with it [the flying corps] near Biggin's Bridge on the forks of the Cooper —was fortunate enough to come upon the enemy by surprise; and, charging them suddenly with that vigor and promptitude which ever marked his character, he routed and dispersed the whole. Whereby he got possession of about four hundred dragoon horses with all their appointments, fifty wagons laden with arms, clothing, and ammunition, and one hundred prisoners, the precipitation with which the enemy had fled and the swampiness of the ground having prevented the slaughter which might else have probably ensued, and facilitated the escape of the rest.

By this very spirited and opportune stroke, which was achieved with the loss of only three men and five horses killed and wounded, Colonel Tarleton was enabled to mount his Legion much better than they were when they left New York, and a free unembarrassed pass over that branch of the Cooper was given to Colonel Webster in his rear, while general terror and dismay were spread through the disaffected in that part of the country. The passes over the other branches of that river being likewise seized immediately after, Colonel Webster lost no time in extending his arms into the district of St. Thomas across the forks of the Wando, by which he drew within his embrace most of the principal roads leading to Charleston. For, though he was certainly too weak to intercept every communication, he was equal to the keeping at bay any body of the enemy that might be in motion from thence or the northward until a sufficient reinforcement from the part of the army before the town (holding the string to a very large bow) could be sent to his support. The Admiral had also promised me to move a naval force into Sewee Bay and Spencer's Inlet to deter the enemy from attempting anything by the lower roads.

We had long expected to see some of the King's ships pass into the Cooper, agreeable to the Admiral's repeated assurances.[13] And the

13. On Apr. 20 Clinton sent the following oral message to Arbuthnot: "Passage of the Cooper was such an object that I thought no opportunity should be missed. But all I wanted was vessels sufficient to command the Cooper. . . . I did not want operation in the Cooper, I only wanted communication with a corps I had in St. Thomas." The Admiral's response was further evasion and indecision, and two days later Sir Henry despaired of real cooperation. "In appearance we were the best friends. But I am sure he is false as hell, and shall behave in consequence." *Ibid.*, fols. 22v–23, 25v–26.

batteries of the trenches were held in readiness at his request, from day to day, to throw their whole fire of shot and shells toward the wharves of the town on that side, in order to lessen the annoyance to the ships expected from thence. But, various impediments having been discovered by him which protracted that measure to the present hour, I was obliged to strengthen the corps under Colonel Webster as soon as the arrival of the reinforcement from New York [14] put it into my power to detach for that purpose. The command of the troops beyond the Cooper was consequently now given to Earl Cornwallis, and the positions His Lordship was requested to take with them soon deprived the garrison of Charleston of all hopes of succor from without and greatly lessened my apprehensions of its escape.[15]

But I was still very desirous of having an armed force in those waters, to remove every possibility of such an event and to facilitate the transportation of supplies to our troops in that quarter, which were liable to be constantly intercepted by the galleys and armed boats from the town. I therefore made use of every argument I could think of to impress the Admiral with conviction of its importance, but I could only obtain from him reiterated promises that he would very shortly comply with my desire—notwithstanding which I had the mortification to be disappointed, as no attempt was *ever* made by him to send ships into the Cooper to the end of the siege. I do not, however, mean to insinuate that Admiral Arbuthnot had not very sufficient reasons for declining it. I am ready to admit the possibility of its being so; and I have therefore thought it right to insert in the appendix all the necessary extracts from our correspondence on the subject, that the reader may be as capable of judging of them as I was.[16]

14. *Clinton's note:* Consisting of the Forty-second Regiment, Queen's Rangers, Prince of Wales' Volunteers, Volunteers of Ireland, and Hessian Regiment of Dittfurth, amounting to 2566 rank and file effectives, of which 1863 were fit for duty.

15. Personal considerations undoubtedly influenced Clinton in making this move. In a memorandum on Apr. 3 André had suggested that Cornwallis ought to be detached as soon as possible. On the 10th Sir Henry had felt impelled to tell Arbuthnot "the situation I was upon with Lord Cornwallis, and that I thought [it] hard, as Lord Cornwallis had withdrawn his advice totally from me, that any of my plans should be made known to him or he [be] privately consulted by others." By the 26th, three days after the Earl had left, Clinton was convinced that he was mismanaging the detachment. "I repent that I sent him. He will play me false, I fear; at least Ross will." "Journal of the Siege," fols. 13v, 28.) Capt. Ross, Cornwallis' aide-de-camp, later played an important part in the breach between the two Generals; see Willcox in *Am. Hist. Rev.*, 52, 9–10, and below, p. 339 n. 13.

16. Clinton did not provide this appendix. Extracts of the relevant correspondence, between Apr. 23 and May 4, are filed in the CP under the latter date. They contain little more, however, than what Sir Henry subsequently quotes in the text, p. 170.

But the number of men I was thereby reduced to the necessity of detaching from me, and the different posts I was obliged to occupy in the islands on my south flank (in order to shut every door of escape on that side, and preserve a ready communication with my magazines), had reduced the troops immediately before the place to such a handful that, notwithstanding the very liberal reinforcement sent me by General Knyphausen from the northward, we had scarcely a relief for the indispensable duties of the trenches. And the severity of duty occasioned thereby would consequently have given me much uneasiness, had not their unremitting zeal supported them with cheerfulness through a labor which they saw was unavoidable as long as the Cooper remained unoccupied by an armed naval force, and [had not] the rapid advances they made in their approaches flattered me with the prospect of a speedy and successful issue.

Mr. Lincoln had on the 21st proposed to me *to enter into the consideration of terms of capitulation.* His letter being addressed to me singly without noticing the Admiral, I pointed out to him the impropriety of the neglect, and desired that one of my aides-de-camp might be permitted to pass with a letter to the ships to request a conference with him.[17] The articles proposed by the rebel General were, however, so much beyond what we thought he had a right to expect that we immediately rejected them, and hostilities were renewed.

The enemy, having by this time remounted their cavalry, had begun to assemble again under the cover of some Continental infantry which had lately joined them from Virginia. But they kept in general to the northward of Santee River, and only made occasional irruptions into different parts of the country for the purposes of harassing the loyalists and encouraging their own friends. In one of these excursions a body of light dragoons, commanded by a Colonel White, had ventured to cross the river to our side and, having fallen in with a small party of our mounted light infantry, [had] carried them off and had returned to the banks of the Santee, where they waited for craft to recross it. It fortunately happened that Lord Cornwallis had that morning sent Lieutenant Colonel Tarleton with part of the Legion cavalry on a patrol to the northward, who, hearing of the capture of the light infantry and the enemy's intention to repass at Lanneau's Ferry, pressed

17. "Lincoln gave for reason," Sir Henry remarks in one of his loose notes, "that the Admiral was so far off he did not consider him as forming part of the siege." For Lincoln's proposals of Apr. 21, and the other transactions leading to the American surrender, see Anonymous, *Original Papers Relating to the Siege of Charleston, 1780, Mostly Selected from the Papers of General Benjamin Lincoln, in the Thomas Addis Emmet Collection, Lenox Library, New York, and Now First Published* (Charleston, 1898), pp. 41–55.

forward thither with the utmost celerity. And, finding them dismounted and crowded together close to the water side, being off their guard in consequence of their distance from Lord Cornwallis' posts, he attacked them with his usual spirit and success (just as a flatboat had put off with the prisoners) and soon routed the whole, putting to the sword between thirty and forty and bringing off seven officers and sixty dragoons. Colonels White, Washington, and Jameson, with some troopers, escaped by swimming the river; but most of the rest, it is supposed, were either drowned in the attempt or perished in Hell Hole Swamp, to which they had fled on the first of the charge. About 100 dragoon horses, with all their appointments, fell into Colonel Tarleton's hands on this occasion. And our men who had been taken prisoners (Mr. Lovet Ashe commanded them), seeing the Legion descending the hill to the attack, immediately threw the rebel guard out of the boat and, rowing back to the shore, rejoined their friends.

On the same day that this happened Captain Hudson of the navy, who had by the Admiral's order landed with 500 seamen and marines on the east end of Sullivan's Island to assist in an attack intended by the King's ships on Fort Moultrie, having luckily intercepted a small party of rebels which was sent from thence to observe his motions, was encouraged by the intelligence they gave him to summon the fort without waiting for the Admiral's cooperation. The rebel officer who commanded, not knowing his force and being alarmed by seeing another party take post on Mount Pleasant,[18] looked upon his escape as impossible, and, having only a few militia with him for the defense of the place) the Continentals being withdrawn to Charleston), thought it better to accept the honorable terms offered him than risk the consequence of an assault. He therefore immediately surrendered his garrison to Captain Hudson, and we had the pleasure of seeing the British flag flying in the fort the next morning.[19]

Judging that these two events, as they removed every hope of either escape or succor, might probably dispose the garrison of Charleston to surrender, and the guns being now mounted in the batteries of the third parallel near the edge of the canal (which was drained almost dry), I sent an aide-de-camp to General Lincoln with a renewal of the offers we had made him on the 21st of April. The enemy was, however, not yet sufficiently humbled to accept them; and, as we were equally

18. *Clinton's note:* This was a detachment sent thither by Lord Cornwallis, under the command of Major Ferguson.
19. Arbuthnot was particularly pleased at the surrender, because he believed that it ended all possibility of a French attempt to relieve Charleston by sea. Clinton pointed out in reply that, if there had been any such possibility, the Americans would never have unguarded the fort. "Journal of the Siege," fol. 36v.

averse from agreeing to those he proposed, I ordered the batteries to open. We were now so very near that their effect soon reduced the besieged to the necessity of closing their embrasures. And under cover of the fire from our Jägers, light infantry, and grenadiers (who shot down every head the instant any appeared above the works) our troops gained the counterscarp of the outwork that flanked the canal, then passed the canal itself, and carried a sap close to the very ditch of the place.

Matters were now arrived at that extremity that the assault was prepared for.[20] And I hope I shall be pardoned for noticing a very singular discovery it gave rise to. Admiral Arbuthnot had on the 23d of April told me that *"whenever I should think it necessary to make a general assault against the enemy's works, he was willing to draw up every ship he had against them, and under cover of the fire endeavor to cut through the boom across the main channel and pass a sufficient force into the Cooper."* And in a subsequent letter he pressed me to let him know *"in what manner I thought the ships of war could most effectually cooperate with me on that important occasion."* I had, in consequence, taken the liberty of suggesting to the Admiral that, "should the enemy wait the assault, *the manner in which His Excellency could best cooperate with us would be, as he proposed himself, by laying ships against the town either in Cooper or Ashley River, as the impression of their fire and their preventing succors coming from the lower parts of the town to the lines would favor our attack very much —signals being concerted to desist at a proper moment, that no annoyance might be given to the King's troops."*

The reader, therefore, will of course be as much surprised as I was at reading the following answer from him: *"Unless it is intended to land a body of troops under the fire of the ships' guns, I confess it would be against my judgment to place the ships against the enemy's batteries, circumstanced as they are, merely for a diversion. However, when the moment arrives, the ships will at least by their movements indicate such a design to the enemy, which will answer the purpose you propose, that of keeping the men at the batteries on this side from opposing you."* [21] Fortunately, however, we had no occasion to put the ef-

---

20. "I begin to think," Clinton wrote to Cornwallis on May 6, "these people will be blockheads enough to wait the assault. *Je m'en lave les mains."* Cornwallis answered the next day that, if the city were stormed, he hoped to be allowed to take part. "Perhaps you may think that on an occasion of that sort you cannot have too many officers."

21. The extracts, in the order in which they appear, are either quotations from or paraphrases of the following: Arbuthnot to Clinton, No. 1 of Apr. 23, May 2; Clinton to Arbuthnot, [May 1]; Arbuthnot to Clinton, May 4.

ficacy of the Admiral's *indicatory* movements to the proof, as General Lincoln judged it most prudent not to abide the assault and now acquiesced in the terms he had two days before rejected—and which many important considerations at the present moment rendered it advisable for us still to grant.[22]

By this very important acquisition there fell into our hands seven generals and a multitude of other officers, belonging to ten Continental regiments and three battlions of artillery, which, with the militia and sailors doing duty in the siege, amounted to about six thousand men in arms. The rebel Lieutenant Governor, the council, and other civil officers became also our prisoners; and four frigates, several armed vessels, and a great number of boats, with four hundred pieces of ordnance, five thousand stand of small arms, and a vast quantity of gunpowder with other naval, artillery, and military stores were delivered up with the town to His Majesty's arms. We had, moreover, the great additional satisfaction to find that this very complete success had occasioned the shedding of much less blood than could well have been expected from so long and obstinate a resistance, the loss sustained by the King's troops in killed and wounded amounting to only 268, and that of the enemy not much exceeding 300.

The articles of capitulation, too, were framed in the mildest spirit of moderation throughout, with a view of convincing those misguided people that Great Britain was more inclined to reconciliation than to punishment, as by it [the capitulation] the Continental troops and sailors alone were required to remain prisoners of war until exchanged, the militia being permitted to return to their respective homes as prisoners on parole. The like terms were also granted to the civil officers and other citizens of every denomination, whether they bore arms or not, whereby the persons and property of all who surrendered were alike secured from molestation as long as they continued peaceable and observed the paroles they had given.

Was I fully to indulge the very high sense I entertain of the merits of the general officers and staff and, indeed, of all the officers and privates of the different corps—foreign, British, and provincial—which composed the army at this siege, I should scarcely know where to stop, and might be led on to attempt naming almost every officer on

---

By this time—more than a year before the Admiral surrendered his command—Sir Henry had already "determined never to serve with such an old woman." "Journal of the Siege," fol. 42v.

22. *Clinton's note:* Brigadier General Dalrymple had arrived on the 10th of May with letters from Lord George Germain, cautioning Sir Henry Clinton and the Admiral against a considerable French armament which might be daily expected on some part of the North American coast. [See below, p. 177.]

the expedition. Lest, therefore, I should happen unintentionally to omit any whose services may claim more particular notice, I shall beg leave to offer them collectively that praise which the closest attention to military discipline, a patient sufferance of extraordinary duty and labor, and a distinguished knowledge of their profession most justly deserve. Nor must I neglect in this place to gratefully acknowledge my obligations to the officers and crews of the King's ships for the very great assistance I received from them, particularly to Captain Elphinstone and the officers and seamen acting under him on shore, whose professional abilities and indefatigable activity and zeal greatly facilitated the approaches of the troops to the object of our attack, and who also contributed their aid to the reduction of the place by a spirited and judicious management of the works they had the charge of.

I think it, moreover, my duty to declare that, had it not been for the few heavy guns and ammunition lent me by Admiral Arbuthnot (though dealt out with a sparing and sometimes a seemingly reluctant hand), my advances must have been greatly retarded and my success rendered perhaps doubtful. For much time must undoubtedly have elapsed before the artillery and stores which were lost in the ordnance ship that foundered on the passage could have been replaced from the different garrisons I sent to for a fresh supply. And the enemy might have so improved the opportunity as ultimately to have defeated every purpose of the campaign. And, indeed, it must be confessed those resources were at best but precarious. For, though too much praise cannot be given to the Governors of East Florida and the Bahamas, as well as to Sir George Rodney and Major General Vaughan, for the readiness with which they had the goodness to comply with my requests, yet many unforeseen or unavoidable circumstances might have intercepted their good intentions (as actually did happen to those of the latter), whereby the operations against Charleston might have been greatly impeded, had I not been more fortunate in the receipt of the supplies I had solicited from other places.

CHAPTER 12

The Establishment of Cornwallis' Command in South Carolina, May to June, 1780

The immediate favorable consequences of the taking of Charleston and the effect of Sir Henry Clinton's subsequent proclamation. Three important moves directly made into the back country to take advantage of this disposition of the people, and Major Ferguson appointed inspector of militia. His instructions. Sir Henry Clinton offers to Lord Cornwallis every additional force he can wish; His Lordship is perfectly satisfied with what he has and declines any more. Sir Henry Clinton recommends that Lord Cornwallis may be appointed joint and separate commissioner. The greatest part of South Carolina submits before Sir Henry Clinton embarks for New York, and Lord Cornwallis soon after tells him that General Williamson's submission has put an end to all further resistance. Admiral Arbuthnot anxious to get to the northward; proposed expeditions to the Chesapeake and Cape Fear suspended in consequence.

The appointment of Commissary of Captures proved to have originated with Sir Henry Clinton and not with Lord Cornwallis, as claimed by His Lordship and asserted by Commissioners of Public Accounts, His Lordship having only obeyed Sir Henry Clinton's orders by reviving the appointment in December after neglecting to do so for four months. Great advantages resulting to the public from that establishment. Singular conduct of the Admiral with respect to the division of prizes taken at Charleston, of which the army has never yet received any share. Sir Henry Clinton's reasons for issuing his proclamation of the 3d of June. Directs a board of police to be formed in Charleston for the administration of justice until civil government can be revived.

Lord Cornwallis' very singular conduct toward Sir Henry Clinton both before and after the arrival of His Majesty's refusal of his request to resign the chief command to His Lordship. Sir Henry Clinton, notwithstanding, leaves His Lordship in the command of the southern district with every power, civil and military, that he can give him. Recommends him to the Minister to be joined in the commission for restoring peace, that no time might be lost in the revival of civil government, and fetters His Lordship with no other instructions than to hold the safety of Charleston and the tranquillity of South Carolina as the principal objects of his attention, after the securing of which he is left at liberty to attempt the recovery of North Carolina. And, to prepare for it, it is recommended to His Lordship to lose no time in establishing a small post on Cape Fear River, to encourage and relieve our friends in the district of Cooper Creek.

WHEN THE royal army first entered the Province of South Carolina, the smallness of its force and the vast preparations I saw the enemy was making for the defense of Charleston dissuaded me very strongly from engaging in any detached operations that might lessen the numbers I had drawn together for besieging that capital. I also judged it to be imprudent, for many obvious reasons, to encourage the friends of government to take any steps which might expose them to the malevolence of their enemies before I was fully certain of success, or a stroke of consequence had already taken place against the town whereby a permanent establishment might be attained to enable me to afford them proper protection. Therefore, before that was actually our situation, it appeared unnecessary to say more to the inhabitants of the province by way of proclamation than to announce the benevolent import of the commission with which the King had vested me, and to desire them to remain quietly at their plantations. With a view also of securing the neutrality of the disaffected, numbers who had been taken prisoners (and several who had voluntarily surrendered themselves as such before the capitulation) were dismissed to their respective homes upon their paroles.

But, as soon as Charleston was possessed by the King's troops and Lord Cornwallis had informed me Williamson's surrender had put an end to all opposition,[1] these motives for caution no longer subsisted. For I had not only procured a very defensible fortress as an asylum for the friends of government to resort to and where they were sure of finding most perfect security, but I had by that event disarmed most of the rebel militia and imprisoned almost the whole of the state and Continental troops in the province, whereby the further operation of the royal forces was much facilitated and a prospect opened of restoring tranquillity and order to the country. Accordingly, I did not now hesitate to call upon all His Majesty's loyal subjects to join the King's standard and assist his troops in re-establishing peace and good government.[2]

Besides the handbills distributed on this occasion I issued also a

1. During the siege of Charleston Gen. Williamson, with a force of some 300 men, had remained idle in the western part of the state; soon after Lincoln's capitulation he also surrendered. His inactivity and supineness gave rise to suspicions of treason.

2. See the extract from Clinton's handbill, May, 1780, below, pp. 440–441.

proclamation, denouncing the severest punishments against those who should still persist in their treasonable practices and promising the most effectual countenance, protection, and support to the King's faithful and peaceable subjects, together with a restoration of their former civil government whenever the situation of the country would permit it. The purport of these handbills and proclamation, together with the news they conveyed, had soon the most happy effects, as numbers with their arms came in every day to headquarters from the remotest parts of the province, many of them bringing in their former oppressors.[3]

And in a very little time nothing appeared to be wanting toward the entire suppression of rebellion but the occupying a few strong posts in the upper country, and the putting arms into the hands of the King's friends for their defense against the straggling parties of rebels who might be still lurking amongst them. To accomplish this end I requested Lord Cornwallis to march up the north side of Santee River to Camden, where I understood a body of rebel troops were collecting with an intention of making a stand there; and I directed Lieutenant Colonel Balfour to move with another corps up its southern shore toward the district of Ninety-six, while a third was put in motion on the Savannah River in Georgia. I had it also in prospect, by Lord Cornwallis' march across the Santee, to cut off the retreat of some rebel troops who, I heard, were advancing to Georgetown, and [I] had applied to the Admiral to pass his galleys into the Pedee with the Legion, to threaten a landing in that quarter. But, as it was judged inexpedient to do so, I gave up that hope and could only expect from it their dispersion and the submission of the town.[4] I likewise appointed Major Ferguson of the Seventy-first Regiment, a very zealous, active, intelli-

3. "Their hearts, poor fellows, are British, though their language is not the most correct. . . . All the rebel grandees are [also] come in. They put on a good face. They own honestly they have been always in arms against us. They confess their dread of the back-country people, who, they say, are all up to join us, as well in North Carolina as South. Their jealousy[?] of their late government, their hopes of a better under us, and [their] conviction that the rebels can never recover this country have induced them to surrender themselves. They seemed at first to boggle at the idea of arming against the Congress, but with respect to the French and Spaniards they seem to say they are willing to join most heartily against them. In the northern provinces this is all I would ask; but we seem so totally masters here that I insisted on their being ready on the first call. The[y] found argument themselves to reconcile their disaffection (as they call it) to Congress, by saying it could no longer protect them. As I had nothing material to lay to their charge but *rebellion at large*, I have received them and embodied them—under loyal officers, however. The citizens of Charleston have some time since shown the same disposition, and the Admiral and I shall probably admit them." [Clinton to Eden,] May 30.

4. Clinton evidently means that the move, if made without naval cooperation, would have resulted only in the capture of Georgetown, not of the American troops, and was therefore not worth making.

gent officer, to be inspector of all militia troops in the southern district, with instructions and authority under Earl Cornwallis to embody and discipline them.[5]

These several movements were intended to awe the disaffected and receive their submissions, give spirits to the King's friends, and promote the arming of a trusty militia for the internal defense of the province. And, to give them the fullest effect, the Forty-second Regiment and the light infantry were advanced to Monk's Corner to be at hand to act as circumstances should require, or even to join Lord Cornwallis, should there be any truth in the reports then circulating of a considerable force approaching South Carolina from the northward. In short, I offered to His Lordship all he wished of every sort, as I had the greatest expectations from these detachments, and was determined they should not be stinted.

I had soon, however, the satisfaction to be informed by him that he had troops sufficient and that the latter were unnecessary,[6] and to see all my measures throughout the course of this expedition crowned with the most flattering success. For, before I took my departure for New York, Georgetown and almost the whole country between the Pedee and Savannah had submitted without opposition. The remaining rebel southern force, under a Colonel Buford, had been overtaken by the cavalry and mounted infantry of the Legion, under Lieutenant Colonel Tarleton, at Waxhaws (in their retreat from Camden) after a rapid march of one hundred and five miles in fifty-four hours, and the greatest part of it annihilated and their whole artillery taken. And Lord Cornwallis soon after assured me that the submission of General Williamson at Ninety-six had put an end to all resistance in every district of South Carolina.

The accounts which were daily brought in to Lord Cornwallis as well as myself from North Carolina were likewise very encouraging. And I very much wished, in consequence, to have sent a small force into Cape Fear River to establish a tenable post there for the en-

5. See Clinton's instructions to Ferguson, May 22, below, p. 441.
6. Clinton's meaning is merely that he offered to have the force at Monk's Corner join Cornwallis, but that the Earl declined the offer. The troops rejoined Clinton and sailed for New York. See Banastre Tarleton, *A History of the Campaigns of 1780 and 1781, in the Southern Provinces of North America* (London, 1787), pp. 76–77; Benjamin F. Stevens, ed., *The Campaign in Virginia, 1781. An Exact Reprint of Six Rare Pamphlets on the Clinton-Cornwallis Controversy* (2 vols., London, 1888), *1*, 211–212; Bernhard A. Uhlendorf, ed., *The Siege of Charleston with an Account of the Province of South Carolina, Diaries and Letters of Hessian Officers from the Von Jungkenn Papers in the William L. Clements Library*, University of Michigan Publications, History and Political Science, *12* (Ann Arbor, 1938), 101.

couragement and supply of the King's friends inhabiting the Highland settlement about Cross Creek [Fayetteville], and to have also occupied two others between Albemarle Sound and the waters of Virginia, agreeable to my plan of '76 explained in a former chapter.[7] But the Admiral['s] determining not to delay collecting his fleet at New York, in consequence of the intelligence we had lately received from administration, obliged me not only to suspend those intentions but even to lay aside for the present a very important move into Chesapeake Bay,[8] which I had intended should have immediately succeeded the reduction of Charleston.

Indeed, the intelligence was of so serious a nature (no less than the sailing of a very considerable armament from Brest for North America) that we thought it right to hasten the conclusion of the siege with as much expedition as possible, lest its premature arrival might not only overset all we had done to the southward, but even endanger every post in possession of the King's troops to the northward.[9] And, as the season of the year would in a short time put a stop to offensive operations in the Carolinas and my presence might be wanted at New York, I prepared with all diligence to finish the arrangements I had proposed for the security and good government of the province we had reclaimed, that I might be able to accompany the Admiral thither with such troops as Lord Cornwallis and I had agreed might be safely and commodiously spared from its defense in the present emergency.[10]

The abundance of cattle and rice which the army found in deserted plantations in the course of its progress through South Carolina afforded me an opportunity (which I must beg leave to say I never neglected during the course of my command) of easing very consider-

7. See above, pp. 27–28.

8. *Clinton's note:* This plan had been some time formed, with a view of laying hold of the neck of land between the Chesapeake and the Delaware, to which Sir Henry Clinton was strongly invited by the great number of friends the King had in that district who offered to take up arms in support of government, and the facility with which that fertile tract of country might have been held, in defiance of the whole strength of the continent and even of a temporary naval superiority on the side of France.

9. The intelligence from London was a letter from Germain to the Lords of the Admiralty, Mar. 15, forwarded by them (below, pp. 439–440). Germain said nothing on the crucial point of the enemy's destination, which Clinton did not know until after he had returned to New York (below, p. 195); the dispatch also gave the French twelve sail of the line, whereas they actually had seven. This exaggeration made Clinton and Arbuthnot understandably anxious about their voyage to New York. Sir Henry proposed sailing in two convoys at different times, to minimize the disaster that would result from meeting the enemy at sea. Clinton [to Arbuthnot], May 28.

10. *Clinton's note:* The British grenadiers and light infantry, the Forty-second Regiment, Hessian Grenadiers and Jägers, and provincial regiment of Queen's Rangers.

ably the burdens of the public by the great saving made thereby in crown rations,[11] and of benefiting the soldier by directing the usual stoppages from his pay for provisions to be appropriated to his use at the end of the campaign. For this purpose *I* constituted *Commissaries of Captures* to take charge of and issue to the troops all fresh provisions that should be taken from the enemy, whereby every possibility of abuse in the Commissary General's department was guarded against, and full credit for the expenditure of captured provisions secured to government. This was only reviving what I had been in the habit of practicing in '76 and '77 whenever I acted on detached commands and took the field, being then a subordinate officer, and what I had again established by general orders as commander in chief in the campaign of '79. And I was so sensible of the benefits accruing from this arrangement *that I left my orders with Lord Cornwallis* to renew the establishment whenever he took the field.

The reader will consequently admit that I had great reason to be astonished when I found on my return to England in 1782 that, whatever little merit there may have been in this measure, the whole of it was claimed by Lord Cornwallis [and] ascribed to Earl Cornwallis by the Commissioners of Public Accounts in their seventh report, after an examination of His Lordship upon oath; [12] and that even an implied censure was passed by those gentlemen on myself for neglecting to apply remedies to abuses asserted to be then existing in the Commissary General's department, while His Lordship is loaded with praises for issuing an order to prevent them.[13] Now, had these abuses really existed in the southern army as the Commissioners of Accounts

11. *Clinton's note:* It appears by the report of a board of field officers who met at Charleston in July, 1782, to inspect the Commissaries of Captures' accounts, that 1,000,000 of rations of fresh provisions had been issued by them to the army, navy, and hospitals. It may be consequently inferred that a saving accrued from thence to the nation of at least £125,000.

12. *Clinton's note:* Extract from the Commissioners' seventh report: "To prevent provisions taken from the country, and either not paid for or paid for at a ceratin price, from being charged to the account of the public, either at all or at a greater price than they were purchased at, he (*Lord Cornwallis*) *appointed Commissaries of Captures,* who collected provisions from the country and gave receipts for them to those persons only who were friends, and delivered out those provisions to the troops without taking receipts for them, by which means those receipts only given to the proprietors of the provisions could be brought in charge against the public."

13. *Clinton's note:* Another extract from the same report: "But we found *at one period only* orders relative to the point immediately under our consideration. *These orders were issued by Lord Cornwallis,* are dated the 23d December, 1780, and contain matter very important to the subject before us. These orders are leveled at abuses *at that time existing,* and these abuses all tend to the defrauding of the public for private emolument. We are, therefore, of opinion *that the orders of the 23d December, 1780, should be put in force forthwith throughout the whole army.*" [For Cornwallis' order see below, p. 483.]

were pleased to assert, I must in justice to myself insist that their existence could arise only from Lord Cornwallis' neglecting to enforce the standing orders I had left with him, the perusal of which will, I humbly presume, evince that any new order on the subject was at least superfluous.[14]

I could not, consequently, but be much hurt when I read that part of the report which relates to this subject because, their reports having been very well received by the public, any censure they imply must make impressions difficult to be erased. I therefore lost no time in offering myself to those gentlemen for examination. And, when I failed in my endeavors to induce them to do me justice, I took the liberty of soliciting the Minister's (Mr. Pitt['s]) support to a motion which I prevailed upon a friend to make in Parliament for authorizing them to revise their seventh report, that my attention to the expenditure of the public money during my having the chief command in North America might undergo a full and candid examination, and [that] the public, whose steward I ever considered myself to be while I held that station, [might] be undeceived in the opinions they must have naturally formed respecting my economy from the partial and unjust representation given of it by the Commissioners—clearly on *ex parte* evidence, although the fullest and most authentic information was within their reach and had, indeed, been offered to them by the highest authority. I am sorry, however, for the sake of justice to add that the motion had not, contrary to my expectations, the *Minister's support,* and was of course overruled, under idea that it would be giving them too much power. But surely, as they had censured upon partial information, they should have been allowed to acquit or rather commend on general information.[15]

I had it, moreover, in my wish, and was not without hopes I should

---

14. Sir Henry here refers in a note to a nonexistent appendix, in which he intended to give his order of Feb., 1780, for establishing the system, a letter from the Treasury thanking him for doing so, and a letter of protest from him to the Commissioners of Public Accounts. His order does not seem to be extant. The Treasury letter, however, proves his point, because it is dated before the order from Cornwallis that purportedly established the system; Clinton published this letter in his *Observations on Mr. Stedman's History of the American War* ([London, 1794], pp. 11–12) and his protest to the Commissioners as *A Letter from Lieut. Gen. Sir Henry Clinton, K.B., to the Commissioners of Public Accounts, Relative to Some Observations in Their Seventh Report, Which May Be Judged to Imply Censure on the Late Commander in Chief of His Majesty's Army in North America* (London, 1784). For Sir Henry's further attempts to vindicate himself from this censure see below, pp. 242–243, 363–367; Stevens, *Clinton-Cornwallis Controversy, 1*, 48–55.

15. The last two words of this sentence are part of an addition in Clinton's hand, and are so abbreviated that they cannot be deciphered with any certainty.

have it in my power, to obtain for the officers and soldiers under my command some small douceur out of the large quantity of public stores and other valuable commodities obtained from the enemy by the capitulation of Charleston and during the siege, to remunerate them in some sort for the severity of the service which they had so cheerfully and honorably gone through, and to repay the extraordinary expenses they had sustained from the excessive dearness of every necessary and comfort of life. For, although I had from the first moment of my engaging in this contest refused—and was determined never —to draw to myself the smallest advantage from prizes taken in so unnatural a war, yet I was ever of opinion that the troops had a very fair claim to them.

But, when upon Charleston surrendering an equitable division of those [prizes] now taken was proposed to the navy (who alone, *it seems, are authorized by law to share prize money*), the Admiral was not inclined to admit the army to any proportionate share; and the captains of the King's ships thought the navy had a right to at least half, although their proportion in numbers did not amount to a third. The matter was therefore referred, with consent of the gentlemen deputed by the captains of the King's ships, to the decision of the King in council. But in the meantime, to our very great astonishment, the navy (who were not a third in number), claiming half, divided among themselves three-fourths—while the poor soldier, who from the nature of services at a siege bore, it is presumable, the principal burden of fatigue and danger, got nothing. For the insignificant remaining fourth (£10,000), which the troops had themselves taken and lodged with their agents until His Majesty's pleasure should be known, continues to this hour in the agents' hands, as they have refused to part with the money and the troops have, unfortunately, no legal power to compel them. So that, notwithstanding the confident assertion of a noted American writer that a *major general's share of prize money obtained in this expedition amounted to upward of 4000 guineas*,[16] I can venture to declare that not an individual in the army that I know of has acquired by it as yet anything but honor. Nor have I the least expectation they ever will, notwithstanding my utmost efforts were not wanting to procure them justice—as the Lords of His

16. *Clinton's note:* "The British on this occasion plundered by system, formed a general stock, and appointed Commissaries of Captures. Spoil collected this way was disposed of for the benefit of the royal army. The quantity brought to market was so great that, though it sold uncommonly low, yet the dividend of a major general was upward of 4000 British guineas." Extract from [David] Ramsay, [*The History of*] *the Revolution of South Carolina,* [*from a British Province to an Independent State* (2 vols., Trenton, 1785), 2, 66–67].

Majesty's Treasury, who alone have the power of enforcing payment, have neglected it, notwithstanding the agents, after using every evasion, have been by law condemned to pay it.[17]

The spirit of rebellion in South Carolina being now very nearly subdued, and numbers of the inhabitants of both town and country daily offering their services and soliciting to be admitted to the condition of British subjects, I judged it proper to release from their paroles all the persons who had surrendered or were taken prisoners before the capitulation of Charleston (excepting such as had served in the military line or were actually in confinement at the taking of that town and Fort Moultrie) and to call upon all the inhabitants of the province indiscriminately to take an active part in settling and securing His Majesty's government. I therefore issued a proclamation on the 3d of June to that purpose, and threatened in it to treat as rebels and enemies to their country all those under the above description who should afterward neglect to return to their allegiance.

This I looked upon as a most prudent measure, because under the sanction of those paroles a great number of inveterate rebels might remain in the country, and by their underhand and secret counsel and other machinations prevent the return of many well disposed persons to their allegiance, or [in] other ways retard the restoration of tranquillity and order. But by thus obliging every man to declare and evince his principles I gave the loyalists an opportunity of detecting and chasing from among them such dangerous neighbors, which they could not with any propriety have attempted as long as those paroles continued in force and the persons sanctioned by them were not guilty of an open breach of their promise. In short, such were the motives by which I was influenced when I formed the resolution of calling in those paroles; and I must say I had every reason to believe, from the state of the province at that period, that the measure would be attended with the happiest effects. But, as I did not remain there myself to watch its progress and assist its operation, I shall not take upon me to disprove the evil consequences ascribed to it since, as from the powers I gave Lord Cornwallis I cannot think myself responsible for them.[18] I may, however, venture to avow the goodness of my in-

17. This issue, like his grievance against the Commissioners of Public Accounts, involved Clinton after his return to England in a long, acrimonious, and unsuccessful wrangle. See his pamphlet, *Memorandums, &c. &c. Respecting the Unprecedented Treatment Which the Army Have Met with Respecting Plunder Taken after a Siege, and of Which Plunder the Navy Serving with the Army Divided Their More than Ample Share, Now Fourteen Years Since* (London, 1794).

18. Stedman, to whom Clinton is presumably referring, argues that those on parole had been in a state of neutrality until the proclamation forced them to

tention and the strong probability there was at the time of its success.

This proclamation was preceded by one also from the commissioners,[19] in which we offered to receive with mercy and forgiveness whoever should immediately return to their allegiance, and upon due experience of their sincerity to grant a full and free pardon for their past treasonable offenses to all who submitted, excepting those who had been polluted by the blood of their fellow citizens. And we again assured His Majesty's faithful and well affected subjects that, as soon as the situation of the province would admit, its inhabitants should be reinstated in the enjoyment of all those rights and immunities which they had heretofore possessed, exempt from all taxation except what their own legislature might find it requisite to impose.

And, as it was universally agreed that no good could possibly be expected (but, on the contrary, much inconvenience and obstruction might arise to the King's service) from the revival of civil government in South Carolina in its present state, I left directions with Lord Cornwallis for the establishing a board of police at Charleston on much the same footing with that at New York, the extent of whose powers I knew, and which had now stood the test of some years. This simple and approved mode of administering justice was, however, soon after entirely changed and another adopted by Lord Cornwallis—which, being a sort of mixed jurisdiction (built partly on the system I recommended and partly on the laws and practices of the civil courts under the old government, many of whose former officers were taken into the administration), His Lordship perhaps thought might give more satisfaction to the people, as more nearly resembling what they had been before accustomed to.

But whether His Lordship was right or not I do not presume to de-

---

choose between nominal loyalty and open rebellion. They complained that their status had been altered without their consent, and the loyalists complained that notorious rebels who took the oath of allegiance were thereby admitted to all the privileges of British subjects. C[harles] Stedman, *The History of the Origin, Progress, and Termination of the American War* (2 vols., London, 1794), 2, 198–199. For further light on the enforcement of Sir Henry's proclamation see Henry Lee, *Memoirs of the War in the Southern Department of the United States* (new ed., revised, London, 1869), pp. 193–194.

19. A commission for restoring peace, similar to that of the Carlisle Commission in 1778, had been issued first to Clinton alone, then to him and Arbuthnot (above, p. 155; Germain to Clinton, Feb. 15). Sir Henry was intensely annoyed to be linked with the Admiral, who was set upon re-establishing civil government in South Carolina as quickly as possible. "In this province it must happen, but I hope gradually. 'Tis too great a blessing to bestow upon them at once; it will intoxicate, as it has done in Georgia." In the next breath Sir Henry threatened to resign unless again made sole commissioner. [Clinton to Eden, May 30.]

termine. And, I confess, I did not signify my disapprobation of the change when it came to my knowledge, as much business had been already done under it, and I did not feel myself altogether competent to judge of its merits. Yet, as its decisions on cases of private property were rather more unlimited than I would willingly have given my sanction to, I must beg leave to rest the responsibility with Lord Cornwallis, though I am free to declare at the same time that I firmly believe both His Lordship and the persons he advised with were actuated in this matter by the very best intentions.

It was mentioned in the preceeding chapter that, as in consequence of my having so strongly solicited the King's permission to return to England it was probable the command of the army would devolve on Lord Cornwallis before the termination of the present expedition, I had constantly consulted His Lordship upon every measure relative to it, and had even yielded to his opinions in many instances from whence no material injury was to be apprehended, though they [his opinions] did not altogether square with my own. This I certainly judged to be a necessary act of prudence under the circumstances I was then placed [in], lest any miscarriage which might possibly happen after my departure should be imputed to some error of mine in the general arrangements of the plan, or to His Lordship's ignorance of the principles on which it was formed. But, I own, I did not at the time foresee all the consequences this step might lead to—though I was prepared to find, as the natural result of my declining power, that, the moment the army should receive a hint of Lord Cornwallis being likely to be their chief, headquarters would be in some degree deserted, and most probably the crowds who usually followed my steps would soon change the object of their homage and swell His Lordship's train. All this happened, of course, as might be expected.

Reports had by some means gone forth that I was to retire, and I believe it was even hinted that I was to be superseded. Lord Cornwallis was consequently, soon after, regarded by a majority of the officers as actually possessed of the command; and even so certain did His Lordship himself seem to be of it that he made no scruple to declare he would assume it as soon as my leave should arrive, let the siege of Charleston be ever so far advanced at the time.[20] This, I must con-

20. At this time each General was in a difficult position. Cornwallis, assuming that the command would soon devolve upon him, advised about a campaign for which he expected to have final responsibility, and of which he was understandably anxious to take charge at the earliest possible moment. Clinton suspected that the Earl's confidence of succeeding him was based on private hints from England. If they were well founded, as André subsequently pointed out, the obvious course was "to make every preparatory operation His Lordship's, lest you might be afterward

fess, hurt me, and was proceeding further than I could have the smallest suspicion of. However, as the promoting His Majesty's service to the utmost of my power was the only object I ever had in view, I was determined to attend to nothing else while I remained in the command. And, though for this reason I probably should not have resigned it into Lord Cornwallis' hands so very suddenly, had my leave reached me at a critical period of the siege, my hope of being indulged in my request to resign the command continued still to be as strong as ever.

The reader may consequently believe me when I assure him that His Lordship's disappointment that my recommendation of him to succeed to me had failed could not be greater than mine, when the American Minister's answer to my application informed me that the King did not wish to see the command of his forces in any other hands. This gracious manner in which His Majesty was pleased to intimate his refusal was certainly exceedingly flattering to me, and perhaps not a little mortifying to the noble Earl whom I had taken the liberty of recommending to succeed me. But whether this or my deviating in one instance from my usual practice of consulting His Lordship (by altering Brigadier General Paterson's destination) had given Lord Cornwallis offense I cannot say; I only know His Lordship's carriage toward me immediately changed. And from this period he was pleased to withdraw his counsels and to confine himself to his routine of duty in the line, without honoring headquarters with his presence oftener than that required.[21]

Symptoms of discontent began also, in a little time after, to appear among the field officers of the British line, which I could not by any

---

criminated for his ill success"; if, on the other hand, the hints were unfounded, "it was essential that yourself should be sole judge of every preparatory operation, as yourself were to be responsible for the consequence." [John André to Clinton, Apr. 3.] André was referring to the situation before Mar. 19, when Clinton had received instructions to retain the command; see Germain to Clinton, Nov. 4, 1779, below, pp. 434–435.

21. The Earl was not acting merely from pique. When he asked in late March not to be consulted on plans, the reason he gave was that he was afraid of responsibility. "Why did he not do this at the first," Clinton wondered, "and not after I had consulted so unreservedly with him?" (Undated Clinton memorandum, filed at the end of May.) The answer that André suggested was that the whole situation changed for Cornwallis as soon as he realized that he was not slated for the command: his previous advice had made him liable for the outcome of the campaign, and he now wished to be quit of his liability. "I think Lord Cornwallis has been influenced hitherto by a degree of ambition industriously set in motion. I believe him now visited by apprehensions of future inquiries, and that His Lordship wishes to give up the former and rid himself of the latter." [André to Clinton, Apr. 3.] Flexner discusses this memorandum (The Traitor and the Spy, pp. 299–300) but misses its point—the effect on Cornwallis of Germain's letter.

means account for. I consequently took an early opportunity of noticing them to Lord Cornwallis, who, to my very great astonishment, told me in answer that he likewise had perceived them *and had himself encouraged them* [*the officers*] *in it, for he could not but think they had great reason to be offended with me for so long withholding my obedience to His Majesty's commands* "to oblige officers who held at the same time commissions in the regulars and provincials to declare their option of the line they chose to serve in and resign one of them" —*which commands he understood I had received some months before.* As I knew that this extraordinary charge had not the smallest foundation (having only by the last packet received the order referred to), and as it must have been notorious to every officer under my command that I had in very strong terms expressed my disapprobation of the late regulations with respect to provincial rank, and was much offended with two officers who had been in my confidence for having given that measure the appearance of my sanction by approving of it when consulted on the subject by the American Minister, I was exceedingly surprised at receiving so unmerited a return for the zeal I had shown for the interests and feelings of the regular officers under my command.

And, although perhaps Lord Cornwallis' conduct *in thus fomenting discontents in an army on actual service against its commander in chief* might very justly call for more serious reprehension, I contented myself with convincing His Lordship that he had been at least most egregiously misinformed by showing to him the Minister's dispatch containing the order, neither the date nor my reception of which could in any shape warrant such an accusation.[22] This I accompanied with an ostensible letter from myself to His Lordship on the subject, which I requested he would do me the justice of showing to the field officers whom he had so imprudently misled.[23] And from His Lordship's promise of doing so without delay, and the contrition he was pleased to express for the very great impropriety of his conduct, I had not the smallest doubt His Lordship would have taken some pains to undeceive

22. Germain to Clinton, Nov. 4, 1779 (received in Apr.), below, pp. 435–436.
23. "As Your Lordship had had occasion to hear of this ill-founded subject of uneasiness, and were candid enough to suffer me to perceive in yourself some degree of acquiescence in the censure given me on this score, I cannot but be anxious to remove such a prepossession, and therefore address to Your Lordship the sole paragraphs in my dispatches from the War Office which relate to this matter, together with my answers. As these must erase from Your Lordship's mind every supposition of the blame so industriously imputed to me being grounded in truth, so I rely on deriving through your means the vindication which you will certainly think it just I should receive. I am happy in thus explaining this affair to Your Lordship, that I shall be first justified where I could least reconcile myself to be censured." [Clinton to Cornwallis,] Apr. 6.

the army. The reader will, therefore, readily judge of my astonishment when I was some time afterward told by one of the field officers who had taken most offense, and was much in Lord Cornwallis' confidence, that he had never seen the letter I wrote to His Lordship, nor did he believe it was ever shown to the army as I expected.

But, notwithstanding these unpleasant instances of Lord Cornwallis' unfriendly disposition toward me, I took no other notice of them than what was necessary to set His Lordship right in matters wherein I conceived it possible he might have been led astray by wrong information. And so far were they from having the smallest influence on my conduct toward him that, upon His Lordship's only hinting to me the awkwardness of his situation as *third* at New York and his consequent wishes to remain in South Carolina, I appointed him to the command of the southern district with the utmost plenitude of power, civil and military, I could give him. And I even recommended it to the American Minister to join His Lordship in the commission with the Admiral and myself, that no time might be lost in reviving civil government in the Carolinas the instant it could be done with any probability of advantage to the King's service.

In short, I cannot charge myself with having omitted anything that was likely to advance the King's interests in this country. And I acted toward Lord Cornwallis, on my leaving him in the command of it, with the same liberality I should expect to have been treated [with] myself had I been left by a superior officer in the like situation, by committing his conduct in most cases to the guidance of his own discretion, and not shackling him with any other instructions than what were necessary to impress on his mind the very great importance of preserving the possessions we had so easily and happily attained.

For this end I requested His Lordship would constantly regard *the safety of Charleston and tranquillity of South Carolina as the principal and indispensable objects of his attention*. When the necessary arrangements for this purpose were completed, and the season suitable to operation in that climate should return, I left His Lordship at liberty, if he judged proper, to make a *solid* move into North Carolina, *upon condition it could at the time be made without risking the safety of the posts committed to his charge*. And I advised His Lordship, by way of preparation against he should be able to attempt the recovery of the latter province, to send a few troops to establish a small post in Cape Fear River as soon as the officer left in the command of the King's ships could spare a sufficient naval force for the service, as such a measure might probably prove in the meantime an encouragement and succor to the King's friends on the upper parts of that river, while

it might tend to prevent the conveyance of assistance to those in rebellion by the inland navigation, and strike a terror into the lower
counties, which were by far the most hostile. It was likewise my intention, as soon as I was relieved from my present apprehensions of a visit
from a superior French fleet, to further assist His Lordship's operations
by taking possession of some suitable and defensible post between the
lower parts of North Carolina and Virginia, in order to at least embarrass and impede the enemy's efforts to oppose him, and where I
could on a future day assemble an armament for the execution of my
plan in the upper Chesapeake.

CHAPTER 13

Developments in the North and Clinton's Return to New York, January to July, 1780

Sir Henry Clinton does not relinquish his hopes of being yet able to strike an important blow to the northward. Severity of the winter at New York. Consequent exposed situation of the King's troops there. Mr. Washington's army in no condition to avail itself of it. Lord Stirling's ineffectual attempt against Staten Island. Subsequent tranquillity of the British posts. General Knyphausen's judicious arrangements, and Brigadier General Pattison's zeal in collecting a respectable militia for the defense of New York. Depressed state of the disaffected colonists. Its causes. Mr. Washington's army being reduced by detachments and desertions, Sir Henry Clinton forms a design of attacking it unexpectedly, in its supine and feeble state at Morristown, before the American General is prepared for taking the field. The frigate which carries his aide-de-camp with the requisite preparatory orders to General Knyphausen unfortunately driven off the coast by our cruisers through ignorance of each other's signals, and arrives a fortnight later than she might have done. Sir Henry Clinton sails from Charleston to New York and unexpectedly finds General Knyphausen already landed with a considerable force in the Jerseys, which alarming the country, and every preparation being consequently made to oppose him, his plan is no longer practicable. Awkward situation of our Jersey corps relieved by Sir Henry Clinton's arrival. It is now ordered to advance and attack the enemy. Washington's rear column driven back. The British troops afterward return unmolested to Staten Island. Sir Henry Clinton gives a camp of rest to his army and prepares 6000 men for immediate embarkation, in hopes an opportunity may offer of employing them to advantage on the arrival of the expected French armament at Rhode Island, for which the Admiral, on his requisition, promises to hold transports in constant readiness.

THE CONQUEST of Charleston, and consequent submission of South Carolina, had given such a shock to the measures of the disaffected colonists that Great Britain was well warranted in the flattering expectations she entertained of soon seeing the war brought to a favorable issue. Nor would she most probably have been disappointed, could the other parts of the general plan which I had formed before my departure from New York have been carried into immediate execution—notwithstanding the present lateness of the season, to which the delays occasioned by the early disasters of our voyage had unavoidably drawn us. However, as I had solicited my recall and recommended a successor who, having approved my scheme of operations, would in all likelihood have adopted it, perhaps my most politic measure would have been to have retired in this hour of our success and not to have exposed myself again to the mortification of that reverse which was naturally to be expected from a long continued naval superiority on the side of the enemy, and [to] a repetition of the neglects I had hitherto experienced. And I must confess that this consideration contributed, with others, to make me lament the refusal [which] my petition for leave to resign had met with from my sovereign, although I shall ever retain a most grateful sense of the gracious professions of His Majesty's good opinion of me with which it was accompanied. But, as it seemed to be his royal pleasure I should remain in the command of his army, it became my duty to submit with all humility to his will. And, although the approach of another considerable French armament obliged me for the present to contract my designs, I did not wholly relinquish my hopes of being able even yet to strike some blow to the northward which might possibly assist our southern success in humbling the rebellious spirit of his American subjects.

While the campaign was carrying on in South Carolina, the northern colonies had experienced the hardest winter almost ever known in that country. The port of New York having been shut up by the frost within a few days after we sailed from thence, all communication with that city by water was, toward the middle of January, entirely cut off, and several new ones opened over the ice, which had soon acquired so firm a consistence that the heaviest cannon could be dragged thereon across the North River to Paulus Hook. And large detachments of cavalry actually marched, and loads of provisions were transported in sleighs, to Staten Island—the first [Paulus Hook] two thousand yards and the last [Staten Island] eleven miles distant from that city.[1]

Thus circumstanced, it is obvious the British posts in that district were on all sides laid open to Mr. Washington's attacks, had his army been in a condition to profit by their very exposed situation.[2] But after the

1. The bracketed insertions are obviously what Clinton meant. The water distance from Manhattan to Paulus Hook was approximately as given, but that from the Battery to Staten Island is less than six miles.
2. Clinton here gives, as a note, a long description of Washington's and Greene's difficulties with the American army, quoted practically verbatim from William

failure of Lord Stirling's attempt against Staten Island in the beginning of the year they suffered no other disturbance for the rest of the winter; but, on the contrary, those of the enemy were kept in perpetual alarm by several successful incursions from our lines. This state of tranquillity was owing in great measure to General Knyphausen's very watchful care, and the alertness of the officers who commanded at the foreposts. Nor must I omit doing justice to the very commendable zeal of Brigadier General Pattison (at that time commandant of New York), who with great industry formed a numerous and respectable militia for the defense of the town out of the citizens, the several navy and army departments, and the crews of the King's ships, traders, and transports. It must be confessed, however, that the services of a large portion of these people could not have been called upon except on such an emergency, when they were absolutely precluded from following their respective occupations by the intenseness of the cold, which had put an end to every other manual labor.[3]

The ruinous distresses resulting from this long and severe winter —added to a general scarcity of bread corn, an almost total disappearance of specie and the enormous depreciation of the paper money which the American Congress had substituted in its place, and the alarming desertion of their troops, with the difficulty of recruiting others—had combined at this period with the diminution of their European credit (by the deprivation of their principal source of remittance in the late loss of Carolina) to depress the friends of independence and make them heartily tired of the war.[4] The knowledge of this state of their affairs naturally suggested the idea that, if I could at so critical a juncture, by a sudden unexpected move, seize upon their grand depot of military stores at Morristown and capture or disperse the force that covered them, not only every plan of cooperation with their expected French reinforcement must be disconcerted, but other happy consequences would probably follow that might ultimately lead even to a general submission of the whole continent.

Wherefore, as I knew that Mr. Washington (whose army lay hutted in that position) had much weakened himself by the different detach-

---

Gordon, *The History of the Rise, Progress, and Establishment, of the Independence of the United States of America: Including an Account of the Late War; and of the Thirteen Colonies, from Their Origin to That Period* (4 vols., London, 1788), 3, 362–363.

3. Clinton's opinion of the New York citizenry was unflattering. "Recollect of what we are composed," he wrote in the spring—"one half of Long Island notorious rebels, one third at least of the city of New York voracious peddlers, who feed upon the vitals of us all." [Clinton to Eden, May 30.]

4. See Fisher, *Struggle for American Independence, 2,* 285–287, 289; Fortescue, *British Army, 3,* 325–326; Wallace, *Appeal to Arms,* pp. 216–217.

ments he had sent to the relief of Carolina, that none of the levies from the different states had yet joined him, and that he was not provided with horses to remove either cannon or stores nor had a single preparation in forwardness for taking the field, my plan was to direct Lieutenant General Knyphausen to hold a sufficient corps in readiness to be crossed to Elizabeth Town Point the instant the fleet from Charleston arrived at Sandy Hook, and to cause the troops that accompanied me in it to be thrown on shore at the same time at Amboy—so that the two corps marching immediately in concert, the one to Chatham, the other to Mordecai's Gap, might have a fair chance of reducing the enemy's General to the hazardous dilemma of either moving out against one or the other, or exposing himself to the united attacks of both by staying in his camp. If he should choose the first, the corps not attacked could easily push between him and his camp, and the one he moved against (being as strong if not stronger than his army) would from superiority of number or advantage of ground most probably defeat him. And, should he determine upon the latter, it certainly was not too presumptuous an expectation that his magazines and army might fall into our possession together. And, if he did neither, all his stores and artillery must have been sacrificed.

Having resolved upon this attempt very soon after I found we were threatened with a superior fleet to our own (by which all operation in Chesapeake was precluded) and I saw the necessity of my returning to the northward, I took the earliest opportunity that offered of sending my first aide-de-camp to New York, that the necessary preparations might privately be put in forwardness for carrying them into execution the instant of my arrival there.[5] And, the troops I had chosen to accompany me being embarked [6] and my arrangements and instructions for the southern district completed, we took our departure for that port on the 8th of June under the escort of Admiral Arbuthnot's squadron. On the 11th the Admiral with his heavy ships separated from the convoy, and I availed myself of that opportunity to send forward also my Adjutant General [André] with such further orders as I judged requisite for conducting my designs with the proper secrecy and expedition.

5. *Clinton's note:* For, having been informed from the commanding officers at New York that they expected a French naval armament to arrive at New York [and] that they were preparing to sink vessels at that bar and other defensive preparations, not having [an] idea they could engage in anything offensive, I did not judge it proper to hint my secret to any but my aide-de-camp, leaving it to his discretion to communicate or not, and to whom he should judge proper.

6. *Clinton's note:* British and Hessian Grenadiers, light infantry, German Chasseurs, Forty-second Regiment, Queen's Rangers, and a detachment of British artillery, amounting in the whole to about 4500.

But—though the last dispatches which I had received from New York had given me to understand that, being in hourly expectation of the arrival of an enemy's fleet, they were preparing to sink vessels on the bar to obstruct its entrance,[7] and I was consequently to suppose they were at this moment confined to the most strict defensive—I had the mortification to hear by a frigate that joined us on our approach to the coast that Generals Knyphausen and Robertson had already entered the Jerseys with a considerable part of the New York force. My plan being therefore thus anticipated, I could not look upon its object as any longer practicable. For, instead of finding Mr. Washington totally *hors de combat* (as I had the greatest reason to expect) and in a state of unsuspecting security in his camp at Morristown, and the bold, persevering militia of that populous province quiet at their respective homes,[8] it was most likely [that] the whole country was now in arms and every preparation made for opposing me with vigor, and that instead of a *coup de main* I should be engaged in operation in Jersey, which did not suit my situation or my objects for the campaign.

This was a most unfortunate *contretemps*, and could not (I humbly presume) have well happened if our ships of war on that station had had common signals to distinguish each other by. For the frigate that carried my aide-de-camp with my orders to General Knyphausen, happening to fall in with some of our cruisers off the port of New York and mistaking them for an enemy, was through a mutual ignorance of signals repeatedly driven off the coast, and thereby retarded in her arrival at least a fortnight longer than necessary, so that neither of the officers I had sent were in time to stop this ill-timed, *malapropos* move—which, General Knyphausen informed me, was undertaken on the ill-founded suggestions of [a] certain American Governor and some other oversanguine refugees, whose zeal (I am free to say) has but too often outrun their prudence in the course of this unfortunate war.[9]

7. Maj. Gen. James Robertson to Clinton, May 29. The original letter is endorsed in the margin, in another hand, "Charleston, July 18," which suggests that it passed Clinton at sea; in that case he presumably received en route either a copy or an oral message. A letter to him from Knyphausen on the same date makes no mention of a projected move, but speaks of awaiting his orders.

Washington was at this time in high hopes of a combined attack on New York as soon as the French fleet arrived. See Fisher, *Struggle for American Independence,* 2, 288–289.

8. *Clinton's note:* "This army, without suffering by desertions, would not have been able to have kept the field but for the assistance of the Jersey militia. Its weakness was occasioned by the numbers who had left it when their enlistment was out, by its not having been joined by a single draft nor received 200 recruits from all the states east of Maryland, and by the troops that had been sent on for the protection of the Carolinas." Gordon's *History [of the Late War, 3,* 371].

9. Loyalists had not only advised Knyphausen to move but had attacked him in

The transports arriving at Sandy Hook in a very thick fog, many of them had run ashore, which somewhat retarded the landing of the troops on Staten Island, where I had ordered them to be disembarked. In the meantime I went over myself to General Knyphausen in the Jersies, where he had been now ten days. I found matters there just as I apprehended, the militia all embodied and that general officer in a manner driven back to Elizabeth Town, menaced by a considerable force that held him at bay, and in appearance rather awkwardly circumstanced for want of a bridge of communication with Staten Island. This was certainly a very unpleasant and mortifying situation, which entirely precluded every idea of the enterprise I had in contemplation. Nothing was therefore now left for me to attempt but to watch some favorable opening for obtaining a partial advantage over the enemy, and ultimately to draw the King's troops out of the Jersies without affront. For, the Secretary of State's intelligence respecting the French armament from Brest being confirmed to me immediately after my arrival by a letter from General Arnold, then with the rebels (who had some time before made me an offer of his services), saying *that a French fleet and army were expected for certain to be at Rhode Island in about three weeks,* I could not in prudence think of engaging in an operation which was likely to be drawn out to any length.

I consequently directed all the troops I had brought with me to be re-embarked as quickly as possible, except the Queen's Rangers, which I added to the corps in the Jersies. And I desired Major General Mathew, supported by Lieutenant General Knyphausen, to advance and attack the rear of Mr. Washington's army, which had turned toward the Clove on the arrival of the fleet from Charleston. This was done partly with a view of retarding the march of the American army in order to give time for the Carolina detachment to get up the North River and, by landing on its western bank, rapidly strike between the enemy and his object. The re-embarkation was not, however, executed with the promptitude the service required, through

---

anonymous letters, presumably for inaction; their principal argument was that the American army was demoralized by the news from the south. (Undated Clinton memorandum, filed at the end of July.) The American governor was William Franklin of New Jersey, who was president of the newly established Board of Associated Loyalists. Clinton had set up this organization at the beginning of the year, in obedience to instructions from London, for the purpose of organizing and managing loyalist raids along the coast. (Germain to Clinton, Apr. 21, 1780 [CP]; Clinton to Germain, Jan. 23, 1781, calendared in Historical Manuscripts Commission, *Report on American Manuscripts in the Royal Institution of Great Britain* [4 vols., London, etc., 1904–09], 2, 237.) He implies that Franklin and his colleagues were already as much of a hindrance as a help, and they later became an acute embarrassment to him; see below, pp. 359–361.

the want of sufficient naval assistance, as the Admiral happened just then to put his fleet under sailing orders. The enemy had consequently time to effect his purpose before the transports could get high enough up the river to prevent him.

General Knyphausen had in the meantime proceeded, agreeable to his orders, in the attack of the enemy; and his *avant garde* under Major General Mathew, coming up with their column at Connecticut Farms, obliged it after a short but spirited contest on both sides to fall back. They then advanced to Springfield, the enemy still retiring before them; but their [the Americans'] numbers and position were judged to be too respectable to encourage any further attempts. One part of my design was, however, answered, which was to impress the enemy with a more respectable opinion of General Knyphausen's strength, and thereby ease his subsequent retreat. Therefore, after resting the troops at Springfield for about three hours, that general officer returned by my orders to Elizabeth Town, and repassed his corps early the next morning to Staten Island (without being molested by the enemy) over a bridge of boats which the engineer had, with the assistance of the Quartermaster General's department, very ably and expeditiously thrown over the sound [Arthur Kill] for that purpose, and which, had he not had a train established, could not have been effected.[10]

The loss sustained by the King's troops in the course of this fruitless excursion was rather more considerable than could have been well apprehended, and much exceeded what my present strength could afford. Had, however, the attack of Mr. Washington's rear succeeded in bringing back his gross or even in retarding its advance, I flatter myself it might have in some degree compensated all by the importance of the consequences. But, fortunately for the rebel affairs, that wary chief acted on this occasion with his usual caution, and by marching his army wide of the river contrived to place every part of it beyond our reach. I had myself attended this move; but, seeing when I got to Haverstraw Bay that there was not the smallest likelihood of my drawing any advantage from pursuing it further, I judged it best to land the troops at Phillipsburg and give them (in the present interval of suspense) a camp of rest, which most of them stood much in need of after an unremitted campaign of fourteen months. For I presume it

10. The failure of the British to press Nathaniel Greene's contingent at Springfield (which puzzled Greene at the time) and their subsequent retirement from New Jersey have been explained by Clinton's fear of the impending French descent on Rhode Island. (Wallace, *Appeal to Arms*, pp. 217–218; Carl Van Doren, *Mutiny in January* [New York, 1943], pp. 25–26.) As Sir Henry makes clear, however, he ordered the advance to Springfield *after* he knew the destination of the French.

will be scarcely necessary to repeat that, after the alarm had been given and the enemy had in consequence collected their militia and procured horses for removing their artillery and stores, it was to no kind of purpose to operate longer in the Jersies, whither I had at first been prompted to go only by the prospect I thought I then had of making a rapid and unexpected move against a discontented army in a supine and enfeebled state, and [by] the consequent hope of thereby accomplishing its total destruction.[11]

I did not, however, propose to remain altogether inactive. For, General Arnold's intimation that the French armament intended to touch at Rhode Island having suggested to me an idea of attacking their troops immediately upon their landing there (should their fleet happen to escape Admiral Arbuthnot's vigilance and his force at the time be superior to that of the enemy), I prepared a select corps with every other necessary apparatus for a sudden embarkation, and requested the Admiral to order transports to be held in constant readiness for the reception of 6000 men on the shortest notice, which he was so obliging to promise me should be complied with.

Nor did I lose any time in communicating to Admiral Arbuthnot the intelligence I had received from General Arnold, that he might be aware of the destination of the French fleet.[12] But, being in a few days after informed by my dispatches from the American Minister that it had actually sailed from Brest and was supposed to be bound for Quebec, and that another lesser armament was preparing to follow, which was destined for either the Chesapeake or Delaware, and this

11. Clinton's whole account of this incursion into New Jersey is confusing because he was confused at the time. The sequence of events shows his groping. Before his return from the south he had planned a coup de main, but on his return he found it hopeless. Although he implies that Knyphausen had spoiled the chance by acting prematurely, he nowhere explains how he himself could have succeeded if he had made the move a fortnight later; instead he impugns, in the text and in his letters at the time, the premises on which Knyphausen had acted—and on which, in essence, his own plan had rested.

When he took command, he attempted to salvage the operation by converting it into a pincers movement, to catch the enemy between British forces on the Hudson and at Elizabeth Town. But his aversion to further campaigning in New Jersey seems to have made him halfhearted: as soon as the river expedition missed its mark, and the Americans offered serious resistance at Springfield, he threw in the sponge. At once he began to minimize the little initiative that he had taken, and to imply that his only purpose throughout had been to extricate Knyphausen from a useless adventure. (Clinton to Germain, No. 2 of July 4.) He is trying to give the same impression in the text.

12. The message was sent orally, perhaps because mentioning Arnold in a letter would have been imprudent. (See Clinton to Arbuthnot, June 22.) The Admiral was skeptical of the intelligence; Sir Henry was not, and later asserted that it was Arnold's most important actual service and major claim to reward. Clinton [to William Pitt, Nov. 17, 1792].

intelligence being accompanied with a promise that 3000 German and British recruits should be sent to me from England by the next convoy, I proposed to him an immediate joint expedition into the Chesapeake for the purpose of anticipating the latter armament.[13]

This I judged might be safely attempted under the persuasion with which the Minister's letters had impressed me, that the first and greater armament would be employed at a distance from us. And I very much wished to secure a small post somewhere in Elizabeth River in Virginia, whereby I might not only have an opportunity of sounding the temper of the inhabitants but also of checking expeditions against the Carolinas by operations on the upper James, and of commanding to a degree the entrance of the Chesapeake.[14] It was, moreover, not improbable that a timely measure of that sort might deter the enemy's ships from entering those waters. The Admiral, however, did not apprehend that the enemy would occupy the bay before us, and was consequently not inclined to spare me a naval escort before he had further information from government by the arrival of Admiral Graves.[15] I was therefore for the present obliged to suspend that scheme, together with every other operation, until the intentions and force of the French might be more clearly developed.

13. Clinton seems to have put a surprising amount of credence in the intelligence from London, contained in two letters to him from Germain of May 3. These dispatches were correct in estimating the main French squadron as seven sail of the line, but in almost every other respect were erroneous.

14. Clinton realized, however, that establishing posts in the Chesapeake might deplete his field army to the point where major operations would be impossible. "It will appear a very mortifying prospect to be reduced to inaction at the hour (should success bring us to it) when an addition of 10,000 men might put a period to the war as far as the Hudson River. How far the being arrived at that point would operate toward the final reduction of the colonies Your Lordship is best able to judge." Clinton to Germain, No. 2 of July 4.

15. See Clinton to Arbuthnot, July 5. Rear Adm. Thomas Graves, with six sail of the line, was racing across the Atlantic against the French squadron under the Chevalier de Ternay. If Graves won, the British would have a great advantage. If the French won, Arbuthnot felt that he would not be able to stir until he was reinforced. (Arbuthnot to Clinton, July 6.) He seems to have turned down Clinton's proposed move to the Chesapeake for an obvious reason, which he was too polite to mention—that in the circumstances it would mean a dangerous, not to say foolhardy, dispersion of force.

CHAPTER 14

The First Attempt against Rhode Island,
July to August, 1780

Some of Admiral Arbuthnot's frigates fall in with the French fleet near the Capes of Virginia on the 5th of July. No further intelligence obtained respecting it until the 18th. Admiral Graves arrives on the 13th, upon which Sir Henry Clinton immediately proposes to Admiral Arbuthnot two plans for attacking the French armament on its arrival at Rhode Island: by the army alone, or by a conjunct attack of both after they had landed, if the first could not take place. The Admiral thinks them premature, as he has not the least doubt of intercepting it with his fleet before it can get there. The Admiral, however, on the requisition of Sir Henry Clinton [in]structs transports for 6000 to be kept in constant readiness. Sir Henry Clinton receives intelligence on the 18th that the French arrived in Newport harbor on the 10th. This he instantly communicates to the Admiral (who had not before heard of it), and renews his former proposals for attacking them. The Admiral acquiesces, and sails thither to judge of their practicability.

Sir Henry Clinton calls in the meantime for the transports, but finds them engaged by the Admiral's order in watering the fleet. Four days thereby lost before they are ready to receive the troops. This and other causes prevent their sailing from Frog's Neck before the 27th. They anchor next day at Huntington Bay to await the Admiral's summons to join him off Newport. Spirited defense of a blockhouse by seventy refugees against two thousand of Mr. Washington's best troops. Admiral intimates through Captain Savage his wishes that Sir Henry Clinton may not proceed to join him. Determined in consequence, at a council of war, to return to Whitestone. The troops relanded there, but everything else remains on board the transports ready for their re-embarkation should the Admiral invite them to another effort.

Mr. Washington crosses the North River with a considerable force and menaces New York but, hearing of Sir Henry Clinton's return, precipitately falls back to the Jersies. The Admiral denies his having told Captain Savage that he wished the General might not proceed, and insinuates that he has kept the sea so long (in anxious expectation of his joining him) that his ships' crews are very sickly, and he is obliged to return into port. The Admiral sends a message to Sir Henry Clinton by Captain Savage, proposing a conference with him at

Gardiners Island. Sir Henry Clinton immediately dispatches two general officers to him by water, and proceeds thither himself through Long Island. When the General arrives at Moriches, he sends forward an express to let the Admiral know of his approach, and arrives the next day at East Hampton. But the Admiral puts to sea the moment he receives his letter, without leaving even a boat to communicate with him. Sir Henry Clinton, thus disappointed, returns to New York and is soon after joined by the general officers he had sent by water, the Admiral having declared to them that he never from the first looked upon [attacking] the enemy as practicable, and that he had no operation to propose, as they were not to be come at. Brief recapitulation of the proceedings in the proposed attack of the French armament. Probable causes of its miscarriage, and the consequences.

NOTHING further of any importance occurred before the 7th of July, when intelligence was brought to the Admiral by two of his cruisers that they had fallen in with a French fleet on the 5th about eighteen leagues from Cape Henry, and supposed by their course that they must be bound for Boston or Rhode Island.[1] As I had no doubt of this being Monsieur de Ternay's squadron, and judging that Admiral Arbuthnot's fleet, upon the junction of the ships under Mr. Graves (who arrived on the 13th), was superior to it, I did not hesitate to propose to him two plans for attacking the French armament, should they unfortunately escape him and arrive at Rhode Island. The one was for the Admiral, immediately after the enemy's arrival there, to mask the entrance of Newport harbor with his large ships while I landed 6000 chosen troops in the Sakonnet under cover of the frigates, and attacked those of the enemy before they could have time to throw up works for their defense. The other was that, in case we should be too late for the first by the enemy being fortified and reinforced, we should according to circumstances both go together into the Narragansett, his fleet [should] anchor between the Conanicut and Rhode Islands, and [we should] then make a joint attack against their ships and troops. And, should neither meet his approbation, I requested a naval force to enable me to make a descent at New London or some other part of the enemy's coast in the sound, in the hope of relieving Canada, which I then judged to be the enemy's object. But the Admiral seemed to look upon both my proposals as premature, and to have such confidence in his own strength (having at this time under his

1. For a detailed discussion of the material of this chapter see William B. Willcox, "Rhode Island in British Strategy, 1780–1781," *Journal of Modern History*, 17 (Dec., 1945), 308–313. That discussion is based primarily upon the CP, and footnote references in this chapter will therefore be limited to additional material.

orders twenty-four ships of war, ten of which were of the line) that he was sure of accomplishing their destruction himself.[2]

But, while we were thus meditating on the means of defeating the enemy's design, their troops had already landed and were fortifying themselves in Rhode Island, the French fleet having arrived there on the 10th. Of this neither Admiral Arbuthnot nor I had received the smallest intimation until the intelligence was brought to me by express on the 18th from the east end of Long Island. This must of course excite surprise, considering the number of fast-sailing cruisers the Admiral had then with him, all which, it is presumable, were immediately after the intelligence of the 7th disposed in proper stations to watch the enemy's fleet. But no further tidings were procured of them from that period to the present moment, when I gave him the first notice of their arrival.

As no plan had been yet concerted between us, I now sent a confidential officer [3] to the Admiral with a renewal of my two former proposals, and I immediately moved the troops destined for this service to the waterside to be ready for embarkation at a moment. For although the enemy had been now nine days on Rhode Island, and I could not consequently flatter myself with as certain success as at first (with my small force against 5000 disciplined French troops covered by works, in a position which General Pigot had not long before defended with only 4000 against 14,000, and those supported by a formidable fleet), yet, as there was a possibility that events might have happened to prevent or retard their operations, I wished to be prepared for taking such advantages as might offer in this very critical and important moment in the war. The Admiral favored me with his answer the next day, saying that he should proceed immediately off Newport and, if it proved possible to put my plan in execution, I should hear from him immediately—advising me in the meantime to embark the troops and go in preference through the sound as far as Huntington Bay, whither, after he had reconnoitered the enemy's fleet, he should dispatch his further wishes.

Upon this I instantly called for the transports which Admiral Arbuthnot had, in consequence of my requisition of the 22d of June, promised me to hold in constant readiness, and was consequently not a little surprised to find by the agents' report (Captains Tomkins and

2. Clinton interlards this chapter with extracts from the correspondence between himself, Arbuthnot, and the agents whom he sent to the Admiral in the effort to concert a plan against the French. The extracts are substantially accurate, although not always verbatim; they cover the six weeks from July 15 to Aug. 31. See below, pp. 443–445, 446–448, 449–450, 451–452, 455.

3. Capt. Thomas Murray; see Arbuthnot to Clinton, July 18, CP.

Chedy) that they were then engaged by his own order in watering the King's ships.[4] This unfortunately occasioned a delay of four days, and obliged us to go to sea at last with less than twelve days' water. Captain Murray in the meantime brought me a letter from the Admiral, to inform me his frigates had clearly perceived eleven ships of the line in Newport harbor and (which I thought at the time somewhat extraordinary after such intelligence) accompanied by a message *that nothing but a hurricane could oblige him to quit the coast and abandon me, should I go in the Sakonnet as proposed.*

My preparations for this expedition had caused a movement in Mr. Washington's army, with a view, it is supposed, of diverting me from my object or at least retarding its taking place. But, the route I had chosen putting within my reach the quickest intelligence of his motions, I knew I could regulate mine according to them at a moment, and they of course suffered no interruption from them. None, however, appeared to have a serious tendency but one; and, as the issue turned out exceedingly honorable to a small body of loyal refugees who garrisoned a stockaded blockhouse on the western shore of the Hudson at Bull's Ferry, almost opposite to New York, it may not be improper to mention it. These poor people were only seventy in number (commanded by a Mr. Ward), who, being usually employed in cutting firewood for the inhabitants of New York for the support of their families, had erected this trifling work to protect them against such straggling parties of militia as might be disposed to molest them, not imagining they could ever become an object to a more formidable enemy. However, on the morning of the 21 July a select detachment from Mr. Washington's army, amounting to nearly 2000 men, under Brigadier General Wayne, suddenly appeared before their post and opened against it a tremendous fire of musketry and cannon. But this gallant band defended themselves with activity and spirit; and, after sustaining the enemy's fire for some hours (by which one face of their little blockhouse was perforated by at least fifty cannon shot and twenty-one of their number killed and wounded) and repulsing an assault on their works, they sallied out and pursued their assailants to some distance, picking up stragglers and rescuing from them part of the cattle they were driving off.[5] Such rare and exalted bravery merited every en-

4. The fleet needed 1500 barrels. The transports, which at this time were under naval control, were ordered down to the bar. Tomkins had previously been warned by Clinton of this danger, and expostulated with the Admiral. But not a ship in the squadron was permitted to come up to New York to water. The navy, by the time it had finished with the transports, "had torn them to pieces." Additional Clinton notes following the "Journal of the Siege of Charleston," fols. 51–51v.

5. Bull's Ferry was on the Jersey shore, some four miles north of Hoboken. The

couragement in my power, and I did not fail to distinguish it at the time by suitable commendations and rewards, to which I had soon after the satisfaction to add the fullest approbation of their sovereign.

The troops were now embarked as soon as the transports could get into Frog's Neck to receive them.[6] But the *Blonde,* which had been appointed for their convoy, having struck on a rock in her passage through the East River,[7] and the winds being for some time contrary, it was the 27th before they sailed; and they consequently did not arrive in Huntington Bay before the next day, when they came to an anchor to wait the Admiral's call to join him off Newport.

As it was impossible from the information which I had hitherto received to form any accurate judgment of either the force or position of the enemy, I had on the 22d, immediately after receiving the Admiral's letter and message by Captain Murray, sent to him Captain Savage (who had been deputy Quartermaster General to the King's troops in Rhode Island) with a few trusty inhabitants of that country, to obtain such intelligence as I could act from. For I own I did not think it very probable that the enemy's army would be now found, after being so long landed, in a situation to be forced by a *coup de main,* the hopes of which had been my principal inducement to propose to the Admiral an attack by the troops alone. And, indeed, this was in some measure confirmed to me by a letter which the Admiral favored me with on the 26th, wherein he said he *could plainly perceive the enemy to be erecting works on the peninsula of Brenton's Neck,* to which he added "and, to say the truth, if I am to judge from a very large encampment on the beach on the south end of Rhode Island fronting the sea, you are to expect some opposition." It is, however, very remarkable that, although the Admiral must from hence have suspected that my proposal of a landing in the Sakonnet for an attack singly by the troops might not be any longer eligible, he did not mention a syllable respecting the

---

episode is described in a letter from Washington of July 26, below, pp. 445–446; another account, differing considerably from Clinton's in detail, is in Stokes, *Iconography of Manhattan,* 5, 1113.

6. *Clinton's note:* The troops embarked were: the flank companies of the Guards, two battalions of light infantry, two battalions of British grenadiers, four battalions of Hessian Grenadiers, Twenty-second, Thirty-seventh, Thirty-eighth, Forty-second, and Forty-third British Regiments, Hessian Regiments of Du Corps and Landgrave, three hundred Jägers, one hundred and thirty artillery, twenty light dragoons, in all about sixty-seven hundred rank and file. The general officers were the Commander in Chief, Majors General Mathew, Leslie, and Kospoth, Brigadier General Leland, Quartermaster General Dalrymple, Colonels Gunning and Howard of the Guards (volunteers).

7. The *Blonde,* a fifth rate of thirty-two guns, ran on the rocks of Corlaer's Hook, apparently as the result of carelessness. Stokes, *loc. cit.*

other [proposal] of a conjunct operation by the Narragansett, his only offer even now being that "he will undertake to prevent the shipping from coming out to impede my landing in the Sakonnet." [8]

Captain Savage rejoined me in Huntington Bay on the 30th, without having been able to put on shore any of the people he carried with him, or to procure any further intelligence respecting the enemy than we had before. But the report that officer made me of his conversation with Admiral Arbuthnot having given me to understand that it was his earnest desire I should not proceed in the proposed attack because the enemy's troops were now strongly covered by works and a powerful artillery [and] that the first part of my plan appeared to be impracticable, and the letter he brought me from him only referring me to this report without taking any notice of the second part [of my letter] (wherein a joint attack of the enemy's armament by the King's ships and troops had been submitted to his consideration) or containing the slightest offer of active cooperation on the side of the navy,[9] I judged it useless for us to remain any longer in the open Bay of Huntington, where the transports might be exposed to danger from hard gales of wind and other casualties. I therefore submitted the circumstances of our situation, with Captain Savage's report, to the consideration of a council of war. And it being the unanimous opinion that it would be most conducive to His Majesty's service for the troops to return to Whitestone, where they would be nearer to frustrate any design of Mr. Washington (who was then crossing the North River) and almost equally apportée to obey the Admiral's summons to join him off Newport, I immediately communicated to him the result of our deliberations and prepared to carry them into immediate execution.

For, as eighteen days had now elapsed since the French troops had actually landed in Rhode Island and no certain intelligence had even yet been procured of their operations, there did not remain the smallest probability that the army could be any longer a principal in the execution of whatever plan might be hereafter adopted for their annoyance. Consequently nothing was left for me but to renew my offers to the Admiral of my most hearty concurrence in any conjunct

8. See Clinton to Arbuthnot, July 22, and Arbuthnot to Clinton, July 23, below, pp. 444–445.

9. Clinton agreed that he should not go to Rhode Island if Arbuthnot's intelligence were correct. "I could get none of my own. For, though I sent seven or eight people who could be depended upon, Captain Hawkes of the *Iris* did not think proper to land them and bring them off, for fear of losing a boat. And my aide-de-camp of course would not send them to certain sacrifice without [being] assured that Captain Hawkes would at least attempt to bring them off." (Clinton [to Eden], undated and filed at the end of August.) For Savage's report of his unsuccessful reconnaissance and interview with Arbuthnot, July 30, see below, pp. 446–447.

operation which his subsequent knowledge of the enemy's situation might induce him to suggest.[10] And, to enable him to obtain every possible information for this purpose, I sent back to him the people whom we had ineffectively attempted to land in the enemy country, accompanied as before by Captain Savage, to whom was now added Major DeLancey, one of my aides-de-camp, on whose judgment and report I knew I could safely depend. The disembarked troops were directed, in the meantime, to remain in the neighborhood of Flushing while everything else for the expedition remained on board the transports at Whitestone, that there might not be any delay in their reembarkation should the Admiral find it expedient to invite us to another effort.

They were likewise in this position more at hand, as noticed before, for acting against Mr. Washington—who, supposing that the British armament was actually gone to Rhode Island, had thrown a very considerable force to the east side of the North River, and advanced with it to the Croton, from whence he was preparing, as I heard, to make a move against New York. But we soon afterward discovered that the instant he received intelligence of our having relanded on Long Island he fell back to his former camp in the Jersies.[11]

Matters continued in this state of uncertainty until the 10th of August, when I was favored with a letter from Admiral Arbuthnot in which he absolutely denied his having told Captain Savage that "he wished he could stop my proceeding"—which, constituting the chief purport of that officer's report, to which he had referred me, had entirely influenced our late measures. On the contrary, he was now pleased to declare that he never officially knew the enemy's strength, and only told Captain Savage *that, if upon his report I judged my force insufficient to warrant an attempt upon them, he thought it better not to come;* and concluded with insinuating that, having kept the sea so

10. Clinton to Arbuthnot, July 30, below, p. 447.
11. *Clinton's note:* Before it was known that a further attempt against Rhode Island was impracticable, and while every mind was anxiously full of the issue of the present expedition, a singular event happened which has every appearance of being intended to stop it. This was no less than an attempt to poison the Commander in Chief, as two gentlemen of his family and himself were seized one day immediately after dinner (and drinking only one glass of wine each!) with violent sickness, attended with convulsive spasms and other strong symptoms of poison. And Dr. Morris, Physician General to the Army (who fortunately happened to be within call, and to whose care and attention they owed their recovery), having analyzed the remains of the liquor, declared that it was strongly impregnated with arsenic. There were several circumstances, also, accompanying this transaction which prove it was done with a view of stopping the expedition. But, as the affair could not at the time be traced to its source, we cease making any further comments upon it.

long in anxious expectation of my joining him off Newport that his
fleet was become sickly, he should repair for a few days to Gardiners
Island Bay to land his sick and take in a fresh supply of water. I own
the contents of this letter altogether greatly astonished me, as I could
not well doubt the veracity of the officer I had sent to him. But I judged
it best in the present important moment to suppress the feelings which
so unaccountable a proceeding must naturally excite, lest the King's
service should suffer from any misunderstanding between us. And I
therefore contented myself with telling the Admiral in my answer that
I was persuaded his zeal for the service would have led him to offer
active cooperation on the part of His Majesty's ships had he seen the
propriety of such a measure.[12]

Captain Savage after this returned to me again on the 13th, with a
proposal from Admiral Arbuthnot to meet him at Gardiners Island.
And a letter received from him at the same time by General Robertson gave me to understand that from some important discoveries he
had lately made he saw an opening for a joint enterprise against the
enemy. I was therefore induced to request Major Generals Mathew
and Dalrymple to proceed round by water to consult with and receive
his commands, and on the 15th I set out myself by land through Long
Island to concert with him in person the most likely means of annoying the French armament, and to be at hand to assist in carrying
whatever we should resolve on into immediate execution. I had it
likewise in intention, in case the expedition against Rhode Island should
prove inexpedient, to lay before the Admiral the plan of a desultory
move I had in contemplation against the stores and shipping at Philadelphia, should he be disposed to assist me with the requisite naval protection.

When I reached Moriches, I sent forward a party of light dragoons
with a letter to apprise him of my being so far advanced on my way
to meet him; and I arrived the next day at East Hampton.[13] But, after
thus exposing myself and suite to the inconveniences and hazards of
posting 120 miles in the most inclement and sickly season of the year
through the excessive heats of that climate,[14] I had at last the mortification to find I had taken this long journey for nothing, the Admiral having been pleased to put to sea with his fleet that very morning—im-

12. Arbuthnot to Clinton, Aug. 3, and Clinton to Arbuthnot, Aug. 11, below, pp.
447–448, 449.
13. Moriches is about two miles north of Moriches Bay, on the southern coast
of Long Island. East Hampton is near the end of the island, some thirty-five miles
east of Moriches.
14. *Clinton's note:* Sir Henry Clinton's coachman was killed on this journey by
a *coup de soleil,* and most of the party suffered very much from the extreme heat
of the weather.

mediately after receiving my letter of the preceding day to announce my approach—without leaving me even a boat to communicate with him.

I had long borne with a variety of disappointments from Admiral Arbuthnot, which I imputed to the capriciousness of age, and had on that account endeavored as much as possible, by falling in with his humors, to keep matters in proper train. But this last extraordinary treatment of his colleague in commission was rather too indecent to be suffered to pass unnoticed. I therefore complained to him of it in such terms as I judged consistent with the King's service and my own dignity.[15] And, being persuaded that the war could never be carried on to any effect (while all our land operations depended so entirely on the zealous cooperation of the navy) unless the chief in that line was cordial in his assistance and firmly steady in the execution of such conjunct operations as might be agreed upon, I looked upon it as an indispensable duty to my country and my own fame to lose no time in laying before His Majesty's Ministers a candid representation of the many instances wherein the Admiral, in my opinion, had failed to cooperate with me with the liberality and animation which I judged requisite to attain the objects I had in view, as well as to preserve a proper openness of communication and union of sentiment between the chiefs of the two services. For which momentous reasons I humbly requested that His Majesty would be graciously pleased either to remove me from the command of his American army or to appoint some other officer to the head of his fleet on that service in whom I might place more confidence than it was possible for me to have in Admiral Arbuthnot. And, as Brigadier General Dalrymple happened to have been employed by me in several negotiations with the Admiral and was consequently, from his own knowledge, fully competent to supply administration with every requisite information on the subject, I requested he would be the bearer of my dispatches to the Secretary of State, and charge himself with the delivery of this very important communication.[16]

Thus ended, *re infecta*, an expedition which had given the greatest

15. His dignity got the upper hand of his indignation only after a struggle. See below, p. 449 n. 36.

16. Clinton here has a reminder to include "my letter and the answer from the Minister, as it shows my conduct was approved." Sir Henry's letter was that of Aug. 25 (below, pp. 454–455). His request for his own or the Admiral's removal (and for changes not mentioned in the text) was conveyed orally by Dalrymple to Germain, and then put into writing for the King and cabinet. Lord George's answer scarcely constituted approval: in one breath Arbuthnot's removal was promised, in the next Clinton was given permission to resign the command to Cornwallis. See Germain to Clinton, Oct. 4, 13, below, pp. 462, 467–468; Willcox in *Journ. of Mod. Hist., 17,* 316–317.

alarm to the enemy and from which, I own, I had once promised myself the most decisive and important consequences. I cannot, however, affirm that my success would have been absolutely certain with
the army alone, unassisted by active cooperation of the fleet, had I
fortunately even met Monsieur de Rochambeau on his landing in
Rhode Island. Much less was I from entertaining very flattering expectations that between five and six thousand disciplined French troops,
after having had time to cover themselves by works and to be reinforced, were likely to be caught in a situation liable to be forced by
a *coup de main* singly of the army. But, as my knowledge of the ground
convinced me that a landing might be attempted in the Sakonnet without the smallest risk in retreat in case of failure, I thought the enterprise
worth the trying. Nor was I without hopes that, when Admiral Arbuthnot had fully reconnoitered the position of the enemy's ships, he might
be tempted to adopt my proposal of a double attack by the Narragansett.
It happened, however, that various delays arising from many causes
rendered the first impracticable; and, as the Admiral had never favored
me with his opinion of the latter, I concluded he looked upon the
enemy's force as too strong to be attempted.

Being conscious, therefore, that I had done everything in my power
to forward His Majesty's service on this important occasion, I should
have probably not thought it necessary at this distance of time to have
troubled the reader with so full a detail. But, as Admiral Arbuthnot
took no small pains to impress his friends with a persuasion that his
ships were always ready for the attack and that its not being carried
into execution was principally owing to my not joining him off Newport, I thought it right to remove every possibility of doubt respecting
my conduct by laying before the public the most material parts of our
correspondence.

These will, I flatter myself, incontestably prove that I very early
formed the design of attacking the French troops on their landing in
Rhode Island, and officially requested Admiral Arbuthnot to order
transports to be kept in constant readiness for the reception of six thousand men; that, as soon as Mr. Graves arrived, I laid before the Admiral two plans of attack, which were received by him with indifference because he thought his ships alone capable of destroying the
French armament; that my proposals were renewed the moment I
heard of their being actually landed there; that, though he did not
now decline them, he deferred speaking to either until he could better
judge of their expediency; that notwithstanding his promise the transports were not ready for the troops when I called for them, owing to
his having himself employed them in watering his fleet; that a con-

siderable delay was thereby occasioned; that, although his fleet had been for several days off Newport, he either did not obtain the slightest knowledge of the enemy's strength and situation, or, if he did, he did not choose to communicate it to me; that, after so much time had elapsed as dissipated every idea of an attempt singly by the army, and they could consequently be no longer regarded as a principal, he not only uniformly evaded giving an opinion on that part of my plan wherein a conjunct operation by the Narragansett was *repeatedly submitted to his consideration* but, on the contrary, intimated to my confidential messenger (to whom he referred me) that he wished he could stop my proceeding; that he afterward denied his having done so, and, when the troops were relanded in Long Island in consequence of Captain Savage's report, he requested an immediate meeting to confer with me upon some important discoveries he had made; that I immediately posted one hundred and twenty miles by land to comply with his request; that, the instant he heard of my approach, he suddenly put to sea with his fleet and left me at the extremity of Long Island without even a boat to communicate with him; and that, so far from his ever having had any object in view or enterprise to propose, he at last declared to Generals Mathews and Dalrymple that he never from the first saw the least opening for either a single or conjunct attack of the enemy. And, upon my still pressing him for a positive answer, he acknowledged in a letter to myself that, not having the least knowledge of the natural strength of Rhode Island, he looked upon any proposals from him for operation as improper, but if any had come from me he would have informed me whether he thought the fleet could take a part. This part of the Admiral's letter (out of delicacy while we were acting together) I did not answer, as the reader will observe that the only answer I could make was that I had in almost every letter proposed to him that, if we should arrive too late for the army to act alone, I not only proposed a cooperation of the fleet under his command but pointed out the Narragansett Passage particularly.

On the other hand I am unwilling to ascribe the failure of this enterprise to any particular cause, though I must acknowledge it to have been my firm opinion that we should scarcely have been disappointed of success had Mr. Graves fortunately reached New York six days sooner than he did,[17] or even had Admiral Arbuthnot contrived by his frigates to have obtained timely information of the French fleet's

17. *Clinton's note:* Admiral Graves having fallen in with and taken on his passage a French East Indiaman, it was suspected by administration at this time that this circumstance contributed to the delay which afterward proved to be fatal. [The suspicion was unfounded; see Willcox in *Journ. of Mod. Hist., 17,* 308–309.]

arrival, and his transports had been ready as promised for the immediate reception of troops. But, let what will have been the cause, this nation will ever surely have reason to lament that anything intervened to prevent either [attack], as there is little doubt that our not being able to crush this reinforcement immediately on its arrival gave additional animation to the spirit of rebellion, whose almost expiring embers began to blaze up afresh on its appearance.[18]

18. "It has revived a dying cause. Washington has raised an army, and the whole continent seems alive upon it." (Clinton [to Newcastle], undated and filed at the end of August.) Sir Henry admitted at the time that the whole blame might not rest with the navy: he himself should perhaps have been more prompt in communicating his plan to Arbuthnot. See Clinton [to Eden], undated and filed at the end of August; the key sentence is deleted in the draft.

CHAPTER 15

The First Chesapeake Expedition and the Arnold Conspiracy, August to September, 1780

Alarming accounts from South Carolina. Sir Henry Clinton determines to send an immediate expedition into the Chesapeake to make a diversion in Lord Cornwallis' favor, and applies to Admiral Arbuthnot for naval support. The low state of his provisions, [the] inadequate number of his field army at New York, and the threatening clouds which begin to gather in all quarters excite in Sir Henry Clinton the deepest uneasiness.

Hints respecting a plan for laying hold of the peninsula between Chesapeake and Delaware, which he has long wished to possess on account of its many local advantages, its being easily defensible even against a temporal naval superiority, and its abounding with friends to the British government; plenty of provisions and perfectly healthy. The design communicated to the Secretary of State, together with the present situation of American affairs and his opinion of the utter impossibility of carrying on the war without reinforcement.

Sir George Rodney arrives at New York with ten sail of the line. Sir Henry Clinton immediately lays before him a state of public affairs, with the particulars of the last attempt against Rhode Island, and offers to join him in any enterprise he may judge their united force equal to. Troops embarked for an expedition to the Chesapeake.

The British Adjutant General, sent at General Arnold's request to meet that officer on particular business, is taken on his return and carried prisoner to the American camp. General Arnold escapes to the British lines. Major André condemned by the Americans as a spy and punished with death, to the disgrace of humanity. His eulogium and character.

I BEGAN about this time to receive the most alarming accounts from the southward,[1] which seemed to call for the utmost exertion of my power to aid Lord Cornwallis' operations in that district instead of drawing from him a few additional troops for my own to the northward, which we both had once thought practicable. But how it was possible with propriety to spare so far from me any portion of my

1. See Simpson to Clinton, Aug. 13, 1780, below, p. 450.

209

very scanty force—which scarcely amounted to 13,000 men—was a question not easily to be determined, especially when I considered that Mr. Washington had an army in my neighborhood equally strong, with nearly 6000 French troops within his call, and was buoyed up with the promise of the speedy arrival of a considerable addition to them from either Europe or the West Indies. It is true, indeed, that I was likewise promised an addition to mine of 3000 recruits; but none had yet made their appearance, nor had I even any accounts of their being embarked.

Matters were, however, become too critical in that quarter to admit of hesitation. And, as Lord Cornwallis had in his late dispatches explicitly told me *that unless he immediately attacked North Carolina he must give up both South Carolina and Georgia and retire within the walls of Charleston*,[2] I resolved without delay to send an expedition into Chesapeake Bay, with a view of making a powerful diversion in His Lordship's favor by striking at the magazines then collecting by the enemy at the head of James River for supplying the army they were assemblying to oppose him. Immediate application was accordingly made to the Vice Admiral for a naval escort, and I directed a proper force to be in the meantime prepared for embarkation, under Major General Leslie, whom I proposed to entrust with the execution of this important service.

This sudden reverse in the King's affairs to the southward, added to the very inadequate amount of my field force when weighed against that of the two armies opposed to me and the daily indispensable services required from it, together with the very low condition of my provision stores (depending altogether for our daily support on what the Commissary General could purchase from the merchants, as no part of this year's supply had yet arrived), could not but fill my mind with the deepest anxiety. For, instead of the flattering prospect which had opened upon me in the beginning of the campaign of reducing the whole country from the Savannah to the Hudson before winter (which [3] there was some reason to hope would have been the case had no foreign power intervened, and we had been in a situation to have followed up our success at Charleston by carrying our arms immediately after it into North Carolina and the Chesapeake), the most threatening clouds began now to gather round us on every side, which not only precluded all thoughts of enterprise against the possessions of the enemy, but even excited apprehensions for the security of our own.

In short, if Lord Cornwallis with 6000 men could scarcely retain his

2. See Cornwallis to Clinton, July 14, Aug. 6, below, pp. 443, 448–449.
3. The MS, which has been interlined, reads "of which."

hold of South Carolina, when nature had traced a defensible boundary against outward foes and given little resource for domestic insurrection, there was still less reason to expect that with the field army my Whitestone embarkation lately exhibited ([6000,] which was the very utmost I could draw from garrison duty) I could first subdue and afterward protect the neighboring populous tracts, which were circumscribed by no natural impediments and were full of enemies and resource. Nor could reason warrant the hope that from the friends of government who were pining under oppression within the limits of the usurpation any effectual aid could be drawn toward the dispersion of Mr. Washington's army, or the maintenance of the country against him. On the contrary, experience had already shown us that the revolutions fondly expected by means of friends to the British government were merely visionary. These, it must be allowed, however, were undoubtedly numerous; and it is but justice to say that a desultory inroad is no countenance, and to possess a territory requires garrisons. Consequently the accession of friends, unless we could occupy the country they inhabited, would have only added some more unhappy exiles to the list of pensioned refugees.[4]

But there was a district which, being locally friendly to the masters of the sea, I had long had my eye upon and wished much to possess. I mean the peninsula between Chesapeake and the Delaware—a large tract of very fertile land abounding with secure harbors on both its shores, whose inhabitants were numerous and in general strongly attached to Great Britain, and which from the defensible nature of the ground at its gorge [neck] and the general healthiness of its climate, and from its being plentifully provided with supplies for the army and having many other advantages, might be held with their assistance against the united power of the whole continent, and even a temporary French naval superiority in those seas. For it was most plentifully provided with every supply an army could want, had a free access from both the Chesapeake and the sea, and had many other advantages which rendered it a most eligible post. But without at least 6000 men, in addition to what I then had, no attempt of the sort could be thought of under my present circumstances. Consequently I could only represent its importance,[5] together with a sketch of the plan I had formed should government be disposed to augment my army and secure my operations in that quarter from being molested by another visit from a superior fleet.

4. This paragraph is taken almost verbatim from Clinton to Germain, No. 1 of Aug. 25, which provides the figure inserted in brackets.
5. See Clinton to Germain, Aug. 25, below, pp. 454–455.

This I strongly represented in my present dispatches to the Secretary of State, stating, however, without reserve the many difficulties under which I labored, together with the absolute impossibility of carrying on the war without speedy reinforcement.[6] I thought it my duty also to remind him that, although we should be so fortunate to arrive at this point, it was to be feared that a glance upon the returns of the army under my command (divided into garrisons and reduced by casualties) on the one part, with the consideration of the task yet before us on the other, might only renew the too just reflection which I had repeatedly before made, that we were still by some thousands too weak to subdue this formidable rebellion.

For the official letters which I received about this time from Lord George Germain, dated in June, had given me to understand that the British recruits were only then beginning to embark, and that, although only part of those from Germany had arrived, sufficient transports had not been yet provided for their reception.[7] This unexpected intelligence did not, of course, greatly brighten my prospects with respect to the issue of the war. But the very flattering approbation of my past conduct with which it was accomplished could not fail to animate my exertions in the service of my King and country to the utmost stretch of the very feeble means with which I was armed.

I was, however, not a little concerned to find that, although His Lordship was perfectly acquainted with the weakness of my powers and the considerable foreign interference I had to contend with, together with the probably consequent rapid increase of Mr. Washington's army, he was still disposed to entertain the most confident expectations of my success in Chesapeake and that it would contribute, with the reduction of Carolina, to the complete recovery of all the southern provinces in the course of the campaign.[8] Nor was I without my apprehensions that the raising people's hopes so much beyond what real appearances authorized might add to the dejection the public would suffer when the present real state of affairs should come to their knowledge, and of course considerably shake that small degree of favor in which the late conquest of Charleston had fortunately placed me. My anxiety was, of course, still further increased by seeing my hands in a manner tied up by the distance at which the Admiral was from me, and the small pittance of provisions to which I was now

6. See Clinton to Germain, Aug. 30, below, p. 455.
7. Germain to Clinton, June 7.
8. Germain to Clinton, July 4 (below, p. 442). Sir Henry lumps the Minister's letters of June 7 and July 4, presumably because they reached him together on Sept. 1. Germain repeated much the same opinion of the importance of the southern campaign in his letter of Sept. 6, below, p. 457.

reduced—both which at the present moment put it absolutely out of my power to forward the expedition to the Chesapeake with that dispatch which the urgency of our affairs in Carolina seemed to require, and for which everything on my part had been for some time fully prepared.

While my thoughts were thus occupied in ruminating on my very unpleasant situation,[9] I was most agreeably surprised by the very unexpected appearance of a fleet of ten sail of the line from the West Indies, which arrived off the Hook on the 13th of September under the command of Sir George Rodney. So very respectable an addition to Mr. Arbuthnot's force (not only giving us a most decided naval superiority on the American coast, but inviting and opening secure roads to enterprise) soon struck the utmost dismay into the disaffected colonists and very justly filled the minds of the King's friends with the highest joy and expectation. Nor was it long before the effects it had on the rebel counsels became visible, as the inimical states began immediately to relax in their augmentations of Mr. Washington's army, which, on the contrary, diminished daily by desertion; and their vaunted preparations for attacking New York after the expected junction of the second division of the French reinforcement were no more talked of. Indeed, many circumstances combined to render the present moment favorable for attempting something against them, and I was determined not to let it slip me.

Wherefore no time was lost in laying before Sir George Rodney my former plans for attacking the French force at Rhode Island, together with such authentic information as I had since received respecting the enemy's present situation, and in offering to him every possible *secondary assistance* of the army if he or Admiral Arbuthnot should now think any attempt against them practicable.[10] Indeed, the late brilliant victories and splendid fame of that spirited and active naval chief had inspired me with such implicit confidence in his judgment and zeal that I should not have hesitated to follow his lead in the prosecution of any plan he might have had to propose for the public good. And I was equally well assured of his animated cooperation and support in the execution of whatever I should offer, with the same view, to his consideration.

With this facile disposition and temper on both sides, every possible success was to be expected from our mutual exertions. We had consequently several very unreserved consultations together on the present critical posture of American affairs, the result of which was

9. See Clinton [to Eden], Sept. 1, below, p. 456.
10. See Clinton to Rodney, Sept. 18, below, pp. 457–458.

[the decision] that the French had been too long in possession of Rhode Island, and were too strongly reinforced by the rebels, to leave the smallest probability of success from a desultory move against them with the handful of troops my present strength could supply. We therefore mutually agreed not to attempt it, but to direct our united powers to the accomplishment of a very important enterprise which had long been the subject of my contemplation, and which I only waited for such an opportunity as the present to prosecute to effect.[11] The juncture appeared also to be most peculiarly and critically favorable, as the recently received intelligence of Lord Cornwallis' victory over the rebel southern army under Gates had spread terror and dismay through the country, and the attention of everyone within and without the lines was closely drawn to an armament I was just then assembling for an expedition to the Chesapeake,[12] the object of which (having been for some time talked of and known) had naturally lulled suspicion to sleep with respect to any other.

About eighteen months before the present period Mr. Arnold, a major general in the American service, had found means to intimate to me that, having cause to be dissatisfied with many late proceedings of the American Congress, particularly their alliance with France, he was desirous of quitting them and joining the cause of Great Britain, could he be certain of personal security and indemnification for whatever loss of property he might thereby sustain.[13] An overture of that

11. For the effects of Rodney's arrival on British planning see Willcox in *Journ. of Mod. Hist.*, *17*, 313–315. That discussion overlooks the fact that the unexpected reinforcement was in one way detrimental: it put out of the question a projected Franco-American attack on New York, and thereby precluded Sir Henry's scheme for trapping the attackers. On this point see Clinton to Germain, Oct. 11, below, pp. 463–464.

12. *Clinton's note:* Corps embarked were the Guards, Regiment of Bose, Eighty-second, Thirty-fourth, Fanning's [and] Watson's light infantry, Jägers, detachment of Seventeenth Dragoons, artillerymen (100), refugees, guides, pioneers, etc.—in all, 2800 rank and file.

13. The remainder of the chapter, beginning with this sentence, is the only substantial passage in the MS that has been printed—first, apparently, in Philip Henry Stanhope, Earl Mahon, *History of England from the Peace of Utrecht to the Peace of Versailles, 1713–1783* (7 vols., London, 1836–54), 7, Appendix, vii–xi, and frequently since. The accompanying extracts from the correspondence about André (below, pp. 457, 458–461) are omitted by Mahon but have been published elsewhere. The most complete description of Sir Henry's role in the affair is in his dispatch to Germain of Oct. 11 (printed below, pp. 462–466, from the draft in the CP), which does not seem to have been previously published in full. The other relevant correspondence is contained in Carl Van Doren, *Secret History of the American Revolution* (New York, 1941), chaps. viii–xv and appendix. The fullest modern accounts of the conspiracy are in Van Doren, in Flexner (*The Traitor and the Spy*, chaps. xxi, xxiii–xxviii), and in Willard M. Wallace, *Traitorous Hero: the Life and Fortunes of Benedict Arnold* (New York, 1954), chaps. xix–xx, xxii–xxv.

sort, coming from an officer of Mr. Arnold's ability and fame, could not but attract my attention; and, as I thought it possible that, like another General Monk, he might have repented of the part he had taken and wish to make atonement for the injuries he had done his country by rendering her some signal and adequate benefit,[14] I was of course liberal in making him such offers and promises as I judged most likely to encourage him in his present temper. A correspondence was after this opened between us under feigned names, in the course of which he from time to time transmitted to me most material intelligence, and with a view (as I supposed) of rendering us still more essential service he obtained in July, 1780, the command of all the enemy's forts in the Highlands, then garrisoned by about 4000 men.

The local importance of these posts has been already very fully described in the last volume of this history [chapters iii and vii]. It is therefore scarcely necessary to observe here that the obtaining possession of them at the present critical period would have been a most desirable circumstance, and that the advantages to be drawn from Mr. Arnold's having the command of them struck me with full force the instant I heard of his appointment. But the arrival of the French armament, the consequent expedition to Rhode Island, and the weakness of my own force (together with the then daily increase of Mr. Washington's) obliged me to wait for some more favorable opportunity before I attempted to put that gentleman's sincerity to the proof.[15]

In the meantime, wishing to reduce to an absolute certainty whether the person I had so long corresponded with was actually Major General Arnold, commanding at West Point, I acceded to a proposal made me to permit some officer in my confidence to have a personal conference with him, when everything might be more explicitly settled between us than it was possible to do by letter. And, as he required that my Adjutant General, Major André (who had chiefly conducted the correspondence with him, under the signature of John Anderson), should meet him for this purpose on neutral ground, I was induced to consent to his doing so from my great confidence in that officer's prudence and address. Some attempts toward a meeting had been accordingly made before Sir George Rodney's arrival. But, though the plans had been well laid, they were constantly frustrated by some untoward accident or other, one of which had very nearly cost Mr. Arnold his life.

14. The comparison with Monk came originally from Arnold in his first overtures to Clinton; see Van Doren, *Secret History*, pp. 198–199.
15. The foregoing paragraph is omitted in Mahon.

These disappointments made him, of course, cautious. And, as I now became anxious to forward the execution of my project while I could have that naval chief's assistance, and under so good a mask as the expedition for the Chesapeake (which enabled me to make every requisite preparation without being suspected), I consented to another proposal from General Arnold, for Major André to go to him by water from Dobbs Ferry in a boat which he would himself send for him under a flag of truce.[16] For I could have no reason to suspect that any bad consequence could possibly result to Major André from such a mode, as I had given it in charge to him *not to change his dress or name on any account,* or possess himself of writings by which the nature of his embassy might be traced; and I understood that after his business was finished he was to be sent back in the same way.

But, unhappily, none of these precautions were observed. On the contrary, General Arnold, for reasons which he judged important or perhaps (which is the most probable) losing at the moment his usual presence of mind, thought proper to drop the design of sending Major André back by water and prevailed upon him—or rather compelled him, as would appear by that unfortunate officer's letter to me [17]—to part with his uniform, and under a borrowed disguise to take a circuitous route to New York through the posts of the enemy under the sanction of his passport.[18] The consequence was, as might be expected, that he was stopped at Tarrytown and searched; and, certain papers being found about him concealed, he was (notwithstanding his passport) carried prisoner before Mr. Washington, to whom he candidly acknowledged his name and quality. Measures were of course immediately taken upon this to seize General Arnold. But that officer, being fortunate enough to receive timely notice of Major André's fate, effected his escape to a King's sloop lying off Teller's Point and came the next day to New York.

I was exceedingly shocked by this very unexpected accident, which not only totally ruined a most important project which had all the appearance of being in a happy train of success, but involved in danger and distress a confidential friend for whom I had, very deservedly, the warmest esteem. Not immediately knowing, however, the full extent of the misfortune, I did not then imagine the enemy could have any motive for pushing matters to extremity, as the bare detention of so valuable an officer's person might have given him a great power and advantage over me. And I was accordingly in hopes that an official

16. See Arnold to André, Sept. 15, below, p. 457.
17. See André to Clinton, Sept. 29, below, p. 460.
18. See Arnold to Clinton, Sept. 26, below, p. 460.

demand from me for his immediate release, as having been under the sanction of a flag of truce when he landed within his posts, might shorten his captivity, or at least stop his proceeding with rigor against him. But the cruel and unfortunate catastrophe convinced me that I was much mistaken in my opinion of both his policy and humanity. For delivering himself up (as it should seem) to the rancor excited by the near accomplishment of a plan which might have effectually restored the King's authority and tumbled him from his present exalted situation, he burnt with a desire of wreaking his vengeance on the principal actors in it. And consequently, regardless of the acknowledged worth and abilities of the amiable young man who had thus fallen into his hands, and in opposition to every principle of policy and call of humanity, he without remorse put him to a most ignominious death—and this at a moment when one of his generals was by his own appointment in actual conference with commissioners whom I had sent to treat with him for Major André's release.

The manner in which Major André was drawn to the enemy's shore —manifestly at the instance and under the sanction of the general officer who had the command of the district—and his being avowedly compelled by that officer to change his dress and name and return under his passport by land were circumstances which, as they certainly very much lessen the imputed criminality of his offense, ought to have at least softened the severity of the council of war's opinion respecting it, notwithstanding his imprudence in having possessed himself of the papers which they found on him, which, though they led to a discovery of the nature of the business that drew him to a conference with General Arnold, were not wanted (as they must have known) for my information. For they were not ignorant that I had myself been over every part of the ground on which the forts stood, and had of course made myself perfectly acquainted with everything necessary for facilitating an attack of them. Mr. Washington ought also to have remembered that I had never in any one instance punished the disaffected colonists within my power with death, but on the contrary had in several [instances] shown the most humane attention to his intercession, even in favor of avowed spies. His acting, therefore, in so cruel a manner in opposition to my earnest solicitations could not but excite in me the greatest surprise, especially as no advantage whatsoever could be possibly expected to his cause from putting the object of them to death. Nor could he be insensible—had he the smallest spark of honor in his own breast—that the example, though ever so terrible and ignominious, would never deter a British officer from treading in the same steps whenever the service of his country should require his exposing himself to the like danger in such a war. But the subject affects me too deeply to proceed, nor can my heart cease to bleed whenever I reflect on the very unworthy fate of this most amiable and valuable young man, who was adorned with the rarest endowments of education and nature and, had he lived, could not but have attained to the highest honors of his profession!

CHAPTER 16

Developments in the Chesapeake and the Carolinas, June to December, 1780

Three thousand British and German recruits arrive at New York. General Leslie's expedition sails. Admiral Arbuthnot sends three victualers he met at sea to Halifax without consulting the General, although he knew the army at New York was in danger of starving. Distressed state of the revolters. General Leslie arrives in the Chesapeake. Great advantages expected from his operations; but that general officer does not find it expedient to move immediately against the enemy's stores at Richmond and Petersburg, as suggested in his instructions, but stops at Portsmouth and lands his troops. Proposed expedition against Philadelphia laid aside for want of naval support, the King's ships having suffered from a storm. The rebels recover their spirits on hearing the news of Major Ferguson's defeat. Embarkation for Canada and loss by storm.

The Commander in Chief under no apprehensions for South Carolina, the army in that province amounting to 11,306 effectives, but his own at New York unequal in number to that of the enemy and in want of everything. A short account of Lord Cornwallis' operations in the southern district. Propriety of leaving His Lordship discretionary powers and permission to report to the Secretary of State. His orders, however, positive not to make any move beyond the borders of Carolina which can endanger the safety of Charleston or that province. The invasion of North Carolina is Lord Cornwallis' own suggestion, and only permitted by Sir Henry Clinton from his entire confidence in His Lordship's prudence. But the Commander in Chief very strongly recommends to His Lordship to previously seize a post in Cape Fear River, for the purpose of forwarding his supplies and supporting and encouraging the King's friends. Supposed consequences of His Lordship's slighting this precaution.

Dangerous dispersed state of the British posts on the frontier before the Battle of Camden. Obviated by Lord Rawdon's prudence. Gates' army defeated and dispersed. Sumter's corps dispersed also, immediately after, by Tarleton. Lord Cornwallis advances to Charlottetown. The affairs of South Carolina begin to assume the most flattering appearances, but everything thrown back into rebellion by the defeat of Major Ferguson, whom Lord Cornwallis had detached into Tryon

*County. This obliges Lord Cornwallis to fall suddenly back, and call
General Leslie's detachment to a nearer cooperation.*

THE UNFORTUNATE discovery of my design put an end, of course, to
the proposed move up the North River. Major General Leslie being
therefore immediately ordered to proceed with the embarked troops
agreeable to their original destination, they sailed from the Hook on
the 17th of October (the English fleet with the promised recruits
having arrived there two days before), and the armament cast anchor
in the Chesapeake on the 20th.

It has been already noticed that the very low state of our provision
stores was one of the causes which retarded my dispatching this expedition. I had, however, very early solicited Admiral Arbuthnot to
spare me convoys for some empty victualers which I wished to send to
Halifax and Charleston for a small supply, which I knew those garrisons could spare; and he had the goodness to tell me in his letter of
the 11th of September that he had appointed the *Rainbow, Camilla,*
and *Galatea* for that service. Two days after this the Admiral requested
I would spare him 500 head of cattle for the use of his fleet, which, I
own, somewhat surprised me from its coming so immediately after
I had laid open to him our distresses. I complied, notwithstanding,
with his requisition as far as I was able, reposing the most confident
hopes (on his recent promise respecting the convoys) that our wants
were in a train of being soon relieved. The reader will from hence
judge of my astonishment when I discovered, immediately after the
expedition had sailed, not only that the empty victualers had not yet
proceeded on their respective voyages but that Admiral Arbuthnot,
having accidently appeared at the Hook the day the English fleet arrived
there, had ordered away to Halifax three army victualers that accompanied it, thereby depriving us of this unexpected temporary relief
—which he very well knew was not wanted by the garrison of Halifax,
and had come most opportunely to remove the apprehensions of famine
which his own unaccountable neglect had excited in me for the troops
under my immediate command.[1]

But, notwithstanding this important service had been so long protracted, the present very distressed state of the disaffected colonists
(which fortunately came to my knowledge by the capture about this
time of their Hartford mail[2]) flattered me with the hopes that General

1. See Clinton to Arbuthnot, Oct. 29, and Arbuthnot to Clinton, Nov. 1, below,
pp. 469, 471.
2. See the address of the American general officers to their states, undated, and
Alexander Hamilton to Isaac Sears, Oct. 12, below, pp. 461–462, 466–467.

Leslie would even yet reach the upper James at a most critical moment not only to intercept the supplies for Gates' army (Petersburg and Richmond being the principal depots from whence all his convoys moved to him at Salisbury, by Taylor's Ferry on the Roanoke), but to increase and accelerate the confusion which began everywhere to appear in the rebel counsels. But my expectations were unfortunately frustrated by that general officer's considering it expedient to stop, contrary to the tenor of his instructions, at Portsmouth, in consequence of some intelligence he had received that the people of the country, having early notice of his coming, had thrown up batteries on the narrow parts of the river to obstruct his passage, and that the inhabitants of Nansemond suspected he was come to distress them.[3] All which, however, turned out in the sequel to have no foundation, and to have been probably suggested by interested persons merely to stop his proceeding further.

It had been my intention, as signified before, to have likewise dispatched another expedition into the Delaware for the purpose of destroying the military stores and magazines collected at Philadelphia, and with the hopes of further easing Lord Cornwallis by giving ample employment (in conjunction with General Leslie's operations on the upper James) to the three adjacent provinces, and thereby preventing their forwarding succors to Gates' army in Carolina.[4] But a violent storm, having so shattered the King's ships about this period that the Admiral could not spare frigates to accompany it, obliged me with much regret to relinquish that design, and to confine myself to the watching Mr. Washington's intentions—which, by his not detaching a man to the southward, seemed to be still turned toward New York.[5]

Indeed, the rebel affairs soon after this began to assume quite another face, the news of Major Ferguson's misfortune [6] having again revived their hopes and suddenly raised them, like that of Trenton, from the despondency into which they had been before thrown. However, as the force under Lord Cornwallis, when he should be joined by the recruits I was now sending him, would amount to 11,306 effectives, I flattered myself I had nothing to apprehend for the safety of South Carolina, which I had no doubt His Lordship, after his late check, would of course make the principal object of his attention, and postpone to some more favorable juncture his proposed attack of North

3. See Clinton's instructions to Leslie, Oct. 12, and Leslie to Clinton, Nov. 4, below, pp. 467, 472–473.
4. See above, p. 204.
5. See Clinton to Arbuthnot, Nov. 1, below, pp. 471–472.
6. The death of Ferguson and the destruction of his detachment in the Battle of King's Mountain, Oct. 7.

Carolina. But I must own I was not so much at my ease with respect to my own situation, as I wanted money, provisions, powder, and spare arms, as well as many other ordnance stores—in short, almost everything—while the army under my immediate command ([which] amounted on the 1st of November to 12,865 fit for duty) was scarcely adequate even to the defense of New York, had Mr. Washington attacked it after Sir George Rodney's departure with all the force he appeared to have it then in his power to bring against me.[7]

But, as Lord Cornwallis' operations in the southern district will be found from this period to have given the principal bias to those to the northward, and indeed to the subsequent fate of the war, it may not be impertinent to insert in this place a succinct relation of His Lordship's proceedings, with their consequences, from the time he took upon him that command to the present moment.

Although it has been the fashion to censure me for giving a subordinate general permission to report to and correspond with the Minister (it being supposed that from thence alone arose that clashing of plans which I so much complain of in my narrative [8]), I am persuaded that the slightest reflection on the distance and difficulty of communication between Charleston and New York will point out the propriety as well as the necessity of vesting the officer who commanded in the southern district not only with a liberty of sending the quickest and most direct intelligence of important events to His Majesty's ministers but, in most cases civil and military, with a discretionary power of acting according to the impulse and urgency of the present moment. These, I acknowledge, I conferred on Lord Cornwallis in the fullest latitude—except with respect to Charleston, the safety of which he was positively directed never to risk—not only from my great desire of omitting nothing which I thought likely to promote the King's service, but from the high sense I then entertained of His Lordship's zeal and abilities. If, therefore, it may appear that His Lordship has in any one instance abused the confidence I thus liberally reposed on him, he alone must be answerable to his country for the consequences, not his Commander in Chief, who could neither suspect nor guard against such misfortunes.

Having premised this much, I shall beg leave with the same candor to offer my sentiments on the tendency of His Lordship's subsequent conduct, without, however, considering myself as more responsible

7. See Clinton to Germain, Oct. 31, below, pp. 470–471.

8. *Narrative of Lieutenant-General Sir Henry Clinton, K.B., Relative to His Conduct during Part of His Command of the King's Troops in North America, Particularly to That Which Respects the Unfortunate Issue of the Campaign of 1781* (London, 1783), reprinted in Stevens, *Clinton-Cornwallis Controversy, 1,* 5–58.

or interested in the event than any other subject of the British Empire. It appears by Lord Cornwallis' letter of the 30th of June that the submission of General Williamson at Ninety-six had put an end to all resistance in South Carolina and that, having in consequence stationed his troops at certain distances along the frontier to cover the raising and establishing a militia, he went to Charleston and was then engaged in adjusting the civil and commercial arrangements of the province. He further tells me that the great scarcity of provisions in North Carolina and the heats of the summer would oblige him to postpone offensive operations until the beginning of September, when he proposed to begin his march into that province, having in the meantime recommended it to our friends there to remain quiet until the King's troops should be ready to give them effectual support. This invasion of North Carolina had been from the first a very favorite object with His Lordship, from a persuasion, as he tells me in the same letter, that the possessing that province would prove an effectual barrier for South Carolina and Georgia, and enable him to spare a part of his troops for operations in the Chesapeake.[9]

I own that, though I wished every necessary measure might be taken for more clearly ascertaining the entire submission of South Carolina and securing to us a fast hold of that most valuable province before he marched any considerable part of the King's troops beyond its borders, yet, being equally ignorant with His Lordship of the amount of the force which de Kalb was drawing together for attacking him, I did not in my instructions restrict His Lordship from acting offensively *except when it might be inconsistent with the security of Charleston, which he was ever unequivocally ordered to regard as a primary object.* Accordingly I contented myself with *recommending to him the mode —by galleys and a few troops up the Cape Fear River—as the most eligible for giving succor to our friends in North Carolina at that season.*[10]

And, indeed, I was so very sensible of the utility and importance of this measure that I should have carried it into execution myself before I left the southward, could the proper naval assistance have been spared for it. For I am persuaded that, if His Lordship had done so immediately, not only the misfortune which soon after happened to a body of loyalists under Colonel Moore might have been avoided,[11] but de Kalb would have probably found it difficult to advance even a day's march

9. Stevens, *Clinton-Cornwallis Controversy, 1*, 223–225.

10. The instructions are in Clinton to Cornwallis, June 1, *ibid.*, pp. 213–214; the advice to move into the Cape Fear is in the same to the same, June 8, CP. For a discussion of the differing strategic ideas of the two Generals at this time see Willcox in *Am. Hist. Rev., 52*, 6–7.

11. See Ward, *War of the Revolution, 2*, 706–708.

through that province. Nor could the scattered debris of General Gates' army have possibly escaped the vigilance of the King's friends whom the having such an asylum and support, to fly to in case of a check, would have undoubtedly encouraged to rise and fall upon those affrightened stragglers in their precipitate flight from the Battle of Camden.[12] But from the neglect of this precaution the enemy's army was permitted to receive supplies by water by Albemarle Sound, to roam unmolested in search of food for nearly six weeks through that famished country, and to encourage by its presence the disaffected of both provinces to reassemble in arms and throw everything back into rebellion. In short, the revolt became soon after so general that it is only wonderful we suffered so little from it, especially as the King's troops were at that time confined in small posts over an extended frontier, each of which was liable to be carried, one after the other, had the enemy managed with common ability and address, and [had] the danger not been partly obviated by Lord Rawdon's vigilance, whose very officer-like conduct on this emergency does him the highest honor.

Lord Cornwallis was now hurried away from Charleston by intelligence from Lord Rawdon that the rebel forces under Gates, having penetrated into South Carolina, were advanced to within a small distance of Camden. And two days after His Lordship joined the King's army he obtained a most complete victory over the enemy, whose militia had very early in the action flung away their arms; and every other corps was so broken and dispersed that their Commander in Chief had scarcely a single attendant to accompany his flight to Charlottetown [Charlotte], from whence he posted with the utmost precipitation to Hillsboro.[13] This very brilliant success against so great a superiority of numbers was almost beyond hope. But Lord Cornwallis' conduct certainly merited it, nor can too much be said in praise of His Lordship's ready decision to meet rather than wait the enemy's attack under his then circumstances, as well as the presence of mind and promptitude with which he availed himself of General Gates' injudicious attempt to change the disposition of his army at the moment of coming into action—a maneuver which must have been extremely hazardous with the best troops but [from which], with such militia as the chief of his was composed of (whom all writers speak so slightingly of), nothing but ruin could be expected. That officer was consequently punished for it as he deserved.[14]

12. Clinton here quotes in a note the remarks about the North Carolina loyalists in Cornwallis' letter to him of Aug. 6, below, p. 448.
13. Cornwallis to Germain, Aug. 21, below, pp. 452–454.
14. I.e., punished by being defeated. Although Congress ordered a court of inquiry on Gates, it never convened.

The victory of Camden and the entire dispersion of Sumter's corps two days after by Lieutenant Colonel Tarleton had certainly greatly humbled the disaffected in South Carolina, and seemed to promise a restoration of tranquillity to every part of that province.[15] And, indeed, there is every reason to believe this might have been the case could Lord Cornwallis have attended somewhat longer to that alone, and no unlucky check had intervened on our side to revive the spirits of the revolters and put them again in motion. But His Lordship was, of course, desirous of extending the consequences of his success as far as and as expeditiously as possible. He therefore immediately dispatched messengers into North Carolina with directions to the King's friends to take arms, and promised that he would march thither without loss of time to their support, his intention being, as he tells me in his letter of the 23d of August, to endeavor to get as soon as possible to Hillsboro, and there assemble and try to arrange the friends who were inclined to arm in our favor, and so form a very large magazine for the winter of flour and meal from the country, *and of rum, salt, etc., from Cross Creek*—in short, to engage in *solid* operations in North Carolina in support of them.[16]

However, we find these flattering appearances were not in the sequel realized to the expected extent. For His Lordship very soon after tells me the indefatigable Sumter is again in the field. And the disaffection of the country east of Santee is so great that the account of our victory could not penetrate into it—any person daring to speak of it being threatened with instant death.[17] There quickly followed, likewise, a very serious insurrection at the ceded lands in Georgia, which was stirred up by a Colonel Clarke, who had actually attacked and very nearly carried the British post at Augusta; and corps of mounted rebel

---

The text at this point contains the following paragraph, which Clinton seems to have deleted: "Nor should I here omit paying to Lord Rawdon my small tribute of applause, for so judiciously remaining on his ground when the King's troops to his right pursued the enemy's left on their breaking—as by attempting to force the enemy's left [an error for "right"], composed as it was of their best troops, strongly posted, he risked a check; whereas, by remaining on the defensive till Lord Cornwallis completed the rout of the enemy's left, he ensured a victory which otherwise might have been doubtful."

If Sir Henry meant to delete this passage because he doubted its accuracy, he was well advised. It is wrong on every count. Rawdon did attack repeatedly; he was counterattacked by the Americans under de Kalb, and barely held his own until he was rescued by the British right and Tarleton's cavalry. See Ward, *War of the Revolution, 2,* 725–730.

15. *Ibid.,* pp. 733–734; Wallace, *Appeal to Arms,* pp. 213–215.

16. "him" in the MS. For the text of the letter see Stevens, *Clinton-Cornwallis Controversy, 1,* 259.

17. *Ibid.,* pp. 261–262.

militia still ranged the country, to the great annoyance of the loyal-ists.[18] It consequently appeared to His Lordship necessary to remain on the frontiers of South Carolina somewhat longer than he at first proposed, that he might take measures for rooting out these lurking remains of rebellion before he moved. With this view, he judged it proper to punish the late revolters with the utmost severity, by seques-tering the lands and property of those in rebellion, and giving orders that all the militia who had enrolled themselves in the King's service, and had afterward deserted and been taken in arms against us, should be forthwith executed. His Lordship had been likewise induced to remove a number of the principal citizens from Charleston to St. Augustine in East Florida "on account of the extreme insolence of their behavior upon the advance of Gates' army, the threats with which they had in the most daring manner endeavored to intimidate our friends, and the correspondence which they had constantly kept up with the enemy, which rendered either *that* or *their close confine-ment* absolutely necessary for the security of that important post." [19]

It was, therefore, the middle of September before Lord Cornwallis began his proposed march. And His Lordship soon after reached Charlotteburg [Charlotte], where it was his intention to halt until the sick he had left behind should be able to join him, having some time before detached Major Ferguson into Tryon County with the small remains of his own corps and a few hundred of the Ninety-six militia "to keep alive the spirits of the King's friends in North Carolina and prevent their being damped by the slowness of his motions." [20]

This leads me, of course, to mention an event which was immediately productive of the worst consequences to the King's affairs in South Carolina, and unhappily proved the first link in a chain of evils that followed each other in regular succession until they at last ended in the total loss of America. That noble General had been very early of opinion that the South Carolina militia had not sufficient confidence in themselves to be trusted without regular troops; and, indeed, sev-eral of the militia corps that were raised on the frontier, he seemed to think, had given such repeated proofs of cowardice and treachery that no reliance could be placed on them. His Lordship had, moreover, informed me in one of his letters, dated August 29, 1780, *that, though Major Ferguson told him he could depend upon a corps of militia he had with him for doing their duty and fighting well, he was sorry to say*

18. Rawdon to Leslie, Oct. 24, below, pp. 468–469. The "ceded lands" were territory that the Creek Indians had ceded to Georgia by the Treaty of Augusta in 1773.

19. The source of the quotation cannot be located, but the substance is in Corn-wallis to Germain, Sept. 19, Stevens, *Clinton-Cornwallis Controversy, 1,* 267–268.

20. Cornwallis to Clinton, Dec. 3, *ibid.,* p. 303.

"that his own experience as well as that of every other officer was totally against him." [21] We shall consequently be naturally surprised to find His Lordship, notwithstanding the decided opinions he had just given to the Minister and me on this subject, immediately detaching Major Ferguson with this very corps into Tryon County, to the west of the Catawba at a very considerable distance from his army, and there leaving them for several weeks without making the smallest move to sustain them. The result was that a body of mountaineers from the back settlements, being encouraged by the extreme distance and large branches of that impracticable river which lay between Lord Cornwallis' post at Charlottetown and this devoted detachment, pursued rapidly on horseback and, coming up with it on King's Mountain, so overpowered it by numbers that after a sharp contest, in which that valuable officer and several of his men lost their lives, they carried off the whole party with about 14,000 stand of small arms—an article they then very much wanted and which was beginning to grow extremely scarce with us, owing chiefly to the army's wanton destruction of them after the Battle of Camden.

It does not appear how early Lord Cornwallis was informed of the danger with which Major Ferguson was threatened, but the extracts of intercepted letters in the notes [22] seem to imply he had sent His Lordship notice of it some days before his misfortune. Yet on the other hand it is presumable, from Lieutenant Colonel Tarleton's not being detached to sustain him before the 10th of October, that either His Lordship did not hear of it in time or that he did not look upon it as very serious.[23] It is, however, a matter much to be lamented that during the whole of His Lordship's command he was certainly too apt to

21. *Ibid.*, p. 263. Clinton adds, in a note, a sentence from Cornwallis' letter to him of Sept. 22 that is omitted in the extract printed in Stevens: "As I have found the militia fail so totally when put to the trial in this province, *I am determined* to try provincial corps alone in the next."

22. Ferguson to Cornwallis, *ca.* Sept. 6, and Cornwallis to Ferguson, Sept. 23, below, pp. 456, 458.

23. *Clinton's note:* Extract from Lieutenant Colonel Tarleton's *History*, [p. 165:] "*On the 10th of October* Earl Cornwallis gave orders to Lieutenant Colonel Tarleton to march with the light infantry, the British Legion, and a three-pounder to assist Major Ferguson." This is Colonel Tarleton's account. Yet Lieutenant Colonel Balfour writes to Sir Henry Clinton, in a letter dated 20 October, that "*my last letters* from Lord Cornwallis are dated on *the 7th instant, when he was ignorant of Ferguson's affairs.* Although suspecting a stroke might be made against him, *he had* detached the Legion to support him, *who were within a very short distance of him when the action happened.*"

How are these two stories to be reconciled? We may at least infer from the latter that Colonel Balfour felt the impropriety of Lord Cornwallis' not sustaining Ferguson, and wished to give the best gloss he could to His Lordship's conduct. [Part of the last sentence is deleted in the MS without substitution; the italics are presumably Clinton's throughout, although Balfour's letter is not extant.]

THE AMERICAN REBELLION

risk detachments without proper support, which is the more to be wondered at as Lexington, Bennington, Danbury, and Trenton were recent instances which His Lordship could not have forgot (and some on the enemy's part also), without referring to those of which every military history is full. And, surely, never was the trite apothegm *that the greatest events often proceed from little causes* more fatally confirmed than by the present check—which, though in itself confessedly trifling, overset in a moment all the happy effects of our successes at Charleston and His Lordship's glorious victory at Camden, and so encouraged that spirit of rebellion in both Carolinas that it never could be afterward humbled. For no sooner had the news of it spread through the country than multitudes of disaffected flew to arms from all parts, and menaced every British post on both frontiers, "carrying terror even to the gates of Charleston." [24]

When Lord Cornwallis first heard of this misfortune and the effect it was likely to have on South Carolina, he suddenly abandoned the post at Charlottetown and returned with his whole force to that province. But the precipitancy with which this retrograde movement was made contributed, I fear, not a little to make the revolt more general [25] and to increase the despondency of the King's friends, especially in North Carolina, where the loyalists whom His Lordship's presence had encouraged to show themselves, being exposed to persecution and ruin by his retreat, threw away forever after all their confidence of support from the King's army. This, however, it is presumed, might have been obviated had we had at the time a respectable post at Wilmington (as I had long before recommended to His Lordship), to which the loyalists of that province might resort with their effects whenever they were likely to be borne down by their enemies. [26]

The instant I heard of Major Ferguson's defeat, I foresaw most of the consequences likely to result from it. And I accordingly sent immediate instructions to Major General Leslie to hold himself in readiness for a sudden move to Cape Fear River, [27] though I was not with-

24. Cornwallis to Clinton, Dec. 3, below, pp. 476–477.

25. *Clinton's note:* "Owing to the badness of the road, the ignorance of the guides, the darkness of the night, or *some other unknown cause*, the British rear guard destroyed or left behind near twenty wagons loaded with supplies for the army, a printing press, and other stores belonging to public departments." *Vide* Tarleton's *History*, page 167.

26. Cornwallis hoped to establish such a post. See Rawdon to Leslie, Oct. 24, below, pp. 468–469.

27. Clinton to Leslie, Nov. 2, below, p. 472. Clinton adds a note referring to his original instructions of Oct. 12 (below, p. 467), where he recommended raiding Richmond and Petersburg and establishing a post on the James—"what Leslie did not but Arnold did effect with half his force." For this subsequent expedition under Arnold see below, chap. xvii.

out hopes that the destruction of Gates' magazines at Petersburg (which I had flattered myself General Leslie would have struck at by the 20th) might put it out of that officer's power to avail himself of this unfortunate *contretemps*. It pleased me, therefore, to find that I had so far anticipated the wishes of Lord Cornwallis—who, as Lord Rawdon informed me, had himself requested that general officer to remove thither with his whole detachment.[28] But, unfortunately, none of my expectations or wishes succeeded. For it soon after appeared that His Lordship had changed his mind, and sent him counter orders to go into the port of Charleston for the purpose of joining him at Winnsboro.[29]

This disappointment gave me, I own, a good deal of concern. Because, though it was by no means my wish to see His Lordship re-enter North Carolina before he had totally subdued the rebel country between Pedee and Santee and had restored tranquillity to the rest of South Carolina, yet the pressing necessity of immediately attending to the forlorn situation of our friends there and, if possible, of recovering their confidence before they were entirely lost to us seemed to render the measure of securing a post on Cape Fear River absolutely necessary; and I consequently did not doubt His Lordship was equally sensible of its importance and would have lost no time in employing at least a part of the Chesapeake detachment on that service.[30] Indeed, Lord Rawdon had informed me "that Lord Cornwallis was resolved to remain for the present in a position which might secure the frontiers without separating his force," and that, though His Lordship foresaw all the difficulties of a defensive war, yet he thought they could not "be weighed against the dangers which must have attended an obstinate adherence to his former plan." [31]

But in a subsequent letter he tells me on further consideration His Lordship, reflecting on the difficulties of a defensive war and the hopes which I would probably build on his success in that quarter, had thought it advisable not only to recommend to General Leslie a cooperation in Cape Fear River, but even to make it his request, being more particularly induced to invite him to that point from a supposition that I would not want those troops during the winter, and because

28. Rawdon to Leslie, Oct. 29, Stevens, *Clinton-Cornwallis Controversy*, 1, 277–280.
29. Cornwallis to Clinton, Dec. 3, *ibid.*, p. 308 (omitted in the extract printed below); see also Willcox in *Am. Hist. Rev.*, 52, 8–9.
30. Rawdon to Leslie, Oct. 31, below, p. 470.
31. Rawdon to Clinton, Oct. 29, Stevens, *Clinton-Cornwallis Controversy*, 1, 279. "If His Lordship felt thus before the loss of Ferguson and all his light troops," Clinton adds in a note, "how must he have felt after?"

they might join me from thence "in the spring scarcely later than should they, on the approach of that season, sail from any part of the Chesapeake." [32] And Lord Cornwallis himself points out those to be his wishes in so clear a manner [33] that I could not possibly have any suspicion of His Lordship's so suddenly altering them until I accidentally discovered he had done so, by opening some letters from Charleston directed to Major General Leslie on His Majesty's service. By these it further appeared that the greatest apprehensions were now entertained for the safety of South Carolina, and that the immediate junction of General Leslie's detachment was judged absolutely necessary to enable His Lordship to repel the invasion with which that province was threatened.[34]

The King's affairs before this misfortune were going on in the happiest train. The spirit of disaffection in the southern colonies had received a rude shock by Gates' defeat; and the appearance of Sir George Rodney's fleet in the harbor of New York, together with the distresses and discontents which at this time prevailed in Mr. Washington's army, had cast a desponding gloom over those to the northward. This was still further increased by my preparations for a descent in the Chesapeake, which I found by intercepted letters had spread the greatest alarm among the enemy.[35] So melancholy a reverse was consequently afflicting in proportion as it was totally unexpected. Nor was I insensible to the extreme mortification Lord Cornwallis must have suffered from seeing himself exposed to such serious alarm by the return of an army which he had not three months before, as he thought, so completely annihilated that not even a guard of six men could be collected to cover its General's flight to Hillsboro.

I am, however, clearly of opinion that the unpromising turn which our affairs took at this time in South Carolina was the natural consequence of Major Ferguson's disaster and Lord Cornwallis' sudden retreat from Charlottetown. For a general panic and despondency appear to have immediately seized the militia and almost every other loyalist in that province. Nor were matters likely to be recovered by the subsequent operations of His Majesty's regular troops, who in some detached skirmishes had been sometimes worsted, or came off at least with doubtful success which, furnishing the enemy with plausible pretenses for crying victory, soon encouraged the whole country to flock in arms to General Sumter, who, by these means and the junc-

32. Rawdon to Clinton, Oct. 31, Stevens, *Clinton-Cornwallis Controversy, 1,* 284.
33. Cornwallis to Leslie, Nov. 12, below, p. 474.
34. See Balfour to Leslie [Nov., 1780], below, p. 471.
35. The letters are those referred to above, p. 220 n. 2.

tion of Branan, Clarke, etc., had now formed a very respectable force to the southwest of the Broad River. General Smallwood likewise had advanced early in November with about 2000 men and encamped between Charlottetown and the borders of South Carolina, where it was confidently reported he was joined by General Gates with 1200 Continentals and 300 cavalry.

The necessity of driving back this army and maintaining a superiority on both his flanks was Lord Cornwallis' inducement (as he tells me in his letter of December the 3d) to relinquish the proposed descent in Cape Fear River and draw General Leslie to a closer cooperation with the troops under his own immediate command. That general officer arrived accordingly, with the detachment under his command, in the port of Charleston on the 14th of December. And the Guards, Regiment of Bose, and Jägers [36] marched immediately after their landing to join the royal army at Winnsboro, where Lord Cornwallis was preparing for his second invasion of North Carolina by the upper roads, His Lordship having allotted for this service the brigade of Guards, Twenty-second and Thirty-third Regiments, the two battalions of the Seventy-first, Jägers, Regiment of Bose, the cavalry and infantry of the Legion, and the North Carolina Regiment, while six British, three German, and nine provincial battalions were left for the protection of Charleston and the frontier of South Carolina in his absence, under the direction of Colonel Lord Rawdon and Lieutenant Colonel Balfour, the latter of whom had the charge of the capital as commandant.

The reinforcement under General Leslie which was thus added to the service of the Carolinas consisted of a brigade of Guards, Hessian Regiment of Bose, provincial King's American Regiment, a battalion of light infantry selected from all the provincial corps in the New York district, a detachment from the German Jägers, and detachments from the Seventeenth Light Dragoons, and British and German artillery, amounting in the whole to about 2233 of as good troops as any general officer need wish to take with him into the field. Besides these they were accompanied by the remains of the flank and two other companies of the Eighty-second Regiment, and the small debris of the Eighty-fourth (forming together between them three or four hundred men), with the former of which Major Craig afterward held the lower district of North Carolina in obedience to His Majesty's government for several months, and afforded protection to all the loyalists of that

36. *Clinton's note:* Fifteen hundred and thirty rank and file; *vide* General Leslie's letter to Lord George Germain, December 19, 1780 [printed in Tarleton, *History*, pp. 242–243].

province who fled to him after Lord Cornwallis' dereliction of the Carolinas.

Yet His Lordship is pleased to tell me in his letter of the 22d of December (even before he had himself seen a single man of this reinforcement) that the *species* of troops which composed it "are, exclusive of the Guards and Regiment of Bose, *exceedingly bad*." To account for so extraordinary a declaration would have, therefore, greatly puzzled me had not His Lordship furnished me with a clue in the same letter, by saying "I think it but justice to the troops serving in this district to state the fact, lest the services performed by the southern army should appear inadequate to what might be expected from the *numbers* of which it may appear to consist." [37] By which it would seem that His Lordship himself had his doubts respecting the propriety of turning his face to the north before the tranquillity of the south was restored or the defenses of Charleston, which had been thrown down by his order, were rebuilt, as such conduct must undoubtedly appear to be contrary to the words of his instructions, which unequivocally directed His Lordship to make no move of the troops under his command that could endanger that important post. His Lordship might also have had a foreboding of the train of evils which were to attend his subsequent operations, and wished to prepare in time this plausible excuse for them. For how else is it possible to reconcile so underground a condemnation of these unreviewed troops with the ardent thanks which His Lordship had but a few weeks before sent me, through Lord Rawdon and in his own letters, for the *very effectual measures I had taken to forward his operations and the ample manner in which I had complied with his wishes*, as what I had sent was more than he expected and full as much as I could spare? [38]

37. Stevens, *Clinton-Cornwallis Controversy*, 1, 313.
38. Rawdon to Leslie, Oct. 24, and Cornwallis to Clinton, Dec. 3, below, pp. 468–469, 476–479. Other reasons, connected with the home government, may also have underlain the change in Cornwallis' attitude; see Willcox in *Am. Hist. Rev.*, 52, 9–10.

CHAPTER 17

The Second Chesapeake Expedition and the Feud with Arbuthnot, November to December, 1780

Present state of circumstances prevents Sir Henry Clinton from immediately replacing the Chesapeake corps on Major General Leslie's removal to Carolina, but he determines to do it as soon as he can risk one for that service. Admiral Arbuthnot proposes to detach six ships of the line to the West Indies. Sir Henry Clinton remonstrates against his weakening his squadron, and points out the pernicious consequences likely to follow the enemy's obtaining a naval superiority on the American coast. The Admiral consents at last to retain the whole of his present force.

Brigadier General Arnold directed in consequence to proceed without delay to Virginia. Sketch of the instructions given to him, and Sir Henry Clinton's chief objects in sending expeditions to the Chesapeake. No idea, however, entertained of engaging at present in solid operation in that quarter, which is explicitly communicated to Lord Cornwallis. *Sir Henry Clinton's principal reasons for choosing Brigadier General Arnold to command this expedition. But Lord Cornwallis is left at liberty to appoint another general officer to it should His Lordship see expedient, and he is accompanied by Lieutenant Colonels Dundas and Simcoe, with whom he is to consult before he undertakes any operation of moment. Another rebel mail captured, which contains important information and shows the present enterprise to be very critically timed. Expedition fleet sails from Sandy Hook on the 20th December [and] meets with bad weather, which separates four ships from the convoy, having on board above 400 troops; and the Brigadier arrives in Hampton Roads on the 30th with the remainder— with which, though scarcely amounting to 1000 men, he immediately proceeds up James River and destroys a valuable foundry and all the public stores he can meet with, to a very considerable amount.*

No definite promise even yet received from administration respecting reinforcements, but very liberal assurances that attention will be paid to all Sir Henry Clinton's requisitions and that Admiral Arbuthnot, whose want of cordial cooperation Sir Henry Clinton had complained of, will be immediately removed from the command in North America to that at Jamaica. The refugees enter into articles

233

of association, and a board of directors formed by the King's order for the conduct and management of their affairs.

SIR GEORGE RODNEY's fleet being about to depart for the West Indies when I received Major General Leslie's information of his intention to remove to Carolina with the troops under his command, together with the then situation and strength of Mr. Washington's army, were circumstances that put it absolutely out of my power to immediately replace the Virginia detachment, though I was still fully sensible of the great advantages likely to arise from our possessing a naval station in the lower district of that province and [from] the pursuing my original plan of striking at the enemy's depots at Petersburg and Richmond, which the general officer I sent thither had been unfortunately diverted from.[1] I was determined, however, to do it, the instant circumstances should admit of my risking a corps for that service and Vice Admiral Arbuthnot be disposed to supply the requisite naval protection. For, although that officer appeared to be perfectly willing to comply with my wishes in this point, yet I could not with prudence hazard an expedition from my army under its present circumstances unless I could be assured of the means of sustaining the few troops that might be spared for it, should they be menaced by a superior force.

And this was what the Vice Admiral certainly could not warrant as long as he persisted in his resolution of quitting Gardiners Bay and detaching Rear Admiral Graves to the West Indies with six ships of the line—as his remaining force would have been thereby reduced considerably below that of Monsieur de Ternay at Rhode Island, who would assuredly not have failed, in conjunction with Mr. Washington, to avail himself of such an opportunity to strike at our uncovered posts. Besides, by thus obtaining the command of the sound the enemy might have easily thrown across it to Long Island any number of the French troops they pleased, which, with the numerous disaffected they would find there, might soon render our situation at New York very critical. These considerations obliged me, therefore, to suspend that enterprise for a while, as well as totally to lay aside another which I had in contemplation up the Delaware; and it was not without much difficulty and trouble that I could convince the Vice Admiral of the

1. Rodney left on Nov. 16, after a two-month stay that had accomplished nothing; Clinton hoped that he would return in the spring as Arbuthnot's successor. The remaining British naval forces were occupied in blockading the French at Rhode Island, and Sir Henry was unwilling to detach to the Chesapeake because he was again obsessed with the danger of an American attack on New York. See Willcox in *Journ. of Mod. Hist.*, 17, 314–316, 318 and n. 58; Clinton to Germain, Nov. 12, below, p. 473.

evil tendency of the measures he was going to pursue. He was, however, at last pleased to yield to the force of my reasoning against his weakening his squadron.[2]

And Brigadier General Arnold was consequently, immediately after, ordered to proceed to the Chesapeake with about 1800 men, with similar instructions to those I had given to Major General Leslie, but rather more positive with respect to the establishing a post at Portsmouth on Elizabeth River, which that officer had represented as "*the key to the wealth of Virginia and Maryland*"; and [Leslie] had left the works he threw up there entire, in hopes of our reoccupying the same ground.[3] He [Arnold] was likewise directed to prepare materials for building a number of boats, etc., and to collect a naval force as soon as possible in Albemarle Sound, for the purpose of annoying the enemy's communications and trade and securing means of intelligence, or even of a retreat for his detachment in case a superior French fleet should take a temporary possession of the Chesapeake.[4]

In short, my chief objects in sending expeditions to the Chesapeake were for the present, as suggested before, to endeavor to destroy the stores collected at the head of James River for the supply of Gates' army, and to lay hold of some convenient post at its mouth for covering frigates—from whence we might obstruct the enemy's trade in those waters and, by commanding that noble river, prevent their forming depots on its banks for the service of Carolina, and consequently [their] moving in any considerable force to the southward of it. But I must say that I had not at this time the smallest idea of engaging in solid operations there for the particular purpose of conquering Virginia, as my resources were certainly by no means equal to an attempt of that magnitude, which it will appear that I ever considered as most hazardous without the support of an assured permanent superiority by sea. And these sentiments had been explicitly communicated to Earl Cornwallis at the time I sent Major General Leslie thither.[5] Nor did the copies of my instructions to Brigadier General Arnold which were now transmitted to His Lordship intimate that they had undergone the smallest change.

It may likewise be not improper to mention here that I was induced to select Brigadier General Arnold for this service from the very high

2. See the correspondence between Clinton and Arbuthnot, Dec. 9–13, below, pp. 479–481; Willcox in *Journ. of Mod. Hist.*, *17*, 317–318.

3. Leslie to Clinton, Nov. 19, Stevens, *Clinton–Cornwallis Controversy*, *1*, 299.

4. See Clinton's instructions to Arnold, below, pp. 482–483. Clinton presumably explained in conversation several of the points mentioned in the text; they are not included in the instructions, or in his only extant letter to Arnold in Virginia.

5. Clinton to Cornwallis, Nov. 6, below, p. 473.

estimation in which he was held among the enemy for active intrepidity in the execution of military enterprises, and from a persuasion that he would exert himself to the utmost to establish an equal fame with us in this first essay of his capacity. I had it also in prospect that the confidence I thus appeared to place in an officer who had acted against us might be a strong incitement to other able leaders of the rebel army to desert their cause and seek employment in that of the King, where their advantages and emoluments were likely to be so infinitely more considerable and certain. I left it, however, in Lord Cornwallis' option to continue that officer in the command of the Chesapeake corps or not, as he should see expedient; and I had the precaution to guard against the consequences of my happening to be mistaken in my opinions by sending with him two officers whose judgment and steadiness I was assured of, whom he was directed to always consult previous to his engaging in any operation of moment.[6] But Brigadier General Arnold's active and spirited conduct on this service fully evinced that my caution was more prudent than necessary, and that he very justly merited the high military character his past actions with the enemy had procured him.

I was also further incited to expedite the present expedition by accounts that had been published by the rebels of a check which another of Lord Cornwallis' detachments under Major Wemyss was said to have lately received,[7] in expectation that the success I flattered myself would attend this move might help to counteract the exultations of the enemy, and prevent the pernicious effect they might otherwise have in precipitating the defection of South Carolina. The capture of another rebel mail had, moreover, opened to me some knowledge of the arrangements of Congress for raising an army for the war, which I found had created much discontent among their officers and were likely soon to be followed by a considerable diminution of their present force.[8] From all which I was persuaded that I had not much opposition to apprehend, and that a fortunate blow in the Chesapeake at this critical moment might be followed by the happiest and most decisive consequences.

The expedition fleet sailed accordingly from Sandy Hook on the 20th of December, and arrived in Hampton Roads on the 30th—except three transports with between four and five hundred troops on board, which

6. Clinton to Cornwallis, Dec. 13, and instructions to Arnold, Dec. 14, below, pp. 481–483.
7. See Cornwallis to Clinton, Dec. 3, pp. 477–478.
8. See Sullivan to the President of the Council of New Hampshire, Nov. 15, 19, Pickering to Trumbull, Nov. 20, Lee to Gordon, Nov. 21, and Lyman to Wanton, Nov. 24, below, pp. 474–476.

did not reach the place of their destination before the 4th of January. Brigadier General Arnold, however, looking upon his success to depend more upon expedition than numbers, did not hesitate to proceed immediately up James River with what he had; and in the space of a few days, with scarcely 1000 men, he effected the destruction of a valuable foundry for cannon, etc., seven miles above its falls, a large quantity of public stores, and a great number of vessels richly laden, in that river and the Appomattox, thereby spreading terror and alarm through the country and doing a most essential injury to the enemy and their allies.

In this situation were our affairs at the close of the year 1780, without my having received the smallest reinforcement to the army under my immediate command (which did not now exceed 11,929 rank and file [9]) or any definite promise upon which I could venture to form an operative plan for the ensuing campaign. I had, however, the satisfaction to receive from the American Minister the most liberal assurances that the King and all His Majesty's confidential servants were strongly disposed to comply with all my requisitions, as far as the ability of Great Britain could enable them, and that His Majesty, being sensible of the inconveniences which must arise to his service from the want of confidence between the Commanders in Chief of the land and sea forces, had been graciously pleased to appoint Admiral Arbuthnot to relieve Sir Peter Parker in the command of Jamaica, and that another flag officer would be immediately named to the command in North America.[10]

Toward the close of this year I received a letter from His Majesty's Secretary of State for American Affairs, with the King's commands to employ the zeal of his faithful refugee subjects within the British lines in annoying the seacoasts of the revolted provinces and distressing their trade. And Governors Franklin and Martin, together with Messrs. Ruggles, Wanton, Cox, Ludlow, Lutwische, Rome, and Leonard be-

9. *Clinton's note:* Distribution and strength of the army in North America on the 31st December 1780:

	Rank and file fit for duty:	Effectiveness:
At New York and posts depending	11,929	15,780
Under the command of Lord Cornwallis	9107	13,382
West Florida, Nova Scotia, Bermudas, and Providence	3948	4998
	24,984	34,160

10. Germain to Clinton, Oct. 4, 13, below, pp. 462, 467–468.

ing approved by His Majesty, I forthwith gave to those gentlemen and others a commission for forming themselves into a board of directors for the conduct and management of this business, and to recommend to me such persons as they should judge proper to receive commissions for commanding the loyalists who should associate under them. I think it proper, however, to mention that, having no other concern in the institution of this board than the following the orders I had received and complying with its requisitions for armed vessels, boats, ordnance, ammunition, provisions, etc., as far as my abilities and the service admitted, I neither claim merit from nor do I consider myself as responsible for any of its transactions, which shall be faithfully recorded in the course of this history whenever they lead to consequences that deserve notice.

CHAPTER 18

The Revolt of the American Line and the Cowpens Campaign, January, 1781

Discontents in Mr. Washington's army. Pennsylvania line revolts, and demands of Congress their arrears of pay and clothing and their discharges according to the terms of their enlistment. Sir Henry Clinton moves his elite to Staten Island, to be in readiness to cover a junction with him should they be so disposed, and sends out messengers to offer payment on that condition of all their demands without requiring any other return besides their allegiance. One messenger too many is sent; he is discovered. The revolters deliver up his [Clinton's] messengers to General Wayne and enter into treaty with a committee of Congress. Part of the Jersey Brigade follow the example of the Pennsylvanians. Their grievances accommodated in the same way. Some observations on the cheerfulness with which the King's troops went on this service at a most rigorous season of the year.

A very curious anecdote respecting the good will, discipline, and zeal of the British army, and the complete order and state of readiness in which the Quartermaster General's trains were found on this very sudden and unexpected emergency. This mode of supply first established by Sir William Howe, afterward adopted by Sir Henry Clinton. Much preferable to the old one of depending upon the country. Reasons why. Illiberal advantage taken of the great expense attending it to accuse Sir Henry Clinton of inattention to economy. This shown to be without foundation, as well as the insinuation by the Commissioners of Public Accounts, in their seventh report, that abuses actually existed in the Commissary General's department and that no steps had been taken to prevent them before Lord Cornwallis' orders of the 23d of December, 1780—as orders to similar effect had been issued by Sir Henry Clinton and Commissaries of Captured Cattle appointed by him in July, '79, and February, '80, by which above a million of rations had been saved to the public even before he left Carolina in June, '80.

The disturbances in the American army critically favorable to Brigadier General Arnold's expedition. He arrives in Virginia. Celerity and success of his operations. Establishes a post at Portsmouth.

Comparative view of the acting strength of the British and American armies on the frontiers of South Carolina. That under Lord Corn-

wallis nearly 6000; Greene's only 2300, of which 1200 are militia. The latter detaches Morgan, with almost half his force, to the distance of 150 miles from him. Lord Cornwallis, hearing that Morgan was moved toward Ninety-six, orders Lieutenant Colonel Tarleton to pass the Broad River and intercept him. The intelligences proves premature, that officer being still on the Pacolet. Lieutenant Colonel Tarleton proposes to Lord Cornwallis to advance to the westward above Morgan while His Lordship moves at the same time with the main army on the east side of the Broad River, and then to attack and drive him over that river on His Lordship.

The main army and Tarleton's detachment move accordingly in cooperation. But Lord Cornwallis halts on the 15th at Turkey Creek, twenty-seven miles from the latter. Tarleton, supposing His Lordship in a situation to cooperate, attacks Morgan at Cowpens, who is inferior to him in infantry in the proportion of four to five and of cavalry of one to three, and has no artillery, of which he has two threepounders. Is most unexpectedly defeated and loses his guns, the colors of the Seventh Regiment, and full 600 men. Shameful behavior of his cavalry (except the Seventeenth Dragoons), who refuse to charge and escape by flight. Probability that this misfortune would not have happened, and that the enemy would have been destroyed, had Lord Cornwallis not have halted, but had [he] moved on to cooperate as had been concerted.

IT WAS SUGGESTED in the preceding chapter that the intelligence furnished by a mail lately taken from the enemy had given me every reason to expect that a considerable decrease would soon happen in Mr. Washington's army. This important event took place, as I had foreseen, at the commencement of the present year. For their troops, having suffered for some time under grievances which the Congress had not the ability to redress—such as the want of pay, clothing, and even food—began at last to complain loudly of them; and, as the term for which most of them had been enlisted was expired, they now insisted on their immediate discharges, with arrears of pay and full retribution for all deficiencies through the depreciation of their paper money. Great discontents had likewise arisen from various causes among the officers, who, having made two ineffectual applications for redress, were much out of temper, so that matters were every day drawing to a crisis. And on the 1st of January, 1781, the whole Pennsylvania line actually seceded from their officers and marched off from Morristown with six fieldpieces, with a determination to demand justice from the American Congress at Philadelphia.

News of this revolt having reached me on the morning of the 3d, I immediately judged it probable that the least wrong step taken by the rebel rulers on such an emergency might be the means, with proper encouragement, of driving the mutineers in to us. Orders were accordingly immediately dispatched to Major General Phillips, who commanded the British elite, and to the officers commanding the Hessian Grenadiers and Jägers to hold themselves in readiness to march at a moment's notice. And, the event being fully confirmed the next day, the troops under orders were directed to proceed to Denyses Ferry on Long Island, from whence they were on the 5th passed over to Staten Island that they might be apportée to act as occasion should require—three messengers having been sent off to the revolters by different routes, with offers of protection and pardon and full liquidation of all their demands, without requiring any other return but allegiance and submission to the British government.[1]

I had, I confess, no particular reason to suppose the mutineers intended to join us. But, as it was impossible for me to judge what measures they meant to pursue, I thought the experiment was worth the trial, as I might thus be prepared either to afford them asylum should they be so disposed or, if not, to circumvent them should they happen to approach within my grasp. For the slightest advance further on my side, before either of these events, would have probably only precipitated an accommodation. They, however, removed to a distance from us and, by delivering up my messengers to General Wayne, soon discovered their real intentions.[2] For having met a committee of Congress at Trenton on the 9th, who consented to the discharge of nearly half their number and promised to satisfy their other demands, matters were so adjusted by the 15th that the rest agreed to readmit their officers and return to their duty. Part of the Jersey brigade also was

1. Clinton's proposals, dated Jan. 4, are given below, pp. 484–485.
He implies, here and elsewhere in the text, that he had little hope of the revolt; during the negotiations, however, he was in fact most optimistic. On the 7th he anticipated that the mutineers would march into Pennsylvania and swell their ranks with the disaffected there; he thought that they might then be induced to move toward the Chesapeake, where Arnold was on hand to head them. They could never, he was convinced, make their peace with Congress. Time was therefore on his side, and all he had to do was make clear his good will and wait on developments. (Clinton memorandum, [Jan. 7].) By the 12th he was more guarded but still cheerful. "I dare do nothing more than favor the revolt and offer asylum. One step beyond—till I know their temper exactly, or [their] wishes—might mar all and reunite them to their late tyrants. My situation is critical. Washington's is equally so. I have, however, all to hope, he everything to fear." Clinton to the Duke of Gloucester, Jan. 12, a photostat volume in the CP.
For the detailed story of the revolt, and Sir Henry's part in it, see Van Doren, *Mutiny in January.*
2. *Clinton's note:* [The] mutineers were saved to the state by the temperate, cautious good conduct of Congress and Washington, notwithstanding any want of either in us.

242 THE AMERICAN REBELLION

tempted a few days after to seek redress in the same way; and I made them the same offers (without, however, any great hopes of success), which proved equally ineffectual.

Indeed, I should have scarcely taken the trouble of noticing the transaction had it not been for the opportunity it gives me of mentioning, to their honor, with how much alacrity and zeal the King's troops exposed themselves on this occasion to all the severities of a very rigorous season, though most of them had enlisted on much the same terms with the revolters (for three years or during the war), but had very properly and zealously submitted to the opinion of the Commander in Chief that the option lay in the King. Nor should I here omit doing justice to the complete order and readiness in which we found the army trains under the management of the Quartermaster General's department, as this instance alone would be sufficient to evince how greatly the mode of supplying wagons, etc., first established by Sir William Howe and adopted by me was to be preferred to the old one of pressing them from the country farmers when wanted. For, had we now been obliged to depend upon the latter, it would have been impossible to move the troops with the suddenness and celerity the service required, even if a sufficient number could have been collected and their proprietors been as eager to serve government as the contrary was notorious in many. And it would have been equally so to preserve that secrecy which is so essential to the success of every military enterprise, and the want of which would have assuredly marred my design in the present one though every other circumstance had been most favorable.

However, I am not unapprised that advantage has been taken of the great expense necessarily attending this contract to misrepresent me as a profuse squanderer of the national wealth,[3] without considering that the mode in question did not only not originate with me but that the state of the war as well as the constant uncertainty of my continuance in the command (having repeatedly entreated leave to resign it) rendered it imprudent, if not impossible, for me to alter it even if I had had doubt of its advantages, or had reason to think otherwise of it than I did. But the word economy was then thrown out as a tub to the whale, and is since become a popular stalking-horse, behind which designing blunderers generally take their stand, the more easily to mislead the public opinion and conceal their own enormities. And I sincerely wish that this nation may not, when it is too late, ultimately find it so greatly to its cost.

3. By the Commissioners of Public Accounts. See Clinton's *Narrative* in Stevens, *Clinton-Cornwallis Controversy*, 1, 49–50 and nn.

For my part, I do not pretend to greater infallibility and circumspection than other men. But I do aver that I never neglected to avail myself of the information of every officer whose experience I judged capable of throwing light upon such matters, and that I made use of every precaution that occurred to myself to prevent either waste or embezzlement of the public money. Some of these have been, I believe, of use, particularly my constituting Commissaries of Captured Cattle in July, 1779, and February, 1780, by which the advantages of feeding the army gratis on the resources of the enemy were secured to the nation as well as the soldier and sailor when on conjunct expeditions, and about a million of crown rations saved to the public before I left Carolina in June, 1780—each of which [rations], by the time it was used by the troops, could not have cost the public less than half a crown. I do not, however, presume from hence to arrogate merit to myself, as I did no more than my duty. But it is to be supposed that Lord Cornwallis thought the idea had some merit, or he would not have endeavored to fasten it to himself by the orders said to be issued by His Lordship on the 23d of December, 1780, and [by] his examination before the Commissioners of Public Accounts, which had an evident tendency to impress those gentlemen with an opinion of his having been the first who applied a remedy to abuses said to be actually existing in the Commissary General's department, although His Lordship was conscious that those abuses could not have existed had my standing orders been continued in force and duly observed, and that in reviving the appointment of Commissaries of Captures on his taking the field in Carolina in September, 1780, he only acted in obedience to the instructions he received from me, when I left His Lordship in that command, to appoint such officer whenever any part of his army took the field.[4]

These disturbances in Mr. Washington's army were critically favorable to our operations in the Chesapeake, as they prevented that officer's immediately detaching troops to disturb Brigadier General

4. Clinton here gives a letter from the deputy Quartermasters General in New York of Aug. 17, 1781 (below, pp. 557–559), and the extract already quoted (above, p. 178 n. 13) from the seventh report of the Commissioners of Public Accounts. To the latter he appends the following note: "These gentlemen seemed to have looked for them [orders] only from Lord Cornwallis. Had they received papers offered to them by the Treasury, had they examined Sir Henry Clinton as they had done Lord Cornwallis, or the officers of the departments then in England, they would have seen orders of the same effect as those of Lord Cornwallis, of prior date to his Lordship's [by] eighteen months. They would have seen the Treasury letter of thanks to Sir Henry Clinton for preventing such abuses, in February, 1780. And they would have avoided the censure that was afterward passed on their conduct by Mr. Pitt, who on reading that letter acknowledged to Sir Henry Clinton 'that the Commissioners of Accounts had been exceedingly remiss.'"

Arnold in the execution of the service he was sent upon. For it appears by the Brigadier's report [5] that he landed at Westover, on James River, on the fourth day of the Pennsylvania revolt; and, as he did not meet with the smallest opposition on his march from thence to Richmond and afterward to Westham, seven miles above the falls, the facility of his operations may be in some measure imputed to this cause. Here the King's troops destroyed twenty-six pieces of cannon, three hundred and ten barrels of gunpowder, a magazine of oats, and various other stores, together with a very fine foundry for cannon, and at Richmond a valuable rope-work, with all its materials and stock, a large depot of Quartermaster's stores, and several warehouses filled with rum, salt, sailcloth, and other goods. After the performance of this important service, and marching sixty-six miles in three days (under an almost constant rain the whole time), this handful of men returned without molestation to their boats, which they reached on the 7th.

Brigadier Arnold was here joined on the 9th by the troops in the missing transports, and on the next day the whole began to fall down the river to carry into execution the other services he had in charge. By this time different bodies of militia had assembled near the banks of the river, under Baron Steuben and others, with a view of annoying him in his progress. But, as they generally dispersed as soon as any troops were thrown on shore to attack them, this active officer reached Portsmouth on the 20th without having suffered any material loss, and immediately began to establish a post for the security of his detachment by taking up Major General Leslie's ground and completing and enlarging the works he found there.

About the time of Brigadier Arnold's arrival in Virginia General Greene, having succeeded Gates in the command of the enemy's southern army, was encamped with a very small force on Hicks Creek, on the east side of the Pedee.[6] He had, a short time before this, detached Brigadier General Morgan with all his light troops—which formed nearly half his strength—to the westward of the Wateree, to encourage the South Carolina militia to assemble, and to watch the motions of the royal army at Winnsboro and Camden while Brigadier General Marion traversed the lower parts of the province at the head of a small corps of mounted militia, for the purpose of picking up intelligence and persecuting the loyalists. Consequently the

5. Arnold to Clinton, Portsmouth, Va., Jan. 21, 1781 (received Feb. 1), in "Correspondence with Brigr. General Arnold" (a letterbook in a slip case in the CP entitled "Correspondence with Arbuthnot, Arnold, Leslie, and Phillips"), pp. 4–10.

6. In the remainder of this chapter Clinton draws heavily, for opinions as well as details, upon Tarleton's *History*, pp. 208–222.

enemy's regular southern army, which did not in the whole much exceed 1000 Continentals, being thus separated into two parts at too great a distance to be able to cooperate to any effect, was certainly not in a situation to encourage any hopes of success from its operations. Yet we shall soon see to our astonishment these two trifling corps, through mismanagement on one side and a series of fortunate occurrences on their part, evade the pursuit of the royal army and (though at this time at least 120 miles wide of each other) effect a junction and gain the ascendant over it—though, if we consider its appointments and discipline, it may [be] fairly deemed to have been greatly superior to both of them even after they were joined and reinforced, and from its position between them their junction appeared to be almost impossible.

But this will be best illustrated by a comparative view of the two armies, taken from authentic returns of their respective commanders. By one of General Greene's, dated the 8th of December, we find that of the enemy consisted of nine hundred and forty-nine Continentals, ninety cavalry, sixty artillery, and twelve hundred and eight militia —in all, twenty-three hundred and seven rank and file fit for duty. Of these, four hundred and seventy infantry and seventy light dragoons were afterward detached under General Morgan to the westward of the Wateree, and on the 29th of December this latter officer sent forward Lieutenant Colonel Washington with the cavalry and two hundred militia to harass the district of Ninety-six. In opposition to this small force Lord Cornwallis lay at Winnsboro with about two thousand troops, and General Leslie was on the march to join him with fifteen hundred, while the posts of Camden and Ninety-six, in his neighborhood, were garrisoned by between two and three thousand more—so that the army His Lordship had under his own immediate command at this juncture could not consist of less than fifty-five hundred most respectable troops, besides a numerous militia. It must be confessed, however, from His Lordship's account of them that no great dependance could be placed on the latter, though it is presumable that those of the enemy, having equally experienced the ennervating effects of a sickly southern climate and a want of many supplies the B[ritish] had from C[harles]ton, could not be much more formidable.

While the three armies lay in the positions just described, Colonel Washington's move being reported to Lord Cornwallis with some exaggerations, His Lordship suspected that Morgan's whole detachment had marched to Ninety-six, and accordingly ordered Lieutenant Colonel Tarleton to immediately cross the Broad River with his own corps and the first battalion of the Seventy-first to compel him to fall back. That officer had not, however, proceeded above twenty miles to the westward of the river before he received certain intelligence that Morgan still remained in his camp on the Pacolet. Ninety-six being consequently in security, he very properly halted to wait for his baggage, and communicated his reasons to Lord Cornwallis, submitting at the same time his opinion that, if His Lordship would advance with the main army along the east side of the Broad River toward King's Mountain at the time His Lordship should appoint for the movement of the light corps, Morgan could not possibly pass the fords of Catawba or escape being destroyed by the one or the other. This plan being exactly, it appears by Colonel Tarleton's history, conformable to Lord Cornwallis' own ideas and design, notice was in consequence sent by Lord Cornwallis to Lieutenant Colonel Tarleton that the army would begin its march on the 7th. The light troops under Colonel Tarleton moved accordingly on that day. But, being obliged to edge considerably to the westward on account of the waters [7] and consequently having a greater distance to move than Lord Cornwallis' army, whose course lay almost due north, that officer had great reason to suppose the latter could easily keep pace with him and be always near enough to cooperate to effect.

This was not, however, exactly the case. For Lord Cornwallis, being delayed by waiting for the reinforcement under Major General Leslie, advanced for some days very slowly. But His Lordship took care to inform Lieutenant Colonel Tarleton of his motions from time to time until the 14th, when he reached Bull Run, and then intimated to that officer that, General Leslie being now clear of the waters, he had nothing further to retard his cooperation. Lieutenant Colonel Tarleton had this day passed the Enoree and Tiger Rivers, and immediately sent word to Lord Cornwallis that he should endeavor to cross the Pacolet by stratagem—as all the fords were guarded by Morgan—and then strike at the enemy in order to force him over the Broad River. It appears also that he requested His Lordship at the same time to proceed up its eastern bank without delay, that he might catch Morgan's corps on its passing.

The passage of the Pacolet was effected by the light troops on the morning of the 16th. And, as Lieutenant Colonel Tarleton had not received any letter or order from Lord Cornwallis since that of the 14th, and was from thence persuaded His Lordship was in a situation to cooperate as had been preconcerted, he did not hesitate to move the next day against the enemy's corps, which he found drawn up

7. Swamps, which were swollen by heavy rains.

ready to receive him at a place called Cowpens, about six miles to the west of Broad River.[8] [He did not hesitate] more especially as the number and species of troops that composed it were greatly inferior to his own, which consisted of the cavalry and infantry of the Legion, fifty dragoons belonging to the Seventeenth Regiment, the Seventh Regiment and first battalion of the Seventy-first, with two three-pounders, making in the whole full one thousand men, of which three hundred were cavalry. But of this powerful arm Morgan had not much more than a hundred, and he was entirely without artillery. Consequently Lieutenant Colonel Tarleton's expectation of success was not ill founded.

This disposition for the attack seems likewise to have been perfectly judicious. Yet, though the enemy's militia were driven back and everything seemed to promise him victory in the beginning of the action, it was suddenly wrested from him by an unexpected fire from the Continentals while the King's troops were charging and sustaining [it] in that loose, flimsy order which had ever been too much the practice in America,[9] whereby his whole corps was thrown into a shameful confusion from which they could never afterward be recovered. And all the cavalry, except the detachment from the Seventeenth Light Dragoons and the chief of the officers, forsaking their leader, fled with precipitation from the field of battle. The consequence was that all the rest of his command, with the two three-pounders, the colors of the Seventh Regiment, and 800 stand of small arms, fell most disgracefully into the enemy's hands.

We have here, unfortunately, another fatal instance of the ruinous effect of risking detachments without being in a situation to sustain them, or [of] promising and not affording support. I fear we sometimes run too great hazards in our endeavors to escape small affronts, for we often by it bring upon ourselves more pernicious disasters than those we wish to shun. It must be acknowledged, however, that, from the very great superiority and advantages which Lieutenant Colonel Tarleton's detachment unquestionably had over the troops under General Morgan, Lord Cornwallis had on this occasion every reason to be perfectly free from apprehension that anything sinister could happen to

8. *Clinton's note:* "The guides were immediately consulted relative to the ground which General Morgan then occupied, and the country in his rear. These people described both with great perspicuity. They said that the woods were open and free from swamps, that the part of Broad River just above the place where King's Creek joined the stream was about six miles distant from the enemy's left flank, and that the river, by making a curve to the westward, ran parallel to their rear." [Tarleton, *History*, p. 215.]
9. See above, p. 95 n. 16.

it. Yet, as a plan of cooperation had been concerted between them, and the advantages to be reaped from Lieutenant Colonel Tarleton's expected success in either defeating Morgan or driving him over Broad River so greatly depended on His Lordship's being near the fords, ready to fall upon him in his crossing, we naturally seek for His Lordship's reasons for being so tardy in his progress after General Leslie had got out of the swamps. For His Lordship appears to have been in a hurry to get on, from his having ordered meal to be delivered to the troops on the 14th to serve them to the 18th inclusive.

But, though they marched the next morning with a view (as presumed) of cooperating, and reached Turtle [Turkey] Creek on the 16th, they there stopped and halted to the 19th. Now, though His Lordship's movements had been hitherto slow—having taken full ten days to march forty miles—yet, had this halt not taken place, as His Lordship was then only twenty-seven miles from Cowpens, it is possible that with a little exertion he might even yet have been within cooperating distance of Lieutenant Colonel Tarleton's corps on the day of action; and the fatal consequences, at least, of that defeat might have been prevented. For Morgan in that case would either not have fought, or, if he had, there can be little doubt he would have been most severely punished for his temerity, as the troops under Colonel Tarleton would have probably acted with more confidence. And every door of escape might have consequently been thus shut against him; or he would at least have been forced so high up the country as to have rendered his subsequent junction with Greene impossible, whereby most probably both corps might have been effectually crushed; or Lord Cornwallis at least must have recovered all the troops, etc., taken by Morgan.[10]

10. Clinton here included in his text a long quotation from Tarleton's narrative of the battle, and then deleted part of it with the comment that "I do not think it becomes me to enter into these little details." He presumably intended to delete the entire passage, and it has therefore been omitted. So has a note in which he quotes from Ramsay, who adds virtually nothing. For these accounts see Tarleton, *History*, pp. 215–218; Ramsay, *History of the Revolution of South Carolina*, 2, 196, 198–199. For modern descriptions see Carrington, *Battles of the Revolution*, pp. 541–546; Wallace, *Appeal to Arms*, pp. 232–234; Ward, *War of the Revolution*, 2, 755–762; Fisher, *Struggle for American Independence*, 2, 382–387.

CHAPTER 19

The Franco-American Offensive against Arnold
in the Chesapeake, January to March, 1781

[A disaster to three of Arbuthnot's ships gives the French temporary
naval superiority. They send a small detachment to the Chesapeake,
and Washington detaches troops; Clinton consequently prepares to
reinforce Arnold, but waits to learn Arbuthnot's plans. The entire
French squadron sails to the Chesapeake, followed by the British.
The battle of March 16 ends the enemy offensive. The reinforcement
sails from New York, under Major General Phillips, and joins Arnold.
Cornwallis decides to invade North Carolina. Clinton's criticism of
this decision.] [1]

THE INCLEMENT season of the year and the very reduced state of
the force under my own immediate command, after the detachments
I had so liberally made from it in support of Lord Cornwallis, certainly
forbade for the present all active operations on the side of New York.
An event also happened, soon after the return of the troops from their
late excursion to Staten Island, which had at first a very alarming appearance, and seemed to render our situation there—but more so in
the Chesapeake—extremely critical. Rear Admiral Graves, on whom
the command of the King's ships in Gardiners Bay devolved during the
Vice Admiral's absence, having in consequence of intelligence that
three line-of-battle ships had sailed from Rhode Island sent an equal
force from the British squadron to pursue them, the latter was unfortunately overtaken by a violent gale of wind, in which the *Culloden*
was lost, the *America* supposed to have shared the same fate, and the
Bedford dismasted. But the French ships, by returning into port in time,
luckily escaped its fury.[2]

1. Clinton's table of contents is missing from chaps. xix–xxi.
2. Arbuthnot, in New York at the time, had warned Graves that the French
were about to sail. When on Jan. 20 they did so, Graves was in a quandary. Although he did not know his superiors' intentions, he realized that he had to act in
order to protect the vulnerable British detachments to the southward. "I incur
every risk which accompanies ill success," he pointed out to Arbuthnot on the 21st.
"Were I, therefore, prudently to wait Your Excellency's instructions, the evil might
be done, the flattering prospect before us quite blasted, and myself exculpated."

Consequently this misfortune evidently transferred the naval superiority in these seas from us to the French, and thereby not only exposed the British squadron in its crippled state to an attack from that of the enemy, but our post at Portsmouth to most imminent danger had they united with the rebels in a combined move against it while Admiral Arbuthnot was incapable of affording the necessary succor. This was assuredly a most afflicting blow to the Vice Admiral; and I must do him the justice to say that, notwithstanding the extreme rigor of the weather, no exertions of his were wanting to recover the respectability of his force. All the stores of the *Culloden* were with much labor and diligence saved; and, jury masts being got into the *Bedford* and the *America* having rejoined him, his fleet was by the 9th of February made equal in number, and something superior in quality, to that of the enemy.

It appears that, as soon as Mr. Washington heard of the disaster of the British ships, he immediately proposed to Monsieur de Rochambeau a conjunct expedition against Brigadier General Arnold's corps in Virginia. But, instead of the French going thither directly with their whole fleet as the American General had proposed, they sent on the service only a sixty-four-gun ship and two frigates.³ This little squadron sailed from Newport on the 8th of February; but it is presumed Admiral Arbuthnot remained ignorant of it, as it does not appear that he sent after them or took timely measures to counteract their operations. And, indeed, the first I heard of it was by another letter from General Arnold, which did not reach me before the 19th.⁴ But I had two days before

---

(Quoted by Willcox in *Journ. of Mod. Hist.*, 17, 318; the letter, however, is there ascribed to Arbuthnot instead of Graves, and the French detachment that inspired it is confused with the ships detached on Feb. 8.) Arbuthnot sailed for Gardiners Bay on the 22d, and the same day the French put back to Newport. That night a hurricane lashed New York and the whole of Long Island. It forced the Admiral to put in at City Island for two days, and destroyed most of the shipping in the sound. Off Gardiners Bay the *Bedford* tried to ride it out in the dark, and was saved only when her crew dismasted her. The *Culloden* drove ashore on Long Island, but her crew escaped. The *America* disappeared; she was blown south to Virginia, and in early February limped home in need of major repairs. *Ibid.*, p. 319 and n. 60; Arbuthnot to Clinton, Jan. 24, 29; Stokes, *Iconography of Manhattan*, 5, 1125.

3. See Washington to Lund Washington, Mar. 28, below, p. 503. The French naval commander was now Capt. Sochet Destouches; de Ternay had died in the previous December.

4. See the postscript (dated the 14th) in Arnold to Clinton, Feb. 13, Stevens, *Clinton-Cornwallis Controversy*, 1, 326.

The sequence of naval moves leading to the battle of Mar. 16 is confusing in Clinton's account. The first French detachment, on Jan. 20, was to search for an expected convoy; the disaster to the pursuing British ships encouraged the French to make a second detachment: a sixty-four and two frigates sailed on Feb. 8 and reached the Chesapeake on the 14th. Clinton prepared a relief expedition. But Arbuthnot, instead of escorting it, merely ordered some frigates north from Charleston; one of these, the *Romulus*, was captured by the French as they returned to

received a letter from the Admiral recommending a Mr. Brenton, who left Rhode Island on the 9th and brought information that all the French line-of-battle ships were preparing to sail on an expedition with 1300 troops, the destination of which was supposed to be the Chesapeake.[5] The Admiral had also written by the same opportunity to Lieutenant General Robertson in the following strong words: "The moment is arrived in which *our enemies may receive a mortal blow, and an end put to this business if we follow it up with spirit. If this opportunity is lost we deserve whatever may result from it.*" [6]

From Mr. Brenton's intelligence, and General Arnold's information that his post was blocked by three French ships of war, I was persuaded that a very serious stroke was meditating by the enemy against our possessions in that quarter. Orders were therefore immediately issued that the British and Hessian Grenadiers, the light infantry, the Forty-second and Seventy-sixth Regiments, with that of Prince Charles, and a detachment of artillery should prepare for embarkation. I sent a confidential officer [to] the Admiral with my request that he would have the goodness to explain to me, through him, the hint contained in his letter to General Robertson, accompanied with the strongest assurances of my being ready to meet his wishes and cooperate with him to the utmost of my power.[7] But the reader will judge of my astonishment at receiving for answer that his ideas were communicated to General Robertson from report that Brigadier General Arnold had penetrated near 200 miles in Virginia with a very small detachment, and that Lord Cornwallis was then on or near the southern frontier of that province; and that no reserve whatsoever was intended on his part to me.[8] He further told me

Newport, where they arrived on the 25th. Meanwhile Washington had detached troops under Lafayette to the Chesapeake, and on Mar. 8 the entire French squadron left Rhode Island. Arbuthnot sailed two days later, overtook the enemy, and on the 16th fought a battle that ended the Franco-American offensive against Arnold. Clinton, in the dark about these final developments, sent his reinforcements on the 20th, while the French were at sea returning to Newport. See Robert Beatson, *Naval and Military Memoirs of Great Britain, from 1727 to 1783* (2d ed., 6 vols., London, 1804), 5, 215–220; W. L. Clowes, ed., *The Royal Navy: A History from the Earliest Times to the Present* (7 vols., London, 1897–1903), 3, 488–493; Georges Lacour-Gayet, *La Marine militaire de la France sous le règne de Louis XVI* (Paris, 1905), p. 358; Willcox in *Journ. of Mod. Hist.*, 17, 318–321.

5. William Brenton, a prominent Rhode Island loyalist. His intelligence report is filed in the CP under Feb. 12.

6. Arbuthnot to Robertson, Feb. 13; the Admiral's letter to Clinton was of the same date.

7. See Clinton to Arbuthnot, Feb. 17, below, p. 488.

8. I.e., that he was not withholding information, as Sir Henry's immediate inquiry had implied. Arbuthnot's idea was that a small reinforcement would probably permit Arnold to join Cornwallis, and would certainly enable him "to cut up the enemy in Virginia and to disable them from deriving any decisive advantages from a cooperation with the French at Rhode Island." Arbuthnot to Clinton, Feb. 21.

that he had just heard that a line-of-battle ship and some frigates sailed from Rhode Island some days since, and therefore proposed the expediency of an *immediate embarkation of my troops, which he would escort with his whole force to the Chesapeake—to which end he requested they might immediately rendezvous at Sandy Hook, off which he should call for them as soon as possible.*[9]

I own this precipitation of the Admiral greatly alarmed me, as it was by no means certain that the whole of the French fleet intended to leave Newport. And, should ours quit Gardiners Bay while theirs remained there, everything was to be apprehended for the safety of all of our supplies of provisions, troops, and stores for the campaign, whose arrival on the coast we were in hourly expectation of. I therefore immediately sent an express to him to request that he would give this matter a serious consideration, or that he would, after sending a proper force to clear the Chesapeake, *at least stop at New York* should he be still determined to quit his present station. His answer to this was that his letter to me and orders to the senior port officer were intended to save time, that the destination of the French fleet to the Chesapeake admitted of little doubt, and that he could not stop from pursuing them, if they sailed, *for any unimportant consideration.* The Admiral seeming by this to have misconceived my letter, I again explained my wishes to him and submitted to his consideration the propriety of his following the enemy unencumbered, should they really sail; and, after he had fixed them, [I said that] I would upon notice immediately send an adequate land force after him, for which I requested he would order a sufficient convoy.[10]

Soon after this I received undoubted intelligence that Mr. Washington was detaching a considerable force under the Marquis de Lafayette to the southward. And, as I had every reason to judge it was intended to cooperate with the French ships already in the Chesapeake, I dispatched a runner to apprise Brigadier General Arnold, that the officer commanding the King's ships there might send cruisers up the bay to intercept or retard it in its passage.[11] The troops I had held in readiness were now ordered to embark, and I requested the senior officer in the port of New York to assemble the King's ships off the Hook. And, communicating without delay to the Vice Admiral what I had

9. See Arbuthnot to Capt. Russell at New York, Feb. 21, below, pp. 488–489.
10. Clinton to Arbuthnot, Feb. 28, below, pp. 489–490.
11. I.e., to retard Lafayette's force on its way by water down the bay. Clinton's actual letter made only a vague reference to "watching" this force; his purpose in writing was to assure Arnold that the Admiral, unencumbered, would follow the French if they sailed with Rochambeau's troops. Clinton to Arnold, Mar. 1, in "Correspondence with Arnold" (CP), p. 34.

done, I submitted to him with all deference the expediency, if he had not already done it, of his immediately detaching a naval force superior to that of the enemy now in the Chesapeake, and coming with the rest of his squadron off the port of New York, that I might have an opportunity of acting with or consulting him in the present emergency.[12] The French ships had, however, sailed in the meantime from Hampton Roads (where they had been at anchor unmolested for five days without attempting anything), and got into Newport on the 25th of February with the *Romulus*, man-of-war, which they had captured off the Capes of Virginia in her return thither from Charleston.

On the 5th of March I received a letter from the Admiral, dated the 2d, to inform me that in consequence of intelligence of the French fleet having sailed for the Chesapeake *he should proceed instantly with the squadron off Sandy Hook, to escort any reinforcement I proposed sending to General Arnold;* and on the 7th another, dated the 4th, to say he *should move immediately with the ships, sending a frigate to reconnoiter Rhode Island in passing, and regulate his measures by what was discovered there with respect to calling off the Hook; but, should he not call, the* Richmond, Orpheus, *and* Savage *were to proceed with the reinforcement.* This last was accompanied by a letter to Lieutenant General Robertson *to tell him that he must take care of Long Island Sound, because it was out of his power to protect it any longer, having neither vessels nor men for the purpose;* and likewise an order of the same date to Captain Hudson, requiring him to proceed with the convoy and transports to Chesapeake Bay *with all possible expedition*— but, should I decline sending any reinforcement, *directing him positively to join him with the King's ships in the Chesapeake with all possible dispatch.*[13]

These letters and orders, being so apparently opposite to each other, placed Captain Hudson and me in a very unpleasant and awkward situation. For, as by those to me I was to suppose the enemy already in possession of the Chesapeake, I could not of course venture to let the troops sail until I should hear further from the Admiral. On the other hand, Captain Hudson having every reason from his to think *the Admiral* in the Chesapeake, it was difficult for him to avoid complying with so positive an order to join him there without delay. And, should both or either act according to the spirit of the order and the Admiral not have sailed (as turned out to actually be the case), both troops and convoy might run into inevitable destruction. Under this dilemma

12. Clinton to Capt. Russell, Mar. 2–3; Clinton to Arbuthnot, Mar. 1.
13. Arbuthnot's three letters were all on Mar. 4; those to Clinton and Robertson are in the CP, that to Hudson below, p. 491.

I took the liberty of advising Captain Hudson to suspend his compliance a little longer, in the hope of our soon hearing again from the Admiral or having more light to conduct us. This he was so obliging to accede to—though with some hesitation, lest he should draw censure on himself, as the orders to him did not admit of a second construction.[14] And it turned out very fortunate that he did so; for, the French fleet having sailed from Rhode Island on the 8th of March, his three ships (being ignorant of it and supposing ours before him in the Chesapeake) might have else most probably fallen into their power.

Admiral Arbuthnot, having now completed the rigging of the *Bedford*, followed the French fleet into the Chesapeake on the 10th. Of this I received notice from him on the 14th. And, being anxious that the reinforcement should get to its destination as soon as possible, lest the combined movement of the enemy might not only injure us in that quarter but affect the operations of Lord Cornwallis in Carolina, I requested Captain Hudson to sail with it from the Hook without delay, advising him, however, to proceed with caution and feel his way as he went, as the safety of the embarked troops was certainly an object of the greatest importance to us in the present state of our affairs.[15]

The detachment which was made from my army on this occasion consisted of two battalions of light infantry, the Seventy-sixth Regiment, that of the hereditary prince,[16] and a detachment of artillery, the whole something exceeding 2000 men—which, with the troops already in Virginia, were put under the command of Major General Phillips, who was directed to take them under his orders and endeavor if possible to effect a junction with Brigadier General Arnold on Elizabeth River. The principal objects pointed out to that general officer in his instructions were, after he had relieved Brigadier General Arnold from the dangers which then threatened him, to make such movements of his troops (consistent with the security of the post on Elizabeth River) as he should judge most likely to effectually assist Lord Cornwallis' operations, by destroying any magazines the enemy might have at Petersburg or on James River or by interrupting the course of supplies to the Carolinas. And, when that object was fulfilled, he was left at liberty to carry on desultory expeditions to any part of the Chesapeake he should think most conducive to His Majesty's service. He was likewise permitted, if the Admiral, disapproving Portsmouth, should require a fortified station for his large ships either at Yorktown or Old

14. Clinton to Arbuthnot, Mar. 8, and Hudson to Clinton, Mar. 9, below, pp. 492–493; Clinton to Hudson, Mar. 8, CP.
15. Clinton to Hudson, Mar. 14.
16. The Prince of Hesse.

Point Comfort, to take possession thereof if either could be acquired and maintained without great risk or loss. *But, should the objections be such as he thought forcible, he was, after stating those objections, to decline it until solid operation should take place in Chesapeake.* It was implied also in those instructions that he would in June be called, with the far greater part of the troops, to a junction with Sir Henry Clinton at New York.[17]

Although the French fleet had two days' start of the British, Admiral Arbuthnot, unencumbered with transports, by pursuing with that zeal and celerity which the greatness of the exigency required had the happiness to overtake them before they entered the Chesapeake. And, though his action of the 16th was certainly not so decisive as might have been expected from the superiority of his force,[18] yet, as he compelled them to return into port without effecting their purpose, he is very justly entitled to the merit of having entirely disconcerted the present enterprise of the enemy against His Majesty's ships and troops in Virginia—which, it must be confessed, could not have well failed had it been undertaken seven weeks sooner. Nor is it unworthy [of] notice that, had not the reinforcement under Major General Phillips been detained at Sandy Hook by contrary winds until the 20th, it would have most probably met the enemy's fleet in its return to Rhode Island and fallen a sacrifice, notwithstanding all my precaution.[19] But, every barrier being now happily removed, General Phillips was enabled to effect a junction with the corps under Brigadier General Arnold on the 27th, and landed his troops in Elizabeth River as soon as accommodations could be prepared for their reception.[20]

I had every reason to expect that the most favorable consequences to

17. See Clinton's instructions to Phillips, Mar. 10, below, pp. 495–497.

18. *Clinton's note:* Copy of the French and British line of battle on the 16 March 1781: French: *Duc de Bourgogne* (coppered), eighty-four; *Le Neptune* (coppered), eighty; *Conquérant*, seventy-four; *Provence*, sixty-four; *Ardent*, sixty-four; *Jason*, sixty-four; *Eveillé* (coppered), sixty-four; *Romulus*, forty. British: *London*, ninety; *Royal Oak*, seventy-four; *Bedford*, seventy-four; *Robust*, seventy-four; *America*, sixty-four; *Prudent*, sixty-four; *Europe*, sixty-four; *Adamant*, fifty (all coppered). [The *Neptune* was actually a seventy-four, the *Romulus* a forty-four, and the *London* a ninety-eight; see Clowes, *The Royal Navy, 3,* 492 n.]

19. His only precaution seems to have been delay. He finally sent the troops, with grossly inadequate naval protection, at a time when the French squadron was at sea and Arbuthnot's whereabouts were unknown. For once, in other words, he took a calculated risk. See above, p. 250 n. 4.

20. Clinton here deletes some four pages of text and notes about his bickerings with Arbuthnot, and explains the deletion in a marginal comment: "I acquit the good old Admiral. His want of memory often occasioned these mistakes, and I fear he was oftener led into them by his designing secretary [William Green]—of whom I need say no more than that he embarked soon after the war [as] supercargo of an American ship to China."

Lord Cornwallis' operations would be the result of these repeated expeditions to the Chesapeake. And, indeed, the enemy themselves have acknowledged that the obstructions thrown before the preparations for the support of their southern army were to be reckoned among the greatest misfortunes which the American cause had suffered from, . . . as it effectually kept back the raising of recruits and every other supply.[21] Yet we have to lament that even these were insufficient to counteract the pernicious effects of an obstinate perseverance in an ill-timed plan, which the then state of the two Carolinas pointed out to be impracticable.[22] But, as the many difficulties attending the mutual communication between Lord Cornwallis and me left me for months in a total ignorance of his actual situation, they obliged me of course to content myself with placing an implicit confidence in His Lordship's judgment by rendering it impossible for me, through want of information, to either order or advise.

And His Lordship had, moreover, repeatedly declared that he would not suffer his invasion of North Carolina to endanger the safety of any of the posts behind him, as he should (after giving our friends there a fair trial, and finding them less numerous or forward than he expected) return in time and secure the province I had committed to his charge —the militia of which he acknowledged to have been so disheartened by Ferguson's misfortune that not 100 could be collected in the whole district of Ninety-six; and he did not think that even these would make the least resistance if attacked.[23] Wherefore I had certainly every reason to be persuaded that Lord Cornwallis would never lose sight of the general instructions I left with him when I appointed him to that command, by which he was clearly and positively directed constantly to look upon the safety of Charleston and its depending province as the chief object of his care, and not to engage in any offensive operation by which they might be endangered.

It is, however, to be suspected that the mortification occasioned by Lieutenant Colonel Tarleton's defeat got the better of His Lordship's prudence, and that through his eager desire of recovering the British prisoners from Morgan, and revenging on him that affront, His Lordship forgot for the moment not only the *dismantled,* open, exposed

21. A paraphrase of Gordon, *History of the Late War, 4,* 62. The omission is of the word "it," presumably inserted by error.

22. Clinton here cites Rawdon's letter to him of Oct. 29, 1780 (below, pp. 469–470), to prove that Cornwallis had considered the invasion of North Carolina impracticable before the Battle of Cowpens. For a discussion of the Earl's subsequent change of mind and "obstinate perseverance" see Willcox in *Am. Hist. Rev., 52,* 10.

23. Cornwallis to Clinton, Dec. 3, 1780, Stevens, *Clinton-Cornwallis Controversy, 1,* 303.

state of Charleston and the numerous rebellious parties which at that
time infested South Carolina,[24] but even the incapacity of acting to
any effect in so exhausted a country, [an incapacity] to which he was
about to reduce the troops immediately with him by destroying his
wagons and stores. I am, however, far from condemning this part of
His Lordship's conduct. The bait was certainly tempting. And, though
we have to lament that his efforts to seize it were not more early exerted (when they must have succeeded), yet they might have been
perhaps praiseworthy as well as justifiable, when he did attempt it, had
His Lordship not suffered himself to be drawn on beyond the banks of
the Yadkin.

There, I humbly presume, His Lordship should have stopped (after
he found the enemy had evaded his grasp, and when he might have
reflected that what he had done to enable him to make this rapid
move against Morgan . . . [had] deprived Morgan of the means of
following it up), and given up for the present his northern pursuits at
least until the re-establishment of the King's interests in South Carolina,
which had been greatly shaken by the late disasters and their consequent effect on the minds of both friends and enemies, might have
rendered the resumption of them more promising. Had His Lordship
there closed his campaign, restored order in South Carolina, and by an
establishment at Wilmington endeavored to recover the lost confidence of our friends in North Carolina, Sir Henry Clinton's plan for
the campaign (approved by government till they were misled by the
false glow of Lord Cornwallis' victory of Guilford, and reapproved in
July when His M[ajesty's] cabinet ceased to see through that medium
which had deceived them) . . . would have had a fair trial. And,
whether it had been offensive or defensive (for it consisted of two parts),
it must have succeed[ed] at a period of the war when negative victory
would have increased American despondence.[25]

It is true Lord Cornwallis told me in his letter of the 18th of January
that, *notwithstanding this unexpected and extraordinary event [Cow-
pens], nothing but the most absolute necessity should induce him to
give up the important object of the winter's campaign*—which, as far as
could be collected from His Lordship's preceding letters, was *to drive
back the enemy's army and, after keeping for a considerable distance on
the west of the Catawba, to pass that river and the Yadkin, and to trust*

24. Cornwallis to Clinton, Jan. 6, 1781, below, p. 485.
25. The preceding paragraph is an insertion, largely in Clinton's hand at its
more difficult; but precisely where he meant to insert it is not clear. The first
omission is apparently of an ampersand, the second of "if it," neither of which makes
sense in context. The final parenthesis, deleted in the MS, is restored for the sake
of clarity.

to events for the direction of his future steps.[26] But, circumstanced as I was at the time of my receiving these intimations of His Lordship's disaster and intentions, it was impossible for me from that distance either to advise or assist him. Matters were, therefore, necessarily left to take their course. And, trusting to His Lordship's abilities, I could only flatter myself with the hope that by his exertions he might overtake and annihilate Morgan, and possibly on his return meet and disperse Greene's corps, and afterward establish himself in some healthy situation among our friends in North Carolina, in order to facilitate, with their assistance, the recovery of that province.

And I candidly own that, as long as His Lordship's march into North Carolina bore the appearance of a *solid* move to give the experiment of supporting friends there a fair trial, he carried with him my approbation, as also my acquiescence to his reasons for making it—though I knew that South Carolina was not at the time in the most eligible state of tranquillity.[27] But, after His Lordship's acting force was considerably diminished by the entire destruction of his light corps and he had divested himself of the means of securing food and other necessary supplies to his troops, and was consequently no longer in a condition to inspire either confidence or respect or to subsist his army except by marauding, I am persuaded every impartial military man will join with me in regarding his longer perseverance in the enterprise as a most rash and injudicious measure, replete with inevitable ruin to his army if it was defeated, and likely to be productive of many pernicious consequences (without the chance of one single advantage to the King's service) even though he should be so fortunate as to gain a victory. The observation is, however, hazarded with all deference; and the reader may be better able to judge of its propriety after he has perused the account of this memorable pursuit which he will find impartially detailed in the following chapter.

26. Clinton here refers in notes to Cornwallis' letters to him of Dec. 3, 1780, and Jan. 6, 1781. The relevant portions of these letters, and of that of Jan. 18, are printed in Stevens, *Clinton-Cornwallis Controversy, 1,* 303, 316, 319, 321.
27. See Cornwallis to Clinton, June 30, Sept. 22, 1780, below, pp. 442, 458.

CHAPTER 20

Cornwallis in North Carolina, January to April, 1781

[*Cornwallis pursues Morgan unsuccessfully after the Battle of Cowpens. Junction of Morgan and Greene, who retreat into Virginia. Cornwallis abandons the pursuit and falls back to Hillsboro; Greene recrosses the Dan. The Battle of Guilford. Cornwallis retires to Cross Creek; Greene pursues, and then moves toward South Carolina. Cornwallis withdraws to the coast at Wilmington. Clinton's criticism of the Earl's generalship.*]

SOME OF the fugitives from Cowpens having reached Lord Cornwallis' camp on Turkey Creek in the night after the action, and the very disgraceful defeat suffered on that day being confirmed by Lieutenant Colonel Tarleton the next morning, His Lordship immediately caused the corps under Major General Leslie to join him, and began his pursuit of General Morgan on the 19th with his whole line.[1] But, having advanced only thirty-one miles in three days, and consequently finding that he made rather too slow a progress by this course, His Lordship committed the wagons, heavy baggage, and women to the care of a large escort under Brigadier General Howard, who had orders to follow the next day; and His Lordship pressed forward with his remaining force on the 22d, in the hope of catching the enemy in his passage of the Broad River at the upper fords. But this had been unfortunately effected before His Lordship could reach them; and the celerity of General Morgan's movements, together with the swelling of creeks, which much impeded the march of the British troops, baffled likewise all His Lordship's efforts to overtake him in his flight to the Catawba.

Lord Cornwallis, being stopped by the south fork of that river (after gaining only thirty-six miles in three days more), determined to re-

---

1. Most of the events recounted in this chapter have been covered by modern historians. See for example Carrington, *Battles of the Revolution*, pp. 547–566; Fisher, *Struggle for American Independence*, 2, 389–416; Fortescue, *British Army*, 3, 364–375; Wallace, *Appeal to Arms*, pp. 234–239; Ward, *War of the Revolution*, 2, 763–797.

assemble his army there and prepare it for lighter action, by destroying all superfluous baggage and even all his wagons except such as were indispensable for the accommodation of sick and wounded and the transport of ammunition and hospital stores. The completing this business caused a halt of three days, and the pursuit was renewed on the 28th. In the meantime the rains had rendered the North Catawba impassable, and all its fords for more than forty miles upward from its fork had been seized by the North Carolina militia under General Davidson, supported by the retreating corps under Morgan—who, having reached the river on the 28th, immediately sent forward his prisoners to Virginia, by orders of General Greene, and made a stand on its eastern bank, that the troops who were hastening from the Pedee might have time to join him. For, as soon as General Greene had heard of Lord Cornwallis' pursuit, he immediately ordered the part of the army under himself to decamp from Hick's Creek and make forced marches without baggage up the Yadkin, while he rode one hundred and fifty miles across the country with a small escort, to meet the light troops under Morgan and direct their movements so as to effect a junction of the two corps either at Charlotte or Salisbury, as circumstances should admit. And [he] arrived at their camp at Sherrill's Ford in the night of the 31st.

Lord Cornwallis' army, having proceeded by short marches so as to give the enemy equal apprehension for several fords, had reached within a small distance of this branch of the Catawba the same day. And, detaching part of his troops with the wagons and heavy artillery under Lieutenant Colonel Webster to make every demonstration of forcing a passage over a ford six miles higher up, His Lordship marched at one o'clock the next morning with the Guards, Regiment of Bose, Twenty-third Regiment, and two hundred cavalry to McCowan's Ford, which he fixed on as the spot for his real attempt. The morning being dark and rainy and the roads bad, the head of the column did not arrive at the bank of the river before daybreak; and from want of the fieldpieces (one [of] which had broken down and the other was rendered useless) the enemy, who appeared in force on the opposite side, could not be cannonaded.[2]

The Guards, however, notwithstanding the prospect of a formidable opposition, with great gallantry entered the ford, which was upward of 500 yards wide. And, though the current was rapid and they were in many places up to their middles, they marched steadily across amidst

2. In his whole account of the preliminaries to the Battle of Guilford, and particularly here, Clinton is drawing upon Cornwallis to Germain, Mar. 17, Stevens, Clinton-Cornwallis Controversy, 1, 355–362.

a constant and heavy fire, without being provoked to return a single shot. The flank companies of the Guards, who first reached the opposite shore, immediately formed; and, [they] having in a few minutes killed or dispersed all that opposed them, the rear of the column got over without annoyance. Lord Cornwallis now detached the cavalry and Twenty-third Regiment to pursue the militia, who, on seeing their General and some other officers drop, had fled in every direction.[3] And Lieutenant Colonel Tarleton, leaving the infantry and pressing on with the cavalry for about ten miles, was so fortunate to fall in with about three hundred of the fugitives, whom he charged and dispersed with very little loss.

Morgan's corps, which lay at Beattie's Ford opposite to Lieutenant Colonel Webster, now fell back and left him a free passage, which that officer immediately availed himself of. And, getting over all his baggage, artillery, and stores (though greatly impeded by the continuance of the rain and swelling of the river), he joined the rest of the army with his detachment soon after dark. All the fords had been in the meantime abandoned by the enemy, and General Morgan's corps immediately pushed forward as fast as it could to the Yadkin. This precaution having given it, of course, a considerable start of the royal army, which was not prepared to follow before seven the next morning, the whole effected their escape over that river without any other loss than that of a few wagons which the Guards came up with on the evening of the 3d at its Trading Ford. Here the royal army was again stopped by a sudden rise of the waters, which had only just fallen (almost miraculously) to let the enemy over, who could not else have eluded Lord Cornwallis' grasp, so close was he up to their rear notwithstanding the numberless difficulties he had to struggle with, in this latter race of thirty-eight miles, from swelled creeks and bad roads.

Lord Cornwallis' great exertions had hitherto certainly merited every praise. Nor can too much be said in commendation of the firm alacrity with which the troops under him bore up against and surmounted difficulties not frequently the lot of a superior army—being often without provisions and ever without covering, or even rum, to comfort them under the hardships of a long fatiguing march through all the inclemencies of a cold and rainy winter. It must be confessed, indeed, that the enemy too had their share of distress. But it should be at the same time recollected that every step they took drew them nearer to their magazines and friends, from whence they were assured that all their wants would be most amply supplied. On the contrary, the King's troops were now advanced into an exhausted, hostile country above 200 miles

3. The American commander (who was killed) was Brig. Gen. William Davidson.

from theirs, without the means of collecting supplies and even beyond the chance of finding refreshment of any sort.[4] Under such circumstances as these, and after having been already twice disappointed of his object by events the repetition of which was constantly to be expected at that season of the year in a country so intersected with water, it is presumable His Lordship might have thought himself justified in relinquishing his fruitless pursuit and returning to restore tranquillity to South Carolina, whose friendly plantations were at this time everywhere ravaged by the enemy's mounted militia and plunderers, and whose safety was even endangered by his absence.[5]

But Lord Cornwallis was still, unfortunately, tempted to endeavor *by rapid marches to get between General Greene and Virginia*—though he knew the present impracticable state of the Yadkin would force him to take a circuit of at least fifty miles before he could pass its two branches at the upper fords, while the enemy, on the contrary, by having already passed [the river] and thereby holding the string of the bow, had every advantage he could desire for accomplishing his escape. Therefore, after halting two days at Salisbury to collect a small supply of provisions, His Lordship put his troops again in motion on the 6th. And, having passed as he proposed at the upper fords, he pressed on by forced marches to the banks of the Dan, which he reached on the 15th, thus completing a route of nearly one hundred and eighty miles in the short space of ten days.

The detour which Lord Cornwallis was obliged to make having afforded the Americans some little time to breathe, General Greene was thereby enabled to effect a junction of the the two divisions of his army. This was accomplished near Guilford Court House on the 7th; and, as he knew that it must take Lord Cornwallis some time to pass the Yadkin, he ventured to halt there for two days in order to arrange his further proceedings and afford refreshment to his fatigued and almost famished troops. These, including Continentals, riflemen, and cavalry, amounted to about 2000, but they were worn down and dispirited. The American General judged it, consequently, prudent to retire over the Dan. He accordingly began his march for this purpose on the 10th, placing a select body of light troops to cover his rear and harass and retard Lord Cornwallis in the pursuit.

4. *Clinton's note:* Copy of Lord Cornwallis' orders, dated the 28th [and 29th] of January, 1781: [28th:] "The supply of rum for a time will be absolutely impossible, and that of meal very uncertain. To remedy the latter it is recommended *either to bruise the Indian corn* or to endeavor *to rasp it after it has been soaked.*" [29th:] "As the provisions will *probably be very irregular,*" etc.

5. See Balfour's letters to Clinton on conditions in South Carolina, Jan. 31, Feb. 13, 14, 24, Apr. 7, May 6, and Rawdon's of Mar. 23, below, pp. 486–487, 489, 501, 507, 520.

But even this little delay might have proved fatal. For Lord Cornwallis had made so great expedition that he was then within less than
forty miles of him, and the light corps of the two armies had a smart
rencontre the day after. However, though they were frequently after
this so near as to have almost daily skirmishes, the Americans managed so judiciously that little impediment was given to the progress of
their main army, whose entire passage across the Dan was completed
(with that of the light troops) on the night of the 14th. And its General
lost no time in soliciting the government of Virginia to send him without delay every necessary supply and reinforcement.[6]

Lord Cornwallis pushed on his troops twenty-three miles the next
day, in full expectation of still catching the chief part of the enemy on
the south side of the river, as his intelligence had assured him that it
was impossible to procure flats [flatboats] anywhere on its banks sufficient for their transportation, and his own route had cut them off
from all the fords that were practicable. His Lordship's disappointment
and mortification must have been, therefore, extreme when he was informed, on his arrival in the evening at Boyd's Ferry, that the light
troops which formed their rear guard had got over the night before,
and that the baggage and main body had passed the preceding days
at that and a neighboring one [i.e., ferry]. The enemy had secured all
the craft on the opposite side of the river. And, as Lord Cornwallis'
force was but ill suited to enter by this quarter so powerful a province
as Virginia, His Lordship determined on the 16th to march back to the
camp he left on the morning before and, halting there a day, to proceed on to Hillsboro (which by this course is sixty-two miles from that
part of the Dan), where he arrived on the 20th after passing two
branches of the Hycootee and three creeks in his route.

Here His Lordship made a halt of five days, and invited by proclamation all loyal subjects to repair with arms and ten days' provisions to
the King's standard and to stand forth and take an active part in assisting him to restore order and constitutional government.[7] And, hearing
that a considerable body of friends resided between Haw and Deep
Rivers, His Lordship detached Lieutenant Colonel Tarleton on the 23d
with 200 cavalry, 100 Jägers, and 150 infantry to favor their assembling
and joining the royal army. His Lordship was also further induced to
take this route by his desire of communicating with a small post Lieutenant Colonel Balfour had established at Wilmington by his order in the
latter end of the last month, under Major Craig of the Eighty-second,

6. See Greene to Jefferson, to von Steuben, and to Washington, Feb. 15, below,
p. 487.
7. The proclamation is printed in Stevens, *Clinton-Cornwallis Controversy, 1,*
327.

that he might learn whether it was practicable to get supplies from thence for his army up the Cape Fear River to Cross Creek.

General Greene, having in the meantime been joined by about 600 Virginia militia and procured some refreshment for his troops, formed the resolution of recrossing the Dan in order to prevent Lord Cornwallis from gaining a footing in North Carolina. With this view he had sent Lee's Legion over that river on the 18th, with orders to lay near the British camp and watch His Lordship's motions. The light troops of his army passed it [the Dan] on the 21st, and he himself followed with the main body the next day. News of this reaching Lord Cornwallis on the 24th, he immediately dispatched an order to Lieutenant Colonel Tarleton to join him as soon as possible.

And this officer, upon hearing that a Continental force was expected in the neighborhood, had sent that morning to a family of the name of Pyle (who had assembled a considerable number of followers in consequence of Lord Cornwallis' invitation) to join him at an appointed rendezvous without delay. But their leader, in his route to obey the summons, unfortunately falling in with a body of the enemy's cavalry which he mistook for the British Legion, his party was surrounded and most of them cut to pieces.[8] This unlucky circumstance did infinite mischief to the royal cause throughout North Carolina, which had been before considerably damped by the preceding misfortunes and the cruel persecutions which followed, together with the present distressed and scanty appearance of the King's troops which His Lordship had now brought to their support—who seemed to stand more in need of assistance themselves than to be capable of affording any to others.

Though Hillsboro was the appointed rendezvous for the friends of constitutional government to assemble at, Lord Cornwallis moved from his present position as soon as the detachment rejoined him, and, crossing the Haw, encamped on Alamance Creek about thirty miles west of that town. The reasons assigned by His Lordship for this move were that he had here a prospect of being better supplied with forage, and could more conveniently assist his friends on the approach of the enemy.[9] But the loyalists, looking upon it as little short of a retreat and an explicit confession of the enemy's superiority, were ever after very shy of showing any disposition to join the King's troops.

General Greene, being joined by a number of riflemen from the west-

8. Fisher, Struggle for American Independence, 2, 402–403; Ward, War of the Revolution, 2, 778–779.

9. Cornwallis to Germain, Mar. 17, Stevens, Clinton-Cornwallis Controversy, 1, 360–361.

ern waters,[10] had in the meantime advanced his little army to within
a few miles of the British camp. But afterward [he] fell back to the
Reedy Fork, twenty miles north of it (which being at no great distance
from the fords of the Dan, a retreat was thereby secured in case of extremity); and his cavalry and light troops were advanced some miles in
his front, to watch Lord Cornwallis and harass his foragers. The two
armies continued in these positions five days; and their vicinity to each
other produced, of course, frequent skirmishes, with various success.

At last Lord Cornwallis, being informed that the enemy's advance
was posted carelessly at separate plantations for the convenience of
subsisting, formed the design of surprising them—or at least of driving them in—and seizing some opportunity of attacking General
Greene's army. For this purpose His Lordship's whole line was put in
motion on the morning of the 6th of March. But, though the enemy's
light troops were at first driven in with precipitation and loss, the
frequent stands made by them at different passes and the length of
the pursuit (eighteen miles) so wasted the day that nothing was effected against their main army, which fell back as that of the British
approached, having always in its power thereby to avoid a general action. And this was clearly General Greene's intention until he could be
joined by the Virginia reinforcements, who were then on their march
toward him.

Lord Cornwallis, being thus disappointed of the blow he expected
to give the enemy, and finding it difficult to subsist his troops in that
devoured country, came to a resolution of immediately inclining toward
the communication with his shipping in Cape Fear River, from a desire of easing the sufferings of his army, which now began to be in
want of every kind of supply. And he was not without hopes that the
loyalists of that district might be disposed to join him when they saw
their country covered by his presence. In pursuance of this plan His
Lordship recrossed the Reedy Fork and marched in a southwest direction for twenty-five miles toward Deep River, where he halted for one
day. This unfortunately afforded General Greene an opportunity of
recrossing the Haw, to meet the supplies and new levies which were
coming to him from Virginia and Hillsboro—which being completely
effected by the 11th, he was now in a condition to face His Lordship and
even bring him to action.

His Lordship, however, renewed his march on the same day. And,
as his army crossed a branch of Deep River on the 13th, its rear was attacked by the enemy's light troops, which were, however, repulsed with

10. A common but ill-defined term for a trans-Appalachian region in what is
now Kentucky, Tennessee, West Virginia, Virginia, and North Carolina.

loss. The next day His Lordship received information that the enemy's main army, which was reported to consist of nine or ten thousand men, was marching to attack him, and that it was advanced to Guilford, within twelve miles of his camp. This determined His Lordship to meet rather than wait for the enemy. And, having accordingly sent off the wagons, with the baggage and sick, under a proper escort to Bell's Mill on Deep River, he marched with the rest of the troops on the 15th at daybreak, to attack them either on the road or in their encampments.

The American army in the field, by the accounts since given us, consisted of forty-two hundred and forty-three infantry, of which only fourteen hundred and ninety were Continentals, the rest militia, with four pieces of cannon and about two hundred cavalry. Lord Cornwallis', by his own returns, [consisted] of thirteen hundred and sixty infantry and two hundred cavalry, with six pieces of cannon; so that disparity does not appear to be very great if we take into account the different quality of the troops which compose each army. For the behavior of the southern militia was so uniformly bad during the whole war that their presence in action would never be regarded as adding much to the strength of the corps they happened to side with—on the contrary. But the circumstances under which each army was now going to fight were certainly widely different. For, should that under Lord Cornwallis happen to be defeated, its destruction was inevitable. But General Greene had so judiciously chosen his ground that he had no very serious misfortune to apprehend should he lose the day, because he had several large fordable rivers and a country of friends behind him to cover his retreat, through which he very well knew His Lordship could be in no condition to follow him.

The action began at about half after one in the afternoon, and appears to have been well disputed on both sides for nearly two hours, when the enemy were obliged to retire from the field of battle with the loss of all their artillery and about thirteen hundred stand of small arms. But, it not being in Lord Cornwallis' power—from the excessive fatigue of his troops—to pursue beyond the Reedy Fork, and their retreat being covered by a compact body of cavalry, which had suffered nothing in the action, there were only a very few prisoners taken. With respect to the loss of the two armies in killed and wounded, it is supposed upon the whole to have been nearly equal, amounting to between five and six hundred each.[11] Greene therefore imputes his de-

11. These figures seem to be unfounded. The returns that Clinton cites give American losses as 265 killed and wounded, British as 506; the most modern estimates are virtually the same. (Below, p. 498 n. 58; Wallace, *Appeal to Arms*, p. 239; Ward, *War of the Revolution*, 2, 793.) Clinton's total of American casualties is

feat to the superior discipline of the King's troops, though it is to be suspected that he owes it also in great measure to much the same cause to which Gates did his in the Battle of Camden—viz., placing the North Carolina militia in front, and their running away on the first fire.[12] It is, however, but justice to say that nothing could possibly have been more honorable to the British arms than the spirited and judicious exertions of both officers and men on this day. Though we have to lament that no other advantage could be derived from its success than an unmolested retreat to Cross Creek, which it might perhaps have been too hazardous for Lord Cornwallis to have attempted in the face of such numbers before they received a handsome check (which this must be allowed to have been, rather than a complete victory), the advantages of which were manifestly transferred to the enemy the moment the door was thrown open for their army's re-entrance into South Carolina.

Lord Cornwallis' army being worn down by the hardships and fatigues of a march of 600 miles (in which, as he himself describes it,[13] it *had forded several large rivers and numberless creeks, several of which would be reckoned large rivers in any other country in the world, without tents or covering against the climate, and often without provisions*), and nearly one-third of its number being now sick and wounded, another action with the enemy was by no means desirable. Therefore, as the troops had been two days without bread and the country about Guilford was so totally destitute of subsistence that no forage could be procured from a nearer distance than nine miles, His Lordship found himself under the disagreeable necessity of leaving above seventy of the worst of the wounded to the humanity of the enemy and removing the remainder, along with his troops, by easy marches to Cross Creek, where he flattered himself he should find the necessary supplies (which he had ordered to be sent him from Wilmington) and receive such an accession of strength, by a junction of numbers of the King's friends in that country, as might enable him to undertake further operations.

The march thither was accordingly commenced on the third day after the action. And His Lordship distributed in his route a proclamation to announce his late victory over General Greene's army, and to call upon all loyal subjects to stand forth and take an active part in restoring

---

1311, of British 532. This, however, is highly misleading, because it includes almost 1000 American militia who were "missing"—and presumably lived to fight another day.

12. See Greene to the President of Congress, Mar. 16, and Cornwallis to Germain, Mar. 17, below, pp. 497–501.

13. In a portion of the letter just cited that is not included in Clinton's extract; see Stevens, *Clinton-Cornwallis Controversy, 1,* 368.

good order and government, promising at the same time that, whatever men in arms (except murderers) should surrender themselves before the 20th of April and give a military parole, they should have permission to return to their respective homes and be protected in their persons and properties.[14] But His Lordship's proclamation, as might have been expected under his then miserable circumstances, produced no effect. For, according to His Lordship's own account of the matter, many of the inhabitants rode into his camp, shook him by the hand, said they were glad to see them and to hear they had beaten Greene, and then rode home again. Nor could he get 100 men in all the Regulators' country to stay with him even as militia.[15]

General Greene, who had fallen back after the action to the ironworks on Troublesome Creek about ten miles from Guilford, no sooner heard of Lord Cornwallis' retreat than he put his troops in motion to pursue them with all possible expedition. But the roads were so deep and the weather [so] bad that he did not reach Ramsay's Mills on Deep River (a distance of only ninety-three miles) before the 28th, the day on which His Lordship had left them. Finding, therefore, that the royal army, by having passed the river and removed their bridge, had too much the start to be easily overtaken, and its being almost impossible for him to subsist his men much longer in that route,[16] he wisely determined to give over the pursuit and return to South Carolina, after a few days' longer stay at the mouth of Deep River to collect a small supply of provisions and to ascertain His Lordship's ultimate destination. This latter measure answered also another very important purpose, for it kept His Lordship for some time in ignorance of the course he proposed to take and made him apprehend that he was still inclined to follow him, which induced His Lordship to force his troops on at the rate of sixteen, seventeen, and eighteen miles a day—a pace but very ill suited to their then crippled state and naked condition, being encumbered with above six hundred sick and wounded and almost without a shoe to the soldiers' feet.

When Lord Cornwallis arrived at Cross Creek, he had the mortification to find that no supplies had been sent up for his army from Wilmington on account of the distance and impracticability of the Cape Fear River, and that the inhabitants of that friendly district, though ready to afford every assistance in their power, were not much inclined to join him. After halting, therefore, for one day to collect provisions, His Lord-

14. The proclamation, dated Mar. 18, is printed in *ibid.*, p. 371.
15. Cornwallis to Clinton, Apr. 10, below, p. 508. For the Regulators see above, p. 25 and n. 15.
16. See Greene to the President of Congress, Mar. 23, 31, below, pp. 502, 503.

ship resumed his route to the coast. And by an accelerated march of ninety miles in six days he had the pleasure of getting the men under cover at McLeane's Bluff, opposite to Wilmington, on the 7th of April, where he immediately began to dispose of his sick and wounded and procure the necessary stores and refreshments for his troops.

I shall beg leave to close this detail by mentioning a few circumstances which may possibly assist the reader in his reflections on the propriety and consequences of this ill-fated invasion and pursuit. When Lord Cornwallis first communicated to me his intentions of invading North Carolina, he told me he had troops sufficient not only for the recovery of that province and securing the tranquillity of those to the southward of it, but even to spare 3000 men from them to assist me in my operations to the northward even before General Leslie with 2500 had joined. And in a letter to His Lordship of the 6th of November, which he received on the 3d of the following month, I told him that the arrival of a French armament at Rhode Island had hurt the King's affairs very much; and that, Mr. Washington's force being greatly increased in consequence, it would not be in my power for the present to detach more from my army than I had already done. His Lordship was not, therefore, to expect any addition to either his own or the Chesapeake corps until I should happen to be reinforced, of which I then saw no immediate prospect. In that letter I also told His Lordship the kind of services which I expected from the expedition under Major General Leslie and that, should it succeed in obliging Gates to fall back by seizing his depots at Petersburg, and consequently facilitate His Lordship's advance, it was then my wish (if His Lordship continued in the resolution of penetrating into North Carolina, which, though I had never disapproved, I had never recommended) *that he might establish a post at Hillsboro and feed it from Cross Creek by means of the Cape Fear River, agreeable to the plan I had formerly recommended to him if ever he should determine on a march into North Carolina.*[17]

Now we have seen that too little caution in Lord Cornwallis' first attempt lost him 1000 men and obliged him, instead of sparing me any troops, to draw to himself the 2000 which I had sent into the Chesapeake to make a diversion in his favor, and which were replaced imm[ediate]ly by [an]other 1000. It was consequently to be presumed that, before His Lordship made his second, he would have not only sent into the Cape Fear River a force adequate to the securing a communica-

17. The parenthesis in the final sentence is Clinton's later addition. His extract of this letter (below, p. 473) omits most of what is in the text, but he is paraphrasing accurately; the complete dispatch is in "Correspondence with Cornwallis" (a slip case in the CP containing a five-volume series of letterbooks), 3, 30–35.

tion between Cross Creek and the sea, but that he would have clearly ascertained the possibility of such a measure, as his success and even safety absolutely depended upon it. And indeed (though delicacy, together with my confidence in His Lordship's abilities, restrained me in this instance, as in many others, from binding him down by positive orders) I could not doubt that he would pay at least that attention to my recommendations which my station was entitled to, or their importance merited.

It appears, notwithstanding, that no descent whatsoever was made in the Cape Fear River until above three weeks after His Lordship decamped from Winnsboro, and then only by a small detachment of three hundred men belonging to a very young corps; and that neither Lieutenant Colonel Balfour [18] nor His Lordship knew that the river was impracticable before his army reached Cross Creek—after a march of one hundred and thirty miles after the Battle of Guilford, through a devoured country, with one-third of its diminished number sick and wounded, and in want of almost everything necessary to its convenience and existence. Wherefore, having already hazarded an opinion respecting the imprudence of His Lordship's passing the Yadkin, I shall venture to trespass still further by expressing my surprise that, when His Lordship saw that no good whatsoever resulted from all his exertions and that every post we held in South Carolina and Georgia was likely to be endangered by General Greene's return to the southward, he did not, upon being disappointed of his expected supplies at Cross Creek, immediately return from thence to Camden (being a better road and not much farther than that to Wilmington) as the most likely means of obviating the pernicious effects of his ill-judged pursuit and subsequent retreat. And, indeed, the only way we have to account for so extraordinary a proceeding is the dread His Lordship seems to have had of being attacked by the American army while he was encumbered by the care of so many wounded, and his firm persuasion that Greene was still at his heels.[19]

In short, after the most impartial review of Lord Cornwallis' two invasions of North Carolina, the only inference we can draw from them is that without adequate encouragement or the smallest certainty of being joined by any considerable number of the King's friends in

18. See Balfour to Germain, Mar. 24, 1781, below, p. 502.
19. This "firm persuasion" may have existed only in Clinton's mind. He based it, as he explains here in a sentence that he later deleted, upon a statement in Cornwallis' letter of Apr. 10 that Greene had been at the mouth of Deep River four days before (below, p. 509). The statement in itself scarcely warrants Sir Henry's conclusion.

that province [20]—for I do not find that His Lordship received either promises or invitations from them after Ferguson's defeat and His Lordship's subsequent retreat from Charlottetown—His Lordship withdrew from South Carolina (before the defection occasioned by the late disasters was overcome) the chief means of its security and defense, in direct disobedience of the orders left with him by his Commander in Chief; and that, after forcing the passage of several great rivers, fighting a bloody battle, and running eight hundred and twenty miles over almost every part of the invaded province at the expense of above three thousand men, he accomplished no other purpose but the having exposed, by an unnecessary retreat to Wilmington, the two valuable colonies behind him to be overrun and conquered by that very army which he boasts to have completely routed but a week or two before.[21]

Wherefore, though we may be ever so much disposed to admire Lord Cornwallis' rapid marches so far as they are indicatory of His Lordship's firm intrepidity, activity, and perseverance (qualities without doubt essential to the composition of a great commander), yet, when we have seen the exertion of these qualities followed only by the ruin of a fine army and the ultimate loss of an opulent and important province, which His Lordship was particularly instructed and had repeatedly promised to secure from danger, I fear we can only lament so destructive a misapplication of his talents without being warranted, by even the splendor of victory, to ascribe the smallest military merit to such conduct.

20. See Rawdon to Clinton, Oct. 29, 1780, below, pp. 469–470.
21. Sir Henry made it clear at the time that he was disappointed in the outcome of the campaign; see his letter to Cornwallis of Apr. 30, below, p. 517.

CHAPTER 21

Phillips and Arnold in Virginia, April to May, 1781

[*Clinton's difficulty in getting information about the southern campaign compels him to rely upon rumor and conjecture. He plans operations in the Chesapeake area and against West Point, and consults with Phillips and Arnold. Cornwallis' dispatch of April 10 arrives from Wilmington; Clinton's difficulty in interpreting it. Phillips raids Virginia; reinforcements are sent him from New York.*]

THE GREAT difficulty of communication between the different distant posts of the army under my command, from the want of small ships of war for that service,[1] kept me a long time in ignorance not only of Lord Cornwallis' proceedings after the unfortunate affair of Cowpens (where, it seems, he lost all his light troops, and consequently the means of making such a march in such a country), but even of the real state of South Carolina, and the pernicious effect his distant northern march was likely to have on the tranquillity of that province. The substance of vague reports respecting it had been, indeed, transmitted to me from time to time by Lieutenant Colonel Balfour, who also intimated to me that the enemy had taken advantage of the distant removal of so large a portion of the troops I had left there to excite an alarming spirit of revolt among the disaffected, and to plunder and distress the friendly, inhabitants. But no report whatsoever was made to me by that officer of the *then dismantled state of its capital* in consequence of *his* [*Cornwallis'*] *having thrown down the old works to make way for new ones*, a measure that surely ought not to have been undertaken without my concurrence, or at least my knowledge! [2]

1. See Clinton to Germain, Feb. 28, below, p. 489. In mid-April Sir Henry was still trying to get frigates for his dispatches to Cornwallis; see his letter to Arbuthnot of Apr. 11 and his memorandum of Apr. 12, CP.
2. *Clinton's note:* [I was] ignorant also that he had ordered part of the old works of Charleston to be leveled and others to be raised, [and] that that very important post was consequently exposed during his absence—[on] an expedition undertaken contrary to Sir Henry Clinton's positive orders and to every military principle.
Another note, misplaced two pages earlier and dated March, 1791: I do not

272

But my ignorance probably saved me from many an uneasy hour, as the extreme scantiness of the defensive to which I was now reduced at New York put it absolutely out of my power, had I known it, to add a man to those I had already detached to the southward. And I could consequently only trust to His Lordship's abilities and activity for extricating South Carolina and Georgia from the imminent danger to which his perseverance in pursuing the objects of his winter campaign had exposed them, while I flattered myself with the hope that these imprudent risks might possibly be at last recompensed by the annihilation of General Greene's army and consequent submission of North Carolina.

And, though the rumors which were now circulating among the enemy respecting the Battle of Guilford did not altogether sanction so favorable a conclusion, yet (as they warranted a belief that the King's troops had gained a complete victory and obliged General Greene to retrograde toward Virginia) I could not doubt but the most salutary consequences to the King's affairs in that district would immediately follow,[3] as I had no reason to have the smallest suspicion of the reduced and miserable condition to which His Lordship's acting force was now worn down. Nor did Lord Rawdon, who from his vicinity was of course a more competent judge, seem to be less sanguine in his expectations of the event.[4]

It appeared also not improbable that the rebel rulers in Virginia would, as soon as they saw their own country exposed to the operations of so large a force as General Phillips was now acting with in that province, instantly call back the succors they had sent to Greene's army, and thereby oblige that General either to disband his remaining troops or retire over the Roanoke, which could not fail to accelerate the restoration of order in South and the reduction of North Carolina. Under these persuasions, therefore, and the great probability I then had of my being speedily reinforced by six regiments from Europe and the West Indies, together with one thousand recruits—which my aide-de-camp, Colonel Bruce, had just brought me information from

---

find the exact period when Lord Cornwallis ordered or permitted any of the works of Charleston to be leveled, but I am surprised indeed that he should have done so at any time without informing Sir Henry Clinton—and particularly at a time when he had determined on an offensive expedition in North Carolina, and consequently when Charleston (which he had been ordered always to consider as a primary object) was exposed, which it was from January, '81, till May, '81, as appears by Lord Rawdon's letter to Lord Cornwallis [of May 24, 1781, below, pp. 521–522].

3. See Clinton to Phillips, Mar. 24, below, pp. 502–503.
4. Rawdon to Clinton, Mar. 23, below, p. 501.

the American Minister were certainly to be added to the army under my command, and whose arrival either at New York or Charleston was hourly to be expected—I began to prepare for carrying into execution two important plans which I had long digested, and whose success in the present state of the rebel affairs could not, I thought, fail of finishing the war in the most advantageous and honorable manner.

Though my prospects from the first of my command had certainly hitherto been dark and gloomy, from the acknowledged inadequacy of my force and the impossibility of my placing any sort of confidence in the cooperation of the naval chief with whom I was associated, and I had in consequence repeatedly implored His Majesty's permission to resign the command of his American army, yet (having now received the strongest assurances from his Minister that Admiral Arbuthnot would be immediately removed to the Jamaica station and another admiral appointed in his room,[5] and the contents of a rebel mail lately taken having convinced me that the affairs of the enemy were in such a desperate state that nothing seemed to be wanting to compel the entire submission and reunion of America to Great Britain but the barely avoiding misfortune on our side for only a few months longer, without even the assistance of any capital loss on theirs) I must confess that I now for the first time became sanguine in my hopes. And, as I knew that the addition of the promised reinforcements (with what I expected to be able to draw from Lord Cornwallis after the successful close of his operations to the southward) would secure me from all risk, I only waited their arrival to open the campaign to the northward with every hope of the fullest success.

Upon casting my eye over the map of the Chesapeake, I had been long since struck with the very commodious and defensible situation of a tract of country lying between that bay and the Delaware, and containing about one hundred square miles, the entrance into which by land is greatly narrowed by the near approach of Elk River to Wilmington Creek, and its gorge being in a manner commanded by an eminence called Iron Hill, nearly midway between the two waters. A proper fortification thereon seemed capable, with a few good troops joined to the armed loyalists of the district, of effectually shutting the door in front, and securing a retreat in case of misfortune from behind. The inhabitants of this noble peninsula amounted to about a twelfth part of those in the thirteen colonies, and were reported to me from very

5. See Germain to Clinton, Oct. 13, 1780, below, p. 467. In fact Lord George had said nothing about removing the Admiral "immediately," and Sir Henry was skeptical about when or even whether the vague promise would be fulfilled; see his letters to Germain, Apr. 5, 30, 1781, below, pp. 507, 516–517.

good authority to be in general attached to the British government (many of them from local reasons probably), and a very respectable number of them ready on invitation to take up arms in its support. Its climate is benign and most of the habitable situations remarkably healthy, while its numerous plantations yielded annually, as reported to me, above 1,300,000 bushels of grain besides 12,000 hogsheads of tobacco, and abounded so amply in black cattle, sheep, and hogs, as well as forage, that they could have conveniently fed a very considerable army even without the aid of foreign resources.

Moreover, the numerous safe harbors which open from its shores into both bays afforded a facility of communication and retreat which scarcely any temporary naval superiority on the side of the enemy could interrupt. And its peninsular situation would, while we commanded the waters that washed it, secure to us all exports from Virginia and Maryland by the Chesapeake, and great part of the produce of Pennsylvania and the Jersies usually exported by the Delaware, so that the maritime communication of these four provinces with the rest of the world must have been in a great measure under our control as long as we could retain this neck of land in our possession—which, there was little doubt, the numerous friends we already had there, and the multitudes of refugees who most probably would have been tempted by the mildness of the British government to have flocked thither from all quarters, might have soon rendered permanent.

The very numerous important advantages, military, political, and commercial, which were likely to result to Great Britain from the possession of this very valuable district are too obvious to require detail; and I was by no means insensible of them. But the attempt was not to be made without conviction of its infallible success, lest inevitable ruin to our friends there might accompany the mortification of disappointment. I had, therefore, in August, 1780, stated to the American Minister my opinions and wishes on this subject, and at the same time told him that with a reinforcement of 6000 men and security against a superior fleet and a foreign army I should have little doubt of being able to reduce it to obedience, but that I did not think a less force than 4000 in addition to the militia of the district could screen it, after conquest, from insult.[6] My plan was at that time honored with His Majesty's approbation, and Lord George Germain assured me in his answer that every exertion should be made to send me the supplies and troops I

6. Clinton to Germain, Aug. 25, 1780, below, p. 454. Sir Henry's scheme was remarkably similar to other proposals submitted to Germain in 1779–80, for which see George W. Kyte, "Some Plans for a Loyalist Stronghold in the Middle Colonies," *Pennsylvania History, 16* (July, 1949), 11–14.

required, of which he would inform me more particularly by my aide-de-camp, Colonel Bruce.[7]

To prepare, therefore, against the moment in which I might be enabled to act, measures were immediately taken to secure a small naval post in the Chesapeake, to cover the King's cruisers and to supply a fit rendezvous for more serious operations. But Lord Cornwallis' subsequent losses, obliging him to withdraw the force destined for this service, not only retarded its execution, but greatly diminished my means of accomplishing the plan I had formed. Another small detachment of 1000 was, however, soon after sent there. And, Colonel Bruce arriving on the 17th of March with assurances that I might for certain expect in addition very soon six old regiments and one thousand recruits, I ventured to reinforce the corps in Virginia with two thousand men under the orders of Major General Phillips, to whom I very fully explained my intentions of seizing the peninsula between Chesapeake and Delaware, together with my plan for a combined move to that purpose, that he might turn it in his thoughts on the spot, and give me his and Brigadier General Arnold's opinions upon it.[8] I took an early opportunity also of *again* communicating my design to the American Secretary.[9]

Accordingly, after the Major General had effected his junction with Brigadier General Arnold and had an opportunity of consulting with that intelligent officer, he lost no time in transmitting to me their joint ideas respecting the practicability of the operations which I had proposed to him.[10] The result [i.e., purport] of which was that, as the enemy was reported from very good authority to have 3000 militia under General Muhlenberg about Suffolk and the Northwest Landing [and] about 1500 more under General Weedon in the neighborhood of Williamsburg, and [as] the Marquis de Lafayette lay with about 1500 Continentals at Annapolis (but where he was blocked up by the British cruisers), they did not think it expedient for the Major General with his present force to engage in the move up the Chesapeake; but, if I would add to it 1600 more troops such as the British grenadiers and Forty-second Regiment, that they should have no doubt of being able not only to carry Lafayette's corps, but afterward to cooperate with me in the project against the lower counties.

For under the circumstances stated it would certainly require every man he had to garrison Portsmouth and its dependent posts, and give

7. Germain to Clinton, Oct. 13, 1780, below, pp. 467–468.
8. See "Substance of opinions given to Maj. Gen. Phillips," *ca.* Mar. 10, 1781, below, pp. 493–495.
9. Clinton to Germain, Apr. 5, below, p. 506.
10. Phillips to Clinton, Apr. 3, 15, below, pp. 504–505, 510.

at the same time support and communication to such a naval armament in Currituck and Albemarle Sounds as might be necessary for commanding the interior waters of North Carolina from Virginia to Cape Fear. But, if Lord Cornwallis' actual situation did not require an immediate cooperation on this extensive plan, they were of opinion *that the post of Portsmouth was a very improper one* merely as a station to cover frigates, etc., on account of the *weakness of its situation and the large number of troops its extensive works would demand for its defense,* as in that point of view the occupying Mill Point, Norfolk, and some corresponding station appeared most likely to answer—whereby the vessels lying within them in Elizabeth River might possibly be protected because, one [post] being forced, a retreat would be left open by the other two; and it must require a large force indeed to attack the three posts at once.[11]

Besides the proposed move against the Delaware Neck I had it likewise in contemplation to blend with it the attempt of a blow against West Point forts in the Highlands, should Brigadier General Arnold, from his knowledge of that post, think success practicable without the loss of much time and [should] the state of the enemy's and my own force be such as to encourage it.[12] At any rate, however, I judged that the bare appearance of the attempt might draw thither all the troops Mr. Washington could collect, and consequently greatly facilitate the combined operations against the Eastern Neck. For this purpose I requested to have the Brigadier's and Major General's ideas with respect to the practicability of the attempt, and the time when they thought the Chesapeake corps might be at liberty to assist in it. For it had been

11. *One of Clinton's loose notes:* All seem agreed that Hampton Roads was the best for large ships and for small also, for these could always take advantage of winds and tides and escape an enemy laying in Chesapeake; for in Lynnhaven Bay they could not lay in bad gales at northwest or north or northeast. Old Point Comfort, which protects Hampton Road, always had been fortified, might easily be [again], and commanded within good distance a narrow, winding channel from [the] sea; whereas it was very broad near the fort, and would have given full scope for large ships to have acted in. Had Lord Cornwallis been there instead of Yorktown, I really believe—by sinking a few transports in the narrow channel—he must have been safe; and he might from thence have passed his army over to the Portsmouth side. The enemy's fleet in that case must have retired to the entrance of York or Potomac or Rappahannock (for in Lynnhaven Bay they could not ride in safety), while ours might have warped in to Hampton Road or, with a fair wind and tide, led in between the sunken vessels.

12. Clinton to Germain, Apr. 5, below, pp. 505–506, and Clinton to Phillips, same date, Stevens, *Clinton-Cornwallis Controversy,* 1, 392. Clinton's inquiry of Arnold was in cipher, and is apparently not extant. Arnold was extremely guarded in his reply, on the ground that he knew nothing of the changes at West Point since the previous September; but he was certainly not enthusiastic about the scheme. See Arnold to Clinton, Apr. 16, in "Correspondence with Arnold" (the letterbook in the CP already cited), pp. 53–57.

my intention, as may be seen in my instructions to General Phillips, that, as soon as the objects of his expedition were accomplished and the heats should put an end to operation in that quarter, both he and General Arnold should return to me and bring with them the light infantry and two other corps.[13]

And immediately upon my receiving the Major General's opinions on the posts in Elizabeth River I left him at full liberty to change them for any others which he might think more eligible, since from his local knowledge he must be a more competent judge than I could possibly be, [I] having been there but for a moment; and it was, as I told him, by no means my wish to bury the elite of my army in Nansemond and Princess Anne. For I had no other object in view by occupying that station than to protect the King's ships which might occasionally sail from thence to cruise in the waters of the Chesapeake and command its entrance, and this I supposed might be very well accomplished by a garrison of less than 1000 men.[14] I consequently left it to General Phillips' discretion to act in this matter as he should judge best for the King's service.

But, by the time I had received Major General Phillips' answers to my letters, the face of affairs to the southward had undergone such a change that, weak as I was, I found I should most probably be obliged to send another considerable detachment to the Chesapeake, instead of drawing any troops for the present from thence or receiving that assistance from Lord Cornwallis which I had before so sanguinely expected. For the *Amphitrite*, frigate, arriving at New York on the 22d of April, brought me a letter from His Lordship—dated at Wilmington the 10th—giving me to understand that, although his victory at Guilford (which he reckoned one of the bloodiest of the war) was very complete, he was compelled by the distresses of his army to leave the back parts of North Carolina and retire to that place, *where he was disposing of his sick and wounded and procuring supplies of all kinds to put the troops into a proper state for taking the field;* and that he was impatiently looking out for the expected reinforcements from Europe, part of which would be indispensably necessary to enable him to act offensively *or even to maintain himself* in the upper country, where alone he could hope to escape the fatal sickness which had so nearly ruined his army last autumn.[15] His Lordship was likewise pleased to

13. Instructions to Phillips, Mar. 10, and Clinton to Phillips, Mar. 24, below, pp. 495–497, 502–503.

14. The paragraph to this point is a paraphrase of Clinton to Phillips, Apr. 11, except that in the original Sir Henry speaks of a garrison of only five or six hundred men. Stevens, *Clinton-Cornwallis Controversy, 1,* 403–404.

15. *One of Clinton's loose notes:* Does not this letter distinctly imply that His

inform me that he was *anxious to receive my commands with respect to the operation of the summer*, and to express his wishes that the Chesapeake might become the seat of war—even, if necessary, at the expense of abandoning New York—*for, until Virginia was subdued, our hold of the Carolinas must be difficult if not precarious.*[16]

It was certainly very unfortunate that Lord Cornwallis had not time by the present opportunity to explain himself more fully on the state of the two Carolinas, and the plan he proposed pursuing either for the reduction of North Carolina or the securing our remaining possessions to the southward of it—which last appeared to be the object most immediately pressing. For, had I now been clearly informed on this very important subject, I might possibly have been able to regulate my measures so as most effectually to aid either, until the inclemency of the season should put an end to military operations in that climate. But all that I could gather from His Lordship's letter was that he was preparing to take the field and march into the back country, undetermined, however, whether he should act on the offensive or defensive, but at all events clearly intimating that he should be under a necessity of detaining at least part of the expected reinforcement from Europe, and consequently that he could not spare any portion of the Carolina army to assist in the summer campaign to the northward.

I was very reluctant, however, to relinquish entirely the enterprise I had planned for the Eastern Neck, though I clearly saw it was impossible now to pursue it in all its parts. Therefore, as the probable inference to be drawn from Lord Cornwallis' letter was that His Lordship had no offensive object in view and would soon seize some healthy, defensible post in the back country which might cover South and awe North Carolina, I flattered myself that I should even yet be able to avail myself of the chief, if not the whole, of the regiments coming

---

Lordship had not the least idea of coming northward, but of retiring to the back country to avoid [the] sickness of last year?

16. See below, pp. 509–510. These strategic ideas Clinton of course rejected. His private comment was pungent: "If the Chesapeake had become the seat of war, and New York evacuated to enable us to carry it there, it certainly would have been the speediest way of finishing the war. For the whole army could probably have been annihilated in one campaign, commencing in July." (Sir Henry's marginal note in the letter.) His comment to the government was more moderate: he conceded that the possession of Virginia would be enormously important, but doubted that it was possible; "conquest alone will be of little moment unless we can retain what we conquer, which I think cannot be done in so large and populous a province as Virginia until the inhabitants themselves are disposed to join us— which we cannot hope for, as they are, I believe, almost universally hostile." He therefore wanted no more than a naval base; from it the fleet might command the entrance of the bay, while the army operated near Head of Elk to cut off enemy supplies to Virginia and the Carolinas. Clinton to Germain, July 13.

from Ireland. And with them and the whole of the Chesapeake corps (except the small garrison which the post in Elizabeth River might require for its defense) and the six regiments from West Indies promised, added to what could be spared from New York, I was determined if possible to give the experiment a fair trial.

With this view I requested Major General Phillips to put everything in forwardness for commencing his part of the move by the *20th of May* or, at farthest, the *1st of June*, by which time I expected to be able to enter the Delaware with a cooperating corps from New York.[17] And about 1800 men were in the meantime embarked under Colonel de Voit for the Chesapeake to enable the Major General to comply with my wishes. Wishing, moreover, to lose no time in my preparations, I had very early in April solicited the Vice Admiral to order transports to be held in readiness for the reception of 3500 men, which he not only complied with but promised to appoint a proper convoy to escort them. But, receiving intelligence in the meantime that the French fleet and a number of transports with troops on board were upon the point of sailing from Rhode Island, the reinforcement for the Chesapeake was necessarily detained until the British squadron was in a condition to secure it from danger.

Major General Phillips, when he received Lord Cornwallis' dispatches by the *Amphitrite*, had been for some days embarked with 2000 men waiting for settled weather to proceed up James River, with a view of making some diversion in His Lordship's favor, supposing him to be at that time establishing himself, after his victory at Guilford, in the back parts of North Carolina. But, finding by His Lordship's letter of the 10th of April that any efforts to that purpose were now no longer necessary, he made only a desultory excursion, merely to distress the enemy and keep the troops employed until he could have time to receive final instructions from either Lord Cornwallis or me for his further proceedings. Accordingly, after exploring the neighborhood of Williamsburg and Yorktown and destroying the shipyard, vessels, warehouses, etc., in the Chickahominy, the Major General landed at City Point on the 24th of April, and marched the next day to Petersburg. Here the troops destroyed 4000 hogsheads of tobacco and some vessels they found on the stocks; and, after burning a range of barracks and a quantity of flour at Chesterfield and taking, sinking, and

17. This is not entirely accurate. Clinton suggested that Phillips begin operations by June 1 unless Cornwallis needed his force before then. May 20 was Sir Henry's terminal date for sending reinforcements to Virginia; if waiting for a convoy delayed the troops longer than that, they would go up the Delaware for a junction with Phillips near Head of Elk. Clinton to Phillips, Apr. 30—May 3, below, pp. 518–519.

burning a considerable number of ships and brigs richly laden at Osborne's,[18] they proceeded to Manchester, where and at Warwick they burned several warehouses with large quantities of tobacco and flour, a number of vessels of different sorts, and a range of public rope-walks and storehouses. After doing the enemy this very essential injury, with scarcely any opposition and consequently very little loss, the Major General re-embarked and fell down the river again as low as Hog Island, in expectation of meeting the reinforcement from New York with orders to proceed to Annapolis, etc. But, receiving here a letter from Lord Cornwallis to desire he would facilitate his junction with him at Petersburg,[19] he immediately returned up the river and marched again into that town on the evening of the 9th of May.

In the meantime, the King's ships (whose compliment of men had been greatly reduced by sickness and other causes) having taken on board a detachment of 560 troops which I had spared the Admiral at his request, the transports joined the squadron from Staten Island. And on the 13th of May the whole sailed together for the Chesapeake, where the reinforcement arrived within a few days after without accident, as the report of the French ships having sailed from Rhode Island turned out to be premature.

18. Arnold to Clinton, May 12, below, p. 520.
19. Cornwallis to Phillips, Apr. 24, below, pp. 512–513.

CHAPTER 22

Cornwallis' Move to Virginia and Greene's to South Carolina, April to May, 1781

Little reason the Commander in Chief has to expect, from his letter [of] 10th April, that Lord Cornwallis will quit the Carolinas. His consequent astonishment at hearing, by that of the 24th, that he has marched from Wilmington to Virginia, so contrary to the most clear and positive orders and his own promises. Great danger to which the southern provinces and even Charleston must be exposed by this move. His Lordship's reasons in support of it contradictory and unfounded. Lieutenant Colonel Balfour reprehensible if he neglected to represent the distracted state of South Carolina in consequence of His Lordship's move to Wilmington, and the exposed state of Charleston works, and to forward Sir Henry Clinton's letters (or the substance of them) to Lord Cornwallis at Wilmington—as he had read them, and promised to do so, and was not without several safe opportunities. These letters, etc., all but forbid His Lordship's march into Virginia; consequently the substance of them could not, as His Lordship says, have prompted him to that measure.

Recapitulation of instructions left with Lord Cornwallis when invested with the command of the southern district. His Lordship also expressed himself to be perfectly satisfied with the amount of the forces allotted for that service. His Lordship's disobedience of positive orders clearly shown. Though His Lordship knew Sir Henry Clinton had no wish to commence solid operations in Virginia, and was warned by him of the danger of it and had acknowledged it himself (both which had been also strongly represented to the American Minister), Lord Cornwallis recommends that plan, notwithstanding, to the American Minister; and the Commander in Chief is positively ordered to support it with his whole force.

Lord Cornwallis' and Sir Henry Clinton's plans compared. The former inexpedient from climate and season, and replete with danger without a superior covering fleet, or place of arms till that fleet should arrive. The latter offensive and defensive. The offensive safe against the consequences of a temporary naval superiority, and the country destined for the scene of action remarkably healthy and adapted to either defense or retreat. The defensive, in case the other should be found inexpedient, founded upon the distressed state of the enemy

282

[*and*] *the determination of France not to support them beyond the campaign* [*of*] *'81, which promises, if we can escape affront for a few months longer, to secure us every* effect of the most decisive victory. *This plan once approved by His Majesty, but that of Lord Cornwallis now preferred to it. Reflections thereon. Sir Henry Clinton's plan is reapproved in September—alas, too late.*

General Greene invades South Carolina; is defeated at Camden by Lord Rawdon, who afterward evacuates that post and falls back to Monk's Corner. His reasons for so doing, in a letter to Lord Cornwallis, ought to have operated on that general officer. Forts Watson, Orangeburg, Motte, Granby, and Dreadnought surrender to the enemy; Ninety-six and Augusta invested by them. In short, almost every post in both provinces are lost and upward of 1000 troops taken or killed since Lord Cornwallis' dereliction of Carolina, to which alone these misfortunes may be justly ascribed. His Lordship persists still in his move to Virginia, even after he hears of Lord Rawdon's victory, and joins General Phillips' army at Petersburg.

BEFORE I knew of Lord Cornwallis' retreat to Wilmington, the enemy's account of the Battle of Guilford had induced me to flatter myself that His Lordship's success among our friends in North Carolina (which was the principal object of his march into that province) might have been such as to have restored both the Carolinas to tranquillity. And I had in consequence submitted to His Lordship the propriety, *in that case,* of his coming in a frigate to Virginia and directing such troops to follow him as could be best spared.[1] His Lordship did not, however, receive this letter before his arrival there. And, even after I had received His Lordship's letter of the 10th of April, I own I thought it not impossible that he might avail himself of that invitation to go thither—upon a visit by himself, without carrying troops—as it offered him a good opportunity of consulting personally with Major General Phillips and concerting their future cooperations. For the intimations His Lordship then favored me with did not give me the smallest reason to suspect that he could, or was disposed to, spare a man from the service of the Carolinas before reinforcements should arrive from Europe. I waited, therefore, with anxiety to receive His Lordship's next dispatches, in the hope that they might enable me to form some judgment respecting his expectations and future intentions, and from thence arrange the operations of the summer upon some decided and permanent plan, because my extreme ignorance of His Lordship's real situation and the delay in the arrival of the promised reinforcements had kept everything hitherto suspended in the air, though all my schemes had been

1. Clinton to Cornwallis, Apr. 13, below, p. 510.

long since maturely digested and every preparation [was] in forwardness for carrying them into execution the instant I should be enabled to do so.

These promised and long-expected dispatches from His Lordship were at last brought to me by the *Speedy*, packet, on the 22d of May, dated at Wilmington the 23d and 24th of the preceding month.[2] But how great was my disappointment and astonishment when, instead of hearing that His Lordship's army was, upon being refitted, marched back into the country to protect friends (as he had promised to do) or for the purpose of occupying some healthy and defensible position for the security of at least South Carolina (as His Lordship had also before promised,[3] and [as] his letter to me of the 10th intimated was then his intention), I found he had come to the fatal resolution of abandoning both Carolinas to their fate and flying into Virginia, to save the corps immediately under himself, as he says, from being hemmed in and cut off by General Greene's army, should it return upon him after succeeding against Lord Rawdon! And this at a moment when His Lordship could not be ignorant, as clearly appears by the tenor of all his letters, that the state of South Carolina was most distressing, that the enemy's parties were everywhere, that the communication by land with Savannah no longer existed, that Colonel Brown was invested at Augusta, that Colonel Cruger was in the most critical situation at Ninety-six—in short, that the defection of that province was so universal that the officers to whom His Lordship had entrusted it declared they did not know any mode short of depopulation to retain it.[4]

But this was not the whole of the danger which at this time, to His Lordship's knowledge, threatened the important post whose security he was most strictly enjoined by my instructions never to lose sight of on any account. For it is scarcely to be credited that Lieutenant Colonel Balfour, the commandant, could have been so reprehensibly inattentive to his duty as to neglect informing Lord Cornwallis,[5] as well

2. Cornwallis to Germain, Apr. 23, to Clinton, the same date, to Phillips, Apr. 24, below, pp. 511–513.
   The *Speedy* belied her name. The *Amphitrite* had taken only twelve days to deliver Cornwallis' letter of Apr. 10.
3. Cornwallis to Leslie, Nov. 12, 1780, below, p. 474.
4. A paraphrase of Balfour to Clinton, May 6, below, p. 520.
5. *Clinton's note:* Indeed, I am convinced that was not the case by the different dispatches sent to His Lordship by Colonel Balfour between the 7th and the 10th, which last His Lordship received the 22d, and by which he was informed of the very distressed and critical situation of the whole province. I cannot doubt but that among other things he informed His Lordship of the exposed state of Charleston, as he described it to Lord Rawdon a fortnight afterward and as he had described it to Major Benson on the 7th of April—on which day that gentleman, as he informed me, had been detached by Colonel Balfour to Lord Cornwallis by land

as Lord Rawdon, that "from the little reason he had to apprehend this serious invasion, *the old works of Charleston had been in part leveled to make way for new ones, which were not yet constructed;* that his garrison was inadequate to oppose any force of consequence; and that the disaffection of the townspeople showed itself in a thousand instances"; and consequently that, if His Lordship should withdraw his army to a distance from the province, any misfortune happening to Lord Rawdon's corps might entail the loss not only of that fortress but of all South Carolina and Georgia, and everything else we possessed south of the Chesapeake.[6] Yet, in the face of these very serious and alarming opinions of the two principal officers upon the spot,[7] His Lordship was pleased to tell the American Minister that *he looked upon Charleston as safe from any immediate attack,* and Major General Phillips that *he could be of no use on his arrival there, "there being nothing at present to apprehend for that post."* But His Lordship's letter to me exposes his apprehensions by telling me that *the undertaking sat heavy on his mind,* and *the situation in which he left South Carolina added much to his anxiety.* And indeed His Lordship informs General Phillips that *he fears "the worst of consequences may happen to most of the troops out of Charleston."* [8]

This being so, how are we to account for His Lordship's adopting a measure, hastily and with precipitation, which so clearly militates against the positive orders of his Commander in Chief, and which could not in all appearance fail of precipitating most of the misfortunes they were intended to obviate, and which even himself seems at that time to have apprehended? For the reason which His Lordship's letter to me assigns for it—*there being no prospect of speedy reinforcement from Europe*—appears to be the strongest that can be adduced for His Lordship's immediate return to Charleston by any means that presented themselves. And I have been since informed from indisputable authority (Major Benson told me he was sent to Lord Cornwallis) that

to inform His Lordship of the distressed state of the province from Greene's invasion: that, if His Lordship did not immediately relieve it, the province must be lost; that Charleston could not be saved unless His Lordship returned to South Carolina; that, in the hope he would do so by the Waccamaw, he [Balfour] had sent galleys, etc., into that river and occupied Georgetown.

6. The quotation is from Balfour's statement (see Rawdon to Cornwallis, May 24, below, p. 522); the remainder of the sentence is largely Clinton's.

7. Clinton comments in a note that Rawdon's letters could have left Cornwallis in no doubt about the danger to South Carolina. This, like the text, is misleading. Before he left Wilmington, the Earl knew of the danger in a general way, and perhaps specifically from Balfour; there is no evidence, however, that he had direct word from Rawdon until after he had committed himself to Virginia.

8. The quotations are from the letters cited on p. 284 n. 2.

Lieutenant Colonel Balfour, dreading the appearance of the cloud which was ready to burst upon him, had most earnestly solicited His Lordship to return to South Carolina, telling His Lordship at the same time that he had possessed himself of Georgetown and had placed armed vessels in the Waccamaw in order to facilitate his doing it by that route, whereby he might have *preserved his cavalry and avoided the necessity of embarking in transports,* which he looks upon as so very disgraceful and ruinous.

But there is still another reason given by Lord Cornwallis for this extraordinary step, which appears to be equally unaccountable with the foregoing. His Lordship tells Lord George Germain in his letter of the 23d of April that he had just received an express from Charleston with information that a frigate was arrived there with dispatches from the Commander in Chief, notifying to him that Major General Phillips had been detached into the Chesapeake with a considerable force, with instructions to cooperate with his army and put himself under his orders. Now I know of no ship lying at that time without Charleston Bar that had dispatches from me to His Lordship unless it be the *Jupiter,* letter-of-marque, which sailed from New York on the 20th of March. Major Amherst of the Sixtieth Regiment went passenger in that ship; and, being entrusted with my dispatches, he delivered to Lieutenant Colonel Balfour my letters for Lord Cornwallis (dated the 2d, 5th, and 8th of March) and a copy of my instructions to General Phillips, which that officer acknowledges the receipt of in his letter to me of the *7th of April* by the *Amphitrite,* man-of-war, wherein *he promises to forward them to His Lordship by the way of Wilmington whenever an occasion offers.*[9] We are therefore to conclude that either the whole or the substance of these letters—for Lieutenant Colonel Balfour opened and read them —had been forwarded to Lord Cornwallis by some one of the several safe opportunities that offered between the 7th of April and the 23d, as the distance between Charleston and Cape Fear is not above twelve hours' sail.[10]

9. For Balfour's letter see Stevens, *Clinton-Cornwallis Controversy, 1,* 393. Sir Henry explains, in a note that is otherwise mere repetition, that Maj. Benson did not get through to Wilmington, but that Balfour must have sent the same message by water.

The Colonel had two good opportunities. His letter to Clinton went by the *Amphitrite,* which stopped at Wilmington to pick up Cornwallis' dispatch to Clinton of Apr. 10; almost a fortnight later Balfour sent a resumé of Clinton's dispatches to Cornwallis, presumably by the *Speedy,* and the Earl received it on the 22d. *Ibid.,* pp. 395, n. 1a, 420.

10. *Clinton's note, later in the chapter, belongs here:* There never was a doubt with me but that he knew the contents on the 9th, by the *Amphitrite.* The precipitation was therefore occasioned by the apprehension of their arrival; for it seems they were sent by the *Careysfort,* frigate, who arrived at Wilmington a few hours after Lord Cornwallis had left it, and proceeded from thence to Chesapeake.

Consequently, as these letters would have informed His Lordship that I was under very great alarm for Brigadier General Arnold's corps (which was blocked up at Portsmouth by a French naval force superior to that he had with him) and that Major General Phillips was embarked with a reinforcement and waited the event of a naval action between the two fleets *to be* detached thither to his relief, I cannot conceive how His Lordship could have been encouraged by them or the substance of them to attempt a junction with Major General Phillips in Virginia—as, on the contrary, they all but forbid such a measure.[11] For those letters left it very uncertain whether General Phillips would go thither or no; and, should Brigadier General Arnold's corps have fallen or be still invested, nothing but ruin could follow to that under His Lordship's own command should he undertake it.

Besides, His Lordship would have seen by my instructions to General Phillips (a copy of which was enclosed in those dispatches) that it was my intention to call back to New York both that officer and Brigadier General Arnold, with a considerable portion of the troops under their orders, as soon as the objects of the expedition he was going on should be fulfilled. And consequently His Lordship ought by no means to have looked northward, at least before he had an opportunity of hearing from me, as there appeared to be no small probability that he might disconcert my plans for the campaign by doing so. And all my former correspondence with His Lordship (particularly my letter of the 6th of November [12]) had clearly evinced that, so far from proposing *to commence solid operation in the Chesapeake before I should be reinforced*, I did not even think any operation there safe unless we were certain of a permanent naval superiority.[13]

Besides, as His Lordship's letter of the 10th told me he was anxious to receive my commands (being as yet totally in the dark as to the intended operations of the summer), it is natural to conclude he would have at least waited to receive them before he commenced a march *of such serious import to the general conduct of the war*, which must cut off all communication between us for several weeks, and consequently put it absolutely out of my power to dispose of His Lordship's force before, perhaps, the moment for employing it to advantage might be past.

11. Extracts of Clinton to Cornwallis, Mar. 2, 8, below, pp. 490–492.
12. Below, p. 473.
13. At this point Clinton originally had a paragraph of conjecture that Cornwallis, before leaving Wilmington, had received Phillips' letters to him of Apr. 4 and 8, telling him that the danger in the Chesapeake was ended. Sir Henry deleted the paragraph with the following comment: "He could not have received them. If he had, they would have been acknowledged in his letters of the 22d and 24th April; and, indeed, they must have prevented his going to Virginia, as they would have convinced him that Sir Henry Clinton had determined against *solid* operations in that province."

There can be little doubt that the conquest of Charleston, with the entire capture of its numerous garrison and the large quantity of arms and military stores of all sorts found within its walls, struck terror into the rest of the province and contributed greatly to its subsequent submission. The preserving, therefore, that valuable fortress from insult became of course my first concern. And to enable Lord Cornwallis, whom I had invested with the command of the southern district, to do so, as well as to extinguish every remaining spark of rebellion and discontent among the inhabitants, I recommended it most strongly to the American minister to add His Lordship to the peace commission, that he might have the power of catching the favorable moment for restoring civil government, should His Lordship at any time discover that such a measure was likely to gratify the wishes of the people and secure their attachment to Great Britain. And, to preserve the public tranquillity and protect the King's friends, I left with His Lordship such a force as he was himself so perfectly satisfied with that he in a manner forbade my leaving him a man more, saying he had enough not only for the defense of South but the reduction of North Carolina.

But, had I known in time that the fortifications of Charleston had been thrown down by his order (in which state they lay from January to May), I should certainly have forbid His Lordship's second invasion of the latter province until that important hold of the other had been put into a proper posture of defense—though I must at the same time confess, as I have already more than once in the course of this narrative, that, trusting to His Lordship's abilities and zeal, I gave him a great latitude of power to act in most things according to his own discretion. Consequently I do not claim a right of blaming His Lordship for not always following the plans which I recommended to him, when he happened to think too close an attention to them incompatible with his actual situation and circumstances, though time might afterward have shown they were the best that could have been adopted. But, as I judged it necessary in one instance (which was, I believe, the only one) to tie His Lordship down by *positive orders*, I humbly presume I had a right to expect implicit obedience to *them*, such being universally admitted among military men to be an indispensable duty of subordinate officers. Wherefore, having by my written instructions to Lord Cornwallis *clearly and positively directed His Lordship to regard the security of Charleston as a primary object, and not to make any offensive move that should be likely to endanger it*,[14] and it being

14. Clinton's formal instructions say that the security of Charleston is a primary object, and his covering letter refers to it as the principal object (Stevens, *Clinton-Cornwallis Controversy*, 1, 214–215). In both the emphasis is positive—on the Earl's

an incontestable fact that his move into Virginia exposed that post to the most imminent danger, I am extremely sorry I am obliged in this place to assert that His Lordship *disobeyed my orders and acted contrary to his duty in doing so.*[15] And, indeed, His Lordship himself seems to have been aware of some such inference by the pains he took, in his letters of that period and his subsequent writings, to inculcate a belief that he did not look upon Charleston to be in any kind of danger.

Whether the idea that the conquest of Virginia was a necessary preliminary measure to facilitate the reduction of the Carolinas originated with Lord Cornwallis or the British cabinet is a question which cannot easily be resolved without a reference to His Lordship's correspondence with the American Secretary. For, as the whole of that correspondence has not yet appeared before the public, we can reason only from that part of it which was read in the House of Lords. [It is, however, possible that His Lordship's very sudden resolution of marching into that province may have been induced by the intelligence he probably received from Europe by the February mail, as it is not unlikely his friends there would have informed His Lordship by that opportunity that I was much discontented with my situation, and had solicited leave to resign the command of the army to him unless I was reinforced and Admiral Arbuthnot should be speedily removed. And His Lordship might have wished, in consequence, to be near enough to receive the marshal's staff from my hand while I remained in that humor, lest anything might intervene (if it was delayed) to divert me from it. It was therefore, I suppose, with a view to prepare me for the step he was going to take that His Lordship told me in his letter of the 10th of April that, until Virginia was in a manner subdued, "our hold of the Carolinas must be difficult, if not precarious." The same might likewise have dictated the opinion given in that of the 18th to Lord George Germain "that a serious attempt upon Virginia would be the most solid plan, because successful operations might not only be attended with important consequences there, but would tend to the

---

acting offensively as long as the town is safe, rather than on his not acting unless it is safe.

15. In one of his loose notes Clinton summarizes his grievances against the Earl. They were "that Lord Cornwallis disobeyed my formal orders when he marched in January, '81, into North Carolina, [and] that it was contrary to all military principle to do so without his light troops; that he was guilty of a second disobedience when he moved to Wilmington, and to a third when he marched into Virginia; [that he was] not justified in weak[en]ing the works of Charleston without acquainting me; and, with respect to the dispatches, [that] Lord Cornwallis and Colonel Balfour must take the charge between them of their not being sent to Lord Cornwallis by various safe opportunities."

security of South Carolina and ultimately to the submission of North Carolina."] [16]

But, until I received Brigadier Arnold's letter of the 12th of May enclosing a copy of Lord Cornwallis' letter to General Phillips,[17] I own I did not imagine it possible for His Lordship to attempt precipitating me into his plan by thus joining the corps in the Chesapeake, without consulting me or allowing me time to prevent him, or that he would engage in what he calls himself a desperate move. (Lamenting he is about to do it without hearing from the Commander in Chief—knowing of his dispatches coming to him, however, and expecting them every hour—he notwithstanding marches.) Nor could it ever enter my head that the cabinet in England would adopt the limited opinions of a subordinate general in preference to those of a commander in chief, and order the latter to follow them without even leaving him an option of acting otherwise should he judge them inexpedient or dangerous. Both these, however, as will be shown in the sequel, have since happened; and it may consequently be not disagreeable to the reader to have an opportunity of comparing the merits of each plan. For this purpose, then, I shall now take the liberty of laying a short sketch of them both before him with all the precision and candor in my power.

Lord Cornwallis' plan, as far as we are capable of judging of it from his letters to Lord George Germain, General Phillips, and me, appears to have been to evacuate New York (thereby abandoning all our friends in that extensive district, opening a wide door for the enemy to wrest Canada from us, and relinquishing the only winter harbor, except Halifax, which the King's ships on the American station had to retire to) and remove the whole army from thence to the sickly Province of Virginia (whose inhabitants were abundantly numerous and almost universally hostile), for the purpose of carrying on solid operation there until that province should be entirely subdued. For the commencement of this grand effort His Lordship had selected the month of June, a period when the deadly epidemics of that sickly climate begin to rage and all military enterprise ought of course to cease, as General Washington repeatedly declares; and [he had chosen to act] before we had any certainty, or even a promise, of a covering fleet—without which I had repeatedly told His Lordship as well as the Minister (in which they had agreed with me) that all operations in the Chesapeake must be exposed to the utmost hazard.[18]

16. For Cornwallis to Germain, Apr. 18, see Stevens, *Clinton-Cornwallis Controversy*, *1*, 417–418. The bracketed portion of the paragraph is deleted in the MS, and restored because of its bearing on the controversy.

17. Cornwallis' letter of Apr. 24 reached Phillips on May 7; it was forwarded by Arnold on May 12 with a covering letter printed below, p. 520.

18. See below, pp. 506, 525, 536, 540.

The country His Lordship had chosen for his scene of action is so destitute in itself of the means of subsisting an army that magazines of all kinds must be formed before it could have been put in motion. These of course required *a respectable place of arms* in communication with the sea (which we had not yet secured) to cover the necessary depots (to be drawn from New York) which would consequently be wanted to feed it from a temporary naval superiority of the enemy, which might otherwise in a very few days famish the troops and, according to Lord Cornwallis' expression, render their arms useless. And, should such a melancholy catastrophe take place, there was no retreat left for the miserable few which (by abandoning the greatest part of the army, together with all our artillery, ships, stores, friends, etc.) might possibly be lightened and accommodated for so arduous an enterprise but by a march of some hundred miles through a devoured, hostile country at the most unhealthy season of the year, when the rays of the sun are more fatal than even a superior and victorious foe.

Such was the plan which Lord Cornwallis thought proper to recommend to His Majesty's Ministers on his own limited and partial information, in opposition to the sentiments of the Commander in Chief that had been maturely formed from general, extensive knowledge and circumstances greatly beyond the reach of His Lordship's confined situation as a subordinate officer, and which, being repeatedly represented by him to His Lordship, seemed to have been received by him with acquiescence and conviction long before he commenced his march into Virginia.[19]

The plan which the Commander in Chief had proposed to carry into execution, as soon as success or the season should have put an end to operations in the Carolinas, was of two sorts, offensive [and defensive. It was offensive] on the Delaware Neck between the Chesapeake and Delaware Bays, supported by a corresponding station on the Susquehanna or Potomac Rivers, in all which districts we had at that time, from various causes, many friends ready to join the King's army on its arrival among them. Their situation is remarkably healthy at all seasons and perfectly safe from being affected by a temporary naval superiority of the enemy, which had been ever my constant dread; subsistence for the troops [was] to be readily had from the enemy's

19. *Clinton's note:* Lord George Germain, to do him justice, had been forced— by a part of His Majesty's cabinet ever hostile to Sir Henry Clinton and his plans because Sir Henry had pointed out the impracticability of the war unless reinforced and the sea part otherwise commanded, and (unless this was attended to) had refused to take any responsibility. Lord Cornwallis, on the contrary, had offered more favorable terms. Lord George Germain had seen the danger of *all* Lord Cornwallis' plans after Cowpens. This was explained to Sir Henry Clinton by Mr. Hamilton, and confirmed by Colonel Conway in a message from Lord George Germain to Sir Henry Clinton. [See Conway to Clinton, Dec. 5, 1781, below, pp. 589–590.]

neighboring depots of flour, etc., besides the abundant produce of the country; strong defensive positions [were] to be found almost every mile they were to march, and in case of necessity a secure retreat to New York [was] open for them either by land or water.

And, to preserve the comparison as nearly as possible in all the principal points, this plan would have more certainly and effectually obstructed the course of supplies from the northern to the southern colonies than even that of Lord Cornwallis (could it have been successful), since the proposed position on the Susquehanna, intersecting their usual great road, would have absolutely forbade all communication between them except by a tedious detour behind the Allegheny Mountains. And even this would have been most probably broken up, or rendered at least precarious, by an expedition which I had requested General Haldimand (through Major General Riedesel) to send out from Canada by the River Ohio, for the purpose of exciting and encouraging the Indians to take up arms and, together with the King's friends who were said to be numerous in those parts, fall upon the back settlements of Pennsylvania and Virginia and act in cooperation with His Majesty's troops in the upper Chesapeake.[20] And I am tempted to observe in this place that, had it been positively known in time that Sir William Howe was to have gone up the Chesapeake in 1777, this might possibly have been the best plan of cooperation for the northern army. At any rate I have little doubt that, had Lord Cornwallis only remained where he was ordered, or even after his coming into Virginia had our operations there been covered by a superior fleet as I was promised, Vermont would have probably joined us; [21] and then these several expeditions would have taken place, and have had a fair and complete trial.

Such, in short, was the offensive plan I had formed should I be reinforced as the Minister promised me, and could I have been at liberty to employ the troops under Major General Phillips as I intended. It was to have opened early in June with an attempt upon the shipping, public stores, and the infant Continental Bank just then forming at Philadelphia,[22] and to have proceeded afterward to the other

20. In the summer of 1781 Clinton sent Riedesel to Haldimand with a plan for cooperation from Canada. Riedesel, on reaching Quebec, embodied the plan in a memorandum dated Sept. 25 (below, pp. 574–576). The date makes it obvious that Clinton did not expect assistance from the north until the campaign of 1782.

21. When Congress refused to recognize Vermont as a state, Ethan and Ira Allen made overtures to the British. These negotiations, authorized by Germain and conducted primarily through Haldimand, began in 1780 and continued for the next two years.

22. The Bank of North America. Robert Morris had been appointed superintendant of finance in Feb., 1781; in May he submitted to Congress his plans for

points in succession, as success or encouragement might suggest.

But, if the reinforcement should happen to be too long delayed or till it did arrive, it was the Commander in Chief's determination to leave only a small corps covered by works in Elizabeth River, merely to afford shelter to the King's cruisers in the Chesapeake and yield some little protection to the few loyalists of those parts—which, as being too insignificant an object, he was sure the enemy would never attempt unless they should happen to be superior by sea. After this it was proposed to assemble our whole force at New York and remain upon the defensive, as the Commander in Chief was then fully persuaded (and it has since clearly appeared that he was right) that rebellion in America was at its last gasp; and a very few more months' escape from disaster on our side promised us every good effect of the most decisive victory, by insuring to Great Britain the future dependence of the revolted colonies on a firm and permanent basis. For it was well known at the time that the French would not (we now say could not) assist the Americans beyond the [campaign of] '81, and that America without such assistance could not resist.

[But what could avail all my toil and anxiety, in thus watching the course of events and guarding against every possible contingency, to promote the interests of my King and country if the confidence of those who alone could give them effect was transferred to another, and measures of a direct opposite tendency from those I had planned pursued, which it was impossible for me either to bias or prevent? For I have the best foundation for believing that Lord Cornwallis, having very early intelligence of my desire to quit the command and the disposition of a junto in His Majesty's cabinet not to oppose it, had insinuated to those in power that means were not wanting to finish the rebellion, and that he himself would be responsible for all consequences in undertaking it with the force then in America, without asking for more. On the contrary I had all along, in the most serious language, declared that we were by many thousands too few and that, unless they could supply me with considerable reinforcements and a superior covering fleet and another naval chief, the thing was impossible. It may be therefore inferred that His Lordship's terms were too grateful to the cabinet of that day (whose existence, depending upon success, was

---

the bank, but it did not open until the following January. For details of the genesis, development, and collapse of Clinton's scheme for the Delaware see George W. Kyte, "A Projected British Attack upon Philadelphia in 1781," *Pennsylvania Magazine of History and Biography*, 76 (Oct., 1952), 383–393; the article does not include Sir Henry's revival of the idea in September and in 1782, for which see below, pp. 339–340, 343 n. 22, 358, 572, 577–578, 596, 598–599.

liable to be crushed by the least adverse turn of the war in which they were responsible) not to be listened to by it with avidity.

His Lordship, being consequently (it is presumed) flattered with an almost certainty of succeeding to the command, naturally beheld every step he advanced northward as placing him so much nearer that great object of his ambition. And it was this, most probably, that incited His Lordship's Tartar move into North Carolina (at a time even when the state of Charleston forbid such a move) after the loss of all his light troops at Cowpens and the destruction of his wagons, train, etc., etc., had deprived him of the only means wherewith he could expect to establish himself in that province, or give solid support to the King's friends who might be inclined to join him. And on the like principle may we venture to account for His Lordship's desperate action at Guilford, his precipitate retreat after it to Cross Creek, and subsequent march to Wilmington in preference to Camden, that he might *there* prepare for his pretermined move into Virginia as soon as Greene's foreseen invasion of South Carolina should open a door for his escape thither—which he was apprehensive that officer's return to North Carolina, either with or without success against Lord Rawdon, might possibly (if he delayed it) put out of his power.] [23]

Having thus premised what appeared to me necessary for elucidating what is to follow, I shall now resume my narrative. And it would have given me the greatest happiness if there had been no occasion in the course of it to notice the pernicious effects which this most unnecessary and consequently reprehensible dereliction of South Carolina very soon had on the welfare of all His Majesty's concerns in that province, and the ruin which it ultimately brought upon His Lordship's own corps and that of the district on which he forced himself, by prematurely inducing operations there to which neither the season nor our powers were at that time adapted.

When General Greene was satisfied that Lord Cornwallis had decidedly bent his course toward the seacoast, he immediately determined to invade South Carolina, wisely looking upon it as the most likely step he could take to do away with any evil impression which the defeat of Guilford might have occasioned, and to reap the advantages which the present defenseless state of that province obviously offered to him. For this purpose he began his march on the 5th of April from Deep River, whither he had followed the royal army in its retreat;

23. The bracketed paragraphs are lightly deleted in the MS; they are restored because they are one of Clinton's clearest statements of his solution to the mystery of Cornwallis' conduct. For a modern discussion of this mystery see Willcox in *Am. Hist. Rev.*, 52, 12–15.

and, detaching Colonel Lee's Legion to join General Marion in an attack of the British post at Wright's Bluff [Fort Watson], he proceeded with the rest of his force to Camden, before which place he presented himself on the 19th.

Lord Rawdon, not having had the smallest intimation of Lord Cornwallis' march to Wilmington and consequently not suspecting that Greene's army could possibly be at liberty to return into South Carolina, had happened to weaken his post by detaching a considerable part of his best troops, under Lieutenant Colonel Watson, for the purpose of dispersing the plunderers that infested the eastern frontier and cooperating with Lord Cornwallis wherever he might be engaged. And, though His Lordship had sent orders to recall Colonel Watson immediately upon hearing of Greene's advance, this officer's movements were too rapid to admit of his joining him before His Lordship found himself under a necessity of repelling the enemy's attack in the best manner he could with the small force he had. And indeed the position which Marion had taken near the high hills of Santee now precluded all hopes of the detached corps' being able to get to him.

Hearing, therefore, that General Greene had sent off all his militia to bring up his artillery (which was a day's march in his rear), Lord Rawdon determined to avail himself, if possible, of that favorable conjuncture, and attack the enemy before their return. By arming everything that could carry a firelock, His Lordship was enabled to march out with nearly one thousand men, sixty of whom were mounted as dragoons. With this force and two six-pounders he marched from Camden on the morning of the 25th, leaving his redoubts to the care of the militia and the sick. And by a circuitous route falling in with the left flank of the enemy, who were strongly posted on Hobkirk's Hill about two miles distant in his front, His Lordship was fortunate enough to come upon them so unexpectedly that, though their artillery had joined before the attack began, their rout was immediately decided. But, the enemy's very great superiority in cavalry not admitting of an extended pursuit, only a few prisoners were taken.[24] But this was perhaps the most important victory of the whole war, for defeat would have occasioned the loss of Charleston (in the then open state of the works of that capital), the Carolinas, and Georgia.

The American General being thus disappointed of his first great object, which would have ensured the accomplishment of every other, he relinquished his design of carrying Camden by assault and adopted the more prudent one of reducing it by blockade. He therefore immediately sent off a reinforcement to Marion on the road to Nelson's

24. Rawdon to Cornwallis, Apr. 26, below, pp. 513–515.

Ferry; and, crossing the Wateree with the rest of his army, he disposed his troops in such a manner as he judged would cut off all supplies from the garrison. Lord Rawdon, being in the meantime joined by Lieutenant Colonel Watson's detachment, which arrived on the 7th of May, and failing in his efforts to bring the enemy to a second action, determined upon evacuating Camden altogether and retiring within the Santee. For His Lordship was convinced that it would be impossible as well as unprofitable to retain that post much longer, as the defection of the country was become general and all his posts on the communication by which alone he could draw his subsistence were daily dropping into the enemy's hands.

This was consequently effected on the morning of the 10th, the works having been destroyed and the baggage, etc., sent off the preceding night; and everything was safely past the river at Nelson's by the evening of the 14th.[25] From hence His Lordship commenced his march that night and proceeded on to Monk's Corner, where he encamped his army, as being in His Lordship's opinion a proper position for covering those districts from which Charleston drew its principal supplies, and from whence he could best improve any favorable occurrence or guard against any untoward event.

In the meantime General Greene, having by his detached corps under Sumter, Marion, Pickens, and Lee obtained possession of Forts Watson, Orangeburg, Motte, Granby, and Dreadnought with all their garrisons, artillery, and stores, advanced himself against the important post of Ninety-six, while Pickens and Lee moved against that of Fort Cornwallis at Augusta, which were the only strongholds we had now remaining in Carolina and Georgia except Charleston, Savannah, and Georgetown. So that in the short space of five weeks from the appearance of General Greene's army before Camden we lost or evacuated almost every post we possessed in the Carolinas and Georgia with provisions and stores to an immense amount and upward of 1000 troops killed, wounded, or taken—all which heavy misfortunes we might most certainly have escaped had Lord Cornwallis fortunately either marched his army back to Camden after the Battle of Guilford or even retired to Charleston by the Waccamaw after he had refitted at Wilmington. But His Lordship, for reasons best known to himself, was determined to approximate to a nearer communication with New York and, it would seem, listened to nothing that tended to divert him from it.

Accordingly, notwithstanding he was by this time fully apprised of

25. Rawdon to Cornwallis, May 24, below, pp. 521–522. For a modern account of this phase of the campaign in South Carolina see Ward, *War of the Revolution,* 2, 797–815.

Lord Rawdon's danger and the alarming situation of every post we held in South Carolina and Georgia, and could not be ignorant of the defenseless state of Charleston at that very instant (all which nothing but His Lordship's immediate return to the southward could in all appearance possibly save), and notwithstanding he had so immediate a prospect of knowing my wishes with respect to the future operations of the campaign (as he had just heard a frigate lay at Charleston with dispatches for him, and it could not be long before he might receive my answer to his letter of the 10th)—I say, notwithstanding these very cogent reasons for His Lordship's not undertaking a move so full of doubt and ruin and which, being through an exhausted, barren, and hostile country, presented infinitely more difficulties and hazards to his army than either of the roads to Camden or Georgetown—yet was His Lordship in such a hurry to get into Virginia that, disregarding them all, the attempt was to be made, in opposition to every principle of policy as well as duty, and in defiance of every event and consequence.

In pursuance, therefore, of this (as his Lordship himself acknowledges) hasty and precipitate resolution, he marched from Wilmington toward the close of the month of April with all the force he could take with him, amounting to about sixteen hundred men (including one hundred and eighty dragoons) and four pieces of cannon, although according to his letter to me of the 23d neither his cavalry nor infantry were in readiness to move, *the former being in want of everything, and the latter of everything but shoes.*[26] And, bending his course to the lower fords of the Roanoke by the shortest route, he effected a junction with the army at Petersburg on the 19th of May, from which not even the news of Lord Rawdon's success against Greene (which had reached him early in the month, and which he had announced to the army before he had passed the Roanoke) had force to turn him—telling Colonel Tarleton when he heard it *that he still looked northward if possible.*[27]

Lord Cornwallis found the army at this place under the orders of Brigadier General Arnold, Major General Phillips having died a few days before His Lordship's arrival. That officer, it is presumed, did not

26. Cornwallis to Clinton, Apr. 23, Stevens, *Clinton-Cornwallis Controversy, 1,* 424.

27. Cornwallis to Tarleton, May 8, Tarleton, *History,* p. 331; see also Cornwallis to Phillips, May 8, *ibid.,* p. 332. Clinton is arguing that Cornwallis had decided to go to Virginia in the hope of diverting Greene from South Carolina, and lost his reason for going as soon as he heard of Rawdon's victory, which made such a diversion needless. The argument is absurd. It ignores the fact that Rawdon was in as much danger after the battle as before, and consequently abandons the solid ground on which Sir Henry usually rests his criticism of Cornwallis' move.

fail to communicate to His Lordship without delay everything he knew relative to the operations in which it was my intention to employ the Chesapeake army whenever it was at liberty to act. But, whether he did or not, they were shortly after very fully explained to His Lordship by my letters, addressed to Major General Phillips, which His Lordship informed me in his of the 26th he had opened and read. Consequently His Lordship was apprised of my intended plan for the summer campaign before he put his troops in motion. And, as he acknowledges that he regarded himself as standing in General Phillips' place and to be equally bound by the orders under which he found him acting, it is presumable His Lordship ought at least to have waited for my final determination before he engaged in any move that might interfere with or retard its execution.

CHAPTER 23

Cornwallis and Lafayette in Virginia, May to July, 1781

Prefatory exordium. Commander in Chief's reasons for not taking serious notice of Lord Cornwallis' late improper conduct. Communicates to him the operations concerted with the late General Phillips, and recommends them strongly to His Lordship's adoption; leaves him, however, at liberty to act as he judges best for the King's service. Cautions him against the danger to which operation in Chesapeake is exposed unless we remain masters of the sea. Advises him, in case he declines joining in those recommended, to seize some healthy, defensible post on the Williamsburg Neck and, after fortifying it, retain in Virginia no more troops than what may be wanted for its defense.

Great want of small arms. Repeated requisitions made to the Board of Ordnance for them, but [Clinton] does not know whether any are even shipped. Expects, however, that both them [sic] and the promised reinforcement will arrive soon. Prepares in the meantime to embark on the expedition as soon as he hears Lord Cornwallis is ready to cooperate. Is disappointed, as Lord Cornwallis has not only disapproved of every part of his plan, but has set off in pursuit of Monsieur Lafayette, which cuts off all communication with His Lordship for some weeks. Expecting every hour to receive the King's permission to resign the command to Lord Cornwallis, he acquiesces.

And, supposing from His Lordship's letter that his excursion will not last long and he is consequently considerably advanced in the defensive recommended to him, he again calls His Lordship's attention to the proposed move to Philadelphia, etc.—and, if he still declines, requests that he will send to New York all the troops he can spare, taking them in succession according to a list sent him. Reasons for these precautions: a rebel mail taken; New York threatened. The force the enemy may collect for such an object. Strength of the garrison not great. Not alarmed for that post.

More apprehensive for the Chesapeake. Anxious to hear Lord Cornwallis is well covered in some defensible post there, lest de Grasse should join Barras and thereby become superior to Arbuthnot. Minister's assurances to the contrary. An express sent to Sir George Rodney to request he will watch his [de Grasse's] motions and follow him to America. Lord [sic] Rodney assures Admiral Arbuthnot that he will follow de Grasse and cover our operations.

Substance of intelligence from the rebel mail. Sir Henry Clinton prepares to strike a blow against Philadelphia, and requests reinforcement from Lord Cornwallis. Washington appears in force before Kings Bridge, but falls back next day to White Plains, where he is joined by the French troops from Rhode Island. Enemy's force being collected on the east side the Hudson favorable for the proposed expedition.

Lord Cornwallis misconceives the General's orders, and hastens to abandon the Williamsburg Neck that he may be able to send him the troops required, having not yet seized any post there. Expedition suspended in consequence. Strictures on Lord Cornwallis' conduct.

I AM NOW entering upon a period of my command the detail of which will require the most impartial and candid precision, as on it in great measure depends a clear and distinct knowledge of the real sources from whence Great Britain may possibly be said to derive the heaviest misfortune which ever befell her as a nation; and justice demands that the culpability, if there is any, may fall only where it is strictly merited. Although I shall ever regard it as a circumstance most peculiarly unfortunate to myself to have had a command at a time so replete with ruin to my country, yet—the consciousness not only of my not having committed any very capital blunders but, on the contrary, of my having acted throughout the whole course of that command to the utmost extent of the powers with which I was armed securing me from all occasion of imputing the smallest blame to myself—I never suspected it could ever become necessary for me to criminate others in defense of my reputation. I contented myself, therefore, with sincerely lamenting (in common with all those who are interested in the welfare of this nation) that such a deplorable and depressing event had happened, and ascribing it in general to its most obvious causes—viz., the assurances given of proper naval support, and the want of it—without deeming it necessary to call in the collateral ones, some of which were perhaps equally deserving.

But, Lord Cornwallis having (for reasons perhaps only known to himself) thought proper in an official public letter to throw out several implications and even assertions which, if they were true, [would] have involved me [most justly] in the censure,[1] and His Lordship having after his arrival in England (notwithstanding my explanation to him on this subject at New York, by which he there appeared to have been convinced) industriously propagated the same sentiments and thereby excited prejudices against me, I found it absolutely necessary upon my

1. "Would" and "most justly" have been deleted in the MS.

return to Europe to endeavor to obviate the odium with which I saw myself threatened. I consequently then submitted to the public a succinct narrative of my conduct in the fatal campaign of '81, which in some degree opened the eyes of prejudice with respect to the causes of the catastrophe that closed it. And my subsequent observations on His Lordship's reply, adducing a few more incontrovertible proofs and illustrations, served to convince many that much wanton injustice had been done me.[2]

But, an ampler and more detailed account seeming to be still wished for to throw proper light upon many matters which it was impossible to explain sufficiently in those limited and hasty publications, and [I] having employed the leisure hours of my subsequent retirement in collecting from the mass of important and original information in my possession the necessary materials for that purpose, they are here arranged in chronological order merely to gratify the lovers of historic truth, without my having the smallest desire of indulging resentment against any man, as I have most carefully avoided the adding in these sheets anything that can reflect on the conduct of the noble Earl who was my second in command or of other officers (except in one instance) more than what has already appeared before the public and remains unrefuted to this hour. And I most solemnly declare that it would have given me the greatest pleasure that nothing of that nature had been at all necessary. But my own conduct could not in many instances have been accounted for unless I told the whole truth; and those on whom it may seem to bear hard have nothing, I presume, but their own imprudence to blame for the consequences.

Although I had every reason to be exceedingly hurt at Lord Cornwallis' quitting the Carolinas without my approbation and even contrary to my orders, and had the most alarming apprehensions for the consequences,[3] yet, having in consequence of Admiral Arbuthnot's informing me that he had not yet received any official intimation of the King's pleasure respecting his removal decidedly assured the Secretary of State that I would resign the command of the army to Earl Corn-

2. After the surrender at Yorktown Cornwallis, on parole, returned briefly to New York and then sailed for England. Sir Henry followed him home the next spring, but the pamphlet war between them was delayed for a year. The Earl's "official public letter" to Clinton, of Oct. 20, 1781, is printed below, pp. 583–587. For the conversations between the two Generals in New York see their exchange of letters between Nov. 30 and Dec. 10 in Stevens, *Clinton-Cornwallis Controversy*, 2, 218, 220–224, 240–247, and Clinton to Germain, Dec. 6, below, pp. 590–591. The three pamphlets to which Sir Henry refers, all published in 1783, were his *Narrative*, Cornwallis' *Answer*, and his *Observations* on the answer; they are reprinted in Stevens, *Clinton-Cornwallis Controversy*, 1, 1–131.

3. See Clinton to Cornwallis, Aug. 2, below, pp. 553–554.

wallis unless the Vice Admiral should be recalled by the next packet,[4] and it being consequently uncertain how soon that event might take place, I judged that this was not a time for me to take *any serious notice* of His Lordship's conduct; but that it might be better for the King's service at the present juncture to let it pass off, and avail myself of His Lordship's presence for conducting the operations in the upper Chesapeake which were to have been entrusted to the late General Phillips. I therefore very strongly recommended that plan to His Lordship's adoption, leaving him, however, at liberty to act as he should judge best for His Majesty's interests, but with a caution of *the danger to which operation in Chesapeake must be necessarily exposed the moment we ceased to be masters of the sea.* From this motive I advised His Lordship to secure as soon as he could some defensible position for his army, and not to retain more troops in Virginia than what might be absolutely wanted unless His Lordship should find it expedient to concur with me in the measures I had concerted with the late Major General Phillips [5]—having likewise in a former letter very fully expressed my dissent from His Lordship's sentiments respecting the facility of conquering that province, or even the propriety of engaging in an operation of any continuance there at the present advanced season of the year.[6]

I must confess, however, that, although I was very anxious to commence my operations on the Delaware Neck and in the upper Chesapeake, there was an article wanting to qualify me for the undertaking even more essential at the present moment than the promised reinforcement. This was a sufficiency of small arms and ammunition, without an ample supply of which to put into the hands of our numerous friends in those districts it would have been unavailing—as also ruinous to themselves—to invite them to join us; and I was fully convinced

4. Clinton to Germain, Apr. 30, below, pp. 516–517.

"It is now eight long months since the Minister's letter was dated by which it appears that His Majesty was graciously pleased to . . . say that Admiral Arbuthnot should be removed to Jamaica. Overwhelmed with such gracious condescension, I labored through some months with the most impracticable naval chief that ever conducted a fleet—and [with] every risk for want of cordial communication, not to say worse, and at a time when the most serious and hearty exertions of the navy were so materially requisite. I waited from day to day, from packet to packet, in hopes of relief, but in vain. . . . Being thus circumstanced, I determined immediately to quit the command. A glimpse, however, of probable active cooperation in this quarter, which I thought might require my presence, determined me to wait if possible still another packet." Clinton to the Duke of Gloucester, May 6, a photostat volume in the CP.

5. Clinton to Cornwallis, May 29, below, pp. 524–525.

6. Clinton to Cornwallis, Apr. 30, Stevens, *Clinton-Cornwallis Controversy, 1,* 443. The dissent "very fully expressed" there is in a single sentence, followed by another that gives Phillips and Cornwallis discretion to act as they think best.

that, unless we could be assured of their effectual aid, the attempt could never be attended with any prospect of success. These had been repeatedly solicited from the Board of Ordnance, both by the commanding officer of artillery and myself. But I was still ignorant of their having even been shipped, and, having been obliged to disarm the New York militia to furnish the few spare arms I had sent with the different expeditions to the Chesapeake, there was scarcely a single firelock now left for this service. But, not doubting that proper attention would have been paid at home to my requisitions and that the arrival of both them and the troops I expected could not be much longer delayed, I was determined to put everything I had in motion the moment I should hear from Lord Cornwallis that he approved of my plan and was ready to cooperate in it.[7]

But I had soon the mortification of finding my wishes again counteracted by this noble peer. For, having thought proper to disapprove of every part of my plan (which he very freely told me he apprehended would do more harm than good to the cause of Britain),[8] His Lordship immediately engaged in a project of his own—which, putting it out of my power to communicate with him for several weeks, would have most effectually defeated my intentions had I even been inclined to exercise my authority and enforce his obedience to them. This line I could not, however, at present pursue with the smallest propriety, as the next packet might possibly bring me His Majesty's permission to deliver over the command to His Lordship. I therefore submitted to the necessity he had thus imposed upon me. And, being persuaded from the general tenor of his letter that the little excursion he was going on *would not occupy him more than a week at most*, and that His Lordship would immediately after *dismantle Portsmouth* and, having *found some more proper post for a harbor and place of arms* (which all agreed was absolutely necessary when we had not, or till we had, a covering fleet), . . . employ [9] his troops in fortifying it, I contented myself with again recommending the move to Baltimore and the Delaware Neck, etc., to his consideration and assuring him that, whatever alterations he might judge proper to make in the Virginia stations, they would receive *my fullest approbation*. But, if he should not be inclined to adopt my plan of operation, I requested that His Lordship would in that case send to New York all the troops he could spare from the ample defense of whatever post he had chosen, and [from] such occa-

7. See Clinton to Germain, June 9, below, pp. 528–529.
8. Cornwallis to Clinton, May 26, below, p. 523.
9. "And employ" in the MS.

sional desultory movements by water as might present themselves for breaking in upon the enemy's communications and destroying their magazines, etc.[10]

These precautions appeared to me necessary for several very forcible reasons, the principal of which was that, as the sickly season in Virginia was approaching fast and Lord Cornwallis had above 7000 men there (the chief part of them the elite of my army), I was anxious to withdraw from thence as many troops as possible until the season for acting there should return, lest the epidemics of that country should happen to lay hold of them and rob me of their services for the rest of the campaign. We had likewise, about this time, authentic information of a considerable armament having sailed from France, great part of which was said to be destined for North America. And some letters from General Washington and several principal officers belonging to the French armament at Rhode Island, that were found in one of their mails just fallen into our hands, gave me to understand that the enemy had in a grand conference come to a resolution of attacking New York with all the force they could collect.

I was well aware that for such an object as the siege of New York Mr. Washington would find no difficulty in assembling what number of troops he pleased. The Continentals immediately under himself at this period amounted to about 6000, the French troops at Rhode Island having been lately recruited to about 6000 more; and these, with the Jersey, Connecticut, and Massachusetts levies, might form an army of 20,000 men. My own force in the New York district was certainly very inadequate to this, not exceeding 9,997 fit for duty, besides about 1500 militia belonging to that city, unarmed. I had, however, such confidence in the zeal and discipline of the troops I commanded that I should have been in no pain for the issue of such an attempt as long as our fleet remained superior to that of the enemy, and preserved the communication open between me and the Chesapeake, as its cooperation would most probably effectually disconcert the enemy's operations either against me or Lord Cornwallis, whose situation I was much more apprehensive for than my own. And [I was] consequently very anxious to hear that His Lordship was properly covered by works in some healthy, defensible post that might secure him, at least for a time, against the effects of such a temporary event—should such a misfortune[11] happen to us notwithstanding the positive and repeated assurances of the Minister to the contrary, and the precaution which Admiral Arbuthnot and I had taken to dispatch intimations of the enemy's intentions to Sir

10. Clinton to Cornwallis, June 11, below, pp. 529–532.
11. I.e., a temporary inferiority at sea.

George Rodney in the West Indies, and his promises in consequence.[12] The letters we had so fortunately intercepted being written immediately after the conference held at Wethersfield between Generals Washington and Rochambeau on the operations of the approaching campaign, they had brought everything into one distinct point of view, and thereby clearly developed to us the enemy's distressed situation and prospects. It was consequently easy to discover from them that, our operations in the Chesapeake under Generals Phillips and Arnold (for Lord Cornwallis did not arrive until long after) having greatly alarmed Mr. Washington, his chief wish had been to induce the French army and navy to join him with their whole force in an attempt against our posts there. But the consideration of their naval inferiority, the large body of troops at present collected in that quarter, and the approaching inaptitude of the time of year for military movements to the south of the Delaware were judged sufficient reasons for deferring that undertaking until a more convenient season.

It seemed to have been therefore unanimously agreed that the French troops should immediately join Mr. Washington on the North River, and that, their battering train and other heavy artillery being lodged under a guard at Providence until wanted, Monsieur Barras' squadron should remove from Rhode Island to Boston for security, and there wait the Count de Grasse's arrival from the West Indies. In the meantime Mr. Washington proposed that preparations should be made for besieging New York without delay, having judged it to be much weakened by the several large detachments lately sent from thence to the southward, and being persuaded that the holding up of such an object to the people would not only give fresh vigor to their cause (toward which a visible languor began universally to prevail) but would likewise spirit up the eastern states to contribute the much wanted supplies of provisions and troops, in the collecting of which they had been hitherto most alarmingly tardy.[13]

But the most interesting piece of intelligence which this capture procured us was an intimation from the court of France that this was the last campaign in which the Americans were to expect assistance of either troops or ships from that nation, as she began to be apprehensive that

12. See Germain to Clinton, Jan. 3, Apr. 4, Clinton to Rodney and to Vaughan, June 28, below, pp. 483–484, 505, 532–534. Sir Henry sent three simultaneous letters to Rodney, in addition to a copy of his letter to Vaughan. Rodney made no "promises in consequence," because he had sailed for Europe before the letters arrived; he did send assistance, but it was inadequate. See Willcox in *Journ. of Mod. Hist.*, 17, 325, and in *Am. Hist. Rev.*, 52, 21–22.

13. See Washington to Sullivan, May 29, and to Lund Washington and Parke Custis, May 31, below, pp. 525–527. In early May the Comte de Barras arrived from France and superseded Destouches in command of the Rhode Island squadron.

her own exigences would put it out of her power to continue her support if the war should be protracted much longer—thereby strongly pointing out to us the policy of avoiding all risks as much as possible, because it was now manifest that, if we could only persevere in escaping affront, time alone would soon bring about every success we could wish.[14]

The very critical situation of our affairs to the southward would have certainly induced me to have proceeded to the Chesapeake myself, that I might expedite the necessary arrangements in that quarter either for a temporary defensive or [for] the move I had proposed to the head of the bay, whichever might be found most expedient when I got there; and indeed I had applied to the Admiral for a proper conveyance to carry me thither for this purpose. But General Knyphausen's precarious state of health (who was the only officer to whom I could entrust the command in my absence) and our late discovery of the enemy's designs against New York made my own presence there indispensable. I was consequently compelled of necessity to confide altogether to Lord Cornwallis' acquiescence with my ideas respecting that business. And, trusting that His Lordship might, by the time he should receive my dispatches, be pretty nearly established in his works at York (which from his letter of the 26th of May appeared to be the post he intended to occupy), I wrote to His Lordship again on the 15th of June to request he would embark a part of the troops mentioned in my letter of the 11th, beginning with the light infantry, and send them to me with all possible dispatch. And, . . . when [15] the Admiral should be able to send him more transports, I desired he would send to New York what part of the remainder he could spare from the defense of his posts, as I did not judge it advisable at present to leave more troops in that unhealthy climate than what might be absolutely wanted for a respectable defensive and desultory water excursions.[16]

In the meantime, as the trade of Philadelphia appeared to be almost the only resource on which the enemy depended for supplies of all kinds, and [as] the hard money which it procured them from the

14. This episode is still an enigma. The intercepted letter on which Clinton based his conclusions was from Rochambeau to Luzerne, the French Minister at Philadelphia; enclosed in it was an extract from the instructions sent to Rochambeau by his government in March. Neither the letter nor the enclosure said or implied what Clinton states in the text, but he unquestionably thought that they did. The only explanation seems to be that the documents were wrongly deciphered in New York. For a fuller discussion of the problem see Willcox in *Journ. of Mod. Hist.*, 17, 322–323 and nn. 82–86.

15. "And, that when" in the MS.

16. Cornwallis to Clinton, May 26, Clinton to Cornwallis, June 15, below, pp. 522, 532.

Havana (amounting in a very short time, as was reported to me, to half a million of dollars) had encouraged the farmers to flock to market with their produce and was beginning to give life and vigor to all their measures, I had proposed to the Admiral a plan for shutting up that port and attempting such a blow against the place itself as might disperse the Congress, ruin public credit, and totally overset their schemes and preparations for the campaign.[17] And I now only waited the arrival of the light infantry from the Chesapeake, and such other troops as Lord Cornwallis might spare me, to proceed on the expedition. For, having heard nothing from His Lordship since the 26th of May, I could not doubt but the close of his move against Lafayette and the completion of his defensive would very soon enable him to assist me with sufficient for the purpose.

But I was sorry to find, by a letter which I received on the 26th from Major General Leslie, that His Lordship was not returned on the 17th, and that he did not then even know where he was.[18] However, as the three regiments from Cork had arrived at Charleston on the 3d, and the drafts for the Guards and part of the recruits had disembarked at Portsmouth, I was still in hopes that Lord Cornwallis would yet have sufficient time to cover himself, so as to be able to send me something with which I might make the attempt before de Grasse could come upon the American coast.[19] For, Mr. Washington's force being by this time assembled on the east side of the Hudson, it is obvious I could not venture to undertake that enterprise before I should receive a reinforcement from the Chesapeake, as I might otherwise risk the extensive post of New York by detaching too largely from it. And, indeed, it was not long before the American chief let me know he was apportée to seize any advantage that should present itself, as he appeared in considerable force before my foreposts on the 3d of July, when a smart skirmish took place between his *avant garde* and about 200 Jägers supported by some refugees.[20]

Upon my hearing that the enemy's army was so near me, I immediately rode out to Kings Bridge to observe their motions and catch at any advantage that might offer. But I soon saw that nothing could be attempted—without risking a general action—with the troops on duty

17. The Admiral was Rear Adm. Thomas Graves. Arbuthnot had at last been ordered home (not to Jamaica); he actually sailed on July 4. For a description of Clinton's design against Philadelphia see his letter to Germain of July 3, below, pp. 537–538.

18. Leslie to Clinton, June 17, below, p. 532.

19. Clinton to Leslie, June 23, below, p. 532.

20. See Carrington, *Battles of the Revolution*, pp. 619–620; Douglas S. Freeman, *George Washington, a Biography* (5 vols., New York, 1948–52), 5, 297–299.

in the lines, as I had not time to bring up more, Mr. Washington having fallen back the next day to the White Plains.[21] There he formed a junction on the 6th with Monsieur de Rochambeau's corps from Rhode Island, both together now composing an army greatly superior in number to everything I could muster at New York, and consequently not to be injured by any direct move in my power to make against it.

Everything at this time appeared to be in the fairest train for securing success to the blow intended against Philadelphia. And so very certain was I of Lord Cornwallis' defensive being in the forwardness I expected that a frigate was dispatched to him on the 1st of July, with orders for the troops to sail from Hampton Roads in forty-eight hours after she should depart from thence with His Lordship's answer [22]— the armament from New York being ready to start from the Hook the instant she should appear off the harbor, in order to meet that from the Chesapeake in its approach to the Delaware. But it was unfortunately my fate to be once more disappointed. For, the officer I had sent to Lord Cornwallis with my letters of the 11th and 15th of June returning to me on the 8th [of July] with one from His Lordship in answer, I had the mortification to find that, so far from being considerably advanced in the defensive I had recommended to him (and even strongly enforced the necessity of, by suggesting the great probability of our receiving a visit in the hurricane months from Count de Grasse with ships and troops), His Lordship had not even yet thought of it, having wasted the time since he wrote to me last (26th May) in an unmeaning and unprofitable ramble through Virginia, whereby a full month of the very best season of the year was totally lost.

But what I was most alarmed at in this letter was His Lordship's telling me he was preparing to retire immediately to Portsmouth and send me 3000 troops, as he did not think it was in his power, consistent with my plans, to make safe defensive posts at York and Gloucester. And he even proceeded so far as to intimate that he looked upon any defensive whatsoever in Chesapeake as nugatory, and he consequently submitted it to my consideration whether it was worth while to hold a sickly, defensive post in that bay, which would be always exposed to a sudden French attack, and consequently whether it would not be more for the King's service to withdraw everything from thence to New York without loss of time.[23]

21. Clinton, in other words, dared not risk a general action with the troops he had in the lines, and did not have time to reinforce them before Washington fell back.

22. Clinton to Cornwallis, and to the officer commanding the troops embarked in the Chesapeake, July 1, below, p. 537.

23. Cornwallis to Clinton, July 8, below, p. 541.

From hence I saw clearly that, as His Lordship had before pretty well convinced me that as long as I indulged him with the·smallest latitude he was determined to combat my opinions and reject my ideas, he was now desirous of showing me that whenever I should presume to circumscribe him by more explicit injunctions he could evade my wishes by misconceiving them.

Having subjoined in the notes copies of my two letters to Lord Cornwallis dated the 11th and 15th of June (which were the only letters on this subject His Lordship had *then* received, and in which I had referred him to two others, of the 29th of May and 8th of June, which had not yet reached him),[24] the reader will be as competent as His Lordship or me to determine whether those letters did not explicitly and unequivocally direct him—in case he should still continue to reject the plan I had concerted with General Phillips and recommended to His Lordship for a move to Baltimore, etc., and an attack on Philadelphia, and which plan the Minister seemed clearly of opinion he would adopt on receipt of these letters—*to lose no time in making choice of some healthy, defensive station on the Williamsburg Neck, either at Williamsburg or York, and fortifying it.* And [whether they did not direct that,] having *afterward* reserved of the 7000 men with him as many as he should think necessary for its ample defense and [for] desultory water excursions during the summer months, he would send me (of the 3000 which I judged might remain after that service was provided for) what he could spare, taking the corps in succession as I named them. And whether His Lordship's compliance with any part of the order contained in my letter of the 15th did not manifestly depend upon his being actually in the situation which I presupposed him to be as expressed in that of the 11th, *covered by works in a healthy position at Williamsburg, Yorktown, or any other spot His Lordship might have chosen on the Williamsburg Neck, from the ample defense of which he could spare me 3000 of the 7000 men I supposed he had then with him.* And whether His Lordship was not clearly cautioned to wait the receipt of my letters of the 29th of May and 8th of June before he executed it, as they contained suggestions more explanatory of my wishes, which might possibly render it unnecessary for His Lordship to send me any part of his force.[25]

These being admitted, I beg leave to ask by what ingenuity it is possible to twist the meaning of the only letters His Lordship had then re-

24. For Clinton to Cornwallis, May 29, June 8, 11, 15, see below, pp. 523–525, 528–532.

25. However unclear these conclusions may have seemed to Cornwallis and may seem to the modern reader, Clinton was convinced at the time that his dispatches were pellucid. See his letter to Germain, July 13, below, pp. 544–545.

ceived so as to extort from them an order which, he says, from its unconditional nature *left him no explicit alternative between complying
with the requisition they contained, or engaging in operations in the
upper Chesapeake?* Or how *could his choice of a healthy situation be
at that time controlled by either the imminent danger of New York or
the important effects I expected from the expedition against Philadelphia* [26]—since nothing, surely, could have been more guardedly expressed [than my requisition] or [more] explicit than the *conditions*
under which the requisition was made? And, with respect to the expedition against Philadelphia having influenced His Lordship's determination, whoever will be at the trouble of reading the letter will see that
no intimation whatsoever is given in it of my intending to send an expedition thither from New York—the advantages likely to result from
a successful enterprise against that place being therein blazoned very
clearly with no other view than that of inciting His Lordship to undertake it.[27] And that His Lordship himself viewed it in this light is plain
from His Lordship's answer, wherein he takes great pains to account
for his not approving the scheme and looking on the project as totally
inexpedient if not impracticable, concluding in these remarkable words:
"*however*, my opinion on the subject is of no great importance, as it
appears from Your Excellency's dispatches that in the execution of these
ideas *a cooperation was intended from your side which now could not
be depended upon, from the uncertainty of the permanency of our naval*

26. *Clinton's note:* Extract from Lord Cornwallis' reply to Sir Henry Clinton's
Narrative, page 9:
"Whoever reads the correspondence will see that, since Sir Henry Clinton had
declared positively in his first and in several subsequent dispatches against the plan
of reducing Virginia, no explicit alternative was left to me between complying
with the requisition (contained in his letters of the 11th and 15th of June) of
such troops as I could spare from a healthy defensive station, or engaging in operations in the upper Chesapeake. *For, whilst he stated in such strong terms the
imminent danger of New York or the important effects which he expected from the
expedition against Philadelphia,* I did not think myself authorized to detain any
part of the troops he so earnestly required, merely upon my opinion of the difference
of the quality of the air of Williamsburg, York, or Portsmouth—from the latter of
which only, as it was already fortified, I could afford an immediate detachment.
Accordingly, that I might be enabled to comply with those orders of the 11th and
15th of June, I passed James River (my remaining force being insufficient to
fortify and maintain a post on the Williamsburg Neck) and embarked the troops
required with all possible dispatch." [Stevens, *Clinton-Cornwallis Controversy, 1*,
72–73.]
27. Clinton refers to his letter of June 11, in which he described the opportunity
in Pennsylvania but, in the next breath, implied that the operation was not feasible
(below, p. 531). If he meant that it was not feasible for him from New York, he
certainly did not say so. This is a striking example of his self-deception about his
use of the English language.

superiority and your apprehensions of an intended serious attempt upon New York." [28]

In short, after Lord Cornwallis had read my instructions and opinions to Major General Phillips, he must have known that I had never any idea of beginning solid operations in Virginia till North Carolina was restored to order [and] till we were certain of a covering fleet (or in the summer months, as I looked upon the climate as too unhealthy and the inhabitants as too universally hostile to promise success from such a measure); and that I had consequently no other intention in occupying a post there (after cooperation with His Lordship's own movements in North Carolina should cease) than to prevent the enemy, if possible, from shutting that door against us, and to secure a naval station and place of arms in the Chesapeake from whence we might afterward start, in proper season, on such services as might present themselves. His Lordship was also informed by them that I had concerted with that officer two very important movements, in which great part of his army was to be employed; and that, if circumstances should happen to render either inexpedient, it was my determination *to leave only about 1000 men in Virginia* in some post such as Mill Point (which that number would be sufficient to defend) unless the Admiral should require a station in the Chesapeake for his large ships, in which case I desired him to secure either York or Old Point Comfort *if either should be found to answer, and could be put in a proper posture of defense within the time we had a chance of doing it in; but if not that he was to relinquish all views of a naval station* for line-of-battle ships, and content himself with the one proposed in Elizabeth River—as I wished to withdraw from thence all the troops I could, as well to avoid the sickness then prevalent there as to lessen the injury we might possibly sustain from a temporary naval superiority on the side of the enemy, should the French West India fleet pay those waters a visit in the hurricane months.

Now, as His Lordship had declared against joining in either of the plans concerted with his predecessor, and knew that I was averse from commencing solid operation in Virginia in the month of June, was it not his duty immediately upon his assuming the command of the Chesapeake army to have attended to my next object, and [to] have looked out without loss of time for such a post as I had described to Major General Phillips and fortified it? But instead of doing this (as he himself had proposed in his letter of the 26th of May) we find His Lordship, the instant he sees himself at the head of another army, forget every in-

28. Cornwallis to Clinton, June 30, below, pp. 535–536.

struction under which he acted and, recommencing his favorite rapid marches, repeat over again in Virginia the very same scene he had just ceased acting in South Carolina—and, I am sorry to add, to every whit as little purpose. The consequence was that, when he was called upon for the portion of his army which he knew it was the intention of the Commander in Chief to employ on important services to the northward, he found himself in no condition to part with it, having most imprudently wasted that time which he ought to have employed in preparing for such a demand.

Wherefore I hope no military man will think me presumptuous in declaring my opinion that, *as His Lordship was not in the healthy defensive place of arms on the Williamsburg Neck* in which I very evidently presupposed him to be at the time he received my letters of the 11th and 15th of June, it was his indispensable duty to have immediately looked out for one. And, if he thought that it could not be secured *hors d'insulte* before the hurricane months (when de Grasse's visit was expected) if he sent me the troops I asked for, His Lordship ought not to have thought of sending a man to New York until he should receive my further orders in consequence of his report; nor could he be in any degree warrantable, before then, in withdrawing his army from the Williamsburg Neck.

The reader will, I am persuaded, pardon me for detaining him thus long on this single transaction when he considers what great influence it had on all the events that followed. For it cannot have escaped his observation that, had not Lord Cornwallis adopted this very precipitate measure, his works on the heights of York might have been begun nine weeks sooner than they were; and that, having consequently had sufficient time to find out the strong as well as the weak points of his position and to discover and obtain ample supplies for *all his wants of entrenching tools, provisions, and heavy artillery and ammunition,* His Lordship would most probably have been better prepared for the reception of the enemy. And, had that been fortunately the case, I will not do His Lordship so much injustice as to suppose we should at this day have to lament the ruinous issue of their combined move against him.

CHAPTER 24

The Second Attempt against Rhode Island and the Crisis in the Chesapeake, July to September, 1781

Pensacola taken, East Florida threatened. Three regiments from Cork arrive at Charleston; scarcely any other post left in Georgia and the two Carolinas beside that fortress and Savannah. Expedition to Phila-delphia suspended. Commander in Chief alarmed at hearing that Lord Cornwallis had done nothing toward securing a healthy defensive post in Virginia, as there are now only six weeks left to do it in before de Grasse may be expected; Portsmouth a weak post and too unhealthy to be retained. Contrary to the King's express commands to withdraw the troops, it could not be done for want of transports; Lord Cornwallis is therefore ordered, at the Admiral's desire, to seize Old Point Com-fort and fortify it to cover a naval station in James River, and is left at liberty to retain all the troops for that service. [Clinton is] tempted to run this risk by the Minister's assurances that Sir George Rodney would watch de Grasse and follow him.

Reasons for not complying with Lord Cornwallis' request to be sent to Charleston. Though Admiral Arbuthnot is recalled, Sir Henry Clinton is still determined to resign the command, as soon as he can, to Lord Cornwallis. His reasons. New York put into a better posture of defense. Proposed expedition against the French squadron at Rhode Island and heavy train at Providence. Everything settled with the Admiral for its taking place when reinforcement arrives. Admiral goes suddenly to sea. Present alarming and mortifying situation.

Lafayette attacks Lord Cornwallis at Jamestown and is repulsed. A glorious opportunity lost; reflections upon it. His Lordship rejects Old Point Comfort, and seizes York and Gloucester to cover a naval station in York River. Sir Henry Clinton thinks it possible, notwith-standing, that His Lordship may yet stay at Portsmouth and send to New York the troops asked for, and sends an advice vessel to meet them with orders. But, finding His Lordship has actually decided on his removal to York, he acquiesces, under a supposition that His Lord-ship has reason to think well of the post, since he reports it to be capable of giving effectual protection to ships of the line.

Comparative strength of the British and rebel armies. Reasons against attacking Washington. Twenty-four hundred German recruits arrive at New York on the 11th of August. Admiral returns on the 16th, implying that he is ready for expedition. Sir Henry Clinton immediately renews his offer for a conjunct move against Rhode Island. The Admiral, in answer, says two of his ships want refitting; the expedition in consequence deferred. Washington forages near Kings Bridge. Bridges prepared to throw over the Harlem. He falls back, recrosses the North River, and encamps at Chatham, menacing Staten Island. Reasons for believing the naval superiority on our side. Confirmed by Sir Samuel Hood, who arrives at Sandy Hook on the 28th with fourteen sail of the line, which he declares are equal to all that de Grasse can bring or send. Rhode Island expedition immediately determined on. News arrives that night that Barras sailed from thence on the 25th.

The allied armies decamp from Chatham on the 29th and march for Trenton. Sir Henry Clinton suspects from this that Washington expects the cooperation of a powerful French fleet in the Chesapeake. Still confides in the assurances and promises given him that our fleet will be superior. The idea that he was deceived by Mr. Washington's maneuvers clearly refuted. Rear Admiral Graves sails on the 31st with nineteen sail of the line, two fifties, and fourteen frigates. Reasons for thinking Lord Cornwallis' works are in some forwardness. Officers of rank lately come from thence report favorably of his position and its defensibility. Letter from His Lordship on the 6th that de Grasse is in the Chesapeake and forty boats with troops went up James River on the 1st of September. Four thousand troops embarked at New York to be ready for starting the instant the Admiral clears the Chesapeake of the enemy's ships. An expedition sails to New London, which is burnt, with several ships and a great quantity of naval stores and valuable merchandise.

IF CHANCE has really any influence over the affairs of men (though I am more inclined to think that their good and bad success has and ever will depend, under Providence, on the prudence or folly with which they are managed), the tide of fortune with respect to the British interests in America was now very evidently beginning to turn against us. Spain had completed her conquest of West Florida by the capture of Pensacola in May,[1] though this remaining hold of that valuable province might have been preserved to us somewhat longer by the presence there of even a single frigate had Sir Peter Parker, who commanded the squadron on the Jamaica station, been properly attentive to my repeated solicitations for this small mark of his watchful regard over that important possession, which it was certainly no longer in my power to assist in any other way. East Florida, expecting that

1. See Fortescue, *British Army*, 3, 351–352.

her turn would come next, was under daily apprehensions of the enemy's approach. And, although the three regiments from Ireland had arrived in Charleston most opportunely to enable Lord Rawdon to raise the siege of Ninety-six (which had been a long time in most imminent danger, and was hitherto saved by the vigilance and gallantry of Lieutenant Colonel Cruger, who commanded there), yet, as His Lordship was soon after obliged to withdraw the garrison from thence, and Augusta had before fallen into the enemy's hands, all our late extensive possessions in the valuable provinces of South Carolina and Georgia were now in a manner reduced to the two maritime ports of Savannah and Charleston.[2] For we can scarcely be said to possess a country from whence our army is incapable of driving that of an enemy, where the hearts of the inhabitants are mostly against us, and in which we have not one place of refuge for the few friends we may have in it to fly to from oppression.

I must, however, confess that, when we reflect on the very respectable number of troops we had at this time in those provinces (very little short of 10,000 effectives) and the very trifling body of Continentals opposed to them (not much exceeding 1000), it is with difficulty we can credit the feeble and precarious tenure by which we seem to have held them. But Lord Cornwallis' fatal dereliction of Carolina at so critical a period had made too deep an impression to be easily effaced. It totally depressed and disheartened all those friends of the British government who had been hitherto zealous in its cause. Even the troops appear to have almost lost their confidence; and the disaffected, increasing daily in number, grew proportionately bold and active. In short, the moment the army had been withdrawn from the frontier to the necessary defense of the capital (which, from its then dismantled state, was open to a sudden assault of the enemy), everything in that country was lost to Britain. For rebellion became in consequence of it [the withdrawal] universally triumphant; and, had she [rebellion] gained the most decisive victory, it could not have more immediately turned the popular stream against us, which was perhaps from thenceforth irresistible.

At a period when our southern possessions were in the deplorable situation I have just stated, and our military powers so changed from the state in which Mr. Washington described them to be in the March preceding,[3] the reader will not be surprised at the very great alarm into

2. See Rawdon to Cornwallis, June 5, Balfour to Clinton, July 20, and Gould to Clinton, Sept. 30, 1781, below, pp. 527, 550–552, 578–579; Ward, *War of the Revolution,* 2, 813–825.

3. See Washington to Benjamin Harrison, Mar. 27, 1781, below, p. 503.

which Lord Cornwallis' letter threw me.[4] Therefore, although the enterprise I was about to embark on certainly held out an assurance of the most important advantages, yet (when I now saw that it could not be undertaken but at the expense of risking all hold of the Chesapeake, the loss of which must inevitably precipitate that of everything else remaining to the southward of it) I did not hesitate to suspend my design for the present, though I had, in my confidence of its immediately taking place, already raised the hopes of administration by informing the American Minister that everything was ready for its instant execution. But our time began now to be contracted within very narrow bounds, as the French West India fleet, if it was to visit us at all, might be expected on the American coast before the end of August, and we had got far advanced into July—so that through Lord Cornwallis' unfortunate neglect of my instructions to his predecessor, and recommendations to himself, little more than six weeks remained for securing some healthy, tenable hold of Virginia before we might be interrupted very powerfully by the enemy.

For as to Portsmouth, which was the only post we as yet held there, it had been already condemned by Major General Phillips and His Lordship as indefensible, from the extensiveness of its works and its being likely to prove a grave to the large garrison they would require from its extreme unhealthiness at that season of the year. And, on the other hand, had I not been myself convinced of the necessity of our retaining a post in that province, the positive commands I had just received from His Majesty through his American Minister would have prevented the evacuation which Lord Cornwallis advised, as they absolutely forbade my withdrawing a man from thence until that province was subdued.[5] But, had I not been restrained by either of these and

4. The letter of June 30, in which Cornwallis announced that he was falling back on Portsmouth, and urged Clinton to abandon the Chesapeake and permit him to return to South Carolina. See below, pp. 535–536.

5. These "positive commands" are the outstanding mystery of Clinton's term as commander in chief. He buttresses his assertion about them in the text by an extract of Germain's letter to him of May 2 (below, pp. 519–520). Elsewhere he says that they were contained in "another letter" from Germain (Stevens, Clinton-Cornwallis Controversy, 1, 467, n. 17); he presumably means that of June 6, to which he later added in a note what appears to be the order in question in Lord George's own words (below, p. 527 and n. 68). Those words are not in the original letter, or in that of May 2, or in any other that has come to light. They apparently do not exist.

The order may have been sent, of course, in a letter that has since disappeared. But two considerations virtually preclude this possibility. In the first place Sir Henry stored documents as a squirrel stores nuts; it is almost inconceivable that he would have destroyed or mislaid such a crucial dispatch. In the second place he disobeyed the order if he ever did receive it; yet his correspondence of the period gives no hint that he was conscious of disobedience—as he had been,

the evacuation had been in other respects ever so eligible, it was at that time totally impracticable, because—so far from having sufficient transports to bring away all the troops and stores, together with a long train of refugees who, from the apparent certainty of our continuance there, had taken shelter under our wings—it was with some difficulty that the Admiral could collect enough [transports] even for the small portion of them [troops] which I had directed to be embarked for the expedition.

Thus circumstanced, I had no alternative but to endeavor to provide the best I could in so short a time for the health and safety of the force I was directed to leave there. Therefore, as Rear Admiral Graves had declared to me that the King's large ships could not possibly remain in North America in the winter unless they had a port in the Chesapeake for the large ships to retire to, and that he consequently requested that Old Point Comfort might, if possible, be fortified in order to cover them in that of Hampton Roads in James River (which from his own knowledge and the Commodore's *they* recommended), and Major General Phillips having formerly intimated to me that *it seemed a point which a small force might defend and the shipping have scope to act in,* I immediately directed Lord Cornwallis to examine and fortify it; and left His Lordship at liberty, if he should judge it necessary, to retain all the troops he had with him until it was accomplished, this appearing from His Lordship's letter to be indispensable for giving the requisite celerity to the works.[6]

And I was encouraged to run that risk from Lord George Germain's having, in his letters of the 4th of April and 2d of May, assured me that Sir George Rodney would be watchful of the Count de Grasse's motions and not give him time to do me any material injury before he came to my succor—the more especially, too, as we had still six weeks to the good before we might expect his arrival, and I had in my letter of the 18th of May cautioned the American Minister of the great probability of his paying us a visit in the hurricane months, and again most strongly marked the danger to which operation in Chesapeake would be exposed without our having a permanent naval superiority there. I did not, however, neglect on the present occasion most strictly to enjoin Lord Cornwallis to expedite his defensive as fast as possible and not to retain a man afterward more than what should be absolutely requisite

---

acutely, at Bunker Hill and on the retreat to New York in 1778. The conclusion seems inescapable, though it is certainly fantastic, that the "positive commands" were a later figment of his imagination. For a fuller discussion of this point see Willcox in *Am. Hist. Rev.*, 52, 19–20 and nn. 65–67.

6. See Clinton to Cornwallis, July 11, below, pp. 543–544. The Commodore referred to was Graves' second in command, Edmund Affleck.

for the services I pointed out to him, having very fully explained to His Lordship, in another letter I had written to him on the 8th, the motives of my anxiety for securing a naval station in the Chesapeake for large ships, and my disapprobation of that of Portsmouth for the cogent reasons before given me by both Major General Phillips and His Lordship.[7]

But, it may possibly be here asked, why did I again risk the fate of the war and my own reputation, at so critical a moment, in the hands of an officer who had so repeatedly counteracted my wishes and evidently evaded or misconceived my orders, as another delay or misconception at the present advanced season might have inevitably induced the most fatal consequences from there being no time now left for rectifying them? And why did I not rather immediately comply with the request Lord Cornwallis made me in his letter of the 30th of June *to be sent back to Charleston,* as it offered so obvious and easy a mode of removing His Lordship out of the way of doing me further injury, without the necessity of coming to an open rupture? I must acknowledge that these are questions of some moment, and I will endeavor to answer them satisfactorily.

It has been before noticed that, having determined to resign the command of the army to Lord Cornwallis unless the next packet should remove Vice Admiral Arbuthnot from that of the navy, I had patiently submitted to the vexations and disappointments which I had hitherto suffered from His Lordship's conduct, on account of the doubt I was in how soon I might be obliged to do so. The April and May packets were, however, now arrived; and that obstacle was most certainly removed by the Vice Admiral's having received by them the King's leave to return to Europe. But the letters which that opportunity brought me from the Secretary of State were of such a nature as to excite in me a still more determined resolution to avail myself of the conditional permission which His Majesty had before graciously granted me,[8] by giving up the command to Lord Cornwallis the instant the cloud which at that time menaced the posts of New York and the Chesapeake was dispersed. For, being convinced by them that I had lost the confidence of His Majesty's Ministers, I judged it was time to retire from a com-

7. See below, pp. 541–542.

8. On June 26–27 Clinton received a batch of eleven letters from Germain, ranging in date from Jan. 31 to May 2 (Clinton to Germain, July 3). Two of these were calculated to rouse Sir Henry's ire. That of Mar. 7 praised Cornwallis in a way that was invidious, and pointed out that Washington's army was smaller than even the provincial force in the British service (Stevens, *Clinton-Cornwallis Controversy, 1,* 335). That of May 2 went much further in preferring Cornwallis' strategy to Clinton's, and its tone would have given a less sensitive man than Sir Henry ample cause to resign; see below, pp. 519–520.

mand which I could no longer hold with benefit to my country or honor to myself.

That command had been clogged with too many embarrassing and mortifying circumstances for any general officer to be very ambitious for retaining it. My zeal for the King's service and the hopes I had of His Majesty's protection had, however, induced me hitherto to struggle through all difficulties. But, when I saw my plans (which had once received His Majesty's approbation) now rejected and others proposed by Lord Cornwallis substituted in their place, and myself directed to support them with my whole force—in short, when I saw that His Majesty's Ministers were permitted to slight my representations and to listen to the crude and oversanguine suggestions of interested, uninformed persons in preference to the well-weighed opinions of his Commander in Chief, who from his situation must not only possess the best means of information, but be more interested than any other man whatsoever in turning it to the advantage of his country—I began to apprehend I had lost that support which alone could have animated my exertions for the public service under a continuance of such very unmerited and improper treatment; [9] and I was therefore determined to retire.

This, however, though ever so ardently desired, could not be done while a formidable army hung over the important post immediately under myself, and a considerable French armament was hourly expected on the coast to assist in a combined attack against either New York, Chesapeake, or Charleston. And, as Lord Cornwallis was to be my successor, I wished to keep His Lordship near me, that I might meet with no delay in surrendering to him the command whenever I should be at liberty to part with it.

I therefore lost no time in transmitting to Lord George Germain my free sentiments on the present state of the King's interests in America and my sense of the cruel injustice that had been done me in suspecting it possible for me not to do everything in my power to bring the war here to an honorable conclusion. But, as my letters of that period seem

9. Clinton presumably means that he had hoped to retain the support of the King, despite Germain and the other Ministers, but that the hope was now dispelled. He felt completely at odds with the cabinet; "'tis not that Ministers are displeased with my conduct, but [that] they know I have no reason to be pleased with theirs, and that I cannot submit to serve on their terms, [which are] *an entire confidence in them without putting any in me.* Perhaps my presumptive successor may offer to accept on any [terms]; but I think I know him too well to believe he will long submit to the treatment I have on many occasions met with, and which nothing but the high veneration I have for my royal master and zeal for his service could have induced me to submit to." Clinton to the Duke of Gloucester, Aug. 18, a photostat volume in the CP.

to have convinced the Minister that he had been rather too precipitate, and may convey the best idea of my feelings at the time, I have taken the liberty of subjoining them in the notes, for the reader, if he thinks necessary, to refer to, that I may save both him and myself the repetition of a vindication which I am not conscious that my conduct in that war has the smallest occasion for.[10]

Although the enemy's menaces of attacking New York had not induced any very great apprehensions for my posts in that district, I thought it, however, right to provide against contingencies and make such additions to the works as the engineers judged necessary for the defense of the place.[11] And, as these required the employment of a large number of hands, the diminution they of course occasioned in my acting force (which at most did not exceed 4000 men) made me more sensibly feel the want of the reinforcement I had solicited from Lord Cornwallis.

For, having received the most authentic intelligence that the French battering train and stores—which were thought too unwieldy to admit of removal but by water—had been left at Providence, that Monsieur Barras' squadron remained at Rhode Island (the works of which had been dismantled) totally unprotected except by about 400 militia and a small number of French convalescents, and that large magazines of various military stores were then forming at Philadelphia, I was most desirous of striking at all or some of these depots before they could be put into motion against me. And, could the Rhode Island squadron be fortunately destroyed at the same time, I had no doubt but every hope and expectation of the enemy must be effectually frustrated. But, as neither the three regiments from the West Indies nor the German recruits that had been promised me were yet arrived, these important enterprises could not well be attempted with my present force while Mr. Washington lay with his army so near me; and all prospect of my hands being strengthened by a detachment from the Chesapeake was now vanished. I was, notwithstanding, very unwilling to relinquish such tempting objects. And, though it was probable the expected German troops might not render me equal to both expeditions, I was determined to attempt at least the one against Rhode Island immediately after their arrival; and, should we be successful in that, I had it in intention —if circumstances should encourage me—to proceed afterward on the other.

My plan was nearly the same with the one I had offered the year

10. Clinton left no such notes. Only two of his letters to Germain are relevant; in that of July 13 he attacked Cornwallis' conduct, and in that of July 18 he defended his own. See below, pp. 544–546, 547–550.

11. The engineers' report on the defenses is contained in Alexander Mercer to Maj. DeLancey, July 3, below, p. 538.

before to Vice Admiral Arbuthnot. And, the eight-inch howitzers, frames, and forges for heating shot, etc., remaining still on board the transports, everything was ready for moving at a moment. My arrangements had likewise been settled with Rear [Admiral] Graves, immediately after the naval command had devolved upon that officer; and it was then concerted that this expedition should take place toward the conclusion of the other against Philadelphia, as the appearance of reinforcing the armament on that service might have effectually covered the design.[12] But, being disappointed (as I have said) of the troops from the Chesapeake, I was obliged to defer my intentions until the arrival of those either from Bremer Lehe or the West Indies, when the Rear Admiral promised to accompany me with his squadron. In the meantime, in consequence of some intelligence by a sloop-of-war from Europe, he thought proper to sail suddenly with all his ships to the northward; and every operation was of course necessarily suspended until his return.

Nothing, certainly, could have been more alarming as well as mortifying than my situation at the present crisis—the most important advantages presenting themselves hourly, of which I could not avail myself for want of force; the enemy's army parading on the heights on my front for two days, and no possibility of my stirring against it was I in ever so great force, as I had not an armed vessel to cover either of my flanks and Mr. Washington had, by an unexpected move, masked the only *débouché* (over Kings Bridge) I then had to the continent. And, should the Count de Grasse happen to arrive on the coast in the Admiral's absence, everything was to be apprehended, not only for all the distant posts of my army, but even for those at New York. And, to complete this melancholy picture, a letter I had just received from General Vaughan gave me to understand that, of the three regiments which the American Minister had assured me I was to receive from the West Indies, *only one* could be now spared me, and this only as marines to the fleet; and it was uncertain when a conveyance could be obtained for even that. So that my whole hopes of a reinforcement rested on the speedy arrival of about 2600 German draftees and recruits, and such troops as Lord Cornwallis might possibly be able to send me after he had completed the small naval post I had directed him to establish for covering Hampton Roads in James River—for the present distracted state of South Carolina precluded every idea of drawing a man from thence.

It happened unfortunately, also, that the *Solebay*, frigate, which car-

12. See Clinton to Graves, July 6, and Graves to Clinton, July 9, below, pp. 539, 542–543. This design against Rhode Island and the factors that frustrated it are described by Willcox in *Journ. of Mod. Hist.*, 17, 326–331.

ried my letters of the 8th and 11th of July to Lord Cornwallis, did not arrive in the Chesapeake before the 20th. And, His Lordship having, contrary to my expectations, persevered in his resolution of abandoning the Williamsburg Neck, my orders for the fortifying Old Point Comfort found him with his whole force on the south side of James River, which he had passed on the 7th after he had repulsed an attack made upon him by a part of the Marquis de Lafayette's army the preceding evening.[13] (I must give His Lordship full credit for his judicious conduct in thus drawing Lafayette into a scrape, though he and his friends very assiduously and falsely assign my orders as a reason of his not having followed the blow.[14]) So that my proposed defensive there suffered all the additional delays necessarily consequent of these untoward circumstances. However, everything might have even yet ended well had His Lordship thought proper to have acted according to the written letter of my orders, and not to his—I must say—erroneous conception of their spirit.

And I hope I shall be pardoned for observing in this place that, although Lord Cornwallis passed James River so precipitately at a most critical moment lest any time, as he gave out, should be lost in sending to New York the troops called for, he had no sooner effected their transportation than (on some vague intelligence, which afterward turned out to be of no importance) he detached a part of those required for the *first embarkation* to a great distance up the country, from whence their return could not be expected for many days.[15] Which circumstance, otherwise of trifling moment, strongly marks that His Lordship most probably did not regard my orders for the reinforcement to be so very positive and unconditional as to admit of no alternative *short of immediate compliance,* and therefore naturally leads to this obvious question: Why, then, did His Lordship neglect to avail himself of the opening—which was so fortunately presented to him after the successful brush of the 7th—for striking a decisive blow at Lafayette's corps the next morning, which His Lordship had declared to me in his letter of the 30th of June (written in answer to the one that contained that requisition) he would lose no favorable opportunity of trying? But our reflections on the partial consequences of this inconsiderate step make but a feeble impression when our attention is so forcibly arrested by

13. See Clinton to Cornwallis, July 8, 11, 15, and Cornwallis to Clinton, July 8, below, pp. 541–542, 543–544, 546–547.

14. Modern historians have also emphasized the influence of these orders upon the Earl's conduct. See Louis R. Gottschalk, *Lafayette and the Close of the American Revolution* (Chicago, 1942), pp. 264–267.

15. Cornwallis to Clinton, July 17, Stevens, *Clinton-Cornwallis Controversy,* 2, 79; Tarleton, *History,* pp. 358–359.

the more general and ruinous effects of His Lordship's conduct throughout every part of this most fatal campaign!

Lord Cornwallis was pleased to tell me, in his answer to my letters of the 8th and 11th of July, that, having caused the ground and channel to be surveyed and sounded, he found that a work on Old Point Comfort would neither command the entrance nor secure His Majesty's ships at anchor in Hampton Roads in James River; and that he consequently should, in obedience to the spirit of my orders, take measures with as much dispatch as possible to seize and fortify York and Gloucester in York River.[16] Now, in the letters stated, the order extended only to the establishing a post at Old Point Comfort to cover Hampton Roads in James River; and no latitude whatsoever was given for fortifying York and Gloucester in York River—of which, as a naval station, I had relinquished every idea, and I consequently only mentioned York as a place he was at liberty to occupy in conjunction with Old Point Comfort if he should judge it an additional security to that post. But, although the order does not expressly say that His Lordship might reject Old Point Comfort upon discovering that it would not answer the Admiral's and my purpose in proposing it, I do not mean to insinuate that such a discretion was not implied. It certainly *was so*.[17]

And, if Lord Cornwallis thought that York and Gloucester, though fortified, would have been dangerous defensive points, was it not most probable that His Lordship would have immediately recurred to General Phillips' papers for my further sentiments on this subject before he engaged, after so many delays, in the fortifying a post which he reported would require such a deal of time and labor? For my instructions to that general officer would have clearly informed His Lordship *that, though the Admiral should propose Yorktown or Old Point Comfort as a naval station, he was not to take possession of either unless they could be acquired and maintained without great risk or loss; and that he was absolutely to decline doing so if his objections were such as he thought forcible.*[18]

And so impressed was I with the possibility of His Lordship's dis-

16. Cornwallis to Clinton, July 27, below, pp. 552–553.
17. Clinton's argument is difficult to follow. The gist of it is that Old Point Comfort, with or without Yorktown and Gloucester as outposts, was always his first choice; although he left Cornwallis free to reject it, and with it the whole idea of a major base in the Chesapeake, he never expected him to select Yorktown and Gloucester instead. In fact, however, Sir Henry said different things at different times. His two letters to the Earl of July 11 clearly emphasized the importance of Old Point Comfort; the memorandum of his conversations with Phillips, on the other hand, suggested just as clearly a preference for Yorktown if it could be made secure. See below, pp. 493–494, 543–544.
18. From Clinton's instructions to Phillips, Mar. 10, below, p. 496.

approving the position I had recommended to him, and availing himself of the latitude there given him of contenting himself in such a case with Mill Point or some other small work for securing the King's cruisers in Elizabeth River, and of His Lordship's being thereby induced to send me the reinforcement I solicited, that upon the Admiral's sailing to the northward on the 21st I had actually dispatched a vessel to cruise for it off the Delaware, with directions to Major General Leslie to bring the troops in that case to Sandy Hook.[19] But I had not the most distant idea that His Lordship could be disposed to seize York and Gloucester, after the opinion he had just before given me of the difficulties he was likely to meet with in rendering them safe defensive posts;[20] though I own, before I had received His Lordship's letter, I had every reason (as well as His Lordship, as appears by his letter of the 29th May) from the report of others to think well of them.

However, as I found that His Lordship had decided to remove the troops thither and *now* looked upon the place as a harbor in which he could give *effectual protection to ships of the line*, the mistakes and delays I had hitherto experienced deterred me from attempting *another* alteration. I therefore permitted His Lordship to act without interruption according to his present plan, not in the least doubting that he would, as he promised, use the utmost dispatch possible in fortifying the two posts—which were *now clearly become his own choice*—and send me afterward all the troops he could spare from their defense.[21]

Before the German recruits arrived, my New York army consisted of only two battalions of British grenadiers, six other British battalions, eleven Hessian, and four provincial corps, in all about ninety-three hundred men dispersed in different posts within a circuit of one hundred miles. And of these, according to formal opinion given by all the general officers in council, 6000 at least must be indispensably set apart for the necessary duties and defense of the city and its dependencies, etc.[22] That of General Washington, including the French troops from

19. Clinton to Leslie or the officer commanding the expedition from the Chesapeake, July 23, below, p. 552.
20. Cornwallis to Clinton, June 30. In his letter of July 27 the Earl reiterated that Yorktown and Gloucester would be difficult to fortify, of limited use, and dangerous; in almost the same breath he announced that he was going to fortify them, *faute de mieux*, because Clinton required a post. See below, pp. 536, 552–553; for a discussion of the need and requirements for a naval base, and the process by which Cornwallis selected Yorktown, see Willcox in Am. Hist. Rev., 52, 17–20.
21. See Clinton's long explanation to Cornwallis, Aug. 2, below, pp. 553–556.
22. "For it was by all agreed that—should I march out, meet Washington and Rochambeau, take them and their army, and find this city burned on my return—I should be their prisoner in a few weeks. . . . I fear that 500 men, landed [on Manhattan] at night, might in a short time do such damage as would in its consequence be most fatal." Clinton memorandum or draft of a letter, entitled "My Plan," filed under Aug. 16.

Rhode Island, amounted to about 11,000 regulars. Yet it has been insinuated that I ought in the first place to have tried to prevent the
junction of Monsieur de Rochambeau's and Mr. Washington's corps;
and, failing in that, their united force ought to have been attacked while
it lay encamped between the Bronx and the North Rivers in front of
the White Plains, within sixteen miles of my lines at Kings Bridge.[23]

I shall not affront any intelligent military man so much as to suspect
he can think it possible for 4000 men—the utmost with which I could
have advanced—to have prevented 7000 from effecting a junction with
4000, even had the intelligence of their movements been ever so early
and exact, and the junction attempted ever so near my posts. It will be
consequently sufficient to observe that it was effected at many miles'
distance from them, and might have been made behind the mountains,
at a still much greater distance, had the enemy had the smallest apprehension of being interrupted. And, with respect to my neglect of
attacking their united force, the censure is equally erroneous. For Mr.
Washington could not have been removed from the very strong position he had taken by an attack in front without great loss, which must
have precluded all possibility of following the blow in a country every
200 yards of which furnishes strong defensive positions. And to have
marched out and retreated afterward, without attempting anything,
would have been to the enemy equal in its consequences to a victory.
In short, a victory to us could not have been decisive, a defeat too much
so; and to have assembled the troops wantonly from such a distance
(which must have taken days to accomplish, and have greatly retarded
our works) would in my opinion have been a most injudicious measure.[24] Having no reason to doubt that, if the enemy had a plan, it was
against New York in conjunction with a fleet, would I have been justified in moving out to attack the enemy's army assembled, and risk the
fate of the American war upon so uncertain an event as a victory against
such a superiority in such a country, and where victory on my part
would not be decisive, but defeat entirely so?

But, when I was joined on the 11th of August by a reinforcement of
about twenty-four hundred German recruits, I looked upon my powers

23. "I was astonished . . . that there was a single person calling himself a
soldier that could . . . have displayed so much ignorance. Whoever he or they
may be, if such are their ideas I must be free to own I should tremble for the army
they command; and I should be cautious how I trusted even a detachment to
them. You know enough of them to see that 'tis the fashion . . . to criticize every
movement. I confess, when I was second in command, I did so; but I never did
it till I had had all the reasonings for it, and had given mine to my chief." *Ibid.*

24. "Having every reason to expect a siege and intending otherwise, at all
events, to leave this place with as small a garrison as possible in the autumn, all
the troops were encamped to work at the different works. To have moved them
without an object would have delayed us much." *Ibid.*

as so respectably increased that—although I had no intentions of running any risks with Mr. Washington that might impede or prevent my views against Rhode Island and Philadelphia—yet (having made preparations for throwing two or three bridges over the Harlem) I should have probably tried a brush with him had he foraged in the loose way he had done on the 15th, and a favorable opportunity offered anywhere near my lines.[25]

Rear Admiral Graves did not return to Sandy Hook before the 16th. I then immediately renewed my offer for a conjunct operation against the French squadron at Rhode Island if he thought himself to be in sufficient force to mask the great harbor, which was all that I would require of him. But, though he had approved my plan and wished much [for] its execution—nay, offered on his return to proceed—two of his large ships unfortunately were found to be wanting repair, which obliged him to postpone his assistance until they could be refitted.[26]

Finding in the meantime that Mr. Washington's army had foraged within six miles of me on the 17th, and expecting that he might do so still nearer about the 20th and, perhaps, advance to his old ground on the heights above our lines, I had ordered three bridges to be laid ready, and meant to have passed the Harlem with about seven thousand men (which I had collected for the purpose) in the night of the 19th, with a hope of possibly catching some partial advantage even though it should bring on a general action, as I could not possibly suffer much from it so very near my own works and [with] three bridges, besides that of Kings Bridge, in my rear. But on the 19th the enemy suddenly broke up their camp and retired; and, in a few days after, the allied army passed the North River and took a position in the neighborhood of Chatham, which seemed to threaten Staten Island.

This, together with a letter from Sir George Rodney to Admiral Arbuthnot [27] (which arrived on the 27th of August and was opened by Commodore Affleck), confirmed me strongly in the opinion I had before formed from the Secretary of State's letters and all accounts from

25. "There is but one plan that can terminate favorably [?]: cross the Bronx with a corps sufficient to bait Washington's whole force that could be collected in forty days, place yourself upon his communications with North Castle, etc., destroy his bridges on Croton; and then he is forced to pass the Bronx upon you, and attack you on your own terms, or break up his army with a *sauve qui peut* over the fords of Croton. If all the reinforcements I expected had arrived in time, this, *entre nous*, was my plan. But it was not possible with the force I had. . . . And we may recollect also that he who passes the Bronx does not easily repass it in the presence of an enemy of equal force." *Ibid.*

26. See Clinton to Graves, Aug. 17, 18, 24, and Graves to Clinton, Aug. 18, 21, below, pp. 559–561.

27. Of July 7; see below, pp. 539–540.

the rebel country, that we had no danger to apprehend from the force under de Grasse—since it was not to be supposed possible that Sir George Rodney would have disobeyed the orders sent him *to be watch-ful of that officer's motions,* and it was consequently clear from this conduct that he looked upon the force with Sir Samuel Hood as amply sufficient to counteract them.

However, I did not relax in my admonitions to Lord Cornwallis to be as expeditious as possible in his defensive, and to send me every man he could spare from it when completed. And I was consequently sorry to find by his letters that the evacuation of Portsmouth could not take place before the 21st, and that he could not until then say how soon it might be in his power to spare any troops.[28] But, concluding from General Washington's late move that he had suspended for the present his intentions of besieging New York and might possibly (after taking a defensive station at his old post of Morristown) detach to the southward, I desired His Lordship in a subsequent letter to keep with him all the troops then in Virginia, intending in addition to forward to him (by the ships that had been some time waiting for convoys to carry his provisions, stores, etc.) the recruits and convalescents belonging to His Lordship's army, being all that I dared as yet venture to send him lest the enemy's maneuvers might prove only a feint to deceive me.[29] For, as I had every reason to be certain of our having a naval superiority, I could not entertain the most distant suspicion that Mr. Washington really intended to march his army to the Chesapeake, where I knew it was impossible for such a number of troops to be fed without his having the command of those waters.

Everything having been long since prepared for the expedition to Rhode Island, and its execution only suspended until some necessary repairs could be done to the *Prudent* and *Robust,* the troops destined for that service were embarked immediately upon Sir Samuel Hood's arrival on the 28th of August with fourteen sail of the line; and it was our determination to have gone thither the next day. But we had the mortification to find that this most important enterprise had been un-fortunately too long delayed, as intelligence brought me that evening over Long Island assured us that Monsieur de Barras' squadron, with transports, storeships, etc., had sailed from Newport on the 25th for the Chesapeake. This circumstance, when added to information re-ceived on the 31st that the allied army had suddenly broke up its camp on the 29th and was marching toward Trenton, would have made me suspect that the French armament expected by the enemy from the

28. Cornwallis to Clinton, Aug. 16, below, p. 557.
29. Clinton to Cornwallis, Aug. 27, below, p. 562.

West Indies was much more respectable than I apprehended, had not Sir Samuel Hood assured me in his letter of the 25th that "*the force he had with him was equal fully to defeat any designs of the enemy, let de Grasse bring or send what number of ships he might in aid to those under Barras.*" [30] And, if I really was deceived, it was in fact this, together with previous repeated, positive promises from the American Minister of the most ample naval support, not Mr. Washington's and Rochambeau's false communications, boats, bridges, or batteries, that deceived me—not, however, into a belief that New York was, but into a certainty that Lord Cornwallis' posts in Virginia could not be, his object. For I will appeal to Mr. Washington himself whether he would ever have engaged in operation against them with his whole army had he not been *certain* of having that naval superiority which I had the strongest reasons for thinking I had, until I received Mr. Graves' account of his action with de Grasse on the 5th of September. [31]

For, the moment Mr. Washington crossed the North River, I concluded he had dropped his design against New York for the present. But, under the persuasions that influenced me, I could not from thence infer he proposed moving his whole force to the southward, though I judged it possible he might send a detachment thither. And, if his position near Chatham excited any conjectures in me respecting his intentions, they only caused the movement of a few troops toward Staten Island in order to obviate the possibility of an affront in that quarter. In short, I will not pay Mr. Washington's understanding so bad a compliment as to suppose he thought it necessary to deceive me, whatever deception policy might have required with respect to his own people; for he too well knew I was in no capacity to interrupt his march to the southward whenever he pleased to make it.

My whole force at that period did not, even after the arrival of the recruits, exceed 10,000 men. And it has been already shown that half of these would be required for the defense of New York in case of a forward move, [and] of course considerably more in an oblique one. [32] This indispensable deduction reducing my acting army to at most 4000, the American General could never have entertained any apprehensions from being followed by that number. But to have landed such

30. See below, p. 562.
31. On the naval background of Clinton's planning see Willcox in *Journ. of Mod. Hist.*, 17, 327–330, and in *Am. Hist. Rev.*, 52, 20–26.
32. This is another interesting sidelight on Clinton's obsession with the safety of his base. A flanking movement against Washington, he argues, would open New York to attack and therefore require a large garrison, whereas in a direct frontal movement the British army itself would screen the town. How the Americans, if they were being attacked in flank, would be free to assault Manhattan he does not explain.

a handful in the Jersies, supposing I had every requisite naval support and assistance, in face of works only seven miles distant from his camp at Chatham is an absurdity which I am persuaded that officer never suspected me capable of, and consequently could have no inducement to guard against—as he might have met me, had he chosen it, with four times the number I could have possibly thrown on shore if I had had boats to have landed my whole force at once. And, if he chose to continue his march to the Delaware, how was it in my power to have stopped him even with twice as many troops as he had? The impracticability of such an attempt appeared evidently in '76, when Lord Cornwallis pursued him in Jersey—and even came up with his rear guard—without bringing him to action.

But the real truth of the matter is that, circumstanced as I happened to be, there was no move within my power which could be of the least use to Lord Cornwallis but *the direct one of joining him in Virginia*. This was the *unanimous* opinion of *all* the general officers under me and Lord Cornwallis, as well as my own. Consequently *I would not have attempted any other if I could;* and, in fact, I *could not if I would.* Therefore, with respect to the misfortunes that followed, I can with firmness aver that no part of my conduct, either before or subsequent to the arrival of de Grasse, is in the smallest degree responsible for them. Nor can their rise be deduced from other causes than those which I have endeavored to explain in the foregoing sheets, namely, *Lord Cornwallis' coming into Virginia contrary to orders, and forcing operation there at an improper season; the American Minister's directing me to support those operations, although I had early apprised him of their danger, and his positively promising me a superior fleet to cover them; and, finally, Sir George Rodney's neglecting to bring or send his whole fleet thither for that purpose, according to the orders sent him from Europe.*

Rear Admiral Graves and Sir Samuel Hood sailed for the Chesapeake on the 31st, with nineteen sail of the line, two fifties, and fourteen frigates, under the fullest confidence of their being at least equal to the united force of de Grasse and Barras, even though the former should be arrived there before them and have joined the latter. From hence, and the information I received from Lord Cornwallis by a runner on the 30th that Portsmouth was evacuated and the stores and troops brought from thence to Yorktown, and that, the engineer *having finished his survey and examination of the latter and proposed his plan for fortifying it,* His Lordship looked upon it as judicious and ordered it to be executed (giving me hopes at the same time that the works, both there and at Gloucester, would be in a tolerable state of defense *in about six weeks,* and that he could spare 1000 men from everything but labor), I was persuaded I had no cause for apprehension respecting the safety of our posts in Virginia, although the accounts from the Jersies in the 2d of September confirmed the report of the allied army's having marched to the Chesapeake with strong expectations of meeting there a considerable French armament to cooperate with it.[33]

The very favorable accounts also which I received from Colonel Robert Conway, Major Desmond[?], Major Du Buy, and other officers just arrived from Virginia, as well as His Lordship's own sentiments of it, gave me every reason to be perfectly satisfied with the defensibility of the ground he had occupied. For, although His Lordship had neglected to transmit to me the engineer's survey and plan of his proposed works as he had promised, I could not have the smallest doubt that the position was in every respect proper, after His Lordship had informed me *it could give effectual* protection to ships of the line and the plan for fortifying it had received his approbation—since a position easily turned or works *liable to be carried by a land attack* d'emblée [34] cannot well come under *that description,* and fortifications erected without necessity on ground commanded and enfiladed can never be deemed *judicious.*

But, when I heard from His Lordship on the 6th that Count de Grasse's fleet was within the capes and that forty boats had gone up James River with troops on the 1st,[35] Mr. Washington's design in marching to the southward remained no longer an object of doubt. I was still, however, persuaded that the naval superiority lay on our side. And I accordingly, without loss of time, embarked 4000 choice troops in the hope that the Admiral would very soon open a passage for me into York River, not doubting that by effecting a junction with Lord Cornwallis I should have it in my power to make the American General repent his enterprise. For, judging His Lordship's army (from his returns of the 15th August) to be full 7000 strong, I flattered myself that with this addition we should be able to face the enemy's combined army even in the field and, by possessing the rivers, attack or harass it at pleasure.[36]

As I was disappointed of the blow which I intended against Rhode Island, I was unwilling that the preparations for that service should be

33. See Cornwallis to Clinton, Aug. 22, and Clinton to Cornwallis, Sept. 2, below, pp. 560–561, 563.
34. I.e., at the first attempt.
35. Cornwallis to Clinton, Sept. 4, Stevens, *Clinton-Cornwallis Controversy,* 2, 151.
36. Clinton to Cornwallis, Sept. 6, below, p. 564. For Cornwallis' return of Aug. 15 see below, pp. 556–557.

wholly lost, without some attempt being made to annoy the enemy's coasts and [some] endeavor to cause a diversion somewhere. Wherefore, soon after the departure of the fleet for the Chesapeake, I detached Brigadier General Arnold with about 1500 men, with directions to endeavor to bring off or destroy the prize vessels, traders, or privateers, together with naval and other stores, said to be collected at New London to a very large amount. This service was accomplished by that officer with his usual spirit and address. But, having been unfortunately detained for some hours off the harbor by contrary winds before the transports could beat up, the enemy, being thereby apprised of his destination, had time to get several vessels under sail and escape with them up Norwich River. All the rest, with a very great quantity of naval stores and valuable European and East and West India commodities, were destroyed. However, in effecting this the town was unfortunately burned, contrary to the Brigadier's intentions; and we had, moreover, to lament the loss of some excellent officers and rather too many men in an attack on Fort Griswold, a very strong work, which was carried by assault in a most spirited manner by the Fortieth and Fifty-fourth Regiments under the command of Major Montgomery and Lieutenant Colonel Eyre. The first [was] killed and the latter very badly wounded before the troops entered the works, which the enemy defended with great obstinacy at the expense of eighty-five of their number killed and sixty wounded.[37]

37. Arnold's report is contained in his letter to Clinton of Sept. 8, below, pp. 565–567. For modern accounts of this notorious episode see Fisher, *Struggle for American Independence*, 2, 483–484; Ward, *War of the Revolution*, 2, 626–628.

CHAPTER 25

The Siege and Fall of Yorktown, September to October, 1781

The idea that Sir Henry Clinton was deceived by Mr. Washington's maneuvers examined and refuted. Determined at a council of war, upon the allied army's decamping and marching to the southward, that the joining Lord Cornwallis with all the force that can be spared from New York is the best and only plan which can be adopted for his relief. No reason yet to doubt on which side the naval superiority lies. The want of it the principal cause of the subsequent misfortune. Lord Cornwallis' neglect and misconception of orders have served to aid and precipitate it. His Lordship's reasons for not attacking in detail the besieging army as it was collecting against him, and not endeavoring to save as much of his own as he can by flight, examined and answered. Sir Henry Clinton's reasons for believing Lord Cornwallis' post capable of sustaining a longer siege. His Lordship's exterior position described from accounts given of it by French and British engineers.

The Admiral's letter after his action of the 5th of September causes the first suspicion of the enemy's naval superiority. But Barras' being supposed to have been in it excites an hope that Admiral Digby's arrival may transfer it again to us. These hopes destroyed on the 23d by Lord Cornwallis' letter of the 17th, saying de Grasse has thirty-six sail of the line. Admiral Digby arrives at New York the next day with three ships of the line. Affairs appearing now to be very seriously alarming, it is determined in a council of flag and general officers to embark 6000 troops in the fleet, when refitted, and endeavor to force a passage through the enemy for their junction with Lord Cornwallis.

Admiral gives hopes he will be ready to sail about the 5th of October. Sir Henry Clinton receives on the 10th of September His Majesty's approbation of his plan for the campaign, with orders to execute it— alas, too late! And the Minister writes that he may not resign the command to Lord Cornwallis. The attempt to relieve Lord Cornwallis by forcing a passage with twenty-five sail through thirty-six examined and defended. Hint sent to His Lordship by Major Cochrane to try to save what he can if the least apprehensive that the fleet cannot arrive in time.

Fleet sails at last on the 19th, but finds on its arrival off Chesapeake

332

that His Lordship had surrendered on that day. His Lordship's abandoning his exterior position before he is forced from it unfortunate, as by holding it until then his defense might have probably been protracted until the arrival of succor. His Lordship's reports of his post favorable until his letter of 12th of October. The probable cause of his then discovering its weakness. Lord Cornwallis' letter of 20th of October sent to the Minister entire, without comment, from delicacy to His Lordship. Certain assertions in that letter, with their consequent implications, shewn to be erroneous or unfounded, which His Lordship afterward acknowledges.

BOTH FRENCH and British writers have rashly suggested that, being deceived by Mr. Washington's maneuvers into a belief that the siege of New York was his object, I had probably neglected taking proper steps to obviate the more immediate danger that threatened my posts to the southward.[1] I flatter myself, however, that the reader is by this time convinced that there was not the smallest foundation for either opinion. For it has been shown in the preceding chapters that I had very early represented to His Majesty's Ministers the danger to which operations in the Chesapeake were likely to be exposed unless we had a fleet there sufficiently strong to cover them; but that, in consequence of an opinion given to them by Lord Cornwallis that the conquest of Virginia would effectually facilitate and secure the recovery of the Carolinas,[2] positive directions had been sent me by His Majesty's command to employ my whole force on that service until it was accomplished, accompanied by the strongest assurances that my operations there should be protected by a naval force superior to what the enemy could bring against me. And, because a place of arms was previously indispensable for covering the King's ships in the Chesapeake and the requisite depots of supplies for the army to be assembled there, I was consequently obliged to direct His Lordship to look out for a proper one and fortify it.[3]

The unexpected delays which unfortunately protracted this neces-

---

1. See Jean Baptiste Donatien de Vimeur, Comte de Rochambeau, *Relation, ou Journal des opérations du Corps Français sous le commandement du Comte de Rochambeau, Lieutenant-Général des Armées du Roi, depuis le 15 d'août* (Philadelphia, 1781), pp. 1–2; Stedman, *History of the American War*, 2, 397.

2. A paraphrase of Cornwallis to Germain, Apr. 18, Stevens, *Clinton-Cornwallis Controversy*, 1, 417–418.

3. This is highly misleading. Clinton had been interested in establishing a post in the Chesapeake months before Cornwallis suggested the conquest of Virginia, and had urged either Portsmouth or Yorktown on a succession of commanders. See Clinton to Leslie, Oct. 12, and to Arnold, Dec. 14, 1780, Clinton's conversation with Phillips, *ca.* Mar. 10, and to Phillips, Mar. 10, 1781, below, pp. 467, 482–483, 493–496.

sary measure to so late a period have likewise been impartially detailed, together with the strong reasons I had for relying on the repeated promises made me by both Ministers and Admirals that Sir George Rodney would be watchful of the Count de Grasse's motions and bring or send me timely succor to prevent his doing me any mischief. The natural inference, therefore, to be drawn from these premises is that I was well warranted in thinking [that] we had a naval superiority and that the Chesapeake was consequently the most eligible theater I could wish to meet Mr. Washington on—though it was scarcely to be hoped that he would venture to commit his army in those waters, where my having the command of them must give me so many advantages over him, and where he must find it almost impossible to feed it at such a distance from the source of all his supplies.

But, when I saw that Mr. Washington had marched, notwithstanding, decidedly thither, I concluded he was influenced by some confident assurances sent him by the Count de Grasse, and that consequently nothing I could do would divert him from pursuing that measure until he was convinced they were fallacious. Wherefore the joining Lord Cornwallis in York River as soon as possible, with all the force that could be spared from New York, was determined unanimously in full council to be the best and only plan which could be adopted under our present circumstances. And, as long as an apparent possibility remained of our carrying it into execution, no other could certainly be thought of lest it should impede or interfere with this; for we had not as yet the smallest cause to entertain even doubts on which side the naval superiority lay.

But why [was it that] we had it not? Let those who may be more immediately concerned answer, as it is no business of mine to assert either that the Admiral commanding in the Leeward Islands was remiss in his attention to de Grasse's motions, or that the Lords of the Admiralty could have furnished Mr. Digby with a larger force than three ships, and have sent him to North America earlier in the season than they did. All that I shall presume to declare is that, had either the one or the other been fortunately more attended to, Lord Cornwallis' army could not have been lost, and the United States of America would in all probability have composed a part of the British Empire at this hour.

But, while I thus impute the misfortunes that followed to our want of the promised naval support, I must not conceal that there were other causes which materially contributed to accelerate their approach and augment their magnitude. Several of these have been already noticed; and I most sincerely wish that I had no occasion to add to their number. But a strict regard to truth and the duty of the task

I have imposed upon myself oblige me to be explicit. And, was I really conscious that any errors of mine had a share in promoting the catastrophe, I solemnly declare I would not hesitate to reveal them.

Notwithstanding that Lord Cornwallis' extraordinary neglect and misconception of my orders had caused the seizing a naval post on the Williamsburg Neck to be delayed until the 1st and 2d of August, there happened to be yet time enough between that period and de Grasse's arrival to have put the works of York in a very respectable state of defense. So far, however, was this from being the case that I am credibly informed not a spade had been stuck into the ground His Lordship stood siege on (except a redoubt to secure his own quarters) until the appearance of the French fleet roused him, although he had been long before cautioned against such an event, and had every reason to expect its arrival much sooner than the 31st of August.

The works on the Gloucester side had been indeed begun soon after the troops landed there. But, as the heights of York (being the commanding ground) were to cover them, these ought certainly to have been attended to first, because they alone could secure the tenability of the post. As I never saw either York or Gloucester, I cannot presume to hazard an opinion on the advantages or demerits of their situation. But, had the latter been such as to have excited the smallest apprehension for its defense, there can be no doubt Lord Cornwallis would have reported them to me, at least after he had examined the survey of the ground which (as would appear from His Lordship's letters) his engineers had been eighteen days completing—a time surely most ample for discovering its defects if it had any! On the contrary, all His Lordship's letters to me until that of the 16th of September (which I did not receive until the 23d) were either couched in such language as tended to impress me with the most favorable ideas of it, or were totally silent on the subject.[4]

At the time when Lord Cornwallis was informed that the Count de Grasse had entered the Capes of Virginia with forty sail of large ships, His Lordship was ignorant of Sir Samuel Hood's arrival—and consequently could have no hopes of receiving succor by means of Mr. Graves' seven ships of the line, which were the utmost he could then count upon. Therefore, as His Lordship had now so little probability of being able to render his post tenable before he should be attacked in it,

4. See Cornwallis to Clinton, Aug. 12, 16, 22, 31, Sept. 2, 8, 16–17, below, pp. 556, 557, 560–561, 563, 565, 571. These letters do not indicate that the engineers took eighteen days to complete the plan; Cornwallis first refers to it on the 16th, and speaks of it as finished four days later. Clinton subsequently persuaded himself that it was never made at all: Stevens, *Clinton-Cornwallis Controversy*, 2, 137 nn. 4–5; below, pp. 347–348 and n. 31.

we are at a loss to account for his not attempting to cut up Monsieur St. Simon's 3000 enervated troops, on their landing within a few miles of him on the 1st of September, or by placing himself between them and Lafayette's small corps of Continentals to prevent their junction (which did not take place until several days after) and strike at either or both as occasion offered, it being obvious that success even against the one or the other must have retarded the enemy's operations against him, and perhaps induced their relinquishing them altogether.[5]

But, when His Lordship saw the enemy's fleet return triumphant after their action on the 5th of September and Barras' squadron of eight ships of the line (who it seems had not been in the action) join them, his prospects of relief must have totally vanished, or become at least so evanescent that we cannot cease wondering at His Lordship's supineness in waiting to be attacked in his half-finished works by the powerful army he then knew was assembling and must very shortly appear before them, while such an opportunity offered for extricating himself by one bold effort, and to which he was so strongly invited by every circumstance of his situation. For the troops under the Marquis de Lafayette, even after St. Simon's junction with him at Williamsburg, were in numbers as well as quality much inferior to the acting force under His Lordship.[6] A sudden and rapid move might have consequently annihilated or dispersed that corps, in which case General Washington could not easily afterward have collected another army to have faced His Lordship even in the field. But, had accident or timely intelligence enabled the Marquis to evade the blow, still an escape up the country

5. To understand the criticism that follows, the outline of events must be borne in mind. De Grasse arrived in the Chesapeake on Aug. 30 and sent St. Simon's marines, whom he had brought with him from the West Indies, up the James to join Lafayette. Graves and Hood left New York on the 31st, met the enemy and were repulsed in the Battle of the Capes on Sept. 5, played hide-and-seek with de Grasse for almost a week at sea, and then retired to New York. Meanwhile de Barras, from Rhode Island, had slipped into the Chesapeake, so that de Grasse on his return had a combined fleet of thirty-six of the line. Cornwallis knew this crucial fact by Sept. 17, but did nothing. Washington's and Rochambeau's army arrived by Sept. 26, and the trap closed.

For a critical discussion of Clinton's points, and an attempt to apportion the responsibility of the various British commanders for the subsequent disaster, see Willcox in Am. Hist. Rev., 52, 27–35.

6. This is debatable. St. Simon brought Lafayette 3100 marines; before Washington's arrival the total Franco-American force amounted to some 5500 regulars, with 3000 militia in the vicinity as reserve, and 3000 more expected. (Gottschalk, Lafayette and the Close of the American Revolution, pp. 297, 300.) Against this force Cornwallis, by abandoning his posts and putting every man into the field, might have brought at most 6000 regulars and a reserve—by Clinton's reckoning —of 1500 to 2000 marines, sailors, and armed loyalists; see below, pp. 556–557, 564.

was open, as there was nothing at that time in Virginia which could have prevented His Lordship from marching to the southward with every man of his army that was capable of moving. And surely the general officer who but a few months before had so readily determined to abandon, without the least necessity, an important post whose safety was committed to his charge and fly into Virginia at every hazard (whither no one duty or object called him), in opposition to orders that were too explicit to admit of discretionary deviation—I say that the general officer who acted thus, at the risk of interfering with the plans of the Commander in Chief and of forcing him into operation he could not be prepared for and had always declared against, cannot be supposed to have had many scruples of etiquette about waiting for discretionary power to authorize his retiring from thence, even with the sacrifice he must have made, when he had two such good objects as the saving the chief part of his gallant army from otherwise inevitable destruction—for such it must have then appeared to His Lordship—and the recovering a valuable province which his late wanton dereliction had thrown back into rebellion and very nearly lost.

All this time I was so confident of our naval strength, and Lord Cornwallis' capacity for retaining his post at least as long as his provisions lasted, that I kept 5000 select troops ready in transports for joining him the instant I should hear that Admiral Graves had cleared the Chesapeake of the enemy's ships and a safe passage was opened for their going thither.[7] For several experienced, sensible officers of rank who had lately left His Lordship at Yorktown were clearly of opinion, which they delivered in council, *that the position he was in might be defended with the troops he then had against twenty thousand assailants for at least three weeks after opened trenches.* And indeed the plans of the ground about Yorktown taken by both English and French officers, which I have since seen, seem strongly to favor this opinion and show that it was not ill founded, as they all represent the exterior position which Lord Cornwallis first occupied to be a space of ground somewhat higher than that round it, between *two impracticable ravines* ascending from the river and not four hundred yards asunder at their extremity, and commanding not only the approaches from the country but, as Mr. Washington expresses it in his letter to Congress, in a near advance all the rest of His Lordship's works in front of the town.[8]

But, when I received the Admiral's letter of the 9th of September

7. Clinton to Graves, Sept. 8, below, p. 567.
8. Washington to the President of Congress, Oct. 1, Fitzpatrick, *Writings of Washington,* 23, 158.

favoring me with an account of his action on the 5th, I confess my faith in our naval superiority began to waver.[9] However, as I flattered myself (and the Admiral still believed it) that Barras' squadron composed part of the French fleet on that day, I was still inclined to hope that Admiral Digby's arrival, which was hourly expected, and the addition of the *Prudent* and the *Robust*, which were now refitted, would soon turn the scale in our favor and enable me to join His Lordship with such a body of troops as might not only dissipate every appearance of danger, but even procure some decisive advantage over the enemy.[10]

This very unpleasant state of doubt, indecision, and hope continued until the 23d, when the arrival of Lord Cornwallis' letter of the 16th and 17th of September informed us that Barras' squadron had not been in the action of the 5th, and that his junction with the Count de Grasse augmented the French fleet to thirty-six sail of the line.[11] So unexpected a naval superiority on the side of the enemy—which far exceeded everything we had in prospect—was not a little alarming, and seemed to call for more than common exertion to evade the impending ruin. I consequently solicited an immediate conference in full council with the flag officers of the fleet (which had arrived at Sandy Hook on the 19th), when it was unanimously resolved that above 5000 troops should be embarked in the King's ships as soon as they could be refitted, and every possible effort made to form a junction with the army at Yorktown. A letter was consequently dispatched to Earl Cornwallis, with the approbation of the council, to inform him of their resolution *and that there was every reason to hope we should start from New York about the 5th of October*, to which I had an opportunity of adding that Admiral Digby was just arrived with three ships of the line.[12]

But I must confess that, after I was thus fully apprised of the enemy's

9. For Graves' letter see below, p. 567.
10. Clinton to Graves, Sept. 14, and minutes of councils of war of Sept. 14, 17, and 19, below, pp. 569–572.
Sir Henry's optimism is understandable. The British had fought the battle of Sept. 5 with nineteen ships of the line, de Grasse with twenty-four out of the twenty-eight that he had brought from the West Indies. Neither Clinton nor Graves yet knew that there were twenty-eight. They assumed, until they heard from Cornwallis on the 23d, that Graves had engaged the entire French force in American waters—sixteen of the line under de Grasse, plus de Barras' eight from Rhode Island. Hence the hope put in the *Prudent*, the *Robust*, and the three ships that Digby was known to be bringing with him: if the French had only twenty-four, these additions would give the British equality. In actual fact the enemy had thirty-six, and Graves had been forced to destroy one of his ships after the battle, so that the odds were overwhelming.
11. For Cornwallis' letter see below, p. 571.
12. Minutes of the councils of war of Sept. 23 and 24, below, pp. 573–574; Clinton to Cornwallis, Sept. 24, Stevens, *Clinton-Cornwallis Controversy*, 2, 159–160.

strength and informed by the Admiral of the crippled condition of his fleet, I should not have been greatly displeased to have heard that Lord Cornwallis had made his escape to Carolina with everything he could take with him.[13] For I could not well comprehend the meaning of His Lordship's declaration in his letter of the 16th that, *if he had no hopes of relief*, he would rather risk an action than defend his half-finished works, but [that], as I said Admiral Digby was hourly expected and *promised every exertion* to assist him, he did not think himself justifiable in putting the fate of the war on so desperate an attempt—as, upon recurring to the letters His Lordship referred to, I could not find that I had promised in them any exertions but *my own*, which I told him must depend upon Admiral Graves' success against de Grasse. But, the Admiral's efforts having failed, and it appearing from His Lordship's postscript of the 17th that he knew the French ships of the line then investing his post were at least one-third in number more than we had any probability of even after Admiral Digby should join us, it was manifest His Lordship *could have no hopes of relief*.

Wherefore I was convinced, by his desiring me to *be prepared to hear the worst*, that upon this intelligence His Lordship had resumed his first idea of forcing his way through the enemy before Mr. Washington's junction with Lafayette, and retiring to the southward. But I happened to be single in this opinion, as all the other general officers in council judged the expression *worst* to mean something more serious than *retreat* arising from the unfinished state of His Lordship's works. It was accordingly proposed to their consideration whether a movement into Jersey, threatening Philadelphia, might not be made, provided it could be done without the risk of impeding the principal object we had in view, which was an attempt to join His Lordship in York River. But the general officers were unanimously of opinion that no de-

13. For Graves' letter see below, pp. 572–573. Sir John Jervis, Clinton's old friend, agreed most emphatically with him that Cornwallis ought to have attempted escape the moment de Grasse sailed out to meet Graves; see Marie Martel Hatch, ed., "Letters of Captain Sir John Jervis to Sir Henry Clinton, 1774–1782," *American Neptune*, 7 (Apr., 1947), 105–106.

To judge by later evidence, which is oral but reasonably direct, Cornwallis did decide to make the attempt, and was then dissuaded from it by Alexander Ross, his aide-de-camp and closest friend. "Tarleton told me (the 2d of April, 1786) that on St. Simon's landing he went to reconnoiter him; that he proposed to Lord Cornwallis to attack him, that Lord Cornwallis approved, and [that] they were to have marched that night, as it was only twelve miles; that Colonel Ross said that on receipt of my letter[s] of the 2d and 6th September it became improper, as I therein gave assurances of exertions of fleet and army to succor Lord Cornwallis, and therefore no risk was to be run; [that] Lord Cornwallis was at last brought over to that opinion, and the attack did not take place." A loose sheet in Clinton's hand, filed under T in "Notes" (alphabetized), CP.

lay whatsoever should be hazarded as long as we had reason to expect the fleet would be ready to receive us.[14] And indeed I readily concurred with this opinion, from my being perfectly convinced that nothing but a direct move to the Chesapeake and our being able, after forcing the French fleet, to effect a junction with His Lordship could be now of the least use toward saving the posts of York and Gloucester, or even a part of Lord Cornwallis' army.

I had on the 10th of September the satisfaction of receiving from Lord George Germain His Majesty's sanction and acquiescence in the plan of operations which *I* had proposed for the present campaign.[15] This plan had, indeed, been before honored (as before mentioned) by the royal approbation; but, before I was prepared for carrying it into execution, subsequent orders having apparently given a preference to another recommended to the Minister by Lord Cornwallis, obedience to them partly obliged me to suspend my intentions, and was unfortunately one of the causes which induced the very critical situation in which we now were. However, my personal feelings were certainly very highly gratified by the information that the King had been most graciously pleased to approve *my plan*, and that my constantly zealous exertions to promote the service were still honored by my sovereign's confidence and support, which his Minister's letters by the April and May packets had alarmed me with the apprehension of having lost. But I must, notwithstanding, never cease to lament that this information came, alas, too late. For, had the American Secretary been (at the time he wrote those letters) equally explicit and condescending,[16] and not forced me into measures for which I was not prepared and which I had constantly represented to be extremely hazardous without the support of a covering fleet, I trust the disposition of my army would have been such on de Grasse's arrival that, had he brought with him twice

14. See the minutes of the council, Sept. 26, below, pp. 576–577. Clinton, at least in his official correspondence, was not so optimistic about the chances of the rescue expedition as he implies here and in later pages. "I presume I may be justified," he wrote to Germain on Sept. 12 (CP), "in having at present the most serious apprehensions. . . . Should the French fleet prove superior to ours [and] remain in the Chesapeake, and Mr. Graves does not find it expedient to attack them now or when Admiral Digby joins him, I own I shall despair of being able by any means to relieve the army there as long as circumstances continue in that situation."

15. Germain to Clinton, July 7, 14, below, pp. 540, 546.

16. The meaning is perhaps that all would have been well if Germain's earlier letters had been as "explicit" in leaving discretion to Clinton and as gracious ("condescending") as those of July. Sir Henry's references in this paragraph to the Minister's "positive commands" not to remove troops from Virginia are far vaguer, it should be noted, than when the "commands" were first mentioned. See above, p. 316.

the force he did, he could not have done me any essential injury.[17] This, however, was not a time for vain lamentations. Matters were approaching fast to a crisis which no longer admitted the measuring forces with the enemy, but called for the most animated exertions in both fleet and army to oppose them. And, although the disparity of strength between the two fleets was indisputably too great for us to be sure of success, I was confident that the vast importance of the stake we were going to contend for, as it fully justified the attempt, would not fail to nerve our efforts in the execution. And, should we be fortunate enough to relieve Lord Cornwallis, it was my firm resolution immediately after to resign into his hands a command which had hitherto produced to me nothing but the most painful anxiety and disappointment.[18]

I know there are some persons who regard this attempt to relieve the army in Yorktown by forcing a passage to it through the French fleet as a chimerical project, because they doubt the possibility of twenty-five sail of the line and two fifties being able to penetrate a compact line of thirty-six sail in the advantageous position de Grasse had taken, or of afterward escaping being all captured, supposing it possible for them to have effected it.[19] This being purely a naval question, I confess that I am by no means competent, as a landsman, to decide upon it. I shall

17. Clinton's logic seems to be confused by hindsight. If he had been supported by the government, he would presumably have put his own plan into execution— and been caught in the midst of it by de Grasse's arrival. The result might have been equally disastrous, and he implied as much at the time. In a letter to Germain on Sept. 12 (CP) he acknowledged that the only moment when his design would have had a good chance of success was when he first suggested it to Cornwallis; "and, indeed, I am far from saying positively that he was in force sufficient to have given it a fair trial. The events, also, since that period may give us reason to apprehend that, though we had succeeded in the attempt, it might now have proved detrimental not only to ourselves, but to those friends of government who might have been induced to declare for the King's interest."

18. This paragraph is taken with slight alteration from Clinton to Germain, Sept. 7 (below, p. 565). The final sentence, however, is elaborated in the letter: Sir Henry is convinced that Germain expected him to resign on receiving the Minister's letters of Mar. 7 and May 2, "which I should certainly have done had not the circumstances of this post been such at the time as to render such a measure highly improper."

19. As an illustration of this viewpoint Clinton here quotes at length from a contemporary pamphlet. The quotation is extremely verbose, and its argument can best be summarized. It is that the British fleet, if it had sailed before the *Torbay* and *Prince William* joined on Oct. 11, would have consisted of only twenty-three ships of the line and two fifties. Opposed to it the enemy had thirty-six ships of superior strength, well situated at the mouth of the York. Only gross carelessness on de Grasse's part could have permitted the British to pass to the south of him, run up the James, and then land 7000 men unmolested. Even if they had achieved this feat, what could have prevented their ships and troops from being bottled up in the James? [W. Graves,] *Two Letters from W. Graves, Esq; Respecting the Conduct of Rear Admiral Thomas Graves, in North America, during His Accidental Command There for Four Months in 1781* (4th issue, London, 1783), p. 37.

therefore only, in answer, observe that, had Commodore Symonds and the other sea officers with Lord Cornwallis not deemed the attempt practicable, we may presume that His Lordship would not have suggested it to me as the only means by which I could assist him; and that the flag officers of the fleet, who were present when this matter was debated in council, were all clearly of the opinion that thirty-six ships of the line could not, in the position the French fleet had taken between the Middle Ground and Horseshoe Flats, prevent even twenty-three from passing (with a leading wind and tide) into either York or James River.

The reasons given were that, the enemy's ships being unable—from the violence of the tide and great swell of the sea that runs in that channel—to avail themselves of the springs upon their cables, their broadsides could not be brought to bear on ships approaching them end on; and, after a passage should be effected, they would not dare suddenly to weigh anchor for the purpose of following, lest they should be driven on shore. On the other hand, our fleet might bring up in the meantime near, but not too near, the mouth of York River, where—the space being better calculated for its smaller number, and the tide being less violent than without—our ships could resist the attack of the enemy by having the free use of their springs; after which the troops might be put into boats and landed, under the cover of frigates, on either side of the river as circumstances should determine. And with respect to the subsequent capture of our fleet (which the disapprovers of this project seem chiefly to apprehend) no idea of the sort was stated at the council of war, from whence it may be inferred that the naval gentlemen then present did not look upon the probability of such an event as very alarming.[20]

As for myself, I confess I only looked toward effecting a junction with Lord Cornwallis without material loss, having such confidence in the experience, discipline, and gallantry of our united force (which would have amounted to at least 11,000 choice troops, headed by most excellent officers) as not to entertain the smallest doubt of our being able afterward to have dislodged Mr. Washington—whose army

20. This is presumably a reference to the council of war of Sept. 24, the first at which Graves and Digby were present. The points Clinton makes are not in the minutes of this or any other council, but may have been brought out in informal discussion. Sir Henry assumes that the Admirals' silence bred assent; in fact they were far from optimistic about the enterprise. They would scarcely have agreed, therefore, with the note that he appends at this point: "The enemy's fleet could not attack ours in their position near the entrance of the York River, when we had all the advantages they had not in the outer position, and where—even had they succeeded—they must have run ashore in York River."

amounted in the whole to little more than 15,000 by our account, having of these innumerable sick, and nearly half of that number [being] composed of southern militia and St. Simon's sickly corps from the West Indies. This being once effected, I trust we should have then found but little difficulty in at least placing our fleet in security until that of the enemy were obliged to return to the West Indies, supposing that our united efforts should happen to prove unequal to more.[21]

Sir Samuel Hood said at the council of war that the ships under him wanted but little preparation, and would be all ready in a day or two. And Admiral Graves, from returns made him that morning, had hopes the fleet would be in a condition for sailing by the 5th of October. That nothing, however, might be wanting to expedite our departure, the King's ships were immediately supplied by the army departments with lumber, boards, ammunition, howitzers, and every other assistance in their power, and the artificers of the ordnance were set about preparing the additional fireships for service, so that not a doubt remained with myself of our sailing from the Hook the first favorable spurt of wind after the day named by the Admiral. But, as we could not exactly ascertain Lord Cornwallis' actual situation, every precaution was taken in wording the letter to apprise him of our intentions, lest His Lordship might be tempted, by trusting too much to our punctuality as to time, to let slip an opportunity of effecting something by himself.

And I had soon the mortification to find that this precaution was not unnecessary, as the Admiral wrote me on the 28th of September that the fleet could not be ready sooner than the 8th; and at a council held on the 30th he was pleased to say he could not promise it would be ready before the 12th of October. All these disappointments were accordingly communicated from time to time to Lord Cornwallis; and Major Cochrane, of the Legion, was sent to His Lordship on the 3d of October with a sketch of the plans we had formed for effecting the junction with him, accompanied by a hint for him *to do what he could to save at least part of his army should he have the least reason to apprehend we could not arrive in time.*[22] In short, notwithstanding all our

21. Sir Henry was obsessed, at the time and afterward, with the idea that the enemy would have thrown in the sponge as soon as the British fleet, inferior as it was, got inshore of the French. "All declare [that], if we had once got possession of the bay, Washington would have given up, considering the risks de Grasse ran in his anchorage without. It is certain he would have sailed for [the] West Indies the 20 October." [Clinton to Newcastle,] Oct. 3–16, 1781.

22. See Clinton to Cornwallis, Sept. 30, and the minutes of the council of war of Oct. 2, below, pp. 578, 579–580. Clinton was for once enthusiastic about the spirit and exertions of the navy, "which to a landsman must appear equal to anything ever attempted." But the fleet had been badly damaged by the battle and by storm; he was not at all confident that it would be ready in time to save Corn-

anxiety and efforts to save our posts in the Chesapeake, we had the misfortune to see almost every succeeding day produce some naval obstruction or other to protract our departure.[23] And I am sorry to add that it was the afternoon of the 19th before the fleet was fairly at sea.

All the letters I had received from Lord Cornwallis since that of the 17th September, being written in better spirits,[24] confirmed me in the persuasion his former ones had inculcated that *he could hold out as long as his provisions lasted,* which I knew (indeed he says so) might by management be to some part of November; and I consequently had no suspicion that His Lordship could be yet reduced to extremity. But I was not a little apprehensive that the sailing of the fleet being unfortunately protracted to so late a period might have given the enemy time to advance their approaches so close to his works (especially since His Lordship had unaccountably given up his exterior position) that we should probably find on our arrival that the difficulties of effecting a junction by the York River were become too great to be surmounted, and we should consequently be obliged to attempt it by the James. I had therefore settled a plan of operations with the general officers of my army previous to our embarkation (and which I endeavored to communicate to Lord Cornwallis) for cooperating with His Lordship by that door in case the others should be closed against us, though I own I had little hopes of effecting more by that means than the probably saving a part of His Lordship's army.[25]

In the meantime, however, the abandoning the exterior position— without the aid of which the post of York became much weaker— discovered to His Lordship many infirmities in that he had retired to which he did not seem to have adverted to before, else he certainly would have taken some earlier opportunity of reporting them to me than by his letter of the 12th of October, which was delivered to me on the 16th. This letter, in the most desponding language, informed me that nothing could possibly save him but a successful naval action and a subsequent junction with him in York River; *for in such works, on disadvantageous ground, he could not hope to make a long resistance.*[26] This

---

wallis, or that Graves could overcome the odds. Sir Henry expected, if the Admiral could not promise to sail by Oct. 8 or 10, to abandon the whole venture and march against Philadelphia, in the hope of drawing off Washington and his Continentals to the Delaware and giving Cornwallis another chance to escape. Clinton memorandum [Sept. 30].

23. See Graves to Clinton, Oct. 17, below, p. 582.
24. Cornwallis to Clinton, Sept. 29, Oct. 3, below, pp. 577, 580.
25. See the minutes of the council of war of Oct. 10, below, pp. 580–581.
26. The Earl's letter was written on Oct. 11; see below, p. 581 and n. 92.

was certainly placing the post of York in a different point of view from any in which it had been shown to me before. For His Lordship had informed me in his letter of the 27th of July that the posts of York and Gloucester would give *effectual protection* to line-of-battle ships; again, in that of the 16th of August, that the engineer was forming a plan for fortifying the ground that covered the harbor; and, in the one of the 22d, that the engineer had finished his survey and proposed his plan of the fortifications, which appeared *judicious,* and he had in consequence ordered to be executed.

Now, as Lord Cornwallis had not thought proper to favor me with a sight of his engineer's survey and plan (though he had promised it) and I had nothing but the above reports and the favorable opinions of some officers of rank who had lately come from thence to guide my judgment, how was it possible for me to suspect His Lordship could be of opinion that *disadvantageous* ground was capable of giving *effectual* protection to any harbor, or that he could regard *any plan for fortifying such ground as judicious and approve of it*—since they involve manifest contradictions which there is no possibility of reconciling? But the real fact I believe to be this: the ground in itself, taken altogether, was not *disadvantageous* until His Lordship had made it so by unnecessarily giving up to the enemy, without even a struggle, those strong points from whence it was afterward commanded and enfiladed. And, although His Lordship had very injudiciously neglected his defenses on the York side until an enemy fleet arrived to invest him, yet—as Mr. Washington had afforded him nearly six weeks afterward before he opened a battery against them—I am humbly of opinion that, *had his plan of fortification been judicious* and the works he had time to throw up been properly defended, such an army as His Lordship commanded ought not to have been reduced to extremity at sixteen, much less *eight,* days opened trenches, let the assailants or their artillery have been ever so powerful.

Consequently we had every reason to hope we should even yet be in time to try our exertions in His Lordship's favor.[27] Our disappointment was therefore as unexpected as it was afflicting when we heard, on our arrival off the Capes of Virginia, that Lord Cornwallis had sur-

27. "I had . . . my moments of agitation when I embarked my little army on board an inferior fleet, and put the fate of this war upon so unequal a conflict as it must have been in every respect—although it appears from the position we found the French fleet in that, if His Lordship had been able to keep his first position till our arrival, there would have been every prospect of brilliant success; and, even in the situation he was [in] after they had got upon the same ground with him and round his left flank, we should have saved great part of his army, with loss perhaps of part of mine." Clinton to the Duke of Gloucester, Dec. 28, 1781, a photostat volume in the CP.

rendered his posts and army by capitulation into the hands of the enemy on the very day on which we sailed from Sandy Hook, being the eighth after the first battery was opened against him.[28]

After this very plain and candid detail the reader will without doubt be as much astonished as I was when he sees in Lord Cornwallis' public letter on this event several *implications* and even unfounded assertions with an apparent intent of throwing the blame of the misfortune which befell him upon my shoulders.[29] [I was] especially [astonished] since I had never shown any desire of criminating His Lordship, either his plan or the execution; and he was consequently under no necessity of accounting for this unfortunate catastrophe in any other way than by imputing it in general to its most obvious cause, *the inferiority of our naval support, to which alone,* indeed, I had myself ascribed it in the report I made of it to Lord George Germain before I had received Lord Cornwallis' letter of the 20th of October, which I shall now beg leave to examine—I hope for the last time, as it gives me infinite concern that I was ever compelled to notice it at all.[30]

Lord Cornwallis has thought proper to *assert* in this letter, and his subsequent explanations of it, that the ground about Yorktown *was in general so disadvantageous and subject to enfilade* that no person, after *once seeing it, could ever think of erecting works there;* and that this had been always his own uniform opinion of that post, but the orders which he had received to seize a station for covering large ships were so positive and unconditional that he did not esteem himself at liberty to disobey them. Therefore, in compliance with what he judged an indispensable duty, he took possession of York and Gloucester as the only naval station he knew or heard of in Virginia that could receive ships of the line and afford them protection. And, when he found he was to be attacked in it in so unprepared a state by so powerful an army and artillery, he would have endeavored to make his escape to New York upon the arrival of General Washington's troops at Williamsburg—or to have risked an action with the enemy's whole combined force—rather than have attempted its defense, *had I not assured him in my letters that every possible means would be tried by navy and army to relieve him.* The obvious design of which appears to have been to inculcate a belief that Lord Cornwallis *was forced into an untenable post by the Commander in Chief's orders, notwithstanding his having*

28. An extract of the articles of capitulation is given below, pp. 582–583.
29. A rephrasing is interlined in the MS: "letting the blame in some degree slide upon my shoulders."
30. Cornwallis to Clinton, Oct. 20, and Clinton to Germain, Oct. 29, below, pp. 583–588.

represented its defects; and, after His Lordship saw himself likely to be attacked in it and overpowered, that he was prevented from endeavoring to escape with his army by the delusive hopes of effectual and timely relief which had been uniformly promised him, and that consequently Sir Henry Clinton, not His Lordship, is responsible for the issue.

The whole of this transaction has been already so fully and impartially explained that I need only refer the reader to the preceding pages, and letters annexed, to convince him that neither the letter nor the spirit of my orders ever obliged Lord Cornwallis to occupy York and Gloucester, as *the letter* clearly commanded him *to examine Old Point Comfort in James River and fortify it,* and *their spirit*—as explained in my instructions to the deceased General Phillips, which His Lordship acknowledges he was bound to act under—not only left him at liberty to reject, but absolutely forbade his occupying, *either Old Point Comfort or York if the objections to them should be such as he thought forcible.* Wherefore it is clear that his possessing York and Gloucester and removing the station to York River was altogether His Lordship's *own free and voluntary act*—and, I am sorry to add, in direct disobedience of a positive order, since it appears from his own confession that His Lordship always viewed that post in an unfavorable light, and *the objections against it must consequently have been such as he thought forcible.*

But, if this was actually the case and His Lordship really *never saw that post in a favorable light,* what could induce His Lordship to tell me that *he could in it afford effectual protection to ships of the line,* since the erecting batteries in a situation of that description would only furnish an enemy with the means of destroying them? And was it not rather His Lordship's indispensable duty to have lost no time in transmitting to me a plan of the ground with his own opinion upon it, since he could not be ignorant that I had no personal knowledge of the place? And, having no means of forming a judgment respecting it but from the report of others, I must be supposed to regard His Lordship's not doing so at least as an implied commendation, especially as His Lordship was pleased to tell me, by the opportunity which I expected would have brought me his engineer's survey and plan agreeable to His Lordship's promise, that he had himself examined them and, thinking the plan for the fortifications *judicious,* he had ordered it to be executed. But whether His Lordship was right or not in his judgment I can only infer from the event. For, when I requested to be indulged with the favor of seeing this plan after Lord Cornwallis came to New York, His Lordship informed me that the only plan he had was destroyed by the bursting of a shell. And his engineer, Captain Sutherland, to whom he referred me for a sight of his, very honestly confessed that *he had never surveyed the ground they stood siege on, and consequently had no plan.*[31]

Lord Cornwallis appears to be equally unfortunate in his assertions that he was prevented from endeavoring to escape to New York or attacking General Washington's army *by my assurances that every possible means would be tried by navy and army to relieve him,* and that he was induced to retire within the works of the town (from the very strong position he had taken in front of them) by the information he received from me on the 29th of September *that the relief would sail about the 5th of October,* because neither the one nor the other of these assertions happens to be founded. For with respect to the first my letters will show (and his of the [2] December acknowledges it) that I did not promise His Lordship *the exertions of the navy,*[32] having only told him that I had four thousand men embarked ready to sail to his assistance the instant I should hear from Admiral Graves (who, I informed him, was gone to the Chesapeake with nineteen sail of the line) that he had driven the enemy's ships from the bay and the passage to him was open. Now His Lordship, at the time he says he received these assurances, knew that Mr. Graves had failed in his attempt, and that the enemy blocked up his post with thirty-six sail of the line. Upon what, therefore, could his Lordship build his hopes of relief? Certainly not upon my assurances or information, as I had very clearly explained to him our whole strength and expectations, and His Lordship was consequently much more competent than I was to judge of our naval capacity. In short, [it is true] that I did not, as he asserts, give him *assurances* of the exertions of the navy before Washington had joined Lafayette nor till three days after, [and] that I consequently did not prevent his attacking or retiring.

And in the second instance I must take leave to say that the information received from me was nothing near so positive as His Lordship states it, my words being *"there is every reason to hope we shall start from hence about the 5th of October."* But—admitting it to have been ever so positive, and that His Lordship had ever such strong reasons to believe that nothing could intervene to prevent our sailing on that day, [and] that we would arrive in two days more off Chesapeake Bay, and the next day force the enemy's superior fleet—how could *either*

---

31. "The fact is that ground was never surveyed, nor never fortified or intended to be, till Lord Cornwallis found my surmises were well founded that de Grasse was come in Chesapeake in force and that he should be attacked. All *now* agree on that." The Clinton memorandum in "Notes" cited above, p. 339 n. 13.

32. Cornwallis to Clinton, Dec. 2, Stevens, *Clinton-Cornwallis Controversy, 2,* 221–223.

[assurance of relief] induce His Lordship to relinquish a position which, from its strength, must have taken the enemy some days to force him from, and thereby (without even waiting to be attacked) give up to them ground which, according to Mr. Washington's letter to Congress, *commanded in a near advance all the rest of his works*, and might enable the enemy to shut the only door by which the relief he was so confident of could possibly join him?

I am also extremely sorry to observe that there is yet another small mistake in this letter which I feel it incumbent upon me to rectify. For, though I am persuaded Lord Cornwallis meant nothing more by the suggestion than to account in some degree for the flimsiness of his works, it has certainly the appearance of—and may possibly be regarded by those who read it as—an implied charge against me of *neglecting to supply His Lordship in time* with the requisite quantity of entrenching tools for constructing the defenses I had directed him to raise. The passage alluded to is this: "our stock of entrenching tools, *which did not much exceed 400 when we began to work in the month of August*, was now much diminished." By his engineer's (Captain Sutherland's) returns, dated the *23d of August*, he had at *that time 992 entrenching tools;* and, as he then made a demand for only 500 additional spades and shovels (having a sufficiency of pickaxes, felling axes, hand hatchets, and wheelbarrows), I own I was not apprehensive that our being prevented from sending them to him by the arrival of the French fleet could have occasioned much distress, as I was told that the neighboring plantations might readily furnish an ample number of hoes and shovels to serve as a substitute. Therefore the scantiness of His Lordship's works cannot in justice be imputed to a deficiency in that article. On the contrary, I am afraid it will be found upon examination that the place was not *lost for want of either works [and] guns or entrenching tools*, but from an *injudicious disposition of the one*, and perhaps *too late* an exertion of the other.

However, although I had every reason to be exceedingly hurt at the apparent tendency of this letter, yet I had too much delicacy either to omit or make comments on its objectionable passages until I could have an opportunity of hearing Lord Cornwallis' explanation of them and conversing with himself on the subject. I therefore lost no time, after I received it, in transmitting a copy of it entire to the Secretary of State without a single remark, as I did not in the least doubt that (being fully competent to the task from his having had early reports of all the transactions in the Carolinas and Virginia, and being possessed of my whole correspondence with Lord Cornwallis) he would, if he should find there was the smallest occasion for it, at least explain such parts of the letter as seemed to want clearing up with respect to me, lest they might otherwise impress the public with prejudice against me.

And, when I afterward pointed out to Lord Cornwallis the several improprieties I have noticed and the little foundation there was for many of His Lordship's assertions, he told me—as I conceived it, in extenuation—*that his letter of the 20th of October was written under great agitation of mind and in great hurry amidst frequent interruptions,* that there might be mistakes, etc.; and His Lordship seemed in other respects to be so sensible of them that I did not wish to press him further at that time in consideration of his recent misfortune, though his disavowal was not altogether so explicit and direct as I expected from His Lordship's liberality and candor. But I made not the least doubt that, on his arrival in England, His Lordship would formally disclaim every suggestion in that letter that tended to my prejudice if he found the passages I complained of were likely to have that effect. But I am extremely concerned—more, however, for His Lordship's sake than my own—that I have occasion to say that Lord Cornwallis, on the contrary, took infinite pains to support his implications and fix the public prejudice so strongly against me before my return that it was with difficulty anything in my vindication would be listened to afterward. And, what may appear still more extraordinary, even the Secretary of State, although he was sensible they had not the slightest foundations to support them, suffered them to have their course without taking any one step to do me justice, by either explanations of his own or publishing an official letter which I had written to him expressly for that purpose.[33]

33. Clinton to Germain, Dec. 6, below, pp. 590–591.

CHAPTER 26

Minor Operations, 1781–82

All the loyalists and refugees greatly alarmed by the tenth article of the capitulation of Yorktown. Sir Henry Clinton endeavors to keep those at New York quiet until Lord Cornwallis' arrival. [They are] not satisfied with His Lordship's reasons. Measures taken by Sir Henry Clinton to pacify them. He even offers to permit the revival of civil government in New York Province. Governor and council think it inexpedient at the present crisis.

Everything lost in the southern provinces except Savannah and Charleston. Battle of Eutaws. King's army falls back to the Quarter House near Charleston. Miserable state in which General Leslie finds the King's affairs in South Carolina on his arrival, and his desponding report of them. Requests to be reinforced by some old regiments. Council of war deliberates upon it. Cannot be granted, but he is left at liberty to withdraw the garrison from Savannah if necessary. Sir Henry Clinton under no apprehensions for that place or Charleston unless an enemy's fleet arrives to cooperate with Greene. Holds 2000 men in readiness to send thither if wanted. East Florida and the Bahamas attended to, and the necessary orders given for their security.

No events worth noticing have happened to the northward during the winter. An ineffectual meeting of commissioners at Elizabeth Town upon exchange of prisoners, etc. Projected move up the Delaware. General officers object to it at the present crisis. An officer dispatched to the Leeward Islands with offers of 2000 men for the relief of Brimstone Hill or the defense of Jamaica.

Resolution of House of Commons against offensive war with America. Sir Henry Clinton receives the King's command to conform to it. Joshua Huddy, a rebel captain, prisoner of war, [is] taken from the provost at New York by Captain Lippincott, an Associated Loyalist, and hanged in the Jersies in retaliation for one White, an Associator. Sir Henry Clinton orders a general court martial to try Lippincott for the murder. General Washington threatens to retaliate. Reflections on this business.

Sir Henry Clinton's friends, unknown to him, solicit the King's leave for his return to England. Sir Guy Carleton sent to New York to relieve him. Receives from him the command on the 8th of May. Various difficulties and mortifications Sir Henry Clinton has struggled through during its four years' continuance. The King most graciously approves of his whole conduct. Slights from Ministers and an implied, unmerited censure from Commissioners of Public Accounts. Conclusion.

THE [ENEMY'S] having wrested from us with so much facility the very important hold of the Chesapeake, which had cost us so much labor and expense to attain, and captured the entire army on that service (amounting, with the sailors and marines of the attendant ships, to little short of 9000 men) were—besides being losses in themselves of the most serious magnitude to us—subjects of such splendid triumph to our enemies and humiliating disgrace to the British arms that every real friend to this country throughout the whole extent of North America felt the blow with the deepest anguish and dejection. But, when the terms of capitulation were publicly known, it is impossible to describe the indignation, horror, and dismay with which the American refugees who had either taken up arms in our cause or flown to us for protection read the *tenth article* of that convention, *whereby* they considered themselves as not only most cruelly abandoned to the power of an inveterate, implacable enemy, to be persecuted at the discretion of party prejudice and resentment, but even as excluded from the same conditions of surrender with their fellow soldiers whenever it should happen to be their unfortunate lot to act with the King's troops in the defense of fortified places.[1]

The Board of Associated Loyalists at New York addressed me immediately on this subject through their president, Governor Franklin.[2] And it was with some difficulty I could restrain their clamors until the arrival of Lord Cornwallis, who I hoped would be able to explain his conduct in this matter to their satisfaction. But, His Lordship's plea of *necessity* and his having secured the *Bonetta,* sloop, as an asylum for the escape of the most *obnoxious* being insufficient to calm their apprehensions (or heal the wounds inflicted on their personal feelings by the word *punished,* which seemed to *admit guilt,* and *a consequent right* in the revolted colonists to prosecute them in their civil courts for acts of allegiance to their lawful sovereign), I thought it proper to endeavor to remove their fears for the future by issuing an order to the different

1. See Lt. Col. Clarke to Clinton, Savannah, Dec. 20, below, p. 591. The significance of the tenth article was the victors' refusal to promise that loyalists who surrendered in York and Gloucester should not be punished for having joined the British cause; see below, pp. 582–583.

2. In early November Clinton assured Gov. Franklin, orally and by letter, of his anxiety to alleviate the loyalists' fears. The Board answered on the 14th, over Franklin's signature, that the only way to do so was to proclaim publicly that they would receive, in any future capitulation, the same terms as regular troops, and to threaten retaliation for any harm done to those already captured. See Franklin to Clinton, Nov. 14, and minutes of the Board of Associated Loyalists for Nov. 8 and 14, 1781, filed at the end of Feb., 1782, CP.

posts of the army under my command, directing them to pay the same attention in all cases and in every event whatsoever to the interests and security of the loyalists within their respective districts that they did to those of the King's troops under their orders, and not to suffer or admit any distinction or discrimination to take place between them on any occasion.[3] And I had the happiness to find that this had in great measure the desired effect, especially as it was soon after honored by His Majesty's most gracious approbation and confirmation.[4]

There were, however, some oversanguine gentlemen [5] who advised me on this occasion to issue a proclamation threatening the enemy with retaliation in kind for every injury they inflicted on the loyalists for joining the King's army. But a punishment of that nature appertained more properly to the civil jurisdiction and could not, consequently, be inflicted without opening the courts of law; for to threaten them in my capacity of commander in chief would have been unavailing and nugatory while so many of our troops were prisoners in the enemy's power. And, being desirous of showing every possible attention to the interests and feelings of those unfortunate men who had relinquished their all and were now drawn into a most alarming situation for their attachment to the constitution of Great Britain, I offered to permit the revival of civil government in the New York district if retaliation was thought indispensable, and the civil courts should be judged by the crown lawyers to be equal to the inflicting of the necessary punishments. For, although I had never yet seen the moment proper for such a measure while that province was involved in the operations of war (which must ever suffer many obstructions and even disappointments when clogged by the control of civil jurisdiction), yet the loss of all the loyalists acting with our troops was a matter of too serious moment to admit of hesitation, had that been likely to be the consequence of our not being armed with the same civil weapons of terror which the enemy had the power of using against us. But Lieutenant General Robertson, the Governor of New York (after having consulted the principal refugees and civil officers of the province), being of opinion that the revival of civil government would be inexpedient at the present juncture, and all the general officers and the Admiral concurring in the same sentiments, the idea was of course dropped.[6]

Not knowing to what part the enemy might direct their next stroke,

3. See the minutes of the council of war of Jan. 17, 1782 (containing Clinton's circular letter), below, pp. 592–593.
4. Germain's letter of Jan. 2 was approbation and confirmation only in principle, but Clinton immediately broadcast it to the loyalists. See Clinton to Germain, Mar. 14, below, pp. 597–598 and nn. 99–100.
5. The members of the Board of Associated Loyalists; see above, p. 352 n. 2.
6. See the minutes of the councils of war of Jan. 17 and 23, below, pp. 592–594.

and having after the departure of Sir Samuel Hood's fleet everything to apprehend for the safety of our remaining posts if the Count de Grasse should winter in the Chesapeake for the purpose of cooperation with the Americans, I lost no time in taking every necessary measure within my power for their preservation. I did not, however, look upon New York to be in any kind of danger as long as I could retain its present garrison, which amounted to about 12,000 men. But, should the exigence of the service in other places oblige me to diminish that number, it was the unanimous opinion of all the general officers with me —as well as my own—that the distant situation of its numerous points of defense might expose it to hazard from a vigorous attack by sea and land.

We were, indeed, soon after eased of part of these apprehensions by hearing that the French fleet had sailed for the West Indies, which in great measure insured to us tranquillity for the rest of the winter. But we had the strongest reasons to expect a powerful combination against us in the spring or beginning of summer, which it was equally prudent to guard against. And the miserable state of our southern possessions gave me cause to suspect that the storm might first burst on that quarter; for in Georgia we held nothing but the neck of land between Ebenezer and Savannah, and in South Carolina little else besides Charleston. But that fortress was now in a condition to stand a formal siege, and its garrison very ample for its defense.

As, after the arrival of the three regiments from Ireland, the command in South Carolina must have fallen upon an officer altogether deficient in the local knowledge requisite for conducting the service in that country, I had directed Lord Cornwallis to detach thither Lieutenant General Leslie to obviate that inconvenience.[7] But, various accidents having prevented or put off his voyage until His Lordship's surrender, I sent him thither while we lay off the Chesapeake, and invested him with the same command and power in the southern district which Lord Cornwallis had held until he was taken prisoner. Consequently the military affairs in that quarter since Lord Rawdon's departure for Europe had been hitherto conducted by Colonel Gould of

7. After Rawdon's departure the ranking officer in South Carolina was Col. Paston Gould, who had arrived in early June in command of the reinforcements from Ireland. He had remained at Charleston waiting for Leslie, and did not take command of the field army until after the Battle of Eutaw Springs. (Gould to Clinton, Sept. 30, below, pp. 578–579.) Meanwhile Clinton had promoted him to brigadier general.

Leslie was detached by Cornwallis to Charleston in late July, recalled by Clinton, detached by Clinton at the end of August and again recalled, then finally sent at the end of October. Stevens, *Clinton-Cornwallis Controversy*, 2, 108; Hist. MSS Com., *American MSS in the Royal Institution*, 2, 326, 344.

the Thirtieth Regiment as senior officer, and the civil department as before by Lieutenant Colonel Balfour as commandant of Charleston. But, little having happened there subsequent to that period besides the Battle of Eutaws, I did not think it necessary to interrupt the detail I have just closed by attending minutely to chronological order.

Lieutenant Colonel Stewart of the Buffs, who succeeded Lord Rawdon in the command of the King's army at Orangeburg, having judged it expedient to approach Charleston for the purpose of covering a convoy of provisions which was on its march to him from that place, had fallen back to the Eutaw Springs, within sixty miles of it, that he might be so much nearer his supplies and disencumber himself of his numerous sick. In this position he was rather unexpectedly attacked on the 8th of September, about nine in the morning, by General Greene —who had, as he advanced, surprised and taken about 300 men (belonging to the flank battalion and the Buffs) who happened to be that morning collecting of roots in front of the line. This considerable loss weakened Colonel Stewart's numbers, which he reports to have been before that greatly inferior to those of the enemy (who had, moreover, the advantage of having a body of well appointed cavalry, in which the King's army was very deficient); the action was, notwithstanding, disputed with great obstinacy for near two hours.

However, the fortune of the day was very near being decided at one time in favor of the enemy. For, the left wing having been tempted to advance too far in pursuit of the militia in their front, and falling back afterward in some disorder, they were charged in their confusion by the enemy's cavalry, and several of them taken prisoners. But a heavy and well directed fire from a detachment of New York Volunteers (whom the Lieutenant Colonel had previously posted in a house to cover his left flank) fortunately checked the pursuit and gave time to the broken troops to rally and form; and the right wing, charging the enemy in flank at the same time by a rapid move to their left (after repulsing the attack in front), obliged them to give way on all sides, leaving behind them two brass six-pounders, two hundred dead, and sixty prisoners. Their cavalry, however, enabled them to retire without pursuit. But the victory was purchased dear, the King's troops having lost in killed, wounded, and missing 792 out of 1396—the gross amount, according to those in the action.[8]

Colonel Stewart was therefore induced to fall back, on the 11th, to the neighborhood of Monk's Corner, where he was joined the next morn-

8. See Stewart to Cornwallis, Sept. 9, below, pp. 567–569; Fisher, *Struggle for American Independence*, 2, 440–444; Ward, *War of the Revolution*, 2, 826–834, where the British casualties are given as 866 out of 2000.

ing by the Thirtieth Regiment from Charleston under Major General Gould. The enemy had likewise fallen back to their former camp on the high hills of Santee. And in these positions the two armies continued, without any transaction of moment happening on either side, until the approach of the enemy's reinforcements from Virginia. This inducing General Greene to recross the Santee and advance to the southward, Lieutenant General Leslie (who arrived in Carolina on the 8th of November) judged it advisable for many reasons to order the royal army to fall back nearer Charleston.

And, indeed, the accounts that general officer now sent me of the state of his district were upon the whole very alarming—East Florida and Georgia in no force to resist a serious attack, and the troops in South Carolina greatly dispirited and so reduced in number by the captures of the enemy, sickness, and other casualties as to be barely adequate to the defense of the capital, which he was apprehensive might consequently disable him from yielding them [Florida and Georgia] the requisite assistance when called upon. In short, the whole country [was] against us except some helpless militia, with a number of officers, women, children, Negroes, etc.; and the expense of supporting the multitudes of ruined refugees that were daily driven into his lines [had] become almost intolerable.[9]

As soon as this information reached me, I judged it right to submit General Leslie's report to the consideration of all the general officers in a full council of war. And, they being unanimously of opinion that (as it appeared from the returns laid before them by the Adjutant General that the rank and file fit for duty in South Carolina amounted to 4576, those in Georgia to 691, and those in East Florida to 456, and the sick and wounded in the whole to 2283, besides 1341 prisoners) there was no necessity at present for sending thither a reinforcement, and that it would be imprudent to diminish the present garrison of New York (which was not more than adequate to its defense), I consequently declined immediately complying with the Lieutenant General's requisition for a few old regiments. But I ordered all the absent officers and recruits belonging to the southern corps, amounting to about 550 men, to be sent to him without delay. And with the advice of the council I left him at liberty to withdraw the garrison of Savannah or not, according as he should judge it expedient from the magnitude of the force collecting against it (as we did not think that the post of Savannah alone was of sufficient importance to risk the loss of the Governor and council, the troops, artillery, and stores there, together with the loyalists

9. Leslie to Clinton, Nov. 30, below, pp. 588–589.

and refugees under their protection), in case there should be a manifest probability of its falling into the enemy's hands.[10]

Such was the melancholy state of the southern district at the commencement of the year '82. And, although Lieutenant General Leslie in some measure removed the alarm excited in me by his late report of the troops' wanting confidence (by his telling me in a subsequent letter that he only meant to say that the greatest proportion of the corps with him, not having been inured to service, consequently wanted that confidence felt by an army accustomed to victory, and that "the unfortunate fall of Lord Cornwallis could not fail of holding out a gloomy presage to a young army just entering upon real service"), yet his evacuating John's Island on the enemy's advance, and his thinking it necessary to confine himself within a very contracted defensive, still indicated too strong a sense of the weakness of the force under his command for me to promise myself anything very flattering from the operations in that quarter.[11] I was, however, not in the least apprehensive for Charleston, and not much so for Savannah, as I was persuaded that Greene would never attempt either (notwithstanding he had now, since Wayne joined him from Virginia, nearly 3000 Continentals) unless either a French or Spanish fleet should arrive on the coast to cooperate with him. But, that I might be prepared against every contingency, I held 2000 men in readiness for instant embarkation, that I might have it in my power to act with celerity and vigor as exigencies in that quarter might require.[12]

Having thus provided as well as I could for the security of Charleston and Savannah, East Florida and the Bahamas became the next objects of my care; and I was consequently not inattentive to them. For the general officer commanding in the southern district had, in obedience to my orders, supplied St. Augustine with such stores as were wanted, and sent his principal engineer thither to put the fortifications in a proper state of defense. He had collected also, from the regiments under his orders, one hundred and seventy invalids to complete the two companies of the garrison battalion on the Bahamas to their complement of one hundred men each, which, with the cannon and stores demanded

10. Minutes of the council of war of Dec. 17, Council Book (CP); Clinton to Leslie, Dec. 20, below, pp. 591–592.
11. The quotation is from Leslie to Clinton, Feb. 2, 1782, "Correspondence with Lieutenant General Leslie" (in a slip case entitled "Correspondence with Arbuthnot, Arnold, Leslie, and Phillips," CP), p. 94. John's Island was threatened by Greene's army and evacuated in January: Leslie to Clinton, Jan. 29 (a different letter from that of the same date in the Appendix), *ibid.*, pp. 87–88.
12. Minutes of the council of war of Jan. 6, 1782, Council Book.

by the Governor, waited only for a convoy to be transported thither as soon as possible.[13]

The severity of the winter having for some months put a stop on both sides to all military operations in the northern district, the few incidents that occurred within that interim are of too trifling consequence to merit the reader's notice. These consisted principally of overtures made me by General Washington for the appointment of commissioners to obviate past difficulties in settling an exchange of prisoners, liquidating the expense of their maintenance, and making solid arrangements for their future provision. Major General Dalrymple and Mr. Elliott, the Lieutenant Governor of New York, were accordingly named by me to confer with Major General Knox and Mr. Morrison [14] on the part of General Washington. But this meeting ended, like all the others, without anything effectual being determined on, owing as usual to the enemy's objecting to the inadequacy of my powers.

It had, however, been long an object of contemplation with me—and was now very much my wish, in consequence of some late intelligence —to make a desultory move up the Delaware to endeavor to take or destroy the shipping, military stores, flour, etc., collected there, and eventually to bring off part of Lord Cornwallis' army, whose place of confinement was not far distant from Philadelphia. But, as the expediency of the measure at the present juncture did not strike some of the general officers whom I consulted upon it as forcibly as it did me, the enterprise did not take place.[15]

Our attention was next turned to the relief of Brimstone Hill in the Island of St. Christopher, supposed to be at that time invested by a powerful French armament, or the sending 2000 men to the island of Jamaica, in case that important possession should be threatened with an attack and our fleet in those seas be superior to that of the enemy. I therefore dispatched an officer to the Leeward Islands for intelligence, and to make offers from me of such assistance as might at the time be in my power to send thither.[16]

But I might have spared myself the trouble of forming plans for

13. Leslie to Clinton, Feb. 18, "Correspondence with Leslie," p. 118.

14. "Mr. Morrison" was in fact Gouverneur Morris. (Washington to Clinton, Dec. 6, 1781, Fitzpatrick, *Writings of Washington*, 23, 373.) For further light on the British side of these negotiations see the minutes of the councils of war of Dec. 31, 1781, Jan. 23, Apr. 8, 1782, Council Book.

15. Minutes of the councils of war of Mar. 8, 10, 28; the first two are in the Council Book, and the third is printed below, pp. 598–599.

16. Clinton to the commanding officer in the Leeward Islands, Mar. 13, below, pp. 596–597. The council of Mar. 10 decided that no troops could be spared from New York, but that the approach of summer would make possible detaching 2000 from South Carolina under the conditions stipulated in the letter.

prosecuting further offensive operations against the revolted colonists, as a resolution had before this period passed the House of Commons for putting an immediate end to all offensive war on the continent of North America. And a copy of it was forthwith transmitted to me by the Secretary of State, with His Majesty's commands that I should regulate my future conduct by it and conform in every respect, as nearly as possible, to the wishes of his faithful Commons.[17] Therefore, as the military transactions of my command cannot be supposed to have been very interesting, I shall here close my narrative of them, and only detain the reader while I relate an extraordinary outrage which happened about this time, through the unauthorized violence of the Associated Loyalists at New York, and had like to have been attended with the most serious and distressing consequences.

I have already noticed that, in obedience to the King's commands transmitted to me by his Secretary of State, I had constituted certain gentlemen therein named a Board of Directors of Associated Loyalists, for the purpose of forming into armed companies and troops (for the annoyance of the revolted colonists) such loyal refugees as pleased to associate under them, and of issuing from time to time regulations and orders for their guidance and government, subject, however, to the control of the Commander in Chief, to whom all their proceedings were to be regularly reported and from whom the commissions for the officers recommended by them were to issue, in order to sanction their operations and entitle them to the usual advantages when taken prisoners by the enemy.[18] A prison was also allotted to them for the confinement of the prisoners captured by their parties, and the power of exchanging or releasing them vested in themselves, but under the express condition of not putting to death or otherwise maltreating, by way of retaliation, any of the enemy who might happen to fall into their hands.

Having by these means guarded, as I thought, against all improper enormities, I did not judge it necessary to require constant reports of the prisoners taken at different times by the Associators, or how they disposed of them. I was consequently greatly surprised and shocked when I heard in the course of common rumor that one Joshua Huddy, a captain in the rebel service who had been taken prisoner by the Associators and lodged for several days in their own prison as a prisoner of war, had been delivered with two other prisoners of war to Richard Lippincott, a captain of Associators, by virtue of a written order from

17. The resolution of the House of Commons (printed below, pp. 595–596) was transmitted to Clinton with a covering letter of instruction by Welbore Ellis, Germain's successor, on Mar. 6; see "Secretary of State to Clinton" (three volumes in a slip case, CP), 3, 210–211.

18. See above, p. 192 and n. 9.

the Board of Directors dated the 8th of April, ostensibly for the purpose of being exchanged for three Associators [who were] prisoners with the enemy; and that, these prisoners being carried by him into the Jersies under this pretense, Joshua Huddy was there murdered and left hanging, with a label on his breast to signify he was thus treated in retaliation for one White, an Associator said to have been murdered not long before by the rebels.

This was so audacious a breach of humanity and the usual customs of war, and such an insult to the dignity of the British arms and my own command, that I should have esteemed myself extremely deficient in my duty had I neglected to take notice of it. But, as the royal sanction from whence the Directors derived their existence as a board had rendered them respectable, I judged it right, out of delicacy, to address myself first to them, and to desire that they would immediately make the necessary inquiries into the circumstances stated and report the result to me, that proper steps might be taken for punishing the delinquents and preventing such atrocities in future. For I could not conceive it possible that those gentlemen would have authorized such an act of barbarity or wished to screen the offenders. But, receiving only evasive answers from them (which were both unbecoming the serious importance of the subject and deficient in that respect which I thought due to my station), I caused Captain Lippincott to be arrested to prevent his escape. And, having submitted all the information I was able to obtain respecting the affair to the consideration of a council of war composed of the general and other principal officers of all the Hessian, British, and provincial corps in the garrison, I directed a general court martial to be convened, in consequence of their unanimous opinion, to try Lippincott for the murder of Huddy.[19] Therefore, as the members of that court martial were selected from the most dignified ranks in the British and provincial lines in order to secure impartial justice to all concerned, I have not the least doubt that—had I remained in the command until their proceeding had been closed—both friends and enemies would have been perfectly satisfied, and neither the humanity, justice, nor dignity of this nation would have been committed by the result of their decision.

But, in taking a retrospective view of this business, I acknowledge that allowances should be made for the actions of men whose minds may have been roused to vengeance by repeated acts of cruelty com-

19. For a modern description of the affair see Freeman, *Washington*, 5, 412–414, 419, 425. Clinton brought the matter before councils of war on Apr. 26 and 27; on the latter day he received Germain's notification that his request to resign had been accepted.

mitted by the enemy on their dearest friends and connections. Such sanguinary effects of their resentment might, however, have introduced a system of war horrid beyond conception; and I am really sorry to observe there were many circumstances accompanying this transaction which would almost warrant a suspicion that it was done with a view of precluding all future reconciliation between Great Britain and the revolted colonies. Having, therefore, most probably long thirsted after indiscriminate retaliation, and finding that I was disinclined to sanction it by my having refused to issue a threatening proclamation in consequence of the tenth article of the capitulation of Yorktown, these gentlemen appear to have taken this bold step for the purpose of forcing that measure.

And, indeed, the progress through which the unfortunate victim was led to his death (by passing him through all the army prisons at New York and ultimately lodging him in one of the King's ships, [where he was] ill treated and whence he was taken afterward to execution) seemed to indicate a premeditated design of involving the navy and army as well as themselves in the guilt. The time they had chosen, too, for this deed sanctions in some measure such a surmise, as this extraordinary action happened while the enemy's commissioners and mine were negotiating an exchange of prisoners and other matters of importance at Elizabeth Town. For, had the enemy in the first burst of their resentment seized upon either of my commissioners (who were gentlemen of rank then in their power) and put him to death in retaliation for Huddy, there is no saying how horrible might have been the consequences. To guard, therefore, against the enemy's having recourse to any such violent modes of redress, and to assert as far as I could the justice and honor of the British nation, I told General Washington in my answer to his threats of retaliation that I had already ordered the person accused of the murder to be tried before the receipt of his letter, and that I looked upon his interference in a business of this nature to be very improper, as my own sense of what was right and abhorrence of cruelty—not his menaces—must be the guides of my conduct.[20]

When my friends in England saw what effects Lord Cornwallis' letter was likely to have on the minds of the public, and how all concerned were striving to avail themselves of it in my absence to avoid the odium of the late misfortune in the Chesapeake and fix it on me, they very earnestly petitioned His Majesty (unknown, however, to myself,

20. See Washington to Clinton, Apr. 21, Fitzpatrick, *Writings of Washington,* 24, 147; Clinton to Washington, Apr. 25, [John Almon,] *The Remembrancer; or, Impartial Repository of Public Events* (17 vols., London, 1775–84), *14,* 156.

and at that time contrary to my wishes) to permit me to return home.[21] Sir Guy Carleton being in consequence sent out to New York to relieve me, I had the happiness of resigning to him on the 8th of May the chief command of His Majesty's forces in North America—a command which I had neither solicited nor coveted but accepted (merely as an act of duty) with reluctance, and which I was afterward compelled to retain for four years, although I had each year prayed to be released from it from the thorough conviction of the impossibility of my doing anything very essential toward extinguishing the rebellion without more troops than I had the direction of, and a cooperating naval force constantly superior to that of the enemy.

For, immediately after I received the command from Sir William Howe, nearly half of my best troops were detached by order to the West Indies and on other distant services, from whence they never returned to me afterward. Reinforcements of troops and ships had been, indeed, most amply promised me. But neither came to answer essential purpose; and my posts were, notwithstanding, insulted or menaced almost each year of my command by powerful French fleets, three of which were greatly superior to that of the King cooperating with me. And the few scanty supplies of troops with which my army was sometimes fed always arrived so late in the season that they were in general of very little service, and the first importation brought with them a jail distemper which soon sent half of my army into the hospitals. To this may be added that, in consequence of the distance we were from our sources of supply and perhaps [in consequence of] some little inattention to our wants, I was more than twice during my command reduced to the verge of starving.

So that, when I look back on the constantly diminishing strength of my own army (which weakened, of course, in proportion to our conquests, and was never properly adequate even to the defense of the extensive and numerous posts it occupied) and the daily increasing

21. This brief description ignores the struggle that had been going on for months within the cabinet. Although Germain was still professing good will and respect for Clinton in early December (after receiving the news of Yorktown), by the end of the month he was saying that Sir Henry could not intend to remain in command after writing him the letter of Sept. 7. The King also assumed that Clinton wished to come home, and suggested Carleton as his successor. Germain, who detested Sir Guy, answered that in that case he himself could scarcely continue in office. His resignation thus became tied to Clinton's, and only the Prime Minister could decide the question. Lord North, even more dilatory than usual, took six weeks to conclude that both must go. On Feb. 6 Clinton's resignation was accepted by Lord George, who then resigned himself and was replaced by Welbore Ellis. See Clinton to Germain, Sept. 7, Conway to Clinton, Dec. 5, 1781, and Germain to Clinton, Feb. 6, 1782, below, pp. 564–565, 589–590, 595 and n. 97; Dalrymple [to Clinton], Dec. 30, [1781,] CP; Fortescue, *Correspondence of George III,* 5, 297–362, *passim.*

numbers, confidence, and discipline of that belonging to the enemy, together with the great aids they were frequently receiving both in ships and troops from France and Spain, I only wonder that we did not meet with a serious affront sooner. I am, however, happy in the reflection that I did my duty in concealing nothing from administration—having repeatedly warned them of our critical situation and given it unequivocally as my opinion that, unless they could furnish an army capable of crushing the rebellion at once, they had nothing but a ruinous, protracted war to expect, and that it might be wiser in that case to withdraw the troops altogether and leave the further prosecution of it to the navy.

It would certainly have been a most fortunate circumstance for me, and I might have perhaps managed better, had I never been promised these reinforcements, but [been] told at once that none could be sent to me. For, being ever zealous to put the troops in motion the instant I could muster a force sufficient to act with, I was constantly making preparations and forming plans of operation, the execution of which depended upon their arrival. But, when disappointment obliged me (as was almost constantly the case) to lay my projects aside, or adopt others more suited to my abilities, or even to become inactive, I was immediately accused of indecision—not infrequently, perhaps, by the officers under me, as well as others who were ignorant of the true cause. And, the malicious and discontented in England being thereby furnished with ample subject for abuse, the inflammatory paragraphs inserted by them in the public prints and magazines contributed, of course, to prepare the minds of the people for receiving those impressions to my prejudice which the unfounded implications and assertations in Lord Cornwallis' letter were calculated to effect.

I have consequently no small reason to lament that I could not return to Europe immediately after the reduction of Charleston, as all this might by that means have been avoided; and I should most probably have still gloried in what the success of His Majesty's arms then procured me—that first and greatest object of a soldier's honest ambition—the unanimous applause of an ever just and grateful country! But I have not forgot (on the contrary, I shall ever remember it with the most dutiful gratitude) that my sovereign has done me the honor to approve my conduct during every period of that difficult command, both through his Ministers and in his closet, and has also been graciously pleased to intimate that all my plans for managing the war while I conducted it either *had* or would have succeeded if they had been suffered to take place.

I hope, however, for pardon if (impressed as I am with the greatest deference and respect) I humbly presume to whisper a complaint that certain Ministers have been permitted to mark my military character with slights, and that a *respectable* board, whose labors in the service of the public have been in other respects meritorious, has designed to step out of the obvious line of its duty for the sole purpose of glancing a most unmerited censure at me by asserting that abuses actually existed in the extraordinary expenses of the army under my command tending to defraud the public for private emolument, and obliquely insinuating that nothing was ever done toward their detection or prevention until their notoriety obliged Lord Cornwallis to take notice of them in his public orders of the 23d of December, 1780. These orders the Commissioners of Public Accounts have introduced into their seventh report, and have regarded as so judicious and important that they there declare it to be their opinion that they "should be put in force forthwith throughout the whole army." They have likewise ascribed to Lord Cornwallis alone the merit of having appointed Commissaries of Captures to collect provisions from the country and deliver them to the troops in order to prevent their being charged to the public by the Commissary General either at all or at a greater price than they were purchased at, as had been the custom.[22]

I shall not take upon me to say that this order was not issued by Lord Cornwallis, although it has never been reported to me, nor have I been able to find it in a copy sent me from the Adjutant General's office of His Lordship's public orders, nor does any officer of the regiments at that time serving in America under His Lordship of whom I have made the inquiry recollect his having seen it in the regimental orderly books. But, whether the order has existence or not as His Lordship's, the reader will, I make no doubt, be greatly surprised to hear that this order, which the Commissioners have pronounced necessary to be immediately put in force throughout the whole army, is little more than a repetition of standing orders of the very same tendency which had been issued by me long before I vested Lord Cornwallis with the command of the southern district, and which—being repeated while His Lordship was serving in the same camp with me and [being] still in force—would of course have precluded the necessity of any new order from His Lordship on that subject had he seen mine properly attended to, as he was directed to do and [as] was undoubtedly his duty. And, with respect to the appointment of Commissaries of Captures, the complimenting Lord Cornwallis with the merit of it will appear equally strange when it is known that certain gentlemen were commissioned by me for that office on the 14th of February, 1780, that they executed the duties of

22. See above, pp. 177–179, 242–243 and nn.

it all the time the army was acting under my command, and that I
left orders with His Lordship to revive it whenever he took the field.
For, judging it possible (though I had no knowledge of the fact) that
all the fresh provisions taken from the enemy might not always have
been carried to the public credit, I fell upon this method as the most
likely I could devise to prevent frauds of that nature. And from that day,
at least as long as my orders were obeyed, all the fresh provisions taken
from the enemy were issued to the troops by the Commissaries of
Captures alone, by which means, I am credibly informed, a considerable
saving accrued to the public, to the amount of at least one million of
crown rations.

It must be obvious that the time of a commander in chief, under the
circumstances in which I found myself during the whole space of my
command, was too much occupied by the various important matters,
civil as well as military, that were incessantly demanding his most
serious attention to admit of his watching over the disbursements of
the different departments of his army with the assiduity and precision
which their intricacy and multiplicity required. But I must in justice
to myself declare that I was not altogether neglectful of so essential a
duty, though I have not thought it necessary to blazon to the public
what I have done, nor have the Commissioners of Public Accounts flattered me with their compliments upon it. But the Lords of His Majesty's
Treasury will do me the justice to acknowledge that my attention to
economy in several instances has been marked by their approbation,
and that I very early in my command solicited Their Lordships to give
me an *effective* Commissary of Accounts to take the load of inspecting
into the management of the public expenditures off my mind. After
Their Lordships had complied with my request and that officer began
to act, I appointed the most respectable and best qualified boards of
investigation which could be procured in that country to assist him in
examining the disbursements of the different departments from the
beginning of the war to nearly its close, for the purpose of detecting
abuses (if any existed) and pointing out to the Commander in Chief
every possibility of retrenchment and reform—having, at least in this
instance, been so fortunate as to anticipate one of the measures which
the Commissioners themselves have since recommended in their seventh
report.

Finding also, upon my coming to the command, that the army was
supplied with wagons, horses, boats, vessels, etc., by contract made by
my predecessor, Sir William Howe, (and being obliged, from the uncertain duration of the war as well as my own continuance in the
command, not to venture upon any innovation) I ordered musters to

be taken of the respective articles of supply, as being in my opinion the most effective check that could be interposed against abuses and frauds in the contractors. And, as my regular reports of all these transactions had been from time to time transmitted to the Lords Commissioners of His Majesty's Treasury, and Their Lordships had been pleased through their Secretary to honor me with their fullest approbation and thanks, I could not doubt that the Commissioners of Public Accounts had availed themselves of this mass of information, so much preferable from its authenticity to any other, and which had been so particularly recommended to them by Mr. Robinson, then Secretary of the Treasury.

Being conscious, therefore, that I had done everything in my power to defend the public from rapine and profusion, I flattered myself on my arrival in England that I should have met with applause from that board, especially when they saw that most of the precautions recommended by themselves had been before taken by me. But the reader will readily judge of my disappointment and chagrin when I discovered, upon reading their report, that I was on the contrary held up by them to the public as an object of censure. Supposing it, however, impossible that this could have arisen from anything but misinformation, I immediately offered myself to those gentlemen for examination, in the hope they would, upon being convinced they had been led into an error, readily consent to a revision of their report in order to do me justice. But, to my great astonishment, I had the mortification to be told by them *that their report, being before Parliament, could not be revised without an order from the legislature.*

To this seeming evasion of rendering justice to a man they must be conscious they had injured I beg leave to add another instance of prejudice almost equally striking. When the Commissioners were investigating this particular object of their seventh report, they were told by the Secretary of the Treasury that Sir Henry Clinton had transmitted to Their Lordships several important papers, the inspection of which would be essentially necessary for their information with respect to the business then before them, and [were] desired that they would include those papers in their precept. But they repeatedly refused the papers offered to them, saying they wanted no other besides those they had issued their precept for. This conduct appears to me so very indefensible that I am almost afraid to trust my pen upon the subject, for I cannot even yet believe it possible that gentlemen of such respectable character, and whose former reports had universally met with so favorable a reception from the nation, could have been so prejudiced by party as to lend themselves for a moment to forward any temporary purpose whatsoever. Yet how can we account for such glaring appearances of partiality?

Being foiled in this quarter, I next submitted my case to the Chancellor of the Exchequer [William Pitt], and entreated his support to a motion which I proposed making through a friend to the House of Commons, either that I might be heard at their bar or the seventh report be sent back to the Commissioners with orders for a revision. The motion was accordingly made; but, not meeting with the support which I expected, it of course failed. And, I am sorry to observe, the injury remains unredressed to this hour.

APPENDIX

Extracts of Correspondence and Other Documents
Chronologically Arranged, 1776–82.

EDITOR'S NOTE

CLINTON embellished his narrative with a running frieze of footnotes, which are sometimes so bulky that they conceal his text. They are of two types. The first is his own comments and those of contemporary writers; these have been printed with the editor's notes in the text. The second is extracts from letters and reports in Sir Henry's files. These he cites, occasionally several times over, as the need of the moment dictates and with little regard to their dates; to have reproduced them as they appear in the manuscript would have resulted in gargantuan footnotes and chronological chaos. They have therefore been reordered by date and printed in the Appendix that follows. At times Clinton did not provide extracts that he promised, and at others he failed to mention documents that bear directly on his story. To remedy such omissions a few letters from among his papers have been added and a few excerpts expanded. But these are rare exceptions; the Appendix in general is the notes that he intended to publish.

When headings are in brackets, they have been supplied by the editor; otherwise they are Sir Henry's. Many of the letters, as shown by citations at the ends of the extracts, have already been published in whole or in part. Where there is no citation, the unpublished original or a copy is in Clinton's papers; two exceptions, printed from his marginal notes, are so indicated. In every other case the extract has been collated with a printed or manuscript copy, and significant variations have been noted. Foreign phrases and the names of ships have been italicized by the editor. All other italics, unless the contrary is stated, are additions that Clinton imposed afterward upon the letters of others as well as his own. Although these italics seem, like Queen Victoria's, so profuse as to be meaningless, they were actually his attempt to bring out particular meanings that he thought were in the record.

Extract of Sir Peter Parker's letter of the 25th of June [1776].

If we should be so fortunate as to take possession of the fort, you will see the Union hoisted. I have enclosed some signals that I have appointed, relative to the landing of the seamen and marines of the squadron, that you may know what I am about. I shall make some of the *signals* [1] when the battery is silenced (though I should not mean to land), and row to the westward agreeable to your desire. [2]

Notice of Lieutenant General Clinton's letter to Lord George Germain, dated July 8th, 1776, from the camp at Long Island; published in London, August 24.

It appears by Lieutenant General Clinton's letter to Lord George Germain, dated July 8th, 1776, from the camp on Long Island, Province of South Carolina, that Sir Peter Parker and the General, having received intelligence that the fortress erected by the rebels on Sullivan's Island, the key to Charleston harbor, was in an imperfect and unfinished state, resolved to attempt the reduction thereof by a *coup de main;* and that, in order that the army might cooperate with the fleet, the General landed his troops on Long Island, which had been represented to him as communicating with Sullivan's Island by a ford passable at low water; but that he, to his very great mortification, found the channel, which was reported to have been eighteen inches deep at low water, to be seven feet deep—which circumstance rendered it impossible for the army to give that assistance to the fleet in the attack made upon the fortress that the General intended, and which he and the troops under his command ardently wished to do. [*Gentleman's Magazine and Historical Chronicle, 46* (1776), 381.]

Clinton's comment: Can this be called an extract of my letter, of which the following is a copy?

Camp on Long Island, Province of South Carolina.

My Lord,

A few days after I had dispatched my letter to Your Lordship of the 3d of May informing you of the arrival of the fleet in Cape Fear River (a duplicate of which is herewith annexed), the *Nautilus*, sloop of war, arrived from the northward and brought me a letter from Major General Howe, dated at Halifax, from whom I had not heard for four months before (his dispatches by the *Glasgow*, man-of-war, having been thrown overboard in an engagement with the rebel fleet). From the general purport of his letter it did not appear to me that he ex-

1. *Clinton's note:* The Commodore acknowledges he did not make any signal.
2. *Clinton's note:* The following short observation I beg leave to make: Sir Peter Parker proposed the plan. I acquiesced, and offered my little assistance. And our object was only to take possession of Sullivan's Island [and] leave a frigate or two to keep it till operations could be carried on with propriety in that climate, which was not the case when we were there.

pected or called upon me for any immediate assistance at the opening of the campaign, nor did he name either the time or place of joining him; but rather seemed, on the contrary, to intimate his wishes that some operations might take place in the southern colonies, and pointed out Charleston in the Province of South Carolina as an object of importance to His Majesty's service.

Previous to the receipt of this letter my intentions were, as Your Lordship will have observed, to have proceeded to Chesapeake Bay. But, having received some intelligence at that time that the works erected by the rebels on Sullivan's Island, the key to Charleston harbor, were in an imperfect and unfinished state, I was induced to acquiesce in a proposal made to me by the Commodore, Sir Peter Parker, to attempt the reduction of that fortress by a *coup de main*. I thought it possible at the same time that it might be followed by such immediate consequences as would prove of great advantage to His Majesty's service. I say immediate, My Lord, for it never was my intention at this season of the year to have proceeded further than Sullivan's Island without a moral certainty of rapid success.

With this object in view we sailed from Cape Fear on the 31st of May, and within a few leagues of Charleston were joined by the *Ranger*, sloop of war, with the remainder of the transports from England belonging to this fleet—by which conveyance I received Your Lordship's dispatches of the 3d March signifying to me His Majesty's pleasure "that if, upon the arrival of the armament at Cape Fear, I should be of opinion, upon a mature consideration of all circumstances, that nothing could be soon effected that would be of real and substantial service and advantage, or that the making any attempt would expose His Majesty's troops to great loss from the season being too far advanced, and that there would be a hazard of disappointing the service to the northward, that I do in that case proceed immediately to join Major General Howe with my whole force, leaving, however, a regiment or two if the purpose therein referred to could be effected." And, being of opinion that the object before me came within Your Lordship's description and might be soon accomplished, I came to a determination to proceed.

Unfortunately delays of various kinds have intervened, some occasioned by contrary winds and storms and other circumstances, so as to protract the operations of the fleet to a much more distant period than was at first expected, and to forebode that those of the army would be converted from a *coup de main* into something too much like a formal siege. By these delays difficulties were daily increased upon me. However, upon weighing every circumstance, Lord Cornwallis agreed with me in opinion that we could not more effectually cooperate with the fleet than by taking possession of Long Island, the situation of which was represented to communicate with Sullivan's Island by a ford passable at low water, and with the main by a creek navigable for boats of draft. This was accordingly done by assembling our whole force there on the 16th of June excepting a few recruits, who were left on board the transports by way of deception.

It became naturally our first business to ascertain the ford and its situation. But to our unspeakable mortification a channel, which for some time before was reported to have been only eighteen inches deep at low water, was now found to be seven feet—a circumstance, I am told, not uncommon on this sandy coast. But by this discovery Your Lordship will perceive that our operations from Long Island were rendered more limited and confined. And, although my situation gave jealousy to two different objects (the main and Sullivan's Island), as I had not boats for above six or seven hundred men, I was reduced to one attack without being able to favor that by ever so small a diversion on the other [object].

Thus circumstanced, *I took the first opportunity* of acquainting the Commodore that from this discovery I was apprehensive that it would not be possible for the troops to take the share in the attack I once flattered myself they would have been able to have done— still, however, assuring him that, whenever he should think proper to begin his attack, I would make every possible diversion in his favor, or send him two battalions to act on his side in case he and the general officer appointed to command them should be of opinion they could be protected in their landing and employed to advantage. In answer to which it seemed to be understood that I should give the best support I could, and we waited only for a wind to begin the attack.

At this time, though the rebels had an entrenchment and battery on the point of the island on which I intended a landing, I thought such a disposition might be made with the light ordnance I had on shore with me as would dislodge them and cover the landing of the troops. But, unfavorable winds preventing the attack of the fleet for some days, they removed from this station and took up some very strong ground 500 yards back, in a much more extended front than the narrow spit of land on which they had at first placed themselves, having a battery on their right and a morass on their left, raising their former work and making it a glacis or esplanade to that more retired. This, My Lord, defended and sustained by three or four thousand men, was a formidable appearance, and such a one as a small army in boats, advancing singly through a narrow channel, uncovered and unprotected, could not attempt without a manifest sacrifice.

My attention was therefore drawn toward an attempt on their battery on Heddral's Point, by landing within three miles of it. I accordingly made my request to the Commodore that some frigates might be directed to cooperate with me in that attempt, to which he assented. But, as my operations depended in a great measure upon those of the fleet, it was impossible to decide positively upon any plan.

It was about eleven o'clock in the morning on the 28th of last month when we discovered the fleet going upon the attack of the battery on Sullivan's Island. But, as they did not appear (when they brought up) to be within such a distance as to avail themselves of the fire from their grapeshot or musketry, I was apprehensive no impression would be made upon the battery. I likewise saw that the three frigates supposed to have been destined to cut off the rebel communication with Heddral's Point, and to favor my attack upon that battery, were aground immediately after the four leading ships had taken their stations.

I made every demonstration, every diversion by cannonade, while the sands were uncovered. I ordered small armed vessels to proceed toward the shore, but they all got aground; and the troops were disposed of in such a manner as to be apportée to attempt a landing either on Sullivan's Island or the main, as circumstances during the attack should appear to make necessary.

The cannonade of the fleet continued without any favorable appearances till night. Expecting, however, that it would be renewed in the morning, I made the best disposition I could of the small ordnance we could collect, to enable me if necessary, whilst the tide suited, to have made one effort on Sullivan's Island—an attempt contrary, I must confess, to every military principle, and justifiable only in cases of the success or distress of the fleet, to support the one or relieve the other. But at break of day, to our great concern, we found the fleet had retired, leaving a frigate aground, which was afterward by orders set on fire. In this situation any feeble effort of ours could answer no good purpose. And, finding the fleet had suffered considerably and that the Commodore had no intention of renewing the attack, I proposed to him that as soon as possible I might proceed with the troops under my command to the northward. They are now in great health, but I fear will not remain long so in this climate. We shall sail in a few days for New York, where I hope they will arrive in good time to do that service which, from a variety of difficulties, they were prevented rendering here.[3] [All but the opening and closing sentence is printed in Sir Henry Clinton, *Narrative of Co-operations*, pp. 10–15.]

Extract of a letter from Sir Peter Parker to Mr. Stephens, Secretary of the Admiralty, dated within Charleston bar, July 9th, 1776 [published in London, August 24].

It having been judged advisable to make an attempt upon *Charleston*,[4] in South Carolina, the fleet sailed from Cape Fear on the 1st of June, and on the 4th anchored off Charleston bar. The 5th sounded the bar and laid down buoys preparatory to the intended entrance of the harbor. The 7th all the frigates and most of the transports got over the bar into Five Fathom Hole. The 9th General Clinton landed on Long Island with about four or five hundred men. The 10th the *Bristol* got over the bar with some difficulty. The 15th gave the Captains of the squadron my arrangement for the attack of the batteries on Sullivan's Island, and the next day acquainted General Clinton that the ships were ready.[5] The General fixed on the 23d for our joint attack; but the wind, proving unfavorable, prevented its taking effect. The 25th the *Experiment* arrived and next day came over the bar, when a new arrangement was made for the attack. The 28th, at half an hour after nine in the morning, informed General Clinton by *signal*[6] that I should go on the attack.

At half an hour after ten I made the signal to weigh, and about a

3. *Clinton's note:* Not thinking that Sir Peter Parker had been sufficiently explicit in his public letter and without meaning at that time to ask any other questions respecting it, I thought the few following necessary:

Did I not, two days after the army landed on Long Island, finding there was no ford, make known my difficulties? Did I not, from that circumstance, say the troops could not cooperate as at first intended? Did I not offer troops, through General Vaughan, to act on your side if you saw any service on which they might be employed to advantage? Was it not intended that the three frigates which got aground were to have assisted my probable operations on the Mount Pleasant side?

In addition to the above questions I thought likewise that part of his public letter, in the following words, required a little explanation: [the passage cited is from Parker's letter of July 9, p. 377, beginning "for the fort was then totally silenced" and ending "His Majesty would have been in possession of Sullivan's Island."]

Respecting the fact whether the fort was silenced and evacuated, for reasons obvious I do not give a public opinion. But, admitting it was silenced, etc., I asked him: Did Sir Peter Parker expect that the army under my command at seven miles' distance, or the sailors and marines which he told me were practiced for the purpose, should take possession of Sullivan's Island? Sir Peter Parker's answer to the foregoing queries [are given in his letter of Jan. 12, 1777, below, p. 379].

4. *Clinton's note:* Sullivan's Island, the key to Charleston harbor.

5. *Clinton's note:* 16th, army landed; 18th, reported that there was no ford.

6. *Clinton's note:* Saw no signal, though we had many officers looking for it, who had seen it whenever made on the preceding day.

quarter after eleven the *Bristol, Experiment, Active,* and *Solebay* brought up against the fort. The *Thunder,* bomb, covered by the *Friendship,* armed vessel, brought the salient angle of the east bastion to bear northwest by north; and Colonel James, who has ever since our arrival been very anxious to give the best assistance, threw several shells a little before and during the engagement in a very good direction. The *Sphynx, Actaeon,* and *Syren* were to have been to the westward to prevent fireships or other vessels from annoying the ships engaged, to enfilade the works, and, if the rebels should be driven from them, to cut off their retreat if possible.[7] This last service was not performed owing to the ignorance of the pilot, who run the three frigates aground. The *Sphynx* and *Syren* got off in a few hours, but the *Actaeon* remained fast till the next morning, when the Captain and officers thought proper to scuttle and set her on fire. I ordered a court martial on the Captain, officers, and company; and they have been honorably acquitted. Captain Hope made his armed ship as useful as he could on this occasion, and he merits everything that can be said in his favor.

During the time of our being abreast of the fort, which was near ten hours, a brisk fire was kept up by the ships, with intervals; and we had the satisfaction, after being engaged two hours, to oblige the rebels to slacken their fire very much. We drove large parties several times out of the fort, which were replaced by others from the main. About half an hour after three a considerable reinforcement from Mount Pleasant hung a man on a tree at the back of the fort, and we imagine that the same party ran away about an hour after; for the fort was then totally silenced and evacuated for near one hour and a half. But, the rebels finding *that our army could not take possession,*[8] about six o'clock a considerable body of people re-entered the fort and renewed the firing from two or three guns, the rest being, I suppose, dismounted. About nine o'clock, it being very dark, great part of our ammunition expended, the people fatigued, the tide of ebb almost done, no prospect from the eastward, and no possibility of our being of any farther service, I ordered the ships to their former moorings.

Their Lordships will see plainly by this account that, if the troops could have cooperated on this attack, His Majesty would have been in possession of Sullivan's Island. But I must beg leave here to be fully understood, lest it should be imagined that I mean to throw the most distant reflection on our army. I should not discharge my conscience

7. *Clinton's note:* And to assist our intended operations on the main.
8. *Clinton's note:* Read Sir Peter's letter to me [of Jan. 12, 1777] in answer to my queries.

were I not to acknowledge that such was my opinion of His Majesty's troops, from the General down to the private soldier, that, after I had been engaged some hours and perceived that the troops had not got a footing on the north end of Sullivan's Island, I was perfectly satisfied that *the landing was impracticable* [9] and that the attempt would have been the destruction of many brave men without the least probability of success. And this I am certain will appear to be the case when General Clinton represents his situation.

The *Bristol* had forty men killed and seventy-one wounded, the *Experiment* twenty-three killed and fifty-six wounded, and both of them suffered much in their hulls, masts, and rigging; the *Active* had Lieutenant Pike killed and six men wounded, and the *Solebay* eight men wounded. Not one man who was quartered at the beginning of the action on the *Bristol's* quarterdeck escaped being killed or wounded. Captain Morris lost his right arm and received other wounds, and is since dead; the master is wounded in his right arm, but will recover the use of it. I received several contusions at different times, but, as none of them are on any part where the least danger can be apprehended, they are not worth mentioning. Lieutenants Caulfield, Molloy, and Nugent were the lieutenants of the *Bristol* in the action. They behaved so remarkably well that it is impossible to say to whom the preference is due, and so indeed I may say of all the petty officers, ship's company, and volunteers. At the head of the latter I must place Lord William Campbell, who was so condescending as to accept of the direction of some guns on the lower gun deck. His Lordship received a contusion on his left side, but I have the happiness to inform Their Lordships that it has not proved of much consequence. Captain Scott of the *Experiment* lost his left arm, and is otherwise so much wounded that I fear he will not recover.

I cannot conclude this letter without remarking that, when it was known that we had many men too weak to come to quarters, almost all the seamen belonging to the transports offered their service, with a truly British spirit and a just sense of the cause we are engaged in. I accepted of upward of fifty to supply the place of our sick. The masters of many of the transports attended with their boats, but particular thanks are due to Mr. Chambers, the master of the *Mercury*. All the regiments will be embarked in a few days. The first brigade, consisting of four regiments, will sail in a day or two under convoy for New York; and the *Bristol* and *Experiment* will, I hope, soon follow with the remainder. [*Gentleman's Magazine, 46,* 380–381.]

9. *Clinton's note:* Did I not tell him that on the 18th?

[Sir Peter Parker to Clinton.] Newport, Rhode Island, 12th January [1777].

Dear Sir:

In a late conversation with you, relative to my public letter on the affair of Sullivan's Island, you seemed to feel hurt at some parts of it. And, as nothing could be further from my wishes than that anything I had omitted to say concerning that business should affect you disagreeably, I will candidly own that I now perceive, from what passed then between us, that I have not mentioned some circumstances which appear necessary in explaining your conduct. And I flatter myself you will readily excuse these omissions, as I imagined our public letters would have appeared together. However, it is sufficient for me that you think an explanation of circumstances necessary, and I am sure it is my wish that what I shall now say may be fully satisfactory.

The three frigates were intended, besides performing the services mentioned in my letter, to have cooperated with you off of Heddral's Point. You certainly made known your difficulties, and in your letter of the 18th of June to General Vaughan you say that, as there is no ford, "the Generals concur with me in opinion that the troops cannot take the share they expected on the intended attack." Some conversation passed between General Vaughan and myself relative to troops, but I did not think it material; and I was so extremely ill on my bed during the whole time that I could not attend to it, and am therefore obliged to refer you to the General for the particulars. I certainly did intend, as appears by my letter of the 25th of June, to have attempted taking possession of the fort with the seamen and marines, but I could not have planned the doing it with about 300 men without the prospect of speedy support from you; and I saw, soon after the attack began, that from a variety of circumstances you could not take any effectual step for that purpose. I most sincerely hope that this explanation will content you, having the honor to be, with due regard, P. Parker.

[Clinton to Burgoyne. October 6, 1777.]

Not having received any instructions from the Commander in Chief relative to the northern army, and ignorant of even his intentions concerning its operations (except his wishes it may get to Albany), Sir Henry Clinton cannot presume to send orders to General Burgoyne. But he thinks it impossible General Burgoyne could really suppose

Sir Henry Clinton had any idea of penetrating to Albany with the small force he mentioned to him in his letter of the 11th September. What Sir Henry Clinton offered in that letter he has now undertaken. He cannot by any means promise himself success, but hopes the move may be serviceable to General Burgoyne, as his letter of the 21st intimates that even the menace of an attack will be of use. [Partly printed in Anderson, *Command of the Howe Brothers*, p. 261.]

Memorial from the American officers, prisoners of war in Long Island, to the Honorable the Congress of the United States of America [read in Congress May 26, 1778].

Your memorialists are once more under the necessity of addressing you on the subject of their wants and sufferings, in which it is unnecessary to repeat the length of captivity, the keen sensations incident to a long separation from their dearest connections, or the waste of some of the choicest years of life in inactivity and indolence. Since the 20th of May last we have received no public supplies. Those received then have long since been entirely expended, even though managed with the most attentive frugality. Our clothing [is] worn and wearing out, our board since that time unpaid, many of our landlords scrupulous and uneasy on that account and threatening to withhold their scanty provisions and turn us out to shift for ourselves. Did the distress end here, we should not have put it in the power of mankind to charge us with the epithet of impatient or clamorous. But, unhappily, disease and mortality rages among us. The physician, the medicine, and almost every other comfort necessary for the sick and dying is wanting or out of our reach to attain.

The feelings these melancholy circumstances naturally produce are greatly exaggerated when we consider that overtures for our exchange on liberal principles, and in our humble opinion not disadvantageous to America, have been offered by the British Commander in Chief without success. The policy on which they were rejected is too deep for us to explore, especially as the late proceedings in this business—in which we were the principal objects and most materially interested—have been hitherto concealed from our view. And it adds peculiar poignancy to our grief and astonishment to hear that exchanges, partial and in direct prejudice to us, have been ordered to be made in favor of some officers lately taken to the southward. The laudable ambition of promotion in due line is a principal incitement to military virtue. Release from long bondage and captivity in the same just order is certainly the indisputable right of the unfortunate captive.

The recital of these our sufferings and sensations is extorted from us with extreme reluctance. We have borne them with silent patience as long as they were tolerable. Conscious that we have served our country from an early period with fidelity and a real affection for her interests, we conceive we have a just claim to her support and relief from our present difficulties. Strongly impelled by these considerations, your memorialists present this address to the justice and humanity of Congress. And, whether an exchange shortly takes place or we be doomed to pass another winter in gloomy captivity, reasonable and competent supplies will be absolutely necessary, which we earnestly request Congress will order to be paid into the hands of the Commissary General of Prisoners or American agent for our use as speedily as possible. [No copy in the CP; printed from Clinton's note.]

Extract of a letter from Lord George Germain to Sir Henry Clinton. May 4, 1778 (received July 1st).

Intelligence having a few days ago been received of the sailing of a French squadron from Toulon on the 13th of last month, consisting of eleven ships of the line (one of fifty guns) and six frigates, commanded by Count d'Estaing, with one thousand land forces on board besides the complement of seamen, destined as is supposed for North America, this packet is dispatched to give Lord Howe and you the earliest information of this event. A squadron of thirteen ships of the line will sail from Spithead, under the command of Admiral Byron, in a day or two in quest of Monsieur d'Estaing; and it is hoped they will arrive in time to prevent his doing any mischief.

[Extract of] General Lee's letter to General Washington, dated camp, Englishtown, June 28th [30?], 1778.

Your Excellency must give me leave to observe that neither yourself nor those about your person could, from your situation, be in the least judges of the merits or demerits of our maneuvers. And, to speak with becoming pride, I can assert that to these maneuvers the success of the day was entirely owing. For I can boldly say that—had we remained on the first ground, or had we advanced, or had the retreat been conducted in a manner different from what it was—the *whole* army and the interests of America would have risked being sacrificed. [*Lee Papers, 2,* 436, where the letter is dated by Lee July 1 and by the editors June 30.]

Extracts from Mr. Washington's letter to the [President of] Congress immediately after the Battle of Monmouth [July 1, 1778].

On the appearance of the enemy's intention to march through Jersey becoming serious, I detached General Maxwell's Brigade in conjunction with the militia of that state to intercept and impede their progress by every obstruction in their power, so as to give time to the army under my command to come up with them and take advantage of any favorable circumstances that might present themselves. The army having proceeded to Coryell's Ferry and crossed the Delaware at that place, I immediately detached Colonel Morgan with a select corps of 600 men to reinforce General Maxwell, and marched with the main body toward Princeton.

The slow advance of the enemy had greatly the air of design, and led me with others to suspect that General Clinton, desirous of a general action, was endeavoring to draw us down into the lower country, in order by a rapid movement to gain our right and take possession of the strong grounds above us. This consideration,[10] and to give the troops time to repose and refresh themselves from the fatigue they had experienced from rainy and excessive hot weather, determined me to halt at Hopewell Township, about five miles from Princeton, where we remained till the morning of the 25th. On the preceding day I made a second detachment of 1500 chosen troops, under Brigadier General Scott, to reinforce those already in the vicinity of the enemy, the more effectually to annoy and delay their march.[11]

The next day the army moved to Kingston. And, having received intelligence that the enemy were prosecuting their route toward Monmouth Court House, I dispatched 1000 select men under Brigadier General Wayne, and sent the Marquis de Lafayette to take the command of the whole advanced corps, including Maxwell's Brigade and Morgan's light infantry, with orders to take the first fair opportunity of attacking the enemy's rear. In the evening of the same day the whole army marched from Kingston (where our baggage was left) with intention to preserve a proper distance for supporting the advanced corps, and arrived at Cranbury early the next morning.

The enemy in marching from Allen's Town [Allentown] had changed their disposition, and placed their best troops in the rear, consisting of

10. *Clinton's note:* This evidently proves Mr. Washington studied to avoid a general action.

11. *Clinton's note:* Abstract of the troops detached from Mr. Washington's main army: Maxwell's Brigade, 1000; Scott's detachment, 1500; Morgan's d[etachment], 600; General Dickinson's militia, 800—[a total of] 3900 men.

all the grenadiers, light infantry, and chasseurs of the line. This alteration made it necessary to increase the number of our advanced corps,
in consequence of which I detached Major General Lee [12] with two
brigades to join the Marquis de Lafayette at Englishtown. The main
body marched the same day, and encamped within three miles of that
place. Morgan's corps was left hovering on the enemy's right flank, and
the Jersey militia under General Dickinson on their left. The enemy
were now encamped in a strong position, with their right extending
about a mile and a half beyond the Court House, in the parting of
the roads leading to Shrewsbury and Middletown, and their left along
the road from Allen's Town to Monmouth, about three miles on this
side the Court House. Their right flank lay on the skirt of a small wood
while their left was secured by a thick one, a morass running toward
their rear, and their whole front covered by a wood and for a considerable extent toward their left, with a morass. In this situation they halted
till the morning of the 28th.

Matters being thus situated, and having had the best information
that, if the enemy were once arrived at the heights of Middletown (ten
or twelve miles from whence they were), it would be impossible to attempt anything against them with a prospect of success, I determined
to attack their rear the moment they should get in motion from their
present ground. About five in the morning General Dickinson sent an
express to inform me that the front of the enemy had begun their march.
I instantly put the army in motion, and sent orders to General Lee to
move on and attack them unless there should be very powerful reasons
to the contrary, acquainting him at the same time that I was marching
to support him and, for doing it with greater expedition and convenience, should make the men disencumber themselves of their packs and
blankets.

After marching five miles, to my great surprise and mortification I
met the whole advance corps retreating. I proceeded immediately to the
rear of the corps, which I found closely pressed by the enemy, and gave
directions for forming part of the retreating troops, who by the brave
and spirited conduct of the officers, aided by some pieces of well served
artillery, checked the enemy's advance and gave time to make a disposition of the left wing and second line of the army upon an eminence
and in a wood a little in the rear, covered by a morass in front. On this
were placed some batteries of cannon by Lord Stirling, who commanded the left wing, which played upon the enemy with great effect

12. *Clinton's note:* The corps under this General consisted of the before-mentioned
3900, to which had been added Wayne's detachment (1000) and the two brigades
that accompanied him (2000), the whole amounting to 6900.

and, seconded by parties of infantry detached to oppose them, effectually put a stop to their advance.

General Lee being detached with the advanced corps, the command of the right wing for the occasion was given to General Greene. For the expedition of the march and to counteract any attempt to turn our right [13] I had ordered him to file off by the new church, two miles from Englishtown, and fall into the Monmouth road a small distance in the rear of the Court House. On intelligence of the retreat he marched up and took a very advantageous position on the right. The enemy, by this time finding themselves warmly opposed in front, made an attempt to turn our left flank; but they were bravely repulsed and driven back by detached parties of infantry.[14] They also made a movement to our right with as little success, General Greene having advanced a body of troops with artillery to a commanding piece of ground, which not only disappointed their design of turning our right but severely enfiladed those in front of the left wing. In addition to this General Wayne advanced with a body of troops, and kept so severe and well directed a fire that the enemy were soon compelled to retire behind the defile where the first stand in the beginning of the action had been made.

In this situation the enemy had both their flanks secured by thick woods and morasses, while their front could only be approached through a narrow pass. I resolved nevertheless to attack them, and for that purpose I ordered General Poor with his own and the Carolina Brigade to move 'round upon their right, and General Woodford on their left, and the artillery to gall them in front. But the impediments in their way prevented their getting within their reach before it was dark. They remained upon the ground they had been directed to occupy during the night, with intention to begin the attack early in the morning; and the army continued lying upon their arms in the field of action, to be in readiness to support them. In the meantime the enemy were employed in removing their wounded, and about twelve o'clock at night marched away in such silence that, though General Poor lay extremely near them, they effected their retreat without his knowledge.[15]

13. *Clinton's note:* Nothing, surely, can show more apprehension and caution, or more strongly mark the defensive plan Mr. Washington had adopted the moment he found himself attacked.

14. *Clinton's note:* These were the light infantry under Sir William Erskine, who retreated by order as mentioned in the text.

15. *Clinton's note:* It does not appear very probable that nearly 7000 men, with the accompanying wagons, artillery, and cavalry, could move off without being heard by troops who lay so near them. But the fact is that, after the line was put in motion, it halted on the road near an hour until the Thirty-third Regiment recovered their packs and blankets, which they had left the day before on almost the very ground said to be occupied by General Poor. And it was twelve o'clock

They carried off all their wounded except four officers and about forty privates, whose wounds were too dangerous to permit their removal. The extreme heat of the weather, the fatigue of the men from their march through a deep, sandy country almost entirely destitute of water, and the distance the enemy had gained by marching in the night made a pursuit impracticable and fruitless. It would have answered no valuable purpose and would have been fatal to numbers of our men, several of whom died the preceding day with heat. Being fully convinced by the gentlemen of this country that the enemy cannot be hurt or injured in their embarkation at Sandy Hook, and unwilling to get too far from the North River, I put the troops in motion early this morning and shall proceed that way, leaving the Jersey Brigade, Morgan's corps, and other light parties to hover about them, [to] countenance desertion, and to prevent their depredations as far as possible.[16] [Fitzpatrick, *Writings of Washington, 12,* 140–146.]

Extract of a letter from Lord George Germain to the general officer commanding in West Florida. Whitehall, July 1, 1778 (received by Clinton July 28, 1779[17]).

As the command of the navigation of the Mississippi and of the communication from thence to the Indian nations in the southern district is essential to the security of His Majesty's possessions in West Florida and to the protection of the King's faithful subjects and their property, and also of great importance to the trade of this country, it is determined immediately to establish a considerable post upon that river. The situation that appears most proper for the purpose is the entrance of the Mississippi into the Iberville at or near the place where Fort Bute stood. I am therefore to signify to you the King's command that you do with all convenient dispatch proceed to the Mississippi, taking with you such part of the troops under your command as you shall think necessary and the proper persons in the engineer's depart-

---

at noon before the reconnoitering parties of the enemy ventured into the village of Freehold—this taken from the report of the British officers and surgeons who were left there with the wounded.

16. Clinton here appends a note that Lee and Washington, in their correspondence, plainly indicate an American retreat to Englishtown after the action, "though they have both taken pains to hide it by misdating some of their letters. And, indeed, Baron Steuben's evidence confirms it." Steuben's testimony (below, p. 390, n. 18) bears on a quite different point, and the rest of Sir Henry's assertion seems to be equally groundless.

17. *Clinton's note:* Is it *meant* [i.e., was it intended] that Sir Henry Clinton did not receive till July, '79, a copy of a letter to an officer acting under him sent by Lord George Germain [in] July, '78?

ment, together with such ordnance and a proportion of stores as may be wanted and can be spared from Pensacola, and there lay out and erect a fort, etc., capable of being defended by a garrison of 300 men, etc.

Governor Chester acquaints me that the works which Mr. Durnford had been constructing at Pensacola were fallen into ruin as soon as finished, and that he had directed him to provide other materials and set about other works for the defense of the place. It is, however, His Majesty's pleasure that you should take these works also under your direction; and I have acquainted Governor Chester that nothing of that nature is to be undertaken or carried on in the province, nor any troops raised, but by your orders.

[Extract of the Commissioners to Germain. July 7, 1778.]

The decided rejection given by the Congress to all terms of accommodation short of independence leaves no room to hope that any success will attend the Commission with which we are honored. And we conceive that, if there should not appear a possibility of our attaining any of those ends that are the objects of our mission, it will be our duty to return home rather than subject ourselves to the imputation of being a useless and great expense to our country, and the high trust reposed in us to contempt and indignities. [Stevens, *Facsimiles, 11,* No. 1116.]

Copy of a letter from Major John Butler to Lieutenant Colonel Bolton, dated Lacuwanack [Lackawanna], 8th July 1778:

Sir:

On the 30th of June I arrived with about five hundred Rangers and Indians at Wyoming, and encamped on an eminence which overlooks the greatest part of the settlement; from whence I sent out parties to discover the situation and strength of the enemy, who brought in eight prisoners and scalps. Two loyalists who came into my camp informed me that the rebels could muster about eight hundred men, who were all essembled in their forts.

July 1st. I marched to the distance of half a mile of Wintermoot's Fort, and sent in Lieutenant Turney with a flag to demand immediate possession of it, which was soon agreed to. A flag was next sent to Jenkins' Fort, which surrendered on nearly the same conditions as Wintermoot's, both of which are enclosed. I next summoned Forty Fort, the commandant of which refused the condition I sent him.

July 3d. Parties were sent out to collect cattle, who informed me that the rebels were preparing to attack me. This pleased the Indians highly, who observed they should be upon an equal footing with them in the woods. At two o'clock we discovered the rebels upon their march, in number about four or five hundred. Between four and five o'clock they were advanced within a mile of us. Finding them determined, I ordered the forts to be set on fire, which deceived the enemy into an opinion that we had retreated.

We then posted ourselves in a fine, open wood, and for our greater safety lay flat on the ground, waiting their approach. When they were within 200 yards of us, they began firing. We still continued upon the ground, without returning their fire, till they had fired three volleys. By this time they had advanced within 100 yards of us; and, [they] being quite near enough, Sucingerachton ordered his Indians, who were upon the right, to begin the attack upon our part, which was immediately well seconded by the Rangers on the left. Our fire was so close and well directed that the affair was soon over, not lasting above half an hour from the time they gave us the first fire till their flight.

In this action were taken 227 scalps and only 5 prisoners. The Indians were so exasperated with their loss last year, near Fort Stanwix, that it was with the greatest difficulty I could save the lives of those few. Colonel Denison, who came in next day with a minister and four others to treat for the remainder of the settlement of Westmorland, assures me that they have lost one colonel, two majors, seven captains, thirteen lieutenants, eleven ensigns, and two hundred and sixty-eight privates. On our side are killed one Indian [and] two Rangers, and eight Indians wounded.

In this incursion we have taken and destroyed eight pallisaded forts, and burned about one thousand dwelling houses, all their mills, etc. We have also killed and drove off about 1000 head of horned cattle, and sheep and swine in great numbers. But what gives me the sincerest satisfaction is that I can with great truth assure you that, in the destruction of this settlement, not a single person has been hurt of the inhabitants but such as were in arms. To those, indeed, the Indians gave no quarter.

I have also the pleasure to inform you that the officers and Rangers behaved during this short action highly to my satisfaction, and have always supported themselves through hunger and fatigue with great cheerfulness.

I have this day sent a party of men to the Delaware to destroy a small settlement there, and to bring off prisoners. In two or three days I shall send out other parties for the same purpose. If I can supply myself with provisions, I shall harass the adjacent country and prevent them from getting in their harvest.

The settlement of Scoharg [Scoharie] or the Minisinks will be my next objects, both of which abound in corn and cattle, the destruction of which cannot fail of greatly distressing the rebels. I have not yet been able to hear anything of the expresses I sent to the Generals Howe and Clinton. But, as I sent them by ten different routes, I am in hopes that some of them will be able to make their way to them and return.

In a few days I do myself the honor of writing to you more fully, and send[ing] you a journal of my proceeding since I left Niagara. [CP, filed under Sept. 15.]

[Extract of the Commissioners to Germain. July 26, 1778.]

But, under the present aspect of affairs, to persist any longer in our pacific advances either to the Congress or to the people at large would be to expose His Majesty and the state of Great Britain to insults of which we should be sorry to furnish the occasion. [Stevens, *Facsimiles, 11,* No. 1122.]

Extract from General Lee's defense at his court martial [August 9, 1778].

The plain was extensive and appeared to me unembarrassed. I had set out in the morning with the idea that it was His Excellency's intention that I should strike some partial blow. There were, indeed, some expressions let fall by the General which at the instant conveyed to me an idea that he had adopted new sentiments, and that it was his wish to bring on a general engagement. It remained with me for some moments, but was entirely banished by what subsequently passed. For, when instead of permitting me to arrange the troops I had brought up near the main army, as I had proposed, he ordered me to march them to three miles in the rear of Englishtown, I was more confirmed than ever in the original idea I set out with, viz., *that it never was his intention to court or hazard a general engagement.* The several councils of war held both in Pennsylvania and on this side the Delaware on the subject of the operations to be pursued in the Jersies reprobate[d] the idea of risking a general engagement, as the advantages to be gained by victory were not to be put in competition with the evils which might result from defeat. And, if I recollect right, the most sanguine of these councils only recommended the cutting off their rear or covering party, or perhaps the demolition or surprise of their baggage.

I flattered myself that the nature of the country (as far as I had a right to judge from its aspect) would secure us from any material disgrace. In these hopes and on this principle I immediately planned and ordered the following attacks: General Wayne with seven hundred men and two pieces of artillery to attack in rear, General Durkee with Varnum's Brigade to make the left flank attack, and Colonel Morgan, I concluded, would attack their right flank. We marched with great rapidity till we emerged from the wood into the plain. About this time a party of our light horse was driven in by those of the enemy toward the spot where Colonel Butler was, who repulsed them by his fire.

The enemy's force was considerably larger than I had been taught to expect. A column of artillery with a strong covering party, both horse and foot, presented themselves in the center of the plain. Another much larger appeared, directing their course toward the Court House on the right. As this column, if it had turned our right, *must have put us into the most dangerous* situation, I immediately ordered three regiments under the Marquis de Lafayette to incline to the right and meet them, and detached Captain Mercer to General Scott, then in the wood on the left, with orders for him to remain where he was as a security to the left flank.

A few minutes afterward I was surprised upon observing that Colonel Oswald, with the artillery, was retiring toward the ravine. And I was preparing to return to the left when I was informed that General Scott had abandoned the wood on the left, and that the whole of the troops were retiring from that quarter. This intelligence astonished as well as disconcerted me. In this state, too, I observed the Marquis de Lafayette had fallen back; and, I confess, circumstanced as we were, I was not sorry for it, although to this day I am ignorant by what means it was brought about. I now had thoughts of taking a position on the hither (western) margin of the ravine, but a variety of circumstances soon determined me to abandon all thoughts of this position. And, upon a favorable report made me of another in my rear, I ordered the battalions and guns to file off toward it. But upon a nearer view I found it an execrable one, there being a ravine and morass in our rear over which there was alone one passage, and that a very narrow one —this being the very place General Dickinson had before pointed out to me in the following emphatic terms: "*General Lee, you may believe me or not, but if you march your party beyond the ravine now in your rear, which has only one passage over it, you are in a perilous situation.*"

I now applied my whole attention to the conducting the troops from this position, having previously ordered General Maxwell into the wood to our left and rear to secure our retreat across the morass. From this point of action to the eminence where we found General Washington I appeal to those near me whether I did not seem more solicitous for the safety and honor of the troops than for my own person. The instant General Washington came up and issued a single order, I considered myself in fact reduced to a private capacity. And, if any disorder arose from this moment, it may, I think, be attributed rather to a clashing of orders than to any want of judgment in me.

When he permitted me to reassume the command on the hill we then were upon, he gave me directions to defend it in order to give him time to make a disposition of his army on the eminence in the rear. I here established a battery and took post myself, and sent orders to Colonel Ogden (who had drawn up in the wood nearest the bridge in our rear) to defend that post for the purpose of covering the retreat of the whole over the bridge. The battalions that were here, having sustained with gallantry and returned with vigor a very considerable fire, were at length successively forced over the bridge. The rear I brought up myself. I there addressed General Washington in these words: "*Sir, here are my troops; how is it your pleasure I should dispose of them? Shall I form them in your front, align them with your main body, or draw them up in the rear?*" His answer was, "*Arrange them in the rear of Englishtown Creek.*" [18] [*Lee Papers, 3,* 182–183, 187–190; Clinton has rearranged and sometimes misquoted the extracts.]

Extract of a letter from Lord George Germain to Sir Henry Clinton. Whitehall, 2d September 1778 (received 22d December).

The distresses of the King's loyal American subjects who have been driven from their habitations and deprived of their property by the rebels has been an object of attention with His Majesty and Parliament from the first appearance of the rebellion; and very considerable sums have been expended in furnishing them with a temporary support. But, as their number is daily increasing and it is much to be apprehended (if a reconciliation does not soon take place) that scarcely any who retain their principles will be suffered to remain in the revolted provinces, it is judged proper in that event that a permanent provision should be made by which they may be enabled to support themselves and their families without being a continual burden upon the revenue of Great Britain.

18. *Clinton's note:* Baron Steuben's evidence likewise proves that General Washington had no intention of bringing on a general engagement. His words are: "*After I had arranged General Lee's corps in the rear of Englishtown Creek, I was joined by General Paterson with three brigades from the second line.*" [See *Lee Papers, 3,* 96.] Now, as the second line composed the chief part of the army with which General Washington says he stopped the advance of the British, how came these brigades to be sent so far into the rear at the moment he wished to bring on a general action?

The tract of country that lies between Penobscot River and the River St. Croix, the boundary of Nova Scotia on that side, offers itself for the reception of these meritorious but distressed people. And it is the King's intention to erect it into a province, and that each of them should there receive a grant of the same quantity of land (provided it does not exceed 1000 acres) as they have been deprived of in any of the revolted provinces, subject to the like quitrent and the like conditions of settlement as the lands in Nova Scotia were granted under at the first establishment of that province. But it is His Majesty's gracious intention not to make any demand from them of quitrent for ten years after the date of the grants, and application will be made to Parliament for their support and assistance in making their settlements until it may be expected they will be in a condition to subsist themselves.

As the first step toward making this establishment it is His Majesty's pleasure, if peace has not taken place and the season of the year is not too far advanced before you receive this, that you do send such a detachment of the troops at Nova Scotia, or of the provincials under your immediate command, as you shall judge proper and sufficient to defend themselves against any attempt the rebels in those parts may be able to make during the winter to take post on Penobscot River, taking with them all necessary implements for erecting a fort, together with such ordnance and stores as may be proper for its defense, and a sufficient supply of provisions.

Besides the reasons I have already mentioned, the security of Nova Scotia and the coast fishery, and the obtaining possession of a country abounding with mast timber and naval stores, are strong inducements for the adoption of this measure. And, if my information be well founded, a safe and commodious harbor for the King's ships will be also thereby obtained. [Calendared in Hist. MSS Com., *American MSS in the Royal Institution, 1,* 284.]

[Extract of the Commissioners to Germain. September 5, 1778.]

It is certain that the idea, which is carefully propagated, that a short interval will extort from Great Britain the concession of independence contributes much to enable the leaders of the rebellion to persist in their claim. The exertion of His Majesty's government in sending a powerful squadron to support the armament already on this coast has, in consequence of the late time of its departure from Great Britain and of its tedious and unfortunate voyage, failed of the full effect that might have been expected from it. Meantime the instructions of 21 March last, fixing the destination of the army and navy to services which could not be executed in the face of a superior enemy at sea, have at the same time (in the expectation of their being carried into execution as soon as circumstances could possibly admit) suspended all offensive operations on this continent, and occasioned an embargo of four months on all the ships in this port [New York] to secure a sufficient quantity of vessels to carry off the troops, stores, goods, and such inhabitants as may be unwilling to trust to the clemency of the enemy in case that measure [withdrawal to Halifax] shall be adopted. Under these appearances of weakness, or of a fixed plan to abandon our possessions here, *our cause has visibly declined;* and nothing less than the sense we have of the importance of our trust, and a resolution not to give way to despair while there remained the slightest hope of eventual success from exertions, could have made us lose any opportunity of quitting a situation in which our services are likely to be of so little avail to His Majesty's affairs.

It is, however, difficult for us to believe that an object of so much consequence as that of holding at least the seaports of this continent by some tie of dependence and friendship (an object which involves not only the ascendant which Great Britain has hitherto held in the navigation of the Atlantic, but likewise the *preservation of the fisheries and even of the West India Islands*) is to be given up without a proportionate struggle, where the effects of a determined perseverance might afford reasonable hopes of success. And yet, if the troops now here, instead of being recruited from home to complete their present establishment, are to be weakened by detachments for different and distant services, we (and indeed the whole people of America) must give way to this opinion. And, as we shall on that supposition have no part to take but that of returning to England, so we cannot doubt that persons of every description here, however well affected, will (if they can be received by the assumed governments of their respective colonies) make their peace upon any terms. And the whole will fall into the hands of France, with every circumstance that can tend to secure the dependence of this people on that power, notwithstanding the natural antipathy that has hitherto prevailed against it. [Stevens, *Facsimiles, 11,* No. 1144.]

Extract of a letter from Sir Henry Clinton to Lord George Germain. New York, October 8th, 1778.

I have the honor to inform Your Lordship that, the Admiral [Byron] having at length been able to appoint a convoy, I shall in a few days have it in my power to obey His Majesty's instructions by detaching the troops for the expedition to the West Indies. And I shall further send, agreeable to those [instructions] received from Your Lordship, 1000 men to Pensacola and 2000 to St. Augustine. For these garrisons I have employed foreign troops and provincials, whose loss to this army will not be so much felt. But, as the treaties with the former and the understood stipulation with the latter have precluded my sending them to the West Indies, I have been forced to send 5000 British effective rank and file upon that service, a dismemberment which is severe indeed!

After a wound, in my humble opinion, so fatal to the hopes of any future vigor in this army I trust, My Lord, you cannot wish to keep me in the mortifying command of it. I fear it is not in the power of Great Britain to restore to me the force I lose by the detaching those ten British regiments. They are the very nerves of this army. The British who remain with me are, to be sure, equal to them in every respect. But their number will be too small to animate the overproportion of foreigners, etc., who, though they may be faithful, etc., cannot be supposed to be equally zealous. This I have said, My Lord, on the supposition that you mean to reinforce me, which, however, I am not authorized to think is your intention. I have had still a further drain from me by the necessity of sending nearly 700 men to replace the marines at Halifax and 300 to garrison Bermudas and the Bahama Islands. Were all the troops that remain with me of the first stamp, their scanty numbers would stifle any hope that might arise from the consideration of their valor. You cannot, I am confident, My Lord, desire that I should remain a mournful witness of the debility of an army at whose head, had I been unshackled by instructions, I might have indulged expectations of rendering serious service to my country.

I trust, My Lord, that I have done my duty zealously in a command at least unsolicited by me. I have followed my instructions strictly and punctually whensoever I could well warp my circumstances to them. True, indeed, as to the manner of evacuating Philadelphia I ventured to deviate from my orders. But by that deviation I think I may say I rescued the honor, perhaps the existence, of the army as well as the interests of my country. His Majesty, upon whose goodness I repose my hopes, will, I doubt not, make an allowance for my feelings; and, when I apply to Your Lordship to request his gracious permission for my resigning this command, I do it in the fullest confidence that my royal master cannot look upon that desire as proceeding from want of ardor for his service, but will attribute it to the conviction that I am no longer in a situation to promote his interests. [*Ibid.*, No. 1175.]

[Extract of the Commissioners to Germain. October 15, 1778.]

The present state of the war enables the Congress still to maintain an influence and power they owe at this time much more to their possession of the sword than to any remains of popular affection and confidence. We thought it our duty, before we retire from the exercise of a trust with which we have been so far ineffectually honored, to make a final and most solemn trial of the powers with which we are vested and to leave, if possible, in this continent an impression rather of the benevolence and spirit of Great Britain than of weakness and want of system. The time, too, seemed particularly seasonable for this attempt, as we have good reason to believe that much reciprocal disgust subsists at this moment between the people of the colonies in general and the subjects of their pretended ally. It is also obvious that the distresses and difficulties of the war must be every hour more reluctantly suffered in proportion to its being understood that all past grievances and future apprehensions, real or imaginary, are equally removed. The benevolent purpose shown by His Majesty and his Parliament has so far appeared unsuccessful, *but has certainly had its effects.* For there is good reason to believe that *the spirit of revolt is much abased,* that *the Congress is becoming an object rather of awe than of confidence to the people,* and that *the French connection is generally disliked. [Ibid., 12,* No. 1178.]

[Report of Mr. Jonathan Clarke, deputy Commissary of Accounts. October 25, 1778.]

Mr. Clarke has the honor to wait upon His Excellency Sir Henry Clinton with the Continental accounts of supplies for the troops of the Convention, and to ask the favor of His Excellency's commands thereupon.

Mr. Clarke prays leave to report upon the accounts that the several articles charged in them were purchased with the bills of credit of the Congress, under their present depreciated state. That General Heath asserts that he is restrained by a resolution of Congress from receiving payment in the same currency, and that he must insist upon specie without any allowance for the depreciation of their own bills. That General Heath refuses permission to Mr. Clarke to purchase supplies in the country for that army. That, by the mode of payment required by General Heath, the amount of the accounts will be more than three times the real cost of them, as four and five Continental dollars can be purchased with a Spanish dollar, and in that proportion for other species of money. That the more the paper money falls in value the higher are the charges of the army, and the greater the advantage arising to the Congress from the money expended by the army.

Mr. Clarke has it in charge from Major General Phillips to submit it as his opinion to His Excellency, with the greatest deference and respect, that payment of the accounts or the sending money into that country for the payment of the troops (except a few thousand pounds for the officers) will be attended with ill consequences to His Majesty's service, as he conceives one great inducement to detain the troops in the country is to possess themselves of the specie sent among them, and to avail themselves of the advantage gained by supplies. That sending them the specie or the payment of their accounts has a very great tendency to raise the credit of their paper currency, which at present is in a distressed situation and of less value than it has ever been yet. That, upon refusing the payment of the accounts, probably the Congress will declare the Convention at an end and the army to be prisoners of war. That, as their present demand amounts to £103,057 sterling, and this for six months only, the expense of the army still increasing and the prospect of their release [being] so distant, it is also respectfully submitted how far it is an object to preserve the army in its present situation. That the Convention, which was made for the benefit of government and the army, has by the violation of it operated to their disadvantage and put them in a worse situation than prisoners of war, as well on account of the expense as the prospect of release. That, as the Congress have detained the troops to answer their own purpose, whether there is not the greatest justice that the army should be maintained by them.

Major General Phillips prays His Excellency to be assured that he has exerted himself in every possible way to keep the troops together, as well by orders to them, by threats and by promises, as by remonstrating against the many arts that have been industriously used by the enemy to induce them to desert. (There have been recruiting parties at the barracks for that purpose, and upon his remonstrating the measure has been disclaimed and in some degree checked.) That, if it is the wish of His Excellency that the same line of conduct should be continued by Major General Phillips, he will with pleasure pursue it, or any other which His Excellency shall please to suggest.

It is the duty of Mr. Clarke also to report to His Excellency that it is the opinion of Major General Riedesel that, if the payment of the German troops is suspended, he shall lose his soldiers by desertion. It is the opinion of Major General Phillips that it will not operate in the same degree upon the British regiments, and great numbers of the men will find their way to the royal army. [Calendered in Hist. MSS Com., *American MSS in the Royal Institution, 1,* 319.]

[Extract of the Commissioners to Germain. November 15, 1778.]

Notwithstanding these effects and other appearances of uncontrolled power in the Congress, *the accounts we have received of a general inclination of the people in favor of the British offers and in opposition to the French connection are still confirmed by the most frequent and most credible reports.* The dislike of the people to the present measures of the rebel rulers arises in part from the distresses to which they are exposed in the war from the continuing depreciation of the paper money and the asperity of their present government.

We must, however, remark that, as the cause of His Majesty and of Great Britain on this continent has from the circumstances we have mentioned at present the appearance of decline, we must expect— unless it be speedily and effectually supported—a very rapid decay of its strength by the ruin of all those who are proscribed under the usurped governments, and by a general defection of all those who can make their peace by submitting to the present usurpations. And it is not to be doubted that the rebel rulers, when left without the pressure of our arms, may find leisure and security sufficient to soften the asperities of their government into a system which may remove the present jealousies and distresses of the people and confirm them in the habits of their new situation so much that, when the present current of power has had time to wear down and deepen its new channel, the work of turning it will become daily more difficult and at last impracticable. [Stevens, *Facsimiles, 12,* No. 1215.]

[Extract of the Commissioners to Germain. November 27, 1778.]

We take this occasion, in justice to Sir Henry Clinton as well as our-selves, to observe that during the five months in which we had the honor of acting with His Excellency we experienced on his part, with-out any intermission, the utmost unreserve, and that cordial zeal to promote the public service which might have essentially contributed to the success of our mission if success had been in any degree obtain-able. (Signed) Carlisle, William Eden. [*Ibid.,* No. 1227.]

Extract of a letter from Lord George Germain to Sir Henry Clinton. Whitehall, December 3d, 1778.

The great military talents so discoverable in all your movements, the readiness you have shown to execute the King's commands, and the strict and punctual manner in which you have obeyed your instructions in preparing and sending off the detachments as soon as the Admiral had provided the proper convoys have given His Majesty additional satisfaction, and consequently would have increased the royal regret were you to quit a command, your exercise of which has redounded so much to your own honor and the public advantage. His Majesty has therefore commanded me to acquaint you that he cannot at present comply with your request, and to assure you that you may rely upon every means being employed to augment your force—so as to enable you to act offensively—that the circumstances of affairs will admit. And, although it may not be possible by the utmost exertions to increase your army to its former number, His Majesty has such entire reliance upon your zeal and ability, and upon the valor and discipline of the corps which remain with you, that he cannot entertain a doubt but that the war will be conducted in such a manner the next campaign as shall reflect particular honor upon you and be productive of great advantage to the public.

The disposition and employment of the troops will be, as it was always intended they should be, left to your judgment. For every measure that I may have suggested was submitted to you to execute or not as you should think most fit, and by no means intended to shackle you in your operations, except the instances of the evacuation of Philadelphia and the sending off the detachments ordered by His Majesty's instructions of the 21st of March. And I can assure you it was with much regret those measures were adopted by His Majesty and all his confidential servants, and the chagrin which it was foreseen those orders would occasion to the General and the army made no inconsiderable ingredient in our concern. But the intelligence we had received of the intentions of France, and the necessity of providing for the immediate security of our West India possessions, would not allow of an alternative; and I am persuaded you now join us in opinion that those measures were unavoidable.

Extract of a letter from Lord George Germain to Sir Henry Clinton. Whitehall, 23d January, 1779 (received 24th April).

The presence of three of the Commissioners, at a time when a perfect knowledge of the real state of affairs in America was so necessary in order to the forming a right judgment of the measures which were most fit to be adopted, was a circumstance that afforded much satisfaction to the King and all His Majesty's confidential servants. And meetings with them were appointed, and every information has been received from them that their situation has enabled them to collect, and their opinions heard upon every important point respecting the mode of conduct to be pursued toward the revolted colonies. When this was done, the situation and resources of this country, the necessity of vigorous exertions against France, the attention due to the security of all His Majesty's possessions, and the protection to be given to our commerce were likewise taken into our consideration and, blended with the American affairs, became the complex subject of frequent and most serious deliberations, the result of which, insofar as your command is concerned, I am now to acquaint you with.

And, in order to your being more fully possessed of the King's wishes and intentions respecting the employment of the forces under your orders in the present year, I will state to you the outlines of the plan for the future conduct of the war in North America submitted to the King, and which His Majesty has thought fit to approve. But at the same time I am commanded to say to you that His Majesty has such entire reliance upon your wisdom, zeal for his service, and great military abilities that he leaves it to your judgment to make such alterations, either in the plan itself or in the mode pointed out for its execution, as (from your knowledge of many circumstances which cannot be known here) you shall conceive to conduce more immediately and effectually to the attainment of the great end of all His Majesty's measures, the reestablishment of legal government in the revolted provinces.

It is most earnestly to be wished that you may be able to bring Mr. Washington to a general and decisive action at the opening of the campaign. But, if that cannot be effected, it is imagined that with an army of about 12,000 men in the field under your immediate command you may force him to seek for safety in the Highlands of New York or the Jerseys, and leave the inhabitants of the open country at liberty to follow *what the Commissioners represent to be their inclinations,* and renounce the authority of the Congress and return to their allegiance to His Majesty—which would obviate the chief objection to the reestablishment of civil government in New York, as a majority of counties in the province could send members to the assembly, and the ancient constitution could be restored in due form.

It is also intended that two corps of four thousand each, assisted by a naval force, should be employed upon the seacoasts of the revolted provinces, the one to act on the side of New England and New

Hampshire and the other in the Chesapeake Bay, and by entering the rivers and inlets, wherever it was found practicable, seize or destroy their shipping and stores and deprive them of every means of fitting out privateers or of carrying on foreign commerce. A considerable diversion will likewise be directed to be made on the side of Canada by a succession of parties of Indians, supported by detachments of the troops there, alarming and harassing the frontiers and making incursions into the settlements.

What opportunities may present themselves in the course of the campaign for extending your operations cannot now be foreseen. But *it surely is not too much to expect* that your force will be so much increased by new levies, under the encouragement now given them, as to enable you to strengthen the corps you appoint *to attack Virginia and Maryland,* so as to give protection to the loyal inhabitants of Jersey or the lower counties on Delaware in any attempt they may be disposed to make, in the absence of the rebel army, to deliver themselves from the tyranny and oppression of the rebel committees and to form a force sufficient to withstand any efforts of the Congress to continue them under its authority.

The reinforcement intended to be sent out to you early in the spring to enable you to effect these important services will consist of Colonel MacDonell's Highlanders and the Edinburgh Regiment, of 1000 each; the remainder of MacLean's Regiment, which is 400; 3000 British recruits, etc.—making in the whole an addition of about 6600 to your present force, which appears from your last returns to be upward of 22,000 effectives at New York and Rhode Island.[19] And, as the proposed augmentation of the British regiments will extend to those in America, some further addition may be expected in the course of the summer. [All but the first paragraph is printed in Johnston, *The Storming of Stony Point,* pp. 27–29.]

[Extract of Germain to Clinton (a second letter). January 23, 1779.]

The King, anxious to show every mark of his royal favor to those of his faithful subjects who have taken arms in support of his government in America and do serve in the provincial corps which are raised in that country, and as a reward for their faithful services and spirited conduct upon many occasions, is graciously pleased to order that, for

19. *Clinton's note:* Strength of the army at New York and Rhode Island on the 1st of January, 1779 (rank and file): In New York and posts adjacent, fit for duty, 13,830; effectives, 16,611. Rhode Island, fit for duty, 5071; effectives, 5895. Total fit for duty. 18,901; effectives, 22,506.

the future, all officers of provincial corps that are or may be raised in America shall have the same rank which the provincial officers who served in that country in the late war enjoyed under the command of Lord Amherst: that is to say, when they are on service with the British officers they shall take rank as juniors of the rank to which they belong.

And as a further encouragement to his provincial officers His Majesty is graciously pleased to order that such of them as shall happen to be wounded in action, so as to lose a limb or be maimed, shall be entitled to the same gratuity of one year's advanced pay as officers of his established army, being so wounded, are entitled to receive.

It is likewise His Majesty's pleasure that you publish and make known to his provincial corps, as also to all others his loyal subjects in America, his gracious intention to support and protect them. And, in order more amply to reward those who have suffered the loss of their property on account of their loyalty and have taken arms in His Majesty's service and exerted themselves in raising and completing American corps, as also those who in future shall in like manner exert themselves, His Majesty has resolved to distinguish such provincial regiments as shall be completed to the same number and proportion of men and officers as the present establishment of the British regiments of foot, and shall be recommended by his commander in chief as being properly officered and fit for service, by making the rank of the officers permanent in America and allowing them half pay upon the reduction of their regiments, in the same manner as the officers of British reduced regiments are paid. [Calendared in Hist. MSS Com., *American MSS in the Royal Institution, 1,* 375.]

Extract of a letter from Lord George Germain to Sir Henry Clinton. March 3d, 1779 (received 29th April).

Rear Admiral Arbuthnot is appointed to command the American squadron, and will sail with four ships of the line and some small ones as soon as the troops arrive at Portsmouth, and take the whole under his convoy. And I have the satisfaction to assure you that the Admiral goes out with the strongest desire to cultivate and maintain the most perfect harmony between the fleet and army, to cooperate with you in every measure for the King's service, and [to] give every facility and assistance in the transportation and accommodation of the troops you may think proper to employ in attacking the seacoasts and in carrying on the war according to the mode I have, in my secret and confidential letter, pointed out to you.

Extract of a letter from Lord George Germain to Sir Henry Clinton. April 1st, 1779.

Besides the reinforcement which goes from hence, it is His Majesty's intention to comply with your wishes and still further increase your force by returning to you the whole of that fine body of men you sent under Major General Grant to the West Indies, so soon as the season for offensive operations there is over. And, that no time may be lost, I have dispatched orders to Major General Grant that, if no event happens that may afford a prospect of employing the troops with advantage in offensive operations before the approach of the hurricane season, he do return to New York or whatever part of the continent of America you shall direct him to come to, with all he thinks may be spared after providing for the security and defense of St. Lucia and the other West India Islands during the season in which it is unfit to carry on any offensive operations.

Extract of a letter from Lord George Germain to Sir Henry Clinton. 11th April [1779].

After I had closed my dispatches and Major Drummond had proceeded with them to Portsmouth, Lord Cornwallis went to court and made an offer of his services to the King, which you will not doubt His Majesty was graciously pleased to accept; and His Lordship is to return to his former situation of second in command to you. As you are well acquainted with Lord Cornwallis' military merit and services, his return to America cannot but be highly pleasing to you; and your having so able an officer to second you in your operations and share with you the cares and fatigue of so extensive a command will, I hope, be an additional motive for your remaining in it—if any motive could be wanting to induce you to continue with satisfaction in a command, your exercise of which has already redounded so much to your own honor, has been so beneficial to the public and so repeatedly approved by the King. [Calendared in Hist. MSS Com., American MSS in the Royal Institution, 1, 415.]

Extract of a letter from Sir Henry Clinton to the British commissioners for settling a cartel with those of the enemy at Amboy. New York, 18th April 1779.

I agree in sentiment with you that this conference was solicited by Congress merely to still the clamors of their officers, their real indifference for whose fate appears clearly through every step of their proceedings. With this conviction, possibly the most becoming step would be to break off instantly, and spurn the idea of further negotiation with a people who invariably meet you with such ungenerous resolutions. But a just tenderness for the sensations of our officers and soldiers in their hands, and even a desire to prove to those of the enemy, prisoners with us, how averse we are from taking any unworthy advantage of the severity of their situation, oblige me to attend to two or three articles on which the enemy ground their principal subterfuges. [Calendared in *ibid.*, p. 420.]

[Extract of Germain to Clinton. April 22, 1779.]

The wind being contrary ever since the arrival of the transports with the troops at Portsmouth, Admiral Arbuthnot has not yet been able to get out to sea. His detention gives me an opportunity of acquainting you that His Majesty has been graciously pleased to appoint you to the command of the Seventh or Queen's Regiment of Dragoons, late General Sir George Howard's; and it is with the most sincere pleasure that I congratulate you upon this fresh mark of His Majesty's royal favor and approbation of your services. [Calendared in *ibid.*, p. 422.]

Copy of a letter from Sir Henry Clinton's commissioners to Colonels Davies and Harrison, commissioners on the part of General Washington. Amboy, 22d April 1779.

Gentlemen:

With a patience inspired by our anxious wishes to effect the end of our mission and supported by the duties of personal politeness, we have waited three days to receive your assent or negative to the proposals we offered you on Monday. As they are determinate and unalterable, so we hope they are clear. In the first case we can only require a decisive answer. Should they be deficient in perspicuity, we shall be happy to explain them. We present to you on our part terms unpropped by argument and resting only on the basis of their equity. Should you not be inclined to acquiesce in them, we trust you will not on your side detain us for the purpose only of entering at large into your motives, especially as we have Sir Henry Clinton's orders to bring this negotiation to a speedy conclusion and to return to New York so soon as we are convinced there are no hopes of success. We are, etc. (Signed) West Hyde, John André. [Calendared in *ibid.*]

Copy of a letter from General Washington's commissioners to Colonel West Hyde and Captain John André, commissioners on the part of Sir Henry Clinton. Amboy, 22d April 1779.

Gentlemen:

We are very sensible of your personal politeness through the whole of our negotiation, and should be extremely unwilling you should indulge an idea that in any instance we would wish to detain you unnecessarily. We affect not delay, but, actuated by the warmest desires to accomplish the humane purposes of our appointment, we have paid the closest attention to the proposals you have offered. We have found them extensive and important in their consequences, involving a variety of interests, which necessarily required much consideration. With a truly anxious zeal we have endeavored to accommodate them to our mutual advantage and that of the prisoners, and are sensibly distressed to find ourselves unexpectedly restricted to a bare assent or negative to your proposals. Should they, however, be finally determinate and unalterable, as you express, we have only to lament that they are such as we cannot accede to without manifest injury to our country and incurring the disapprobation even of our unfortunate prisoners themselves. We are, etc. (Signed) William Davies, R. H. Harrison. [Calendared in *ibid.*, p. 421.]

Extract of a letter from Lord George Germain to Sir Henry Clinton. Whitehall, May 5, 1779 (received 21 July).

The favorable appearance His Majesty's affairs now put on in America have made me extremely anxious for the departure of the reinforcement of troops and ships which I acquainted you in my letter of the 1st of April were then in readiness to sail, but were detained until the 1st instant by contrary winds at St. Helen's. A circumstance fell out the next day which, I am afraid, will occasion a little more delay. But it is only on that account to be lamented, for on every other it is to be esteemed most fortunate, *and does great honor to Admiral Arbuthnot's good sense and spirit,* and I trust will furnish the occasion of giving a severe blow to the enemy.[20]

Some accounts from France seem to intimate an intention to throw some French troops into Canada by the way of the River St. Lawrence, and an embarkation that has been some time preparing to sail under the convoy of five ships of the line, commanded by Monsieur la Motte-

20. *Clinton's note:* An advice boat falling in with Admiral Arbuthnot that was carrying to England intelligence of the French attack of the Island of Jersey, the Admiral sent his convoy into Torbay and sailed thither for its relief.

Picquet, has been pointed out as intended for that purpose. The rebel agents affect to say the ships and troops are destined to act against you, and there are some appearances which give so much countenance to such a supposition that I think fit to mention it to you, that you may be on your guard in case Admiral Arbuthnot should not arrive before them. The troops are embarked in seven large transports and in the ships of war, and are said to consist of about 3000 men.

[Clinton to Germain. May 14, 1779.]

My Lord:

I have issued to the provincial troops His Majesty's most gracious regulations in their favor. The order was so positive that I did not dare to hesitate, Your Lordship's dispatch No. 21 [of October 8, 1778] having put me upon my guard in that respect to suffer any motive, howsoever pressing, to betray me into a suspension of orders from home.

Had any degree of latitude been left to me, I should have suggested some objections, particularly in the case of granting rank to provincial field officers immediately after those of their respective ranks in the British service, so contrary to the establishment fixed by Sir William Howe. This measure has given great discontent to the field officers of the regular regiments, which is not balanced by any advantage gained upon the minds of the provincials. For the latter never expected that indulgence nor, I believe, even wished it. They had entered the service upon a different condition, with which they were well satisfied. They were advanced to stations to which many of them could not possibly upon other terms have aspired and, conscious of their own inexperience, never aimed at commanding men who had passed years in the sole study of their profession.

I shall now meet with constant difficulty in employing the provincials. It is to be wished that they should always be mixed with the regular troops, and should be employed in active service. But, were that system pursued, the command of important detachments would, by the present regulation, so often devolve upon heads entirely unequal to the task that I shall be obliged on many occasions to sacrifice the advantage I should otherways reap from their knowledge of the country.

The promise of half pay will prove a very powerful incitement, but it is clogged in such a manner that I fear it will lose much of its effect. I imagine that the various formation of the different provincial corps has escaped Your Lordship. Many of them (the light corps especially, which include cavalry) are scarcely reducible to the establishment of the British regiments. I shall, therefore, as I am restricted to that standard, be much at a loss how to recommend any corps in that predicament, howsoever it may distinguish itself.

There is another point to which Your Lordship does not appear to have adverted. The provincial corps, when scarcely half their number has been raised, have always been led into the field and exposed to all the casualties of service. It is hardly to be expected that those battalions should ever be completed, whilst they are subjected to a continual drain almost as copious as their resources. I need only instance the Queen's Rangers. That corps has enlisted at least a thousand men; their present strength is [blank in MS] rank and file. They have twelve captains, exclusive of the field officers, each of whom has raised the number of men requisite to entitle him to his commission. That number will not accord to the proposed establishment, and what can I do with the supernumeraries? The whole provincial line is overofficered; and the professional merit of some, with the connections of others, render it scarcely possible to remedy the fault.

I have entered into these circumstances, My Lord, that the consideration of them may incline Your Lordship not to judge precipitately upon any steps which I may think it necessary to take for better modeling the provincial line. Should any plan be fixed upon to mold that body into a more serviceable form, it cannot avoid being detrimental to some individuals, and may therefore excite misrepresentation. I have always understood that the provincial corps were entirely at the disposal of the commander in chief, to be incorporated or dissolved as the service, in his judgment, might require. I am happy in saying that the present state of the provincial forces will fully vindicate the measures I have hitherto pursued in that respect, but I should wish to have His Majesty's pleasure how far my powers in that particular are henceforth to extend.

I have the honor to be, etc. [Calendared in Hist. MSS Com., *American MSS in the Royal Institution, 1*, 434.]

[Extract of] Sir Henry Clinton to Lord George Germain [a second letter]. New York, May 14th, 1779 (received the middle of June).

It shall be my endeavor to draw Mr. Washington forward, before he is reinforced, by indirect maneuvers. If he gives in to my views, no effort shall be wanting to strike at him whilst in motion. But, if he persists in keeping his present post, I must not flatter myself that it will be easy to gain any advantage over him or to carry into extent, as I certainly should wish, the measures which Your Lordship appears to recommend.

From what I have said, My Lord, you will see the part which I have taken. Since I am ordered to remain in the command, Your Lordship may depend during this campaign upon the most active exertions that my powers can supply. But I must lament that my happiness is sacrificed to prevent the partial inconvenience which might have arisen from a change. Had public opinion required that I should stay in the command, more attention would surely have been paid to my situation. [*Ibid.*, p. 435.]

Extract of a letter from Commodore Sir George Collier to Sir Henry Clinton. *Rainbow*, off Portsmouth, 16th May 1779 (received 20th May).

Our success and the present appearance of things infinitely exceed our most sanguine expectations; and, if the various accounts the General and myself have received can be depended on, the most flattering hopes of a return to obedience to their sovereign may be expected from most of this province. You are too good a judge, sir, of the very great importance of the post ["pass" in the original] we now hold to render my saying much upon that subject necessary. Permit me, however, as a sea officer to observe that this port of Portsmouth is an exceeding safe and secure asylum for ships against an enemy, and is *not* to be forced even by great superiority. The marine yard is large and extremely convenient, having a considerable stock of seasoned timber besides great quantities of other stores. From these considerations, joined to many others, I am firmly of opinion that it is a measure most essentially necessary for His Majesty's service that this port should remain in our hands, since it appears to me of more real consequence and advantage than any other the crown now possesses in America; for by securing this the whole trade of the Chesapeake is at an end, and consequently the sinews of the rebellion destroyed.

Extract of a letter from Sir Henry Clinton to General Mathew. New York, May 20th, 1779.

Your letter does not intimate your further views. But one I have just received from the Commodore speaks a desire of prosecuting the blow, which would certainly extend your stay in Chesapeake beyond the time proposed. With respect to the disposition of the three counties, it has been ever friendly; and, if they have declared openly for you, it is an urgent reason for remaining to protect them. But I wish that, *until we had determined to establish ourselves amongst them, the inhabitants had not been invited to join,* lest our circumstances should oblige us to abandon them to the insult and oppression of the rebel faction. In a political light I fear the attachment of those three counties would not be very important either as to example, influence, or internal strength.

Sir George Collier likewise gives very strong opinions as to the importance of the post, which I readily admit, and that great advantages might arise from an immediate establishment there. If you are of the same opinion and can maintain your ground for some time with the troops you have at present, I consent to your stay. I confess, however, I do it with reluctance, as I did expect you at this time to have assisted in the operations which might have taken place in this country. I cannot possibly reinforce you until such time as I myself am reinforced, unless Mr. Washington should detach troops against you. Were I obliged to take that step, it would disable me utterly from attempting anything serious in this quarter. Should you, however, not find the prospect bright, I wish your return as early as possible, leaving a garrison in the fort if Sir George Collier thinks that necessary for the covering of any ships of war he may think proper to leave on that station.

[Extract of Clinton to Germain. May 22, 1779.]

When I was ordered to this difficult command (under circumstances much less eligible than those in which it had been undertaken by my predecessor), I was flattered with the hope of having every latitude allowed me to act as the moment should require. And I trusted that, as I risked much reputation in accepting a charge of no auspicious appearance, the merit of any fortunate arrangement might rest with myself. After I had assumed the command, difficulty arose on difficulty. I, notwithstanding, struggled through them with a zeal and activity which I think Your Lordship cannot arraign. This surely, My Lord, ought to have increased the confidence which I was taught to believe was reposed in me. How mortified then must I be, My Lord, at finding movements recommended for my debilitated army which Your Lordship never thought of suggesting to Sir William Howe when he was in his greatest force and without an apprehension from a foreign enemy!

It is true Your Lordship does not bind me down to the plan which you have sketched for the ensuing campaign. Your Lordship only recommends. But by that recommendation you secure the right of blaming me if I should adopt other measures and fail; and, should I follow that system with success, I appear to have no merit but the bare execution. I had taken the measures of sending troops to Virginia before I had received Your Lordship's desire of doing it; and I should have sent to Georgia long before had I thought a sufficient number of troops could be spared when I was threatened by d'Estaing. Is it to be supposed that I am not upon the watch to profit by every favorable disposition in any quarter of this continent, or to improve any accidental advantage of circumstances?

I am upon the spot; the earliest and most exact intelligence on every point ought naturally, from my situation, to reach me. It is my interest as well as my duty, more than any other person's living, to inform myself minutely and justly of the particular views, connections, state, and temper of every province—nay, of every set of men within the limits of my command; and it is my business to mark every possible change in their situation. Why then, My Lord, without consulting me, will you adopt the ill-digested or interested suggestions of people who cannot be competent judges of the subject, and puzzle me by hinting wishes with which I cannot agree yet am loath to disregard? For God's sake, My Lord, if you wish me to do anything, leave me to myself and let me adapt my effects to the hourly change of circumstances. If not, tie me down to a certain point, and take the risk of my want of success.

The regulation of the provincial rank might surely have been suspended, without detriment to the service, till my sentiments had been heard. For no person could be so well acquainted with what was expedient and requisite in that line as I, who had formed many of the corps, and who had understood that the power was handed down to me from my predecessor of modeling them as I should judge most salutary for the service.

I do not wish to be captious, My Lord. But I certainly have not had that attention paid to my wishes and satisfaction which the weight of my situation, and the hopes which you held forth for me, gave me reason to expect.

Extract of a letter from Major General Grant to Sir Henry Clinton. St. Lucia, May 26th, 1779.

In obedience to a letter received from Lord George Germain, Sir Henry Calder is to remain here with the Twenty-seventh, Thirty-fifth, and Forty-ninth Regiments until he is relieved by the Royal American battalions. The Fourth, Fifteenth, Twenty-eighth, and Forty-ninth [sic] are to embark, under the command of Brigadier General Prescott, and are to proceed directly to New York unless you shall think proper to alter their destination.

Extract from Sir Henry Clinton's letter to Lord George Germain. . . . Headquarters, Phillipsburg, 18 June 1779.

Not having received any accounts whatever from Major General Prevost since his letter of the 16th of April, I have to lament that I can only enclose for Your Lordship's information copies of reports and intelligence lately received from Georgia [in a letter from Peter Paumier]: "Savannah, 23 May '79. On my arrival here I found the General and *the greatest part of the army* were gone on an expedition against Carolina. And, two days since, we have had an express from General Prevost from James Island, where the rebels had destroyed their fort, called Fort Johnson; and [he said] that he soon hoped to be in possession of Charleston."

[Extract of Germain to Major Drummond. June 23, 1779.]

I have received letters from Sir Henry Clinton very different from those I expected. You were a witness to my poor endeavors in making his command not only honorable but agreeable to him. He complains of being not left sufficiently at liberty in the plans of operations, when every caution was used to prevent the least inconvenience to him by anything like positive orders. All was left to his discretion and judgment. But it is impossible, from considering the whole state of this country with respect to foreign nations as well as to America, that government must [not] express a wish in general to what point the operations of the campaign should be directed.

It is fortunate, however, that the attack of Georgia and the expedition to Chesapeake Bay should have been objects both of administration and of the General; and it is the first time that the joining in sentiment has been matter of complaint. He may be very well assured that, whatever merit arises from his success, he will have the entire credit for it. And, if he deviates from any wish I may have expressed and should not meet with success, I shall be the first to allow the justness of his reasons for what he undertook, being fully persuaded that he is too good an officer to adopt any plan till he had a fair prospect of success. And events after that are in no man's power to command.

I was the most surprised at his not approving the regulations about the provincials, as they were founded upon ideas which have since been sent over as proper encouragements by the general officers to whom that matter had been referred by Sir Henry Clinton. As to the rank, it was only what they had enjoyed when Lord Amherst commanded, and then had not been objected to; and I do not recollect that either you or Colonel Innes thought there would have been any objections to what was proposed. And it is impossible for me to have taken more precautions than I did in attempting to have them framed in a manner agreeable to the Commander in Chief. The Commissioners were strong in their opinion that greater encouragements should be held out to the inhabitants of America to engage them in our cause; and I am certain the effect will answer the strongest. expectations if it met with the approbation of Sir Henry Clinton.

Whenever my office is held by any other person, I hope your General may find more satisfaction in corresponding with him. But he will never act with one who is more desirous of doing him justice with the King, and of promoting his wishes both in his public and private situation.

I thought to have written a f[ew li]nes. But I have been insensibly drawn into this long letter, which proves in our present scene of hurry how much I am hurt by the General's discontent.

[Extract of Germain to Clinton. June 25, 1779.]

Give me leave to express to you His Majesty's great satisfaction in the important effects with which the spirited and able execution of the judicious plan you formed for the attacks of the coast of Virginia has already been attended. And I am sanguine enough to expect to hear that still greater advantages have accrued to His Majesty's affairs from the success of that measure.

Your own determination to take the field without waiting for the growth of green forage is conformable to that vigor and zeal which have distinguished your operations in every instance since you were appointed to the chief command. And His Majesty has the firmest reliance that no opportunity will be lost, nor any exertions omitted, for the speedy reduction of the rebellion by destroying the rebel force. And for your particular satisfaction I am authorized to add that it is not the present intention to make any reduction of the forces under your command until the great object of the war in America, the recovery of the revolted provinces, is attained.

The King is not uninformed or insensible of the great pains you have taken to form the provincial corps into useful troops. And I am confident I do not hazard too much in assuring you that whatever regulations you may think proper to make, either by incorporating or reducing the corps, will be approved by His Majesty from the entire confidence he has that you will in all cases do the best for his service. [Hist. MSS Com., *MSS of Mrs. Stopford-Sackville, 2,* 130–131.]

Extract of letter from Brigadier General Wayne to General Washington. Stony Point, 17 July 1779.

At eight o'clock in the evening of the 15th the van arrived at Mr. Springsteel's, within one and a half miles of the enemy, and formed into columns as fast as they came up. The troops remained in this position until several of the principal officers, with myself, had returned from reconnoitering the works. Half after eleven o'clock the whole moved forward. At twelve o'clock the assault was to begin on the right and left flanks of the enemy's works, while Major Murfree amused them in front. But *a deep morass, covering their whole front and at this time overflowed by the tide,* together with other obstructions, rendered the approaches more difficult than were at first apprehended, so that it was about twenty minutes after twelve before the assault began; previous to which I placed myself at the head of the right column, and gave the troops the most pointed orders not to fire on any account but place their whole dependence on the bayonet, which order was literally and faithfully obeyed. Neither the deep morass, the formidable and double rows of abatis, nor the strong works in front and flank could damp the ardor of the troops, who, in the face of a most tremendous and incessant fire of musketry and from cannon loaded with grape shot, forced their way at the point of the bayonet through every obstacle, both columns meeting in the center of the enemy's works nearly at the same instant.[21] [Sparks, *Writings of Washington, 6,* 538.]

[Tryon to Clinton. New York, July 20, 1779.]
Sir:

Having on the 3d instant joined the troops asembled on board the transports at Whitestone, Sir George Collier got the fleet under way the same evening. But, the wind being light, we did not reach the harbor of New Haven until the 5th in the morning.

The first division, consisting of the flank companies of the Guards, the Fusiliers, Fifty-fourth Regiment, and a detachment of the Jägers, with four fieldpieces, under Brigadier General Garth, landed about five o'clock A.M. a mile south of West Haven and began their march, making a circuit of upward of seven miles to head a creek on the western side of the town. The second division could not move till the return of the boats. But, before noon, I disembarked with the Twenty-third, the Hessian Landgrave's and King's American Regiments, and

21. *Clinton's note on American losses:* Two sergeants, thirteen privates killed; one lieutenant colonel, two captains, three lieutenants, ten sergeants, sixty-seven rank and file wounded.

two pieces of cannon on the eastern side of the harbor, and instantly
began the march of three miles to the ferry from New Haven east toward Branford. We took a fieldpiece, which annoyed us at our landing,
and possessed ourselves of the Rock Battery, of three guns, commanding the channel of the harbor, abandoned by the rebels on our approach.
The armed vessels then entered and drew near the town.

General Garth got into the town (but not without opposition, loss,
and fatigue), and reported to me at half past one that he should begin
the conflagration which he thought it merited, as soon as he had secured the bridge between us over Neck Creek. The collection of the
enemy in force, on advantage[ous] ground and with heavier cannon
than his own, diverted the General from that passage. And, the boats
that were to take off the troops not being up, I went over to him; and
the result of our conference was a resolution that with the first division he should cover the north part of the town that night, while with
the second I should keep the heights above the Rock Fort. In the morning the first division embarked at the southeast part of the town and,
crossing the ferry, joined us on the East Haven side—excepting the
Fifty-fourth, which were sent on board their transports.

In their progress of the preceding day from West Haven they were
under a continual fire. But by the judicious conduct of the General and
the alertness of the troops the rebels were everywhere repulsed. The
next morning, as there was not a shot fired to molest the retreat, General
Garth changed his design and destroyed only the public stores [and]
some vessels and ordnance, excepting six fieldpieces and an armed
privateer, which were brought off. The troops re-embarked at Rock
Fort in the afternoon with little molestation; and the fleet, leaving the
harbor that evening, anchored the morning of the 8th off the village of
Fairfield.

The boats being not sufficient for the whole of the first division, I
landed only with the flank companies of the Guards [and] one company of the Landgrave's and the King's American Regiment, with two
fieldpieces, east of the village and southwest of the Black Rock Battery,
which commands the harbor. We pursued our march (under a cannonade without effect) toward the village, but in our approach received a smart fire of musketry. The rebels fled before the rapid advance of the Guards, and left us in possession of it and of the heights
in the west until General Garth, who landed two miles in the south,
joined us with the remainder of the troops in the evening.

Having laid under arms that night, and in the morning burnt the
greatest part of the village to resent the fire of the rebels from their
houses and to mask our retreat, we took boat where the second divi-

sion had landed, the enemy throwing only a weak, scattered fire on our flanks, the Regiment de Landgrave by a very proper disposition having effectually covered our rear.

Wanting some supplies, we crossed the sound to Huntington, and there continued till the 11th and, repassing that day, anchored five miles from the Bay of Norwalk. The sun being nearly set before the Fifty-fourth, the Landgrave's Regiment, and the Jägers were in the boats, it was near nine in the evening when I landed with them at the Cow Pasture, a peninsula on the east of the harbor within a mile an[d] a half of the bridge which formed the communication between the east and west parts of the village [of Norwalk], nearly equally divided by a salt creek. The King's American Regiment being unable to join us before three next morning, we lay that night on our arms.

In our march at the first dawn of day the Fifty-fourth led the column, and soon fell in with the rebel outposts and, driving the enemy with great alacrity and spirit, disposs[ess]ed them of Drummond Hill and the heights at that end of the village, east from and commanding the bridge. It being now but four o'clock in the morning, and the rebels having taken post within random cannon shot upon the hills on the north, I resolved to halt until the second division, landing at the Old Wells on the west side of the harbor, had advanced and formed the junction.

General Garth's division passed the bridge by nine, and at my desire proceeded to the north end of the village, from whence (and especially from the houses) there had been a fire for five hours upon our advanced guards. The Fusiliers, supported by the light infantry of the Guards, began the attack and soon cleared that quarter, pushing the main body and a hundred cavalry from the northern heights and taking one piece of their cannon. After many salt pans were destroyed, whole boats carried on board the fleet, and the magazines, stores, and vessels set in flames with the greatest part of the dwelling houses, the advanced corps were drawn back. And the troops retired in two columns to the place of our first debarkation and, unassaulted, took ship and returned to Huntington Bay. We were waiting only for fresh supplies of artillery and force adequate to the probable increase of the rebels (by the decrease of the objects of their care and the alarm of the interior country) when I was honored on the 13th with your command of the 12th for the return of the troops with the fleet to Whitestone.

The rebels in arms at New Haven were considerable, more numerous at Fairfield, and still more so at Norwalk. Two hundred and fifty Continental troops had now joined their militia, under General Parsons, and together were said to be upward of two thousand. The accounts of their loss are vague. It could not be trifling. The general effect of the printed address from Sir George Collier and myself to the inhabitants,[22] recommended by Your Excellency, cannot be discovered till there are some further operations and descents upon their coast. Many copies of it were left behind at New Haven, and at Fairfield I sent one by the Reverend Mr. Sayre, their Episcopal missionary, under flag to a party in arms, and received the answer of defiance already transmitted.[23]

I regret the loss of two places of public worship at Fairfield, which took fire unintentionally by the flakes from other buildings. And I gave strict orders and set guards for the preservation of that burnt at Norwalk. But it is very difficult, where the houses are close and of very combustible materials (of boards and shingles), to prevent the spreading of the flames. I should be very sorry if the destruction of these two villages would be thought less reconcilable with humanity than with the love of my country, my duty to the King, and the law of arms to which America has been led to make the awful appeal.

The usurpers have professedly placed their hopes of severing the empire in avoiding decisive actions [and] upon the waste of the British treasures and the escape of their own property during the protraction of the war. Their power is supported by the general dread of their tyranny, and the arts practiced to inspire a credulous multitude with a presumptuous confidence in our forbearance. I wish to detect this delusion and, if possible, without injury to the loyalists. I confess myself in the sentiments of those who apprehend no mischief to the public from the irritation of a few in the rebellion, if a general terror and despondency can be awakened among a people already divided, and settled on a coast everywhere thinly inhabited and easily impressible, and to which their property is principally confined.

I should do injustice if I closed this report without giving every praise to the troops I had the honor to command. Sir George Collier cooperated with us in the direction of the armed vessels employed in the descents, and I have the pleasure to add that we had a perfect concert of opinion in the main operations. The loyal refugees possess a zeal which, with their intimate and minute knowledge of the country, will always render them useful on such services. I must not withhold my commendations even from the mariners of the transports, who were gen-

22. Printed in Collier, *Particular Services Performed in America*, pp. 93–95.

23. "Connecticut having nobly dared to oppose the usurpations of an unjust and oppressive nation (as flames have preceded the answer to your flag), we hope they will still continue, as far as in their power, to protect persecuted and oppressed innocence. Samuel Whiting, Colonel." *Ibid.*, pp. 95–96.

erally employed in manning the flatboats and bateaux, and who were as alert as if they had been entitled to national rewards.

I have the honor herewith to transmit Your Excellency a general return of the killed, wounded, and missing on this expedition,[24] and am with all possible respect Your Excellency's most obedient and very humble servant, William Tryon.

[Extract of Washington to the President of Congress. July 21, 1779.]

It has been the unanimous sentiment to evacuate the captured post at Stony Point, remove the cannon and stores, and destroy the works, which was accomplished on the night of the 18th, one piece of heavy cannon only excepted. [Fitzpatrick, *Writings of Washington, 15*, 450.]

[Extract of Clinton to Germain. July 28, 1779.]

The return of Lord Cornwallis to America gives me satisfaction proportionable to the important benefit which the King's service must receive from His Lordship's known professional merit and abilities.

Extract of a letter from Lord George Germain to Sir Henry Clinton. August 5, 1779.

The expeditious and well timed movement up the North River, and the great importance of the posts you by that means so easily got possession of, are fresh proofs of your constant attention to the great objects of your command and of the judicious measures you take for attaining them. They could not, therefore, fail of receiving His Majesty's approbation. And you will give me leave to add that, from the successes with which your operations have already been attended and the very able dispositions you have made, His Majesty entertains the strongest hopes that this campaign will be productive of every great advantage to the public.

The accounts you transmitted of General Prevost's progress,[25] though not authenticated by himself, are highly pleasing. And, from the information I have of the state of South Carolina and the disposition of the majority of the inhabitants, I am sanguine enough to flatter myself with the hope he will find *means to effect the reduction of Charleston,*

24. *Clinton's note:* The loss of the King's troops in the different descents amounted to twenty killed, ninety-five wounded, and thirty-two missing.
25. In Clinton to Germain, June 18; see above, p. 409.

and that the province will be speedily restored to the King's obedience. Vice Admiral Arbuthnot with his convoy will, I trust, before this be arrived with you. The ships and troops he carried out will be a seasonable reinforcement to the fleet and army, and give spirit and confidence to all the King's faithful subjects. And it will make me extremely happy if with their assistance you find yourself in a condition to effect the important services you meditate. Major General Grant acquaints me that, in pursuance of the orders I told you were transmitted to him, he should send back five regiments of the troops he carried to St. Lucia as soon as the Admiral should appoint a convoy; I therefore hope they are also with you by this time.

When the Prohibitory Act was passed, Parliament thought fit to vest the crown with powers to appoint commissioners to grant pardon and restore to peace such as should return to their allegiance. And in pursuance of this power His Majesty has judged it proper that the commander in chief of His Majesty's forces in North America should be possessed of those authorities. A commission appointing you His Majesty's commissioner for the before-mentioned purposes has therefore been prepared and passed under the great seal, and will be transmitted to you by Major General Robertson. [Hist. MSS Com., *MSS of Mrs. Stopford-Sackville*, 2, 135, where the letter is misdated Aug. 3.]

Extract of a letter from Governor Dalling to Sir Henry Clinton. Jamaica, 11th August 1779.

I have the most certain assurances that Count d'Estaing is now at Hispaniola with a strong fleet and powerful army. His descent upon this island may be daily expected. My force here is very inconsiderable, nor will it flatter me with any reasonable hope of preserving this colony to His Majesty without the speediest and strongest reinforcement that can be sent me. I am persuaded nothing further need be said to procure your utmost exertions toward saving this valuable part of His Majesty's dominions.

Extract of a letter from Commodore Sir George Collier to Sir Henry Clinton. *Raisonnable*, in Penobscot Bay, August 19, 1779.

I left the Hook on the 3d instant. After our arrival off the Island Monhegan we lost no time in immediately proceeding up Penobscot Bay. The next morning, 14 August, about eleven in the morning the rebel fleet presented themselves to our view, seeming inclined to dispute the passage. Their resolution, however, soon failed them; and an unexpected and ignominious flight took place. The *Hampden*, of twenty guns, surrendered. All the rest of the rebel fleet, consisting of nineteen sail from thirty-two guns to ten (amongst which was the *Warren*, of thirty-two guns, eighteen- and twelve-pounders), together with twenty-four transports, were all blown up and destroyed. [Hist. MSS Com., *American MSS in the Royal Institution*, 2, 12–13.]

[Extract of Clinton to Germain. August 20, 1779.]

I must beg leave to express how happy I am made by the return of Lord Cornwallis to this country. His Lordship's indefatigable zeal, his knowledge of the country, his professional ability, and the high estimation in which he is held by this army must naturally give me the warmest confidence of efficacious support from him in every undertaking which opportunity may prompt and our circumstances allow.

But his presence, My Lord, affords me another source of satisfaction. When there is upon the spot an officer every way so well qualified to have the interests of his country entrusted to him, I should hope I might without difficulty be relieved from a station which nobody acquainted with its conditions will suppose to have sat light upon me. To say truth, My Lord, my spirits are worn out by struggling against the consequences of many adverse incidents which, without appearing publicly to account for my situation, have effectually oppressed me. To enumerate them would be painful and unnecessary, perhaps improper. At the same time let me add, My Lord, that my zeal is unimpaired; and, were I conscious that my particular efforts were necessary for His Majesty's service, no circumstance of private feeling would raise within me a single wish of retiring from the command.

That, however, is not the case. For I do seriously give it as my opinion that, if *the endeavors of any man are likely under our present prospects to be attended with success, Lord Cornwallis' for many reasons stand among the first*. I have only to lament that I came to the head of this army at a period of difficulty, when the urgency of affairs in different quarters, and matters of more immediate concern, necessarily withdrew from this command the extensive support which its nature required, and which I am convinced it would not otherwise have wanted. I acquiesce in the importance of those objects which have either actually diminished or have prevented the augmentation of my force. Yet I must say that, had even the feeble reinforcement which I am still expecting arrived as early as I thought myself secure would have been the case, I should have found myself enabled to attempt measures perhaps of serious consequences.

Under my present circumstances, if I shall not have fulfilled any expectations which may have been indulged from this army, I trust I shall always find the failure attributed to its just cause—the inadequacy of my strength to its object. The only reinforcement upon which I am now to reckon is two new-raised regiments and the recruits for this army. To counterbalance the advantage I might gain by this, I am obliged to send 2000 men to Canada; and, if the exigency of affairs demands that I should be subjected to General Haldimand's requisition, it likewise obliges me to send him troops of proper discipline. Your Lordship will consequently judge whether, in effect, the balance will remain much in my favor, and whether I have not, moreover, reason to expect that no reinforcement can arrive which will in any manner enable me to act with the necessary vigor.

Thus circumstanced, and convinced that the force under my command at present [26] or that will be during this campaign is not equal to the services expected from it, I must earnestly request Your Lordship to lay before His Majesty my humble supplications that he will permit me to resign the command of this army to Lord Cornwallis. His Majesty's assent to this petition will crown the many favors of which my heart will ever retain the most grateful remembrance. [Johnston, *The Storming of Stony Point*, pp. 138–140.]

[Extract of Clinton to Germain. August 21, 1779.]

Your Lordship will no doubt have been aware that the delay of our expected reinforcements, the waste of the season, and the operations of the enemy in that important interval must naturally have so influenced circumstances as to render utterly unsuitable to the present hour that plan to which the past movements of this campaign have been merely preparatory. I now find myself by many cogent reasons obliged to abandon every view of making an effort in this quarter. The precautions which Mr. Washington has had leisure to take make me hopeless of bringing him to a general action, and the season dissuades me strongly from losing time in the attempt.

The weather will admit of our acting in Carolina in the beginning of October, and many motives call our attention to that point. I am convinced by Sir James Wright's and General Prevost's letters to me that, if we do not conquer South Carolina, everything is to be apprehended for Georgia. We have flattering hopes of assistance from the inhabitants held forth to us; and, though I cannot say I think the conquest would have the same serious influence which would have been the

26. *Clinton's note:* All the troops in New York and posts depending, on the 1st of August, amounted to only 14,682 fit for duty and 18,337 effectives, rank and file.

case at an earlier period of the war, it cannot fail to have important consequences. In order to give the effort a fair trial, it is necessary that the corps destined for that service should get there before Mr. Washington can throw any considerable reinforcement to the southward [and] before, also, any part of the French fleet (which by the junction of la Motte-Picquet may be superior to ours in the West Indies) shall have come upon the coast.

I am therefore employing the army to perfect the defenses of this post, which at all events must be left out of reach of any probable insult. I shall then give the enemy every jealousy to the eastward; and, without losing a moment, the expedition will proceed to South Carolina. Having seized on the stations of Verplanck's and Stony Point on the Hudson River with a view of offensive operations in this country, their principal importance must cease when that design is discarded. And, as without great reinforcements (which we cannot now expect) nothing of consequence can be carried on again in this quarter, I shall probably abandon those posts, not having troops sufficient without hazard and difficulty to maintain them through the winter. [Partially printed in *ibid.*, pp. 140–141.]

Extract of a letter from Brigadier General MacLean to Lord George Germain. Penobscot, August 26th, 1779.

Having received Sir Henry Clinton's directions to establish a post on the River Penobscot, I landed here on the 26th of June with a detachment consisting of 650 rank and file from the Seventy-fourth and Eighty-second Regiments. The difficulties in clearing the wood, landing our provisions and stores, etc., made it be the 2d of July before the intended fort could be marked out. On the 21st of July, when I received information of the sailing of a considerable armament from Boston for the purpose of reducing us, two of the bastions of the intended fort were untouched; and the remaining two, with the curtains, were in no part above four or five feet in height and twelve in thickness, the ditch in most parts not above three feet in depth, no platform laid nor any artillery mounted. However, relying on the zeal and ardor which appeared in all ranks, we laid aside all thoughts of finishing it, and employed ourselves in putting the post in the best posture of defense the shortness of the time would admit. His Majesty's ships *Albany, North,* and *Nautilus* were in the river, the commanders of which joined their efforts to ours for our mutual safety.

On the 25th the enemy's fleet, to the number of thirty-seven sail, appeared in sight; and at two in the afternoon their armed vessels began cannonading our ships of war and a battery of four twelve-pounders, which I had thrown up on the bank of the river for the protection of the shipping. The warmth with which it was returned soon obliged them to retire and anchor off the west end of the peninsula on which they [the twelve-pounders?] were posted. On the morning of the 28th, under cover of a very heavy cannonade, they (to my great astonishment) effected a landing and obliged the advanced picket to retire to the fort. We were now obliged to withdraw all our outposts and confine our attention to strengthening our works.

On the 30th the enemy opened a battery at 750 yards' distance and, a few days after, another 50 yards nearer, from both which they cannonaded us briskly—notwithstanding which our work went on with great spirit. The gorge of one of the unfinished bastions was filled up with logs; and, as our well was in the other, we carried a work of fascines and earth ten feet thick round it. Platforms were laid and artillery mounted, by which we were enabled to return their fire. A sort of *chevaux-de-frise* was carried round the fort and, without that, a tolerable abatis; so that we daily increased in strength, and in a few days were out of all apprehensions of being stormed.

From the 30th of July to the 12th of August the cannonading continued with great spirit on both sides. On the 14th they abandoned their works, on the appearance of a fleet of His Majesty's ships under Sir George Collier. I have, consequently, only to add my congratulations to Your Lordship on the entire destruction of the rebel armament —not one vessel having escaped being either taken or burned, and their army (which at first consisted of from twenty-five hundred to three thousand men) being dispersed and endeavoring to escape through the woods to the westward.[27]

[Extract of Major Drummond and Colonel Innes to Clinton. New York, September 13, 1779.]

In a conference we had with Lord George Germain, His Lordship did us the honor to inform us that it was concluded upon that the provincials should have rank upon the same footing as it was fixed last war by Lord Amherst, and that permanent rank and half pay would be given to the officers of those corps that should be recommended by Your Excellency as deserving this particular mark of the King's favor. His Lordship at the same time wished to know our sentiments, whether we thought this would be agreeable to you, sir, as commander in chief—

27. *Clinton's note:* Total loss of the King's troops twenty-three killed, thirty-five wounded, and eleven missing.

as on this, and indeed on every, occasion it is but justice to His Lordship to acknowledge he showed the greatest anxiety to give you every satisfaction in his power.

The reasons which the Minister has given to Your Excellency might have been sufficient to make us believe that the measure could not have been disagreeable to you. Yet upon this head, sir, we did not presume to speak *positively* or *officially* of your wishes, never having had any instructions from you on that subject. We only assented to what had been done as, in our *private* opinion, it might meet with your approbation. Unhappily we find ourselves mistaken, and have only to lament that the event has not corresponded with our zeal and anxiety for your satisfaction.

[Extract] from Major General Campbell to Sir Henry Clinton. Pensacola, 14th September 1779.

A dispatch I this moment have received from Lieutenant Colonel Dickson informs me that on the 20th *ultimo* the independence of the American states was publicly declared by beat of drum at New Orleans, that on the 29th of the same month two of our transports that were returning from the Amite River (where they had landed a detachment of the Regiment of Waldeck) were seized at Galveztown, and [that] Governor Galvez was marching with a considerable force toward Manchac.[28] [Hist. MSS Com., *American MSS in the Royal Institution*, 2, 31.]

[Extract from Clinton to Dalling. New York, September 16, 1779.]

On the knowledge you have obtained of the enemy's designs I cannot hesitate sending the whole British force which can be spared from this important post. Your Excellency is acquainted with the restriction to which I am submitted with respect to foreigners and provincials. The command will, I believe, amount to near 4000 men under Earl Cornwallis, who with his accustomed zeal offers himself for this service. Admiral Arbuthnot, equally attentive to the importance of the object you represent in danger, contributes nearly his whole force in line-of-battle ships.

28. The Amite River flows into Lake Maurepas, in eastern Louisiana; Galveztown (Galvez) is some twenty miles west of the lake. Manchac was not the present town of that name, but a post at the intersection of the Mississippi River and what is now called Bayou Manchac.

Extract of a letter from Sir Henry Clinton to Lieutenant General Earl Cornwallis. New York, September 23d, 1779.

Respecting the service Your Lordship so handsomely desires to conduct (and which you will not permit me to object to), as I am entirely ignorant of the state of Jamaica, its force, or Governor Dalling's projected defensive, I am a little at a loss how to advise. I do not think it likely that the French should attempt the island before the Spaniards join. And, by all accounts, that can scarcely happen before your arrival. Governor Dalling will of course have collected magazines, and taken some strong position with his whole force near the mountains, in hopes of reinforcement; a junction with him will depend upon intelligence, etc. If that is judged impracticable, an attempt upon the enemy's magazines (which, as it will not be expected, may easily succeed) will relieve Governor Dalling; and, a junction once made, the sooner the enemy is brought to action the better, for reasons most obvious.

You know, my good Lord, how far this expedition to Jamaica interferes with our intended southern move. But I confess I think it more important, and I hope the first is only delayed. I therefore request [that] Your Lordship, as soon as the business at Jamaica is completed, will with the troops under your command (excepting such as you shall judge necessary to leave at Jamaica) join me by the most expeditious route at Savannah, unless West Florida should be threatened—in which case I should think it advisable to send a force to its relief and, if possible, to lay hold of New Orleans, which would undoubtedly give us the Mississippi and all the southern Indians. If West Florida [29] should not be threatened, nor likely to be, I still shall think a reinforcement necessary. It must be of at least 1000 men.

I do not mean to tie Your Lordship down by any orders, but submit the whole to your judgment on the spot, giving only my opinion as things appear to me.[30] Respecting my own [31] operations, they will depend upon my determination to keep or withdraw [from] Rhode Island. At all events, I fear I shall not be able to stir this month.

29. Clinton's autograph draft of this letter here reads "Georgia."
30. Clinton here omits the following sentence in his draft: "If you determine to send troops to West Florida, I must beg leave to name them in course, that the *odium*, if any, may not fall on you."
31. The draft reads "*our* operations."

Extract of a letter from Sir Henry Clinton to Vice Admiral Arbuthnot. New York, 26th September 1779.

After our conversation of this morning I of course think seriously of withdrawing the troops from Rhode Island. On Colonel Stuart's return from thence we shall be able to judge what directions to give for the final evacuation of the place. When I say final, I would submit to you whether it would not be better to keep a small post at Rhode Island, as it will prevent the rebels from getting entire possession of the island without the assistance of the Bourbons. And if, contrary to your opinion, they [the French] should not come on this coast, or should be followed close by Byron, the holding any part of it may be of consequence. This, however, I submit to you.

[Extract of Germain to Clinton. September 27, 1779.]

The very important service you propose to employ a part of the troops under your command in effecting in the month of October is an object of such vast importance that I would not on any account suggest the most distant idea of changing it for any other. The feeble resistance Major General Prevost met with in his march and retreat through so great a part of South Carolina is an indubitable proof of the indisposition of the inhabitants to support the rebel government. The possession of Charleston would therefore, I flatter myself, be attended with the recovery of the whole of that province; and probably North Carolina would soon follow, and present you with a pleasing occasion of exercising the powers His Majesty has invested you with of granting pardon and restoring to the King's peace those valuable countries.

The other enterprise you meditate on the side of Chesapeake Bay cannot, I am persuaded, fail of accelerating the great end of all the King's American measures, the suppression of the rebellion. And I shall hear with particular pleasure that you have found means to establish a post at Portsmouth in Virginia, as that situation appears to be so well circumstanced as a station for the men-of-war and privateers to intercept the trade of that province and Maryland whilst they persist in rebellion, which [trade], with that of Carolina and Georgia, have furnished the Congress with the chief means of purchasing supplies for carrying on the war.

The severe blow Sir George Collier has given to the rebel force at Penobscot, by entirely destroying the shipping employed in the attempt to dislodge Colonel MacLean, must deprive the people of the New England provinces of their great resource from privateering, and prove a considerable security to the navigation of the King's faithful subjects. I was always of opinion that the most effectual mode of distressing those provinces was by destroying their shipping. And it is most honorable for Sir George Collier to have performed more by his spirited and able exertions with his small force than has been effected in any former year of the rebellion, when the force was so greatly superior.

I have heard with great pleasure from Captain Dixon that the dissensions and jealousies among the members of Congress continue to enervate, and that the people's repugnance to serve in their army becomes every day greater. As it may be expected that France and Spain will immediately detach some ships to the West Indies, and as in the winter season our large ships can be of no use in North America, orders are sent out by this conveyance to Admiral Arbuthnot to send three of the line to join the Leeward Island squadron. But they will be replaced early in the spring, when we hope to be better able to spare ships of the line from hence than at present. Should affairs with you have taken so fortunate a turn as that you could think New York and Rhode Island in safety through the winter with smaller garrisons than those you may have in your power to reserve for them after supplying your southern services, the *departure of these ships would furnish a safe conveyance for whatever you could spare during the season of inaction to the northward.* I can take upon me to assure you that such a mark of attention to the security of the sugar colonies would give great pleasure to all ranks in this country. [Hist. MSS Com., *MSS of Mrs. Stopford-Sackville*, 2, 143–145.]

Extract of a letter from Admiral Arbuthnot to Sir Henry Clinton. *Europe*, Sandy Hook, October 6th, 1779.

If Your Excellency recollects, the several conversations which we have had respecting the evacuating of Rhode Island originated in the idea of strengthening the corps that might be employed to the southward; in the course of which I gave it as my opinion that a powerful diversion might be made for their assistance by my entering the Chesapeake and attacking Virginia with the whole of the King's ships and a small number of troops, and that the troops at Rhode Island, in my opinion, might be employed better on this service than remaining at that place, *which hitherto had never been of the smallest use to the navy. And in that idea I still remain.* [Stevens, *Facsimiles*, 10, No. 1010.]

Extract of a letter from Sir Henry Clinton to Vice Admiral Arbuthnot. October 6th, 1779.

I presume, however, to enter so far on a subject on which you are so much more able to determine as to invite you to consider whether, supposing d'Estaing should penetrate into this harbor, Rhode Island would not become an object of the utmost importance for Admiral Byron's fleet, which we may naturally suppose will follow; and whether we should not, by preserving that place, keep him a better harbor than the French could have, and indeed the only one where he could assemble his fleet on this coast. [*Ibid.*, No. 1011.]

Extract of a letter from Sir Henry Clinton to Admiral Arbuthnot. 16th October 1779.

I am honored with your letter enclosing the translated account of the armament under Count d'Estaing. The objects threatened appear from this paper to be Halifax and Newfoundland. You are the best judge whether his original plan may still be pursued at this advanced season. But, should you, sir, think it the most advisable measure to go to Halifax with the fleet under your command, I will on the shortest notice order such a reinforcement to attend you as with the resources of General MacLean will, I conceive by the proportion of troops required, give the harbor, town, dock, and stores all the protection they can derive from the land defenses.

Extract from Admiral Arbuthnot's answer. [Arbuthnot to Clinton.] *Europe,* Sandy Hook, October 18th, 1779.

Notwithstanding the troops are all this day embarked and everything ready to proceed, I am sorry to say (from the first of this succor to Halifax being intended to this instant) the sea has been so rough upon the bar that none of the large ships could encounter with it. Which unfortunate circumstance at this advanced season, together with the length of time since it has been known Count d'Estaing has arrived on this coast, [makes it probable] that he must have either accomplished his purposes, or the boisterous winds which have been experienced in all parts of this coast since his arrival must have compelled him to abandon them.

Those considerations have *induced me to alter my first intention.* And, instead of risking the King's troops at this advanced season to the northward, I have sent a very swift-sailing little vessel with orders to land and by every means to come at the state of Halifax—*which leaves me at liberty to tender my assistance in cooperating with the utmost zeal [in anything] wherein the ships under my command may be useful in future.* [Stevens, *Facsimiles, 10,* No. 1015.]

Extract of an intercepted letter from General Washington to Brigadier General du Portail and Lieutenant Colonel Hamilton, who were sent on an embassy to Count d'Estaing. West Point, 18th October 1779.

I have attentively considered the object to which you have particularly referred, and am now to authorize you (provided the Count will not determine on a cooperation to the full extent of my instructions) to engage the whole force described in my letters to him, comprehending the Continental troops and the militia, in such an enterprise against the enemy's shipping as the Count and you may agree to undertake. In a word, I will aid him in any plan of operation against the enemy at New York or Rhode Island in the most effectual manner that our strength and resources will admit. He has, therefore, nothing more to do than to propose his own plan if time will not permit him to accede to ours, weighing thoroughly the consequences of expense and disappointment. Every proper attention has been given to preparing the necessary number of fascines and such other materials as may be requisite in this quarter. Fascines, gabions, etc., are also held in readiness at Providence in case of an operation against Newport. I had thought of the fireships, and have taken order in this matter. I do not, however, choose to go to the great expense these must run us to, till something is decided with His Excellency Count d'Estaing; but everything relative to it shall be provided so far as to occasion no delay when such matters become necessary. [Fitzpatrick, *Writings of Washington, 16,* 483–484.]

Extract of a letter from Vice Admiral Arbuthnot to Sir Henry Clinton. October 19th, 1779.

When I had the honor to give Your Excellency my opinion with respect to the evacuation of Rhode Island as a post no way useful as a situation for ships of war—and sure I am it was not, nor do I conceive it ever could [have been] under our circumstances at that time. But, if Count d'Estaing has taken Halifax, I would leave it to your consideration whether, if it can be done, the suspension of the evacuation of the island may not take place for a moment, because New York is not a place for large ships. I hope, sir, you understand that I conceive, while we possess Halifax, that I considered Rhode Island as not worth—for any utility to the King's fleet—either the expense of the garrison or the ships of war that has been employed in keeping possession. But without Halifax it becomes another question—which, at the time the idea of abandoning it took place, neither yourself nor your humble servant could foresee. [Stevens, *Facsimiles, 10,* No. 1016.]

Extract from Sir Henry Clinton's answer. [Clinton to Arbuthnot.] New York, October 19th, 1779.

In answer to your proposal that I should recall my orders for evacuating Rhode Island, I have the honor to inform you that as, before, I received my first idea of quitting it from you, so I now follow your opinion in deferring the evacuation until we have some accounts from Halifax.[32] The officer you send tells me he has your orders to send off a ship with my dispatches to Rhode Island before he leaves New York. I have not, therefore, time to hesitate; but send directions, in whatever stage the operations may be, to desist and even reoccupy the debris of the works (which I fear will be already demolished) unless the situation should be so critical as to have had positive information of the approach of the French fleet, or that an enemy should have so situated himself before the post that evident destruction would attend the attempt to keep possession.

In the meantime I should wish speedily to consider with you how far the motives which induced us to withdraw the garrison of Rhode Island are invalidated by the supposed reduction of Halifax. It can hardly be necessary for me to call your attention to the ill consequences which might be apprehended should the French squadron come upon the garrison under the circumstances in which these orders will place them. [*Ibid.,* No. 1018.]

Extract of a letter from Admiral Arbuthnot to Sir Henry Clinton. October 22d, 1779.

I am now ready to leave this place when I have the honor of your dispatches. I beg you will send them, as the wind is now fair, and I wish to go to sea tomorrow. [*Ibid.,* No. 1020.]

[Extract of Clinton to Arbuthnot. October 22, 1779.]

Since you left me this morning I have been considering the situation in which your request to reoccupy Rhode Island has placed me. To do

32. Clinton here omits the following sentence in his original letter in the CP: "The taking this new resolution would have been attended with much less difficulty had I received your hint on the subject earlier."

it before the winter sets in, I fear it will be necessary for me to send reinforcement there; and consequently I can little spare that which goes with you, sir, to Halifax. I will, however, send near 1500 men, exclusive of the Seventh Regiment (which, being the weakest, I request may be sent up from the Hook as soon as possible); Colonel Stuart will proceed with my orders to General Prescott as soon as the frigate you were so kind as to promise for his conveyance arrives. [*Ibid.*, No. 1021.]

Extract from a [second] letter from Sir Henry Clinton to Admiral Arbuthnot. October 22d, 1779.

An expedition to Carolina was a principal object, and one having reference to that (or, indeed, of importance enough of itself) to the Chesapeake was another. From the first we were diverted by the rumor of an attack being intended on Jamaica. The advices of the French fleet being on this coast were, soon after, a reason no less coercive to deter us from our designs; and at this hour the threatened state of Halifax again calls off our attention and our powers. The arguments for attacking the southern settlements would still prevail had not such events intervened; and they will reassume their full force when these shall cease to operate. Permit me then, sir, *to request that we do not relinquish our original and most important projects* until we are so unfortunate as to see them totally impracticable. In this idea let me hope you have it in view, so soon as Halifax shall from the climate or incidents be restored to security, to bring back both the ships and troops in order at length to act.

I would now, sir, trouble you with my own reflections concerning Count d'Estaing's armament. He must be at this time coming to Rhode Island, to this place, or have put into Boston on his way to Halifax. His squadron must else have quitted the coast, or have taken refuge in Boston for the winter. If I may give an opinion in these matters, it is that the season is too far advanced for him to have offensive designs at all on this coast, particularly against Halifax. But, if he has fixed himself at Boston for the winter, or if he has quitted the coast, the strongest reasons exist for directing our thoughts to the southward, both to reinforce what may be weak or to attack what may be unguarded. Georgia and Pensacola chiefly claim our attention as requiring succor, Charleston and New Orleans as points whereby well timed exertions may possibly reap some brilliant advantage. The hopes of a blow against the Spaniard may be connected with the business of relieving Pensacola (by an expedition from Jamaica) with troops which we might deposit there. The relieving Georgia will in like manner go hand in hand with attacking Carolina. Other more desultory operations may also be occasionally undertaken whilst we have ships and troops in those climates. I have thus wished, in taking leave of you, to recite what have been our joint intentions and what has suspended their effect. [*Ibid.*, No. 1023.]

Extract from the Admiral's answer. [Arbuthnot to Clinton.] October 23d [1779].

I will do myself the honor to answer your letter of yesterday's date fully tomorrow, and I hope to Your Excellency's satisfaction—because nothing has ever been nearer my heart than to put an end to this ruinous war as far as my poor abilities could direct the enfeebled force under my command. [*Ibid.*, No. 1024.]

[Extract of Arbuthnot to Clinton. October 24, 1779.]

However flattering the prospect of success to His Majesty's arms might appear on my arrival in this country, the vigilance of the enemy has hitherto frustrated our attempts to promote it. I need not recite the catalogue of our disappointments. But from that time to this instant I have not seen a possibility of more than defensive action, the force of the enemy at sea being so decisively superior to that under my command. Under this circumstance we have made every exertion to secure ourselves, though we remained ignorant of their designs until the dispatches lately taken in the Spanish packet from the Havana gave us the fullest information. The contents of these dispatches have already been communicated to Your Excellency, and Halifax is therein pointed out as a principal object against which d'Estaing's operations are to be directed. Being acquainted therewith and well informed of its naval consequence, it is my duty to make every possible effort for its relief.

But, if Your Excellency has any immediate and more important object in view, I will yet give up my design of going thither, and act in all things conformable to your wishes and intentions to promote the King's service. *I beg Your Excellency will favor me with the particulars of your southern plan of operation* and the time when likely to take place. Your Excellency may rest assured I have not relinquished any part of our original plan of operations, but have only made temporary alterations thereof according to circumstances. And I only·now go upon this service because you have assured me you have no immediate intention to carry it into execution.

With respect to the return to this post of the troops now with me and the ships of the line so soon as Halifax can be considered either from climate or incidents to be in a state of security, I beg leave to observe to Your Excellency that, whenever *it becomes unsafe to enter the port of Halifax, it is equally dangerous to come upon this coast;* but, as far as depends upon me, *the transports shall not want a strong convoy. The ships of the line cannot winter in the port of New York, much less can they come upon the coast near it,* being of all others the most dangerous for large ships. But, if Your Excellency wishes I should cooperate with you in Virginia with the ships of the line, I shall use my utmost efforts to be there at any time you may please to appoint. [*Ibid.*, No. 1025.]

Extract from Sir Henry Clinton's answer. [Clinton to Arbuthnot.] October 24th, 1779.

I will forbear resting upon topics we have already discussed, but give you simply my sentiments upon those matters wherein you hint a wish that I should explain myself further. Until the blow which you suppose impending from Count d'Estaing is averted or decided, I can have no thoughts of offensive operations to interfere with your desire to succor Halifax. From the very industrious researches your cruisers are to make, the fate of Georgia will soon be known. My first wish will be to strengthen that province beyond the fear of insult. Pensacola will claim the same attention. It is not at this time possible to detail further operations, which may be more or less important as the draining our strength by reinforcements may variously affect our powers, or as the proximity or distance of an enemy in force may warrant our undertakings. But the main point in contemplation is, as it has ever been and as it stands confirmed by His Majesty's approbation, *the reduction of Carolina.* This plan I consider as much improved by your project of visiting the Chesapeake. I am in the prospect of meeting you to execute it; nor shall I fail to seize the moment for consulting and acting with you in those seas, either according to our present views or such as we may jointly adopt. [*Ibid.*, No. 1026.]

Extract of a [second] letter from Sir Henry Clinton to Vice Admiral Arbuthnot. October 24th [1779].

In consequence of the orders I had written to General Prescott at your request, to suspend the evacuation of Rhode Island till he received further orders from me, that post must be in a most dangerous situation. I represented this to you, sir, on the 22d, and requested that a frigate might be sent with my further most necessary instructions immediately. You promised that a frigate should be sent up and proceed with Colonel Stuart through the sound. You afterward proposed that he should go down to the Hook and proceed from thence in the *Virginia*. Colonel Stuart, accordingly, was so good to go down to the Hook yesterday morning; and, returning to me this night, tells me that the *Virginia* is in such a state that she cannot proceed to Rhode Island and return here, but must go from thence to Halifax. The Colonel tells me you are pleased to order the *Solebay*. But, as I am informed she cannot be ready for three or four days, I must in the most formal and earnest manner request that you will be so good to order a frigate to proceed with my dispatches to Rhode Island immediately, as I cannot but repeat that an hour's delay in the present state of that place may be most fatal.

Extract from Admiral Arbuthnot's answer. [Arbuthnot to Clinton.] *Europe*, October 25th, 1779.

I understood from Your Excellency's letter of the 22d instant that it was possible your orders to suspend the evacuation of Rhode Island had arrived too late, and hence I concluded it must have already taken place. Notwithstanding the *Delaware*, the only frigate here, is to be employed on a very important service, I have ordered Captain Mason to receive Colonel Stuart on board, and to proceed with him thither as expeditiously as possible.

Extract of a letter from Sir Henry Clinton to Lord George Germain. New York, 29th October 1779.

I request Your Lordship will do me the honor to charge yourself with expressing to His Majesty the very grateful sense I have of the high honor done me, and the increased degree of confidence he has been pleased to repose in me, in the commission he has appointed me to fill. I have ever thought it was essential to our hopes of success in this country that such powers should be vested in those who hold the command in chief.

And in my concern for His Majesty's service I am happy to observe that the commission is made inherent in the command, and will consequently devolve uninterrupted to my successor, should I have obtained His Majesty's most gracious acquiescence in my prayer to be recalled. In the same ardent wish that a unity of plan and vigor in execution may pervade the operations of His Majesty's arms through any change in the commander of his forces, I have strove to interest Lord Cornwallis in the measures I judge most expedient for the King's service, and to avail myself of His Lordship's counsels. It is with the greatest satisfaction I inform Your Lordship that our opinions entirely coincide, and that the operations I shall undertake will probably be such as he would with equal earnestness prosecute. [Calendared in Hist. MSS Com., *American MSS in the Royal Institution, 2, 55.*]

Extract of a letter from Major General Prevost to Sir Henry Clinton. Savannah, November 2d, 1779.

On the certainty of having an attack to sustain, all outposts were called in; and by the 16th of September they were all happily got here. On the 12th the French had landed at Beaulieu, distant about thirteen miles, at the head of Ossirbau [Ossabaw Sound]. The officers and men of His Majesty's ships *Fowey, Rose,* and *Keppel,* armed brig, with cannon, stores, etc., were cheerfully brought on shore by Captain Henry. And to the active service of that gentleman, Captain Brown, and their officers and men, together with the indefatigable industry of Captain Moncrieff, commanding engineer, much of our safety has been owing.

It was the 16th before Count d'Estaing appeared before our lines, and we were then in a tolerable condition to receive him. On that morning he sent us a summons to surrender to the arms of France. You will see the spirit in which our answers were written. We certainly wished to gain a little time: we knew that the troops from Beaufort were near at hand, and Colonel Maitland did actually arrive by noon with the first division, about 400 men; and by the same time next day we had all the rest fit for duty except the Hessian artillery, which by some strange neglect was left behind. The enemy on the 23d at night broke ground opposite the left of our center, and by the time the morning fog of the 24th was cleared off had pushed a sap to within 300 yards of our abatis. On the night between the 3d and 4th of October the enemy began to bombard with nine mortars of eight and ten inches, to which was added by dawn of day the fire of thirty-seven pieces of cannon from their batteries and sixteen from the frigate and galleys in the river. These last had frequently before cannonaded the town and the left and center of our lines. And this firing was kept up with intervals till the 9th, when a little before daylight the enemy advanced to attack our lines.

The firing began upon the right of our center in front of the enemy's trenches, and very soon afterward toward the extremities of our right and left. It was still dark, and rendered more so by a very thick fog, so that it was not easy to judge on the sudden where the real attack was intended or how many. No movement was therefore attempted. The troops waited coolly at their several posts to receive the enemy, those in the lines in readiness agreeable to [an] order to sustain the points of attack wherever they should be by charging the enemy whilst entangled with the redoubts in front. Your Excellency will observe by the plan that on our right, in spite of all a judicious engineer could do, the ground still favored the enemy. A deep and swampy hollow covered his approach to within fifty yards of our works, and at some points still nearer. On our left it was not much dissimilar; and, though the approach was not so well covered nor to such an extent, yet there was a sufficient [approach]; and, being firm and clear, it was rather that on which we thought regular troops would choose to act. Here, therefore, we always expected the French, and only the rebels on the right. A real attack was indeed intended here. But the principal, composed of the flower of the French and American armies and led by Count d'Estaing in person, with almost all the principal officers of either army, was made on the right.

They advanced in three columns. But, having taken a wider circuit than was necessary and gone deeper in the bog, they neither came at the time nor, I believe, in the order they intended. The attack, however, certainly was spirited and for some time obstinately persevered in, particularly on the Ebenezer road redoubt. Two stand of colors were actually planted, and several of the assailants killed, upon its parapet. But here they met with so determined a resistance that they were put at least to a stand. At this critical moment Major Glazier of the Sixtieth, with the Sixtieth grenadiers and a small company of marines, advancing rapidly from the lines, they were thrown into irretrievable disorder. In an instant the ditches of the redoubt and of a battery to its right in rear were cleared, the enemy being driven in confusion over the abatis into the swamp.

It was now daylight, but the fog was not so entirely off as to enable us to judge with certainty of the numbers and further intentions of the enemy in this quarter. From the center to the left the fog was still impenetrably thick; and, a pretty smart firing being kept up there, it was not judged proper to draw together a number sufficient for a respectable sortie to take that advantage of the confusion of the enemy which, had we known, we might have done. We contented ourselves with plying them with our cannon, advancing some fieldpieces to the abatis as long as they were in sight or judged within reach. They retired everywhere in disorder and with precipitation.

Our loss on this occasion was one captain and fifteen rank and file killed, one captain, three subalterns, and thirty-five rank and file wounded. That of the enemy we do not exaggerate when we set it down from 1000 to 1200 in killed and wounded. We buried within and near the abatis 203 on the right, on the left 28, and delivered 116 wounded prisoners, the greater part mortally. They themselves, by permission, buried those who lay more distant. Many no doubt were self-buried in the mud of the swamp, and many carried off. Among the wounded, Count d'Estaing in two places, Count Pulaski (since dead), Monsieur de Fontanges (Major General), and several other officers of distinction.

From this to the 18th, nothing very remarkable happened. The enemy was employed in moving off the cannon, mortars, etc., and embarking the sick and wounded. We continued to be alert and work as formerly. A little firing at intervals, particularly in the night. On the morning of the 18th, the fog clearing up about nine o'clock, we were not displeased to find the enemy had abandoned their works. The French embarked in Augustine Creek; the rebels crossed at Zubly's Ferry.[33]

Our strength Your Excellency will see by the returns. The French land forces, consisting of the Brigade of Dillon, the Regiment of Foix, the Grenadiers, Chasseurs, and Pickets of Armagnac, Agénois, Béarn, and Royal Roussillon, and of their West India corps, with the marines, amounted to about 5500. Of these were landed near 4000 at first, and after at twice [sic] 800 men. They had besides some hundreds of blacks and mulattoes. Their further destination, according to our best information, is: Count d'Estaing with eleven sail of the line to France, four to Brest, and seven to Toulon; Monsieur la Motte-Picquet and five sail to the Chesapeake, Monsieur de Grasse and six sail to Martinique with all the troops. Three or four stout frigates and *flûtes* are to remain some time at least at Charleston. [Calendared in *ibid.*, p. 57.]

Copy of a letter from Lord George Germain to Sir Henry Clinton. Whitehall, November 4th, 1779 (received 19th March 1780).

Sir:

I did not omit the earliest opportunity of laying before His Majesty your letter of 20th of August, in which you express your desire of being permitted to return to England and resign the command of the troops to Lord Cornwallis. Though the King has great confidence in His Lordship's abilities, yet His Majesty is too well satisfied with your conduct to wish to see the command of his forces in any other hands. You have had too recent proofs of His Majesty's favor to doubt of his royal approbation. The reinforcements sent you have been as ample as could be afforded in the present situation of this country, when so many different services must be attended to and when the

33. On the Savannah River near the present Purysburg, S.C.

powerful enemies we are engaged with require the utmost exertions for the protection of this kingdom and for the defense of its extensive dominions. In times like these every officer, every subject, is called upon to stand forth in the defense of his sovereign and of his country. And, if a general declines the service because the force he commands is not adequate to his wishes or may not enable him to extend his offensive operations with that rapidity he might expect, by whom is this country to be served in dangerous and critical situations? Though your army is much diminished, yet you have shown that activity and good conduct can insure success. Your settlement at Penobscot, your expedition to Virginia, your subduing of Georgia, and the late operations under Major General Tryon are recent proofs of what I assert. And I must add that generals gain at least as much honor by their able management of small armies as when they act with a superiority that commands success. If, however, you shall still under the present circumstances wish to retire, upon receiving your final resolution upon that subject I shall lay it immediately before the King; and I should hope that His Majesty, though reluctantly, would comply with your request. I am, sir, etc., George Germain. [Calendared in *ibid.*]

Extract of a [second] letter from Lord George Germain to Sir Henry Clinton. Whitehall, November 4th, 1779 (received April, 1780).

I laid the memorial of several lieutenant colonels and majors of His Majesty's regular troops serving in North America before the King, in which they conceive themselves affected by His Majesty's order, notified the 2d of May last, on the subject of rank lately given to the officers of the provincial troops. Nothing could be further from His Majesty's intentions than that the field officers of the army, who have so much distinguished themselves for their zeal and ability during the present war, should suffer any injury to their respective pretensions from the encouragement necessary to be given to the provincials by restoring them to the rank provincial officers formerly enjoyed, and which is still inferior to what is granted to officers in regiments lately raised here upon a similar footing. But I must observe that officers in the army who have accepted commissions in these new corps have not been allowed to keep their former commissions; and, as I understand much discontent has arisen in America from British officers serving in the provincials and commanding in a superior rank to that they are entitled to in the army, His Majesty thinks proper to order that no officer shall at the same time hold commissions in the regulars and provincials, but that they do make their option in which corps they will serve, resigning the one or the other of their commissions. [Calendared in *ibid.*, p. 58.]

[Extract of Major General Campbell to Clinton. Pensacola, November 7, 1779.]

Since my letter of the 14th September I have nothing to present Your Excellency with but relations of misfortunes, vexations, and disappointments. Lieutenant Colonel Dickson's capitulation on or about the 20th day of September, whereby the territories on the Mississippi lately belonging to Great Britain are now under the dominion of Spain and the troops he commanded incapacitated from serving against Spain or her allies for eighteen months from the date of the capitulation, is too well ascertained by repeated intelligence to admit the smallest doubt of its being fatally true.[34] Don Galvez' previous information of the declaration of war, added to his situation, gave him every advantage over us that he could wish or desire.

I have now to report to Your Excellency the little prospect I have of reinforcement or aid from either inhabitants or Indians in case of Pensacola or Mobile being attacked. There are no militia laws in being within this province to enforce the services of the former, and they seem averse and backward to military duty without they are thereunto compelled by law; and, as to the Choctaw Indians, they seem to be estranged and seduced from our interest. Of the troops that now remain under my command, sixty-three sergeants and seven hundred and twenty-four rank and file are returned fit for duty. But I can assure Your Excellency that above 100 of these are perfect invalids, which Your Excellency may easily conceive when you are informed that only the infirm and unfit for service of the Sixteenth Regiment were left here. Colonel Dickson was permitted and, indeed, ordered to carry with him all such and only such as he judged fit for active service, and in general not one invalid, sick, or infirm was ever sent off from here for the Mississippi.

Your Excellency will hence judge of the expediency and necessity of sending me reinforcements, as I am by the late disaster altogether disabled from executing His Majesty's expectations and commands signified to me in a letter from the Right Honorable Lord George Germain of the 24th of June last. And, indeed, I must even add that, chiefly from want of a naval force and partly from the still unfinished and ruinous condition of this garrison, my state of defense is not very respectable. [Calendared in *ibid.*, p. 59.]

34. See Fortescue, *British Army, 3*, 302.

[Extract of Major General Campbell to Clinton. Pensacola, December 15, 1779.]

I have to report to Your Excellency that, notwithstanding the Right Honorable Lord George Germain's repeated information that whatever was judged necessary to be sent from Great Britain either for the construction or defense of a post to be erected on the Mississippi had been shipped in the *Earl Bathurst*, ordnance store-ship, so long ago as the month of October, 1778, yet on her arrival it appears that not one single article was shipped on board her for this place—notwithstanding we are almost entirely destitute of field artillery, are greatly in want of shot, have only been supplied with powder by seizing on what belonged to merchants (and even that affords but a moderate quantity), are entirely without cartridge paper of every kind, in short are almost run out of a vast number of useful and necessary articles relative to artillery, engineer's department, etc.

Gage Hill, at the distance of nearly a thousand yards from this garrison, entirely commanding it by its greater elevation of nearly sixty perpendicular feet, I have judged it absolutely necessary to erect a small, square log work with demi-bastions on the top of it, the inward area of which consists of one hundred feet square; and the ramparts are nearly about half carried up, so that I am in hopes (notwithstanding the immense[ly] tedious progress in erecting works) to have the platforms laid and the guns mounted on it by the first day of February next. When this work is finished and a few outworks added, I presume to say it will contribute more to the real and effectual security of this place, should it ever be attacked, than all the works [hitherto] erected at Pensacola. I have to acknowledge Your Excellency's attention in furnishing us with provisions to replace those lost in the *Lord Townshend*, victualer. [Calendared in *ibid.*, p. 72.]

Extract of a letter from Admiral Arbuthnot to Sir Henry Clinton. December 23d [1779].

Will you permit me to offer my reasons to enter the Chesapeake, if the weather will permit, previous to our advancing further to the south? We know that some French ships of war are in the Chesapeake, and that the *Fendant* is one of them, of seventy-four guns. Will it not be better to destroy those ships if possible, and thereby secure our rear?

[Extract of Arbuthnot to Clinton. December 25, 1779.]

The wind is now from the northeast and coming on to blow, which has rendered my standing from the land proper and necessary. I shall endeavor in the evening, if the wind proves favorable, to regain the port. But, if I should be disappointed, I leave to escort Your Excellency two forties and two frigates, a force sufficient to protect the armament until you rejoin me off the Capes of the Chesapeake—where, finding myself thus circumstanced, I shall impatiently await you.

Extract from Sir Henry Clinton's answer. [Clinton to Arbuthnot.] *Romulus*, Sandy Hook, December 26th, 1779.

The delay of some of the transports in coming down was occasioned by the necessity of new arrangements, in consequence of seven ships being drove from their anchors by the ice and rendered unfit for sea.

I must still be of the same uniform opinion that no secondary object should make us deviate from the purpose for which we sail. We are invited to it most urgently by the season, and by everything we hear of the enemy's measures. The attention of government is turned to this, and the carrying it into execution is looked for with solicitude.

Permit me, sir, to observe how precarious a hope it is that we shall find ships (or even a ship, having reason to fear us) unprotected by works on shore which we could not force but by siege, or in any situation but at a great distance from the Capes of Virginia. And those circumstances might engage us in operations of a greater extent than our time and our primary design will permit us to think of. Nor would success against one or two ships justify an interruption in the only essential business we have undertaken.

I am sure, sir, you will take in good part my having given you my opinion thus freely. Yet, with all my anxiety to get to the southward, should you by keeping near the shore (which I presume to be your intention) learn anything further on your arrival off the Capes of Virginia to lessen in any material degree the objection I have taken the liberty to offer, I submit the matter to your decision and will cheerfully follow your signal.

[Extract of Clinton to Arbuthnot. March 4, 1780.]

I am honored with your letters of the 1st and 3d instant. I took the liberty some time since of making known to you our distress as to cannon and stores, in a great measure owing to the loss of the *Russia Merchant*, ordnance ship. I have given Major Trail, commanding the detachment of artillery on this service, directions to purchase the powder at Providence. In the meantime, if you can spare us 120 barrels to replace that lost in the *Russia Merchant* and 200 rounds for each of the guns you are so good to let us have, I hope we shall hold out until it arrives. I need not say that whatever further quantity can be spared, from the large ships going probably to New York, will be replaced on their arrival there. In addition to the eight thirty-two-pounders you were so good to spare us, I beg you will permit me to request fourteen twenty-four-pounders and ten nine-pounders, with the same proportion of ammunition; the first you were so good to say should be taken from the *Vigilant*. I am persuaded you [will] forgive my importunity, which your repeated obliging offers of assistance will, I hope, justify.

> Admiral Arbuthnot's answer. [Arbuthnot to Clinton.] March 5th, 1780.

I have just received the honor of Your Excellency's letter requesting 120 barrels of gunpowder and 200 rounds of shot to replace those *said to be lost* in the *Russia Merchant*. Permit me to hope that stores of such consequence were not trusted, at the season we set out for this place, in a ship which the master protested was unfit for sea.

I have sent you four thirty-two-pounders out of each of the seventy-four-gun ships, with one hundred rounds of shot, [and] six twenty-four-pounders with the like stores. The *Lord North* is not at present in a condition to go to Providence. As to convoys or dispatching ships to New York, it is impossible at present to determine.

> Extract of a letter from Lord George Germain to the Lords Commissioners of the Admiralty. Whitehall, 15 March 1780 (received by Sir Henry Clinton and Admiral Arbuthnot May 10th).

From the intelligence lately received there is good ground to believe a squadron consisting of twelve ships of the line and some frigates is to convoy a large body of land forces to North America, and to sail from Brest the end of this month. His Majesty therefore commands me to signify to Your Lordships his royal pleasure that you do, without the least delay, reinforce Vice Admiral Arbuthnot with eight ships of the line. And it is His Majesty's further pleasure that you do immediately dispatch an express to Vice Admiral Arbuthnot acquainting him with what it is apprehended are the designs of the enemy, and directing him to assemble his whole force (or such part of it as he shall judge necessary) at New York, where he will be joined by the intended reinforcement. But, should he in the meantime receive any well authenticated information that the destination of the enemy's force is against Quebec or any of His Majesty's possessions within his command, he is in such case to exercise his discretion with respect to the station most proper for him to take, and to dispatch orders accordingly and appoint cruisers to fall in with the reinforcement and direct it to join him at such station as he shall appoint. But, in all cases, he is *to use his utmost diligence to obtain early advice of the arrival of the enemy on the American coast* or wherever may be their destination. And to that end he is to appoint a sufficient number of cruisers at proper stations, and by means of swift-sailing vessels keep up a constant correspondence and intercourse with the commanders of His Majesty's ships on the Leeward Island and Jamaica stations. [Calendared in Hist. MSS Com., *American MSS in the Royal Institution, 2,* 103.]

[Extract of Arbuthnot to Clinton. March 21, 1780.]

I have such demands for all my force upon this occasion that, unless there is absolute necessity with regard to the ammunition, I am rather inclined to wait the arrival of the *Bonetta* from Providence.

Sir Henry Clinton's answer. [Clinton to Arbuthnot.] March 22d, 1780.

I lament with you, sir, that there should be a cause for depriving you of any part of your force at this hour; and it is with regret I find my call for it to arise from the necessities of the army. The supply of powder, however, from Providence I would endeavor to dispense with until the arrival of the ample provision expected from New York, if according to my request it were possible for you to spare me *200 rounds* of ammunition to each gun you have given me. From your own wants, or the demand I was so free to make not being, I fear, clearly expressed, I have received only 100 shot per gun.

Extracts from the handbill distributed by Sir Henry Clinton's orders among the inhabitants of the upper parts of South Carolina and Georgia [filed in the CP under May 12, 1780].

Those who have families will form a militia to remain at home and occasionally to assemble in their own district, when required, under officers of their own choosing for the maintenance of peace and good order. Those who have no families, and can be conveniently spared for a time, it is hoped will cheerfully assist His Majesty's troops in driving the rebel oppressors and all their miseries of war far from the province. For this purpose it is necessary that the young men be ready to assemble when required, and serve with the King's troops for any six months of the ensuing twelve that may be found requisite, under proper regulations. They may choose officers to each company to command them and will be allowed, when on service, pay, ammunition, and provisions in the same manner as the troops. When they join the army, each man will be furnished with a certificate declaring that he is only engaged to serve as a militiaman for the time specified, that he is not to be marched beyond North Carolina and Georgia, and that, when the time is out, he is freed from all claims whatever of military service, except the common and usual militia duty where he lives.

Extracts from the instructions given to Major Ferguson as inspector of militia [May 22, 1780].

In order to procure the general and hearty concurrence of the loyal inhabitants it is of the first importance to limit their service to a precise term, and to remove all distrust that they may entertain of being drawn into the regular service without their consent. For this purpose you will furnish each of them, when they engage, with a written certificate in the following words:

"By order of Sir Henry Clinton, etc., I do hereby certify that A.B. has joined the British army as a militiaman and not as a regular soldier, and has only engaged to serve any six months of the ensuing twelve that may be required. I further certify that he is entitled to six pence British sterling per day and provisions, during the time of his actual service, and that he is not to be obliged under any pretense to march beyond North Carolina or Georgia. And he is hereby absolutely freed from all further claims of serving with the army after the ———, being the expiration of his term."

You will furnish each man with ammunition and oznabrass for a rifle shirt, and when practicable supply those with arms who have none. Those who are averse to serve on foot may be allowed to serve on horseback at their own expense. In a word, you are to endeavor to derive as much advantage as possible from their services at as little expense as may be. You will pay particular attention to restrain the militia from offering violence to innocent and inoffensive people, and by all means in your power protect the aged, the infirm, the women and children of every denomination from insult and outrage. Beside this body of militia, to act offensively with the army, you will promote the establishment of a domestic militia for the maintenance of peace and good order throughout the country, composed of the men who have families, under their own officers, ready to asemble occasionally in their own districts.

[Extract of Cornwallis to Clinton. June 30, 1780.]

I shall now take the liberty of giving my opinion with respect to the practicability and the probable effect of further operations in this quarter, and my own intentions if not otherwise directed by Your Excellency. I think that with the force at present under my command (except there should be a considerable foreign interference) *I can leave South Carolina in security,* and march with a body of troops into the back part of North Carolina *with the greatest probability of reducing that province to its duty.* And, if this is accomplished, I am of opinion that beside the advantages of possessing so valuable a province *it would prove an effectual barrier for South Carolina and Georgia, and could be kept (with the assistance of our friends there) by as few troops as would be wanted on the borders of this province if North Carolina should remain in the hands of our enemies.* Consequently, if Your Excellency should continue to think it expedient to employ part of the troops at present in this province in operations in Chesapeake, *there will be as many* to spare as if we did not possess North Carolina.

If I am not honored with different directions from Your Excellency before that time, I shall take my measures for beginning the execution of the above plan about the latter end of August or beginning of September, and *shall apply* to the officer commanding his Majesty's ships *for some cooperation by Cape Fear,* which *at present* would be burdensome to the navy and *not of much importance to the service.* [Stevens, *Clinton-Cornwallis Controversy, 1,* 225.]

Extract of a letter from Lord George Germain to Sir Henry Clinton. July 4, 1780.

The glorious and important event of the reduction of Charleston and the destruction or capture of the whole rebel land and naval force that defended it gave His Majesty the highest satisfaction, especially as it was achieved with so inconsiderable a loss of his brave troops, a circumstance which in His Majesty's judgment at all times greatly enhances the value of victory and reflects particular honor on a general. And His Majesty commanded me to express to you his entire approbation of your conduct, and to assure you it had very fully answered the very high expectations he had entertained from your great military abilities and zealous exertion of them in his service. I trust you will still find an opportunity of prosecuting your plan of operations in the Chesapeake, from the success of which (added to the reduction of Carolina) I am sanguine enough to expect the recovery of the whole of the southern provinces in the course of the campaign. The accounts of the happy consequences of your success, though not unexpected, gave His Majesty great satisfaction; and the very judicious and well timed publications you issued after the surrender of Charleston were so well calculated to excite the zeal and give confidence to His Majesty's faithful subjects, and at the same time hold out the terrors of due chastisement to all such as should persist in their revolt, that they could not fail of producing the effects you expected from them and of being approved by the King.

[Extract of Cornwallis to Clinton. July 14, 1780] (received August 24).

De Kalb is certainly at Hillsboro with 2000 Continentals, and said to be preparing to advance to Salisbury. Porterfield is in that neighborhood with 300 Virginians. Caswell with 1500 militia is marched from Cross Creek to the Deep River, and Sumter with the same number [h]as advanced as far as the Catawba settlements. The effects of the exertions which the enemy are making in the two Carolinas will, I make no doubt, be exaggerated to us. But, upon the whole, there is every reason to believe that their plan is not only to defend North Carolina, but to commence offensive operations immediately. [Stevens, *Clinton-Cornwallis Controversy, 1,* 232–233.]

Extract of a letter from Sir Henry Clinton to Admiral Arbuthnot. July 15, 1780.

I have every reason to suppose from the Minister's intelligence that Ternay's destination is Canada, and that they will first assemble at Rhode Island. Now, sir, if I am not much mistaken, should they assemble there we may have the fairest prospect (if you are superior to him, and their land force does not exceed 5000 men) of giving to both a mortal blow. I have two plans, in few words as follows:

Supposing the French fleet and army in Rhode Island, my first plan is for you, sir, to mask the entrance of the harbor with your large ships, and your humble servant, when he receives information from you, to go into the Sakonnet Passage with 5000 men and a sufficient number of frigates to cover my landing. If I succeed against the French army, our joint endeavors against their fleet afterward cannot fail. This must not be attempted without you are sure of blocking up the French fleet (or, in case of a gale of wind at east, you will run into the Narragansett Passage), without which the expedition in Sakonnet may be exposed.[35]

35. Clinton's phrasing is obscure. He means that the French fleet must be prevented from interfering with the landing in the Sakonnet but that, if an easterly

The other plan is, the whole to run into Narragansett, your fleet to anchor between Conanicut and Rhode Island [and] cover a landing and by joint attack against fleet and army—or separate against the army —do the business that way. If either of these succeeds, perhaps it will be the shortest way of putting an end to the Canada expedition, and probably the war. If you are superior to Ternay, either of these experiments may be tried with little risk.

Should you not approve of either of these, I may possibly be tempted to make an effort against New London and Connecticut River, in the hopes of relieving Canada when attacked. But, without you, sir, are so good to give me a considerable naval force, I dare not attempt it. A vigilant or two, some galleys, and three or four small frigates will, I should suppose, be sufficient.

> Extract of Admiral Arbuthnot's answer. [Arbuthnot to Clinton.] *Europe*, Sandy Hook, July 16, 1780.

If they [the French] are inferior to me and their first landing is Rhode Island, I am sure that they will be disappointed, *because I think they cannot escape me. And, if I am superior, of course their whole force must submit.* As to armed ships and galleys to cover your proposed descent in Connecticut River, I have not the means at present to prepare them nor seamen to man them. [Clinton, *Narrative of Co-operations*, p. 23.]

> Extract of a letter from Admiral Arbuthnot to Sir Henry Clinton. July 18, 1780.

I am informed by Captain Murray of the arrival of a French squadron at Rhode Island, and honored with Your Excellency's plan of cooperation in consequence thereof. I shall lose no time in proceeding off that port; and, if it is possible to put your plan in execution, you shall hear from me immediately. [*Ibid.*, p. 25.]

> Extract of a letter from Sir Henry Clinton to Admiral Arbuthnot. July 22, 1780.

Captain Murray delivered me your message intimating that nothing but a hurricane could oblige you to quit the coast and abandon me, should I go into the Sakonnet as proposed. With respect to the enemy's numbers in ships, I hope they are not so great as they may have ap-

---

gale should immobilize the enemy, Arbuthnot might shelter in the Narragansett Passage.

peared. At least I am satisfied that you still consider yourself superior to them, as unless that were the case you would not invite me to join you.

I have much to lament that our information of their arrival at Rhode Island came so late. This intelligence came nine days after the enemy's fleet had arrived and, it was said, troops had been landed. With the most favorable winds and with every other advantage we could not have reached Rhode Island before the 22d. I fear we cannot, as things are, be there by the 24th. I am not without apprehension that, time having been given for fortifying the place and assembling a greater force to it, I shall have before me the prospect of a siege instead of a *coup de main*. To this I should neither in numbers, artillery, or other requisites find myself equal. In the hope, however, of an unexpected stroke, I shall make every effort speedily to join you.

The winds still continue adverse. I have therefore requested a frigate may be dispatched with this letter. Captain Savage goes in her, and from him I expect material intelligence. If the French are not considerably reinforced and have not fortified the post, I shall propose as at first to land in the Sakonnet and (whilst you are anchored without, threatening cooperation) to attack them. If, by having had so much time, they are prepared, that plan must of course be set aside, in which case you may perhaps adopt the second I proposed (of entering by the Narragansett) or some other mode which the knowledge you have now obtained of the state of the enemy may suggest to you. [*Ibid.*, pp. 26–27.]

Extract of a letter from Admiral Arbuthnot to Sir Henry Clinton. *Europe*, off Rhode Island, July 23d, 1780 (received the 26th).

I plainly perceive the French squadron consists of seven ships of the line and four frigates, which are at anchor between Fort [Goat] and Rose Islands in the ship channel. The enemy appear to be erecting works on the peninsula of Brenton's Neck; and, to say the truth, if I am to judge from a very large encampment on the beach on the south end of Rhode Island fronting the sea, you are to expect some opposition. *I undertake to prevent the shipping coming out of the harbor to impede your landing, which shall be covered by frigates.*

Extract of a letter from General Washington to the President of Congress. Headquarters, Bergen County, July 26, 1780.

I detached Brigadier General Wayne on the 20th with the First and Second Pennsylvania Brigades, with four pieces of artillery attached to them and Colonel Moylan's Dragoons. I had it in contemplation to attempt the destruction of a blockhouse erected at Bull's Ferry, which served the purpose of covering the enemy's woodcutters and giving security to a body of refugees, by whom it was garrisoned and who committed depredations upon the well affected inhabitants for many miles round. General Wayne, having disposed of his troops in such a manner as to guard the different landing places on the Bergen shore upon which the enemy might throw over troops from York Island to intercept his retreat, proceeded with the First, Second, and Tenth Regiments and the artillery to the blockhouse, which he found surrounded by an abatis and stockade. He for some time tried the effect of his fieldpieces upon it. But, though the fire was kept up for an hour, *they were found too light to penetrate the logs* of which it was constructed. The troops during this time being galled by a constant fire from the loopholes of the house, and seeing no chance of making a breach with cannon, those of the First and Second Regiments, notwithstanding the utmost efforts of the officers to restrain them, rushed through the abatis to the foot of the stockade with a view of forcing an entrance, which was found impracticable. This act of intemperate valor was the cause of the loss we sustained, and which amounted in the whole to three officers wounded, fifteen noncommissioned officers and privates killed, and forty-six noncommissioned officers and privates wounded. I have been thus particular lest the account of this affair should have reached Philadelphia much exaggerated. [Fitzpatrick, *Writings of Washington, 19,* 260–262.]

Copy of a letter from Admiral Arbuthnot to Sir Henry Clinton. *Europe,* off Block Island, 27 July 1780.

Sir,

Having ordered the *Galatea* to proceed off the harbor with Captain Savage and Captain Hudson of the *Richmond* to reconnoiter the different passages and landings, to the report of these officers I beg leave to refer you for every information respecting the strength and situation of the enemy. I have the honor, etc., Marriot Arbuthnot.

Copy of Captain Savage's report to Sir Henry Clinton. On board the *Galatea,* off Huntington Bay, July 30, 1780.

Sir,

Agreeable to your commands I delivered the dispatches with which I was charged to Admiral Arbuthnot off Rhode Island on the 27th instant. In conversation thereupon *the Admiral expressed his wishes that he could stop your intentions of proceeding,* for that the French had obtained a large rebel force in addition to the 5000 men they had brought with them, and had raised works and mounted a great many pieces of cannon, *so that he thought that an attack might be dangerous.* But yet, if the General (meaning Your Excellency) wished to make an attempt, *he would put you on shore and prevent the French fleet from giving you annoyance. But that it was to be further noticed he, the Admiral, could give no assistance with either guns or ammunition.*

Admiral Arbuthnot proposed that Captain Hudson of the *Richmond* should accompany me in reconnoitering, as far as possible, the entrance of the harbor and position of the enemy for Your Excellency's information. The weather was hazy, yet it could be distinguished that three small encampments were formed upon Brenton's Neck and a large one on the heights over the town of Newport. On the Island of Conanicut a large work was erecting, upon the high ground by the Dumplings Point that forms an entrance of the harbor. Possession also appeared to be taken of a barrack not far distant, and some tents pitched thereby. I have the honor, etc., H. Savage. [Clinton, *Narrative of Co-operations,* p. 28.]

Extract of a letter from Sir Henry Clinton to Admiral Arbuthnot. Huntington Bay, July 30, 1780.

The object before us is so very important that I am persuaded it will make my excuse for entreating you to second my efforts to procure more detailed intelligence than you have as yet received. Should you learn that any opening yet remains *where, with the most active cooperation of the army, we might hope [for] success in a joint attempt,* I beg your speedy communication of it. I will in this case, if you wish it, with all expedition repair to any place you will appoint in company with such general officers as may be near me, in order to meet you, sir, with Rear Admiral Graves, the Commodore [Affleck], and any other officers you would wish to be of this conference, and determine on the means, if they yet exist, of gaining an advantage over the enemy— perhaps the greatest [advantage] that has been within our reach since the commencement of the war. [*Ibid.,* pp. 30–31.]

Extract of a letter from Admiral Arbuthnot to Sir Henry Clinton. *Europe,* off Block Island, 3d August 1780 (received August 10).

I never was here before, and am totally ignorant of the situation of the place. As to the conversation between Captain Savage and myself,

I said no more than, if upon his report you judge your force insufficient to warrant an attempt upon the enemy, I thought it better not to come. Far was my idea from pretending officially to know their strength. For I pledge myself, if I had, you should certainly have received an earlier information of it. *It is sixteen days since I have been about this place, in anxious expectation of hearing from you. The fleet being in a very critical situation with upward of 900 sick, and short of complement,* I shall for a few days repair to Gardiners Island to water and put the sick on shore. [*Ibid.,* pp. 31–32.]

Extract of a letter from Lord George Germain to His Majesty's commissioners [Clinton and Arbuthnot]. Whitehall, August 3, 1780.

The reduction of the whole Province of South Carolina and the concurrence of all our accounts from the provinces in rebellion of *the distress of the inhabitants and their anxious desire to return to the King's obedience, together with the reduced state of Mr. Washington's force, the decay of the power of Congress, and to total failure of their paper money, open a flattering prospect of a speedy and happy termination of the American war.* Your able and vigorous conduct in your respective commands leaves no room to apprehend anything will be wanting to accelerate this happy event that the exertion of great military talents can accomplish.

[Extract of Cornwallis to Clinton. August 6, 1780] (received August 24).

The reports industriously propagated in this province of a large army coming from the northward had very much intimidated our friends, encouraged our enemies, and determined the wavering against us, to which our not advancing and acting offensively likewise contributed. The whole country between Pedee and Santee has ever since been in an absolute state of rebellion. This unfortunate business, if it should have no worse consequences, will shake the confidence of our friends in this province and make our situation very uneasy until we advance. *It may be doubted by some whether the invasion of North Carolina may be a prudent measure. But I am convinced that it is a necessary one and that, if we do not attack that province, we must give up both South Carolina and Georgia and retire within the walls of Charleston.* Our assurances of attachment from our poor distressed friends in North Carolina are as strong as ever. The Highlanders have offered to form a regiment as soon as we enter their country.

An early diversion in my favor in Chesapeake Bay will be of the greatest and most important advantage to my operations. [Stevens, *Clinton-Cornwallis Controversy*, *1*, 236–238.]

Copy of a letter from Admiral Arbuthnot to Sir Henry Clinton. Gardiners Island, August 8, 1780 (received August 13).

Sir:

Captain Savage having communicated the substance of the intelligence he has gained, *I beg to propose to Your Excellency an immediate meeting*, and that in the meantime every measure you may in consequence concert may be put in a state of forwardness, that the result of your and our deliberations may be carried into instant execution. I have the honor, etc., Marriot Arbuthnot.

[Extract of Clinton to Arbuthnot.] New York, 11 August 1780.

I am honored with your letter of the 3d instant. But I shall defer answering it more at large until Captain Savage returns. I must, however, in the meantime beg leave to observe *respecting my first attempt, simply of the troops,* that I could not flatter myself six thousand French troops, after occupying a post such as Rhode Island twelve days, and under a probability of having received considerable reinforcement, could be open to it. *And I am persuaded your zeal for the service would have led you to offer active cooperation on the part of the navy if you had seen the propriety of such a measure.*[36] I must therefore, sir, be free to own I see no prospect in an attempt which, had circumstances combined, would have been most important.

And I must beg leave to repeat that, had Mr. Graves arrived a few days sooner to have enabled Your Excellency to intercept that armament, or us jointly or even the troops alone to have attempted the post of Rhode Island before it was fortified or reinforced, I do think success would have been certain. Nay, sir, had Your Excellency, even as it was, received information a few days after their arrival, and had *transports been ready for the troops,* we might not have been too late. As it is, we have only to lament that concurring circumstances may have put it out of our power. [Clinton, *Narrative of Co-operations*, pp. 32–33.]

36. In place of this sentence Clinton's first draft reads as follows: "And, as you, sir, did not offer the least active cooperation, I am to suppose of course (without reference to your conversations with my aide-de-camp—which I am told I am to look upon as private conversation, but which, I confess, I never can consider as such) that you had none to propose."

[Extract of Clinton to Arbuthnot. New York, August 13, 1780.]

In consequence of your letter by Captain Savage I shall repair myself, or send general officers, to Gardiners Island as soon as possible, to settle any plan of cooperation that can be agreed on in the present situation of the enemy.

I am sure you will forgive my having requested Captain Collins not to move transports till I hear again from Your Excellency, who probably did not consider the delays and inconveniences that might attend the marching troops 120 miles through Long Island.[37] Everything will be ready at Whitestone for a sudden move of the army, but I do not think it right to depart from thence till some plan is fixed, lest by laying at Gardiners Island they [the troops] should give the enemy alarm.

I am ever happy when it is in my power to assist the navy. Perhaps, threatened with a far superior army, it is not quite right for me to part with a battalion at this time to man the fleet.[38] I will, however, sir, endeavor as soon as possible to send one to Your Excellency, but under your promise that prior to the fleet's leaving the coast of America it shall be returned to us. I have directed a general press to take place here immediately, and I think, sir, you might have one on the seacoast of Long Island. [*Ibid.*, pp. 34–35.]

Extract of a letter from James Simpson, Esq., Attorney General of South Carolina, to Sir Henry Clinton. Charleston, 13 August 1780 (received 24 August).

Three months ago I had little doubt but by this time the tranquillity of Carolina would have been re-established and the rebel cause entirely relinquished. I then knew that both Laurens and Rutledge were meditating how they should make their peace. For what reasons they have been delivered from their purpose I am a stranger. But it is very visible that the hopes of rebellious faction here are elevated by something which they either know or apprehend.

37. The Admiral had asked Clinton's approval for moving the transports from Whitestone, where they were exposed to the dangers of navigating the sound, to the safety of Gardiners Bay. (Arbuthnot to Clinton, Aug. 6.) In the bay they would have been safe but useless, and Sir Henry is hinting at this absurdity.

38. Arbuthnot had asked to borrow a regiment, not a battalion. The request is in a part of his letter of Aug. 3 that Clinton does not give in his extract.

Extract of a letter from Admiral Arbuthnot to Sir Henry Clinton. *Europe,* 18 August 1780.

I am this moment honored with Your Excellency's *letter of yesterday.* And, as I am preparing to weigh to cruise for the enemy between Montauk Point and the southward of Nantucket Shoals, I do not think it proper to delay a moment.

Extract of a letter from Sir Henry Clinton to Admiral Arbuthnot. East Hampton, 18 August 1780.

After a journey of 120 miles, made purely upon Your Excellency's invitation requesting an immediate conference, I cannot help being exceedingly surprised at the duplicate I have this day received of your letter of the 17th in answer to mine of the 11th, which was written, sir, at a time—I must beg leave to repeat it—when you had offered no one active cooperation and when, from every account of the enemy's situation, it was evident the army alone could undertake nothing. On my part, sir, the instant I receive the least hint of a probability of the navy's cooperating, which you give me in your letter of the 8th desiring an immediate conference, I overlook every inconvenience and set off to join you with all possible dispatch, riding at this inclement season both night and day. From Your Excellency's conversations which have been related to me, and from your letter to Lieutenant General Robertson, expressing such zeal for a very important enterprise, I could not but be persuaded that I should meet some proposals for a joint undertaking, though it had been retarded to this hour. Much more confident, however, was I that I should have an opportunity of speaking with you, and at least expected to learn the cause which had induced you to leave me in disappointment at the extremity of this island, without a ship of force to receive me or even a boat to communicate with you. [Clinton, *Narrative of Co-operations,* pp. 35–36.]

Copy of a letter from Admiral Arbuthnot to Sir Henry Clinton. *Europe,* at sea, 19 August 1780.

Sir:

I am, by the arrival of the *Galatea* this morning, honored with a conversation with Generals Mathew and Dalrymple, for the substance of which I beg leave to refer you to them.

I have the honor, etc., Marriot Arbuthnot.

Minutes of the conversation referred to above [August 19, 1780].

The Admiral told us he had received a letter from the Commander in Chief (dated the 17th or 18th) from Moriches, and supposed we were come to concert with him some operation against the French fleet and army in Rhode Island. General Mathew made answer, "we come by appointment of Sir Henry Clinton, whom we hoped to have seen on board the *Europe.*" The Admiral told us he meant to enter very fully into the business in question, adding that he was in possession of the most perfect information of the state of things at Rhode Island, arising from his own most minute observation as well as from other means; that the enemy were in great force, covered with a vast artillery, strongly fortified, and the colonies adjacent ready to support them; and that *nothing could be done after the first day of their arrival.* General Mathew told the Admiral that he was empowered by the General to offer three or four thousand men to assist in any operations the Admiral might propose against the enemy. *He answered that he could attempt nothing. The enemy were not to be come at.* [He said] that the idea of an attack by the Narragansett Passage was a mistaken one, the coast opposite to Conanicut Island being mounted with guns to the great prejudice of ships, as the *Renown* had experienced; that the holding Conanicut Island with troops was of no consequence, the channel to the northward being improper for ships of the line to pass by. Therefore he could not undertake that operation.

I then proposed a query if anything could be done by the passage of Brenton's Point, the troops holding the Dumplings? He said no, that the enemy's fleet was too strongly posted—formed in a crescent and flanked by two islands, on which seventy large guns and mortars were mounted, other batteries raking the ships also from different points; that his fleet would thereby be torn to pieces, and would bring up under every disadvantage opposite the enemy. He concluded by saying nothing could be done, *nor was there ever any prospect of it* unless Sir Henry Clinton had an army of eighteen or twenty thousand men to form a regular siege. He expressed his thanks for the offer made, but said it could not be of any use, from the strength and position of the enemy. J. Dalrymple. [Clinton, *Narrative of Co-operations,* pp. 37–38.]

Extract of a letter from Lord Cornwallis to Lord George Germain. Camden, August 21, 1780.

I had now my option to make, either to retire or attack the enemy; for the position at Camden was a bad one to be attacked in, and by General Sumter's advancing down the Wateree my supplies must have failed me in a few days. I saw no difficulty in making good my retreat to Charleston with the troops that were able to march. But in taking that resolution I must have not only left near 800 sick, and a great quantity of stores at this place, but *I clearly saw the loss of the whole province except Charleston, and of all Georgia except Savannah, as immediate consequences, besides forfeiting all pretensions to future confidence from our friends in this part of America.* On the other hand, there was no doubt of the rebel army being well appointed, and of its numbers being upward of five thousand men; and my own corps, which never was numerous, was now reduced by sickness and other casualties to about fourteen hundred fighting men of regulars and provincials, with four or five hundred militia and North Carolina refugees. On the afternoon of the 14th I determined to march at ten o'clock on the night of the 15th and to attack at daybreak, pointing my principal force against their Continentals, who from good intelligence I knew to be badly posted.

I had proceeded nine miles when, about half an hour past two in the morning, my advanced guard fell in with the enemy. By the weight of the fire I was convinced they were in considerable force, and was soon assured by some deserters and prisoners that it was the whole rebel army on its march to attack us at Camden. I immediately halted and formed, and, the enemy doing the same, the firing soon ceased. Confiding in the disciplined courage of His Majesty's troops, and well apprised that the ground on which both armies stood (being narrowed by swamps on the right and left) was extremely favorable to my numbers, I did not choose to hazard the great stake for which I was going to fight to the uncertainty and confusion to which an action in the dark is so particularly liable. At the dawn I made my last disposition, when I perceived that the enemy, having persisted in their resolution to fight, were formed in two lines opposite and near to us. And, observing a movement on their left, I directed Lieutenant Colonel Webster to begin the attack, which was done with great vigor; and in a few minutes the action was general along the whole front.

It was at this time a dead calm with a little haziness in the air which, preventing the smoke from rising, occasioned so thick a darkness that it was difficult to see the effect of a very heavy and well supported fire on both sides. Our line continued to advance in good order and with the cool intrepidity of experienced British soldiers, keeping up a constant fire or making use of bayonets as opportunities offered, and after an obstinate resistance for three-quarters of an hour threw the enemy into total confusion, and forced them to give way in all quarters. At this instant I ordered the cavalry to complete the rout, which was performed

454 THE AMERICAN REBELLION

with their usual promptitude and gallantry; and, after doing execution on the field of battle, they continued the pursuit to Hanging Rock, twenty-two miles from the place where the action happened, during which many of the enemy were slain. A number of prisoners, near 150 wagons, a considerable quantity of military stores, and all the baggage and camp equipment of the rebel army fell into our hands. The loss of the enemy was very considerable. A number of colors and seven pieces of brass cannon, with all their ammunition wagons, were taken. Between eight and nine hundred were killed and about one thousand prisoners, many of them wounded.

The fatigue of the troops rendered them incapable of farther exertion on the day of action. But, as I saw the importance of destroying or dispersing, if possible, the corps under General Sumter, I detached Lieutenant Colonel Tarleton with the Legion cavalry and infantry, in all about 350 men, with orders to attack him wherever he could find him. Lieutenant Colonel Tarleton executed this service with his usual activity and military address. He totally destroyed or dispersed his detachment, consisting then of seven hundred men, killing one hundred and fifty on the spot, and taking two pieces of brass cannon, three hundred prisoners, and forty-four wagons. [Stevens, *Clinton-Cornwallis Controversy, 1,* 250–255.]

Extract of a letter from Sir Henry Clinton to Lord George Germain. 25 August 1780 (received 23 September).

At this new epoch in the war, when a foreign force has already landed, I owe to my country [to declare]—and I must, in justice to my own fame, declare to Your Lordship—that I become every day more sensible of the utter impossibility of prosecuting the war in this country without reinforcement. And I must add that, with every succor I require, unless I have the good fortune to meet in the commander of the fleet a gentleman whose views with respect to the conduct of the war are similar to my own and whose cooperation with me as commissioner and commander in chief is cordial, uniform, and animated, the powers with which the King may in his most gracious confidence entrust me, any more than my own exertions, cannot have their fair trial or their full efficacy.

With the addition of 6000 men, and security against a superior fleet and foreign army, I trust the peninsula between Chesapeake and Delaware might be reduced to obedience. That district is locally friendly to the masters of the sea. But, dependent as its geography has rendered it, a less force than 4000 could not, after conquest, secure it from insult.

I am sensible, My Lord, that men reason often from partiality toward themselves. But there is in my breast so full a conviction of the rectitude of my intentions and of the candor and fairness of my proceedings with Admiral Arbuthnot that, with the strictest scrutiny into my conduct, I can trace the difficulties and clogs the service suffers from want of his cordial, uniform, and animated cooperation to no cause wherein I can impute blame to myself.

[Extract of Clinton to Germain.] August 30, 1780.

By the letters I have lately received from Lord Cornwallis I hold myself powerfully called upon to make a diversion in his favor in Chesapeake Bay. I have prepared for it, and have again made application to the Admiral for naval protection and cooperation. This new drain from my army must throw me upon a very strict defensive indeed, when I have opposed to me so considerable a force compared to my own.

Nor may I build upon the resource of the New York militia when my purpose is to act for any length of time at a distance and in the summer season. The zeal of Major General Pattison, so well followed by a large number of people last winter, discovered the very satisfactory consideration *that in an hour of imminent danger to the city of New York* more inhabitants could be formed than had been perhaps thought of. These, however, consisted in merchants, tradesmen, and persons attached to the different army and navy departments, consisting of sailors, watermen, and others, each having under government or in their own professions their several employments, which could admit of their bearing arms only in case of a blockade or in time of hard frost.

I have requested General Dalrymple to represent to Your Lordship in the strongest terms the distress the army under my command will probably soon be reduced to for want of provisions, not having as yet received a single day's of the present year's supply.

Extract of a letter from Admiral Arbuthnot to Sir Henry Clinton. 31 August 1780.

My want of knowledge of the natural strength of Rhode Island, with which you are perfectly well acquainted, would have rendered improper any proposals of operations from me. Had such come from Your Excellency, I would have spoken at once to the assistance the ships might have given.[39]

39. *Clinton's note:* The absurdity of this latter hint must plainly appear to whoever reads our correspondence. For I not only proposed a conjunct operation of the fleet and army, but repeatedly pointed out the means by which it was to be effected. However, as I did not wish to cause an open breach between us, I now ceased pressing him further on the subject.

Extract of a confidential letter from Sir Henry Clinton to a friend very high in office [William Eden]. New York, September 1, 1780.

It is a pity we could not have followed up the business of the Chesapeake. Something must be done there, and immediately, if the Admiral will now consent. But how to do it is the question. *Entre nous* I now have in rank and file fit for duty about 13,000. Washington has at least 12,000 already, the French nearly 5000 and 3000 more daily expected. The number I have is by no means adequate to the defense of this post, threatened by such a force—notwithstanding General Pattison's militia, from whom I cannot expect much permanent assistance, as they are composed of merchants, traders, shopkeepers, officers, and men of the different civil departments, sailors, etc.

Our success to the southward, had we been in a situation to have followed it up, must have been decisive as far as Hudson's River, as we should immediately have taken possession of Chesapeake Bay if we had had a covering fleet. I wish this southward business had been adopted three years since. We all think so, Lord Cornwallis the first to own it. But I have observed in this war we have sometimes been in the *south* when we should have been in the north, and oftener in the north when we should have been in the south. But, should we ever possess as far as Hudson River, expedition alone against their seaport towns can reduce the northern provinces.

I have now acting with me two major generals and some brigadiers of my own making. I have no money, no provisions, nor indeed any account of the sailing of the Cork fleet, nor admiral that I can have the least dependence on, no army. In short, I have nothing left but hope for better times and a little more attention!

[Extract of] Major Ferguson to Lord Cornwallis, without date [*ca.* September 6, 1780].

A doubt does not remain in regard to the intelligence I sent Your Lordship. They are *since* joined by Clarke and Sumter. I am on my march toward you by a road leading from Cherokee Ford north of King's Mountain. Three or four hundred *good* soldiers, part dragoons, would finish the business. *Something must be done soon.* [Lyman C. Draper, *King's Mountain and Its Heroes: History of the Battle of King's Mountain, October 7th, 1780, and the Events Which Led to It* (Cincinnati, 1881), pp. 207–208; the italics in the final sentence are Ferguson's.]

[Extract of Germain to Clinton. September 6, 1780.]

The capture or destruction of the French ships and troops are objects of the highest importance in our present circumstances and, if they could be effected without paying too dearly for them, could not fail of being attended with the best consequences to the King's affairs both in Europe and America. But of this both you and the Vice Admiral are so thoroughly informed, and the King is so fully assured of the earnest desire of both to do the utmost to promote his service and of your ability to judge what is best and fittest to be done, that whether you determine upon immediately attacking Monsieur de Ternay, if he continues in Rhode Island, or taking such measures as may prevent him from interrupting you in your operations in the Chesapeake and proceed[ing] immediately in your plan for the reduction of the southern provinces is entirely submitted to your judgment. *But, in either case, His Majesty has no doubt but you will find means to recover those provinces to His Majesty in the course of the campaign.*

Extract of a letter from General Arnold, under the signature of Gustavus, to Major André, under that of John Anderson, dated September 15 [1780].

On the 11th at noon, agreeable to your request, I attempted to go to Dobbs Ferry, but was prevented by the armed boats of the enemy, who fired upon us and continued opposite to the ferry until sunset. I will send a person in whom you can confide, by water, to meet you at Dobbs Ferry at the landing on the east side, on Wednesday the 20th instant, who will conduct you to a place of safety, where I will meet you. [Van Doren, *Secret History*, p. 472.]

Extract of a letter from Sir Henry Clinton to Admiral Sir George Rodney. New York, September 18, 1780.

As to land operation against the French at Rhode Island, I must give it as my opinion to you, sir, as I did to Admiral Arbuthnot, that as long as there was appearance of a *coup de main* before the enemy were entrenched and reinforced, I thought an attempt practicable; and with 6000 men I would have made it. But, when I found the enemy had at least fourteen days to prepare against it, I naturally gave up all hopes from a *coup de main*.

Should Admiral Arbuthnot, so considerably reinforced by you, sir, think any attempt still practicable, he will of course report it. And in that case I offer to Your Excellency, as I did to him, every possible secondary assistance of the army. But if Admiral Arbuthnot, reinforced so considerably by you, sir, does not alter his opinion, I am persuaded you will agree with me in mine that we should give our whole attention to the plan I laid before you yesterday—and, finally, in sending an expedition into Chesapeake Bay, as to the necessity and importance of which we are both agreed. I sincerely wish it may be Your Excellency's intention to stay upon this coast at least while there is possibility of the arrival of a superior naval force. I am equally sincere in my wishes that the course of service may bring us together early next year, for I have a pleasure in cooperating with you as I have in assuring you, dear sir, etc.

[Extract of Cornwallis to Clinton. September 22, 1780.]

I then think of moving on my principal force to Salisbury, which will open the country sufficiently for us to see what assistance we may really expect from our friends in North Carolina, and will give us a free communication with the Highlanders, on whom my greatest dependence is placed. [Stevens, *Clinton-Cornwallis Controversy, 1,* 270.]

[Extract of Cornwallis to Major Ferguson, intercepted and] published by the enemy. Warsaw, September 23 [1780].

I have just received yours of the 19th. I heard a report that a Major Davis, who commands a corps of about eighty horse militia, had marched against you. As soon as I have consumed the provisions in this settlement, I shall march with as much expedition as possible to Cross Creek. [Tarleton, *History,* p. 192.]

Copy of a letter from Major André to General Washington. Salem, 24 September 1780.

Sir:

What I have as yet said concerning myself was in a justifiable attempt to be extricated. I am too little accustomed to duplicity to have succeeded. I beg Your Excellency will be persuaded that no alteration in the temper of my mind, or apprehension for my safety, induces me to take the step of addressing you, but that it is to secure myself from an imputation of having assumed a mean character for treacherous purposes or self-interest, a conduct incompatible with the principles that actuated me as well as [with] my condition in life. It is to vindicate my fame that I speak, and not to solicit security. The person in your possession is Major John André, Adjutant General to the British army.

The influence of one commander in the army of his adversary is an advantage taken in war. A correspondence for this purpose I held as confidential in the present instance with His Excellency, Sir Henry Clinton.[40] To favor it I agreed to meet upon ground not within posts of either army a person who was to give me intelligence. I came up in the *Vulture*, man-of-war, for this effect, and was fetched by a boat from the shore to the beach. Being there, I was told that the approach of day would prevent my return, and that I must be concealed until the next night. I was in my regimentals, and had fairly risked my person. *Against my stipulation, my intention, and without my knowledge beforehand,* I was conducted within one of your posts. Your Excellency may conceive my sensation on this occasion, and will imagine how much more I must have been affected by a refusal to reconduct me back the next night as I had been brought. Thus become a prisoner, I had to concert my escape. I quitted my uniform and was passed another way in the night without the American posts to neutral ground, and informed I was beyond all armed parties, and left to press for New York. I was taken at Tarrytown by some volunteers. Thus, as I have had the honor to relate, was *I betrayed*, being Adjutant General of the British army, into the vile condition of an enemy in disguise within your posts.

Having avowed myself a British officer, I have nothing to reveal but what relates to myself, which is true on the honor of an officer and a gentleman. The request I have to make to Your Excellency (and I am conscious I address myself well) is that, in any rigor policy may dictate, a decency of conduct toward me may mark that, though unfortunate, I am branded with nothing dishonorable, as no motive could be mine but the service of my King, and as I was involuntarily an impostor. Another request is that I may be permitted to write an open letter to Sir Henry Clinton, and another to a friend for clothes and linen.

I take the liberty to mention the condition of some gentlemen at Charleston who, being either on parole or under protection, were engaged in a conspiracy against us. Though their situation is not similar, they are objects who may be set in exchange for me, or are persons whom the treatment I receive may affect. It is no less, sir, in a confidence in the generosity of your mind than on account of your superior station that I have chosen to importune you with this letter. I have the honor, etc. John André, Adjutant General. [Sparks, *Writings of Washington*, 7, 531–532.]

40. The purport of these two obscure sentences seems to be that Clinton's negotiation with Arnold was justifiable according to the rules of war, and that André acted as Sir Henry's confidential agent.

Extract of another letter from General Arnold to Sir Henry Clinton. September 26, 1780.

I commanded at the time at West Point [and] had an undoubted right to send my flag of truce for Major André, who came to me under that protection; and, having held my conversation with him, I delivered to him several confidential papers in my own handwriting to deliver to Your Excellency. Thinking it much properer that he should return by land, I directed him to make use of the feigned name of John Anderson, and gave him my passports to pass my lines to the White Plains on his way to New York. [Van Doren, *Secret History*, pp. 360–361, 486–487.]

Extract of a letter from Major André to Sir Henry Clinton. Tappan, 29 September 1780.

I have obtained General Washington's permission to send you this letter, the object of which is to remove from your breast any suspicion that I could imagine I was bound by Your Excellency's orders to expose myself to what has happened. The events of coming within the enemy's posts and of changing my dress, which led me to my present situation, were contrary to my own intentions as they were to your orders, and the circuitous route which I took to return was *imposed*, perhaps unavoidably, *without alternative upon me*. [*Ibid.*, pp. 475–476.]

Copy of the opinion of the board of American Generals on Major André's case, held at Tappan, September 29, 1780.

That he came on shore from the *Vulture*, sloop of war, in the night of the 21st of September, on an interview with General Arnold, in a private and secret manner.[41] That he changed his dress within our lines, and under a feigned name and in a disguised habit [42] passed our works at Stony and Verplanck's Points the evening of the 22d of September; and was taken in the morning of the 23d at Tarrytown in a disguised habit, being then on his way to New York, and when taken he had in his possession several papers which contained intelligence for the enemy.[43] This board, having maturely considered these facts, do also report to His Excellency, General Washington, that Major André, Adjutant Gen-

41. *Clinton's note:* Invited to it by that General!
42. *Clinton's note:* By order of that General!
43. *Clinton's note:* Given him by that General sealed, and [André] ignorant of the contents.

eral to the British army, ought to be considered as a spy from the enemy; and that, agreeable to the law and usage of nations, it is their opinion he ought to suffer death. [Clinton's addition:] Signed by all the members. [From Washington to Clinton, Sept. 30, *ibid.*, pp. 487–488.]

Extract from an address of the general officers in the rebel service to their respective states [early October?, 1780], found in a rebel mail which was intercepted on the 22d of October, 1780.

After having joined our brother officers of the line at large in two ineffectual applications to Congress on the subject, nothing but the purest regard for the safety of the country could impel us to undertake a third essay of this kind. The officers are sensible of the public embarrassments. They have been attentive to the administration of civil as well as military affairs, and forward in suggesting their thoughts on every proper occasion with an honest zeal of promoting the welfare of the army and state. They do not ask for impossibilities from government. But they wish to see that effusion of a liberal heart which it is impossible to exhibit in a state of poverty.

The war appears to us as far from an honorable issue as it has ever done. Our allies, however generous their intentions, have not been able to give us the expected assistance. Perhaps Providence, by repeated disappointments from this quarter, designs to convince us that our help and salvation are, under God, to be derived from our own exertions. There is no ground of hope the enemy will relinquish their object until they find the country prepared to defend itself—that is, until they see an army opposed to them as regular as their own and on as permanent a basis. Our present condition promises them the speedy accomplishment of their wishes. An army consisting of a few inadequate thousands, almost destitute of every public supply, its officers, whose tables once abounded with plenty and variety, subsisting month after month on one bare ration of dry bread and meat, and that frequently of the meanest quality, their families looking up to them for their usual support, their children for the education to which they once had a title—our enemies know human nature too well to apprehend they shall have to contend long with an army under such circumstances.

In faithfulness to our country we make this representation without the solicitation or knowledge of those officers who are the chief objects of it. They, we are assured, are generally determined to resign their commissions at the end of this campaign. Indeed it is impossible for them to continue, let their virtue or inclination be ever so great. And we cannot but express to you that we shall consider the loss of the present body of officers as little short of the dissolution of the army. If the country is competent to its defense without a regular army, no more need be said on the subject. Let ours progress, as it does, to its dissolution. But, on the other hand, if an army well appointed and provided is absolutely necessary, the subjects of it must be made easy and contented with their situation, etc. Signed by Generals Greene, Parsons, Knox, Glover, Stark, Huntington, and Paterson. [(Almon,) *The Remembrancer, 11,* 13–15.]

[Extract of Germain to Clinton.] 4 October 1780.

I have desired Brigadier General Dalrymple to put everything you have given him in charge in writing, which he has done accordingly; and I shall take the first opportunity of communicating his papers to the other Ministers. And by the next conveyance I shall acquaint you with His Majesty's determination in consequence of their advice.

[Draft of] a letter from Sir Henry Clinton to Lord George Germain. New York, October 11, 1780.

My Lord:

About eighteen months since, I had some reason to conceive that the American Major General Arnold was desirous of quitting the rebel service and joining the cause of Great Britain. A secret correspondence which I conceived to be from this officer, which expressed a displeasure at the alliance between America and France, engaged me to pursue every means of ascertaining the identity of the person who was thus opening himself to me, and from whom I had on every occasion received, during the whole of our correspondence, most material intelligence. I was not at first, however, sanguine in my ideas of General Arnold's consequence, as he was said to be then in a sort of disgrace, had been tried before a general court martial, and [was] not likely to be employed; and, whatever merit this officer might have had, his situation, such as I understood it then to be, made him less an object of attention. I apprehended that without employment he might be of more use to me in corresponding than by joining me.

In the course of our communication information was given me that he should certainly (the person who was writing) be again employed in the American service, with an offer of surrendering himself under every possible advantage to His Majesty's arms. The correspondence was continued up to July, 1780, when Major General Arnold obtained the command of all the rebel forts in the Highlands, garrisoned with near 4000 men. And it seemed to me, by the correspondence in question, that it was certainly that officer who made the offers under the description I have given. The getting possession of these posts with their garrisons, cannon, stores, vessels, gunboats, etc., etc., appeared to me an object of the highest importance, which must be attended with the best consequences to His Majesty's service—among others that of opening the navigation of the North River and the communication, in a certain degree, with Albany, as appears by the enclosed copy of a letter from G[eneral] Haldimand to me.

The very particular situation of the campaign at this period will mark of what great import such an event would prove. A French fleet and a considerable land force had arrived at Rhode Island. Mr. Washington had very much augmented his army, and was drawing additional strength to it daily by every strained exertion upon the country and the militia of it. There was great reason, from information, to suppose that an attempt was intended upon New York, that Mr. Washington with his army was to have moved upon Kings Bridge and Morrisania while a corps threatened—perhaps attacked—Staten Island, at the same time that the French would have invaded Long Island and have moved upon New York by that inroad. To have pursued these plans large magazines of every nature must have been formed by the rebels, and it is beyond doubt that the principal rebel depot must have been made at West Point and its dependent forts.

From this description, which I have reason to believe just, will be seen of what great consequence would be the encouraging and closing in with a plan of such infinite effect, if carried into execution, toward the success of the campaign, and that it was to be pursued at every risk and at every expense. My idea of putting into execution this concerted plan with General Arnold with most efficacy was to have deferred it till Mr. Washington, cooperating with the French, moved upon this place to invest it, and till [44] the rebel magazines should have been collected and formed in their several depots, particularly that at West Point. General Arnold surrendering himself, the forts, and garrisons at this instant of time would have given every advantage which could have been desired. Mr. Washington must have instantly retired from Kings Bridge, and the French troops upon Long Island would have been consequently left unsupported and probably would have fallen into our hands. The consequent advantage of so great an event I need not explain.

I had prepared for this serious purpose and for the movements which would have attended upon it everything which my reflection could suggest as necessary upon the occasions, and there were vessels properly

44. "that" in the MS.

manned and of a particular draft of water ready to have improved the designed stroke to the utmost. The important news from South Carolina of Lord Cornwallis having defeated Mr. Gates' army [45] arrived here the latter end of August, and I watched the effect it might have upon Mr. Washington's army. But he did not in the least alter his positions, or send a man to the southward, from whence I was led to imagine this place was still his object—in which, indeed, I was confirmed by intelligence from General Arnold.

At this period Sir George Rodney arrived with a fleet at New York, which made it highly probable that Mr. Washington would lay aside all thoughts against this place. It became, therefore, proper for me no longer to defer the execution of a project [from] which, from the situation of the rebel army and its chief (then about [West] Point), would be derived such considerable advantages, nor to lose so fair an opportunity as was presented [by], and under so good a mask as, an expedition to the Chesapeake, which every person imagined would of course take place. Under this feint, therefore, I prepared for a movement up the North River. I laid my plan before Sir George Rodney and Lieutenant General Knyphausen, when Sir George—with that zeal for His Majesty's service which marks his character—most handsomely promised to give me every naval assistance in his power.

It became at this instant necessary that the secret correspondence under feigned names which had been so long carried on should be rendered into certainty, both as to the person being Major General Arnold, commanding at West Point, and that, in the manner in which he was to surrender himself, the forts, and troops to me, it should be so conducted under a concerted plan between us as that the King's troops sent upon this expedition should be under no risk of surprise or counterplot. And I was determined not to make the attempt but under such perfect security.

I knew the ground on which the forts were placed and the contiguous country tolerably well, having been there in 1777, and had received many hints respecting both from General Arnold. But it was certainly necessary that a meeting should be held with that officer for settling the whole of the plan. My reasons as I have described will, I take for granted, prove the propriety of such a measure on my part. General Arnold had also his reasons, which must be so very obvious as to make it unnecessary for me to explain them.

Many projects for a meeting were formed, and in consequence several appointments made, in all which General Arnold seemed ex-

45. The Battle of Camden, fought on Aug. 16.

tremely desirous that some person who had my particular confidence might be sent to him—some man, as he described in writing, of *his own mensuration*.[46] I had thought of a person under this immediate description, who would have cheerfully undertaken it but that his peculiar situation at the time (from which I could not then release him) precluded him from engaging in it.[47] General Arnold finally insisted that the person sent to confer with him should be the Adjutant General, Major André, who indeed had been the person on my part who managed and carried on the secret correspondence.

A meeting was proposed to be held at a particular place and on neutral ground, on a fixed day and hour. The parties accordingly were on their way to the rendezvous, but an unlucky accident prevented the conference. A gunboat which had been up the river, falling down to the usual station, very near met that in which General Arnold was, who with difficulty escaped and was in some risk of his life. This necessarily put off the matter for some days. The correspondence was obliged to be renewed, and another appointment made to meet at the same spot as first proposed.

The appointment took place, though not exactly as intended, as appears by the narrative which I have the honor to transmit herewith to Your Lordship; and it proved a most unfortunate one respecting the general plan, and a most fatal one to the Adjutant General, Major André—who was taken prisoner, tried by a board of rebel general officers, [and] condemned by their sentence to suffer death, which sentence was confirmed and ordered to be put into execution upon this unhappy gentleman by the rebel General Washington. Major General Arnold received intelligence of Major André's being taken just in time to allow him to make his escape, which he did with great difficulty and danger, being pursued by land and by water.

Thus ended this proposed plan of a project from which I had conceived such great hopes, and from whence I imagined would be derived such great consequences. The particulars respecting the ill-fated ending of this serious—I may say great—affair shall be detailed in a narrative wherein all papers and letters connected with it will be inserted.[48] As this very commendable step of G[eneral] Arnold is likely to produce *great* and good consequences, I have thought it right to appoint him col[onel] of a reg[iment], with the rank of brigadier gen-

46. Arnold to Beckwith, June 7, 1780, Van Doren, *Secret History*, pp. 263–264.
47. Maj. Gen. William Phillips, who had been captured at Saratoga and was on parole in New York; see *ibid.*, pp. 212–213, 269, 277.
48. Printed in *ibid.*, pp. 482–495.

[eral] of p[rovincial] forces. I must beg leave to refer Your Lordship to him for other particulars and information.[49]

The unexpected and melancholy turn which my negotiation with General Arnold took, with respect to my Adjutant General, has filled my mind with the deepest concern. He was an active, intelligent, and useful officer, and a young gentleman who promised to be an honor to his country as well as an ornament to his profession. Therefore, as he has fallen a sacrifice to his great zeal for the King's service, I judged it right to consent to his wish that his company, which he purchased, may be sold for the benefit of his mother and sisters. But I trust, My Lord, that Your Lordship will think Major André's misfortune still calls for some further support to his family, and I beg leave to make it my humble request that you will have the goodness to recommend them in the strongest manner to the King for some beneficial and distinguishing mark of His Majesty's favor.[50] [Partly printed in Winthrop Sargent, *The Life and Career of Major John André* (Boston, 1861), pp. 256–257.]

> Extract of a letter from Colonel Hamilton, aide-de-camp to General Washington, to Isaac Sears, Esq., of Boston [October 12, 1780], found in a rebel mail which was intercepted on the 22d of October, 1780.

It is necessary we should rouse and begin to do our business in earnest, or we shall play a losing game. It is impossible the contest can be much longer supported upon the present footing. We must have a government with more power. We must have a tax in kind. We must have a foreign loan. We must have a bank on the true principles of a bank. We must have an *administration different from Congress, and in the hands of single men* under their orders. We must, above all things, have an army for the war, and on an establishment that will interest the officers in the service. The states must sink under the burden of temporary enlistments, and the enemy will conquer us by degrees during the intervals of our weakness.

Clinton is now said to be making a considerable detachment to the southward. *My fears are high, my hopes low.* We are told here there is to be a congress of the mutual powers at the Hague for mediating a peace. *God send it may be true; we want it.* But, if the idea gets abroad, 'tis ten to one if we do not fancy the thing done, and fall into a profound sleep until the cannon of the enemy awakens us next campaign.

49. A reference to Arnold's long letter to Germain, *ibid.*, pp. 372, 375–377.
50. The concluding paragraph is omitted in Clinton's draft, but is in the extract of the finished letter that he gives in his note.

This is our national character. [Henry Cabot Lodge, ed., *The Works of Alexander Hamilton* (12 vols., New York and London, 1904), 9, 224–225.]

Extract from Sir Henry Clinton's instructions to Major General Leslie. Headquarters, October 12, 1780.

You will be pleased to proceed with the troops embarked under your command to Chesapeake Bay. And upon your arrival you will pursue such measures as you shall judge most likely to answer the purposes of this expedition, the principal object of which is to make a diversion in favor of Lieutenant General Earl Cornwallis, who by the time you arrive there will probably be acting in the back parts of North Carolina. The information you shall procure on the spot, after your arrival at your destined port, will point out to you the properest method of accomplishing this. But, from that which I have received here, *I should judge it best to proceed up James River as high as possible, in order to seize or destroy any magazines the enemy may have at Petersburg, Richmond, or any of the places adjacent,* and *finally* to establish a post on Elizabeth River. But this, as well as the direction of every other operation, is submitted to Earl Cornwallis, with whom you are as soon as possible to communicate, and afterward to follow all such orders and directions as you shall from time to time receive from His Lordship. [Stevens, *Clinton-Cornwallis Controversy*, 1, 270–271, where the letter is dated October 10.]

[Extract of Germain to Clinton. October 13, 1780.]

His Majesty has been pleased to direct me to acquaint you that he is so sensible of the inconvenience which must arise to his service from the want of confidence between the Commanders in Chief of the land and sea forces that His Majesty has been pleased to appoint Admiral Arbuthnot to relieve Sir Peter Parker in the command at Jamaica; and another flag officer now on the list will be immediately named to the command in North America. You may be further assured that such a reinforcement of troops as can be spared from this country, and from the extensive operations in which it is engaged, will be sent to you, together with as many recruits as can be collected toward completing your army.

I have now explained to you as distinctly as I am able His Majesty's intentions, and how far your requests can be complied with. Such gracious attentions on the part of His Majesty must lead me to conclude that you will, with pleasure and satisfaction, wish to continue in the command. But, should you notwithstanding desire to return home, His Majesty in that case (though unwillingly) permits you to resign the command of his forces to Lord Cornwallis, leaving with His Lordship, or transmitting to him, all instructions and other papers which may be necessary for his conduct and information. [Calendared in Hist. MSS Com., *American MSS in the Royal Institution, 2,* 191.]

Extract of a letter from Colonel Lord Rawdon to Major General Leslie. October 24, 1780.

Major Ferguson, with about 800 militia collected from the neighborhood of Ninety-six, had previously marched into Tryon County to protect our friends who were supposed to be numerous there, and it was intended that he should cross the Catawba River and endeavor to preserve tranquillity in the rear of the army. A numerous army now appeared on the frontiers, drawn from Nolachucky and other settlements beyond the mountains, whose very names had been unknown to us. A body of these, joined by the inhabitants of the ceded lands in Georgia, made a sudden and violent attack upon Augusta.[51] Major Ferguson, by endeavoring to intercept the enemy in their retreat, unfortunately gave time for fresh bodies of men to pass the mountains and to unite into a corps far superior to that which he commanded. They came up with him and, after a sharp action, entirely defeated him. Ferguson was killed, and all his party either slain or taken.

By the enemy's having secured all the passes on the Catawba Lord Cornwallis received but confused accounts of the affair for some time, and the delay gave His Lordship great reason to fear for the safety of Ninety-six. To secure that district was indispensable for the security of the rest of the province, and His Lordship saw no means of effecting it but by passing the Catawba River with his army; for it was so weakened by sickness that it could not bear detachment. After much fatigue on the march, we passed the river three days ago. We then received the first intelligence respecting our different posts in this province which had reached us for near three weeks, every express from Camden having been waylaid and some of them murdered by the inhabitants. Ninety-six is safe, the corps which defeated Ferguson having, in consequence of our movements, crossed the Catawba and joined Smallwood on the Yadkin.

In our present position we have received the first intimation of the expedition under your command. From the circumstances which I have detailed, we fear that we are too far asunder to render your cooperation

51. *Clinton's note:* Why did you not let loose the Indians upon them?

very effectual. No force has presented itself to us whose opposition could have been thought serious against this army, but then we have little hopes of ever bringing the affair to the issue of an action. The enemy are mostly mounted militia, not to be overtaken by our infantry nor to be safely pursued in this strong country by our cavalry. *Our fear is that instead of meeting us they would slip by us into this province, were we to proceed far from it, and might again stimulate the disaffected to serious insurrection. This apprehension, you will judge, sir, must greatly circumscribe our efforts.* The Commander in Chief has complied so very *fully and completely* with Lord Cornwallis' request by sending so powerful a force to make a diversion in the Chesapeake that His Lordship fears he should require too much were he to draw you into the more immediate service of *this* district. Should your knowledge of Sir Henry Clinton's desires prompt you to make a trial upon North Carolina, *Cape Fear River* appears to us to be the only part where your efforts are at present likely to be effectual. *A descent there would be the surest means of joining and arming the friends of government, as well as of cooperating with this army.* [Stevens, *Clinton-Cornwallis Controversy*, 1, 272–275.]

Extract of a letter from Sir Henry Clinton to Admiral Arbuthnot. New York, 29 October 1780.

I cannot help expressing my astonishment at hearing that the *Rainbow* and *Camilla*, with their convoy, are still with you. And I must beg leave to observe that whatever fatal consequences may result to this army from the want of provisions I am to impute to this unfortunate circumstance and [to] your sending the three army victualers to Halifax without doing me the honor to consult me—though you knew our distress, and that the garrison there had a greater supply than they wanted. For I have the mortification to inform Your Excellency that I do not at this moment possess one month's provisions with all I can collect, and I do not hear a word of our expected victualers from Cork.

Extract of a letter from Lord Rawdon to Sir Henry Clinton. Camp between Broad River and the Catawba, October 29, 1780.

Orders were therefore dispatched [after the Battle of Camden] to our friends in North Carolina, stating that the hour which they had so long pressed was arrived, and exhorting them to stand forth immediately and prevent the reunion of the scattered enemy. Instant support was in that case promised to them. In the fullest confidence that event was to take place, Lord Cornwallis ventured to press Your Excellency for cooperation in the Chesapeake, hoping that the assistance of the North Carolinians might eventually furnish a force for yet further favorable efforts. Not a single man, however, attempted to improve the favorable moment, or obeyed that summons for which they had before been so impatient. It was hoped that our approach might get the better of their timidity. Yet during a long period whilst we were waiting at Charlotteburg for our stores and convalescents, they did not even furnish us with the least information respecting the force collecting against us.

In short, sir, we may have a powerful body of friends in North Carolina (and indeed we have cause to be convinced that many of the inhabitants wish well to His Majesty's arms); but they have not given evidence enough either of their numbers or of their activities to *justify the stake of this province for the uncertain advantages that might attend immediate junction with them. There is too much reason to conceive that such must have been the risk.*[52] Lord Cornwallis foresees all the difficulties of a defensive war, *yet His Lordship thinks they cannot be weighed against the dangers which must have attended an obstinate adherence to his former plan.* [Stevens, *Clinton-Cornwallis Controversy, 1,* 278–279.]

Extract of a letter from Lord Rawdon to Major General Leslie. 31 October 1780.

Upon further consideration Lord Cornwallis fears that he may not have expressed himself strongly enough with regard to the expediency of the above movement. The difficulty which must attend a defensive war on this frontier, and the fear that he may neglect means which the Commander in Chief expects him to employ, induce Lord Cornwallis to request that you will undertake the descent and operations recommended upon the Cape Fear River. Lord Cornwallis hopes for the most speedy communication of your resolutions on this point. A movement upon our part without the assurance of your cooperation (which, I am to repeat, *can only be effectual in Cape Fear River*) promises but little and hazards much. But this army will be held in constant readiness to act with the utmost vigor in your support.

Extract of a letter from Sir Henry Clinton to Lord George Germain. October 31, 1780.

Your Lordship well knows how often this army has been on the eve of being reduced to the greatest distress for want of provisions since

52. *Clinton's note:* This before Leslie even had joined His Lordship.

I have had the honor to command it. The same melancholy prospect, notwithstanding the many representations that have been made on this subject, again appears in a very alarming degree. It becomes, therefore, highly necessary for me once more to represent to Your Lordship, as the Commissary General has repeatedly done to the Treasury Board, that, unless some measures are speedily adopted to supply us more effectually than we have hitherto been, I have the greatest reason to apprehend that the most fatal consequences will ensue.

Were I to name the many other instances of the service suffering from the arrangements which Admiral Arbuthnot makes without consulting me, Your Lordship would be fully convinced that it cannot go on with any prospect of advantage to the King's interest while we are acting together. For my own part I am so thoroughly persuaded of it that I must beg leave to entreat [that] Your Lordship will have the goodness to attend in a particular manner to the requests I have already made on the subject of myself and Admiral Arbuthnot, and that you will submit them from me most humbly for His Majesty's consideration.

Extract of a letter from Lieutenant Colonel Balfour to Major General Leslie, without date [November, 1780].

I wrote to you a few days ago by the express sloop, and have only to repeat *that the safety of this province now is concerned in your getting as fast as possible near us.* Gates is advancing, as we are told, toward this province and already [is] near it. [Stevens, *Clinton-Cornwallis Controversy, 1,* 301–302.]

[Extract from Arbuthnot to Clinton. No. 3 of November 1, 1780.]

I am most sincerely disposed to regret with Your Excellency that the three army victualers have been sent to Halifax. When the army is in want of any articles of comfort or convenience that I can communicate, I consider myself as a brother. And Your Excellency will do me the justice to be persuaded that I will with pleasure share the last biscuit with you.

Extract of a letter from Sir Henry Clinton to Admiral Arbuthnot. November 1, 1780.

While Monsieur de Ternay continues at Rhode Island, I am to suppose, of course, Your Excellency will make such a disposition of the fleet under your orders as will secure the Sound of Long Island. For, should the enemy possess themselves of it, a detachment of French and New England troops will be passed immediately over to Long Island, where they will be joined by most of the people at the east end of it, who are in general disaffected. And the consequence of such an event would be most fatal, particularly at a time when my great detachments to the southward have so much reduced the army under my immediate command.

Extract from the second instructions from Sir Henry Clinton to Major General Leslie. New York, November 2, 1780.

Should Lord Cornwallis have passed the Yadkin and be advanced toward Hillsboro, I think you cannot act anywhere so well as on James River, approaching sometimes toward the Roanoke but not passing that river without orders from His Lordship. If you have *every reason* to believe that His Lordship meets with opposition at his passage of the Yadkin, *I think a move on Cape Fear River* will operate effectually. I have had much conversation with General O'Hara on this subject. I have given him every information respecting that move, and I trust that after consulting him you will act in the best manner possible to fulfill the *object of all your instructions—a diversion in favor of Lord Cornwallis.* You will, of course, cautiously avoid enrolling any of the militia of Princess Anne or elsewhere, without you determine to establish a post. Those, however, who voluntarily join you must be taken care of. [Stevens, *Clinton-Cornwallis Controversy, 1, 286.*]

Extract of a letter from Major General Leslie to Sir Henry Clinton. Portsmouth, Virginia, November 4, 1780.

We anchored in Chesapeake, after a most favorable passage, and the next day proceeded up as high as Lynnhaven. The day following the shipping proceeded to Sewell's Point. The parties that landed found the inhabitants either unwilling or unable to give any satisfactory intelligence relative to Lord Cornwallis' army. *The principal that could be collected was that the country was acquainted with our destination some weeks before our arrival, which had given them time to take measures to oppose us by erecting batteries on the banks of the narrow parts of James River, fortifying Richmond, and collecting a formidable militia.* I was also acquainted that the people of the country about Portsmouth were in the greatest consternation, being impressed with an idea of our being sent to distress them. The above accounts, the difficulty of the navigation of James River, the want of pilots, our uncertainty with regard to Lord Cornwallis, and the diffidence of the people of the country (who it was dangerous to leave behind us in the opinion they had formed of our intentions) all led us to resolve unanimously that a post ought to be established at Portsmouth *prior* to our penetrating further into the country. [The original in the CP (filed under Nov. 6) differs in numerous minor details.]

Extract of a letter from Sir Henry Clinton to Earl Cornwallis. November 6, 1780 (received by Lord Cornwallis December 3).

However, when I know Your Lordship's success in North Carolina and your determination respecting a post in Elizabeth River, I will then consider what additional force I can spare. If Your Lordship determines to withdraw that post, I shall in that case think your present force, including General Leslie's, quite sufficient. *If my wishes are fulfilled, they are that you may establish a post at Hillsboro, feed it from Cross Creek, and be able to keep that of Portsmouth.* A few troops will do it, and carry on desultory expeditions in Chesapeake until more solid operations can take place, of which I fear there is no prospect without we are considerably reinforced. The moment I know Your Lordship's determination to keep a post at Portsmouth I will, as I said before, consider what additional force I can spare. Once assured of our remaining superior at sea, I might possibly send 2000 more for this winter's operation. With respect to operations in Chesapeake, they are but of two sorts: solid operations with a fighting army to call forth our friends and support them; or a post such as Portsmouth, carrying on desultory expeditions, stopping up in a great measure the Chesapeake and, by commanding the James River, prevent[ing] the enemy from forming any considerable depots upon it or moving in any force to the southward of it. Such, My Lord, are the advantages I expect from a station at Portsmouth, and I wish it may appear to Your Lordship in the same light. God grant us peace with Spain and a reinforcement of 10,000 men, and then Your Lordship may see a speedy end to this unhappy war. [All but the last sentence is in Stevens, *Clinton-Cornwallis Controversy, 1,* 287–288.]

Extract of a letter from Sir Henry Clinton to Lord George Germain. New York, November 12, 1780.

I must also most seriously lament, My Lord, that the present situation in force of Mr. Washington and that of the French will necessarily prevent me from replacing the troops which were in the Chesapeake. And yet I profess, My Lord, to be of opinion that a post established at Portsmouth, on Elizabeth River, would be of great consequence. It is needless to add that my situation becomes weakened by Sir George Rodney quitting this coast.

Extract of a letter from Earl Cornwallis to Major General Leslie. Winnsboro, 12 November 1780.

If you come to Cape Fear River, of which at present I have little doubt, by the help of galleys and small craft (which will be sent you from Charleston) you will easily secure a water conveyance for your stores up to Cross Creek. I will, on hearing of your arrival in Cape Fear, instantly march with everything that can be safely spared from this province—which, I am sorry to say, is *most exceedingly disaffected*— to join you at Cross Creek. We will then give our friends in North Carolina a fair trial. If they behave like men, it may be of the greatest advantage to the affairs of Britain. If they are as dastardly and pusillanimous as our friends to the southward, *we must leave them to their fate and secure what we have got.* If you find it difficult, from contrary winds, to get into Cape Fear River, the entrance of which is not easy to vessels coming from the northward by the projection of the Frying Pan Shoal, it will be very little out of your way to look into Charleston, and you will enter Cape Fear River with every assistance that can be procured from thence. [Stevens, *Clinton-Cornwallis Controversy, 1,* 295–296.]

[Extract of a letter] found in a rebel mail, captured December 8, 1780, [from] General Sullivan to the President of the Council of New Hampshire. November 15 [1780].

A new army is now arranged, and the states called upon for men and specific supplies. A committee is appointed for arranging our finances [and] a loan from France solicited in the most pressing and positive terms, and a regular system will soon take place. Every day's experience proves that many of our distresses arise from a want of power in Congress to carry any of their measures into execution. They send requisitions to the states; some comply, some do not, and the consequence of this is too obvious to need explanation. Hence it is that our army is often ready to perish with hunger and cold. At present we have no money in the treasury. Our army is almost naked, yet we have had clothing sufficient for them at Cape François more than eighteen months, and frigates employed on useless adventures. In short, this season has exhibited a scene of misfortunes scarcely to be equaled in history. Many of them have arisen from unforeseen events, and too many from our own inattention and neglect. General Clinton is about embarking with a large force, I suppose for the southern states, to employ the winter there as he did the last, though I hope not so successfully. [Hammond, *Letters and Papers of Major-General John Sullivan, 3,* 200–204.]

[Extract of Sullivan to the President of the Council of New Hampshire. November 19, 1780 (intercepted with the preceding letter).]

As I was informed that upon the new arrangements of the army there was a contention among the New Hampshire officers for retiring, which gave much uneasiness to His Excellency General Washington, I took the liberty of addressing them in writing, which I hope will meet with the approbation of the honorable assembly. [*Ibid.*, p. 210.]

[Extract of a letter] from Quartermaster General Pickering to Governor Trumbull. November 20th [1780 (intercepted with the preceding letters).]

The particular states have exhausted their funds in purchasing partial supplies; the Continental treasury, of consequence, remained empty. The army has been without pay, but half clothed, and not seldom ill fed. The numerous mischiefs that have flowed from those troops are seriously alarming. The long continued sufferings of the troops have produced many resignations of excellent officers and great desertions among the soldiers. Their distresses will, I fear, be renewed and increased. For, as not a single magazine of provision or forage is yet formed and the subsistence of the troops will depend on daily transportation through the winter (which is ever precarious) and the provisions themselves are yet to be procured, I cannot but be apprehensive of the troops suffering extremely.

[Extract of a letter] from Arthur Lee, Esq., to Reverend Doctor Gordon, November 21, 1780 [intercepted with the preceding letters].

The old leaven prevails so much in Congress that I find great difficulty in obtaining from them simple justice. With regard to their public conduct, from anything I can learn they are too much influenced—if not entirely governed—by a man who in my conscience I think has been stationed among them from the beginning to direct their proceedings to the purposes of our enemy. His intimate connection with Galloway, Deane, and Arnold, his devising the late destructive paper plan, and his now contriving in Congress to frustrate every effectual measure for obtaining a foreign loan are facts perfectly know[n] to that very body on which our fate depends, and in which he sits and sways. It is to be hoped that the virtue and wisdom of Congress will at length recover from the torpor which enables this man to dupe and deceive them.[53]

[Extract of a letter] from General Daniel Lyman to John G. Wanton, Esq. November 24 [1780, intercepted with the preceding letters].

This campaign has stolen away without furnishing materials for either censure or applause. The operations of the enemy have been little more successful. The action at Camden can be considered as nothing more than a promiscuous carnage, and the respite from slaughter only furnished a stimulus for more vigorous exertions. Unable to improve their advantages, and buoyed up by a success which in its operations proved merely ideal, they have been checked in the very commencement of their rapid progress by a handful of determined freemen, their detachments destroyed, and their hopes blasted. This event, though apparently small in the beginning, has been productive of happy consequences.

Extract of a letter from Lord Cornwallis to Sir Henry Clinton. December 3, 1780.

Winnsboro, my present position, is an healthy spot, well situated to protect the greatest part of the northern frontier, and to assist Camden and Ninety-six. The militia of the latter, on which alone we could place the smallest dependence, was so totally disheartened by the defeat of Ferguson that, of that whole district, we could with difficulty assemble 100; and even those, I am convinced, would not have made the smallest resistance if they had been attacked. I determined to remain at this place until an answer arrived from General Leslie (on which my plan for the winter was to depend), and to use every possible means of putting the province into a state of defense, which I found to be absolutely necessary whether my campaign was offensive or defensive.

Bad as the state of our affairs was on the northern frontier, the eastern part was much worse. Colonel Tynes, who commanded the militia of the high hills of Santee and who was posted on Black River, was surprised and taken, and his men lost all their arms. Colonel Marion had so wrought on the minds of the people, partly by the terror of his threats and cruelty of his punishments and partly by the promise of plunder,

53. Probably James Duane, of New York, who at this time was the object of Lee's particular antipathy. (See Edmund C. Burnett, ed., *Letters of Members of the Continental Congress* [8 vols., Washington, 1921–36], 5, 426, n.) Lee was presumably writing to the Rev. William Gordon, the historian of the Revolution.

that there was scarce an inhabitant between the Santee and Pedee that was not in arms against us. Some parties had even crossed the Santee and *carried terror to the gates of Charleston.* My first object was to reinstate matters in that quarter, without which Camden could receive no supplies. I therefore sent Tarleton, who pursued Marion for several days, obliged his corps to take to the swamps, and—by convincing the inhabitants that there was a power, superior to Marion, who could likewise reward and punish—so far checked the insurrection that the greatest part of them have not dared openly to appear in arms against us since his expedition.

The Sixty-third Regiment, under Major Wemyss, had been mounted on indifferent horses of the country, for the purpose of reducing and disarming the Cheraws. It had afterward been sent by Lord Rawdon for the security of Ninety-six. When I sent Lieutenant Colonel Tarleton to the low country, I ordered Major Wemyss to come down to Broad River [and] to keep constantly moving on either side of the river he might think proper, for the protection of the mills from which the army subsisted and for the preservation of the country. Sumter then lay with about three hundred men, partly militia and partly of the banditti who have followed him ever since the reduction of this province, near Hill's Ironworks, between the Catawba and Broad Rivers, about forty miles in our front. Branan, Clarke, and others had different corps, plundering the houses and putting to death the well affected inhabitants between Tiger River and the Pacolet. Major Wemyss, who had just passed Broad River at Bryerly's Ferry, came to me on the 7th of last month and told me that he had information that Sumter had moved to Moore's Mill, within five miles of Fishdam Ford and about twenty-five miles from the place where the Sixty-third then lay, that he had accurate accounts of his position and good guides, and that he made no doubt of being able to surprise and rout him. As the defeating so daring and troublesome a man as Sumter and dispersing such a banditti was a great object, I consented to his making the trial on the 9th at daybreak, and gave him forty of the dragoons which Tarleton had left with me, desiring him, however, neither to put them in the front nor to make any use of them during the night.

Major Wemyss marched so early and so fast on the night of the 8th that he arrived at Moore's Mill soon after midnight. He then had information that Sumter had marched that evening to Fishdam Ford, where he lay with his rear close to Broad River on a low piece of ground. The Major immediately proceeded to attack him in his new position, and succeeded so well as to get into his camp whilst the men were all sleeping round the fires. But, as Major Wemyss rode into the camp at the head of the dragoons and the Sixty-third followed them on horse-back, the enemy's arms were not secured; and some of them, recovering from the first alarm, got their rifles, and with the first fire wounded Major Wemyss in several places and put the cavalry into disorder. The Sixty-third then dismounted and killed and wounded about seventy of the rebels, drove several over the river, and dispersed the rest. The command, however, devolving on a very young officer, who neither knew the ground nor Major Wemyss' plan nor the strength of the enemy (some few of which kept firing from the wood on our people who remained in the enemy's camp, and who were probably discovered by their fires), our troops came away before daybreak, leaving Major Wemyss and twenty-two sergeants and rank and file at a house close to the field of action. In the morning those that were left with a flag of truce with the wounded found that the enemy were all gone; but, on some of their scouting parties discovering that our people had likewise retired, Sumter returned and took Major Wemyss' parole for himself and the wounded soldiers.

The enemy on this event cried victory, and the whole country came in fast to Sumter, who passed the Broad River and joined Branan, Clarke, etc. I detached Major McArthur with the first battalion of the Seventy-first and the Sixty-third Regiment to Bryerly's Ferry, in order to cover our mills and to give some check to the enemy's march to Ninety-six. At the same time I recalled Lieutenant Colonel Tarleton from the low country. Tarleton was so fortunate as to pass not only the Wateree but the Broad River without General Sumter's being apprised of it—who, having increased his corps to one thousand, had passed the Enoree and was on the point of attacking our hundred militia at William's House, fifteen miles from Ninety-six, and where I believe he would not have met with much resistance. Tarleton would have surprised him on the south of Enoree had not a deserter of the Sixty-third given notice of his march. He [Tarleton], however, cut to pieces his rear guard in passing that river, and pursued his main body with such rapidity that he [Sumter] could not safely pass the Tiger, and was obliged to halt on a very strong position at a place called Blackstock's, close to it.

Tarleton had with him only his cavalry and the Sixty-third mounted, his infantry and three-pounder being several miles behind. The enemy, not being able to retreat with safety, and being informed of Tarleton's approach and want of infantry by a woman who passed him on the march and contrived by a nearer road to get to them, were encouraged by their great superiority of numbers, and began to fire on the Sixty-third, who were dismounted. Lieutenant Colonel Tarleton, to save them from considerable loss, was obliged to attack, although at some hazard, and drove the enemy with loss over the river. Sumter was dangerously wounded, three of their colonels killed, and about one hundred and twenty men killed, wounded, or taken. On our side about fifty were killed and wounded. Lieutenant Colonel Tarleton pursued and dispersed the remaining part of Sumter's corps; and then, having assembled some militia under Major Cunningham, he returned to the Broad River, where he at present remains, as well as Major Mc-Arthur, in the neighborhood of Bryerly's Ferry.

Morgan's infantry and Washington with 100 cavalry came down on the 1st in the evening to attack a blockhouse built by Colonel Rugeley, in which he had placed himself with 100 militia. The enemy infantry did not advance within six miles of his blockhouse; but the cavalry surrounded it and summoned him, and he instantly surrendered without firing a shot.

After everything that has happened, I will not presume to make Your Excellency any sanguine promises. *The force you have sent me is greater than I expected, and full as much as I think you could possibly spare* unless the enemy detached in force to the southward. *It is from events alone that any future plan can be proposed.* [Stevens, *Clinton-Cornwallis Controversy, 1,* 303–309.]

[Extract of Arbuthnot to Clinton. New York, December 9, 1780.]

I have already communicated to Your Excellency the King's orders to send five ships of the line, at least, from this station to the Leeward Islands when the season no longer admits of conjunct operation with the army and fleet. The armaments of the enemy said to be on their way against our possessions in the West Indies press my immediate compliance therewith. I accordingly have the honor to acquaint you that I shall give the necessary orders immediately to Rear Admiral Graves to proceed to the Leeward Islands with six ships of the line.

[Extract of Clinton to Arbuthnot. New York, December 9, 1780.]

I cannot avoid referring to Your Excellency's reflection the great consequence your fleet in its present situation in Gardiners Bay is to the King's service here, and that [by detaching] you will give the enemy opportunity of possessing a part of Long Island Sound and beginning operations there which may, in our present situation, prove most fatal. It would assuredly have a most dangerous effect at any time, but particularly so now, when so great a French force as 6000 men are on Rhode Island, ready to undertake any enterprise so soon as their fleet shall be superior here. By all accounts, I look upon this instant as most critical. Washington's army by the 1st of January will be greatly reduced. But, if he can show them a prospect of acting to advantage on Long Island (which your quitting Gardiners Bay will certainly give him), he will not only be able to keep for that purpose his present army, but that will be greatly increased by numbers of militia, whom such a prospect might induce to join him. You are sensible, sir, that the present expedition to Virginia, and such others as from the reasons above mentioned I have in contemplation to undertake, will depend on the aid you can give it in the first instance, and its safety afterward on the *certainty of their not being insulted*—which may, if not must, happen whenever you permit the French fleet to be superior. I will conclude by observing to Your Excellency that, by giving up your present superiority over Monsieur de Ternay, you destroy our present cooperation and prevent any in future during the winter. In short, sir, you give us little to hope and much to fear.

[Extract of Arbuthnot to Clinton. New York, December 12, 1780.]

If Your Excellency will point out a third object [54] for the ships of the line to act, I will join to attain it with the greatest pleasure. But I apprehend the lying inactive in Gardiners Bay the whole winter, if it be practicable (which has not yet been determined), will not be deemed excusable at home when my orders are so absolute to the contrary. I request, therefore, that Your Excellency will furnish me such objects for action as may justify my disobedience of directions so unconditional as these in question.

[Extract of Clinton to Arbuthnot. New York, December 12, 1780.]

I beg leave to observe that I cannot look upon your instructions from the Lords of the Admiralty as unconditional, nor that all conjunct operations are over. Surely, sir, your remaining in Gardiners Bay, masking the enemy's fleet at Rhode Island while your frigates assist in the operations of the army (also very essential to those [troops] under Lord Cornwallis), besides answering many other important purposes, are conjunct operations. And, even if you should think that your fleet cannot lay in safety in Gardiners Bay (which you did not seem to doubt when I had the honor of seeing you last), I think other conjunct operations may be most important in Chesapeake; and I will for the purpose give every assistance in my power.

54. Arbuthnot and Clinton had been discussing, in sections that are omitted, the convoys required for Arnold's expedition and for Leslie's move from the Chesapeake to South Carolina.

[Extract of Clinton to Arbuthnot. New York, December 13, 1780.]

If the advantages a superiority at sea gives were to be transferred from us to the enemy, I should not only lose the hope of the success, but fear for the safety, of the forces that are and may be sent on different and distant expeditions. Far from thinking this the time when co-operation between the fleet and army should cease, I think their conjunct efforts may become at this critical season most necessary, not only for supporting the operations already undertaken but for extending them, should either be necessary. And you must be sensible, sir, nothing can be undertaken should the enemy become masters at sea.

The approach of the winter season may make the continuance of the fleet in Gardiners Bay of less importance than it appears to me to be at the present. And I therefore flatter myself that you will not quit that station before January, by which time it is probable the events of the war to the southward may make it necessary and proper for me to carry on offensive operations in Chesapeake Bay, which I should not dare to undertake without the protection of a fleet superior to that of the enemy. I will request of you, sir, to give this and my other letters on this subject your most serious consideration. And I will hope Your Excellency will give your answer so soon as convenient, as the sailing or not of the expedition under Brigadier General Arnold will depend on Your Excellency's determination.

[Extract of Arbuthnot to Clinton. New York, December 13, 1780.]

I am honored with Your Excellency's letter. I have given it and your other letters upon the same subject a just consideration. I have yielded to Your Excellency's reasons, and to the nature of our situation. I shall not, in consequence, detach the line-of-battle ships to the West Indies, but reserve them to cooperate with Your Excellency according to the objects Your Excellency has proposed. I beg, therefore, that Your Excellency in this assurance will give your final orders for the expedition under Brigadier General Arnold to sail, as no time should be lost at so critical a season. The squadron shall remain in Gardiners Bay as long as the season will admit.

Extract from Sir Henry Clinton's letter to Lord Cornwallis. December 13, 1780 (received January 6, 1781).

Wishing to give Your Lordship's operations in North Carolina every assistance in my power, though I can ill spare it I have sent another expedition into the Chesapeake, under the orders of Brigadier General Arnold, Lieutenant Colonels Dundas and Simcoe. The force by land

is not equal to that which sailed with General Leslie, but I am not
without hopes it will operate most essentially in favor of Your Lordship, either by striking at Gates' depot at Petersburg (which I have
still reason to think is considerable) or finally by taking post at Portsmouth. *If we take post there [and] fortify and assemble the inhabitants,
it ought not afterward to be quitted;* and therefore I cannot suppose
your Lordship *will wish to alter the disposition of this corps without
absolute necessity.* On the contrary, I flatter myself that (*should your
Lordship's success be such* as you will, I hope, *now* have reason to expect) that you will reinforce that corps and enable it to act *offensively.*
When that is your intention, I am to request that the following corps
may in their turn be considered for that service: viz., the troops of
Seventeenth Dragoons, the Jägers, the detachment of the Seventeenth
foot, and the provincial light infantry. I need not tell Your Lordship
that these detachments have left me very bare indeed of troops, nor
that Washington still continues very strong (at least 12,000 men), having not detached a single man to the southward except Lee's cavalry
(about 250). Should Your Lordship at any time judge it expedient to
reinforce the corps under Brigadier General Arnold, you will of course
either continue it under his orders or send any other general officer
you think proper to take command, *whenever you may think such alteration necessary.* [Stevens, *Clinton-Cornwallis Controversy, 1,* 310–312.]

Extract from Sir Henry Clinton's instructions to Brigadier General
Arnold. Headquarters, New York, December 14, 1780.

You will be pleased to proceed with the troops which are embarked
under your command to Chesapeake Bay. And, if a favorable opportunity of striking at any of the enemy's magazines should offer itself,
you are at liberty to attempt it, provided it may be done without much
risk. But, if there should be no prospect of effecting that or any other
partial service, you are as soon as possible to establish a post at Portsmouth on Elizabeth River in Virginia, make known your intention of
remaining there, distribute the proclamations you take with you (which
are to be addressed to the inhabitants of Princess Anne and Norfolk
Counties), and assemble and arm such of those people as you shall
have reason to believe are well affected to His Majesty's government
and are inclined to join you. It is, however, by no means my intention
that you should invite the inhabitants of other districts to join you till
such time as you can establish yourself and afford them the like protection as is held out to those of Princess Anne and Norfolk Counties.

Having sent Lieutenant Colonels Dundas and Simcoe (officers of
great experience and much in my confidence) with you, I am to desire

that you will always consult those gentlemen previous to your undertaking any operation of consequence. You will be able to judge from appearances on your arrival in Chesapeake whether it may be expedient to immediately establish the intended post. Should Lord Cornwallis, who will have been informed of your move, require any cooperation on your part before that is done, you are directed to obey His Lordship's commands. But, after you have established the post, it is my request that you do not undertake any operation with the least risk to that important station unless, after consulting the above-mentioned gentlemen, your reasons should be such as you shall all think sufficient for so doing, or Earl Cornwallis should positively direct.

Copy of the order referred to [by the Commissioners of Public Accounts], supposed to have been delivered to the Commissioners by Lord Cornwallis. Headquarters, Winnsboro, 23d December 1780.

As I consider myself a steward for the public money expended by the troops under my command, I think myself bound by the duty I owe my country to regulate the charges to be made by the different departments. The Commissary General is not to charge government for the complete ration delivered to the soldier unless such ration is supplied from the stores sent from England. Whenever he delivers to them fresh provisions, he must only charge to them the real amount of what he pays for the cattle, for which the receipts of the inhabitants will be his vouchers. The same rule must be strictly observed in the delivery of flour and India meal.[55] [Sir Henry Clinton, A Letter to the Commissioners of Public Accounts, pp. 12–13.]

Extract of a letter from Lord George Germain to Sir Henry Clinton. January 3d, 1781.

The having a secure port in the Chesapeake for our ships to resort to for supplies would enable them to continue on their station and intercept the whole trade of the bay, and thereby deprive the enemy of all remittances through that channel. And the establishment of that post would deter the French from sending any troops there to make a diversion in favor of Washington or Gates, *which there is reason to expect they may do.* For, although the destination of the armament

55. *Clinton's note:* Sir Henry Clinton has not yet met with an officer of Lord Cornwallis' army who can recollect the issuing of the above order. Nor does any such order appear in any of His Lordship's orderly books that have hitherto reached his hands.

484 THE AMERICAN REBELLION

which I formerly told you was preparing last summer for the Chesapeake appears to have been changed, it is highly probable, if they send any troops to North America in the spring—as our intelligence says they intend doing—that they will pursue their former purpose and send a part into the Chesapeake, and secure that important post when they hear we have abandoned it. On all these accounts I regret exceedingly that, as Brigadier General Leslie has been called away, you could not spare a detachment from New York for such important purposes. But I trust you will yet find means of doing it, as the season of the year will secure you against any augmentation of the French force at Rhode Island. But, should you have judged it proper to defer making the detachment, I am commanded to acquaint you that it is the King's pleasure you do carry it into execution whenever the King's service will admit of it. My opinion of the importance of the measure, and of its great tendency to reduce the rebellion, makes me repeatedly press its execution. [Calendared in Hist. MSS Com., *American MSS in the Royal Institution*, 2, 232.]

Copy of the proposals made by Sir Henry Clinton to the Pennsylvania revolters [January 4, 1781].

To the person appointed by the Pennsylvania troops to lead them in the present struggle for their liberties and rights:

It being reported at New York that the Pennsylvania troops and others, having been defrauded of their pay, clothing, and provisions, are assembled to redress their grievances, and also (notwithstanding the terms of their enlistments are expired) [that] they have been forcibly detained in the service, where they have suffered every kind of misery and oppression, they are now offered to be taken under the protection of the British government, to have their rights restored, free pardon for all former offenses, and that pay due to them from the Congress faithfully paid to them (without any expectation of military service, except it may be voluntary) upon laying down their arms and returning to their allegiance. For which purpose, if they will send commissioners to Amboy, they will there be met by people empowered to treat with them, and faith pledged for their security.

It is recommended to them for their own safety to move behind South River; and, wherever they request it, a body of British troops shall protect them. It is needless to point out the inability as well as want of inclination in the Congress to relieve them, or to tell them the severities that will be used toward them by the rebel leaders should they think of returning to their former servitude. It will be proved to the commissioners they may choose to send that the authority from whence this comes is sufficient to insure the performance of the above proposals. [The substance of this document is in Van Doren, *Mutiny in January,* pp. 85–86.]

Extract of a letter from Lord Cornwallis to Sir Henry Clinton. Winnsboro, 6 January 1781.

The difficulties I have had to struggle with have not been occasioned by the opposite army (they always keep at a considerable distance, and retire on our approach) but [by] the constant incursions of refugees, North Carolinians, and back-mountain men, and the *perpetual risings in the different parts of this province.* The invariable successes of all these parties against our militia keep the whole country in continual alarm, and render the assistance of regular troops everywhere necessary. [Stevens, *Clinton-Cornwallis Controversy, 1,* 315.]

Extract from Lord Cornwallis' letter to Sir Henry Clinton. Camp on Turkey Creek, Broad River, 18 January 1781.

Lieutenant Colonel Tarleton conducted his march so well and got so near to General Morgan (who was retreating before him) as to make it dangerous for him to pass Broad River, and came up with him at 8:00 A.M. on the 17th instant. Everything now bore the most promising aspect: the enemy were drawn up in an open wood and, having been lately joined by some militia, were more numerous; but the different quality of the corps under Lieutenant Colonel Tarleton's command, and his great superiority in cavalry, left him no room to doubt of the most brilliant success.

The enemy's line soon gave way, and their militia quitted the field. But, our troops having been thrown into some disorder by the pursuit, General Morgan's corps faced about and gave them a heavy fire. This unexpected event occasioned the utmost confusion in the first line. The Seventy-first and the cavalry were successively ordered up; but neither the exertions, entreaties, nor example of Lieutenant Colonel Tarleton could prevent the panic from becoming general. [*Ibid.,* pp. 319–320.]

Extract from Lord Cornwallis to Lieutenant Colonel Tarleton. January 30, 1781.

The means you used to bring the enemy to action were able and masterly, and must ever do you honor. Your disposition was unexceptionable. The total misbehavior of the troops could alone have deprived you of the glory which was so justly your due. [Tarleton, *History*, p. 252.]

[Extract of Balfour to Clinton. January 31, 1781.]

In the night of the 25th instant a detachment of cavalry from Greene's army, under Colonels Lee and Marion, made an attempt on Georgetown. By the best accounts from Greene's army he was on the 25th to the eastward of the Pedee; and I learn his intentions are to distress this country by making frequent inroads of cavalry into it—one of which, yesterday morning, destroyed the wagons and Quartermaster General's stores at Monk's Corner. Two very enterprising officers, Lee and Marion, are employed on this service. [Calendared in Hist. MSS Com., *American MSS in the Royal Institution*, 2, 240.]

[Extract of Germain to Clinton. February 7, 1781.]

It gave His Majesty particular satisfaction to find you had determined to replace Major General Leslie's detachment in Elizabeth River by one under Brigadier General Arnold, with positive orders to establish a permanent post there. [Calendared in *ibid.*, p. 244.]

Copy of a letter from Sir Henry Clinton to Admiral Arbuthnot. New York, 12 February 1781.

Sir:

I was last night honored with Your Excellency's letter of the 9th instant, and most heartily congratulate you on the safe return of the *America*. I rejoice also much to hear that the weather has been so favorable as to permit your saving everything belonging to the unfortunate *Culloden* (except her hull), which softens in some degree the great severity of her loss. And I hope your sailors will be soon able to recover from the fatigue they have been exposed to on this melancholy occasion. Your own feelings I sincerely sympathize in, and shall be happy to hear that you are perfectly recovered from your indisposition. I have the honor, etc., Henry Clinton.

[Extract of Balfour to Clinton. February 13, 1781.]

Small parties of the enemy are continually making incursions into this province, and threaten greatly to distress it. [Calendared in Hist. MSS Com., *American MSS in the Royal Institution*, 2, 245.]

[Extract of Balfour to Clinton. February 14, 1781.]

I shall, as soon as every necessary arrangement can be made, move a part of this garrison over the Santee, which I hope will free the country between that river and the Pedee of those parties of the enemy which of late have so much infested it, and restore to the lower district of the province that peace they have for some weeks been deprived of. [Calendared in *ibid.*, p. 246.]

[Extract of Nathaniel Greene to Thomas Jefferson. February 15, 1781.]

Almost fatigued to death, having had a retreat to conduct for upward of 200 miles, maneuvering constantly in face of the enemy, to give time for the militia to turn out and get off our stores. [Julian P. Boyd, ed., *The Papers of Thomas Jefferson* (5 vols., Princeton, 1950–52), 4, 615–616.]

[Extract of Greene to Baron von Steuben. February 15, 1781.]

Colonel Williams, with the light infantry, Lieutenant Colonel Lee's Legion, and the cavalry of the First and Third Regiments, has covered our retreat, which he has conducted with great propriety in the most critical situation. Cornwallis' movements are so rapid that few or no militia join us. He marches from twenty to thirty miles in a day, and is organized to move with the same facility as a light infantry corps. Should he continue to push us, we must be finally ruined without reinforcements. [Nathaniel Greene Papers, Clements Library.]

[Extract of Greene to Washington. February 15, 1781.]

The miserable situation of the troops for want of clothing has rendered the march the most painful imaginable, several hundreds of the soldiers marking the ground with their bloody feet. I have not a shilling to obtain intelligence with. Our army is in good spirits, notwithstanding their sufferings and excessive fatigue. [Jared Sparks, ed., *Correspondence of the American Revolution: Being Letters of Eminent Men to George Washington, from the Time of His Taking Command of the Army to the End of His Presidency* (4 vols., Boston, 1853), 3, 234, 236.]

Extract of a letter from Sir Henry Clinton to Admiral Arbuthnot. New York, 17 February 1781.

As the enemy are supposed, from Mr. Brenton's seeming positive information, to have prepared 1300 men for the intended enterprise, I
have directed a very fair proportion of troops to be in instant readiness
to cooperate with any wishes or intentions of yours, to endeavor to
frustrate the designs and attempts of the rebels and their French friends.
And I shall request you will communicate your sentiments to me on
this very important subject, to which I shall pay every possible attention. I should most cheerfully have gone to Gardiners Bay to communicate with you, sir, on objects of such great importance, which
strike your Excellency so very strongly as you have described in your
letter to Lieutenant General Robertson (and which he has thought
proper to refer to me); but I am fearful it might be possible I should
not be so fortunate as to meet you there.

I, however, send to you, sir, Major Robertson, deputy Quartermaster
General, an officer of high trust, and in whom your Excellency may
place the utmost confidence. I am to request of you, sir, most earnestly
to have the goodness to explain to me by Major Robertson what may
be the mortal blow you mention in your letter to Lieutenant General
Robertson the enemy might receive at this instant. And be assured, sir,
I shall cooperate with you to my utmost power in the prosecution of
such plans as may be most likely to produce so happy an effect as a
mortal blow to the enemies of our country.

Copy of a letter from Admiral Arbuthnot to Captain Russell of
the *Beaumont*. *Royal Oak* in Gardiners Bay, 21 February 1781.

Sir:

As it is impossible but Captain Dawson of His Majesty's ship
the *Iris* must have left the port of New York before this time, I address
myself to you to desire that you will get ready with all expedition
possible such transports as His Excellency Sir Henry Clinton purposes
to employ upon a proposed and important service, and that you will
exert yourself as usual to push the whole, upon embarkation, down to
Sandy Hook, where they are to remain until I appear off that place
for them. I desire you will apply to Lieutenant General Robertson
(acquainting him that the measure is absolutely and indispensably necessary) for a general press both afloat and ashore to raise seamen for
the fleet, which I am much in want of. I desire also that yourself, Captain George, and your officers and ships' companies (excepting such as
are charged with stores) will also come down with the transports, to

serve as volunteers on the present service. Not a moment must be lost.
I am, etc., M. Arbuthnot.

[Extract of Balfour to Clinton. February 24, 1781.]

By intelligence brought me yesterday the post of Congaree's has
been for three days invested by seven or eight hundred men under
Colonel Sumter. [Calendared in Hist. MSS Com., *American MSS in
the Royal Institution*, 2, 248.]

Extract of a letter from Sir Henry Clinton to Lord George Germain. New York, February 28, 1781 (received April 25th).

It is much to be lamented that the want of a proper conveyance has
prevented Earl Cornwallis and me from communicating with each
other so often as was requisite to forward the King's service, though
perhaps at no time has this been more necessary, or have there been
so few ships of war to do it. For I am persuaded, if the Admiral had
any that could have been spared from other important services, His
Lordship and I would not have been so long ignorant of each other's
situation. I therefore think it my duty to state the circumstances to
Your Lordship, in the hope that an additional number of frigates will
be sent out to enable the naval commander here to cooperate in services
which I am sure Your Lordship will think very essential. [Calendared
in *ibid.*, p. 251.]

Extract of a letter from Sir Henry Clinton to Admiral Arbuthnot. New York, February 28th, 1781.

I fear, by Your Excellency's letter of the 25th, which I had the
honor to receive last night, that mine of the 23d has been misconceived.
It expressed a hope that you will not think it necessary to quit Gardiners
Bay, or at least this coast, leaving the French fleet behind you at Rhode
Island.

A land force is held in readiness to proceed from hence to the Chesapeake, and may be embarked from hence in a few hours for that purpose. But, as you tell me, sir, your motions must be governed by those
of the enemy, and that you cannot for any unimportant consideration
stop from pursuing the French in case they sail, I would submit to Your
Excellency whether it would not be better, in case they really do sail,
to follow them unencumbered; and, as soon as you have fixed them,
such a land force as I shall think necessary shall join you immediately
after you give me notice. If this meets Your Excellency's approbation,

you will possibly be pleased to order a sufficient convoy for the purpose.

I flatter myself, though you do not mention it, that you have already detached a sufficient force to clear the Chesapeake Bay. For, should the enemy remain too long in possession of it, though our post at Portsmouth is perfectly secure against an army attempting to penetrate from the land side, it is not so from a landing in Lynnhaven or Willoughby Bay. As to the remainder of the French fleet now at Rhode Island, I cannot conceive it will venture to sea, encumbered with transports, while it knows that a superior force of copper-bottomed ships, unencumbered, is ready to follow.

In short, sir, if the whole French fleet and troops in Rhode Island go to the Chesapeake and you follow them, not having it in their power to act against the post at Portsmouth, they will proceed up York River to that town [Yorktown] and there, under the cover of works which were raised last year on each side on very commanding ground to protect the *Fendant* and two frigates that wintered there, perhaps place themselves in a situation in which an attack by your ships alone might not be advisable. Should the French remain at Rhode Island and you continue at Gardiners Bay, I may possibly, if Mr. Washington detaches to Chesapeake, wish to send thither a reinforcement also, for which I am persuaded you will have the goodness to give a convoy.

[Extract of Clinton to Cornwallis. March 2, 1781.]

Your Lordship may probably hear *that the army and navy in the Chesapeake are blocked up by a superior French naval force to that under Captain Symonds.* The first account I had of it was from General Arnold, dated the 14th of February; and I sent it immediately to the Admiral at Gardiners Bay. A day or two afterward I had it confirmed that they were part of the fleet from Rhode Island, which, I have heard since, sailed from thence on the 9th *ultimo*—notwithstanding which I greatly fear he has not sent a naval force to relieve them. *Washington has detached some New England troops under Lafayette and Howe that way.*

If so much time is given, I cannot answer for consequences. Portsmouth is safe at this season against any attack from the Suffolk side, but not so from a landing in any of the bays to the southward of Elizabeth River. I have much to lament that the Admiral did not think it advisable to send there at first, as Brigadier General Arnold's projected move in favor of Your Lordship's operations will have been stopped. *And, if the Admiral delays it too long, I shall dread still more fatal consequences.* I have troops already embarked in a great proportion to that of the enemy; *but to send them under two frigates only, before the Chesapeake is our own, is to sacrifice the troops and their convoy.* Should the troops already embarked for the Chesapeake *proceed* and, when there, be able to undertake any operation in addition to what the Brigadier General proposes, I am confident it will be done. *Major General Phillips will command this expedition. I shall tremble for our post at Portsmouth* should the enemy's reinforcement arrive in that neighborhood before the force which I now flatter myself the Admiral will order a sufficient convoy for arrives. [Stevens, *Clinton-Cornwallis Controversy, 1,* 341–344; the second paragraph is there dated Mar. 5, as it is in Clinton's note, but the original draft indicates that the whole letter was written on the 2d.]

Copy of Admiral Arbuthnot's orders to Captain Hudson. [*Royal Oak,* in Gardiners Bay, March 4, 1781.]

You are hereby required and directed to take the *Orpheus* and *Savage* under your command, and such transports with troops as His Excellency Sir Henry Clinton may judge expedient to send to Virginia to reinforce General Arnold, and to proceed with them to Chesapeake with all possible expedition. But, should the General decline sending any reinforcements to Virginia, you are hereby required and directed positively to join me in the Chesapeake with all possible dispatch, for which this shall be your order.

Extract from Sir Henry Clinton's letter to Earl Cornwallis. New York, March 5, 1781.

I am most exceedingly concerned at the very unfortunate affair of the 17th of January [Cowpens]. From the account Your Lordship gives me of it, I fear our first line has been too impetuous, and that the reserve has sustained the other too nearly and probably in too loose order, and that the enemy has moved against them in that critical situation. [Stevens, *Clinton-Cornwallis Controversy, 1,* 333.]

[Extract of Clinton to Cornwallis. March 8, 1781.]

The Admiral informs me of the return of the French ships to Rhode Island, and of their having taken the *Romulus* and carried her into that place. But, as the Admiral in his letter of the 4th seems to think that *the whole or at least a great part of the French fleet sailed for Chesapeake on the 27th ultimo,* and that he was at that time ready to sail, I flatter myself he is either gone there or has sent a sufficient force to clear the Chesapeake. *The troops under General Phillips have been embarked for some time and are now at the Hook, waiting for the Admiral or a message from him.* General Phillips commands, and I am sure you know his inclinations are to cooperate with Your Lordship; *and you will therefore be pleased to take him under your orders* until you hear further from me.[56] [*Ibid.*, pp. 344–345.]

Copy of a letter from Sir Henry Clinton to Admiral Arbuthnot. New York, March 8, 1781.

Sir:

I am honored with Your Excellency's letter of the 4th, and a duplicate of that of the 2d. By that of the 2d I am to understand it is your opinion that the French fleet is probably gone to Chesapeake and that you shall immediately call at the Hook, by that of the 4th that you are ready to sail and shall determine your motions by appearances at Rhode Island; in case you do not call off the Hook, you have appointed a convoy for the troops destined to reinforce General Arnold. By this I am of course to understand I shall either see or hear from Your Excellency before they proceed to the Chesapeake. I have therfore, sir, submitted to Captain Hudson whether it may not be better to stay till he hears from Your Excellency. For, though I have nothing more at heart than sending a reinforcement to the Chesapeake, I dare not do it until I am assured by Your Excellency the entrance of that bay is ours.

I understand, sir, that the *Chatham* and *Assurance* with their convoys are between this port and Charleston. I need not say of what importance it is to bring these fleets safe into port, and what risk they run if Your Excellency goes with your whole fleet to the Chesapeake, leaving that of the French at Rhode Island. I am sorry to find, by Your Excellency's letter to General Robertson, that you are under the necessity of leaving the Long Island Sound without a single ship. The port of New York will also, I fear, be in the same situation.

You, sir, are certainly the best judge of how the naval force under your command should be disposed of. But I will, however, venture with great deference to suggest to Your Excellency that it has ever been usual to have a naval force in the sound, at the Hook, and in the North River, even when we were in possession of Rhode Island. And, should there be none in either, I fear we shall be liable to insult even

56. *Clinton's note:* A copy of the instructions to Major General Phillips was enclosed in the above letter. [This letter and those of Mar. 2 and 5, together with Phillips' instructions, were sent by the *Jupiter* to Col. Balfour at Charleston, but did not reach Cornwallis; see above, p. 286.]

from the enemy's privateers at all these stations. I have the honor, etc.,
Henry Clinton.

Extract of a letter from Captain Hudson to Sir Henry Clinton.
9 March 1781.

Your Excellency will see by the order from the Admiral that no
time is to be lost in putting it in execution. And if you, sir, think it inexpedient to send a reinforcement to Virginia, I am in that case positively directed to proceed to the Chesapeake with the *Orpheus* and
Savage to join him; and by any unnecessary delay in complying with
his directions I may be subject to great censure. I shall not, however,
take any step without Your Excellency's approbation and advice. But,
if you have no accounts soon from the Admiral, with your concurrence
I shall put the latter part of his instructions to me in execution.

Substance of opinions given to Major General Phillips in several
conversations held with him previous to his embarkation, on
the subject of operations in the Chesapeake. [*Ca.* March 10, 1781;
extract.]

Until I know Lord Cornwallis' success to the southward and what
force can be spared from the southern districts for further operations,
and until the reinforcements expected to this army arrive, such troops
as are in Chesapeake may be employed first in assisting His Lordship's operations, and then in either establishing a *permanent* post near
the entrance of that bay (if the naval commander does not approve of
the one in Elizabeth River) where large ships as well as small may lie
in security during any temporary superiority of the enemy's fleet, *or, if
such a post cannot be found,* in employing what remains of the season
in carrying on desultory expeditions against such towns, stations, magazines, etc., as the enemy may have there (to convince those people,
more by what we can do than by what we really do, that they are in
our power), and finally in pursuing the same plan—supporting friends
—in a more northerly and healthy climate.

With regard to a station for the [protection of the] King's ships I
know of no place so proper as Yorktown, if it can be taken possession
of, fortified, and garrisoned with 1000 men—as, by having 1000 more
at a post somewhere in Elizabeth River, York and James Rivers would
be ours, and our cruisers might command the waters of the Chesapeake. Troops might likewise be spared from these posts to carry on
expeditions during the summer months, when probably nothing can
be risked in that climate but water movements.

But, if the heights of York and those on Gloucester side cannot be so well and so soon fortified as to render that post hors d'insulte before the enemy can move a force against it, it may not be advisable to attempt it. In that case something may be possibly done at Old Point Comfort to cover large ships lying in Hampton Road (which is reckoned a good one, and not so liable to injury from gales at northeast as that of York, particularly in winter). *If neither can be secured,* we must content ourselves with keeping the Chesapeake with frigates and other armed vessels, which will always find security against a superior naval force in Elizabeth River.

At a proper time of the year operations must still go northward, either by a direct movement, stationing your supplies in the navigable rivers which lie favorable for it (in which you are, however, exposed to a temporary naval superiority of the enemy), or by proceeding up the Chesapeake if a force equal to the attempt can be collected. For, when it can, I should propose to take a station threatening all the provinces bordering on Chesapeake with a desultory war, [and to] prevent those provinces from being succored by menacing communications and availing ourselves of a supposed numerous band of friends, who otherwise may be forced to arm against us.

Had we a force sufficient for two movements, that would be best: 4000 men to proceed in transports up to Baltimore, taking a station within a certain distance of the Susquehanna and having vessels always ready for a rapid move with part (or even the whole) to a corresponding station on the Eastern Neck, while a corps of 10,000 men or more, according to the force that can be brought against you, occupies the Eastern Neck and can in its turn succor the western corps. Whether the eastern corps acts alone or in cooperation, it must be in very great force, for reasons obvious. I do not know enough of the neck to say what force, or whether any, can be placed in security. The most advanced station would certainly be the best, particularly at first, to enable our friends (who, we are told, are at Lancaster, Little Yorktown [i.e., York, Pa.], and Chester) to join us. Iron Hill may perhaps be it; and, as marshy creeks run up from Delaware and Chesapeake (the heads of which are not far asunder), many good posts may be found for corps of different strength. For, while we command those bays, there can be no danger of operation against our flanks and rear; and, if the enemy should be superior in one, he cannot be so in both. We should therefore have always communication open. This corps should be very strong indeed, or there should be one acting in favor of it in Jersey.

The preference must be given to that plan against which Washington can bring the least force. He can undoubtedly bring a greater into Jersey than anywhere, as the New England troops may be prevailed on to go there, and they cannot be so easily drawn into the Eastern Neck or even over Delaware. Besides, if Washington moves into Jersey, his meat and flour have both but a short portage. But, once deprived of the eastern counties, his cattle in that case coming chiefly from New England will increase his difficulty of subsistence. For, as we may under those circumstances attempt to occupy King's Ferry, he will be reduced to the detour. I therefore should prefer a single corps in the Eastern Neck, sufficient, however, for the purpose.

As the French have added considerably to Washington's force, I do not think a force less than Sir William Howe had could be sufficient, 15,000 men. But where are they to be found? My *whole* force, rank and file fit for duty, is nearly 24,000. It is presumed Lord Cornwallis will be content with 6000 for the southward, 2000 we suppose in the Chesapeake, 12,000 are required for New York; there remains only 4000 for that operation. I did expect 10,000 men as an augmentation to my present army. Had they come, this project might have taken place. But I am now told I am to expect only 4000, which will not be sufficient. However, once convinced that the French will not send reinforcement and *that we shall be permanently superior at sea* and have an active, cooperating naval commander, I should be tempted to try. But, until all this combines, I dare not. And, if it is delayed too long, our friends in Pennsylvania may be forced from us or cajoled.

If we could hold the Chesapeake by the posts on Elizabeth and York Rivers, Oxford, and Port Penn, and the two eastern on the seacoasts, and threaten our enemies of Virginia and Maryland and protect our friends of all these counties, I think we should in that case leave the French little to induce them to support the war. [Stevens, *Clinton-Cornwallis Controversy, 1*, 430–435.]

Extract from the instructions given by Sir Henry Clinton to Major General Phillips. Headquarters, New York, March 10, 1781.

You will be pleased to proceed with the troops embarked under your command to Chesapeake Bay, and there form a junction as soon as possible with Brigadier General Arnold, whom (and the corps with him) you will take under your orders.

When you shall have formed your junction with Brigadier General Arnold, if you find that General acting under the orders of Earl Cornwallis, you will of course endeavor to fulfill those orders. If this should not be the case, after receiving information respecting his probable situation you will make such movements with the corps then under your orders as can be made consistent with the security of the post on Elizabeth River, or [as] you shall think will most effectually assist His Lordship's operations, by destroying or taking any magazines the enemy may have on James River or at Petersburg on the Appomattox. After which, if it should be thought necessary, you will establish a post or posts at such stations on James River as shall appear best calculated to open the way for, and secure the safety as far as possible of, a rapid movement of troops to give jealousy for upper James River and to interrupt the course of supplies for the Carolinas. The object of cooperation with Lord Cornwallis being fulfilled, you are at liberty to carry on such desultory expeditions for the purpose of destroying the enemy's public stores and magazines in any part of the Chesapeake as you shall judge proper.

If the Admiral, disapproving of Portsmouth and requiring a fortified station for large ships in the Chesapeake, should propose Yorktown or Old Point Comfort, [and] if possession of either can be acquired and maintained without great risk or loss, you are at liberty to take possession thereof. But, if the objections are such as you think forcible, you must, after stating those objections, decline it *until solid operations take place in Chesapeake.*[57]

As to whatever relates to the people of the country, their being received and armed, or it being more for the King's service that they should remain quiet at their houses, or respecting the oaths that should be offered to them, or for your general conduct in matters of this kind, I refer you to my instructions to Major General Leslie and Brigadier General Arnold, copies of which will be given to you. And concerning your return to this place you will receive either my orders or Lord Cornwallis', as circumstances may make necessary. It is presumed His Lordship will be able to spare troops to station at Portsmouth, etc.; but, should that not be the case, you are at liberty to leave either the regiment of [the] *Prince Héréditaire* or the Seventy-sixth, or both, for that purpose under any officer—being a general officer—Lord Cornwallis may choose to appoint.

It is probable, when the objects of this expedition are fulfilled, and that you have strengthened the present works and added such others as you shall think necessary, that you may return to this place. In which case you must bring with you Brigadier General Arnold, the light infantry, Colonel Robinson's corps or the Seventy-sixth, and, if it

57. *Clinton's note:* Read this, my good Lord Cornwallis, attentively—and then say what forced you to take an indefensible station in York River.

should be possible, the Queen's Rangers. The moment you have communicated with Lord Cornwallis and heard from His Lordship, you are to consider yourself as under His Lordship's orders until he or you shall hear further from me. In order that I may be furnished with every information necessary to be communicated to the Secretary of State, to be laid before the King, I am to request that you will from time to time transmit to me such intelligence as you may think interesting to His Majesty's service. [*Ibid.*, pp. 347–350.]

Extract from General Greene's account of the action [at Guilford] in his letter to the President of Congress. Camp at the ironworks, ten miles from Guilford Court House, March 16, 1781.

The army marched from the High Rock Ford on the 12th, and on the 14th arrived at Guilford. The enemy lay at the Quaker Meeting House on Deep River, eight miles from our camp. On the morning of the 15th our reconnoitering party reported the enemy advancing on the Great Salisbury Road. The army was drawn up in three lines: the front line was composed of North Carolina militia, under the command of Generals Butler and Eaton; the second line of Virginia militia, forming two brigades commanded by Generals Stevens and Lawson; the third line, consisting of two brigades, one of Virginia and one of Maryland Continental troops, commanded by General Huger and Colonel Williams. Lieutenant Colonel Washington, with the dragoons of the First and Third Regiments, a detachment of light infantry composed of Continental troops, and a regiment of riflemen under Colonel Lynch, formed a corps of observation for the security of our right flank. Lieutenant Colonel Lee with his Legion, a detachment of light infantry, and a corps of riflemen under Colonel Campbell formed a corps of observation for the security of our left flank.

The greater part of this country is a wilderness, with a few cleared fields interspersed here and there. The army was drawn up on a large hill of ground, surrounded by other hills, the greater part of which was covered with timber and thick underbrush. The front line was posted with two fieldpieces, just on the edge of the woods and the back of a fence which ran parallel with the line, with an open field directly in their front. The second line was in the woods, about three hundred yards in rear of the first, and the Continental troops about four hundred yards in the rear of the second with a double front, as the hill drew to a point where they were posted; and on the right and left were two old fields. In this position we waited the approach of the enemy, having previously sent off the baggage to this place appointed to rendezvous at in case of a defeat.

Lieutenant Colonel Lee with his Legion, his infantry, and part of his riflemen met the enemy on their advance, and had a severe skirmish with Lieutenant Colonel Tarleton, in which the enemy suffered greatly. Captain Armstrong charged the British Legion and cut down near thirty of their dragoons; but, as the enemy reinforced their party, Lieutenant Colonel Lee was obliged to retire and take his position in the line. The action commenced by a cannonade, which lasted about twenty minutes, when the enemy advanced in three columns, the Hessians on the right, the Guards in the center, and Lieutenant Colonel Webster's Brigade on the left. The whole moved through the old fields to attack the North Carolina Brigades, who waited the attack until the enemy got within 140 yards, *when part of them began to fire, but a considerable part left the ground without firing at all. The general and field officers did all they could to induce the men to stand their ground, but neither the advantages of the position nor any other consideration could induce them to stay.*

General Stevens and General Lawson and the field officers of those brigades were more successful in their exertions. The Virginia militia gave the enemy a warm reception, and kept up a heavy fire for a long time; but, being beat back, the action became general almost everywhere. The corps of observation under Washington and Lee were warmly engaged and did great execution. In a word, the engagement was long and severe, and the enemy only gained their point by superior discipline. They, having broke the Second Maryland Regiment and turned our left flank, got into the rear of the Virginia Brigade, and appearing to be gaining our right—which would have encircled the whole of the Continental troops—I thought it most advisable to order a retreat.

About this time Lieutenant Colonel Washington made a charge with the horse upon a part of the brigade of Guards. And the First Regiment of Marylanders, commanded by Colonel Gunby and seconded by Lieutenant Colonel Howard, followed the horse with their bayonets. Near the whole of the party fell a sacrifice. General Huger was the last that was engaged, and gave the enemy a check. We retreated in good order to the Reedy Fork River, and crossed at the ford about three miles from the field of action, and then halted and drew up the troops until we collected most of the stragglers. We lost our artillery and two ammunition wagons, the greater part of the horses being killed before the retreat began and it being impossible to move the pieces but along the Great Road. After collecting our stragglers we retired to this camp, ten miles from Guilford.[58] [Tarleton, *History,* pp. 313–317.]

58. *Clinton's note:* Return of the killed, wounded, and missing of the British troops in the action at Guilford: one lieutenant colonel, two lieutenants, two en-

Extract from Lord Cornwallis' letter to Lord George Germain. Guilford, 17 March 1781.

About four miles from Guilford our advanced guard, commanded by Lieutenant Colonel Tarleton, fell in with a corps of the enemy consisting of Lee's Legion [and] some back-mountain men and Virginia militia, which he attacked with his usual good conduct and spirit, and defeated. And, continuing our march, we found the rebel army posted on rising grounds about a mile and a half from the Court House.

The prisoners taken by Lieutenant Colonel Tarleton, having been several days with the advanced corps, could give me no account of the enemy's order or position; and the country people were extremely inaccurate in their description of the ground. Immediately between the head of the column and the enemy's line was a considerable plantation, one large field of which was on our left of the road, and two others (with a wood of about two hundred yards broad between them) on our right of it. Beyond these fields the wood continued for several miles to our right. The wood beyond the plantation in our front, in the skirt of which the enemy's first line was formed, was about a mile in depth, the road then leading into an extensive space of cleared ground about Guilford Court House. The woods on our right and left were reported to be impracticable for cannon. But, as that on our right appeared the most open, I resolved to attack the left wing of the enemy. And, whilst my disposition was making for that purpose, I ordered Lieutenant MacLeod to bring forward the guns and cannonade their center.

The attack was directed to be made in the following order: on the right the Regiment of Bose and the Seventy-first Regiment, led by Major General Leslie and supported by the first battalion of Guards; on their left the Twenty-third and Thirty-third Regiments, led by Lieutenant Colonel Webster and supported by the grenadiers and second battalion of Guards, commanded by Brigadier General O'Hara. The

---

signs, thirteen sergeants, and seventy-five rank and file killed; two brigadier generals, two lieutenant colonels, nine captains, four lieutenants, five ensigns, two staff [sergeants], fifteen sergeants, five drummers, and three hundred and sixty-nine rank and file wounded; one sergeant and twenty-five rank and file missing. Total five hundred and thirty-two, besides one hundred on the march.

Return of the killed, wounded, and missing of the American troops in the same action: one major, five captains, three subalterns, five sergeants, and sixty-five rank and file killed; two brigadier generals, one major, eleven captains, twelve subalterns, seven sergeants, and one hundred and fifty-three rank and file wounded; one major, four captains, twenty subalterns, seventeen sergeants, eight drummers and fifers, and nine hundred and ninety-six rank and file missing. Total one thousand three hundred and ten. [See above, p. 266 n. 11.]

Jägers and light infantry of the Guards remained in the wood on the left of the guns, and the cavalry in the road, ready to act as circumstances might require.

Our preparations being made, the action began about half an hour past one in the afternoon. Major General Leslie, after being obliged by the great extent of the enemy's line to bring up the first battalion of Guards to the right of the Regiment of Bose, soon defeated everything before him. Lieutenant Colonel Webster, having joined the left of Major General Leslie's division, was no less successful in his front when, on finding that the left of the Thirty-third was exposed to a heavy fire from the right wing of the enemy, he changed his front to the left and, being supported by the Jägers and light infantry of the Guards, attacked and routed it—the grenadiers and second battalion of Guards moving forward to occupy the ground left vacant by the movement of Lieutenant Colonel Webster. All the infantry being now in the line, Lieutenant Colonel Tarleton had directions to keep his cavalry compact, and not to charge without positive orders except to protect any of the corps from the most evident danger of being defeated.

The excessive thickness of the woods rendered our bayonets of little use, and enabled the broken enemy to make frequent stands, with an irregular fire which occasioned some loss and, to several of the corps, great delay—particularly on our right, where the first battalion of Guards and Regiment of Bose were warmly engaged in front, flank, and rear with some of the enemy that had been routed on the first attack, and with part of the extremity of their left wing, which by the closeness of the wood had been passed unbroken. The Seventy-first Regiment and grenadiers and second battalion of Guards, not knowing what was passing on their right and hearing the fire advance on their left, continued to move forward, the artillery keeping pace with them on the road, followed by the cavalry. The second battalion of Guards first gained the clear ground near Guilford Court House, and found a corps of Continental infantry much superior in number formed in the open field on the left of the road. Glowing with impatience to signalize themselves, they instantly attacked and defeated them, taking two six-pounders; but, pursuing into the wood with too much ardor, were thrown into confusion by a heavy fire, and [were] immediately charged and driven back into the field by Colonel Washington's dragoons, with the loss of the six-pounders they had taken.

The enemy's cavalry was soon repulsed by a well directed fire from two three-pounders just brought up by Lieutenant MacLeod, and by the appearance of the grenadiers, of the Guards, and of the Seventy-first Regiment, which, having been impeded by some deep ravines, were now coming out of the wood on the right of the Guards, opposite to the Court House. By the spirited exertion of Brigadier General O'Hara (though wounded) the second battalion of Guards was soon rallied and, supported by the grenadiers, returned to the charge with the greatest alacrity. The Twenty-third Regiment arriving that instant from our left, and Lieutenant Colonel Tarleton having advanced with part of the cavalry, the enemy were soon put to flight, and the two six-pounders once more fell into our hands. Two ammunition wagons and two other six-pounders, being all the artillery they had in the field, were likewise taken. About this time the Thirty-third Regiment and light infantry of the Guards, after overcoming many difficulties, completely routed the corps which was opposed to them, and put an end to the action in this quarter.

The Twenty-third and Seventy-first Regiments, with part of the cavalry, were ordered to pursue. The remainder of the cavalry was detached with Lieutenant Colonel Tarleton to our right, where a heavy fire still continued, and where his appearance and spirited attack contributed much to a speedy termination of the action. The militia with which our right had been engaged dispersed in the woods, the Continentals went off by the Reedy Fork, beyond which it was not in my power to follow them—as their cavalry had suffered but little, our troops were excessively fatigued by an action which lasted an hour and a half, and our wounded, dispersed over an extensive space of country, required immediate attention. The care of our wounded, and the total want of provisions in an exhausted country, made it equally impossible for me to follow the blow next day. The enemy did not stop until they got to the ironworks on Troublesome Creek, eighteen miles from the field of battle. [Stevens, *Clinton-Cornwallis Controversy, 1*, 364–367.]

Extract of a letter from Lord Rawdon to Sir Henry Clinton. Camden, 23d March (received 22d April) 1781.

I have the honor to transmit to Your Excellency the copy of a note which I have this day received from Lord Cornwallis. Generals Sumter and Marion, commanding distinct corps, have made some efforts to excite insurrection in this province and to interrupt our supplies from Charleston. As the enemy are all mounted, we have never been able to force them to a decisive action. They are still in the field, *but the destruction of Greene's army will have a serious effect upon their spirits.* [Hist. MSS Com., *American MSS in the Royal Institution, 2*, 260–261.]

Extract of a letter from Major General Greene to the President of Congress. Buffalo Creek, March 23, 1781.

On the 16th I wrote Your Excellency giving an account of an action which happened at Guilford Court House the day before. I was then persuaded that, notwithstanding we were obliged to give up the ground, we had reaped the advantage of the action. Circumstances since confirm me in opinion that the enemy were too much galled to improve their success.

We lay at the ironworks three days, preparing ourselves for another action and expecting the enemy to advance. But of a sudden they took their departure, leaving behind them evident marks of distress. Our army are in good spirits, notwithstanding our suffering, and are advancing toward the enemy, who are retreating to Cross Creek. [*Pennsylvania Journal*, Apr. 11, 1781.]

Extract of a letter from Lieutenant Colonel Balfour to Lord George Germain. Charleston, March 24, 1781.

However, Lord Cornwallis has at present no design (as I apprehend from his letters) of pursuing him [Greene] on that route, as his army is in the greatest want of *the supplies which have long been waiting for it in Cape Fear River, and which he will receive on his communicating with Cross Creek.*

By His Lordship's letters I learn reinforcements from Pennsylvania and Virginia are daily expected by the rebel army. And I must further beg leave to inform Your Lordship of the exertions of the enemy to raise a force *in this province,* either (as I apprehend) with a view to distress us by frequent interruption of the communications or on a more enlarged idea (if greatly successful) of drawing back Lord Cornwallis' attention to the more immediate protection of South Carolina. [No copy in the CP; printed from Clinton's note.]

Extract of a letter from Sir Henry Clinton to Major General Phillips. March 24, 1781.

I believe that Lord Cornwallis has finished his campaign—and, if report says true, very handsomely—by taking all Greene's cannon and recovering the greatest part of his own men who had been made prisoners by Mr. Greene. If that should be the case, and Lord Cornwallis does not want any cooperation to assist him, and you see no prospect of striking an important stroke elsewhere, I shall probably request you and General Arnold to return to me with such troops as I have already named in my instructions. But all this will depend on the information I shall receive from you, and your opinion respecting the post at Portsmouth and such others as you propose to establish on James River, with their importance, considered either as assisting Lord Cornwallis' operations or connected with those of the navy. [Stevens, *Clinton-Cornwallis Controversy, 1,* 373.]

[Extract of Washington to Benjamin Harrison. New Windsor, March 27, 1781.]

We are now suffering from a remnant of a British army *what they could not in the beginning accomplish with their forces at the highest.* [Fitzpatrick, *Writings of Washington, 21,* 381.]

Extract of a letter from General Washington to Mr. Lund Washington, dated New Windsor, 28 March 1781.

It was unfortunate (but this I mention in confidence) that the French fleet and detachment did not undertake the enterprise they are now upon when I first proposed it to them. The destruction of Arnold's corps would then have been inevitable, before the British fleet could have been in a condition to put to sea.[59] Instead of this the small squadron which took the *Romulus* and other vessels was sent—and could not, as I foretold, do anything without a land force at Portsmouth. [*Ibid.,* p. 386; see also Freeman, *Washington, 5,* 279–281.]

[Extract of Greene to the President of Congress. Deep River, March 31 (30?), 1781.]

On the 27th we arrived at Rigden's Ford, twelve miles above this, and found the enemy then lay at Ramsey's Mill, from which it was imagined they meant to wait an attack. Our baggage was accordingly left under proper guard in our rear, and the army put in motion without loss of time. But we found the enemy had crossed some hours before our arrival, and with such precipitation that they left their dead unburied on the ground. Our men had suffered so much for want of provisions in this exhausted part of the country that many of them fainted on the march, and the difficulty of procuring any immediate supply prevented our further pursuit. [Tarleton, *History,* pp. 320–321.]

59. *Clinton's note:* Does not everything prove the absurdity of operation in Chesapeake without a covering fleet, or respectable place of arms till such arrives?

Extract of a letter from Major General Phillips to Sir Henry Clinton. Portsmouth, 3d April (received 11 April 1781).

If you intend to preserve this post as a station to which Lord Cornwallis may retire (or come to should he be very successful), it must be taken up upon a more extensive plan. It will be necessary, perhaps, to have a post fortified at some good point in Nansemond near to Suffolk, and on our left the Northwest Landing must be possessed in the same manner. The first will prevent any eruption in force from the rebels while we are masters of the sea, and having the Northwest Landing gives support and communication to an armament sent into Currituck and Albemarle Sounds, etc.

It comes then into consideration whether, upon so very uncertain a communication with Lord Cornwallis as appears to us to be the case, Your Excellency will lock up 3400 men at Portsmouth and its dependencies. I will very freely offer my opinion that this post has not been, I should imagine, properly explained to Your Excellency by Generals Mathew and Leslie. The object of the post from its situation respecting James River and the Chesapeake, with its connections with the waters to and in Albemarle Sound and the consequent connections it may have with an army in the Carolinas, are subjects I do not think myself at liberty to touch upon.

I mean to confine myself merely to the locality of the post itself. And under that description I declare I think *the present situation not calculated for a post of force or for one for a small number of troops.* Should it be required by Your Excellency to merely keep a post here, without intending more than a station, I think *Mill Point,* where the old fort stood, well calculated for such a purpose; and it would not require more than a strong battalion, equal to 600 men, effective rank and file, to be the garrison.

In both instances the Chesapeake must be secure. For, even allowing every exertion of defense against a fleet, it would be difficult to preserve the river under the first idea of an extensive plan; under the latter I consider it scarcely to be done. *Old Point Comfort* shall be explored, *as it seems a point which a small force might defend, and the shipping have scope to act in* and, by trying various methods of winds and tides, would be able possibly to escape from even a superior naval force—whereas, *once blocked up in Elizabeth River, the ships must at last fall with the post.* Upon the whole, sir, it may be perceived that I lean in favor of a small post, where the army can assist the navy and the latter have a chance of escaping (supposing a superior force arrive in the bay), and where the post can be maintained with five or six hundred men for some time, even perhaps until some reinforcement, naval and land, might be sent to raise the siege. [Printed, except for the first four sentences, in Stevens, *Clinton-Cornwallis Controversy*, 1, 378–379.]

[Extract of Germain to Clinton. April 4, 1781.]

Our intelligence from France gives us reason to believe no part of the land or sea force that has been so long preparing at Brest will be sent directly to North America. A fleet consisting of twenty-six sail of the line, under the command of the Count de Grasse, and transports with from seven to twelve thousand land forces were ready to sail the 20th of last month; and it is said they did sail the 22d. The lateness of the season will, I imagine, prevent Monsieur de Grasse from undertaking anything against the King's possessions in the West Indies. But it is probable, as soon as he has thrown supplies into the several islands, he will proceed to North America and join the French forces at Rhode Island. *But, as Sir George Rodney's force is but little inferior to his, and he will be watchful of his motions, I am not apprehensive he will give him time to do you any material injury before he comes to your succor.* [*Ibid.*, p. 381.]

Extract of a letter from Sir Henry Clinton to Lord George Germain. New York, April 5, 1781 (received June 23).

I feel myself particularly flattered by the manner in which Your Lordship does me the honor of expressing yourself respecting a plan which, had it succeeded, would certainly have had the most important consequences. And I may with truth presume to say Your Lordship does but justice to my zeal in supposing that I shall not let slip any favorable opportunity of rendering His Majesty and my country so essential a service as the securing, even by a regular attack, the important post of *West Point* whenever the attempt can be made with propriety.

As to Brigadier General Arnold's opinions regarding this business I can only say that, whatever he may have represented to Your Lordship, nothing he has yet communicated to me on the subject has convinced me that the rebel forts in the Highlands can be reduced by a *few days'* regular attack. But, even if that had been my own opinion, to have attempted them when Washington was in the neighborhood with twice the force I could have marched against them (exclusive of the numbers which might have been readily collected in the three populous and warlike provinces adjoining, and the support he might have received from the French armament at Rhode Island) would surely have been so very unjustifiable that I trust the impropriety of the measure under such circumstances must be obvious to Your Lordship. Nor would it have been practicable during the winter months, for reasons equally manifest.

However, if Brigadier General Arnold convinces me now, in the present reduced state of the rebel army, that success is probable—*for to fail would be death to our cause in the present stage of the war*— I shall most likely be induced to make the attempt. I have, therefore, requested that officer to send his plan of operations to me without delay, and to follow or accompany it himself. In the meantime I am preparing for every exertion within the compass of my very reduced force—which, after the several large detachments sent to the southward, amounts to no more than 6275 auxiliary troops, 4527 regular British, and 906 provincials fit for service in the field.

If an attempt upon the forts in the Highlands shall not upon mature deliberation be thought advisable, and nothing else offers in this quarter, I shall probably reinforce Major General Phillips, directing him to carry on such operations as may most effectually favor those of Lord Cornwallis until some plan can be determined on for the campaign. For, until I know His Lordship's success, the force he can in consequence of it spare from the Carolinas, and the certainty of the arrival of the six regiments intended to reinforce us, it will be impossible to decide *finally* upon it. Your Lordship will, however, see by the enclosed opinions what were the operations I had planned for the ensuing campaign, upon the supposition that Lord Cornwallis succeeded in the Carolinas and was able to spare a considerable force from thence.

With the 10,000 men I requested, I should not have had a doubt of success. But in my present reduced state and prospects I dare not flatter myself with any; and, if the French should be still reinforced, Your Lordship will, I am persuaded, judge our situation to be even critical. For, with regard to our efforts in the Chesapeake, Your Lordship knows how much their success *and even the safety of the armament there will depend upon our having a decided naval superiority in these seas.* And I am therefore fully persuaded *that every precaution* will be taken to give me timely notice of the contrary being likely to happen, *as my ignorance of such an event might be most fatal in its consequences.*

The reinforcement I asked for was only what I judged to be barely adequate to the services required; and I most sincerely wish it had been possible to have sent it in the full extent of numbers and in the time I requested, as our prospects in that case would have certainly been brighter. But the present reduced state of Washington, *the little probability there is (I hope) of an augmentation to the French armament,* and the *certainty* there is (*I also hope*) *of the six British regiments and one thousand recruits joining me in a very short time,* together with the *expectations I have of Lord Cornwallis' success in Carolina enabling His Lordship to send me a considerable reinforcement from thence,* render the appearance of my situation less critical. And I shall only add, My Lord, that, whilst the King does me the honor to trust me with the command of this army, I will employ it to the utmost extent of my poor abilities for the promoting his service—taking the liberty, however, to represent, as I think it my duty, *what advantages might be obtained by an additional force and what evils may be apprehended from the want of a sufficient one.*

It gave me great satisfaction to be informed, in Your Lordship's dispatch Number Seventy-one, that Vice Admiral Arbuthnot was appointed to relieve Sir Peter Parker on the Jamaica Station. And I confess that I wait with some impatience for that event taking place, as every land movement in the present stage of the war depends so entirely upon the assistance and cooperation of the navy that, unless it is given in the extent and with the dispatch required, the hoped-for success will but too often escape us. But I shall for the present decline to give Your Lordship any further trouble than to express my gratitude for the gracious attention with which my royal master has been pleased to honor my representations, as I am in the hope of being soon relieved from my anxieties on that subject. *For, unless that shall be the case and the promised reinforcement arrives soon from England, I shall be constrained—though reluctantly—to avail myself of the permission His Majesty has been graciously pleased to give me to resign this command, which I humbly presume I ought to hold no longer than whilst I have a prospect of doing it with advantage to his service and my own honor.* The contrary of which, Your Lordship is sensible, may happen when there is a want of confidence between the commanders in chief of the land and the sea forces. [*Ibid.,* pp. 387–390.]

[Extract of Balfour to Clinton. April 7, 1781.]

In some of my former letters I have had occasion to mention to Your Excellency the inroads which the enemy were daily making into the heart of this province, and the distresses, both to the people of the country and the army, which attended them. I am therefore sorry the occasion still exists for the like informations. [*Ibid.,* pp. 395–396.]

Copy of a letter from Lord Cornwallis to Sir Henry Clinton.
Wilmington, 10 April 1781.

Sir:

I am just informed that I have a chance of sending a few lines
to New York by the *Amphitrite*. But, as it depends upon my being expeditious, I cannot attempt to give Your Excellency a *particular account
of the winter's campaign* or the Battle of Guilford. I have, however, the
satisfaction of informing you that our military operations were uniformly
successful; and the victory at Guilford, though one of the bloodiest of
this war, was very complete. The enemy gave themselves out for nine
or ten (and undoubtedly had seven) thousand men in the field, upward of two thousand of which were eighteen-months men or Continentals. Our force was 1360 infantry rank and file, and about 200
cavalry.

General Greene retreated the night of the action to the ironworks
on Troublesome Creek, eighteen miles from Guilford, leaving us four
six-pounders, being all the cannon he had in the field. The fatigue of
the troops and the great number of wounded put it out of my power to
pursue beyond the Reedy Fork in the afternoon of the action, and the
want of provisions and all kinds of necessaries for the soldiers made it
equally impossible to follow the blow next day. I therefore issued the
enclosed proclamation and, having remained two days on the field of
battle, marched to Bell's Mill on Deep River, near part of the country
where the greatest number of our friends were supposed to reside.
Many of the inhabitants rode into camp, shook me by the hand, said
they were glad to see us and to hear that we had beat Greene, *and
then rode home again.* I could not get 100 men in all the Regulators'
country to stay with us even as militia.[60]

With a third of my army sick and wounded, which I was obliged to
carry in wagons or on horseback, the remainder without shoes and
worn down with fatigue, I thought it was time to look for some place
of rest and refitment. I therefore by easy marches (taking care to pass
through all the settlements that had been described to me as most

60. "These words," Clinton commented, "convey to me what their opinion was
of the effort made to relieve them. And, if they could have expressed their thought,
perhaps they would have said: 'We wish you well, but dare not join you. After
your victory of Camden you ordered us to rise, [and] you came forward to Charlotteburg to receive us. The elite of your militia was soon afterward exposed unsupported and was butchered [at King's Mountain]; our enemies recovered their spirits
and raised an army; you were obliged to retrograde; and we were exposed to the
cruel resentment of our oppressors. You have gained a battle, but you have your-
selves lost considerably. You are not in sufficient strength to support us. You
have no provisions. You must leave us; and, when you do, you leave us to ruin.' "
Clinton to the Duke of Gloucester, May 6, 1781, a photostat volume in the CP.

friendly) proceeded to Cross Creek. On my arrival there I found, to my great mortification and contrary to all former accounts, that it was impossible to procure any considerable quantity of provisions, and there was not four days' forage within twenty miles. The navigation of Cape Fear River, with the hopes of which I had been flattered, was totally impracticable, the distance from Wilmington by water being 150 miles, the breadth of the river seldom exceeding 100 yards, the banks generally high, and the inhabitants on each side almost universally hostile. Under these circumstances I determined to move immediately to Wilmington. By this measure the Highlanders have not had so much time as the people of the upper country to prove the sincerity of their former professions of friendship; but, though appearances are rather more favorable among them, I confess they are not equal to my expectations.

General Greene marched down as low as the mouth of Deep River (where he remained) four days ago. He never came within our reach after the action; nor has a shot been since fired except at Ramsey's Mill on Deep River, where Colonel Malmedy, with about twenty of the gang of plunderers that are attached to him, galloped in among the sentries and carried off three Jägers.

I cannot sufficiently commend the behavior of both officers and men under my command. They not only showed the most persevering intrepidity in action, but underwent with cheerfulness such fatigues and hardships as have seldom been experienced by a British army, and justly merit every mark of favor and reward. The great assistance which I received from Generals Leslie and O'Hara and Lieutenant Colonel Tarleton deserves my warmest acknowledgments and highest commendations.

I am now employed in disposing of the sick and wounded, and in procuring supplies of all kinds to put the troops into a proper state to take the field. I am likewise impatiently looking out for the expected reinforcement from Europe, part of which will be indispensably necessary to enable me either to act offensively or even to maintain myself in the upper parts of the country, where alone I can hope to preserve the troops from the fatal sickness which so nearly ruined the army last autumn.

I am very anxious to receive Your Excellency's commands, being as yet totally in the dark as to the intended operations of the summer. I cannot help expressing my wishes that the Chesapeake may become the seat of war—even, if necessary, at the expense of abandoning New York. Until Virginia is in a manner subdued, our hold of the Carolinas must be difficult if not precarious. The rivers in Virginia are advantageous to an invading army. But North Carolina is, of all the provinces in America, the most difficult to attack (unless material assistance could be got from the inhabitants, the contrary of which I have sufficiently experienced) on account of its great extent [and] of the numberless rivers and creeks and the total want of interior navigation.

In compliance with Your Excellency's general directions I shall dispatch my aide-de-camp, Captain Brodrick, to England with the particular accounts of the Battle of Guilford, of the winter's campaign, and the present state of the province, copies of which I shall have the honor of transmitting to Your Excellency with my next dispatch. I have the honor, etc., Cornwallis. [*Ibid.*, pp. 395–399.]

Extract of a letter from Sir Henry Clinton to Lord Cornwallis. New York, 13 April 1781 (received in Virginia in June).

As it appears even from the rebel account of the action that Your Lordship has gained a victory over Greene, and it is probable he may in consequence have repassed the Roanoke, I beg leave to submit to Your Lordship the propriety of your coming to Chesapeake Bay in a frigate *as soon as you have finished your arrangements for the security of the Carolinas and you judge that affairs there are in such a train as no longer to require your presence,* directing at the same time such troops to follow you thither as Your Lordship is of opinion can best be spared. [*Ibid.*, pp. 405–406.]

[Extract of Phillips to Clinton. April 15, 1781.]

I am free to declare *Portsmouth to be a bad post, its locality not calculated for defense,* the collateral points necessary to be taken up so many that altogether it would require so great a number of troops as no general officer, I imagine, would venture to propose to a commander in chief to leave here for mere defense. [*Ibid.*, p. 407.]

Extracts from Major General Phillips' and Brigadier General Arnold's joint letter to Sir Henry Clinton. Portsmouth, 18 April 1781 (received 28 April).

We are of opinion that, was this corps of troops more in numbers by 1800 or 2000 men, a post in force might be taken at Petersburg, from whence detachments might be made in such strength as to break up entirely Mr. Greene's communication with Virginia.

We now take the liberty of giving an opinion of what may be done in Chesapeake previous to the month of June, supposing all cooperation over with the southern army. And we profess to conceive that, if the Marquis de Lafayette remains with his corps of 1500 men at Baltimore, an attempt may be made upon him, Baltimore, and Annapolis with great probability of success. But it cannot be undertaken, we imagine, without a reinforcement of effective 1600 or 2000 men, and a proportion of heavy artillery. Should the Marquis retire upon the approach of a corps of troops against him, Maryland would be defenseless.

We are of opinion these operations, if undertaken about the first of May, would terminate the latter end of that month, after which it would be in the power of Your Excellency to direct the future operations of this corps of troops—either to make an attempt upon Philadelphia and take posts in the lower counties of the Delaware (for which we apprehend this force sufficient) or to return to New York and operate with Your Excellency's main army for the campaign. [*Ibid.*, pp. 410–412.]

[Extract of Cornwallis to Germain. April 23, 1781.]

I yesterday received an express by a small vessel from Charleston, informing me that a frigate was there (but not then able to get over the bar) with dispatches from Sir Henry Clinton, notifying to me that Major General Phillips had been detached into the Chesapeake with a considerable force with instructions to cooperate with this army and to put himself under my orders. This express likewise brought me the disagreeable accounts *that the upper posts of South Carolina were in the most imminent danger* from an alarming spirit of revolt among many of the people, and by a movement of General Greene's army.

The distance from hence to Camden, the want of forage and subsistence on the greatest part of the road, and the difficulty of passing the Pedee when opposed by an enemy render it utterly impossible for me to give immediate assistance; and I apprehend a possibility of the utmost hazard to this little corps without the chance of a benefit in the attempt. For, if we are so unlucky as to suffer a severe blow in South Carolina, the spirit of revolt in that province would become very general, and the numerous rebels in this province be encouraged to be more than ever active and violent. This might enable General *Greene to hem me in* among the great rivers and, by cutting off our subsistence, render our arms useless. And to remain here for transports to carry us off would be a work of time, would lose our cavalry, and be other ways as ruinous and disgraceful to Britain as most events could be. I have, therefore, under so many embarrassing circumstances (*but looking*

upon Charleston as safe from any immediate attack from the rebels)
resolved to take advantage of General Greene's having left the back
part of Virginia open, and march immediately into that province to
attempt a junction with General Phillips. [*Ibid.*, pp. 420–422.]

[Extract of Cornwallis to Clinton.] 23d of April [1781] (received by Sir Henry Clinton May 22d).

It is very disagreeable to me to decide upon *measures so very important, and of such consequence to the general conduct of the war,*
without an opportunity of procuring Your Excellency's directions or
approbation. But the delay and difficulty of conveying letters, and the
impossibility of waiting for answers, render it indispensably necessary.
My present undertaking sits heavy on my mind. I have experienced
the dangers and distresses of marching some hundreds of miles in a
country chiefly hostile, without one active or useful friend, without
intelligence, and without communication with any part of the country.
The situation in which I leave South Carolina adds much to my anxiety.
Yet I am under the necessity of adopting this hazardous enterprise
hastily and with the appearance of precipitation, as I find there is no
prospect of speedy reinforcement from Europe, and that the return
of General Greene to North Carolina, either with or without success,
would put a junction with General Phillips out of my power. [*Ibid.*,
pp. 424–425.]

Copy of a letter from Earl Cornwallis to Major General Phillips.
Wilmington, 24 April 1781.

Dear Phillips:
        My situation is very distressing. Greene took the advantage of
my being obliged to come to this place, and has marched to South
Carolina. My expresses to Lord Rawdon on my leaving Cross Creek,
warning him of the possibility of such a movement, have all failed.
Mountaineers and militia have poured into the back part of that province; and *I much fear that Lord Rawdon's posts will be so distant from
each other, and his troops so scattered, as to put him into the greatest
danger of being beat in detail, and that the worst of consequences may
happen to most of the troops out of Charleston.*
        By a direct move toward Camden I cannot get time enough to relieve
Lord Rawdon. And, should he have fallen, my army would be exposed
to the utmost danger from the great rivers I should have to pass, the
exhausted state of the country, the numerous militia, *the almost universal spirit of revolt which prevails in South Carolina,* and the strength

of Greene's army (whose Continentals alone are at least as numerous as I am); and I could be of no use on my arrival at Charleston, *there being nothing to apprehend at present for that post.* I shall, therefore, immediately march up the country by Duplin Court House, pointing toward Hillsboro, in hopes to withdraw Greene.

If that should not succeed, I should be much tempted to try to form a junction with you. The attempt is exceedingly hazardous, and many unforeseen difficulties may render it totally impracticable, so that you must not take any steps that may expose your army to the danger of being ruined. I shall march to the lowest ford of the Roanoke, which I am informed is about twenty miles above Taylor's Ferry. Send every possible intelligence to me by the cipher I enclose, and make every movement in your power to facilitate our meeting (which must be somewhere near Petersburg) with safety to your own army. I mention the *lowest ford,* because in a hostile country ferries canot be depended upon. But, if I should decide upon the measure of endeavoring to come to you, I shall endeavor to surprise the boats at some of the ferries from Halifax upward.

Most sincerely yours, Cornwallis. [*Ibid.,* pp. 428–429.]

Extract of a letter from Lord Rawdon to Earl Cornwallis. Camden, 26 April 1781.

On the 19th General Greene appeared before us. I was so weak in troops, considering the extent I had to defend, that I would not risk men to harass him as he advanced. Three days after[ward] the South Carolina Regiment, which I had summoned from Ninety-six, arrived; and, although I had been obliged to abandon the ferry, I fortunately secured the passage of that corps into Camden. At the same time I received a letter from Lieutenant Colonel Balfour, giving me notice of Your Lordship's situation and signifying to me Your Lordship's wish that I should retire within the Santee. The necessity of the measure was obvious, but it was no longer in my power.

The efforts of the enemy to examine our works, and in particular an attempt to destroy our mill, had in the meantime occasioned some skirmishing. From the prisoners whom we made in these excursions I gathered that General Greene's army was by no means so numerous as I had apprehended, but that reinforcement was daily expected by them. The position which Marion had taken near the high hills of Santee precluded the hope of Lieutenant Colonel Watson's joining me; I therefore conceived some immediate effort necessary. And, indeed, I did not think that the disparity of numbers was such as should justify a bare defense.

I had procured information that the enemy, with a view of hazarding an assault, had sent their cannon and baggage a day's march in their rear, but that, abandoning the resolution, they had detached all their militia to bring up again their artillery. Although my intelligence was somewhat tardy, I hoped I should still be in time to avail myself of this conjuncture. By arming our musicians, our drummers, and in short everything that could carry a firelock, I mustered above nine hundred for the field, sixty of whom were dragoons. With this force and two six-pounders we marched, about ten o'clock yesterday morning, leaving our redoubts to the care of the militia and a few sick soldiers.

The enemy were posted on Hobkirk's Hill, a very strong ridge about two miles distant from our front. By filing close to the swamps we got into the woods unperceived and, taking an extensive circuit, came down upon the enemy's left flank. We were so fortunate in our march that we were not discovered till the flank companies of the Volunteers of Ireland, which led our column, fell in with Greene's pickets. The pickets, though supported, were instantly driven in and followed to their camp. The enemy were in much confusion, but notwithstanding formed and received us bravely. I believe they imagined us to be much weaker than we were. Their artillery, three six-pounders, had unluckily arrived a few minutes before the attack began, of which circumstances they gave us notice by heavy showers of grapeshot. I had ordered Lieutenant Colonel Campbell to lead the attack with the Sixty-third and King's American Regiments, which he performed with great spirit. The extent of the enemy's line soon obliged me to throw forward the Volunteers of Ireland also. Those three corps quickly gained the summit of the hill; and, giving room for the rest of our force to act, the rout of the enemy was immediately decided.

We pursued them about three miles. But the enemy's cavalry greatly surpassing ours as to number, horses, and appointments, our dragoons could not risk much; nor could I suffer the infantry to break their order in hopes of overtaking the fugitives. A part of the enemy's cavalry got into our rear, exacted paroles from several officers who lay wounded on the ground from which we had first driven the enemy, and carried off several wounded men, probably with intent to deceive the country people respecting the event of the action. We brought off above 100 prisoners exclusive of a number who, finding their retreat cut off, went into Camden and claimed protection as deserters. The enemy's cannon escaped by mere accident: it was run down a steep hill among some thick brushwood, where we passed without observing it; and it was carried off whilst we pursued the infantry in a contrary direction.

His Majesty's troops behaved most gallantly. I am under great obligations to Lieutenant Colonel Campbell, Major Campbell, Major Fraser, Major Coffin, Captain St. Leger, Captain Kane, and Captain Robinson, commanding the different corps or detachments—as likewise to Lieutenant Laye, commanding the Royal Artillery—for their animated exertions. Major of Brigade Doyle distinguished himself very much, and Lieutenants Rankin and Stark, who acted as my aides-de-camp, deserve my warm praises. I hope this success may give me an opening to get across the Santee, as the spirit of revolt appears strongly in the interior country.[61]

[Extract of Clinton to Phillips. April 26–30, 1781.]

I am favored with your several letters by the *Amphitrite*, man-of-war, and beg you will accept my thanks for the plan of attack you sent me in that of the 16th instant—on which, however, it is now unnecessary to give you any further trouble, as I have for certain reasons been induced to lay aside the enterprise at least for the present.[62]

Lord Cornwallis' arrival at Wilmington has considerably changed the complexion of our affairs to the southward, and all operations to the northward must probably give place to those in favor of His Lordship, which at present appear to require our more immediate attention.

The security of the two Carolinas is certainly an object of the greatest importance, and should at all events be first attended to. Success also against any considerable corps of the enemy which may be collected anywhere within reach, and the taking or destroying their public stores, magazines, etc., are undoubtedly very important advantages. But there is, in my humble opinion, still another operation which, if successful, would be most solidly decisive in its consequences, and is therefore well worth our attention. It is the trying the same experiment, which has hitherto unfortunately not succeeded to the southward, in other districts which have been represented as most friendly to the King's interests.

Virginia has been, in general, looked upon as universally hostile. Maryland has not been as yet tried, but is supposed to be not quite so much so. But the inhabitants of Pennsylvania on both sides of the Susquehanna, [in] York, Lancaster, Chester, and the peninsula between Chesapeake and Delaware, are represented to me to be friendly. There or thereabouts I think this experiment should now be tried.

61. *Clinton's note:* There were two hundred and fifteen killed and wounded and forty-three missing on Lord Rawdon's side in this action; the loss on that of the enemy, by their reports, [was] two hundred and sixty-four.
62. This paragraph is such a far cry from the original that it only approximates its meaning.

But it cannot be done fairly until we have a force sufficient not only to go there but to retain a respectable hold of the country afterward, should it be judged necessary. I wish that our numbers were competent to the occupying two corresponding stations at Baltimore and Elk River, agreeable to what I mentioned to you in the conversations we have had together on this subject. [Stevens, *Clinton-Cornwallis Controversy, 1,* 437, 439.]

Extract of a letter from Sir Henry Clinton to Lord George Germain. April 30th (received 23d June), 1781.

It gives me pain, My Lord, when I feel myself obliged to trouble Your Lordship with my distresses. But my regard to the King's interests and the duties of the very important command he has honored me with cannot but excite in me the most anxious solicitude. Your Lordship will therefore, I am persuaded, forgive me if I recall your attention to the very disagreeable predicament in which I now stand, being on the eve of opening the campaign before I know the naval chief to whom I am to communicate my plans and with whom I am to consult upon the measures to be pursued in the course of our operations.

Eight long months have elapsed since Your Lordship did me the honor of telling me that His Majesty was graciously pleased to listen to my representations and had appointed Admiral Arbuthnot to relieve Sir Peter Parker, and that another flag officer then on the list would be immediately named to the naval command in North America. Being in consequence of this information unwilling to trouble the Vice Admiral with a consultation on operations which his removal from the naval command here would of course prevent his being concerned in, and not having received any intimation from him of his intentions of going to Jamaica, I thought it my duty to endeavor to ascertain what they were.

Therefore, in the presence of a general officer and in the civilest manner I was capable of, I requested that the Admiral would inform me whether he proposed leaving us soon, and gave him my reasons. His answer was that he never had received any official intimation of the King's pleasure respecting his relieving Sir Peter Parker, nor any public letter of a later date than October. As this conversation was subsequent to the arrival of the *Cormorant,* which did not sail from Torbay before the latter end of February, I own I am at a loss to account for what he said.

I shall, however, wait the arrival of another packet, by which if *Admiral Arbuthnot is not recalled, I trust that His Majesty from his gra-*

*cious goodness will pardon me if I avail myself of the permission
he has been pleased to give me to resign this command to Lord Cornwallis.* For I must be free to own to Your Lordship that I cannot place
a confidence in Vice Admiral Arbuthnot, who from age, temper, and
inconsistency of conduct is really so little to be depended on that, was
I to continue to serve with him, I should be constantly under the most
distressing apprehensions of the miscarriage of such enterprises as
we might be engaged in. [*Ibid.*, pp. 447–448.]

> Extract of a letter from Sir Henry Clinton to Lord Cornwallis.
> New York, April 30, '81 [enclosing a duplicate of Clinton to
> Cornwallis of April 13].

The disparity of numbers between Your Lordship's force and that of
the enemy opposed to you in the action at Guilford appears to be very
great. And I confess I am at some loss to guess how Your Lordship came
to be reduced before that event to 1360 infantry. Before I was favored
with Your Lordship's letter the rebel account of the battle had led me,
indeed, to hope that its consequences would have been more decisive,
and that General Greene would have repassed the Roanoke and left
Your Lordship at liberty to pursue the objects of your move into North
Carolina. Under the persuasion, therefore, that you would soon be able
to finish your arrangements for the security of the Carolinas, I submitted
to you in my letter of the 13th instant the propriety of your going in
a frigate to Chesapeake. But, as it is now probable that *Your Lordship's
presence in Carolina cannot be so soon dispensed with,* I make no doubt
that you will think it right to communicate to Major General Phillips
without delay the plan of your future operations in that quarter, together with your opinion how the Chesapeake army can best direct
theirs to assist them. That general officer has already under his orders
3500 men, and I shall send him 1700 more, which are now embarked
and will sail whenever the Admiral is ready.

I was, indeed, in great hopes that your successes in North Carolina
would have been such as to have put it in my power to avail myself of
a large portion of Your Lordship's army, the whole Chesapeake corps,
and the entire reinforcements from Europe for this campaign's operations to the northward of Carolina. But I observe with concern from
Your Lordship's letter that, so far from being in a condition to spare me
any part of your present force, you are of opinion that part of the European reinforcement will be indispensably necessary to enable you to
act offensively, or even to maintain yourself in the upper parts of the
country. [*Ibid.*, pp. 442–444.]

[Extract of Clinton to Phillips. April 30–May 3, 1781.]

If His Lordship proposes no operation to you soon (that is, before the month of June) and you see none that will operate for him directly, I think the best indirect one in his favor will be what you and General Arnold have proposed to me in Number 10 of your joint letter of the 18th instant,[63] beginning with the attempt on Philadelphia. The only risk you run is from a temporary superiority of the enemy at sea. It is, however, an important move, and ought in my opinion to be tried, even with some risk. Give me timely information of your intended move; and, if possible, I will follow you into the Delaware with such a small reinforcement as I can at the time spare.

The reinforcement is embarked and fallen down to Staten Island, where they wait only the Admiral's pleasure for their proceeding to the Chesapeake.

As you seemed to think, before you received Lord Cornwallis' letter, that all direct operation in favor of His Lordship should cease by the end of May, should the expedition not sail from hence before the 20th and I do not hear further from you, I will not send it. For in that case I think the experiment on the peninsula may be tried to more advantage up Delaware than round by Chesapeake—in which case I shall expect General Arnold and you, with such troops as you can spare, to meet me at the Head of Elk or Bohemia and form a junction. I can certainly spare more troops from hence for such a move than I can send to Chesapeake, for reasons obvious.

Pray let me receive General Arnold's and your opinions upon Colonel Rankin's proposals as soon as possible. I confess I am not sanguine; but, if the experiment can be tried without any other risk than from the enemy's superiority at sea, I should wish to do it. Therefore, if General Arnold and you like it, I shall be reconciled to it; and it shall be tried after I know your opinions on it and the enclosed proposals.

If Lord Cornwallis proposes anything necessary for his operations, you of course must adopt it if you can. But, should His Lordship determine on a defensive in the Carolinas, he surely cannot want any of the European reinforcement, and will of course send it to you and all such other as shall arrive. Thus reinforced, if after leaving a sufficient garrison in *Elizabeth River* you can proceed to the peninsula, I think we shall be in force to give this a fair trial. And I may leave you in the command there, *unless things should take a more favorable turn in the Carolinas and Lord Cornwallis' presence there be no longer necessary.*

63. In the final paragraph of the extract printed above, p. 511.

For, *until they do, I should imagine he will not leave the Carolinas.*
[*Ibid.,* pp. 451–455.]

Extract of a letter from Lord George Germain to Sir Henry Clinton. Whitehall, 2 May 1781.

Indeed, had we any doubt of the wisdom of the present plan of pushing the war in that quarter and of *the vast importance of the possession of Virginia,* the conduct of the rebels would confirm us in our judgment. For they could not give stronger proofs of the high opinion they entertain of its importance than by the great efforts they made and the hazards they ran in their attempts to preserve it, as nothing less than the apprehension of the most fatal consequences to their cause from its loss could have prevailed on them to detach so large a part of Mr. Washington's best troops to such a distance. Conceiving, therefore, so highly as I do of the importance of the southern provinces, and of the vast advantages which must attend the prosecution of the war upon the present plan of extending our conquests from *south* to *north,* it was a great mortification to me to find by your instructions to Major General Phillips that it appeared to be your intention that only a part of the troops he carried with him should remain in the Chesapeake and that *he* and General *Arnold* should return to New York, leaving only a sufficient force to serve for garrisons in the posts they might establish in Virginia.

Your ideas, therefore, of the importance of recovering that province appearing to be so different from mine, I thought it proper to ask the advice of His Majesty's other servants upon the subject; and, their opinion concurring entirely with mine, it has been submitted to the King. And I am commanded by His Majesty to acquaint you that the recovery of the southern provinces and the prosecution of the war by pushing our conquests from *south* to *north* is to be considered as the *chief and principal object for the employment of all the forces under your command* which can be spared from the defense of the places in His Majesty's possession *until it is accomplished.* The three regiments from Ireland and the British recruits that went with them are, I trust, well on their way by this time to Charleston. *And, as Sir George Rodney will bring you three more regiments from the Leeward Islands* [64] *before the*

64. *Clinton's note:* Sir George Rodney did not come to America, and sent Sir Samuel Hood thither with only fourteen sail of the line—when de Grasse brought twenty-eight sail. The regiments and recruits from Ireland arrived at Charleston in June; and of the three regiments promised from the West Indies only one very weak one ever joined Sir Henry Clinton's army, and that only for a few days.

hurricane months, the augmentation of your force must, I should think, be equal to the utmost of your wishes. [Ibid., pp. 465–468.]

[Extract of Balfour to Clinton. May 6, 1781.]

I must inform Your Excellency that the general state of the country is most distressing [and] that the enemy's parties are everywhere. The communication by land with Savannah no longer exists; Colonel Brown is invested at Augusta, and Colonel Cruger in the most critical situation at Ninety-six. Indeed, I should betray the duty I owe Your Excellency did I not represent *the defection of this province* [as] *so universal that I know of no mode short of depopulation to retain it.* [Ibid., pp. 472–473.]

Extract of a letter from Brigadier General Arnold to Sir Henry Clinton. Petersburg, May 12, 1781.

The same day, 27 April, I marched to Osborne's with the Seventy-sixth and Eightieth Regiments, Queen's Rangers, part of the Jägers, and the American Legion, where we arrived about noon. Finding the enemy had a very considerable force of ships four miles above Osborne's, drawn up in line to oppose us, I sent a flag to the Commodore proposing to treat with him for the surrender of his fleet—which he refused with this answer, *that he was determined to defend it to the last extremity.* I immediately ordered down two six- and two three-pounders, brass fieldpieces, to a bank of the river nearly level with the water and within one hundred yards of the *Tempest,* a twenty-gun state ship, which began immediately to fire upon us, as did the *Renown* of twenty-six guns, the *Jefferson,* a state brigantine of fourteen guns, and several other armed vessels and brigantines. About two or three hundred militia on the opposite shore, at the same time, kept up a heavy fire of musketry upon us, notwithstanding which the fire of the artillery (under the direction of Captain Fage and Lieutenant Rogers) took such place that the ships were soon obliged to strike their colors and the militia [were] drove from the opposite shore.

Want of boats and the wind blowing hard prevented our capturing many of the seamen, who took to their boats and escaped on shore, but not without first scuttling and setting fire to some of their ships, which could not be saved. Two ships, three brigantines, five sloops, and two schooners, loaded with tobacco, cordage, flour, etc., etc., fell into our hands. Four ships, five brigantines, and a number of small vessels were sunk and burnt. [Tarleton, *History,* p. 336.]

Extract of a letter from Lord Rawdon to Earl Cornwallis. Monk's
Corner, 24 May 1781.

On the 7th May Lieutenant Colonel Watson joined me with his detachment, much reduced in number through casualties, sickness, and
a reinforcement which he had left to strengthen the garrison at Georgetown. By him I received the unwelcome intelligence *that the whole
interior country had revolted,* and that Marion and Lee, after reducing
a post at Wright's Bluff, had crossed the Santee to support the insurgents. Information reached me the same day that the post at Motte's
House (near the mouth of the Congaree) was invested, and batteries
opened against it.

I had been long sensible of the necessity for my retiring within the
Santee. But, while Lee and Marion were in a situation to retard my
march in front at the same time that my rear was exposed to Greene,
I conceived it impracticable without the disgrace of abandoning my
stores—and particularly my wounded—at Camden. The measure, even
now, could only be effected at Nelson's Ferry, which was sixty miles
from me. On the 9th I published to the troops and to the militia my
design of evacuating Camden, offering to such of the latter as chose
to accompany me every assistance that we could afford them. During
the ensuing night I sent off all our baggage, etc., under a strong escort,
and destroyed the works, remaining at Camden with the rest of the
troops till ten o'clock the next day in order to cover the march.

On the night of the 13th I began to pass the river at Nelson's Ferry,
and by the evening of the 14th everything was safely across. We brought
off all the sick and wounded, excepting about thirty who were too ill to
be moved; and for them I left an equal number of Continental prisoners
in exchange. We brought off all the stores of any kind of value, destroying the rest, and we brought off not only the militia who had been
with us in Camden, but also all the well affected neighbors on our route,
together with the wives, children, Negroes, and baggage of almost all of
them.

My first news upon landing at Nelson's was that the post at Motte's
House had fallen. This stroke was heavy upon me, as all the provisions
had been forwarded from Nelson's to that post for the supply of Camden. Immediately on my arrival at this place I dispatched emissaries to
Ninety-six, directing Lieutenant Colonel Cruger to retire to Augusta.
Should Lieutenant Colonel Cruger not have received this order, I fear
his situation will be dangerous. I did not think it practicable to assist
him without running hazards which I judged the general state of the

province would not allow. Beside, I had no deposit of provisions left on the frontier; and, as to the expectation of gleaning them as I advanced (in a wasted country, and surrounded as I should have been by a swarm of light troops and mounted militia), I conceived that my whole force must have been so employed in procuring its daily subsistence that little else could have been effected with it.

I am using every effort to augment our cavalry, in hopes that the arrival of some force *which may put Charleston out of danger* will speedily enable us to adopt a more active conduct. But the plundering parties of the enemy have so stripped the country of horses, and there is such difficulty in getting swords and other appointments made at Charleston, that I get on but slowly in this undertaking.

Lieutenant Colonel Balfour was so good to meet me at Nelson's. He took this measure that he might present his circumstances to me. He stated that the revolt was universal; that, from the little reason to apprehend this serious invasion, the old works of Charleston had been in part leveled to make way for new ones, which were not yet constructed; that his garrison was inadequate to oppose any force of consequence; and that the defection of the townspeople showed itself in a thousand instances. I agreed with him in the conclusion to be drawn from thence, that any misfortune happening to my corps might entail the loss of the province. [Stevens, *Clinton-Cornwallis Controversy, 1,* 481–484.]

Extract of a letter from Earl Cornwallis to Sir Henry Clinton.
Byrd's, north of James River, 26 May 1781 (received June 9th).

The arrival of the reinforcement has made me easy about Portsmouth for the present. I shall now proceed to dislodge Lafayette from *Richmond,* and with my light troops to destroy any magazines or stores in the *neighborhood* which may have been collected either for his use or General Greene's army. From *thence* I propose to move to the *Neck at Williamsburg* (which is represented as *healthy,* and where some subsistence may be procured) *and keep myself unengaged from operations which might interfere with your plan for the campaign until I have the satisfaction of hearing from you.*

I hope I shall then have an opportunity to receive better information than has hitherto been in my power to procure *relative to a proper harbor and place of arms. At present I am inclined to think well of York.* The objections to Portsmouth are that *it cannot be made strong without an army to defend it, that it is remarkably unhealthy, and can give no protection to a ship of the line.*

Your Excellency desires Generals Phillips and Arnold to give you their opinions relative to Mr. Alexander's [65] proposal. As General Arnold goes to New York by the first safe conveyance, you will have an opportunity of hearing his sentiments in person. Experience has made me less sanguine, and more arrangements seem to me necessary for so important an expedition than appear to occur to General Arnold. Mr. Alexander's conversations bear too great a resemblance to those of the emissaries from North Carolina to give me much confidence. And, from the experience I have had and the dangers I have undergone, one maxim appears to me to be absolutely necessary for the safe and honorable conduct of this war—which is that we should have as few posts as possible, and that wherever the King's troops are they should be in respectable force. In regard to *taking possession of Philadelphia by an incursion, even if practicable,* without an intention of keeping or burning it (neither of which appear to be advisable) I should apprehend it would do more harm than good to the cause of Britain. I shall take the liberty of repeating that, if offensive war is intended, *Virginia appears to me to be the only province in which it can be carried on, and in which there is a stake.* [*Ibid.,* pp. 487–489.]

Extract of a letter from Sir Henry Clinton to Earl Cornwallis. New York, May 29, 1781 (received June 26 [66]).

When I first heard of Your Lordship's retreat from Cross Creek to Wilmington, I confess I was in hopes you had reason to consider Greene so totally *hors de combat* as to be perfectly at ease for Lord Rawdon's safety. And after your arrival at Wilmington I flattered myself that, if any change of circumstances should make it necessary, you could always have been able to march to the Waccamaw, where I imagined vessels might have passed you over to Georgetown.

I cannot, therefore, conceal from Your Lordship the apprehensions I felt on reading your letter to me of the 24th *ultimo,* wherein you inform me of the critical situation which you supposed the Carolinas to be in, and that you should probably attempt to effect a junction with Major General Phillips. Lord Rawdon's officer-like and spirited exertions in taking the advantage of Greene's having detached from his army have indeed eased me of my apprehensions for the present. But in the disordered state of Carolina and Georgia, as represented to

65. A code name for Col. Rankin.
66. In a marginal note on a copy in a letterbook (May 26–Oct. 20, 1781, in a slip case entitled "Correspondence with Cornwallis," CP) Clinton points out that he referred Cornwallis to this letter and that of June 8 before calling on him for troops, but that the Earl had received neither dispatch when he crossed the James.

me by Lieutenant Colonel Balfour, I shall dread what may be the consequence of Your Lordship's move unless a reinforcement arrives very soon in South Carolina. Had it been possible for Your Lordship in your letter to me of the 10th *ultimo* to have intimated the probability of your intention to form a junction with General Phillips, I should certainly have endeavored to have stopped you—as I did then, as well as now, consider such a move as likely to be dangerous to our interests in the southern colonies.

And this, My Lord, was not my only fear. For I will be free to own that I was apprehensive for the corps under Your Lordship's immediate orders, as well as for that under Lord Rawdon. And I should not have thought even the one under Major General Phillips in safety at Petersburg, at least for so long a time, had I not fortunately, on hearing of your being at Wilmington, sent another detachment from this army to reinforce him.

I am persuaded Your Lordship will have the goodness to excuse my saying thus much. But what is done cannot now be altered. And, as Your Lordship has thought proper to make this decision, I shall most gladly avail myself of your very able assistance in carrying on such operations as you shall judge best in Virginia until we are compelled (as I fear we must be by the climate) to bring them more northward.

Your Lordship will have been informed of my ideas respecting operations to the northward of the Carolinas by my instructions to the different general officers detached to the Chesapeake, and the substance of some conversations with General Phillips on the subject, which I committed to writing and sent to him with my last dispatch, with directions to communicate it to Your Lordship. By these Your Lordship will observe that my first object has ever been a cooperation with your measures. But Your Lordship's situation at different periods made it necessary for me to vary my instructions according to circumstances. They were originally directed to assist Your Lordship's operations in securing South and recovering North Carolina; their attention was afterward pointed to the saving South Carolina. And now Your Lordship may think it necessary to employ your force in recovering both or either of these provinces, by either a direct or indirect operation. With respect to the first Your Lordship must be the sole judge. With respect to the last you have *my* opinions, which may, however, probably give way to *yours* should they differ from them, as they will have the advantage of being formed on the spot and upon circumstances which at this distance I cannot, of course, judge of. I shall therefore leave them totally to Your Lordship to decide upon, until you either hear from me or we meet.[67]

As I had judged the force I sent to the Chesapeake fully sufficient for all operations there, even though we should extend them to the experiment (mentioned in the conversations referred to) at the *western* head of the Chesapeake about Baltimore, and Your Lordship will perceive it was Generals Phillips' and Arnold's opinion they were sufficient for even that on the *eastern* (which, however, might certainly require a much greater force), it is possible that the additional corps Your Lordship has brought with you may enable you to return something to me for this post. But I beg Your Lordship *will by no means consider this as a call,* for I would rather content myself with ever so bare a defensive —until there was an appearance of serious operations against me—than cramp yours in the least. But, as I said in a former letter, I trust to Your Lordship's disinterestedness that you will *not require from me more troops than what are absolutely wanted,* and that *you will recollect* a circumstance which I am ever aware of in carrying on operations in the Chesapeake, which is *that they can be no longer secure than while we are superior at sea.* But at all events I may at least expect timely information will be sent me of the *contrary* being likely to happen, *and I hope Your Lordship may be able in that case to place your army in a secure situation during such temporary inconvenience.* For, should it become permanent, I need not say what our prospects in this country are likely to be. [*Ibid.,* pp. 493–497.]

Extract of a letter from General Washington to General Sullivan. New Windsor, May 29, 1781.

But the perplexed, distressed, and embarrassed state of our affairs on account of supplies, with which you are well acquainted, the languid efforts of the states to procure men, and the insuperable difficulties in the way of transportation would, I apprehend, have rendered the scheme—however devoutly to be wished and desired—abortive in the first instance. And I must inform you there is yet another obstacle which makes the attempt you have suggested *absolutely impracticable* with

67. In further notes on the copy of this letter in "Correspondence with Cornwallis" Clinton explains why he was polite to the Earl. The government had been persuaded to adopt Cornwallis' strategy by "the victories of Camden and Guilford —which, considering the race of beings he had to contend with, were not more creditable than Plassey." Sir Henry, in consequence, decided to resign "the instant I could with propriety," and therefore left his subordinate complete freedom of action. If the government had not taken the stand it did, "I would have sent His Lordship back by sea" to South Carolina.

the means you propose, but which I dare not commit to paper for fear of the same misfortune which has already happened to some of my letters.

You will have seen before the receipt of this, by my public letter to Congress of the 27th instant, the result of the deliberations of the Count de Rochambeau and myself at Wethersfield. That plan, upon the maturest consideration and after combining all the present circumstances and future prospects, appeared, though precarious, far the most eligible of any we could possibly devise while we are inferior at sea. The object was considered to be of greater magnitude and more within our reach than any other. *The weakness of the garrison of New York,* the centrical position for drawing together men and supplies, and the spur which an attempt against that place would give to every exertion were among the reasons which prompted to that undertaking, and which promised the fairest prospect of success unless the enemy should recall a considerable part of their force from the southward. And, even in this case, the same measure which might produce disappointment in one quarter would certainly, in the event, afford the greatest relief in another. While an opportunity presents itself of striking the enemy a fatal blow, I will persuade myself the concurring exertions of Congress, of the several states immediately concerned, and of every individual in them who is well affected to our cause will be united in yielding every possible aid on the occasion. [Fitzpatrick, *Writings of Washington,* 22, 131–132.]

[Extract of Washington to Lund Washington. May 31, 1781.]

We have heard nothing yet of the detachment, consisting of about 2000 men, which left New York the 13th instant; nor do we know whether those troops were bound for Virginia, North or South Carolina, or elsewhere. A report prevails, and is believed by some, that the enemy are about to quit New York altogether. But I shall withhold my opinion of the matter yet a little longer. If such an event should take place, it will be an evidence in my mind that they expect matters are drawing to a conclusion, and that they have a mind to get as fast hold on the southern states as possible. I have already given you my opinion, in some late letters, with respect to my movable property. After removing the most valuable and least bulky articles, the rest, with the buildings, must take their chance. [*Ibid.,* p. 145.]

[Extract of Washington to John Parke Custis. May 31, 1781.]

The states this way are miserably slow in sending their recruits for the army, and our supplies come in equally tardy. Whether the season and the prospects before them will produce any change I am unable to say. [*Ibid.,* pp. 142–143.]

Extract of a letter from Lord Rawdon to Earl Cornwallis. Charleston, June 5th, 1781.

General Greene invested Ninety-six on the 22d of May. All my letters to Lieutenant Colonel Cruger failed, so that he thought himself bound to maintain that post. Fortunately we are *now* in a condition to undertake succoring him *without exposing a more valuable stake.* On the 3d instant the fleet from Ireland arrived, having on board the Third, Nineteenth, and Thirtieth Regiments, a detachment of the Guards, and a considerable body of recruits. I shall march on the 7th toward Ninety-six, having been reinforced by the flank companies of the three regiments. If I am in time to save that post, it will be a fortunate circumstance. [Tarleton, *History,* pp. 479–480.]

[Copy of Germain to Clinton. Whitehall, June 6, 1781.]

Sir:

After I had closed my letters which go by this conveyance, Captain Brodrick arrived with dispatches from Lord Cornwallis and Colonel Balfour, the contents of which I need not repeat to you, as you will have long since been fully informed of everything that has passed in that quarter. I shall therefore only observe, in addition to all I have hitherto written upon the subject, that I am well pleased to find Lord Cornwallis' opinion entirely coincides with mine of the great importance of pushing the war on the side of Virginia [68] with all the force that can be spared, until that province is reduced (if it be possible to do it) before the season become too intemperate for active operations there. The troops from Ireland will, I hope, have arrived in good time to join His Lordship, or form another army under Lord Rawdon to drive

68. Clinton printed this letter in his *Narrative* of the Yorktown campaign, and in one copy of the pamphlet he made the following MS marginal note: "You are therefore commanded not to take a man from thence and, if you have, to send them back; and [to] go there as soon as the season will permit, with all the force you can spare from the defense of New York." This note was printed by Stevens (*Clinton-Cornwallis Controversy,* 2, 13, n. 5), where it appears to be Sir Henry's restoration of a crucial sentence in Germain's original letter, omitted in the version printed in the *Narrative.* In fact Germain never wrote the sentence; it is pure fabrication. See above, p. 316 and n. 5.

the enemy out of the upper country while Lord Cornwallis and General Phillips are employed in reducing the lower parts. For I plainly see there must be great exertions and constant cooperations of different and powerful corps to effect this most essential service.

I am, sir, your most obedient, humble servant, Germain. [Stevens, *Clinton-Cornwallis Controversy, 2,* 13.]

[Extract of Clinton to Cornwallis. June 8, 1781.]

I enclose Your Lordship copies of some intercepted letters; by these Your Lordship will see that we are threatened with a siege. The enemy had bad information respecting my force. It is not, however, as Your Lordship knows, what it ought to be.

I am persuaded that I need not say to Your Lordship how necessary it is that I should be informed without delay of every change of position in Your Lordship's army. And I am sure you will excuse me for observing *that, had it been possible, upon the arrival of the last reinforcement from hence, for Your Lordship to have let me know your views and intentions, I should not now be at a loss to judge of the force you might want for your operations. Ignorant, therefore, as I am of them,* I can only trust that, as Your Lordship will see by the enclosed letters that my call for a reinforcement is not a wanton one, you will send me what you can spare as soon as it may be expedient. For, should Your Lordship be engaged in a move of such importance as to require the employment of your whole force, *I would by no means wish to starve or obstruct it,* but in that case would rather endeavor to wait a little longer until my occasions grow more urgent *or your situation admits of your detachment*—of which, however, I request to be informed with all possible dispatch. [*Ibid.,* pp. 14–15, 17.]

Extract of a letter from Sir Henry Clinton to Lord George Germain. New York, 9th June, 1781 (receipt acknowledged 14th July).

As Lord Cornwallis will have been informed on the 21st of May of the arrival in Chesapeake of the last reinforcement from hence, and that Vice Admiral Arbuthnot was at sea, I am inclined to suppose from his letters that he will of course proceed immediately against Lafayette. But, should he have unfortunately gone off and escaped him, His Lordship will not, I expect, confine himself to James River; but he will probably *proceed to Baltimore or the Head of Elk, to make trial of that part of my plan against Philadelphia* recommended to General Phillips (as His Lordship will find among that officer's papers, and to which I have referred him), and finally *in support of our supposed friends in Pennsylvania.* But, as Your Lordship will observe, I have left Lord Cornwallis wholly at liberty to pursue such measures as he shall judge best.

I cannot say *until I hear again from His Lordship* what may be the plan most proper to follow at this time. The appearance of so formidable a force in Chesapeake may incline some of those provinces to submit. But, if we have not their hearts—*which I fear cannot be expected in Virginia*—there is reason to believe that on the first turn of fortune (should that be *by the arrival of a superior French fleet*) they will revolt again and render our situation everywhere critical. For my part I am convinced that, unless our friends join us heartily, though we may conquer, we shall never keep. How the experiment has failed in the Carolinas I cannot judge, nor dare I say it will not likewise fail in Pennsylvania. But that is now the only place on this continent left untried; and, if Lord Cornwallis' prospects of another sort are not very certain, *I heartily hope he will decide for this,* which I shall recommend immediately.

But, should His Lordship have reasons for declining it and have no other to propose, I shall probably direct him to take such posts in the Chesapeake as he shall judge proper, keep troops sufficient for desultory water expeditions during the summer (when, according to one of Mr. Washington's intercepted letters, all land operations should cease in that province), and draw what troops can be spared from them to this post, with which I shall act offensively or defensively as circumstances may make necessary. [Calendared in Hist. MSS Com., *American MSS in the Royal Institution, 2,* 288.]

[Copy of a letter from] Sir Henry Clinton to Lord Cornwallis (sent by Ensign Amiel and received by His Lordship on the 26th June). June 11 [1781].

My Lord:

I am honored with Your Lordship's letter of the 26th *ultimo;* and, as I am unwilling to detain the convoy, I shall not have time to write so fully to Your Lordship as I could wish. Respecting my opinions of stations in York and James Rivers, I shall beg leave only *to refer Your Lordship to my instructions to, and correspondence with, Generals Phillips and Arnold, together with the substance of my conversations with the former, which Your Lordship will have found among General Phillips' papers* and to which I referred you in my last dispatch. I shall, therefore, of course, approve of any alterations Your Lordship may think proper to make in those stations.

The detachments I have made from this army into Chesapeake since General Leslie's expedition in October last, inclusive, have amounted to 7724 effectives; and, at the time Your Lordship made the junction with the corps there, there were under Major General Phillips' orders 5304—a force I should have hoped would be sufficient of itself to carry on operation in any of the southern provinces in America, where, it appears by the intercepted letters of Washington and Lafayette, they are in no situation to stand against even a division of that army. I have no reason to suppose the Continentals under Lafayette can exceed 1000; and I am told by Lieutenant Colonel Hill, of the Ninth Regiment, that about a fortnight ago he met at Fredericktown, in Maryland, the Pennsylvania line under Wayne of about the same number, who were so discontented that their officers were afraid to trust them with ammunition. This, however, may have since altered; and Your Lordship may possibly have opposed to you from 1500 to 2000 Continentals and, as Lafayette observed, a small body of ill-armed peasantry, full as spiritless as the militia of the southern provinces and without any service. Comparing, therefore, the force now under Your Lordship in Chesapeake and that of the enemy opposed to you (and I think it clearly appears they have for the present no intention of sending thither reinforcement), I should have hoped you would have quite sufficient to carry on any operation in Virginia, *should that have been advisable in this advanced season.*

By the intercepted letters enclosed to Your Lordship in my last dispatch you will observe that I am threatened with a siege in this post. My present effective force is only 10,931. With respect to that the enemy may collect for such an object, it is probable they may amount to at least twenty thousand, besides reinforcements to the French (which from pretty good authority I have reason to expect) and the numerous militia of the five neighboring provinces. Thus circumstanced, I am persuaded Your Lordship will be of opinion that the sooner I concentrate my force the better. Therefore, *unless Your Lordship after the receipt of my letters of the 29th of May and 8th instant* [69] should incline to agree with me in opinion and judge it right to adopt my ideas respecting the move to Baltimore or the Delaware Neck, etc., I beg leave to recommend it to you, as soon as you have finished the active operations you may be now engaged in, *to take a defensive station in any healthy situation you choose,* be it at Williamsburg or Yorktown. And I would wish *in that case* that, *after reserving to yourself such troops as you may judge necessary for an ample defensive and desultory move-*

69. *Clinton's note:* These two letters were not received by Lord Cornwallis before the 12th July, the originals having been lost.

ments by water for the purpose of annoying the enemy's communica-
tions, destroying magazines, etc., the following corps may be *sent me*
in succession as you can spare them: the two battalions of light infantry,
Forty-third, Seventy-sixth or Eightieth Regiments, the two battalions
of Anspach, Queen's Rangers, cavalry and infantry, remains of the detachment of Seventeenth Light Dragoons, and such a proportion of
artillery as can be spared, particularly men.

Until the arrival of the expected reinforcements from Europe it will
be impossible for me to judge what future operations may be within
my power under my present circumstances. I heartily wish I was able
to spare a second army, after leaving a sufficient defensive for this
important post. But Your Lordship will, I hope, excuse me if I dissent
from your opinion of the manner in which that army should be employed. For experience ought to convince us that there is no possibility of re-establishing order in any rebellious province on this continent without the hearty assistance of numerous friends. *These,* My
Lord, *are not, I think, to be found in Virginia.* Nor dare I positively
assert that under our present circumstances they are to be found in
great numbers anywhere else, or that their exertions when found will
answer our expectations.

But I believe there is a greater probability of finding them *in Penn-*
sylvania than in any except the southern provinces. In these Your Lordship has already made the experiment. It has there failed; they are gone
from us, and I fear are not to be recovered. The only one, therefore,
now remaining is this; *and, if I continue in the command, I am deter-*
mined to give it a fair trial whenever it can be done with propriety. I
am not, however, likely to have a choice of operation, at least for some
time to come.

Nor can I altogether agree with Your Lordship in thinking that a
desultory move against Philadelphia would do more harm than good.
There, My Lord, are collected their principal depots of stores for the
campaign, an immense quantity of European and West India commodities, and no inconsiderable supply of money, which their uninterrupted
trade and cruisers have lately procured them. And from these funds
they are now forming a bank by subscription, which, if it succeeds, may
give fresh vigor to their cause. Could we, therefore, at this moment
seize these important magazines, etc., and overset their schemes and
break up their public credit, the favorable consequences resulting from
such success are too obvious to need explanation. And all this, My Lord,
I have no doubt might have been effected if our reinforcement had arrived in time (and the enemy had no prospect of receiving any), without our either keeping or destroying Philadelphia—the latter of which

is foreign from my inclination, and the former is certainly inadvisable.
I have the honor, etc., H. Clinton. [Stevens, *Clinton-Cornwallis Controversy*, 2, 19–23.]

Extract of a letter from Sir Henry Clinton to Lord Cornwallis.
New York, 15 June 1781 [received June 26].

As the Admiral has thought proper to stop the sailing of the convoy
with stores, horse accouterments, etc., I delay not a moment to dispatch a runner to Your Lordship with a duplicate of my letter of the
11th instant. And, as I am led to suppose from Your Lordship's letter
of the 26th *ultimo* that you may not think it expedient to adopt the operations I had recommended in the upper Chesapeake and will by this
time probably have finished those you were engaged in, I request you
will immediately embark a part of the troops stated in the letter enclosed, beginning with the light infantry, etc. [*Ibid.*, pp. 24–25.]

Extract of a letter from Major General Leslie to Sir Henry Clinton. Portsmouth, June 17, 1781 (received 26 June).

Captain Elphinstone, in the *Warwick*, is arrived at Hampton Road
with a detachment of the Guards, etc., for this army and fifteen victualers. I can hear nothing of Lord Cornwallis since he marched from
Mrs. Byrd's [Westover] the 26th *ultimo*, but I fear he has not fallen in
with Lafayette. I have sent an armed vessel up the Rappahannock to
look for them in case they are near Fredericksburg. When I hear from
His Lordship, I shall forward the contents to New York by advice
vessel. All is quiet here, the whole country taking paroles.

Extract of a letter from Sir Henry Clinton to Major General
Leslie. New York, June 23, 1781.

As I think it probable that the season may have put an end to all operation in Chesapeake except by water, and that Lord Cornwallis will
have embarked a considerable part of his army to join me, I have desired that you may come here with such troops as His Lordship shall
send, if he has not already named you for the command at Charleston
and he can spare you.

Extract of a letter from Sir Henry Clinton to Sir George Rodney
in the West Indies. June 28, 1781.

As Lord Cornwallis' operations in Chesapeake must now cease from
the inclemency of the season, I have called back a part of his force and

have recommended it to His Lordship to occupy defensive stations in York and James Rivers until the season for operations in that climate should return.

Let me hope, my dear Sir George, that, if de Grasse comes here or even detaches in great force (which authentic intelligence confirms he will), you will come here if possible in person, as we have all confidence in you.[70] Should de Grasse come here, he will be most probably encumbered with transports. On the contrary, it is most likely that such reinforcement as General Vaughan may think proper to send us will be embarked in your fleet, a fortunate junction of which with this squadron may give Your Excellency a decided superiority, and an opportunity of ending the affair that way most gloriously. But, should a storm or any unforeseen circumstance prevent that, I am persuaded that our combined efforts will not only render all the enemy's attempts abortive, but ensure success to such operations as we may afterward undertake together. The present situation of our country requires more than common exertions, and you will ever find me ready to assist yours to the utmost of my power.

[Extract of Clinton to Rodney, a second letter. June 28, 1781.]

I have no doubt you will agree with me respecting de Grasse's intention of coming here during the hurricane months, and that this post will be his first object. Now, sir, permit me to suggest to you an idea which forcibly strikes me. Barras is left at Rhode Island with seven ships, all the cannon taken out of the works, and these garrisoned with twelve hundred French and thirteen hundred militia. It is therefore become the same tempting object it was before the French were fortified or reinforced. I need not say how important success against that squadron and port would be while they remain in the state I describe, and there can be no material alteration which I shall not be constantly acquainted with. I ask no more of the navy than to take a station between Conanicut Island and Brenton's Neck, covering my landing either on that neck or under the protection of frigates in Sakonnet Passage. As I have not another set of the intercepted letters copied, I beg you will communicate those enclosed herewith to General Vaughan.

70. "and, I am sorry to say, not the least in this same old gentleman." This clause in the original draft was omitted in the final letter. So were two sentences in an earlier paragraph: if Rodney decides to come in person, "I hope you will give such positive orders to our old Admiral (if he should be still in the command) as he cannot misconstrue and will not dare to disobey. For otherwise I shall fear his doing both." Clinton had known since the previous autumn that Sir George shared his own view of Arbuthnot's incapacity; see Willcox in *Journ. of Mod. Hist.*, 17, 315.

[Clinton] to General Vaughan. June 28th, 1781.

As it is clear from the intercepted letters which Sir George Rodney will communicate to you, and other intelligence which I can depend upon, that the enemy mean to make one great effort against this place, and that de Grasse will probably come here in the hurricane season (if not before) with both ships and troops, I write to Sir George Rodney to express my hope that he will follow him hither in person. And I flatter myself that Your Excellency will make use of the opportunity of his fleet to send me the three regiments which were originally destined to reinforce this army.[71]

Extract of a letter from [Clinton] to Lord Cornwallis. 28 June 1781.

Having for very essential reasons come to a resolution of endeavoring by a rapid move to seize the stores, etc., collected at Philadelphia, and afterward to bring the troops employed on that service to reinforce this post, I am to request that, if Your Lordship has not already embarked the reinforcement I called for in my letters of the 8th, 11th, 15th, and 19th instant and should not be engaged in some very important move, either of your own or in consequence of my ideas respecting operation in the upper Chesapeake, you will be pleased as soon as possible to order an embarkation of the troops specified in the margin,[72] and of the ordnance and other stores, etc., etc., stated in the enclosed paper,[73] *or in as full a manner as Your Lordship can with propriety*

71. *Clinton's note:* Intelligence enclosed to George Rodney and General Vaughan: On the 19th instant (June) a frigate arrived at Newport from Boston in the evening and, after taking ten pilots on board, sailed the next morning; and it is imagined they are bound to the West Indies to pilot a fleet from thence before the hurricane months.

72. Clinton's note of the troops requested is identical in substance with the request in his letter of June 11 (above, p. 531); it is also reproduced in Stevens (*Clinton-Cornwallis Controversy*, 2, 29 n.), where "second battalion" should read "two battalions."

73. *Clinton's note of the enclosed paper:* Artillery, etc., wanted: two eight-inch howitzers (light), two five-and-a-half-inch ditto, two medium brass twelve-pounders, four brass six-pounders (fieldpieces); twelve wagons without the bodies, for transporting boats, etc.; a proportion of carcasses; vessels: the sloop *Formidable*, brigantine *Spitfire*, brigantine *Rambler*, the prize ship *Tempest* (if she can be unloaded and fitted without delaying the transports); as many horses as are necessary for the artillery and wagons; as many of the first twenty-four new boats as Lord Cornwallis can spare (those that have platforms to have cannon mounted in them and completely fitted, if it can be done without delaying the embarkation)— the cannon to be brought in the transports and the boats towed by them; Lieutenant Sutherland of the Engineers, with entrenching tools, etc., for five hundred men. [*Ibid.*, pp. 30–31.]

comply, recollecting that whatever may have been taken too great a proportion of will be immediately returned to you the moment the expedition is over. [Stevens, *Clinton-Cornwallis Controversy, 2,* 29–30.]

Extract of a letter from Lord Cornwallis to Sir Henry Clinton. Williamsburg, June 30th, 1781.

The morning after my arrival here I was honored with Your Excellency's dispatches of the 11th and 15th instant, delivered by Ensign Amiel. By them I find that you think, if an offensive army could be spared, *it would not be advisable to employ it in this province.* It is natural for every officer to turn his thoughts particularly to the part of the war in which he has been most employed. And, as the security at least of South Carolina, if not the reduction of North Carolina, seemed *to be generally expected from me both in this country and in England,* I thought myself called upon, after the experiment I had made had failed, to point out the only mode in my opinion of effecting it and to declare that, *until Virginia was to a degree subjected,* we could not reduce North Carolina or have any certain hold of the back country of South Carolina, the want of navigation rendering it impossible to maintain a sufficient army in either of these provinces at a considerable distance from the coast, and the men and riches of Virginia furnishing ample supplies to the rebel southern army. Your Excellency being charged with the weight of the whole American war, your opinions of course are less partial, and are directed to all its parts. To those opinions it is my duty implicitly to submit.

Being in the place of General Phillips, I thought myself called upon by you to give my opinion with all deference on Mr. Alexander's proposals and the attempt upon Philadelphia. Having experienced much disappointment on that head, I own I would cautiously engage in measures depending materially for their success upon active assistance from the country. And I thought the attempt upon Philadelphia would do more harm than good to the cause of Britain because, supposing it practicable to get possession of the town (which, besides other obstacles, if the redoubts are kept up would not be easy),[74] we could not hope to arrive there without their having had sufficient warning of our approach to enable them to secure specie and the greatest part of their valuable public stores by means of their boats and shipping, which give them certain possession of the river from Mud Island upward. The discriminating [between] the owners, and destroying any considerable quantity of West India goods and other merchandise dispersed through

74. *Clinton's note:* There is a back as well as a front door to Philadelphia.

a great town without burning the whole together, would be a work of much time and labor. Our appearance there without an intention to stay might give false hopes to many friends and occasion their ruin, and any unlucky accident on our retreat might furnish matter for great triumph to our enemies.

However, my opinion on that subject is at present of no great importance, as it appears from Your Excellency's dispatches that in the execution of those ideas *a cooperation was intended from your side which now could not be depended upon, from the uncertainty of the permanency of our naval superiority* and your apprehensions of an intended serious attempt upon New York. I have therefore lost no time in taking measures for complying with the requisitions contained in your dispatch of the 15th instant. Upon viewing York I was clearly of the opinion *that it far exceeds our power, consistent with your plans, to make safe defensive posts there and at Gloucester, both which would be necessary for the protection of shipping.* The state of the transports has not yet been reported to me, but I have ordered the few that are at Portsmouth to be got ready; and, as soon as I pass James River (for which purpose the boats are collecting) and can get a convoy, they shall be dispatched with as many troops as they will contain, and shall be followed by others as fast as you send transports to receive them.

When I see Portsmouth, I shall give my opinion of the number of men necessary for its defense or of any other post that may be thought more proper. But, as magazines, etc., may be destroyed by occasional expeditions from New York, and there is little chance of being able to establish a post capable of giving effectual protection to ships of war, I submit it to Your Excellency's consideration whether it is worth while to hold a sickly, defensive post in this bay, which will always be exposed to a sudden French attack and which experience has now shown makes no diversion in favor of the southern army.

By the letter enclosed you will see General Greene's intention of coming to the northward, and that part of the reinforcements destined for his army was stopped in consequence of my arrival here. As soon as it is evident that our plan is merely defensive here, there can be little doubt of his returning to the southward and of the reinforcement's proceeding to join his army. I still continue in the most painful anxiety for the situation of South Carolina. I have ordered Colonel Gould to proceed, as soon as convoy could be procured, with the Nineteenth and Thirtieth Regiments to New York, leaving the Third Regiment and flank companies in South Carolina. [*Ibid.,* pp. 33–37.]

Copy of a letter from Sir Henry Clinton to Lord Cornwallis.
New York, July 1, 1781 (received by His Lordship July 12th).

My Lord:

For reasons which I think it is unnecessary to mention to you by
this opportunity, I request that whatever troops, etc., Your Lordship
may have embarked for this place may sail forty-eight hours after the
departure from the Chesapeake of the frigate which carries this letter,
and which has orders to return whenever Your Lordship signifies to
the captain of her that the troops, etc., are all on board and ready to
proceed on the intended service.

I have the honor, etc., Henry Clinton. [*Ibid.*, p. 41.]

Copy of a letter from Sir Henry Clinton to Major General Leslie,
or officer commanding the troops embarked in the Chesapeake
for New York. July 1st, 1781.

Sir:

Whenever the troops which Lord Cornwallis shall have embarked
under your orders are ready to sail, it is the Admiral's and my wish that
the frigate which carries this should return to us, and that forty-eight
hours after she leaves the Chesapeake you will, if possible, put to sea
and proceed to the River Delaware, off which you will hover out of
sight until joined by the Admiral, when you will receive further orders.
If this meets you at sea, you will of course proceed as above mentioned
off Delaware, waiting for the Admiral.

I have the honor, etc., H. Clinton.

Extract of a letter from Sir Henry Clinton to Lord George Germain. New York, July 3d, 1781.

You will have observed, My Lord, that it has long been my wish to
seize or destroy the public stores, etc., the enemy have collected at
Philadelphia. The happy consequences which would result from such
a blow successfully given are apparent, as it would not only distress
them for the campaign, but break up their credit and entirely overset their scheme of finance on which they build their principal hopes
of paying their troops and supporting the war. Therefore, as Rear Admiral Graves concurs with me in opinion that de Grasse will probably not arrive on this coast before the first week in August and that
this is the proper moment to make the attempt, I have made every
requisite preparation, and only wait the arrival of the reinforcement

from Chesapeake and the Admiral's assembling his fleet to carry it into immediate execution.

The enemy are just now totally unprepared against this event, as General Washington has collected his whole force on the east side of Hudson's River, where he is joined by about 4000 French, who have left the remainder of their troops at Rhode Island. His Continentals for the campaign I judge to be about 8000, and his militia, which are very numerous, are held in readiness to move when wanted. Lieutenant General Robertson, to whom I have entrusted the conducting the expedition, will have the most positive instructions to guard as much as possible against any injury being done to the town in the destruction of the public stores, etc., which he will not have time, I fear, to take. He will carry with him boats on carriages for passing the Schuylkill, and he will be directed, if he cannot lay hold of Mud Island, to possess himself of certain stations to cover his retreat, particularly a bluff point commanding the Schuylkill about three miles distant from Philadelphia.

[Copy of a letter from Alexander Mercer, commanding Engineer, to Major Oliver DeLancey, Adjutant General. New York, July 3, 1781.]

Sir:

You will be pleased to inform His Excellency the Commander in Chief that we are employed at the following places, viz.:

Kings Bridge: repairing and giving additional strength to the works, and making fascines for such purposes as may be necessary. Hoorn's Hook: making fascines and collecting materials for the fort, batteries, and covering redoubt. Brooklyn: making fascines and collecting materials, etc., and leveling the upper part of the Spiral Redoubt (so that it may be commanded by the fire of the fort), and in repairing and strengthening the whole for the security of the right flank. Paulus Hook: raising and thickening the fronts of the works; repairing and giving additional strength, and preparing additional materials for, an intermediate battery of eight or ten guns. Staten Island: repairing and strengthening the works at Richmond; raising and thickening the front of the Flagstaff Redoubt and producing [i.e., prolonging] the work from the rear to the edge of the cliff, so as to gain two flanks (the rear to remain as a traverse); making fascines and collecting fraising, plank, etc.

I have the honor to be, sir, your most obedient and most humble servant, Alexander Mercer, commanding Engineer.

Extract of a letter from Sir Henry Clinton to Rear Admiral Graves. July 6, 1781.

I am more and more convinced every day of the importance of the move we talked of. And, whenever you, sir, shall think yourself in sufficient force, I shall be ready and willing to undertake my part. It will be much better that we should at least threaten a joint attack, for reasons obvious. There are three plans I should have proposed to your consideration: first, the fleet between Conanicut and Brenton's Neck, the army landing at Brenton's and proceeding against the place from thence; second, the navy either in the above station or near it, the army landing in Sakonnet Passage, covered by frigates, and proceeding to the attack of the town from thence; third (which I proposed to Admiral Arbuthnot last year, and I am apt to think the best), the whole to enter Narragansett Passage, the army to be landed on Rhode Island, army and navy threatening a joint attack [and] the army attacking—but I doubt whether the navy can, except circumstances should make it expedient.

You seemed to think that you should not have a sufficient force for this move until the return of the *Royal Oak*. That in Delaware may therefore proceed. If it succeeds, most important consequences may follow; and it will make a diversion in favor of the other. I expect *3000 men from Chesapeake;* 1000 goes with General Robertson to the Delaware. The instant I know that expedition to be drawing near a conclusion, I will prepare for the other under the mask of reinforcing the Delaware. And, when you appear off this post on your return, I will meet you; and, if circumstances at the time make it expedient, we will proceed with such troops as can be spared from this place.

Copy of a letter from Admiral Sir George Rodney to Vice Admiral Arbuthnot (received and opened by Commodore Affleck at New York on the 27th of July, Rear Admiral Graves being then at sea with his squadron). *Sandwich*, Barbados, 7 July 1781.

Sir:

As the enemy has at this time a fleet of twenty-eight sail of the line at Martinique, *a part of which is reported to be destined for North America,* I have dispatched His Majesty's sloop *Swallow* to acquaint you therewith, and to inform you *that I shall keep as good a lookout as possible on their motions, by which my own shall be regulated.*

In case of my sending a squadron to America, I shall order it to make the Capes of Virginia and proceed along the coast to the Capes of the Delaware and from thence to Sandy Hook, unless the intelli-

gence it may receive from you should induce it to act otherwise. You
will be pleased to order cruisers to look out off the first mentioned
capes, giving them orders to hoist . . . [signals for recognition].

*The enemy's squadron destined for America will sail, I am informed,
in a short time;* but whether they call off at Cape François I cannot learn.
*However, you may depend upon the squadron in America being re-
inforced should the enemy bend their force that way.*[75]

I have the honor to be with great regard, sir, your most obedient,
humble servant, Geo. Brydges Rodney.

To the Commander in Chief of His Majesty's ships, etc., in North
America. [(W. Graves,) *Two letters from W. Graves, Esq.,* p. 10.]

Extract of a letter from Lord George Germain to Sir Henry Clinton. Whitehall, July 7, 1781 [received September 10].

The three regiments and the thousand British recruits from Ireland
were, I trust, arrived at Charleston before your dispatches left New York;
and it would not be long before the twenty-eight hundred Germans were
with you. The arrival of these reinforcements will, I hope, *enable you to
proceed immediately in the execution of your purpose* without waiting
for the three regiments from the West Indies. For I do not expect they
will join you before the season for offensive operations there is over—
when I have reason to believe *the French fleet will push for North
America* and *Sir George Rodney will certainly follow them, to prevent
them from giving you any interruption in your operations.* And, to enable him the better to effect it, Admiral Digby will carry out with
him a reinforcement of three ships of the line to the American squadron. [Stevens, *Clinton-Cornwallis Controversy,* 2, 42–43.]

[Extract of a second letter from Germain to Clinton. July 7, 1781.]

The uneasiness you expressed on a certain occasion must have ceased
long before this reaches you—and, *I trust, in full time to prevent your
resigning the command to Earl Cornwallis.* [*Ibid.,* pp. 46–47.]

75. *Clinton's note:* If they were not reinforced in proportion, there was little
meaning in the assurance given. Sir George Rodney told me since, on publication
[i.e., of W. Graves' pamphlet?], that about the 27th July, convinced that de Grasse
would move with his whole fleet, he dispatched two ships of the line to join Sir
Samuel Hood, and ordered them to call at Jamaica with an *order* to Sir Peter Parker
to detach for the same service *all* his ships of the line except the *Sandwich.* Had
these orders been obeyed, the action of the 5th of September must have been decisive. Nay, had Sir George Rodney (who was with four capital ships within sixty
leagues of the capes three days before the action) joined, it must have been equally
so. But!

Extract of a letter from Earl Cornwallis to Sir Henry Clinton.
Cobham, July 8th, 1781 (received 14 July).

I must again take the liberty of calling Your Excellency's serious attention to the question of the utility of a defensive post in this country, which cannot have the smallest influence on the war in Carolina, and which only gives us some acres of an unhealthy swamp and is forever liable to become the prey of a foreign enemy with a temporary superiority at sea.

About noon on the 6th information was brought me of the approach of the enemy, and about four in the afternoon a large body attacked our outposts. Concluding that the enemy would not bring a considerable force within our reach unless they supposed that nothing was left but a rear guard, I took every means to convince them of my weakness, and suffered my pickets to be insulted and driven back. Nothing, however, appeared near us but riflemen and militia till near sunset, when a body of Continentals, with artillery, began to form in the front of our camp. I then put the troops under arms, and ordered the army to advance in two lines.

The attack was begun by the first line with great spirit. There being nothing but militia opposed to the light infantry, the action was soon over on the right. But, Lieutenant Colonel Dundas' Brigade (consisting of the Forty-third, Seventy-sixth, and Eightieth Regiments), which formed the left wing, meeting the Pennsylvania line and a detachment of the Marquis de Lafayette's Continentals with two six-pounders, a smart action ensued for some minutes, when the enemy gave way and abandoned their cannon. The cavalry were perfectly ready to pursue, but the darkness of the evening prevented my being able to make use of them.

We finished our passage yesterday, which has been an operation of great labor and difficulty, as the river is three miles wide at this place.[76]
[*Ibid.*, pp. 57–59.]

Extract of a letter from Sir Henry Clinton to Lord Cornwallis.
July 8th, 1781 (received July 21).

Being strongly impressed with the necessity of our holding a naval station for large ships as well as small, and judging that Yorktown was of importance for securing such a one, I cannot but be concerned that Your Lordship should so suddenly lose sight of it, pass James River, and

76. *Clinton's note on British losses:* Lost in this action eleven killed, sixty-six wounded, one missing; two horses killed and five wounded.

retire with your army to the sickly post of Portsmouth, where your horses will, I fear, be starved, and a hundred other inconveniences will attend you. And this, My Lord, you are pleased to say [was] because you were of opinion that it exceeded your power, consistent with my plans, to make safe defensive posts there and at Gloucester. My plans, My Lord, were to draw from the Chesapeake (as well for the sake of their health as for a necessary defensive in this important post) such troops as Your Lordship could spare from a respectable defensive of York, Gloucester, or such other station as was proper to cover line-of-battle ships, and from all other services I recommended. But I could not possibly mean that Your Lordship should for this give up the hold of a station so important for the purpose I designed, and which I think Lafayette will immediately seize and fortify the moment he hears you have repassed James River. For though I am to suppose the enemy will be as little able to defend it with 5000 men as Your Lordship judged yourself to be, and may for the same reasons of course be dispossessed, I should be sorry to begin with a siege the operations I am determined to carry on in Chesapeake whenever the season will admit of them.

With regard to Portsmouth, Your Lordship will have seen by my former letters and the papers in your possession that, when I sent General Leslie to the Chesapeake, I only wished for a station to cover our cruising frigates and other small ships. That general officer thought proper to make choice of Portsmouth. But it has ever been my opinion that, if a better could be found, especially for covering line-of-battle ships, it ought to have the preference; and *I think, if Old Point Comfort will secure Hampton Roads, that is the station we ought to choose.* [*Ibid.*, pp. 51–53.]

[Extract of Graves to Clinton. July 9, 1781.]

The squadron will not be in sufficient force until the arrival of the *Royal Oak.* [For] the squadron to anchor before the Great or Rhode Island Passage, without Brenton's Reef, I think very practicable, from whence they may be put in motion to threaten a joint attack or even to push forward and improve any unexpected advantage. The frigates can cover at the same time a descent in the Sakonnet Passage, which answers the second scheme. The position of the squadron which will best countenance a joint attack is most assuredly by placing it off the grand or middle entrance, from whence a descent may be covered by frigates in the Sakonnet or eastern Passage, and the squadron may countenance any effort at another place. I can meet Your Excellency any day at the Hook, only by your letting me know the day before at what time you will be there and allowing for tide, which all sailors must be governed by.

Extract of a letter from Sir Henry Clinton to Earl Cornwallis.
New York, July 11th, 1781.

I am just returned from having a conference with Rear Admiral Graves in consequence of Your Lordship's letter of the 30th *ultimo,* and we are both clearly of opinion that it is absolutely necessary we should hold a station in Chesapeake for ships of the line as well as frigates. And the Admiral seems to think that, should the enemy possess themselves of Old Point Comfort, Elizabeth River could no longer be of any use to us as a station for the frigates. He therefore judges that Hampton Road is the fittest station for all ships, *in which Your Lordship will see by the papers in your possession I likewise agree with him.* It was, moreover, my opinion that the possession of Yorktown, even though we did not possess Gloucester, might give security to the works we might have at Old Point Comfort, which I understand secures Hampton Road. I therefore beg leave to request *that you will without loss of time examine Old Point Comfort and fortify it,* determining such troops as you may think necessary for that purpose and garrisoning it afterward. But, if it should be Your Lordship's opinion that Old Point Comfort cannot be held without having possession of York (for in this case Gloucester may perhaps be not so material) and that the whole cannot be done with less than 7000 men, you are at full liberty to detain all the troops now in Chesapeake, which I believe amount to somewhat more than that number.

Until the season for recommencing operation in the Chesapeake shall return, Your Lordship—or whoever remains in the command there—must, I fear, be content with a strict defensive. And I must therefore desire that you will be pleased *to consider this as a positive requisition to you* not to detain a greater proportion of the troops now with you than what may be absolutely wanted for defensive operations, etc. When, therefore, Your Lordship has finally determined upon the force you think sufficient for such works *as you shall erect at Old Point Comfort,* and the number you judge requisite to cover them at Yorktown and for the other services of the Chesapeake during the unhealthy season, you will be pleased to send me the remainder. Your Lordship will observe by this that I do not see any great necessity for holding Portsmouth while you have Old Point Comfort. For, should a station on Elizabeth River be judged necessary, I think Mill Point will answer every necessary purpose for covering frigates, etc. [Stevens, *Clinton-Cornwallis Controversy*, 2, 62–65.]

[Extract of a second letter from Clinton to Cornwallis. July 11, 1781.]

It is the Admiral's and my wish at all events to hold Old Point Comfort, which secures Hampton Roads. [Ibid., p. 61.]

Extract of a letter from Sir Henry Clinton to Lord George Germain. New York, 13 July 1781.

I only waited for the arrival of a reinforcement which I expected from the Chesapeake to send off the expedition I had prepared against a considerable depot of stores, etc., which the enemy had collected at Philadelphia for the support of the campaign, [an expedition] which I had formed on a supposition that Lord Cornwallis could have spared me at least two or three thousand men from the seven thousand effectives he had in Virginia. But, at the instant when everything was prepared for its moving and I expected the arrival of the troops I called for, I received a letter from His Lordship, dated the 30th *ultimo,* by the enclosed extract from which Your Lordship will perceive that he does not think he will be able to maintain the healthy and important station I had recommended to him if he complies with any part of my requisition—the utmost extent of which did not exceed 3000 men, and of that number I only called for such a part as His Lordship might think he could spare from the ample and respectable defensive of a post in which Brigadier General Arnold's information gave me every reason to suppose 2000 might bid defiance to every effort which could be made against it.

And it further appears from His Lordship's letter that he proposes quitting the Neck of Williamsburg altogether, and retiring with his army to Portsmouth—a measure which I, however, still flatter myself His Lordship may possibly wait to receive my opinion about before he carries it entirely into execution, especially if he should give my requisition another consideration. Therefore, upon finding that not only this was likely to be the consequence of my withdrawing any part of His Lordship's force, but that even the possession of the Chesapeake became a question with him, I immediately gave up all ideas of offensive operation.

I cannot better explain to Your Lordship the reasons I had for undertaking this important service, and the mortification I feel from my not being able to carry it into execution, than by referring you to my correspondence with Lord Cornwallis. By these [enclosed extracts from it] I am persuaded it will appear that, although I certainly wished that Lord Cornwallis should remain upon the defensive in the Chesapeake during the summer months and that he should, in that case, send me for operation here such a portion of his force as he could spare from the amplest and most respectable defensive, I left the posts he was to occupy, as well as the number he was to keep, totally to His Lordship's judgment—only, with respect to the first, recommending to his attention my correspondence with General Phillips, wherein I had suggested the propriety of possessing the heights of York and Gloucester as a proper station to secure a harbor for our line-of-battle ships, [a harbor] which the enemy would probably lay hold of if we did not.

I cannot, therefore, be less surprised than concerned to find that His Lordship, in consequence of my requisition to him for a reinforcement (which he was left at liberty to comply with or not as he might see expedient), has thought proper to retire from a district of so much importance. Nor can I, My Lord, comprehend why, because His Lordship cannot act offensively during the severity of the present season, he should advise the totally giving up the Chesapeake, whereby we should probably have our future operations there to begin with a siege, in case the enemy should take the advantage of our absence and fortify.

As, upon perusing the enclosed correspondence, Your Lordship will perceive that Lord Cornwallis and I differ in opinion with regard to the operations proper to be pursued in the Chesapeake when the season shall make them practicable, it may not be improper in this place to say a few words in explanation of my reasons for not acceding to His Lordship's sentiments, as stated in his letter of the 10th of April, *"that until Virginia is in a manner subdued our hold of the Carolinas must be difficult, if not precarious."* Although I never had a doubt of the important advantages we might derive from the possession of Virginia, I am humbly of opinion that the assistance of friends is absolutely necessary to attain it. For conquest alone will be of little moment unless we can retain what we conquer, which I think cannot be done in so large and populous a province as Virginia unless the inhabitants themselves are disposed to join us—which we cannot hope for there, as they are, I believe, almost universally hostile. I therefore judged it best to content ourselves *at first* with laying hold of a respectable naval station in that province, from whence we might command the entrance and the waters of the Chesapeake, and there carry our arms to the head of that bay, where, I am told, we have many friends, and by whose assistance and proper posts we might endeavor effectually to prevent all supplies of men and military stores being sent from the northward not only to Virginia but the Carolinas—which would certainly, together with the blocking up their trade, greatly facilitate the reduction of those provinces.

Which of these two modes of recovering the Carolinas are most likely to succeed I cannot determine. But the trial of either must now be deferred until the season will admit of operation to the southward. And I can only say that, had Lord Cornwallis been able to have sent me in the meantime any part of the troops I solicited, I should have endeavored to employ them in such offensive operations as the state of the enemy's force would have permitted me, by attempting the destruction of their stores, etc., at Philadelphia, and afterward by taking advantage of any false movements they might be induced to make in consequence of my apparent weakness.

[Extract of Germain to Clinton. July 14, 1781.]

It is with the most unfeigned pleasure I obey His Majesty's commands in expressing to you *his royal approbation of the plan you have adopted* for prosecuting the war in the provinces south of the Delaware, *and of the succors you have furnished and the instructions you have given for carrying it into execution.* The purpose of the enemy was long known here, and Sir George Rodney has been apprised of it and will *certainly* not lose sight of Monsieur de Grasse. I cannot close this letter without repeating to you the very great satisfaction your dispatch has given me, and my most entire and hearty coincidence with you in the plan you have proposed to Lord Cornwallis for distressing the rebels and recovering the southern provinces to the King's obedience. And, as His Lordship (*when he receives your letters of the 8th and 11th of June*) will have fully seen the reasonableness of it, I have not the least doubt but His Lordship has executed it with his wonted ardor, intrepidity, and success. [Stevens, *Clinton-Cornwallis Controversy, 2, 69–72.*]

Extract of a letter from Sir Henry Clinton to Earl Cornwallis. New York, July 15, 1781.

Until I had the honor to receive Your Lordship's letter of the 8th instant I had flattered myself that, upon reconsidering the general purport of our correspondence and General Phillips' papers in your possession, you would at least have waited for a line from me in answer to your letter of the 30th *ultimo* before you finally determined upon so serious and mortifying a move as the repassing James River and retiring with your army to Portsmouth. And I was the more induced to hope that this would have been the case as we both seemed to agree in our opinions of the propriety of taking a healthy station on the neck between York and James Rivers for the purpose of covering a proper harbor for our line-of-battle ships.

As Your Lordship is again pleased to call my serious attention to the question of the utility of a defensive post in Virginia, etc., I must in answer beg leave again to repeat to Your Lordship that it never was my intention to continue a post on Elizabeth River any longer than until the commencement of solid operation in Chesapeake, nor to have there more troops than what might be capable of defending a small work on that river; and that all the general officers who have commanded in the Chesapeake have had my consent to change Portsmouth for a more healthy station if they judged it proper to do so. [*Ibid.*, pp. 73–75.]

Extract of a letter from Sir Henry Clinton to Lord George Germain. New York, July 18, 1781.

As I am conscious that ever since I have had the charge of this arduous and important command I have never relaxed in the most zealous exertions to employ the troops entrusted to me to the best advantage for His Majesty's interests, I cannot but be affected with some observations and expressions contained in Your Lordship's letter marked No. 81,[77] and secret one of the 2d of May, *which seem to insinuate that there was a possibility of my doing more than I have done.* The extracts from my correspondence with Earl Cornwallis which I have had the honor to transmit from time to time to Your Lordship will show that I left in Carolina a very fair proportion of my army, *and such as His Lordship thought sufficient to secure South and recover North Carolina.* With what was left for me to act with in this quarter I took the field immediately upon my arrival here. And, if my intentions against the French armament at Rhode Island were not carried into execution, Your Lordship will, I am persuaded, do me the justice to impute it to the proper cause, of which you have been already fully informed by my letters to Your Lordship and my correspondence with Vice Admiral Arbuthnot on that subject. General Leslie's expedition to the Chesapeake took place soon after; and some unfortunate events in Carolina, calling for still further reinforcement and cooperation, soon reduced this part of my army to a defensive almost as low in number as that Sir William Howe left me in 1777.

77. Germain to Clinton, Mar. 7, 1781, Stevens, *Clinton-Cornwallis Controversy,* 1, 334–336.

It gave me, therefore, My Lord, the most mortifying concern to be told by Your Lordship that the rebel force was now so very contemptible in all parts, and our superiority so vast everywhere that no resistance was to be apprehended to obstruct the suppression of the rebellion, and that it was "a pleasing, though at the same time a mortifying, reflection (when the duration of the rebellion is considered) that the American levies in the King's service are more in number than the whole of the enlisted troops in the service of Congress." [78] By the return of the provincial forces which I had the honor to send Your Lordship their effective strength amounted to 8168, of which only 4300 were fit for duty, and not two-thirds of those were acting against the rebel force. That of Mr. Washington in the service of Congress, taking him in his most reduced state since I have had the honor to command this army (I mean after the revolt of the Pennsylvania line, for that of the Jersey one was of very short duration), amounted to at least 9400 effectives. Lord Cornwallis, moreover, tells Your Lordship that he had 7000 men opposed to him at the Battle of Camden and 10,000 at that of Guilford, at which period also there were above 4000 before Brigadier General Arnold's lines in Virginia. To these I may with great propriety add the militia of the states in the neighborhood of this post, which may, when wanted, be assembled in a very few days to the amount of from 4000 to 8000, and which we have found to be nearly as well appointed and as formidable as the best of their Continentals.

Allowing, therefore, this estimate to be just, instead of the superiority you suppose on our side you will find a very great inferiority even at the period I stated, and which I may venture to assert has since increased above six thousand men and, as they now take even three-months men, will continue to do so every hour while they have a prospect of French reinforcements and the attack of New York is held up to them as an event certainly to take place. And, if Your Lordship will be pleased likewise to cast your eye on the effective number of my regulars, the post I have to defend, and the extensive country I have to reduce, together with the different armies of Washington, Lafayette, and Greene, supported by the cooperation of a French fleet and at least 6000 French troops (all which are at this moment acting against the different stations of my army), I flatter myself you will find that, so far from the rebel force being so very contemptible in all parts and our superiority so vast everywhere, that I have no small claim to applause for obliging the enemy to act with the utmost caution and regard me with a very jealous eye in this quarter, notwithstanding the

78. *Ibid.*, p. 334.

smallness of my force in consequence of the very liberal detachments I have sent to Carolina and the Chesapeake.

But, if our successes in the southern provinces have not answered Your Lordship's expectations, it cannot, I am certain, be imputed to either the smallness of the number I left there or the tardiness or scantiness with which I have since supplied the exigencies of that service. Though I am strongly impressed with the importance of recovering Virginia, I fear the entire reduction of so populous a province is not to be expected from an operation solely there, unless our friends in it were more numerous and were heartily inclined to assist us not only in conquering but keeping it. *It was therefore my intention at a proper season, after securing a safe harbor in Virginia for the King's ships, to lay hold of Baltimore or the Head of Elk, and with the assistance of the loyalists (who I am informed are very numerous in that district) secure proper posts for the intercepting the passage of supplies from Pennsylvania and the northern states to Virginia and the Carolinas.*

I can say little more to Your Lordship's sanguine hopes of the speedy reduction of the southern provinces than to lament that the present state of the war there does not altogether promise so flattering an event. Many untoward incidents, of which Your Lordship was not apprised, have thrown us too far back to be able to recover very soon even what we have lately lost there. For, if as I have often before suggested *the good will of the inhabitants is absolutely requisite to retain a country after we have conquered it,* I fear it will be some time before we can recover the confidence of those in Carolina, as their past sufferings will of course make them cautious of forwarding the King's interests before there is the strongest certainty of his army being in a condition to support them.

I shall therefore most cordially join with Your Lordship in condemning the bad policy of taking possession of places at one time and abandoning them at another, and in the opinion that the war should be conducted upon a permanent and settled plan of conquest by securing and preserving what has been recovered. But, if these maxims have been on any occasion deviated from in the past progress of the war, I must in justice to myself declare that it has never been warranted by my orders, except in the case of Rhode Island. And, if Lord Cornwallis made a desultory move into North Carolina and—*without a force sufficient to protect or provisions to support them—invited by proclamation the loyalists to join him, and afterward found it necessary to quit the friendly districts of that province before he could have time to give them a fair trial,* I am persuaded Your Lordship will acknowledge he did not act under my instructions. Nor were His Lordship's retreat to Wilmington and subsequent move from thence to Virginia in consequence of my orders. For, as I foresaw all the unhappy consequences of them, I should certainly have endeavored to have stopped him could I have known his intentions in proper time. But, though His Lordship's movements (which, it must be confessed, have been as rapid as your Lordship expected) have not, to my sincere concern, been successfully decisive, I am convinced he is—as I hope we all are—impressed with the absolute necessity of vigorous exertions in the service of his country at the present crisis. And, if mine have not been equal to my inclinations, I have little doubt they will be found to be at least equal to my powers.

I shall now, My Lord, beg leave to conclude with the strongest assurances that no man can be more fervently desirous than I am to see an honorable end put to this most burdensome war; and, if I should remain in the command, that no endeavors of mine shall be wanting to execute in the fullest manner the King's pleasure and commands. Of the 10,000 men I solicited only 4000 men were even promised me; and no portion of these, except a few recruits, has yet joined this part of the army. Your Lordship's last letters give me hopes that three British battalions and twenty-six hundred German troops may be immediately expected. If all these arrive, I shall then be able at a proper season to reinforce the Chesapeake corps very considerably. And, if a reinforcement does not likewise come to the French armament already here, such operations may be carried on as may perhaps produce some advantages in the course of the winter. But, if our reinforcement does not come and the French should receive theirs, I think we shall have everything to apprehend. [*Ibid.*, pp. 82–87.]

> Extract of a letter from Lieutenant Colonel Balfour to Sir Henry Clinton. Charleston, 20 July 1781.

No sooner were the necessary arrangements made than Lord Rawdon proceeded with a corps of about 2000 men to the relief of Ninety-six. On his near approach to which post General Greene took the resolution, rather than risk an action with Lord Rawdon, of storming the garrison —in which, however, he was repulsed by the exertions of Lieutenant Colonel Cruger and the very spirited conduct of the troops under him, with the loss, as acknowledged, of at least seventy-five killed and one hundred and fifty wounded (ours being truly inconsiderable both on this occasion and during the siege, which was closely pressed by the enemy). This event, so fortunate in itself and creditable to Colonel

Cruger and his small garrison, took place the 19th *ultimo.* On the succeeding day the enemy's army retired over the Saluda, and on the 21st Lord Rawdon arrived at Ninety-six.

From hence His Lordship proceeded to the Congaree's. For this place General Greene likewise pushed and afterward passed the river with the view of striking at Lord Rawdon (then at Orangeburg) or cutting off the Third Regiment, which was proceeding to join him. But, His Lordship's vigilance and skill frustrating these intentions, on his being reinforced by the corps under Lieutenant Colonel Stewart (who accomplished his junction by a march of twenty-seven miles in one day) and the troops under Lieutenant Colonel Cruger, General Greene found it necessary to fall back with the greater part of his infantry over the Santee. He, however, detached the chief of his cavalry and some mounted infantry against the post at Monk's Corner, where the Nineteenth Regiment and the mounted men of the South Carolina Rangers were stationed. Before this place the enemy appeared in force on the 14th instant; and the next day a party of them came within four miles of this town, having taken near Dorchester several horses in the Quartermaster General's employment and, at the Quarter House, some dragoon ones belonging to the South Carolina Rangers, with a few invalids of that regiment who were left in charge of them and unable to make their escape.

Lieutenant Colonel Coates, finding himself nearly surrounded by the enemy and that their numbers were greatly superior to his, on the 16th instant destroyed the post and stores at Monk's Corner and retreated on the east side of the Cooper toward this. But in his march, being closely pressed by the enemy's cavalry, which were numerous, [he] was obliged to relinquish his baggage and sick, which fell into their hands. On receiving this intelligence Colonel Gould, with about 700 men, marched from hence to sustain the Nineteenth Regiment; and on his approach the enemy retired. But, as Lord Rawdon is come down with a small part of his corps (Colonel Stewart being left in command of the rest) to Goose Creek, I am in some hopes he may be able to intercept any parties of them that may attempt to get off that way. At present it is impossible to ascertain our loss on this occasion, though I fear it will prove rather considerable.

These events, the great force of the enemy (especially of cavalry, in which we are vastly deficient), and the general revolt of the province will, I conceive, even with the present force much circumscribe any future positions we may take. When a freer communication with Lord Rawdon is opened, I shall do myself the honor to inform His Lordship of

Your Excellency's desire to receive from himself an account of the late action near Camden [Hobkirk's Hill].

Copy of a letter from Sir Henry Clinton to Major General Leslie, or [the] officer commanding the expedition from the Chesapeake at sea. New York, July 23, 1781.

Sir:

Should the *Solebay*, frigate, have arrived in the Chesapeake before you sailed from thence, and Lord Cornwallis have received from Captain Stapleton my letter of the 11th instant sent by that opportunity, *and should His Lordship notwithstanding have thought proper to direct you to proceed according to your original destination*, you will be pleased in that case to come with the troops under your command to Sandy Hook and, coming to an anchor within the Hook, there wait my further orders. But, if the *Solebay* had not arrived in Chesapeake and Lord Cornwallis had not received the letter I sent by her before your departure, you will be pleased upon the receipt of this immediately to return to Portsmouth and follow such further directions as you may receive from His Lordship. As corresponding directions with these will be sent to Captain Hudson or the officer commanding the King's ships that compose your convoy by Commodore Affleck, who commands His Majesty's ships at New York in the absence of Rear Admiral Graves, you will of course receive every assistance you want from him in carrying these orders into execution.

I have the honor, etc., Henry Clinton.

Extract of a letter from Earl Cornwallis to Sir Henry Clinton. Portsmouth, Virginia, 27 July 1781 (received August 1st).

You mention Williamsburg and York in your letter of the 11th as defensive stations, but only as being supposed healthy, without deciding on their safety. Williamsburg, having no harbor and requiring an army to occupy the position, would not have suited us. I saw that it would require a great deal *of time and labor to fortify York and Gloucester*, both of which are necessary to secure a harbor for vessels of any burden. And, *supposing both places fortified, I thought they would have been dangerous defensive posts*, either of them being easily accessible to the whole force of this province; and from their situation they would not have commanded an acre of country.

Immediately on the receipt of your ciphered letter [79] I gave orders to the engineer to examine and survey Point Comfort and the chan-

79. Of July 11, 1781; Stevens, *Clinton-Cornwallis Controversy*, 2, 61.

nels adjoining to it. I have likewise visited it with the Captains of the King's ships now lying in Hampton Roads. From their reports, and the survey enclosed, Your Excellency will see that a work on Point Comfort would neither command the entrance nor secure His Majesty's ships at anchor in Hampton Roads. This being the case, I shall, in obedience to the spirit of Your Excellency's orders, take measures with as much dispatch as possible *to seize and fortify York and Gloucester,* being the *only* harbor in which we can hope *to be able to give effectual protection to line-of-battle ships.* [Stevens, *Clinton-Cornwallis Controversy, 2,* 106–108.]

Extract of a letter from Sir Henry Clinton to Earl Cornwallis. New York, August 2d, 1781.

I was last night honored with Your Lordship's letters of the 24th and 27th *ultimo* by Captain Stapleton, and it gives me no small concern to observe by the tenor of them that you are displeased with the opinions I took the liberty of giving in my letter of the 29th of May, respecting the probable consequences of your retreat from Cross Creek to Wilmington, and march from thence to Petersburg. The high opinion I entertained of Your Lordship's military talents, and the respect I had for your situation as second to myself, induced me from the moment you took charge of a separate command to leave you at full liberty to act in it as you judged best for the King's service. And I am persuaded Your Lordship is not insensible that I constantly pursued this line of conduct toward you during all your operations in the Carolinas, aiming at no other merit *than that of diligently attending to your wants and supplying them, whilst I was content to remain here myself upon the very confined defensive to which I was reduced by the large detachments I had sent to the southward in support of your progress.*

Although Your Lordship was, as you have observed, subjected by this means to a certain degree of anxiety and responsibility, it does not appear that I was exonerated of my share of them. I could not, therefore, but be personally and anxiously interested in Your Lordship's successes and disappointments. And, though I have a respect for Your Lordship's judgment and am apt to doubt my own when it differs from it, yet it is certainly a duty I owe to my station as commander in chief to express my dissent from any measure Your Lordship adopts when I apprehend that the consequences may be prejudicial. This being the case, My Lord, with respect to the move taken notice of in my letter of the 29th May (and I most sincerely wish experience had convinced me I was mistaken), I immediately communicated to Your Lordship my sentiments of the event, and how I thought it might have been obviated.

In these it seems I am not so fortunate to have your concurrence. But, I must confess, they are not in the least altered by Your Lordship's arguments, [I] being still of opinion that, under the circumstances in which you describe your troops to be, you could have fallen back from Cross Creek to the Pedee with much greater ease and safety than you could have marched double the distance to Wilmington, through a country which you report to be entirely hostile. And I should suppose Lord Rawdon might have moved to the Pedee without interruption, to join you with every refreshment your army wanted, as there does not appear to have been at that time an enemy between that river and Camden; and, before you reached the Pedee, the country would probably have been so opened that your orders for that purpose might have got to His Lordship with as much expedition and safety as your note did from Guilford after the battle. And with respect to Your Lordship's subsequent move I hope you will pardon me if I continue to dissent from the policy of the measure (though you happily surmounted the danger of it), as I fear *the advantages resulting from your junction with the Chesapeake army will not compensate the losses which immediately followed your quitting Carolina.*

To give a full and satisfactory answer to Your Lordship's letter of the 27th of July will perhaps take up more time than you or I can well spare. But, as Your Lordship appears to be greatly affected by the contents of my letters of the 8th and 11th *ultimo,* I think it a duty I owe to your feelings and my own to say something in explanation of them. I must therefore beg Your Lordship's patience while I state the substance of my correspondence with General Phillips and yourself concerning the stations to be held and operations to be carried on in Chesapeake, etc., which I presume will at least prove that I spared no pains to explain my desires to Your Lordship, though I have perhaps unhappily failed in making them understood.

My instructions to General Phillips, as quoted by Your Lordship, gave him a power to take possession of Yorktown or Old Point Comfort as a station for large ships, if the Admiral should disapprove of Portsmouth and require one. In my letters to that general officer of the 24th of March and 11th of April I desired his opinion respecting the post of Portsmouth and such others as he proposed to establish on James River, with their importance considered either as assisting Your Lordship's operations or connected with those of the navy. And, after having received that opinion, I told him that Portsmouth was by no means my choice, and left him at liberty to change it if he saw proper. And the substance of the conversations with him, as extracted by Your Lordship, go more fully into the advantage of a naval station, pointing particularly to the one at York, being led to the consideration of its utility by the French having two winters ago sheltered their ships under works thrown up there.

From hence, My Lord, I presume it will appear that I very early entertained thoughts of a station in Chesapeake for large ships. And in my letter of the 29th of May I referred Your Lordship to my correspondence, etc., with General Phillips for my ideas on that and other operations which I had in view, leaving you, however, at liberty to follow them or your own as you judged best for the King's service. Having therefore seen afterward, by Your Lordship's dispatch of the 26th of May, that you had considered the papers referred to and that, though you did not think it expedient to attend to Mr. Alexander's proposal and the expedition against the stores at Philadelphia, you had the same objections to Portsmouth as General Phillips, and was inclined to think well of York as a proper harbor and place of arms, I naturally concluded that Your Lordship had entirely concurred with me, not only as to the propriety of laying hold of a naval station somewhere on the Williamsburg Neck, but as to the place. And of course I supposed that Your Lordship would set about establishing yourself there immediately on your return from Richmond, which I expected would be in three or four days after the date of your letter.

Wherefore, imagining you were considerably advanced in your works (for I had no letter afterward from Your Lordship until the one you honored with me of the 30th June), I ventured to solicit you for a part of your force to assist me in the operations I proposed carrying on in this quarter during the summer months, when those in the Chesapeake must have probably ceased. And in doing this, as I was totally in the dark with respect to what was then doing in the Chesapeake, I endeavored as much as lay in my power to avoid all possibility of interrupting the moves you might be engaged in or any object you might have in view—as will, I doubt not, be manifest from my letters to Your Lordship on that subject. These letters, My Lord, are each a link of the same chain and, collectively or separately, were intended to speak the same language, the simple and obvious meaning of which I humbly presume to be this: "I find Your Lordship does not think it expedient to undertake the operations *I* proposed, and you have none of your *own* in contemplation; and, it being probable you have made your arrangements for changing the post of Portsmouth (which you dislike) and have finished your defensive on the Williamsburg Neck (which we both approve of), I request that, of the 7000 men which—as far as I can judge without having lately received any returns—you have, you will reserve as many as you want for the most ample defensive and desultory water expeditions and then send me the rest, according to the enclosed list, in succession as you can spare them."

It is true indeed that several of these letters were not received by Your Lordship until some time after you received those of the 11th and 15th of June, owing to the unexpected[ly] tedious voyage of the *Charon* that carried them. But, if Your Lordship will be pleased to recur to those you did receive, I am persuaded you will find that the letter of the 11th refers you to those of the 29th of May and 8th of June, which it is expressly implied Your Lordship was to read before you executed the order contained in that of the 15th. And your not having *received them* would, I should suppose, have fully warranted at least *the suspension of your resolution to repass James River until you had stated to me your situation and heard again from me.*

After this very candid and ample explanation, My Lord, I have only to assure you that it was not my intention to pass the slightest censure on Your Lordship's conduct, much less an unmerited or severe one. We are both amenable to the censure of a much higher tribunal, should either of us unhappily commit errors that deserve it. Nor had I the smallest right to doubt Your Lordship's readiness to comply with my desires if you had understood them. I had, therefore, only to lament that Your Lordship had mistaken my intentions, and to endeavor to obviate the inconvenience as speedily as possible. And this perhaps was done in more positive language than I had been accustomed to use to Your Lordship. But I had no other object in view than to make myself clearly understood. [*Ibid.*, pp. 109–111, 113–115, 118–119.]

[Extract of Cornwallis to Clinton. Yorktown, Virginia, August 12, 1781.]

The works on the Gloucester side are in some forwardness and, *I hope, in a situation to resist a sudden attack.* Brigadier General O'Hara is hastening as much as possible the evacuation of Portsmouth. As soon as he arrives here, I will send to New York every man that I can spare consistent with the safety and subsistence of the force in this country. [*Ibid.*, p. 125.]

Abstract from Lord Cornwallis' return, dated 15 August 1781.

Present fit for duty, 4847 rank and file; within the district, 543; artillerymen, etc., 568; total fit for duty, 5958. Sick, 1222; wounded, 323; [total,] 1545. Total effectives, 7503—[Clinton's addition:] besides marines of the ships of war and sailors and armed refugees, not less than 1500. [Grand total,] 9003.

[Extract of Cornwallis to Clinton. Yorktown, Virginia, August 16, 1781.]

The evacuation of Portsmouth, with every exertion by land and water, I do not expect to be completed before the 21st or 22d instant. Since our arrival we have bestowed our whole labor on the Gloucester side. But I do not think the works there, after great fatigue to the troops, *are at present—or will be for some time to come—safe against a* coup de main *with less than 1000 men.* After our experience of the labor and difficulty of constructing works at this season of the year, and *the plan for fortifying this side not being entirely settled,* I cannot at present say whether I can spare any troops or, if any, how soon. But, when the garrison of Portsmouth arrives and *the engineer's plan is completed,* I shall apply to Captain Hudson for a frigate *to carry my report of the state of things here,* and to bring Your Excellency's commands upon it. [Stevens, *Clinton-Cornwallis Controversy, 2,* 127–128.]

Extract of a letter from Majors Bruen and Robertson, deputy Quartermaster Generals, to Lieutenant General Robertson, president of a board of general officers and magistrates constituted by Sir Henry Clinton for the investigation and examination of the expenditures of the public money by the different departments of the army under his command. New York, 17 August 1781.

With respect to the mode pursued for the supply of the wagons and horses contracted for the use of the army, we understand that Lieutenant Colonel Sheriff, who was the principal in the department in 1775 and the greatest part of '76, was ordered by the then Commander in Chief, Sir William Howe, to supply those articles for the army as circumstances required *by hiring them at a daily hire according to the usual prices of the country they were had in.* Sir William Erskine was appointed quartermaster general in September, 1776, but did not enter into this part of the business of his department till the 1st of January, 1777, when, having received the Commander in Chief's instructions to pursue the same mode as was customary (by hiring what horses and wagons, etc., he should find necessary for the transportation of the army's provisions, stores, baggage, artillery, ammunition, etc., which he was to procure from the country at a daily hire as Lieutenant Colonel Sheriff, his predecessor, had done), Sir William Erskine did employ a number accordingly, [with] which, [and] with a few horses and wagons of a provision train sent from England under the inspection of Mr. Francis R. Clarke, he endeavored to carry on the business of the army.

But, when it was in contemplation to make a forward move in March following, the train as it then stood was found insufficient, by reason of the country people not choosing to follow the army and their unwillingness to serve government. The wagons sent from England were found to be totally unfit for this country, being too heavy and made of bad materials. The horses were reduced—what with those taken by the enemy, and those lost by disorders contracted during their passage from England, which they never recovered of—to a small number. These circumstances obliged Sir William Erskine to lay their state before the Commander in Chief, proposing at the same time a plan for the better establishing a train that would be equal to the exigencies of the service *by purchasing wagons and horses on government account,* which His Excellency did not think proper to agree to by reason of the recent example given of those under Mr. Clarke—which cost government upward of £100,000 sterling, without performing hardly a day's duty. He said that mode would lead to expenses which could never be ascertained.

His Excellency was therefore pleased to order Sir William Erskine to take that branch under the immediate care and management of his own department, and directed him to *pursue the same plan as was customary for all quartermaster generals in this country to do,* by taking drivers, horses, and wagons into the service as a daily hire *according to the rates that were then established,* indemnifying the proprietors for their horses and wagons (in case of their being lost at sea or taken or destroyed by the enemy) according to their value. Should he find the same inconvenience continue, by the backwardness of the country people to serve, *he should fall upon every method possible, by contracting with one or more men to furnish the number required.*

Sir William Erskine accordingly set about establishing a train, which was done so effectually as not to cause any disappointment to the movement of the troops, as we humbly conceive will be acknowledged by the army at large. And this we chiefly ascribe to those who were employed to purchase the best horses and the best kind of carriages that could be had in the country. There was no expense spared to effect this; and by the uncommon pains, labor, and attention paid to those particulars and by their having an interest in the property of these horses and wagons, they naturally took every care of them.[80] *They have been in constant readiness to attend the movements and duty of the army,* besides giving assistance to the several departments. We presume to say there never was a supply of such magnitude better or more effectually complied with or better arranged than the train of this army, nor can we conceive a more economical plan could have been adopted on the part of government.

Copy of a letter from Sir Henry Clinton to Rear Admiral Graves. New York, August 17th, 1781.

Sir:

I requested the Commodore [Affleck] to make my best compliments to you, but I fear the bad weather will prevent his going to you. I cannot say I credit the reports of the French being on the coast. Should they prove false and there was little probability of their coming for a week or ten days, I think those could not be better employed than in a visit to Rhode Island. The recruits I have lately received and the return of the *Royal Oak* enables me to make this offer. Whenever you think it prudent to attempt it if you determine [on it], I request that Captain Duncan may direct the water movement of the army. I have, etc., Henry Clinton.

Extract of a letter from Rear Admiral Graves to Sir Henry Clinton. *London,* Sandy Hook, 18 August 1781.

In answer to your proposition, I can only assure you by letter what I had the honor to declare in person—that I am ready to concur with Your Excellency in any enterprise where you found a probability of success, and that I would risk the squadron whenever you thought it advisable to risk the army. In the letter I did myself the honor to write yesterday, I acquainted you of the *Royal Oak* having joined and part-

80. *Clinton's note:* Sir William Erskine acknowledged to Sir Henry Clinton, on being question[ed] who were the contractors, that he was one. And, on Sir Henry Clinton's remarking that it sounded odd that contract and contract[or]s should be in the same hands, Sir William Erskine assured him it had ever been the practice in America from General Braddock's time. Sir Henry Clinton, after paying some compliments to Sir William Erskine upon his zeal, ability, and exertion, and upon the state of the train (which he ever found ready, efficient, and complete), repeated that though he thought it sounded odd he should take no notice of it, but that Sir William Erskine must in future day be responsible. As it had been in Sir William Erskine's time and his predecessors', so it continued under Lord Cathcart and General Dalrymple, his successors. Nor was it altered till the war (after the resolution of the authorities) was put on a strict defensive, when the contract was reduced.

ing company again in a fog.[81] The *Robust* is so leaky I am forced to send her to the yard for reparation, and I suspect that her guns and heavy furniture must be taken out to enable the shipwrights to examine as much of her bottom as possible. By this state you will perceive our naval capacity. [Stevens, *Clinton-Cornwallis Controversy*, 2, 129.]

Extract from Sir Henry Clinton's letter to Rear Admiral Graves in answer. August 18, 1781.

Not to dwell too long upon the subject of the expedition to Rhode Island, which we both think important and I am sanguine enough to believe would succeed, I shall only say that I have 3000 troops ready to embark at an instant, and every necessary arrangement prepared. Therefore (as it is probable that the absence of the *Royal Oak* and the condition of the *Robust* and *Prudent*—which I am much concerned at —may occasion some small delay) whenever, sir, you think that the fleet under your command is in number and state equal to the undertaking and you will give me twenty-four hours' notice, everything shall be embarked; and I shall with pleasure accompany you myself on it.

Extract of Rear Admiral Graves' letter to Sir Henry Clinton in answer. 21 August 1781.

How soon the *Robust* will be ready is yet impossible to form a judgment upon, as we cannot yet learn the extent of her defects. The *Prudent* will, I am confident, be ready in much less time; and so will all the other ships, I have not a doubt. The *Royal Oak* is now with us. Your Excellency may rest assured that timely notice shall be given; and, as early as it is possible to determine upon the day, the squadron will be fit to act—for I would not wish that a single day should be lost. The Commodore tells me that the French squadron are preparing for sea, which is a further inducement to be ready to operate against them. [Stevens, *Clinton-Cornwallis Controversy*, 2, 129–130.]

Extract of a letter from Earl Cornwallis to Sir Henry Clinton. Yorktown, 22 August 1781 (received August 30th).

The engineer has finished his survey and examination of this place and has proposed his plan for fortifying it—which, appearing judicious, I have approved of and directed to be executed. The works at Gloucester are now in such forwardness that a smaller detachment than the

81. The purport of the letter, as Clinton points out in an obscurely worded note, was that the fleet was assembling and that, if Sir Henry did not want it kept together for a joint expedition, Graves intended to send out separate ships on cruise.

present garrison would be in safety against a sudden attack; but I make no alteration there, as I cannot hope that the labor of the whole *will complete that post in less than five or six weeks.* My experience there of the fatigue and difficulty of constructing works in this warm season convinces me that all the labor that the troops here will be capable of, without ruining their health, *will be required at least for six weeks* to put the intended works at this place in a tolerable state of defense. And, as Your Excellency has been pleased to communicate to me your intention of recommencing operation in the Chesapeake about the beginning of October, I will not venture to take any step that might retard the establishing of this post. But I request that Your Excellency will be pleased to decide whether it is more important for your plans that a detachment *of 1000 or 1200 men (which I think I can spare from every other purpose but that of labor)* should be sent to you from hence, or that the whole of the troops here should continue to be employed *in expediting* the works. [*Ibid.,* pp. 137–138.]

Extract from Sir Henry Clinton's letter to Rear Admiral Graves. August 24, 1781.

From information I received yesterday, on which I place great dependence, those people expect only a few ships to relieve those at Rhode Island unfit for service. I know your anxiety and my own to put our favorite plan in execution; I sincerely hope that the *Robust* will be ready before the first week in September.

It certainly would be better that you should appear off [Rhode Island] in force sufficient to threaten an immediate attack. *But, if you are only in such force as to mask the harbor,* I am willing to try my part. And I think, from the information I have received, if I succeed in getting possession of Coasters Island and Brenton's Neck and am lucky enough to find cannon in either, I shall be able to annoy the French fleet in the station they have taken; and I hope I am not too sanguine in supposing it possible I may even stir them, and give you a safe anchorage in the harbor. I understand you are coming to town; I shall be happy to consult you.

Extract of a letter from Rear Admiral Sir Samuel Hood to Sir Henry Clinton. Off Cape Henry, 25 August 1781.

I am now steering for Cape Henry in order to examine the Chesapeake. From thence I shall proceed to the Capes of the Delaware and, not seeing or hearing anything of de Grasse or any detachment of ships he might have sent upon this coast, shall then make the best of my way off Sandy Hook. This I have communicated to Rear Admiral Graves in order that he may determine my anchoring or not, as the King's service may require.

I have the honor to send you my line of battle, by which you will see the number and force of His Majesty's squadron under my command. And I trust you will think it equal fully to defeat any designs of the enemy, let de Grasse bring or send what ships he may in aid of those under de Barras. [Stevens, *Clinton-Cornwallis Controversy, 2,* 141.]

Extract of a letter from Sir Henry Clinton to Earl Cornwallis. New York, 27 August 1781.

I cannot well ascertain Mr. Washington's real intentions by this move of his army. But it is possible he means for the present *to suspend his offensive operations against this post* and to take a defensive station at the old post of Morristown, *from whence he may detach to the southward.* On this account, therefore, and because the season is approaching when operation may recommence in the Chesapeake, I request Your Lordship will be pleased to keep with you all the troops you have there.[82] And I will send you such recruits, convalescents, etc., as can go by this sudden opportunity—*which are all that I can at present spare, as this move of the enemy may be only a feint and they may return to their former position,* which they certainly will do if de Grasse arrives. But toward the latter end of next month, when the effects of the equinox are over (for I am persuaded the Admiral will not approve of any water movements till then), if this post should not be threatened, I propose to reinforce the Chesapeake army with all the troops which can possibly be spared, consistently with the security of this important post.

General Leslie has been here some days. He will himself explain to Your Lordship the cause of his coming. I was much concerned to find him in so bad a state of health on his arrival; but, as it is now much altered for the better, he embarks tomorrow to proceed to Chesapeake on his way to Charleston. [*Ibid.,* pp. 142–143.]

82. *Clinton's note:* So far from calling on Lord Cornwallis *à cor et à cri* for troops, as Monsieur Rochambeau terms it, the reader will see I desire Lord Cornwallis to keep all he has with him. [The reference is to Rochambeau, *Relation, ou Journal des opérations du Corps Français,* p. 2.]

[Extract of Cornwallis to Clinton. Yorktown, Virginia, August 31, 1781.]

A French ship of the line, with two frigates and the *Loyalist* (which they have taken), lay at the mouth of this river. A lieutenant of the *Charon* who went with an escort of dragoons to Old Point Comfort reports that *there are between thirty and forty sail within the capes,* mostly ships of war and some of them very large. [*Ibid.,* p. 146.]

[Extract of Cornwallis to Clinton. Yorktown, Virginia, September 2, 1781.]

Comte de Grasse's fleet is within the Capes of the Chesapeake. Forty boats with troops went up James River yesterday, and four ships lie at the entrance of this river. [*Ibid.,* p. 148.]

Extract of a letter from Sir Henry Clinton to Earl Cornwallis. New York, September 2d, 1781.

By intelligence which I have this day received, it would seem that Mr. Washington is moving an army to the southward with an appearance of haste, and gives out that he expects the cooperation of a considerable French armament. Your Lordship, however, may be assured that, if this should be the case, I shall either endeavor to reinforce the army under your command *by all the means within the compass of my power,* or make every possible diversion in Your Lordship's favor.

Captain Stanhope of His Majesty's ship *Pegasus,* who is just arrived, says that on Friday last, in latitude thirty-eight about sixty leagues from the coast, he was chased by eight ships of the line which he took to be French, and that one of the victualers he had under his convoy had counted upward of forty sail more. However, as Rear Admiral Graves (after being joined by Sir Samuel Hood) sailed from hence on the 31st *ultimo* with a fleet of nineteen sail besides some fifty-gun ships, I flatter myself Your Lordship will have little to apprehend from that of the French. Washington, it is said, was to be at Trenton this day, and means to go in vessels to Christian Creek [and] from thence by Head of Elk down Chesapeake. He has about 4000 French and 2000 rebel troops with him. [*Ibid.,* pp. 149–150.]

Extract of a letter from Sir Henry Clinton to Earl Cornwallis.
New York, September 6th, 1781.

I think the best way to relieve you is to join you as soon as possible
with all the force that can be spared from hence, which is about 4000
men. They are already embarked, and will proceed the instant I receive
information from the Admiral that we may venture, or any other intelligence which the Commodore and I shall judge sufficient to move
upon.[83] By accounts from Europe we have every reason to expect Admiral Digby hourly on the coast. [*Ibid.*, pp. 152–153.]

[Extract of Clinton to Germain. New York, September 7, 1781.]

By the enclosed return of the 15th August Your Lordship will be informed of the force Lord Cornwallis had with him at that period, since
which I have no cause to think it has been diminished, but on the contrary that many of his sick have recovered; besides which the Commissary of Prisoners informs me that from the assurances of the rebel
Commissary he judges His Lordship has been joined by about 500 or
600 exchanged men of the troops captured in the unfortunate affair
of Cowpens. His Lordship's former force therefore being good 6000, I am
in hopes it will be increased to nearly 8000 by the addition of these 500,
the sailors and marines of the squadron, and the refugees which have
joined him. The force of the enemy opposed to His Lordship will consist of the French troops arrived with de Grasse (which are reported
to be between 3000 and 4000), those with Washington (4000), the
rebel Continentals (about 4000), and in all probability a very numerous
militia if they can arm them.

This, My Lord, is a very alarming report of our situation; and I therefore cannot sufficiently lament the impossibility there was of sending
me the reinforcement I solicited for, as Your Lordship may now perceive that my requisition was not a wanton one. I have reason also to
be concerned that even what was sent to me could not have been
sent away soon enough to join me at an earlier period of the campaign;
and that, of the three complete battalions which I was told General
Vaughan would certainly send me from the Leeward Islands, only one
very weak one has been yet added to this army. Your Lordship will likewise have observed that, instead of receiving a reinforcement from Lord
Cornwallis, as I had expected last year, I have been obliged to detach in
the whole about eight thousand men to His Lordship, besides leaving

83. The wording is that of Clinton's excerpt. In the original draft, as in Stevens,
the last phrase reads "or that from other intelligence the Commodore and I shall
judge sufficient to move upon."

in Carolina the three regiments which lately arrived there from Ireland.

But this is not a time, My Lord, for vain lamentations. Things appear to be coming fast to a crisis. We are therefore no longer to compare forces with the enemy, but to endeavor to act in the best manner we can against them. And Your Lordship may be assured that with what I have, inadequate as it is, I will exert myself to the utmost to relieve Lord Cornwallis. After which, if I am so fortunate to succeed, I shall avail myself of the permission His Majesty has been graciously pleased to give me of resigning to His Lordship a command which, I am persuaded, Your Lordship expected I would have resigned upon my receiving your message by Colonel Bruce and letter[s] of 7th of March and 2d of May, and which I should certainly have done had not the circumstances of this post been such at the time as to render such a measure highly improper.

I have the honor to be, etc., H. Clinton.

[Extract of Cornwallis to Clinton. Yorktown, Virginia, September 8, 1781.]

The French troops landed at Jamestown are said to be 3800. Washington is said to be shortly expected, and his troops are intended to be brought by water from the Head of Elk. The Marquis de Lafayette is at or near Williamsburg; and the French troops are expected there, *but were not arrived last night.* As my works were not in a state of defense, *I have taken a strong position out of the town. I am now working hard at the redoubts of the place. The army is not very sickly. Provisions for six weeks*—I will be very careful of it. [Stevens, *Clinton-Cornwallis Controversy, 2,* 155.]

Extract from Brigadier General Arnold's report to Sir Henry Clinton. [Long Island Sound, off Plumb Island,] September 8, 1781.

At one o'clock in the morning of the 6th we arrived off the harbor of New London, where, the wind suddenly shifting to the northward, it was nine o'clock before the transports could beat in. From information I had reason to believe that Fort Griswold, on Groton side, was very incomplete; and I found the enemy's ships would escape unless we could possess ourselves of it. I therefore dispatched an officer to Lieutenant Colonel Eyre with the intelligence I had received, and requested him to make an attack on the fort as soon as possible, at which time I expected the howitzer was up and would be made use of.

On my gaining a height of ground in the rear of New London from which I had a good prospect of Fort Griswold, I found it much more formidable than I expected. I observed at the same time that the men who had escaped from Fort Trumbull had crossed in boats and thrown themselves into Fort Griswold; and, a favorable wind springing up about this time, the enemy's ships were escaping up the river, notwithstanding the fire from Fort Trumbull and a six-pounder I had with me. I immediately dispatched a boat with an officer to Lieutenant Colonel Eyre to countermand my first order to attack the fort, but the officer arrived a few minutes too late.

After a most obstinate defense of near forty minutes the fort was carried by the superior bravery and perseverance of the assailants. The attack was judicious and spirited, and reflects the highest honor on the officers of the troops engaged, who seemed to vie with each other in being the first in danger. The troops approached in three sides of the work (which was a square with flanks), made a lodgement in the ditch and, under a heavy fire which they kept upon the works, effected a second lodgement on the fraising—which was attended with great difficulty, as only a few pickets could be forced out or broken in a place, and [the fraising] was so high that the soldiers could not ascend without assisting each other. Here the coolness and bravery of the troops were very conspicuous, as the first who ascended the fraise were obliged to silence a nine-pounder (which enfiladed the place on which they stood) until a sufficient body had collected to enter the works, which was done with fixed bayonets through the embrasures, where they were opposed with great obstinacy by the garrison with long spears.

On this occasion I have to lament the loss of Major Montgomery, who was killed by a spear on entering the works; also of Ensign Whitlock of the Fortieth Regiment, who was killed in the attack. Three other officers of the same regiment were wounded; Lieutenant Colonel Eyre and three other officers of the Fifty-fourth Regiment were also wounded. Lieutenant Colonel Eyre, who behaved with great gallantry, having received his wound near the works, and Major Montgomery being killed immediately after, the command devolved on Major Bromfield, whose behavior on this occasion does him great honor. Ten or twelve of the enemy's ships were burned, among them three or four armed vessels and one loaded with naval stores. An immense quantity of European and West India goods were found in the stores, among the former the cargo of the *Hannah* (Captain Watson) from London, lately captured by the enemy; the whole of which was burned, with the stores—which proved to contain a large quantity of powder, unknown to us. The explosion of the powder, and [a] change of wind soon after the stores were fired, communicated the flames to part of the town, which was, notwithstanding every effort to prevent it, unfortunately destroyed. Upward of fifty pieces of iron cannon in the different works were destroyed, exclusive of the guns in the ships. A very considerable magazine of powder, and barracks to contain 300 men, were found in Fort Griswold.

[Postscript.] Return of the [British] killed and wounded: forty-eight killed and one hundred and forty-five wounded; three of the wounded officers since dead. [A version with slight differences, and misdated Sept. 3, is printed in Isaac N. Arnold, *The Life of Benedict Arnold; His Patriotism and His Treason* (Chicago, 1880), pp. 349–351.]

Extract of a letter from Sir Henry Clinton to Rear Admiral Graves. New York, September 8, 1781.

I have the honor to enclose duplicates of my letters to you and Lord Cornwallis of the 2d instant sent by the *Pegasus,* and of my letter to Lord Cornwallis of the 6th by a runner. By this last you will find that the troops are embarked, and ready for moving to the Chesapeake the instant I hear from you. I am persuaded, therefore, that I need not mention to you, sir, how anxious I am for that honor, or how necessary it is to lose no time in reinforcing the army at York the first moment it becomes possible.

Extract of a letter from Rear Admiral Graves to Sir Henry Clinton. *London,* off Currituck Inlet, September 9, 1781.

I am sorry to inform you the enemy have so great a naval force in the Chesapeake that they are absolute masters of its navigation. The French fleet at sea consists of twenty-four sail of the line (large ships) and two frigates. We met them the 5th coming out of the Chesapeake, and had a pretty sharp brush with their van and part of their center; the rear on neither side was engaged. They appear to have suffered, but not so much as our van. We have been in sight of each other ever since; and for two days they had the wind of us, but did not incline to renew the action. In this ticklish state of things Your Excellency will see the little probability of anything getting into York River but by night, and of the infinite risk to any supplies sent by water. All that I can say is that every resistance the fleet can make shall not be wanting; for we must either stand or fall together.

Extract of a letter from Lieutenant Colonel Stewart to Earl Cornwallis. Eutaw's [Eutaw Springs], September 9, 1781.

Notwithstanding every exertion being made to gain intelligence of the enemy's situation, they rendered it impossible by waylaying the bypaths and passes through the different swamps, and even detained different flags of truce which I had sent on public business on both sides. About six o'clock in the morning of yesterday I received intelligence by two deserters, who left General Greene's camp the preceding evening, about seven miles from this place; and from their report the rebel army consisted of near 4000 men, with a numerous body of cavalry and four pieces of cannon. In the meantime I received information by Major Coffin, whom I had previously detached with a hundred and forty infantry and fifty cavalry in order to gain intelligence of the enemy (as none could be collected by spies), that they appeared in force in his front, then about four miles from my camp.

Finding the enemy in force so near me, I determined to fight them, as from their numerous cavalry a retreat seemed to me to be attended with dangerous consequences. I immediately formed the line of battle with the right of the army to Eutaw Branch, and its left crossing the road leading to Roaches' Plantation, leaving a corps on a commanding situation to cover the Charleston road and to act occasionally as a reserve. About nine o'clock the action began on the right and soon after became general. Knowing that the enemy were much superior in numbers, and at the same time finding that they attacked with their militia in front, induced me not to alter my position unless I saw a certain advantage to be gained by it. For by moving forward I exposed both flanks of the army to the enemy's cavalry, which I saw ready formed to take that advantage, particularly on the left—which obliged me to remove the reserve to support it. By an unknown mistake the left of the line advanced and drove their militia and North Carolinians before them; but unexpectedly finding the Virginia and Maryland lines ready formed occasioned some confusion. It was therefore necessary to retire a little distance to an open field in order to form, which was instantly done under cover of a heavy and well directed fire from a detachment of New York Volunteers, under the command of Major Sheridan, whom I had previously ordered to take post in the house to check the enemy should they attempt to pass it.

The action was renewed with great spirit. But I was sorry to find that a three-pounder posted on the road leading to Roaches' had been disabled and could not be brought off when the left of the line retired. The right wing of the army, being composed of the flank battalion under the command of Major Majoribanks, having repulsed and driven everything that attacked them, made a rapid move to their left and attacked the enemy in flank, upon which they gave way on all quarters, leaving behind them two brass six-pounders and upward of two hundred killed on the field of action and sixty taken prisoners (amongst whom is Colonel Washington), and from every information about eight hundred wounded, although they contrived to carry them off during the action. The enemy retired with great precipitation to a strong situation about seven miles from the field of action, leaving their cavalry to cover their retreat. The glory of the day would have been more complete had not the want of cavalry prevented me from taking the advantage which the gallantry of my infantry threw in my way.

I omitted to inform Your Lordship in its proper place of the army's having for some time been much in want of bread, there being no old corn or mills near me. I was therefore under the necessity of sending out rooting parties from each corps, under an officer, to collect potatoes every morning at daybreak. And unfortunately that of the flank battalion and Buffs, having gone too far in front, fell into the enemy's hands before the action began, which not only weakened my line but increased their number of prisoners. Since the action our time has been employed in taking care of the wounded. And, finding that the enemy have no intention to make a second attack, I have determined to cover the wounded as far as Monk's Corner with the army.

My particular thanks is due to Lieutenant Colonel Cruger, who commanded the front line, for his conduct and gallantry during the action, and to Lieutenant Colonel Allen, Majors Dawson, Stewart, Sheridan, and Coffin, and to Captains Kelly and Campbell, commanding the different corps and detachments; and every other officer and soldier fulfilled the separate duties of their stations with great gallantry. But to Major Majoribanks and the flank battalion under his command I think the honor of the day is greatly due. I hope, My Lord, when it is considered, such a handful of men, attacked by the united force of Generals Greene, Sumter, Marion, Sumner, and Pickens and the legions of Colonels Lee and Washington, driving them from the field of battle and taking the only two six-pounders they had deserves some merit. It will give me most singular pleasure if my conduct meets with the approbation of His Majesty, that of Your Lordship, and my country. [Tarleton, *History*, pp. 508–512.]

Extracts from minutes of a council of war held at New York. September 14, 1781.[84]

Present: General Sir Henry Clinton; Lieutenant Generals Knyphausen and Robertson, Leslie and Campbell; Major Generals Stirling

84. Sir Henry took this extract, and those of the minutes of subsequent councils that he cites, from a MS Council Book, which is now in a slip case entitled "Reports." The draft minutes in the chronological file of the CP differ widely in wording but little in substance; some of them are fragmentary, and they are less reliable because they are not, like those in the Council Book, formal signed copies.

and Paterson; Brigadier Generals Birch and Arnold; Commodore Affleck.

The late correspondence with Earl Cornwallis and Rear Admiral Graves read. Officers lately arrived from Virginia examined.

Following question proposed by the Commander in Chief: "As the Admiral in his last letter says that, the enemy being absolute masters of the navigation of the Chesapeake and having a naval superiority at sea, there is little probability of anything getting into York River but by night and infinite risk to any supplies sent by water, and as the army under Lord Cornwallis may be computed at eight thousand men and it appears from the returns that His Lordship has provisions at full allowance for ten thousand to the end of October, and it is the opinion of the officers lately arrived from Virginia that the post of York may be defended with its present garrison against twenty thousand assailants for at least three weeks, whether it is most advisable to commit a reinforcement of five or six thousand men to the hazards of the sea during our present naval inferiority and endeavor to relieve Lord Cornwallis immediately at all risks, or to wait until we either receive more favorable accounts from Rear Admiral Graves, or the junction of Rear Admiral Digby's squadron affords a more certain prospect of success in the attempt?"

Unanimously resolved it will be most prudent to wait more favorable accounts from Rear Admiral Graves, or the arrival of Rear Admiral Digby.

Extract of a letter from Sir Henry Clinton to Rear Admiral Graves. New York, September 14, 1781.

I was yesterday honored with your letter of the 9th instant. Notwithstanding I am clearly of opinion that a direct move to the Chesapeake and landing troops there is the only one which can effectually assist Lord Cornwallis, I cannot but agree with you that there will be infinite risk in sending supplies at present to York River unless you can force the enemy's fleet. I do not, however, apprehend that His Lordship is, or can be, in any immediate danger, as his numbers, including the sailors and marines of the King's ships and the refugees who have joined him, may be computed at 8000, and he can feed 10,000 at full allowance until the end of October.

By this time you will have been informed that Admiral Digby is on his passage. When you are joined by him, the *Robust*, and *Prudent*, I shall hope you may be able to force the Chesapeake and cover our landing. For I must again repeat that I think nothing can relieve Lord Cornwallis but a landing of troops in Chesapeake. And, should his army fall, I need not say what fatal consequences are to be apprehended. Every exertion, therefore, of both fleet and army, in my humble opinion, should certainly be tried even at great risk; and I flatter myself you will concur with me.

Wherefore, sir, if you approve, I will instantly attend your summons whenever you determine on the attempt and think you can force the enemy into James River or up the Chesapeake Bay, and bring with me all the troops which can be spared from the defense of this post. And then, sir, if you will be so good to land me on either York or Gloucester Neck, I will at all risks endeavor to effect a junction with Lord Cornwallis, provided you will continue in possession of the bay. In which case, if we are succeful and can afterward make an impression on their troops, we may try our joint efforts against their fleet should it be retired into James River.

[Extract of Cornwallis to Clinton. Yorktown, Virginia, September 16–17, 1781.]

[September 16.] I have received your letters of the 2d and 6th. The enemy's fleet has returned. I hear Washington arrived at Williamsburg on the 14th; some of his troops embarked at Head of Elk, and the others arrived at Baltimore on the 12th.

If I had no hopes of relief, *I would rather risk an action than defend my half-finished works.* But, as you say Admiral Digby is hourly expected *and promise every exertion to assist me,* I do not think myself justifiable in putting the fate of the war on so desperate an attempt. My provisions will last at least six weeks from this day. *I am of opinion that you can do me no effectual service but by coming directly to this place.*

[September 17.] Lieutenant Conway, of the *Cormorant,* is just exchanged. He assures me that, since the Rhode Island squadron has joined, they have thirty-six sail of the line. This place is in no state of defense. If you cannot relieve me very soon, you must be prepared to hear the worst. [Stevens, *Clinton-Cornwallis Controversy,* 2, 156–158.]

[Extract of minutes of a council of war held at New York. September 17, 1781.]

[Present: General Clinton; Lieutenant Generals Knyphausen, Leslie, Robertson, and Campbell.]

Read Lord Cornwallis' letter to Sir Henry Clinton, dated the 8th instant and received this day.

Unanimously resolved that it appeared from Lord Cornwallis' letter that His Lordship was under no apprehensions whatsoever, and that his provisions would last very well to the end of October.

Resolved, therefore, that it would be improper to detain the *Robust*, and that the attempt to throw in supplies and reinforcement ought to be deferred until it could be undertaken with less danger than at present.

The two Mr. Goodriches and Mr. Burnley [85] were called in and examined respecting the possibility of subsisting an army in Virginia without having the command of the waters of the Chesapeake. These gentlemen were unanimously of opinion that the difficulties would be great even to Mr. Washington, but almost insurmountable to an army of any considerable numbers who did not possess the good will of the inhabitants.

Therefore unanimously resolved that an army could not act there alone without the communication and cooperation of the fleet. And, until that became practicable, it would be highly improper to add considerably to the numbers already in Virginia.

[Extract of minutes of a council of war held at New York. September 19, 1781.]

Present: the Commander in Chief and Lieutenant Generals as before [on September 17].

Mr. Rankin and other persons examined respecting the situation of the loyalists in the lower counties of Delaware.

The substance of the last letters to the Admiral communicated to the board, and the Commander in Chief informed the general officers that he would propose to the Admiral to take the troops, etc., on board the King's ships as soon as his fleet was ready (either by the junction of Admiral Digby or otherwise) and to endeavor to force the Chesapeake if it should be found practicable. And, if there was left no other means of relieving Lord Cornwallis, he should propose the running up the Delaware and destroying the public stores, etc., at Philadelphia whilst the fleet covered the entrance of the river.

Extract of a letter from Rear Admiral Graves to Sir Henry Clinton. *London*, at Sandy Hook, 21 September 1781.

I beg leave to assure you that, as soon as the fleet can be got into a state for action, I am ready to undertake any service in conjunction

85. The copy in the chronological file of the CP reads "Messrs. Goodrich and Burnley." Hardin Burnley had given Clinton his opinion in writing on Sept. 15. John Goodrich submitted a report on conditions in Virginia on Oct. 7, and "the

with the army that shall be thought advisable. At the same time I should be greatly wanting were I not to apprise Your Excellency that the injuries received by the fleet in the action, added to the complaints of several very crazy ships, makes it quite uncertain how soon the fleet can be got to sea. One ship we have been obliged to abandon, and another is in a very doubtful state.

[Extract of minutes of a council of war held at New York. September 23, 1781.]

Present: General Sir Henry Clinton; Lieutenant Generals Knyphausen, Robertson, and Leslie; and Major General Paterson.

Unanimously resolved that the only probable means which occur [86] of relieving Lord Cornwallis are by a direct movement of the fleet and army to possess the eastern branch of the Chesapeake leading to York, or some other which might open a communication with His Lordship.

Unanimously resolved that Lord Cornwallis' letter of the [16th–] 17th gives every reason to suppose His Lordship's situation is such as to require the most speedy assistance.

Unanimously resolved that the loss of Lord Cornwallis' corps will have the most fatal consequences, and that an attempt to relieve him ought to be made by both fleet and army even at great risk.

Unanimously resolved that this attempt ought not to be delayed many days.

Resolved, therefore, that an immediate conference be requested with the Admiral in Chief and flag officers.

[Extract of minutes of a council of war held at New York. September 24, 1781.]

Present: general officers as before [on September 23] and Rear Admirals Graves, Sir Samuel Hood, and Drake; and Commodore Affleck.

Read Sir Henry Clinton's letters to Earl Cornwallis of the 2d and 6th instant, and the Earl's letters to Sir Henry Clinton of the 22d and 31st August, and 2d, 8th, and 16th–17th instant.

Sir Henry Clinton acquainted the board that it was the unanimous opinion of the general officers, assembled the evening before, that Lord Cornwallis' situation required the most speedy assistance.

Messrs. Goodrich" on Oct. 13; for further light on these brothers see Lorenzo Sabine, *Biographical Sketches of Loyalists of the American Revolution, with an Historical Essay* (2 vols., Boston, 1864), *1*, 480–482.

86. The wording is that of Clinton's excerpt; the Council Book reads "occurred."

His Excellency therefore proposed, and the question was put, whether the troops, etc., designed and held in readiness for this service should (when the fleet was refitted) be put on board the King's ships, and the whole afterward proceed to the Chesapeake and endeavor by every means in their power to form a junction with Lord Cornwallis' army at York. Agreed to.

This being the opinion of the board, [it was] proposed that the following letter should be sent immediately to Lord Cornwallis: "At a meeting of the flag and general officers held this day, in consequence of Your Lordship's letter of the 16th and 17th instant, it was unanimously determined that above 5000 men shall be embarked on board the King's ships, and the joint exertions of the fleet and army shall be made in a few days to relieve you. There is every reason to hope we shall start from hence the 5th of October." [87] Unanimously agreed to.

Resolved that three additional fireships shall be prepared for immediate service, with every possible dispatch.

Signed by all the flag and general officers present.

> [September 25, 1781.] Narration des idées du Général Sir Henry Clinton d'une diversion de Canada, en coöpération avec une expédition que ce général est intentionné de faire par le haut de la baie de Chesapeake, montant les rivières de Potomac et de Susquehanna si haut que possible, laquelle ce général a communiquée en confidence au Major Général Riedesel avec ordre de la communiquer à son excellence le Général Haldimand.

Comme on est sûr, si bien par les intelligences de l'Europe que par les lettres interceptées en Amérique des officiers français du corps de Monsieur Rochambeau à l'envoyé français à Philadelphie, qu'on se désiste entièrement pour le moment présent de toute l'entreprise contre la province de Canada, Sir Henry espère que son excellence le Général Haldimand pourrait épargner 2000 hommes pour faire une diversion par le chemin de Niagara, du lac Erie, et Presqu'isle vers le Fort Pitt, la rivière Ohio, les montagnes d'Allegheny, et jusques aux établissements qui se trouvent dans le dos de la Pennsylvanie et Virginie. L'exécution d'une telle entreprise devait beaucoup faciliter son expédition du haut de la baie de Chesapeake, et l'on s'en promit d'autant plus une heureuse issue parce qu'on prétend d'avoir des nouvelles bien fondées que les habitants le long de l'Ohio sont très prêts à se soumettre

87. Clinton made a few verbal modifications and added considerably to the letter, which was dispatched to Cornwallis the same day and received on Sept. 29. See Stevens, *Clinton-Cornwallis Controversy*, 2, 159–160.

sous le gouvernement de la Grande Brétagne, à condition qu'elle voudrait les séparer entièrement de la Pennsylvanie et la Virginie pour en former une province séparée.

Après avoir arrangé à Niagara tous les magasins nécessaires de provisions, artillerie, d'attirail, etc., on suppose que le corps de Canada pourra passer le lac Erie en bateaux et prendre un poste fixe à Presqu'isle, où il faudrait s'établir tellement par des fortifications qu'une force supérieure ne pourrait pas l'y déloger ni couper sa retraite par eau à Niagara. Comme on se flatte que ce corps peut être renforcé par un bon nombre de sauvages de pays en haut, il est à savoir si, en attendant qu'on s'établit à Presqu'isle, on ne peut pas tenter à se rendre maître (par un coup de main ou par surprise) du Fort Pitt, par un détachement composé de sauvages, chasseurs, quelques compagnies canadiennes, et d'infanterie légère. On s'apercevrait par ce moyen bientôt des sentiments des habitants le long de l'Ohio. Et, si on les trouverait de disposition pour le Roi et qu'ils voudraient défendre eux-mêmes les défilés entre les montagnes d'Allegheny et les Bleus Ridges, on ne risquerait plus beaucoup pour son dos et les flancs, et on pourrait prendre poste à Fort Pitt, en établissant deux postes intermédiaires à Venango et Shenango pour entretenir la communication avec Presqu'isle, ce qui faciliterait en même temps les excursions de sauvages pour faire des dégâts dans le dos de la Pennsylvanie et Virginie.

Si le Fort Pitt ne serait pas à prendre, ni par un coup de main ni par surprise, et si—contre toute apparence—on se trouverait trompé dans les sentiments des habitants le long de l'Ohio de prendre les armes pour le Roi, et que par conséquence on risquerait de s'aventurer dans l'intérieur du pays, il faudrait alors se contenter de garder Presqu'isle dans sa possession (en rendant ce poste aussi formidable que possible) et établir deux postes avancés à Venango et Shenango dans deux rédoutes, dont on pourra soutenir la communication par eau. On fera agir les sauvages en avant ces deux postes, et ruiner tout le pays aussi loin que possible; pourtant [on les fera] agir avec jugement et précautions.

Dans une telle position et avec une telle conduite, l'officier qui commandera le corps de Canada doit attendre le progrès de l'expédition qui se fait du côté de la baie de Chesapeake, et il doit être toujours en connection par des émissaires avec ce général qui commandera cette expédition, faisant tout ce qui sera en son pouvoir de l'assister avec prudence par sa coöpération.

Pour dérober à l'ennemi le vrai but de cette expédition, Sir Henry propose une autre petite excursion qui devait se faire avec un petit corps du côté de la rivière Mohawk par Oswego, pour prendre le fort

Stanwix, ou au moins pour faire la mine de le vouloir prendre. Le corps doit ruiner le pays autant que possible et après un certain temps s'en retourner à Oswego. Si en même temps la flotte sur le lac Champlain avancerait, et que quelques Canadiens (volontaires et rangers) faisaient des excursions vers Ticonderoga et Fort George et, s'il est possible, encore un peu loin, cette triple expédition doit naturellement beaucoup déconcerter un ennemi qui se voit attaqué en même temps dans la Caroline, la Virginie, et le Maryland. Autant qu'une diversion du côté de la province de Canada pourrait possiblement se correspondre en temps avec la sienne, d'autant plus Sir Henry se flatte d'un bon succès. Et, si l'on serait en état de détacher les habitants sur les rivières d'Ohio et Kentucky [et] des autres provinces révoltantes, ce serait peut-être le plus sûr moyen de faire finir la rébellion.

Québec, 25ème septembre, 1781. Riedesel. [A German translation, differing only inconsequentially, is in Max von Eelking, *Leben und Wirken des Herzoglich Braunschweig'schen General-Lieutenants Friedrich Adolph Riedesel* . . . (Leipzig, 1856), pp. 342–344.]

> Extract of a letter from General Washington to the Count de Grasse. Williamsburg, September 26 [25], 1781.

If Your Excellency quits the bay, an access is open to relieve York-[town] of which the enemy will instantly avail themselves. The consequences of this will be not only the disgrace of abandoning a design on which are founded the fairest hopes of the allied forces (after a prodigious expense, fatigue, and exertion), but the probable disbanding of the whole army. For, the present seat of war being such as absolutely precludes the use of wagons (from the great number of large rivers which intersect the country), there will be a total want of provisions unless this inconvenience is remedied by water carriage. This province has been so exhausted by the ravages of the enemy, and by the support already given to our forces, that subsistence must be drawn from a distance; and that can be done only by a fleet superior in the bay. [An extremely free paraphrase of Washington to de Grasse, Sept. 25; Fitzpatrick, *Writings of Washington*, 23, 137.]

> Extracts from minutes of a council of war held at New York. September 26, 1781.

Present: all the general officers as before [on September 23].
The Commander in Chief proposed the following questions:

"Are the board of opinion upon reading Lord Cornwallis' letter of the 16th instant that, had His Lordship not been in hopes of succor, he would have endeavored to force his way through the enemy before General Washington's army joined the Marquis de Lafayette, and [to] retire to the southward?" Unanimously of opinion that it is so implied in that letter.

"Are they of opinion upon reading the latter part of the same letter, dated the 17th, that, His Lordship's hopes of succor being greatly lessened by his hearing that the French fleet consisted of thirty-six sail of the line, he in consequence recurred to his former idea of risking an action, etc.?" The Commander in Chief was singly of opinion yes, the other general officers being of opinion that the expression "worst" in His Lordship's letter of the 17th means something more serious than a *retreat*, arising from the unfinished state of his works.[88]

"Are the board of opinion that, upon the probability of Lord Cornwallis' intentions on the 17th [being] as above stated, and upon the uncertainty of the fleet's being ready exactly to a day, a movement into Jersey threatening Philadelphia might not be made, provided it can be done without risking delay of the principal object—*which is the accompanying the fleet to the Chesapeake?*" The general officers, conceiving that the fleet will be ready to receive the troops on the 3d of next month, are unanimously of opinion that such a move will not be advisable, as a delay would thereby be risked to the principal object above stated.

[Extract from Cornwallis to Clinton. Yorktown, Virginia, September 29, 1781.]

I have ventured these last two days to look General Washington's whole force in the face, *in the position on the outside of my works;* and I have the pleasure to assure Your Excellency that there was but one wish throughout the whole army, which was that the enemy would advance.

I have this evening received your letter of the 24th, which has given me the greatest satisfaction.[89]

I shall retire this night within the works. *And [I] have no doubt, if relief arrives in any reasonable time, York and Gloucester will both be in possession of His Majesty's troops.* Medicines are wanted. [Stevens, *Clinton-Cornwallis Controversy, 2,* 169–170.]

88. Clinton's note reads "arising from his sense of the unfinished state of his works." It is not clear whether the phrase modifies "*retreat*" or "the expression 'worst.'" The italics throughout this extract are in the original.

89. See above, p. 574 and n. 87.

[Copy of a letter from Clinton to Cornwallis. September 30, 1781.]

My Lord:

Your Lordship may be assured that I am doing everything in my power to relieve you by a direct move. And I have reason to hope, from the assurances given me this day by Admiral Graves, that we may pass the bar by the 12th of October, if the winds permit and no unforeseen accident happens.

This, however, is subject to disappointment. Wherefore, if I hear from you, your wishes will of course direct me; and I shall persist in my idea of a direct move even to the middle of November, should it be Your Lordship's opinion that you can hold out so long. But, if when I hear from you you tell me that you cannot, and I am without hopes of arriving in time to succor you by a direct move, I will immediately make an attempt on Philadelphia by land—giving you notice, if possible, of my intention. If this should draw any part of Washington's force from you, *it may possibly give you an opportunity of doing something to save your army,* of which, however, you can best judge from being upon the spot. I have the honor, etc., Henry Clinton. [*Ibid.,* pp. 172–173.]

Extract from Colonel Gould's letter to Sir Henry Clinton. [September 30, 1781.]

I have the honor to acquaint Your Excellency that Lord Rawdon, after his return from Ninety-six, left the charge of the army at Orangeburg to Lieutenant Colonel Stewart of the Third Regiment. Upon His Lordship's embarking for England he resigned the command of the army on the frontier to my direction.

I would immediately have taken the command of the army in person but that, as Lieutenant General Leslie was hourly expected to arrive at Charleston, I remained there to receive his instructions, which I had reason to believe would have ordered me to the northward.

Lieutenant Colonel Stewart, having remained two days on the field of action [at Eutaw Springs], fell back on the 11th instant to Colleton's House, near Monk's Corner, in order to take care of his wounded and refresh his troops. At this place I joined him on the 12th instant and took the command of the army.

On the 14th instant I received intelligence that General Greene had taken post at Martin's Tavern, twelve miles distant from our camp, and had secured with his light troops the difficult pass at Ferguson's

Swamp, four miles in his front, from whence he had in person reconnoitered our position. I moved forward on the evening of the 16th,
with design to bring the enemy to action or force them to cross the
Santee. Upon the first intelligence of our movement Greene quitted
his position and retired hastily to the Santee, where, dividing his force
into three parts, he passed the whole at different ferries nearly at one
time, destroying or carefully concealing on the opposite side all his
boats to impede our pursuit. Having crossed the river, General Greene
moved to the high hills of Santee and took post on very strong ground
at Singleton's Mills, which he occupied before the action.

As I found it impracticable to get up with the enemy before they
had crossed the river; and, as it was not possible to pass the army over
for the want of boats, I took the resolution of falling down the banks
of the Santee toward Murray's Ferry, where alone I could subsist my
army without drawing upon the King's stores at Charleston, the upper
country being totally exhausted. I was further determined to this movement by the reports I received from Lieutenant Colonel Balfour of
the appearance of the French fleet on the coast and the uncertainty of
its destination, as I did not conceive it advisable to be at too great a
distance from Charleston in the event that this province should prove
to be their object. I propose falling down gradually toward Monk's Corner, where I shall remain a few days to clothe some of the troops that
are naked, and to put the whole in a state for the next campaign.

[Extract of minutes of a council of war] held at New York.
October 2d, 1781.

Present: General Sir Henry Clinton; Lieutenant Generals Knyphausen, Robertson, and Leslie; Major General Paterson; and Brigadier
General [the] Earl of Lincoln.

The Commander in Chief told the board that his own ideas were
first to endeavor to force a junction with Lord Cornwallis by the York
River, landing if possible immediately at Yorktown but, if that was
not practicable, landing on the Gloucester side and passing the river
from our post there to York. But, if a landing on either side York
River should be found impracticable, the fleet should run up James
River and put the troops on shore at Newport News and, after communicating with Lord Cornwallis, determine on some mode of effecting a junction with him or saving as great a part of his army as possible.

[He added] that these were only his own suggestions of what might
be proper to be done in case he did not hear again from Lord Cornwallis.
But, should His Lordship favor him with his opinions respecting the

best mode of effecting a junction (as he had requested), he should most probably be guided by them.

Unanimously approved.[90]

> [Extract of Cornwallis to Clinton. Yorktown, Virginia, October 3, 1781.]

I received your letter of the 25th of September last night.[91]

The enemy are encamped about two miles from us. On the night of the 30th of September they broke ground and made two redoubts (about eleven hundred yards from our works) *which, with some works that had been constructed to secure our exterior position, occupy a gorge between two creeks which nearly embrace this post;* they have finished those redoubts, and I expect they will go on with their works this night. *From the time that the enemy has given us, and the uncommon exertions of the troops, our works are in a better state of defense than we had reason to hope.*

I can see no means of *forming a junction with me but by York River.* And I do not think that any diversion would be of use to us. [Stevens, *Clinton-Cornwallis Controversy,* 2, 174–175.]

> Extract from minutes of a council of war held at New York. October 10, 1781.

Present: all the general officers [as on October 2].

Resolved that the three following plans shall be communicated to Lord Cornwallis as soon as possible:

First, in case it shall be found absolutely impracticable to form the junction by going directly to York or from the Gloucester side, and it shall in consequence be determined to proceed up James River, the troops will land at Newport News, from whence they will advance on the James River road to some favorable position in communication with that river, where they will wait until information arrives from Lord Cornwallis or circumstances may make it proper for them to co-operate with His Lordship in effecting a junction of the two armies— which it is at present the opinion of the general officers will be best done without his lines, in preference to an attempt of doing it within.

90. *Clinton's note:* These resolutions [were] communicated to Major Cochrane (with every other requisite information for Lord Cornwallis' guidance), who was dispatched to the Chesapeake the next day in a whaleboat, and joined His Lordship on the 10th. [The note adds that Cochrane carried Clinton's letter of Sept. 30, for which see above, p. 578.]

91. The letter added little to that of the previous day. It is printed in Stevens, *Clinton-Cornwallis Controversy,* 2, 163–164.

Second, the junction with Lord Cornwallis to be attempted by a combined move, this army moving up James River to Jamestown, and His Lordship's up the York River to either Queen's Creek or Cappahosic Ferry, and the two meeting each other as near Williamsburg as they can—thereby putting themselves in a situation to attack the enemy should such an attempt be judged advisable.

Third, to save as great a part of Lord Cornwallis' corps as possible by bringing them off to Jamestown, which may be done by this army giving a jealousy to the enemy from Newport News or Mulberry Island whilst Lord Cornwallis, moving as many of his troops as he can in boats up York River, lands either at Queen's Creek or Cappahosic and makes the best of his way to Jamestown.

His Lordship to be at the same time informed that the above is the opinion of the general officers of what may be proper to be done in case nothing more comes from him. But, if he should suggest other ideas to the Commander in Chief, they will of course be governed by them.

Copy of a letter from Earl Cornwallis to Sir Henry Clinton. Yorktown, Virginia, 12 M., 11 October 1781.

Sir:

Cochrane arrived yesterday. I have only to repeat what I said in my letter of the 3d, that nothing but a direct move to York River—which includes a successful naval action—*can save me.*

The enemy made their first parallel on the night of the 6th at a distance of 600 yards, and perfected it and constructed places of arms and batteries with great regularity and caution. On the evening of the 9th their batteries opened, and have since continued firing without intermission with about forty pieces of cannon (mostly heavy), and sixteen mortars from eight to sixteen inches. We have lost about seventy men, and many of our works are considerably damaged. *With such works on disadvantageous ground, against so powerful an attack, we cannot hope to make a long resistance.*

I have the honor, etc., Cornwallis.

P.S., 5 P.M. Since the above was written, we have lost thirty men.

[P.S.,] October 12. We continue to lose men very fast.[92] [Stevens, *Clinton-Cornwallis Controversy, 2,* 176–177.]

92. This second postscript is a mystery. The original ciphered dispatch and two deciphered copies (filed under Oct. 19 in the CP) conclude with the first postscript. The second, however, is added in the copy entered in the letterbook in "Correspondence with Cornwallis," and in Clinton's note in his history.

Extract of a letter from Rear Admiral Graves to Sir Henry Clinton. *London,* off New York, 17 October 1781.

There has, I hope, been no mistake. For, as we cannot sail until about ten o'clock this forenoon, and can then go but little below Denyses, I would not give you unnecessary alarm; and meant to have sent an officer at eight o'clock, when I should have explained to Your Excellency that all this show of signals and topsails were no other than so many spurs to push forward the lazy and supine. And I am sorry to find that *difficulties go on increasing, and that nothing can turn the current* but being actually at sea.

Extracts from the articles of capitulation between General Washington, Lieutenant General the Count de Rochambeau, and the Count de Grasse on the one part, and the Right Honorable Lieutenant General Earl Cornwallis and [Captain] Thomas Symonds, [R.N.,] Esq., on the other. [October 19, 1781.]

Article 1. The garrisons of York and Gloucester, including the officers and seamen of His Britannic Majesty's ships as well as other mariners, to surrender themselves prisoners of war to the combined forces of America and France. The land troops to remain prisoners to the United States, the navy to the naval army of His Most Christian Majesty. Granted.

Article 4. Officers are to retain their side arms. Both officers and soldiers to keep their private property of every kind, and no part of their baggage or papers to be at any time subject to search or inspection. The baggage and papers of officers and soldiers taken during the siege to be likewise preserved for them. Granted; it is understood that any property obviously belonging to the inhabitants of these states in the possession of the garrison shall be subject to be reclaimed.

Article 8. The *Bonetta,* sloop of war, to be equipped and navigated by its present captain and crew and left entirely at the disposal of Lord Cornwallis from the hour that the capitulation is signed, to receive an aide-de-camp to carry dispatches to Sir Henry Clinton. And such soldiers as he may think proper to send to New York to be permitted to sail without examination when his dispatches are ready. His Lordship engages on his part that the ship shall be delivered to the order of the Count de Grasse if she escapes the danger of the seas, [and] that she shall not carry off any public stores. Any part of the crew that may be deficient on her return, and the soldiers passengers, to be accounted for on her delivery. Granted.

Article 10. Natives or inhabitants of different parts of this country at present in York or Gloucester are *not to be punished* on account of having joined the British army. Answer: this article cannot be assented to, being altogether of civil resort.

Article 14. No article of the capitulation to be infringed on pretense of reprisals. And, if there be any doubtful expressions in it, they are to be interpreted according to the common meaning and acceptation of the words. Granted.

Done in the trenches before York, October 19, 1781. [Tarleton, *History,* pp. 438–442.]

> Extract of a letter from Earl Cornwallis to Sir Henry Clinton. Yorktown, Virginia, 20 October 1781 (received on board the *London* at the Hook, 3d November).

I have the mortification to inform Your Excellency that I have been forced to give up the posts of York and Gloucester and to surrender the troops under my command by capitulation, on the 19th instant, as prisoners of war to the combined forces of America and France.

I never saw this post in a favorable light. But, when I found I was to be attacked in it in so unprepared a state by so powerful an army and artillery, nothing but the hopes of relief would have induced me to attempt its defense. For I would either have endeavored to escape to New York by rapid marches from the Gloucester side immediately on the arrival of General Washington's troops at Williamsburg, or I would, notwithstanding the disparity of numbers, have attacked them in the open field, where it might have been just possible that fortune would have favored the gallantry of the handful of troops under my command. *But, being assured by Your Excellency's letters that every possible means would be tried by the navy and army to relieve us,* I could not think myself at liberty to venture on either of those desperate attempts. Therefore, after remaining two days *in a strong position in front of this place in hopes of being attacked,* upon observing that the enemy were taking measures which could not fail *of turning my left flank in a short time,* and receiving the second evening your letter of the 24th of September informing me *that the relief would sail about the 5th of October,* I withdrew within the works on the night of the 29th of September, hoping by the labor and firmness of the soldiers *to protract the defense until you could arrive.*

Everything was to be expected from the spirit of the troops. But every disadvantage attended their labor, *as the works were to be continued under the enemy's fire;* and our stock of entrenching tools, which *did not much exceed 400 when we began to work in the latter end of August,* was now much diminished. The enemy broke ground on the night of the 30th and constructed on that night and the two following days and nights two redoubts *which, with some works that had belonged to our outward position,* occupied a gorge between two creeks or ravines which come from the river on each side of the town. On the night of the 6th of October they made their first parallel, extending from its right on the river to a deep ravine on the left, nearly opposite to the center of this place and embracing our whole left at the distance of 600 yards.

Having perfected this parallel, their batteries opened on the evening of the 9th against our left; and other batteries fired at the same time against a redoubt advanced over the creek upon our right and defended by about 120 men of the Twenty-third Regiment and marines, who maintained that post with uncommon gallantry. The fire continued incessant from heavy cannon, and from mortars and howitzers throwing shells from eight to sixteen inches, until all our guns on the left were silenced, our works much damaged, and our loss of men considerable. On the night of the 11th they began their second parallel about 300 yards nearer to us. The troops being much weakened by sickness as well as by the fire of the besiegers, and observing that the enemy had not only secured their flanks but proceeded in every respect with the utmost regularity and caution, I could not venture so large sorties as to hope from them any considerable effect. But otherwise I did everything in my power to interrupt their work, by opening new embrasures for guns and keeping up a constant fire with all the howitzers and small mortars that we could man.

On the evening of the 14th they assaulted and carried two redoubts that had been advanced about 300 yards for the purpose of delaying their approaches and covering our left flank, and during the night included them in their second parallel, on which they continued to work with the utmost exertion. Being perfectly sensible that our works could not stand many hours after the opening of the batteries of that parallel, we not only continued a constant fire with all our mortars and every gun that could be brought to bear upon it, but a little before daybreak on the morning of the 16th I ordered a sortie of about three hundred and fifty men under the direction of Lieutenant Colonel Abercromby, to attack two batteries which appeared to be in the greatest forwardness and to spike the guns. A detachment of Guards with the Eightieth Company of grenadiers under the command of Lieutenant Colonel Lake attacked the one, and one of light infantry under the command of Major Armstrong attacked the other; and both succeeded, by forcing the redoubts that covered them, spiking eleven guns, and killing and wounding about one hundred of the French troops who had the guard of that part of the trenches, and with little loss on our side. This action, though extremely honorable to the officers and soldiers who executed it, proved of little public advantage. For the cannon, having been spiked in a hurry, were soon rendered fit for service again; and before dark the whole parallel and batteries appeared to be nearly complete.

At this time we knew that there was no part of the whole front attacked in which we could show a single gun, and our shells were nearly expended. I had, therefore, only to choose between preparing to surrender next day or endeavoring to get off with the greatest part of the troops; and I determined to attempt the latter, reflecting that, though it should prove unsuccessful in its immediate object, it might at least delay the enemy in the prosecution of further enterprises. Sixteen large boats were prepared and, upon other pretexts, were ordered to be in readiness to receive troops precisely at ten o'clock. With these I hoped to pass the infantry during the night, abandoning our baggage and leaving a detachment to capitulate for the townspeople and for the sick and wounded, on which subject a letter was ready to be delivered to General Washington. After making my arrangements with the utmost secrecy, the light infantry, greatest part of the Guards, and part of the Twenty-third Regiment embarked at the hour appointed; and most of them landed at Gloucester.

But at this critical moment the weather, from being moderate and calm, changed to a most violent storm of wind and rain and drove all the boats, some of which had troops on board, down the river. It was soon evident that the intended passage was impracticable, and the absence of the boats rendered it equally impossible to bring back the troops that had passed, which I had ordered about two o'clock in the morning. In this situation, with my little force divided, the enemy's batteries opened at daybreak. The passage between this place and Gloucester was much exposed. But, the boats having now returned, they were ordered to bring back the troops that had passed during the night; and they joined us in the forenoon without much loss.

Our works in the meantime were going to ruin. And, not having been able to strengthen them by abatis nor in any other manner than by a slight fraising (which the enemy's artillery were demolishing wherever they fired), my opinion entirely coincided with that of the engineer and principal officers of the army that they were in many parts very assailable in the forenoon, and that by the continuance of the same fire for a few hours longer they would be in such a state as to render it desperate, with our numbers, to attempt to maintain them. We at that time could not fire a single gun: only one eight-inch and little more than one hundred cohorn shells remained. A diversion by the French ships of war that lay at the mouth of York River was to be expected. Our numbers had been diminished by the enemy's fire, but particularly by sickness; and the strength and spirits of those in the works were much exhausted by the fatigue of constant watching and unremitting duty.

Under all these circumstances I thought it would have been wanton and inhuman to the last degree to sacrifice the lives of this small body of gallant soldiers—who had ever behaved with so much fidelity and courage—by exposing them to an assault which, from the numbers and precautions of the enemy, could not fail to succeed. I therefore proposed to capitulate; and I have the honor to enclose to Your Excellency the copy of the correspondence between General Washington and me on that subject, and the terms of capitulation agreed upon. I sincerely lament that better could not be obtained, but I have neglected nothing to alleviate the misfortune and distress of both officers and soldiers. The men are well clothed and provided with necessaries and, I trust, will be regularly supplied by the means of the officers that are permitted to remain with them.

The treatment in general that we have received from the enemy since our surrender has been perfectly good and proper. But the kindness and attention that has been shown to us by the French officers in particular—their delicate sensibility of our situation, their generous and pressing offers of money, both public and private, to any amount—has really gone beyond what I can possibly describe and will, I hope, make an impression on the breast of every British officer whenever the fortune of war should put any of them into our power. Although the event has been so unfortunate, the patience of the soldiers in bearing the greatest fatigues, and their firmness and intrepidity under a persevering fire of shot and shells that I believe has not often been exceeded, deserved the highest commendation and praise.

A successful defense, however, in our situation was perhaps impossible. For the place could only be reckoned an entrenched camp, subject in most places to enfilade, and the ground in general so disadvantageous that nothing but the necessity of fortifying it as a post to protect the navy could have induced any person to erect works upon it. Our force diminished daily by sickness and other losses, and was reduced when we offered to capitulate on this side to little more than 3200 rank and file fit for duty, including officers, servants, and artificers, and at Gloucester to about 600, including cavalry. The enemy's army consisted of upward of 8000 French, nearly as many Continentals, and

5000 militia. They brought an immense train of heavy artillery, most amply furnished with ammunition and perfectly well manned.

The constant and universal cheerfulness and spirit of the officers in all hardship and danger deserve my warmest acknowledgments. And I cannot sufficiently acknowledge my obligations to Captain Symonds, who commanded His Majesty's ships, and to the officers and seamen of the navy for their zealous and active cooperation.[93] [Stevens, *Clinton-Cornwallis Controversy*, 2, 205–216.]

Extract of a letter from Sir Henry Clinton to Lord George Germain. *London,* off Chesapeake Bay, 29 October 1781.

This is a blow, My Lord, which gives me the most serious concern, as it will in its consequences be exceedingly detrimental to the King's interests in this country and might, I flatter myself, have possibly been prevented could the fleet have been able to sail at, or within a few days of, the time we first expected. At least I am persuaded we should have saved to His Majesty's service great part of that gallant army, together with its respectable chief, whose loss it will be now, I fear, impossible to repair.

When Sir Samuel Hood goes to the West Indies, I am inclined to suppose it probable that, if de Grasse's fleet does not follow him, the enemy's next operations will be against our posts in Carolina and Georgia, which I am apprehensive may fall (as every other certainly will) if they are not succored in time by a superior fleet. These, My Lord, were the ideas I entertained with respect to those in Chesapeake, as I had the honor of suggesting to Your Lordship *even before you honored me with the King's commands to carry on operation there.* And Your Lordship's former letters, as well as your dispatch Number 87,[94] encouraged me to expect that our fleet here would not only have been augmented at least in proportion to that of the enemy, but that our naval reinforcement would have arrived on this coast even before theirs.

Your Lordship will therefore, of course, suppose that my surprise was great when I heard de Grasse had brought with him twenty-eight sail

93. *Clinton's note:* Loss of the British army during the siege: one hundred and fifty-six killed, three hundred and twenty-six wounded, and seventy missing; total, five hundred and fifty-two.

Lord Cornwallis' deputy Adjutant General's return of the troops surrendered at York and Gloucester:

Surrendered at York: 385 sergeants, 165 dummers, 5014 rank and file.

Gloucester:	91	" , 39	" , 936	"	"	" .
	476	" , 204	" , 5950	"	"	" ,

of which about 1900 rank and file were sick.

94. Of July 7, 1781; see above, p. 540.

of the line while Sir Samuel Hood had only fourteen, and one of these in such bad condition that it was found necessary to destroy her at sea soon after the action of the 5th *ultimo*. *To this inferiority*, then, I may with confidence assert, *and to that alone*, is our present misfortune to be imputed. Nor will the evil end here, My Lord. For I beg leave to prophesy, as I did of those [operations] in Chesapeake, that we hold every station we have in this country at risk if the enemy retains a naval superiority in these seas only for a few weeks.

> Extract of a letter from Lieutenant General Leslie to Sir Henry Clinton. Charleston, November 30, 1781 (received December 16th).

I have now the pleasure to inform you of the safe arrival of Major Craig with his detachment from Wilmington, and that they brought off all the loyalists who wished to accompany them. I found the corps under Colonel Stewart, consisting of 1700 infantry and 200 cavalry, posted a few miles above Monk's Corner waiting the movements of the rebel army, which has been on the high hills of Santee since the action at the Eutaws. But upon the approach of their reinforcements from Virginia, which are now near at hand, Greene has moved across the Santee; and I have directed Colonel Stewart to fall down on this side of Goose Creek. This movement I have been led to make, not only to avoid any decisive action, but from the present disposition of the army, which I am with regret obliged to say appears *to want confidence in a great degree*.

The strength of the whole army here is not at present above thirty-five hundred men fit for duty, and those composed of thirty different corps. This great weakness has been owing chiefly to the action at the Eutaws, to a great sickness and the smaller actions which have very frequently happened during the summer, and which have been attended with great losses.

By this Your Excellency will see the impossibility of sparing any large reinforcements to Georgia or Florida. These provinces are certainly by no means in force to resist any attack of a serious nature; but, unless I run great risks here, they cannot be aided from hence. Fearing, however, that Savannah might be the immediate object of Greene (who is now actually in motion), I propose sending the remains of the Seventh Regiment there and making up a corps nearly of 200 men for that place, trusting that they may be able to defend it, if attacked, until reinforcements arrive from Your Excellency—and without which I do not foresee that we can hold any part of the country or go beyond our camp at the Quarter House, as I am clear (without some additional force immediately sent, both in infantry and artillery) the greatest part of our present possessions in this district must inevitably fall.

I have established posts at Stono and John's Island, and will try to keep the islands as long as I can, as our only hope of supplies to this town depends upon them. But the numbers of loyal inhabitants and of helpless refugees, with their women and children, is very great. They are burdens that will soon become very serious, and I must request Your Excellency's instructions respecting the support that I should allow them. And provisions is an object of so great importance that, unless the inhabitants get some supply, they must all leave the town. [Calendared in Hist. MSS Com., *American MSS in the Royal Institution, 2,* 357.]

> Extract of a letter from the Honorable Colonel Robert Conway to Sir Henry Clinton, to whom he was aide-de-camp, dated 5th December 1781, [he] having been sent to England with this General's dispatches.

As it is now more than probable that you are fixed at least for some time at New York, it is necessary that I now acquaint you that I have to the best of my abilities fulfilled the several purposes of my mission: that I, till Lord Cornwallis' failure was known, endeavored as your messenger and representative to prevent despondency in the public without exciting any very sanguine hopes in them; that I have had many opportunities of doing justice to your zeal and exertions in private conversations, the particulars of which—as the names of the persons with whom they have been held—I dare not name even to you on paper. Suffice it to say that people of all ranks, parties, and descriptions ardently wish you to preserve the command you hold in America. And I verily believe that it would have been almost as general a wish had Lord Cornwallis' army proved in offense as well as defense ever so successful.

The Minister, Lord George Germain, to whom on my arrival I scrupled not freely to say in what instances you conceived yourself to have been ill treated by him and to what motives you ascribed such ill treatment, declared to me that you had thoroughly mistaken his wishes as well as conduct with respect to the command—that he had no connection whatever with, or partiality for, the second in command; that he never recommended your having leave to withdraw yourself from America upon any other principle and with any other view than as conceiving you were yourself out of humor, and that the public service was in all cases interested in employing officers pleased with the service they were engaged [on]; and that, as proof of his opinion of your abilities, he had submitted some time ago to the King your reasoning and opinions on Lord Cornwallis' operations in the Carolinas and subsequent move into Virginia as *remarkably* able and just. This much was I desired at the time by His Lordship to repeat to you.

Would to God that, however just your conclusions in that reasoning may have been, your predictions had not been so fully verified by a late melancholy catastrophe!

> Extract of a letter from Sir Henry Clinton to Lord George Germain. New York, December 6, 1781.

I have so often had the honor of delivering the same sentiments to Your Lordship that I must beg your pardon for again troubling you with the repetition that I have ever been of opinion *that operation should not be undertaken in the Chesapeake without having a naval superiority in these seas;* and to the want of it, and perhaps to that alone, are we to impute our late misfortune in that quarter. Therefore, when I did myself the honor of sending you a copy of Lord Cornwallis' letter to me of the 20th of October, I did not think it necessary to trouble Your Lordship with any remarks on some passages of it which might seem to imply *that His Lordship had been forced into a bad post by my orders, notwithstanding he had represented its defects, and had been induced to remain there contrary to his own judgment by the positive assurances I had given him of relief*—especially as Your Lordship was possessed of our correspondence, which could in the fullest manner invalidate every implication of the sort, and [as] I wished to have an opportunity of speaking to Lord Cornwallis before I said anything upon so delicate a subject.

No man, My Lord, can feel more sensibly than I did for the unhappy situation of Lord Cornwallis and his gallant army, whose meritorious conduct, spirit, and zeal on all occasions must heighten our anxiety and concern for their present fate. And therefore, as His Lordship is pleased to tell me that his letter of the 20th of October was written under great agitation of mind and in great hurry, which might possibly have prevented his adverting to the implications which it may be thought to bear, I cannot at present wish to give His Lordship more trouble on the subject; as I cannot doubt, if the passages in that letter should be understood in Europe in any respect to my prejudice, but His Lordship will have candor enough most formally to disavow his having any such intentions. But, if His Lordship, contrary to my expectations, shall not be inclined to do so, I must be obliged, though reluctantly, most earnestly to request Your Lordship to render me that justice which I am persuaded you think me entitled to by publishing this letter.[95] [Stevens, *Clinton-Cornwallis Controversy*, 2, 233–234, 238–239.]

Extract of a letter from Lieutenant Colonel Clarke to Sir Henry Clinton. Savannah, December 20th, 1781.

I am sorry to inform Your Excellency that the tenth article of the capitulation of Yorktown has made a very alarming impression on the minds of the people in general, and that I have just grounds of apprehension that it will amount to so *considerable a defection* of the militia —if our situation should become more critical—as to leave us but very little hopes of any material assistance from them, many having already gone off. [Calendared in Hist. MSS Com., *American MSS in the Royal Institution*, 2, 366.]

Extract of a letter from Sir Henry Clinton to Lieutenant General Leslie. New York, December 20, 1781.

With respect *to the want of confidence* in the army which you mentioned in your ciphered letter, I must entreat that you will order a strict inquiry to be made into the cause of it, and favor me with your opinion thereon. For, as you have not been sufficiently explicit on this subject, I am totally at a loss to conjecture the meaning of it. If it should be owing to a relaxation of discipline in some of the regiments, that may be easily recovered; and I shall of course expect everything from your abilities and the high opinion the troops entertain of you. But I must request, sir, that in future you will have the goodness to be more explicit upon points of such importance. For, as I think it my duty in these times to transmit to administration copies of all letters of consequence which I receive relative to the army under my command, I was under the necessity of sending your last without explanation on either of those material subjects, the strength of your army or the cause of its want of confidence.

In regard to our keeping possession of much of the Province of South Carolina, as it is not to be done with less force than a covering army equal to Greene's, which cannot now be spared, we must therefore content ourselves with the islands which you have so judiciously secured by the posts of Stono and John's Island. I am inclined to think as you do with respect to General Greene's intentions of attacking

95. *Clinton's note:* This letter was, notwithstanding, neither published, nor even produced before the House of Lords when Sir Henry Clinton's correspondence with the Secretary of State was called for.

Savannah. It may therefore be worth our consideration whether the chance of retaining that post alone, now that the rest of the province is gone from us, is an object of sufficient importance to risk, etc. Wherefore I think it right to leave you at liberty to attempt the defense of Savannah or not, as you may from the circumstances stated judge best for His Majesty's service.

It being probable that in the present situation of affairs in Carolina you will not be able to extend yourself to any considerable distance from Charleston, I would recommend to you the measure of reducing the number of your cavalry as low as it can be done with propriety. Such officers and men as belong to the corps in the southern district are directed to proceed thither by the present conveyance.

The Commissary of Accounts sends a deputy by my directions to reside at Charleston, agreeable to your request, with instructions for his conduct which he will lay before you on his arrival, and receive your orders. I must request that you will be pleased to order a particular inquiry to be made respecting the loss of the hospital at Colleton, and transmit a report thereof to me. I have permitted several merchant ships with provisions to take the benefit of the present convoy for Charleston, which I hope will in some degree relieve the inhabitants. With respect to the refugees, whatever orders Lord Cornwallis gave and the Minister approved regarding them must be supported as far as it may be practicable; and for your further information on this head I send you a copy of the instructions I gave to Colonel Morris, the inspector of the claims of refugees in this district, which will show how this matter has been conducted here.

[Extract of the minutes of a council of war held at New York. January 17, 1782.]

Present are the general officers [Clinton, Knyphausen, Robertson, Dalrymple, and Paterson] and Rear Admiral Digby.

The Commander in Chief told the board that he was clearly of opinion that something ought to be done very speedily to confirm the confidence of the loyalists, either by public assurances of protection or by an order to the officers commanding in the different principal posts of New York, Charleston, and Savannah not to propose or accept any terms from the enemy in which the interests and security of the loyalists were not equally attended to with those of the troops. But [he said] that he could not accede to the propriety of his issuing a proclamation threatening retaliation, etc., as proposed by General Robertson at the last meeting [on January 14], because military retaliation would by no means put us upon a footing with the punishments the loyalists apprehended from the rebel jurisdictions, and would be particularly improper at the present hour, when the enemy had so considerable a part of our army in their power.

But, if General Robertson thought a threat of retaliation was requisite to put us on a level with the enemy and quiet the minds of the loyalists, and was of opinion that the civil courts were equal to it, he should have no objection as commander in chief to their being opened in this province whenever he [Robertson] as civil governor represented to him the necessity of it. To which General Robertson made answer that he was not competent to judge of the power of the civil courts, or how far the opening them might be effectual in the case in question; but he would consult those better informed of these matters than himself, and let His Excellency know their opinion.

The board then gave their opinion that, if the Commander in Chief sent the following order to General Leslie and Colonel Clarke, it would most probably satisfy the loyalists, not only in that quarter but every other in rebellion:

"As it is my most earnest and fervent wish to give every possible protection to all His Majesty's loyal subjects, and to remove from their minds every cause of apprehension, I desire that you will endeavor to restore the confidence of those in your quarter by the fullest assurances that the Commander in Chief and every officer under his command *will pay the same attention to the interests and security of all His Majesty's loyal subjects of every denomination and country, in all cases whatsoever, that they do to those of the troops under their orders; and that they will not on any occasion or in any event make the least distinction or discrimination between them.*" [Calendared in Hist. MSS Com., *American MSS in the Royal Institution*, 2, 382.]

[Extract of the minutes of a council of war held at New York. January 23, 1782.]

Present as before [on January 17].

Upon the Commander in Chief's signifying to General Robertson his willingness not to oppose his revival of civil government if he was of opinion that the exercise of civil jurisdiction was absolutely necessary to put us upon a level with the enemy (by opposing the threats of civil punishments to those General Washington seemed to hold out in his answer to the tenth article of the capitulation of Yorktown [96]), the General said that, when he gave an opinion the other day respecting the

96. See above, p. 583.

Commander in Chief's issuing a proclamation threatening retaliation, he had no idea about the revival of civil government, and that he thought the expedient of sending the order agreed to at the last meeting to the different posts of the army was better than the proclamation proposed and would, he believed, answer every purpose of quieting the minds of the loyalists.

Much conversation afterward ensued upon the impropriety of reviving civil government in this province at this time, and of the general inconveniences and obstructions which would accrue from it to the operations of the army whilst the country remained in a state of war—of which every general officer present, together with the Admiral, appeared to be equally sensible, and no one to think differently. They therefore unanimously approved of the measure which had been taken by the Commander in Chief, and agreed that it would be proper to communicate it likewise to Governor Franklin for the information and satisfaction of the loyalists in this place. And General Robertson said that he would, if the Commander in Chief pleased, take the opinion of principal persons amongst them upon it, and let him know what they said. To which the Commander in Chief agreed, and left the General at liberty still to revive civil government if he thought it absolutely requisite for the purposes desired. [Calendared in *ibid.*, p. 385.]

Extract of a letter from Lieutenant General Leslie to Sir Henry Clinton. Charleston, January 29th, 1782.

The army is now well clothed and recovered from its sickness and the fatigue it underwent during the last summer. As you may easily suppose, sir, the people of the country are daily coming in to us to seek that protection which, though entailing a burden on ourselves, is not to be refused them. I regret the heavy and increasing expense of provisions and money incurred by this means, and by the militia now with us; but their misery and helpless situation justifies our attention to them, though perhaps their services are not to be esteemed an equivalent.

The men of the Legion and Lieutenant Colonel Simcoe's corps shall be sent by the first opportunity. The Guards and the very small number of General de Bose's Regiment here are directed to be prepared to embark when ordered. These drafts, Your Excellency will please to recollect, must weaken my effective force, which I conceived was not more than sufficient for the necessary and essential defense of this town and dependencies. I must observe, sir, that (whatever the world may expect from me) Your Excellency, being now perfectly informed of the actual force under my orders as well as of my situation in other matters, *can hope for nothing material from offensive operation.* Every exertion within the power of that force shall be employed wherever an opportunity shall offer. [Calendared in *ibid.,* p. 388.]

[Copy of Germain to Clinton. Whitehall, February 6, 1782 (received April 27).]

Sir:

The Duke of Newcastle having applied to me in your name that I would obtain His Majesty's permission for you to quit the command in North America, that you might return immediately to England, I have the pleasure to inform you that His Majesty has been graciously pleased to comply with your request. And I am to signify to you His Majesty's pleasure that you embark for England the first convenient opportunity, and that you resign the command of the King's forces to Major General Robertson, leaving with him all papers and instructions which may be necessary for his information to enable him to discharge the important trust committed to him. He will, by this packet, receive a commission as commander in chief of all His Majesty's forces in the colonies in North America lying upon the Atlantic Ocean.[97]

I am, sir, etc., George Germain.

Copy of a resolution proposed by General Conway and passed by the House of Commons on the 4th of March, 1782.

Resolved that, after the solemn declaration of the opinion of this House in their humble address presented to His Majesty on Friday last and His Majesty's assurance of his gracious intention, in pursuance of their advice, to take such measures as shall appear to His Majesty to be most conducive to the restoration of harmony between Great Britain and the revolted colonies, so essential to the prosperity of both, this House will consider as enemies to His Majesty and this country all who shall endeavor to frustrate His Majesty's paternal care for the ease and happiness of his people *by advising or by any means attempting the further prosecution of offensive war on the continent of North*

97. Clinton, in an undated and uncatalogued memorandum in the CP, comments that Robertson had long been hoping to get the command, if Sir Henry resigned and Cornwallis was forced out by his own blunders. "The old gentleman had nearly the foresight of his country! Lord Cornwallis did blunder on till he lost his army; I was permitted to resign; and he was appointed Commander in Chief in my absence by Lord George Germain. But Sir Guy Carleton was afterward prevailed on to come out, as he told me, lest I should have set sail and left the command to Robertson."

America for the purpose of reducing the revolted colonies to obedience by force. [*Journals of the House of Commons,* 38 (for 1780–82; 1803), 868.]

[Extract of minutes of a council of war held at New York. March 8, 1782.]

Present: General Sir Henry Clinton; Lieutenant Generals Knyphausen and Robertson; Major Generals O'Hara, Paterson, and Dalrymple; Rear Admiral Digby assisted.

The Commander in Chief suggested to the board that joint operations with the navy against the posts and towns upon the seacoasts of the revolted provinces, for destroying their shipping and stores and obstructing their trade, might have the greatest advantages, and may be necessary to prevent them from acting offensively against us. Under this idea he had long since meditated a move up the Delaware, in the hopes of being able to take or destroy the shipping, military stores, flour, etc., collected there and, by seizing their bank, destroy the enemy's public credit and distract their counsels, and eventually bring off such a part of the prisoners of Lord Cornwallis' army as might be fortunate enough to make use of that opportunity of escaping to him.

The Admiral expressed his opinion that no French fleet would come upon the coast before the latter end of April.

Captain Beckwith [was] called in, and read intelligence lately received from a person at Philadelphia representing the state of the forts, *chevaux-de-frise,* watch boats, guards, etc., and strongly representing the practicability of the attempt.

The council then broke up. [Calendared in Hist. MSS Com., *American MSS in the Royal Institution,* 2, 414.]

Copy of a letter from Sir Henry Clinton to the general officer commanding in the Leeward Islands. New York, March 13, 1782.

Sir:

I dispatch a runner to inform you that, in case our fleet in the Leeward Islands should have had the good fortune to defeat that of France, and you shall have required of me the assistance of troops to enable you to raise the siege of Brimstone Hill, I propose immediately upon the receipt of your requisition to send you 2000 men. But the possibility of sending them will totally depend upon our being at the time in a situation to part with them, and that the Admiral judges they may be risked with such a convoy as he shall be able to give them. I beg leave also to intimate to you that, as this army is from its present diminished state very inadequate to the defense of the King's posts under my care, I dare not venture to part with so considerable a portion of British troops (it being stipulated by treaty that those of our allies shall not be detached from the continent [98]) unless I receive your most positive assurances that these 2000 men shall be returned to me as soon as the above service is accomplished.

I have likewise the honor to mention to you that, should St. Christopher have been recovered and the enemy's armaments have gone down against Jamaica, I shall (under the same provisos) send these troops thither upon being favored with your opinion that such a reinforcement will be wanted there, and that our fleet will certainly be superior to that of the enemy, so that they may move thither without risk and be landed in safety. But, if on the contrary St. Christopher should have fallen and our fleet in the Leeward Islands be inferior to that of the enemy, I certainly shall not judge it advisable to weaken my army by detaching to such a distance, as I think there can be little doubt the enemy's whole force will in that case finally come against these posts.

I have the honor, etc., Henry Clinton.

Extract of a letter from Sir Henry Clinton to Lord George Germain. New York, March 14, 1782.

I was well aware, My Lord, of the dangerous tendency of the tenth article of the capitulation of Yorktown, and took immediate pains to quiet the refugees in this quarter, who began to be very clamorous. But, as I every hour expected the arrival of Lord Cornwallis, out of delicacy to His Lordship I postponed taking any public measures in consequence, or saying anything to Your Lordship on the subject, until I saw him.

What I have since done respecting this business Your Lordship will have been informed [of] by my dispatch Number 153.[99] And I now

98. The treaties by which the British government had hired its German mercenaries. The provision in question is in the ninth article of the agreement with the Landgraf of Hesse Cassel, printed in Friedrich Kapp, *Der Soldatenhandel deutscher Fürsten nach Amerika: Ein Beitrag zur Kulturgeschichte des achtzehnten Jahrhunderts* (Berlin, 1874), p. 258.
This letter is not in the chronological file of the CP. It was approved by a council of war on Mar. 13 and entered in full in the minutes; see the Council Book already cited, pp. 54–56.
99. Clinton to Germain, Jan. 24, 1782 (in Letterbook No. 5 in slip case, "Clinton to Secretary of State, Vols. 4–5," CP). Clinton merely mentioned that he had corresponded with Gov. Franklin, and had sent him a copy of the letter approved by the council of war of Jan. 17 and printed above, p. 593.

have the honor to acquaint you that, immediately on the receipt of Your Lordship's letter Number 96,[100] I signified the contents thereof by letter to Governor Franklin, the President of the Board of Associated Loyalists, that His Majesty's gracious declarations might be communicated to the refugees under their direction and, by printing it, be publicly made known to all the loyalists on the continent, which I judged to be a safer mode of obtaining the end I wished than by a proclamation, which I was afraid might too forcibly attract the attention of the rebels and point out to them the evils we were apprehensive of, and thereby incite them to take advantage of the alarm occasioned by the article in question by terrifying the loyalists with their threats.

> [Extract of minutes of a council of war held at New York. March 28, 1782.]

Present as before [on March 8].

The following question was stated: "Considering the expedition [against Philadelphia] as a combined move of the navy and army, is the object, from the information laid before you, of sufficient importance to justify the attempt?"

"I voted against it at a former council [on March 10] after hearing the information then produced by Major [sic] Beckwith. The intelligence afforded by that gentleman this day has not induced me to alter my opinion. W. Dalrymple."

"I am clearly of opinion that the importance of the object is not sufficient to justify the attempt in the present critical situation of the colonies. J. Paterson."

"I concur in sentiments with Major Generals Dalrymple and Paterson. Charles O'Hara."

"I think the expedition should be undertaken. James Robertson."

"Je crois que maintenant nous sommes dans une situation trop critique pour oser entreprendre cette expédition. Knyphausen."

"I am of opinion that the object would be of importance, and am ready to send such ships as shall be thought necessary. But I wish not to judge of the expediency of sending the number of forces intended from this place at this time. Robert Digby."

"I have received no information that induces me to alter my opinion.

100. Germain to Clinton, Jan. 2, 1782 (in Letterbook No. 3 in slip case, "Secretary of State to Clinton," CP). Germain forwarded the King's assurances of regard and concern for the loyalists, and added the suggestion that they might be encouraged to revolt in any area where they had the possibility of maintaining themselves with minor military support.

I therefore think that the expedition should be undertaken. Henry Clinton." [101] [Calendared in Hist. MSS Com., *American MSS in the Royal Institution, 2, 434.*]

101. Clinton was thus outvoted by four to two, with Digby abstaining. The question had first been put at the meeting of Mar. 10, attended by the same men; the vote had then been three to three, with Digby refusing to express himself at all. In the meantime Knyphausen had changed his mind and joined the opposition.

LIST OF WORKS REPEATEDLY CITED

Alden, John R. *General Charles Lee: Traitor or Patriot?* Baton Rouge, 1951.
——. *General Gage in America: Being Principally a History of His Role in the American Revolution.* Baton Rouge, 1948.
[Almon, John.] *The Remembrancer; or, Impartial Repository of Public Events.* 17 vols., London, 1775–84.
Anderson, Troyer S. *The Command of the Howe Brothers during the American Revolution.* New York and London, 1936.
Carrington, Henry B. *Battles of the American Revolution, 1775–1781: Historical and Military Criticism, with Topographical Illustration.* New York, etc., 1876.
Clark, Jane. "Responsibility for the Failure of the Burgoyne Campaign," *American Historical Review*, 35 (Apr., 1930), 542–559.
[Clinton, George.] *Public Papers of George Clinton, First Governor of New York, 1777–1795, 1801–1804.* 10 vols., New York and Albany, 1899–1914.
Clinton, Sir Henry. *A Letter from Lieut. Gen. Sir Henry Clinton, K.B., to the Commissioners of Public Accounts, Relative to Some Observations in Their Seventh Report, Which May Be Judged to Imply Censure on the Late Commander in Chief of His Majesty's Army in North America.* London, 1784.
——. *Narrative of Lieutenant-General Sir Henry Clinton, K.B., Relative to His Conduct during Part of His Command of the King's Troops in North America, Particularly to That Which Respects the Unfortunate Issue of the Campaign of 1781.* London, 1783.
——. *A Narrative of Sir Henry Clinton's Co-operations with Sir Peter Parker, on the Attack of Sullivan's Island, in South Carolina, in the Year 1776, and with Vice-Admiral Arbuthnot, in an Intended Attempt against the French Armament at Rhode-Island, in 1780.* 4th issue, New York, 1781.
Clowes, William L., ed. *The Royal Navy: A History from the Earliest Times to the Present.* 7 vols., London, 1897–1903.
[Collier, Sir George.] *A Detail of Some Particular Services Performed in America, during the Years 1776, 1777, 1778, and 1779. Compiled from Journals and Original Papers, Supposed to Be Chiefly Taken from the Journal Kept on Board of the Ship* Rainbow, *Commanded by Sir George Collier, While on the American Station during That Period. . . . Printed for Ithiel Town, from a Manuscript Obtained by Him, While in London, in the Summer of 1830.* New York, 1835.
Fisher, Sydney G. *The Struggle for American Independence.* 2 vols., Philadelphia and London, 1908.
Fitzpatrick, John C., ed. *The Writings of George Washington from the Original Manuscript Sources, 1745–1799.* 39 vols., Washington, 1931–44.

Flexner, James T. *The Traitor and the Spy: Benedict Arnold and John André*. New York, 1953.

Fortescue, Sir John W. *History of the British Army*. 13 vols. in 20, London, 1899–1930.

——. ed. *The Correspondence of King George the Third from 1760 to December 1783*. 6 vols., London, 1927–28.

Freeman, Douglas S. *George Washington, a Biography*. 5 vols., New York, 1948–52.

French, Allen. *The First Year of the American Revolution*. Boston and New York, 1934.

Gordon, William. *The History of the Rise, Progress, and Establishment, of the Independence of the United States of America: Including an Account of the Late War; and of the Thirteen Colonies, from Their Origin to That Period*. 4 vols., London, 1788.

Gottschalk, Louis R. *Lafayette and the Close of the American Revolution*. Chicago, 1942.

[Graves, W.] *Two Letters from W. Graves, Esq; Respecting the Conduct of Rear Admiral Thomas Graves, in North America, during His Accidental Command There for Four Months in 1781*. 4th issue, London, 1783.

Hammond, Otis G., ed. *Letters and Papers of Major-General John Sullivan, Continental Army*. New Hampshire Historical Society Collections, *13–15*. 3 vols., Concord, 1930–39.

Historical Manuscripts Commission. *Report on American Manuscripts in the Royal Institution of Great Britain*. 4 vols., London, etc., 1904–09.

——. *Report on the Manuscripts of Mrs. Stopford-Sackville, of Drayton House, Northamptonshire*. 2 vols., London, 1904–10.

Johnston, Henry P. *The Storming of Stony Point on the Hudson, Midnight, July 15, 1779: Its Importance in the Light of Unpublished Documents*. New York, 1900.

[Lee, Charles.] *The Lee Papers*. New-York Historical Society Collections for 1871–74. 4 vols. [New York, 1872–75].

Martyn, Charles. *The Life of Artemas Ward, the First Commander-in-Chief of the American Revolution*. New York, 1921.

Myers, William S., ed. *The Battle of Monmouth, by the Late William S. Stryker* . . . Princeton, 1927.

Partridge, Bellamy. *Sir Billy Howe*. London, New York, and Toronto, 1936.

Ramsay, David. *The History of the Revolution of South Carolina, from a British Province to an Independent State*. 2 vols., Trenton, 1785.

Robson, Eric. "The Expedition to the Southern Colonies, 1775–1776," *English Historical Review*, 66 (Oct., 1951), 535–560.

Rochambeau, Jean Baptiste Donatien de Vimeur, Comte de, *Relation, ou Journal des opérations du Corps Français sous le commandement du Comte de Rochambeau, Lieutenant-Général des Armées du Roi, depuis le 15 d'Août*. Philadelphia, 1781.

Ross, Charles, ed. *Correspondence of Charles, First Marquis Cornwallis*. 3 vols., London, 1859.

Sparks, Jared. *The Writings of George Washington.* 12 vols., Boston, 1858.

Stedman, Charles. *The History of the Origin, Progress, and Termination of the American War.* 2 vols., London, 1794.

Stevens, Benjamin F., ed. *The Campaign in Virginia, 1781: An Exact Reprint of Six Rare Pamphlets on the Clinton-Cornwallis Controversy.* 2 vols., London, 1888.

———. *Facsimiles of Manuscripts in European Archives Relating to America, 1773–1783.* 25 vols., London, 1889–98.

Stokes, I. N. Phelps. *The Iconography of Manhattan Island, 1498–1909.* 6 vols., New York, 1915–28.

Stryker, William S. *See* Myers, William S.

Tarleton, Banastre. *A History of the Campaigns of 1780 and 1781, in the Southern Provinces of North America.* London, 1787.

Van Doren, Carl. *Mutiny in January.* New York, 1943.

———. *Secret History of the American Revolution.* New York, 1941.

Wallace, Willard M. *Appeal to Arms: A Military History of the American Revolution.* New York, 1951.

Ward, Christopher. *The War of the Revolution,* ed. John R. Alden. 2 vols., New York, 1952.

Willcox, William B. "The British Road to Yorktown: A Study in Divided Command," *American Historical Review, 52* (Oct., 1946), 1–35.

———. "British Strategy in America, 1778," *Journal of Modern History, 19* (June, 1947), 97–121.

———. "Rhode Island in British Strategy, 1780–1781," *Journal of Modern History, 17* (Dec., 1945), 304–31.

634

Kelly, British Capt., at Eutaw
Springs, 569

Kennebec River, Me., Clinton's proposed raid on, 1775, 21–22

Kentucky, in proposed campaign of
1782, 576

Keppel, Augustus (subsequently first
Viscount), British Adm., court
martial of, mentioned, 141 n. 11

Keppel, British armed brig, at Savannah, 1779, 432

King George: *see* George III

Kings Bridge, N.Y., British post commanding entrance to Manhattan,
in operations of 1776, xxiii, 40, 44–
45, 47–48, of 1777, 66–68, 79,
82 n. 51, 83, of 1779, 136, 152,
of 1780, 463, of 1781, 307–308,
321, 325–326, 538; mentioned,
105 n. 10, 117

King's County, L.I., American prisoners in, 1777, 69

King's Creek, S.C., in Battle of Cowpens, 247 n. 8

King's Ferry, N.Y., in 1779, 122, 125;
in 1780, 495

King's Mountain, N.C., in campaign
of 1780–81, 246, 456; Battle of,
1780, and its effects, 221 n. 6,
226–227, 508 n. 60. *See also* Ferguson, Patrick

Kingston, N.J., in Monmouth campaign, 382

Kingston. N.Y.: *see* Esopus

Kipp's Bay, N.Y., British landing at,
1776, 45–46, 49

Knighthood: *see* Bath, Order of

Knox, Henry, American Brig. (subsequently Maj.) Gen., address to
the states signed by, *ca.* Oct.,
1780, 461–462; and prisoners of
war, 1781–82, 358

Knyphausen, Wilhelm, Baron von,
Hessian Lt. Gen., in Monmouth
campaign, 92, 93 n. 12, 96, 98,
105; in operations of 1779–80,

158, 162, 168, 190–194, 195 n.
10; and Arnold conspiracy, 464;
illness of, 1781, 306; at councils of
war in New York, 1781–82, 569,
571–573, 576, 579–580, 592–593,
596, 598

Kospoth, Heinrich Julius von, Hessian Maj. Gen., in 1780, 201 n. 6

Lackawanna, Pa., Butler at, 1778,
386

Lafayette, Gilbert Motier, Marquis
de, American Maj. Gen., in Monmouth campaign, 382–383, 389;
in Virginia, 1781, xl, xli, 250 n. 4,
252, 276, 307, 322–323, 336, 339,
348, 490, 511, 522, 528, 530, 532,
541–542, 548, 565, 577

Lake, Gerard, British Lt. Col. (subsequently Gen. and first Viscount),
at Yorktown, 1781, 584–585

Lake Champlain, in campaign of
1777, 70; in proposed campaign of
1782, 576; *see also* Lakes

Lake Erie, in proposed campaign of
1782, 574–575

Lake George, in campaign of 1777,
70, 73 n. 32; *see also* Lakes

Lake Oneida, in campaign of 1777,
70

Lake Ontario, in campaign of 1777,
70

Lakes (Champlain and George),
and communications with Canada,
11–12; in campaign of 1776, 53
n. 29, of 1777, 70, 73–74, 80 n. 45

Lancaster, Pa., loyalists at, 1781,
494, 515

Lanneau's Ferry, S.C., in operations
of 1780, 169

Laurens, Henry, President of Continental Congress, in South Carolina,
1780, 450

Lawrence, Elisha, British Lt. Col.
(New Jersey provincials), on Stat-
en Island, 1777, 68 n. 20

Ontario, Lake: *see* Lake Ontario

Opposition, Parliamentary, and origins of war, 3; and Sullivan's Island fiasco, 37 n. 36; and Clinton's attempted resignation, 1778, 108 n. 16

Orangeburg (Fort Orangeburg), S.C., in campaign of 1781, 355, 551, 578

Orange County, N.Y., mentioned, 1778, 114 n. 1

Orpheus, British frigate, in campaign of 1781, 253, 491, 493

Osborne's, Va., in campaign of 1781, 280–281, 520

Ossabaw Sound, Ga., French landing at, 1779, 432

Oswald, Eleazer, American Lt. Col. (artillery), at Monmouth, 389

Oswego, N.Y., in proposed campaign of 1782, 575–576

Oxford, Pa., in Clinton's plan for 1781, 495

Pacolet River, S.C., in campaign of 1780–81, 246, 477

Parker, Sir Peter, Rear Adm., R.N. (subsequently Adm.), in southern campaign, 1776, xix–xxii, xlvii, 28–37, 38 n. 37, 58 n. 42, 371–379; at Rhode Island, 1776–77, 57; commanding at Jamaica, 1779–81, 134, 143, 154, 237, 314, 467, 507, 516, 540 n. 75; letters from, to Clinton, June 25, 1776, 371–372, Jan. 12, 1777, 379; letter from, to Stephens, July 9, 1776, 376–378

Parliament, Clinton's election to, 1772, xiv, xv; and origins of war, 2–5, 7–9, 15; and efforts to restore peace, 87, 394, 416; and Commissioners of Public Accounts, 179, 366–367; and American loyalists, 390–391. *See also* House of Commons; House of Lords; Opposition, Parliamentary

Paroles, from prisoners of British in southern campaign, 171, 174, 181, 268, 532

Parsons, Samuel H., American Maj. Gen., in campaign of 1777, 68 n. 20, 69, 73 n. 31, 80; in Connecticut raid, 1779, 413; address to the states signed by, *ca.* Oct., 1780, 461–462

Parson's Pass, N.Y., in campaign of 1776, 50

Passaic, N.J.: *see* Acquackanonck

Paterson, James, British Maj. Gen., at Stony Point, 1779, 125; in Charleston campaign, 1780, 160, 162–163, 165, 184; at New York, 1781–82, 569, 573, 576, 579–580, 592–593, 596, 598

Paterson, John, American Brig. Gen., at Monmouth, 390 n. 18; address to the states signed by, *ca.* Oct., 1780, 461–462

Pattison, James, Maj. Gen., R.A. (subsequently Gen.), arrival in America, 1777, 72 n. 29; at Stony Point, 1779, 125; commandant at New York, 1779–80, 190, 455–456

Paulus Hook, N.J., British occupation of, 1776, 47; in campaign of 1777, 63, 67–68, of 1779, 139, 152, of 1780, 189; fortifications of, 1781, 538

Paumier, Peter, quotation from letter from, in Savannah, May 23, 1779, 409

Pedee River, S.C., in operations of 1780–81, 175–176, 229, 244, 260, 448, 477, 486–487, 511, 554

Peekskill, N.Y., in campaign of 1777, 66, 69, 72–73, 78

Pegasus, British frigate, detached by Rodney to New York, 1781, 563; in Chesapeake, 567

Pennsylvania, in campaign of 1777, xxv–xxvii, 62 n. 7, 67 n. 19, of 1781, xxxviii, xl, xlii, xlv, 310 n.

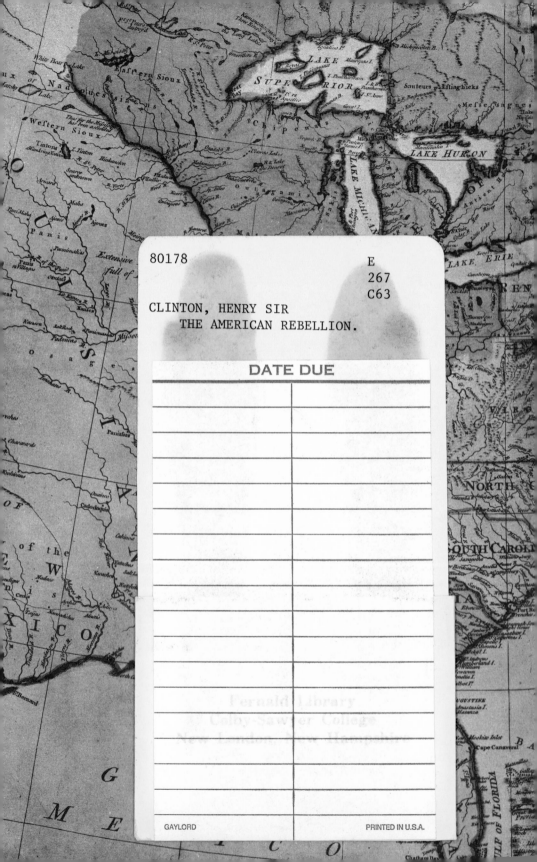

DATE DUE